CRIMINAL PROCEDURE

THIRTY-THIRD EDITION

STEVEN L. EMANUEL

Founder & Editor-in-Chief, *Emanuel Law Outlines*® and
Emanuel Bar Review
Harvard Law School, J.D. 1976
Member (Ret.), NY, CT, MD and VA bars

The *Emanuel Law Outlines*® Series

ASPEN
PUBLISHING

To contact Customer Service, e-mail customer.service@aspenpublishing.com,
call 1-800-950-5259, or mail correspondence to:

Aspen Publishing
Attn: Order Department
1 Wall Street
Burlington, MA 01803

1 2 3 4 5 6 7 8 9 0

ISBN 979-8-8941-0978-7

ABOUT ASPEN PUBLISHING

Aspen Publishing is a leading provider of legal education content and digital learning solutions in the United States and globally. Our innovative products and platforms—designed based on best practices in learning science—engage students and enhance outcomes. From textbooks and audiobooks authored by renowned experts to digital platforms and products like LEAF, Connected eBooks, Connected Quizzing, PracticePerfect, and JD-Next, we empower the next generation of legal professionals with innovative, trusted, and accessible resources.

The Aspen Casebook Series, affectionately known as the "red and black" casebooks among law faculty and students, includes hundreds of highly regarded textbooks across more than 80 disciplines. These range from foundational courses like Torts and Contracts to emerging electives such as Sustainability and the Law of Policing. Our study aids, including the popular *Examples & Explanations* series, help law students master complex topics with clarity and confidence.

Aspen's expertise extends to undergraduate education with our Paralegal, Criminal Justice, and Business Law series, offering the same hallmark quality to a broader audience. JD-Next, our groundbreaking online law school prep course and admissions test, provides a realistic preview of law school, equips students with essential skills for academic success, and evaluates their readiness for legal studies.

Aspen Publishing Is Proud to Be a UWorld Company

Since 2003, UWorld has been a global leader in developing high-quality learning tools for students preparing for high-stakes exams. With a commitment to excellence, UWorld has helped millions of students in undergraduate, graduate, and professional programs in fields such as medicine, nursing, finance, and law achieve their academic and career goals.

Founded by Chandra S. Pemmasani, M.D., during his medical residency, UWorld began focusing on medical education and has since expanded into various academic fields, including law. In 2020, UWorld launched its Legal vertical, starting with its comprehensive Multistate Bar Exam (MBE®) Question Bank, followed by the acquisition of Themis Bar Review, which integrated resources to provide a complete bar exam preparation experience. In 2024, UWorld expanded its offerings by acquiring Aspen Publishing, enhancing its suite of legal education products.

Today, UWorld offers an unparalleled range of study materials that blend active learning methods with expert content, ensuring students and educators can access the most effective resources. From bar preparation to law school success, UWorld is committed to supporting the next generation of legal professionals. Learn more at uworld.com.

About the Author

As a student at Harvard Law School in the 1970s, **Steve Emanuel** wrote concise outlines for his courses and sold them in the law school dining hall to his fellow students. His outlines were such an immediate hit that soon after graduation, Steve quit the practice of law and started his own company to publish the *Emanuel Law Outlines*® series and other study-aid series he helped write.

For more than 40 years, Steve's full-time job has been to update the *Emanuel Law Outlines*® — and other study aids he's written or published, like the *Law in a Flash* series — to reflect changes in the law, in casebooks, and on topics tested in bar exams. Over 2 million copies of study aids written by Steve have been sold. Steve is a retired member of the New York, Connecticut, Maryland, and Virginia bars, and has passed the California bar exam.

Abbreviations Used in Text

A,H,L,L&M — Allen, Hoffmann, Livingston, Leipold & Meares, *Comprehensive Criminal Procedure* (Aspen, 6th Ed., 2025)

A,S,H,L,L&M — Allen, Stuntz, Hoffmann, Livingston, Leipold & Meares, *Comprehensive Criminal Procedure* (Wolters Kluwer, 4th Ed., 2016)

ALI Model Study — American Law Institute, *Model Code of Pre-Arraignment Procedure*

D,M&S — Dressler, Michaels & Simmons, *Understanding Criminal Procedure* (2 vols., Carolina Acad. Press, 2021)

K,K&P — King, Kerr & Primus, *Kamisar, LaFave and Israel's Modern Criminal Procedure* (West Acad. Publ, 16th Ed., 2023)

KLIKK&P — Kamisar, LaFave, Israel, King, Kerr & Primus, *Modern Criminal Procedure* Casebook (West Academic Publ., 15th Ed., 2019)

K&S — Kadish and Schulhoffer, *Criminal Law and Its Processes* (Little, Brown & Co., 6th Ed. 1995)

LIK&K — LaFave, Israel, King & Kerr, *Criminal Procedure* Hornbook (West Academic Publ., 6th Ed. 2017)

S&C — Saltzburg and Capra, American Criminal Procedure (West Publ, 9th Ed., 2010)

SUMMARY OF CONTENTS

TABLE OF CONTENTS

Chapter 3

WARRANTLESS ARRESTS AND SEARCHES

Chapter 4

ELECTRONIC SURVEILLANCE AND SECRET AGENTS

Chapter 5
CONFESSIONS AND POLICE INTERROGATION

Chapter 6
LINEUPS AND OTHER PRE-TRIAL IDENTIFICATION PROCEDURES

Chapter 7
THE EXCLUSIONARY RULE

Chapter 8
THE RIGHT TO COUNSEL

Chapter 9
FORMAL PROCEEDINGS

Preface

Thank you for buying this book.

This new edition includes coverage of a number of cases decided through June, 2025, as well as some new topics. The topics and cases[1] include:

> Recent lower-court cases interpreting the 2018 decision in *Carpenter v. U.S.*, under which government demands for a ***suspect's personal data*** held by a ***non-governmental third-party*** (e.g. a cellphone company) must sometimes be supported by a ***search warrant*** and ***probable cause.***
>
> *Mitchell v. Wisconsin*, holding that police ***do not require a search warrant*** before performing a ***blood-alcohol test*** of a driver who is ***so drunk as to be unconscious***.
>
> ***42 U.S.C. §1983***, a statute that sometimes allows people whose Fourth Amendment or other constitutional rights have been ***violated by a police officer*** to bring a ***civil suit for money damages*** against the officer.
>
> *Samia v. U.S.*, covering the situation in which D1 and D2 are ***tried together*** for the same crime, and the prosecution wants to present to the jury ***a confession by D1*** (who doesn't take the stand) that also ***implicates D2.*** *Samia* makes it much easier for prosecutors to present D1's confession with only ***slight redactions*** of the portions that implicate D2, without thereby violating D2's ***Confrontation Clause rights.***
>
> Claims of ***"selective prosecution,"*** including why it's ***virtually impossible*** for a defendant to successfully assert such claims.

In addition to giving you a comprehensive outline of Criminal Procedure from a constitutional-law perspective, here are some of this book's special features:

> **"Casebook Correlation Chart"** — This chart, located just after this Preface, correlates each section of our Outline with the pages covering the same topic in the five leading Criminal Procedure casebooks.
>
> **"Capsule Summary"** — This is a 105-page summary of the key concepts of the law of Criminal Procedure, specially designed for use in the last week or so before your final exam.
>
> **"Quiz Yourself"** — At the end of nearly every chapter I give you short-answer questions so that you can exercise your analytical muscles. There are 106 of these questions, each written by me.
>
> **"Exam Tips"** — These alert you to what issues repeatedly pop up on real-life Criminal Procedure exams, and what factual patterns are commonly used to test those issues. I created these Tips by looking at literally hundreds of multiple-choice and essay questions asked by law professors and bar examiners. You'd be surprised at how predictable the issues and fact-patterns chosen by professors really are! The Tips are located at the end of nearly every chapter.

I intend for you to use this book both throughout the semester and for exam preparation. Here are

---

1. The cases mentioned are all Supreme Court cases unless otherwise specified.

some suggestions about how to use it:[2]

1. During the semester, use the book in preparing each night for the next day's class. To do this, first read your casebook. Then, use the *Casebook Correlation Chart* to get an idea of what part of the outline to read. Reading the outline will give you a sense of how the particular cases you've just read in your casebook fit into the overall structure of the subject. You may want to use a highlighter to mark key portions of the *Emanuel.*

2. If you make your own outline for the course, use the *Emanuel* to give yours a structure, and to supply black letter principles. You may want to rely especially on the *Capsule Summary* for this purpose. You are hereby authorized to copy small portions of the *Emanuel* into your own outline, provided that your outline will be used only by you or your study group, and provided that you are the owner of the *Emanuel*.

3. When you first start studying for exams, read the *Capsule Summary* to get an overview. This will probably take you about one day.

4. Either during exam study or earlier in the semester, do some or all of the *Quiz Yourself* short-answer questions. You can find these quickly by looking for *Quiz Yourself* entries in the Table of Contents. When you do these questions: (1) record your short "answer" on the small blank line provided after the question, but also (2) try to write out a "mini essay" on a separate piece of paper. Remember that the only way to get good at writing essays is to write essays.

5. Three or four days before the exam, review the *Exam Tips* that appear at the end of each chapter. You may want to combine this step with step **4**, so that you use the Tips to help you spot the issues in the short-answer questions. You'll also probably want to follow up from many of the Tips to the main outline's discussion of the topic.

6. The night before the exam: (1) do some *Quiz Yourself* questions, just to get your thinking and writing juices flowing, and (2) re-scan the *Exam Tips* (spending about 2-3 hours).

My deep thanks to my colleagues Barbara Roth and Troy Froebe for their help in assuring the reliability and readability of this and my other books.

Good luck in your Corporations course. If you'd like any other Aspen publication, you can find it at your bookstore or at **www.AspenPublishing.com**. If you'd like to contact me, you can email me at **semanuel@westnet.com**.

Steve Emanuel

Larchmont NY

October 14, 2025

2. The suggestions below relate only to this book. I don't talk about taking or reviewing class notes, using hornbooks or other study aids, joining a study group, or anything else. This doesn't mean I don't think these other steps are important — it's just that in this Preface I've chosen to focus on how I think you can use this outline.

CASEBOOK CORRELATION CHART

(**Note:** general sections of the outline are omitted from this chart. **NC** = not directly covered by this casebook.)

Emanuel's Criminal Procedure Outline *(by chapter and section heading)*	Allen, Hoffmann, Livingston, Leipold & Meares **Comprehensive Criminal Procedure** (6th ed. 2025)	Kamisar, LaFave, Israel, King, Kerr & Primus **Modern Criminal Procedure** (16th ed. 2023)
CHAPTER 1 **CONSTITUTIONAL CRIMINAL PROCEDURE GENERALLY**		
II. State Procedures & Fed'l Const.	57-104	19-31
III. Steps in a Criminal Proceeding	NC	3-13, 884-1013, 1276-1374
CHAPTER 2 **ARREST; PROBABLE CAUSE; SEARCH WARRANTS**		
II, III & IV. Reasonable Expectation of Privacy; Interests Protected by 4th Amendment; Third-Party Doctrine; Plain View Doctrine	317-412, 474-480, 746-759	213-295, 366-469
V & VI. Probable Cause Generally; Particular Information Establishing Probable Cause	415-420, 427-440	296-309
VII. Search Warrants — Issuance and Execution	412-444	309-323
VIII. Arrest Warrants	500-508	367-371
CHAPTER 3 **WARRANTLESS ARRESTS AND SEARCHES**		
II. Warrantless Arrests	500-508, 672-681	327-331, 367-371
III. Search Incident to Arrest	608-641	360-387
IV. Exigent Circumstances	445-474	327-333
V. The "Plain View" Doctrine and Seizures of Evidence	474-480	219-221
VI. The "Automobile Exception" to the Requirement of a Search Warrant	480-500	352-366
VII. Consent Searches Generally	508-517	436-444
VIII. Consent by Third Persons	518-526	445-453

CASEBOOK CORRELATION CHART (continued)

Emanuel's Criminal Procedure Outline *(by chapter and section heading)*	Allen, Hoffmann, Livingston, Leipold & Meares **Comprehensive Criminal Procedure** (6th ed. 2025)	Kamisar, LaFave, Israel, King, Kerr & Primus **Modern Criminal Procedure** (16th ed. 2023)
CHAPTER 3 **WARRANTLESS ARRESTS AND SEARCHES (cont.)**		
IX. "Stop-And-Frisk" and Other Brief Detention	398-412, 532-594	387-417
X. Regulatory and Other "Special Needs" Searches	528-532, 653-671	427-436
CHAPTER 4 **ELECTRONIC SURVEILLANCE AND SECRET AGENTS**		
I. Historical Background	270-272	NC
II. Fourth Amendment Protection of *Katz*	317-324, 774-759	214-221
III. The Federal Wiretapping And Stored Communications Statutes	740-774	NC
IV. The Use of Secret Agents	774-790	511-518
V. Entrapment	774-790	518-536
CHAPTER 5 **CONFESSIONS AND POLICE INTERROGATION**		
II. Pre-*Miranda* Confession Cases	847-861	537-549
III. *Escobedo* and the Right to Counsel	860-861	549-556
IV. *Miranda* Generally	852-878, 948-954	556-574
V. What is a "Custodial" Interrogation	879-887	574-583
VI. Minor Crimes	NC	NC
VII. What Constitutes Interrogation	887-898	584-593
VIII. The "Public Safety" Exception	946-948	595-601
IX. Warnings Required under *Miranda*	899-915	601-604
X. Waivers and Invocations of *Miranda* Rights	915-946, 965-981	604-622
XI. The *Miranda* Rights of Grand Jury Witnesses	1075-1082	803-805
XII. Other Admissibility Issues Relating to *Miranda*	954-965	731-736

CASEBOOK CORRELATION CHART (continued)

Emanuel's Criminal Procedure Outline *(by chapter and section heading)*	Allen, Hoffmann, Livingston, Leipold & Meares **Comprehensive Criminal Procedure** (6th ed. 2025)	Kamisar, LaFave, Israel, King, Kerr & Primus **Modern Criminal Procedure** (16th ed. 2023)
CHAPTER 6 **LINEUPS AND OTHER PRE-TRIAL IDENTIFICATION PROCEDURES**		
II. Limitation of the Privilege Against Self-Incrimination	257-264, 791-847	23, 737-750
III. The Right to Counsel	131-142	738-745
IV. Exceptions to the Right to Counsel	128-142	745-750
V. Due Process Limitations	136-142	750-762
CHAPTER 7 **THE EXCLUSIONARY RULE**		
II. Standing to Assert the Exclusionary Rule	700-710	454-469
III & IV. Derivative Evidence Generally, and "Independent Source" and "Inevitable Discovery" Exceptions; "Purging the Taint" of Police Illegality	710-731	469-489, 719-731
V. Collateral Use Exceptions	731-735	489-493
VI. Other Exceptions -- The "Good Faith Warrant" and "Knock-and-Announce Violation" Exceptions	294-307	487-489, 493-510
VII. The Right to Sue for Civil Damages (§1983)	308-310	417-427
CHAPTER 8 **THE RIGHT TO COUNSEL**		
II. Right to Retained Counsel of One's Choice	232-239	63, 116-124
III. The Indigent's Right to Appointed Counsel	107-116, 166-168	63-79
IV. Proceedings in Which the Right to Counsel Applies	116-128	73-79, 86-99
V. Stages at Which Right to Counsel Attaches	128-146	79-85
VI. Right to Effective Assistance of Counsel	146-221	125-173
VII. The Client's Right to Control The Defense	179-180, 225-227, 1601	189-199
VII. Waiver of the Right to Counsel	221-231	102-115

CASEBOOK CORRELATION CHART (continued)

Emanuel's Criminal Procedure Outline *(by chapter and section heading)*	Allen, Hoffmann, Livingston, Leipold & Meares **Comprehensive Criminal Procedure** (6th ed. 2025)	Kamisar, LaFave, Israel, King, Kerr & Primus **Modern Criminal Procedure** (16th ed. 2023)
CHAPTER 9 **FORMAL PROCEEDINGS**		
I. Grand jury Proceedings	1039-1105	768-774, 902-928
II. Bail and Preventive Detention	1015-1037	828-851
III. Plea Bargaining	1247-1299	1067-1133
IV. Selective Prosecution	308-310	867-878
IV. Right to Speedy Trial	1108-1129	996-1013
V. Pre-Trial Motions to Suppress Evidence	NC	11
VI. Pre-Trial Discovery	1175-1220	1015-1066
VII. Right to a Jury Trial	1301-1353	1134-1171
VIII. The Trial	1353-1417	1206-1240
IX. Double Jeopardy	1537-1600	1241-1275

CAPSULE SUMMARY

This Capsule Summary is intended for review at the end of the semester. Reading it is not a substitute for mastering the material in the main outline. Numbers in brackets refer to the pages in the main outline where the topic is discussed. The order of topics is occasionally somewhat different from that in the main outline.

CHAPTER 1

CONSTITUTIONAL CRIMINAL PROCEDURE GENERALLY

I. STATE PROCEDURES AND THE FEDERAL CONSTITUTION

A. Meaning of "criminal procedure": The term "criminal procedure" refers to the methods by which the criminal justice system functions. Here are some of the topics that are usually included within criminal procedure:

1. The ***arresting*** of suspects.
2. The ***searching*** of premises and persons.
3. The use of ***electronic surveillance*** and ***secret agents***.
4. The ***interrogation*** of suspects, and the obtaining of ***confessions***.
5. The use of ***line-ups*** and other pre-trial identification procedures.
6. The ***Exclusionary Rule***, and how it affects the admissibility of evidence obtained through methods that violate the Constitution.
7. The right to ***counsel***.
8. ***Grand jury*** proceedings.
9. ***Bail*** and preventive detention.
10. ***Plea bargaining.***
11. The right to a ***speedy trial.***
12. Pre-trial ***discovery.***
13. The ***Double Jeopardy*** clause.

B. Focus on U.S. Constitution: Many aspects of criminal procedure are regulated by the U.S. Constitution, particularly the Bill of Rights (the first ten amendments). As discussed below, most federal constitutional provisions concerning criminal procedure are binding on state proceedings as well as federal ones.

1. **Non-constitutional issues:** The states are free to develop their own procedures for dealing with criminal prosecutions, as long as these do not violate the federal constitution.

C. Applicability of Bill of Rights to states: In deciding how the federal constitution applies to state criminal prosecutions, the Supreme Court follows the ***"selective incorporation"*** approach. Under this approach, not all rights enumerated in the Bill of Rights are applicable to the state, but if ***any aspect of a right*** is found to be so necessary to fundamental fairness that it applies to the states, then ***all aspects*** of that right apply. Thus if a right is applicable in state courts, its ***scope*** is the same as in federal courts. [2]

1. **All but two rights applicable to states:** All Bill of Rights guarantees have been held applicable to the states, except for two. [4] The two Bill of Rights guarantees that have ***not*** been found applicable to the states are:

   a. **Bail:** The Eighth Amendment's guarantee against ***excessive bail*** (so that apparently, a state may choose to offer bail, but may then set it in an "excessive" amount); and

   b. **Grand jury indictment:** The Fifth Amendment's right to a ***grand jury*** indictment (so that a state may decide to begin a prosecution by using an "information" prepared by the prosecutor rather than a grand jury indictment).

D. Raising constitutional claims in federal court: A defendant in a state criminal proceeding can of course raise in the proceeding itself the claim that his federal constitutional rights have been violated (e.g., by the use against him of a coerced confession or the fruits of an illegal search and seizure).

CAPSULE SUMMARY

1. **Federal habeas corpus:** But the state criminal defendant has in some situations a ***second chance*** to argue that the state trial has violated his federal constitutional rights: He may bring a ***federal*** action for a writ of ***habeas corpus***. The defendant may bring a habeas corpus proceeding only after he has been convicted and has exhausted his state appellate remedies. The petition for habeas corpus is heard by a ***federal district court judge***. If the judge finds that the conviction was obtained through a violation of the defendant's constitutional rights, he can order the defendant released (usually subject to a new trial). [5]

   a. **Limits:** There are significant limits on the kinds of arguments a defendant can make in a federal *habeas corpus* proceeding. Here are two:

      i. **Search and seizure cases:** In ***search and seizure cases***, if the state has given D the opportunity for a ***"full and fair litigation"*** for his Fourth Amendment claim (that is, the defendant got a fair chance to argue that evidence should not be introduced against him because it was the fruit of an illegal search or seizure), D may not make this argument in his *habeas corpus* petition, even if the federal court is convinced that the state court reached the wrong constitutional conclusion. [*Stone v. Powell*] [5]

      ii. **Mistakes of law:** Under a 1996 federal statute, a federal court can't give *habeas* relief for a state-court mistake of law unless the state decision was either ***"contrary to"*** or an ***"unreasonable application of"*** some ***"clearly established"*** principle of federal law ***as determined by the Supreme Court***. [5]

      Example: Suppose the Supreme Court has never decided a particular issue of federal constitutional law. The state court decides that issue of law against D. A federal district court cannot give habeas relief even if the court believes (based on, say, federal Courts of Appeals decisions) that the state court erred on that issue of constitutional law.

II. STEPS IN A CRIMINAL PROCEEDING

A. Here is a brief summary of the steps in a criminal proceeding:

1. **Arrest:** When a police officer has probable cause to believe that a suspect has committed a crime, the officer makes an ***arrest***. An arrest may occur either with or without a warrant (most are made without a warrant). Arrest usually involves taking the suspect into custody and transporting him to the police station. [7]

2. **Booking:** At the police station, the suspect undergoes ***"booking,"*** which includes entering information about him into a police blotter, and photographing and fingerprinting him. [7]

3. **Filing complaint:** A prosecutor now decides whether there is enough evidence to file charges; if so, the prosecutor prepares a ***"complaint."*** [7]

4. **First appearance:** After the complaint has been filed, the suspect is brought before a ***magistrate***. In most states, this is called the ***"first appearance."*** Here, the magistrate informs D of the charges, notifies him that he has the right to counsel, and sets bail or releases D without bail. [8]

5. **Preliminary hearing:** If the case is a felony case, a ***"preliminary hearing"*** is held. Again, this is in front of a magistrate, and usually involves live witnesses so the magistrate can determine whether there is probable cause to believe that D committed the crime charged. [8]

6. **Filing of indictment or information:** In the federal system, or in a "grand jury" state, the next step is for a grand jury to hear the prosecutor's evidence and to issue an ***indictment***. In a non-grand-jury state, the prosecutor now prepares an ***"information,"*** reciting the charges. [8]

7. **Arraignment:** After the indictment or information has been filed, D is ***"arraigned"***; that is, he is brought before the trial court and asked to plead innocent or guilty. [8]

8. **Pre-trial motions:** Defense counsel now makes any pre-trial motions. [9]

9. **Trial:** Next comes the ***trial***. If the charge is a felony, or a misdemeanor punishable by more than six months in prison, all states (and the federal system) give D the right to have the case tried before a ***jury***. [9]

10. **Sentencing:** If D pleads guilty or is found guilty during the trial, he is then ***sentenced*** (usually by the judge, not the jury). [9]

11. **Appeals:** A convicted defendant is then entitled to ***appeal*** (e.g., on the grounds that the evidence admitted against him at trial was the result of an unconstitutional search). [9]

12. **Post-conviction remedies:** Both state and federal prisoners, even after direct appeal, may challenge their convictions through federal-court ***habeas corpus*** procedures. [9]

CHAPTER 2

ARREST; PROBABLE CAUSE; SEARCH WARRANTS

I. GENERAL PRINCIPLES

A. Fourth Amendment: The Fourth Amendment to the U.S. Constitution provides, "The right of the people to be secure in their persons, houses, papers, and effects, ***against unreasonable searches and seizures***, shall not be violated, and ***no Warrants shall issue, but upon probable cause***, supported by Oath or affirmation, and ***particularly describing*** the place to be searched, and the persons or things to be seized." [13]

B. Applies to both searches and arrests: The Fourth Amendment thus applies both to ***searches and seizures*** of ***property***, and to ***arrests*** of persons. [14]

1. **Invalid arrest no defense:** Generally, the fact that D was ***arrested in an unconstitutional manner*** makes ***no difference***: a defendant may generally be tried and convicted regardless of the fact that his arrest was made in violation of the Fourth Amendment. [14] However, when evidence is seized as part of a ***warrantless search*** conducted ***incident to an arrest***, the evidence will be excluded as inadmissible if the arrest was a violation of the Constitution (e.g., the arresting officer did not have probable cause to believe that D had committed a crime). [14]

2. **Probable cause for issuance of warrant:** Where a search or arrest warrant is issued, the Fourth Amendment requires that the warrant be issued only based on ***"probable cause."*** This requirement is quite strictly enforced.

3. **Where warrant required:** A warrant is usually ***required*** before a ***search or seizure*** takes place, unless there are "exigent circumstances." An ***arrest*** warrant, by contrast, is usually ***not*** constitutionally required.

4. **Search must always be "reasonable":** Whether or not there is a search warrant or arrest warrant, the arrest or search ***must not be "unreasonable."***

5. **Probable cause for warrantless search or arrest:** But there is ***no*** requirement in the Fourth Amendment that a warrantless search or seizure take place only upon ***probable cause***. This is why police may conduct a brief "stop and frisk" even without probable cause: They are making a Fourth Amendment "seizure," but merely need some reasonable suspicion, not probable cause. (See *Terry v. Ohio*, discussed below.)

CAPSULE SUMMARY

II. THE "REASONABLE EXPECTATION OF PRIVACY"; THE INTERESTS THAT ARE PROTECTED BY THE FOURTH AMENDMENT

A. Two different ways to "search": There are ***two different ways*** in which government may be deemed to have carried out a Fourth Amendment search:

[1] First, government will be deemed to have done a "search" of a defendant if government ***physically intrudes*** on the defendant's personal or real ***property*** (in an attempt to find something or to obtain information). This is a concept of searches as being a form of ***trespass*** on the defendant's property. [*U.S. v. Jones*] [15]

[2] Second, a search will be deemed to occur if the government infringes on the defendant's ***"reasonable expectation of privacy"*** (again, in an attempt to find something or to obtain information). [*Katz v. U.S.*] [15]

We'll consider the second of these types first.

B. *Katz* "expectation of privacy" doctrine: A Fourth Amendment search or seizure only takes place when a person's ***"reasonable expectation of privacy"*** has been violated. [16] [*Katz v. U.S.*]

1. **Waiver of privacy right:** A person's conduct may mean that he has ***no*** reasonable expectation of privacy in a particular situation. If so, no Fourth Amendment search or seizure will result, even if the police are doing something that a non-lawyer would think of as being a "search" or "seizure."

Example: D puts some papers into a public trash bin, unaware that the police are watching his conduct through binoculars. Because a person who disposes of trash normally does not have a "reasonable expectation of privacy" as to the trash, the police do not commit a Fourth Amendment search or seizure when they go through the trash bin's contents and remove the papers belonging to D (and use these in a subsequent prosecution of D).

More precisely, a person will be found to have had a "reasonable expectation of privacy" in some matter only if ***two tests*** are satisfied:

[1] The person exhibited an ***"actual (subjective) expectation of privacy"*** in the matter; and

[2] That expectation is "***one that society is prepared to recognize as 'reasonable***.'"

[*Katz v. U.S.*, concurrence by Harlan]

a. **Contexts:** Some types of evidence that are likely to be found ***not protected*** by any "reasonable expectation of privacy" are:

[1] ***abandoned property***, such as ***trash***;

[2] things that can be seen from the perspective of a person ***stationed on public property*** (e.g., a police officer stands on a sidewalk and looks through binoculars into a window at the front of D's house);

[3] things a person says or does while ***in public*** (e.g., D1 talks to D2 in a restaurant, while a police officer is eavesdropping nearby); and

[4] information the police learn by use of ***other senses*** while the police are in a place they have a right to be (e.g., the police use dogs to ***smell*** odors coming from luggage in a public place and, thus, detect drugs).

C. **Digital databases of personal information:** Vast amounts of sensitive personal data about each American are compiled into huge ***electronic databases*** maintained by private companies. An individual who wishes to make use of modern technology – by talking on a cell phone, making online purchases, sending emails, etc. – has essentially no choice but to allow service providers to amass this sensitive information. If government then demands or requests this information from the service provider that has collected it, ***does the individual have a reasonable expectation of privacy as to the compiled data?***

1. **Tentative answer:** As of this writing (mid-2025), we don't have a full understanding of how the Supreme Court would answer this question. But we *do* know that there is one type of personal data as to which a person definitely *does* have a reasonable expectation of privacy:

Seven days' or more worth of ***"CSLI,"*** or ***"cell site location information."***

2. **What CSLI is:** CSLI specifies, for any particular cell phone at a particular time, ***the precise location of the phone, and thus of the person carrying the phone.*** CSLI is maintained by the wireless carrier from whom the person receives cell phone service. [*Carpenter v. U.S.* (2018), discussed *infra*, C-10.]

a. **Significance:** The significance of the fact that a person has a reasonable expectation of privacy with respect to seven days or more of her CSLI is that if government demands that the cell carrier turn over the person's CSLI, government is ***performing a search*** for Fourth Amendment purposes.

b. Rationale: Here's the reasoning by which the Court in *Carpenter, supra*, concluded that a person has a reasonable expectation of privacy in seven days' or more worth of her own CSLI:

[1] The ***"time-stamped" data*** furnished by CSLI is ***highly revealing***; it "provides an ***intimate window into a person***'s life, revealing not only his particular movements, but through them his '***familial, political, professional, religious, and sexual associations.***'" [*Carpenter*]

[2] While an individual might not have a reasonable expectation that her public movements over a short period of time won't be tracked by traditional human-based methods, the individual *does* have a reasonable expectation that government will not do the sort of longer-term tracking — of ***her every movement, both prospectively and retrospectively, over long periods of time*** — that CSLI permits.

[3] Therefore, when government demands seven or more days' worth of CSLI data about a person from a carrier, government has ***conducted a Fourth Amendment search*** of that person's information.

[*Carpenter*] [34]

D. The property-based "trespass" approach to searches: Apart from government intrusions that infringe on a person's reasonable expectation of privacy, a Fourth Amendment search can occur if government ***physically intrudes*** on a person's property, and does so for the purpose of finding evidence or other information. This is an ***alternative*** path by which a defendant can show that a Fourth Amendment search occurred — if there is a ***physical intrusion by government on a person's property*** coupled with an investigative purpose, a search has occurred ***even if the individual had no reasonable expectation of privacy*** as to the type of information the police end up learning. [18]

Example 1: The police have reason to suspect that D is engaged in cocaine trafficking. Without a valid warrant, they secretly put a GPS tracking device on the underside of a Jeep belonging to D, while the Jeep is in a public parking lot. For 28 days, the tracker sends the government constant wireless signals showing the vehicle's movements over public roads. When D is tried for narcotics trafficking, the government uses the locational evidence from the tracker to show that D visited the "stash house" where large amounts of cocaine were found. D claims that the placement and use of the tracker was a Fourth Amendment search.

Held (by the Supreme Court) for D. The ***mere conducting of a physical intrusion*** by the government — the placing the GPS tracker underneath D's vehicle — was itself ***enough*** to constitute a Fourth Amendment search, ***regardless*** of whether D's reasonable expectation of privacy was ever violated. [These facts are a slight modification of the facts of *U.S. v. Jones*.] [18]

Example 2: Local police get an unverified tip (not constituting probable cause for a search or arrest) that marijuana is being grown in D's house. A "trained canine handler" who works for the police brings his trained drug-sniffing dog, Franky, onto D's front porch. Franky sniffs the base of the front door, and then indicates that narcotics are being stored inside the house. The police use this information to procure a search warrant for the inside of the house, do the search, and find marijuana. D argues that the dog-sniffing on the porch was an illegal Fourth Amendment search, making the ensuing search warrant invalid.

Held (by the Supreme Court), for D. When the government obtains information by physically intruding into a person's "house," a Fourth Amendment search has occurred. A person's "house" for Fourth Amendment purposes includes the area immediately surrounding the physical structure (an area called the "curtilage"; see Par. (D) below), which in this case included the porch. When D hung a front-door knocker, he implicitly gave consent to anyone (including the police) to come on the porch, knock, and wait briefly for a response. But bringing a trained dog onto the porch to try to find incriminating evidence went beyond the scope of this implied consent. Therefore, the dog's sniffing was a physical intrusion into the curtilage portion of D's "house," making the sniffing a Fourth Amendment search whether or not the entry and sniffing violated any ***legitimate expectation of privacy*** on D's part. [*Florida v. Jardines*] [20]

E. Curtilage: For purposes of the "physical intrusion" test (as well as apparently for the "reasonable expectation of privacy" test), the police normally commit a search if they enter or investigate a person's "house." But a person's "house" does ***not include*** all of a person's residential real estate, merely the actual house and what the Supreme Court calls the house's ***"curtilage."*** The curtilage is ***"the area 'immediately surrounding and associated with the home'."*** [*Florida v. Jardines, supra*]

1. **Four factors:** Four factors should be looked to in determining whether a structure or area is or isn't within the "curtilage":

   [1] the ***proximity*** of the home to the area claimed to be curtilage (closer = curtilage);

   [2] whether the area is included within an ***enclosure*** that surrounds the home (enclosed = curtilage);

   [3] the nature of the ***uses*** (domestic vs. non-domestic) to which the area is put (domestic = curtilage); and

   [4] the ***steps taken*** by the resident to ***protect*** the area from ***observation*** by people passing it (more protective steps = curtilage).

   [*U.S. v. Dunn*] [23-23]

   Example: D owns a 190-acre ranch, enclosed by an outer fence. D's farmhouse is surrounded by an interior fence that does not include any other structures. The issue is whether a barn, located about 60 yards from the farmhouse (and outside the interior fence surrounding the farmhouse), is within the farmhouse's curtilage.

   Held (by applying the above four factors), the barn was not within the curtilage. For instance, as to factor (3), the barn was not (as the police knew prior to the start of the episode) being used for any activities related to the home — the police had evidence that drugs were being manufactured in the barn. *U.S. v. Dunn, supra.*

   a. **Open fields:** ***Open fields*** on a farm or ranch (i.e., fields that are not close to the house, and/or are not within the same tight fencing that includes the house) are not part of the "curtilage," and are therefore ***not protected by the Fourth Amendment***. [*Oliver v. U.S.*] [23]

b. **Front porches and garages:** By contrast, *Jardines (supra*, p. C-7) shows that the ***front porch*** of a house *is* within the curtilage. Similarly, a residential homeowner's ***garage***, and her front and back yards (at least if they're enclosed by a fence), will normally be held to be within the curtilage.

c. **Driveway:** A recent case, ***Collins v. Virginia*** (2018), holds that in the case of a ***driveway*** to a house, the portion of the driveway that ***immediately abuts the house*** *is* usually part of the curtilage. [23]

Example: A police officer, Rhodes, suspects that a particular orange-and-black motorcycle has been stolen and is now in the possession of D at D's girlfriend's house. Rhodes drives to the street in front of the house to investigate. From there, Rhodes can see that at the top of the driveway, next to the house and partly visible from under a tarpaulin, there is a parked motorcycle. Now, having probable cause to believe that the partially-visible motorcycle is probably the stolen one, Rhodes walks up the driveway, lifts the tarp, and sees that the motorcycle resembles the stolen orange-and-black one. He uses his hands to examine the cycle, uncovers the vehicle's license plate and VIN, verifies by cellphone that these match the details of the stolen motorcycle, and replaces the tarp. Rhodes then goes to the front door of the house, where he eventually arrests D for receiving stolen property.

Held, when Rhodes went up to the motorcycle and touched it, he was standing in a portion of the driveway that was curtilage. That part was curtilage because it was an enclosure (walls on three sides), it was adjacent to the house, and it was next to an entrance to the house. Therefore, Rhodes was conducting a Fourth Amendment search of D's home, for which a search warrant was required. [*Collins v. Virginia*] [23]

2. **Significance of curtilage:** In sum, the curtilage of a house is ***protected*** against warrantless searches by the police, even if the area is one as to which the homeowner might ***not otherwise have a reasonable expectation of privacy.***

a. **Visibility to public is irrelevant:** If an area is curtilage, it receives this protection against warrantless searches even though a person standing in a public place (e.g., the street) can ***see into the curtilage.***

Example: In *Collins*, *supra*, the portion of the driveway in which the motorcycle was parked was curtilage, even though Officer Rhodes (or any member of the public) could see part of the motorcycle from the street.

F. **Trash and other abandoned property:** ***Trash*** or other ***abandoned*** property will normally ***not*** be material as to which the owner has a reasonable expectation of privacy. Therefore, when a person puts trash out on the curb to be picked up by the garbage collector, the police may ***search that trash without a warrant***. [*California v. Greenwood*] [27]

1. **Trash on one's own property:** But if the owner puts his trash out for collection not on the public street or sidewalk but instead on a portion of his ***own property*** (and the trash collector comes onto the property to retrieve it), the police probably may not enter D's property to inspect the trash. (But they could wait until the collector collects the trash, and search it at the street.) [28]

G. **Some special contexts:**

1. **Jail cell:** A prisoner has no legitimate expectation of privacy in his ***prison cell***. Thus even if an inmate shows that a guard has without justification searched the inmate's personal posses-

sions that are highly unlikely to relate to security issues, the inmate has not made out a Fourth Amendment claim. [*Hudson v. Palmer*] [29]

2. **Guests:** ***Guests*** in a person's house may or may not have a legitimate expectation of privacy in the premises being visited.

   a. **Overnight social guest:** An ***overnight social guest*** normally ***has*** a legitimate expectation of privacy in the home where he is staying. Therefore, the police may normally not make a warrantless arrest or warrantless search of the premises where D is staying as an overnight guest. (But if the owner of the premises consents to a search, the guest is out of luck.) [*Minnesota v. Olson*] [29]

   b. **Social guest not staying overnight:** A social guest who is ***not staying overnight*** probably ***also has*** a legitimate expectation of privacy in the premises, although the Supreme Court has not definitively decided this question yet.

   c. **Business guest:** A guest who is at the premises on ***business*** is ***less likely*** than a social guest to be found to have a legitimate expectation of privacy in the premises. Where the business visit is a relatively ***brief*** one, the court is especially likely to find that there is no legitimate privacy expectation. [29]

      Example: D visits X's apartment for a couple of hours, for the purpose of bagging cocaine that D and X will later sell. The police snoop while the visit is going on. *Held*, the shortness of the visit and the business-rather-than-personal nature of what D did at the apartment meant that D had no legitimate expectation of privacy in the apartment. Therefore, D's Fourth Amendment rights couldn't have been violated, even if *X*'s rights were violated. [*Minnesota v. Carter*] [29]

3. **Searches of passengers in, or non-owner drivers of, a vehicle:** Just as a social guest in another person's home may well have a legitimate expectation of privacy in that home (see *Minn. v. Olson, supra*), so a ***passenger*** in a ***vehicle***, or a ***driver who does not own the vehicle,*** will ordinarily have a reasonable expectation of privacy in the vehicle (and thus have standing to assert a Fourth Amendment violation) if the police stop the vehicle or search it.

   a. **Passengers:** A ***passenger*** in a vehicle that's stopped ("seized") and/or searched, will generally have a reasonable expectation of privacy in the contents of the vehicle. That's true even if the passenger has ***no ownership or possessory interest*** in the vehicle — her mere ***presence*** in the vehicle at the time of the stop or search will generally be sufficient to give her a reasonable expectation of privacy in the vehicle. Consequently, if the stop or search occurs without probable cause (and no exception to the requirement of probable cause applies), the passenger will be able to assert that her Fourth Amendment rights have been violated. [30]

   b. **Driver who is not owner:** Now, consider a person who is ***not the owner of a vehicle*** (call her D), but who is ***driving the vehicle*** at the time it is stopped by the police. Does D's lack of an ownership interest in the vehicle prevent her from having a reasonable expectation of privacy in the vehicle, so as to deprive her of standing to assert that the stop violated her Fourth Amendment rights?

      i. **Authorized use of vehicle:** If the driver D was ***authorized*** by the owner to drive the vehicle, the clear answer is ***"no."*** Just as a social guest in a home normally has a reasonable expectation of privacy with respect to the portion of the home where the owner has authorized the guest to be present (see, e.g., *Minnesota v. Olson*, *supra*, p.

C-9), so the authorized-driver D normally has such an expectation with respect to the car, and therefore has standing to raise the Fourth Amendment argument. [31]

ii. **Unauthorized use – the rental car scenario:** Now, let's assume the non-owner driver D is driving the vehicle ***without authorization*** by the owner. This scenario is most likely to arise when the vehicle is a ***rental car***, and the rental agreement lists someone other than D as the sole person authorized to drive the vehicle. In this scenario, D's standing to assert the Fourth Amendment if the vehicle is improperly stopped is a closer question than in the authorized-use case above. But here, too, the Supreme Court has held that the fact that the rental agreement prohibits D from driving the vehicle will ***not*** normally deprive D from asserting that the stop violated his Fourth Amendment rights. [*Byrd v. U.S.* (2018)] [31]

III. THE "THIRD-PARTY" DOCTRINE: VOLUNTARY DISCLOSURE TO OTHERS AS VOIDING THE EXPECTATION OF PRIVACY

A. **Transfer to third person, generally:** Under the so-called ***"third-party doctrine,"*** when an individual ***voluntarily transfers information to a third party***, the transferor ***enjoys no further Fourth Amendment protection*** as to that information. Where the doctrine applies, government may ***demand that the third party turn the information over,*** even if government not only ***lacks probable cause or a warrant,*** but doesn't even have reasonable grounds for suspecting that the information may be relevant to a criminal investigation.

Example: D, in his dealings with Bank (his own bank), gives Bank access to his checks, deposits, and financial statements. The federal government, acting without a warrant, subpoenas Bank's microfilm copies of these records, and uses the copies to prosecute D. D claims that the government's seizure of these records was a Fourth Amendment search, requiring probable cause and a search warrant.

Held, for the government. D had no reasonable expectation of privacy with respect to these documents. "The depositor takes the risk, in revealing his affairs to another, that the information will be conveyed by that person to the government." [*U.S. v. Miller* (1976)] [33]

B. **Modern digital databases and the third-party doctrine (*Carpenter v. U.S.*)** The key cases applying the third-party doctrine (including *Miller,* above) were decided in the 1970s, ***before*** the ***rise of smart phones, the Internet,*** and other technological advances that allow ***non-governmental third-parties to amass huge amounts of potentially-intimate data about a person.***

1. **Consequence:** During the decades since the 1970s, it became clear that if the third-party doctrine was applied broadly so as to encompass all privately-operated databases fed by these emerging communications technologies, the Fourth Amendment would be no barrier to a vast enlargement of government's surveillance powers.

2. ***Carpenter* changes the rules:** The Supreme Court responded to this danger by dramatically weakening the scope of the third-party doctrine in a major case, ***Carpenter v. U.S.*** (2018). [34] In *Carpenter*, a 5-4 decision, the Court decided that when private cellphone companies compile a digital database of ***"cell-site location information" ("CSLI"),*** the third-party doctrine should ***not*** apply.

a. **Nature of CSLI:** CSLI refers to information — typically held by phone companies — showing the ***location of a person's cell phone*** from moment to moment.

b. **Holding in *Carpenter*:** *Carpenter* held that because CSLI exposes far more private information than, say, the limited bank records in *Miller*, a person ***maintains a reasonable expectation of privacy*** in her own CSLI ***even though the information is held by a third-party.*** (See *supra*, C-5.)

c. **Consequence:** *Carpenter* means that when police officers request at least seven days' worth of a person's CSLI from a wireless carrier, the officers are ***conducting a Fourth Amendment search.*** This means that before the police may even request — let alone demand — this amount of CSLI from the carrier, the police must:

[1] ***demonstrate*** to a judge or magistrate ***probable cause*** to believe that the information sought will reveal evidence of crime or contraband (i.e., they must have probable cause for a search warrant); and

[2] ***obtain the search warrant.*** [35]

3. **The *Carpenter* multi-factor test:** *Carpenter* indicates that the following are the most important factors in determining whether a particular database of an individual's personal information is one as to which the individual has a reasonable expectation of privacy:

[1] whether the information is ***"deeply revealing"***;

[2] whether the information's ***"reach"*** is "***deep,"*** ***"broad,"*** and ***"comprehensive"***; and

[3] whether the ***process*** by which the information is collected is ***"inescapable and automatic."*** [37]

4. **Prior third-party case law not overruled:** *Carpenter* does not officially overturn the third-party doctrine as it existed prior to that case. However, it looks as though the doctrine will be confined to a ***small number*** of situations, those in which the third-party database does not consist of very revealing personal information.

Example: Suppose the police want to demand, from the bank at which X has an account, images of all checks X wrote during a particular time period. The third-party doctrine will probably still apply (exactly as it did in the 1970s-era case of *Miller*, *supra*), because this type of data does not contain hugely intimate details. Therefore, the police will not need a search warrant (or probable cause to believe that the checks will contain evidence of wrongdoing).

C. **Post-*Carpenter* case law:** The Supreme Court has not heard any cases interpreting *Carpenter* since that case was decided in 2018. However, lower courts have had occasion to decide whether *Carpenter* applies to various fact patterns. Here's an overview of some of the scenarios raised by *Carpenter*, and how some courts have decided (or might decide) the applicability of *Carpenter* to those scenarios.

1. **Length of CSLI surveillance period:** A key issue left unresolved in *Carpenter* is the ***maximum length of time CSLI surveillance can last*** before becoming a search that requires a warrant.

a. **Seven days or more:** ***If the surveillance continues for seven days or more***, *Carpenter* itself supplies the answer: that surveillance is ***sufficiently lengthy and intrusive*** that it

automatically constitutes a Fourth Amendment search for which a warrant is required. [39]

b. Less than seven days: But *Carpenter* does not decide whether ***shorter-than-seven-day*** surveillance periods will also be Fourth Amendment searches. A few lower courts have had to decide, post-*Carpenter,* whether obtaining CSLI data ***covering just a few hours*** constitute a search. The courts have ***split*** on this question. [000]

2. Real-time CSLI: The CSLI in *Carpenter* was ***"historical"*** data – the government was asking the wireless carriers to supply location data for a designated time ***in the past.*** But CSLI can also be tracked on a ***"real time"*** basis – that is, law enforcement can and does send a request to a carrier in the form: "Track the location of whatever cell phone is associated with the phone number (xxx) xxx-xxxx for one week starting tomorrow at noon." Is such a seven-days-or-more ***real-time*** (or ***"forward-looking")*** gathering of CSLI necessarily a Fourth Amendment search?

a. Affirmative answer: The answer is almost certainly "***yes.***" Therefore, when the police requisition a seven-day-or-more batch of real-time CSLI data, this seems almost certain to ***be a search.*** [39]

C A P S U L E S U M M A R Y

3. Pole camera surveillance of D's home: Another issue is whether *Carpenter* applies (i.e., whether the police commit a search) when officers install a ***"pole camera"*** to ***monitor the front door of a suspect's house***, in order to track comings and goings there. Typically, the camera is mounted on a ***pole or a tree, usually on public property.*** Since the camera is small and readily hidden, often the suspect does not ***realize*** she is being surveilled, even if the camera operates for multiple months. Here, as in the case of less-than-seven-day CSLI surveillance, courts have ***split*** about whether a lengthy observation by the pole camera constitutes a search. [40]

4. Automatic License Plate Readers: Many jurisdictions use ***Automated License Plate Readers (ALPRs)***, which ***take a picture of every license plate*** that passes by a fixed location on the roadway. Does the use of ALPRs to track the movements of D's vehicle constitute a search under *Carpenter*?

a. Not a search: At least one lower-court case has answered ***"no,"*** given the relatively non-intrusive nature of the ALPR data collection there.

Example: Police suspect that D has been transporting narcotics by car to a co-conspirator on Cape Cod. They know that for D to get there, he will have to cross over one of two bridges, each of which has an ALPR at each end. The police track, for ***2 ½ months***, the time, direction and even lane each time D crossed either bridge.

Held, the surveillance here was ***too limited to constitute a search.*** The police were not "monitor[ing] the ***whole*** of the defendant's public movements, or ***track[ing] enough*** of his comings and goings so as to reveal the ***privacies of life."*** Whatever the dividing line is between a search and a non-search, ***no search occurs*** where the data is "produced by ***4 cameras at fixed locations on the ends of two bridges."*** [*Commonwealth v. McCarthy* (Mass. 2020)] [41]

5. Tracking IP addresses: One common investigative technique is the ***tracking of Internet Protocol (IP) addresses.*** Any computer used to browse a website has an IP address, which is the equivalent of a phone number. Suppose the police learn that some unidentified person has committed a crime by accessing a particular Internet application (which we'll assume here is a messaging app) at a particular time. The authorities submit a subpoena to the operators of the messaging app, asking them to disclose which IP addresses were used (by anyone) to access the app during that period of time. That way, the user/criminal can be identified based on their IP address. Do the police commit a search under *Carpenter* when they ask the messaging-app operator to furnish such a list of incoming IP addresses?

a. **Court answers "no":** In the case described in the following Example, the court answered ***"no"*** on the facts there.

Example: The police (acting without a search warrant or probable cause) request from an application operator all IP addresses that accessed the application during a ***4-day window*** when the crime occurred. Based on this data, the police learn that the relevant address belongs to P, whom they arrest. P argues that the request to the app operator amounted to a search under *Carpenter,* for which a warrant was required.

Held, for the government: the ***degree of intrusiveness*** here was ***so much less*** than that in *Carpenter* that ***no search should be found to have occurred.*** For instance, IP addresses don't convey any ***location information,*** unlike the CSLI information in *Carpenter*. Therefore, the surveillance here ***did not pose the invasion-of-privacy concerns*** that the Supreme Court raised in *Carpenter*, and no warrant was needed. [*U.S. v. Hood* (1st Cir. 2019)] [42]

6. **Does not apply to the contents of emails:** There's one final category of electronic data as to which the rationale of *Carpenter* might conceivably (but probably *doesn't*) apply. That data consists of the actual ***contents*** of a person's ***emails or instant messages***, when maintained on a third party's computer (say, the server of an ISP who handled the message).

a. ***Carpenter*** **doesn't change this:** Emails are, if anything, more likely to be deeply revealing of intimate thoughts than the CSLI data at issue in *Carpenter*. So the Supreme Court would likely hold that the rationale of *Carpenter* dictates that the third-party doctrine ***not*** be applied to the contents of emails, text messages, or other electronic communications. [43]

i. **Consequence:** Therefore, a user who sends an email — even if she knows a copy is going to reside on some third-party computer system — should not be viewed as having thereby surrendered any expectation of privacy in the email's contents. So prosecutors will have to get a search warrant in order to obtain even a small number of emails from a third-party provider of email services.

IV. THE "PLAIN VIEW" DOCTRINE

A. **The plain view doctrine, generally:** In general, the police do not commit a Fourth Amendment search where they see an object that is in the ***plain view*** of an officer who has a ***right to be in the position to have that view***. This is the "plain view doctrine." [43]

Example: While Officer is walking down the street, he happens to glance through the picture window of D's house. He spots D strangling V to death with a stocking. Because D's conduct took place in "plain view" of Officer — that is, Officer perceived the conduct while being in a place where he was entitled to be — Officer can give testimony at D's trial about what he saw, with no Fourth Amendment problem. By contrast, if Officer had without a warrant secreted himself in D's house, then observed the murder, Officer would not be permitted to testify about what he saw, because the view would not have occurred from a place from where Officer had a right to be.

1. **Distinguish from seizure:** The fact that the police may have a plain view of an item does not mean that they may necessarily ***seize*** that item as evidence. Unless the officer is already legally in a place where he can touch the item, the fact that he sees it will not dispense with the need for a warrant to seize the item. (*Example:* On the facts of the above example, the fact that Officer has seen D strangle V with a stocking does not automatically entitle Officer to enter D's house without a warrant and to seize the stocking.) [43]

B. Use of mechanical devices, generally: The "plain view" doctrine will often apply where the police stand on public property, and use ***mechanical devices*** to obtain the view of D or his property. [44]

1. **Flashlights:** Thus if a police officer, standing on public property, uses a ***flashlight*** to obtain a view of D or his property, this will nonetheless be a "plain view" and will, therefore, not be a Fourth Amendment search. [*Texas v. Brown*]

2. **Electronic "beeper":** Similarly, the Court held in 1983 that police may attach a simple electronic ***"beeper"*** on a vehicle, and use the beeper to follow the vehicle along public roads — because any member of the public could see the driver's public movements, the tracking by beeper does not violate the driver's reasonable expectation of privacy, and thus does not constitute a Fourth Amendment search. [*U.S. v. Knotts*] [45]

   a. **More modern tracking technology:** But suppose the police in a post-*Carpenter* era — say in 2020 or later — use a modern-era ***location-tracking device*** such as a ***"cell site simulator"***[1] that enables them to track, cheaply and easily, the movements of a cell phone over long periods of time. Such a device enables far ***deeper and longer surveillance*** than a police officer could perform by visual observation.

      i. **Consequence:** Therefore, it's likely that police use of the simulator device *will* be a Fourth Amendment search for which probable cause and a warrant are required. Thus the situation will need to be analyzed not by the easy-to-satisfy standard used to analyze the old-fashioned beeper in *Knotts* (no expectation of privacy because the person's movements are visible to any public observer), but by the "high-tech devices not in civilian use" standard applied in the "thermal imager" case of *Kyllo v. U.S.*, immediately *infra*, or even by use of the multi-factor test applied to CSLI in *Carpenter v. U.S.*, *supra*, p. C-10.

C. High-tech devices not in general public use: If government obtains special ***high-tech devices, not in general civilian use***, and employs them from public places to gain "views" that could ***not*** be had by the naked eye, the use of such devices will be ***considered a search***. [*Kyllo v. U.S.*] [46]

> **Example:** Drug agents think D is growing marijuana inside his house with the use of high-intensity heat lamps. They therefore obtain a "thermal imager" and point it at the outside of D's house from across the street. The device detects heat escaping from D's house, and shows the relative amounts of heat as black and white images. The images show that D's garage is much hotter than the rest of his house. The agents use this infor-

C A P S U L E S U M M A R Y

---

1. Such a simulator poses as a cell tower, and causes each cell phone in an area to transmit the phone's number and location to the simulator, where government can store and track the information.

mation to get a warrant to search D's house, and find marijuana being grown, as suspected, under lamps in his garage.

Held, the use of the imager here was a Fourth Amendment search, which was presumptively unreasonable without a warrant. Since the device was not in general civilian use, and enabled the agents to learn information about what was going on inside the house, its use does not fall within the plain view exception. [*Kyllo v. U.S.*]

D. Aerial observation: When the police use an ***aircraft*** to view D's property from the air, ***anything the police can see with the naked eye*** falls within the "plain view" doctrine (as long as the aircraft is in ***public***, ***navigable*** airspace). [*California v. Ciraolo*; *Florida v. Riley*] [49]

E. Use of other senses: Probably the same "plain view" rule applies to ***senses other than sight*** (e.g., touch, hearing, or smell).

1. **Smell:** For instance, if a police officer (or a dog being used by an officer) ***smells contraband*** while standing in a place where he has a right to be, no Fourth Amendment search has taken place.

   Example: While D's car is properly stopped for a routine traffic violation, a police officer escorts a trained dog to sniff around the exterior of the car to find narcotics. *Held*, the dog-sniffing was not a Fourth Amendment search or seizure, since the sniffing did not reveal (and could not have revealed) anything as to which the car's owner had a legitimate expectation of privacy. The sniff could only have revealed the presence of contraband, which no one has the right to possess, and as to which there is therefore no reasonable expectation of privacy. [*Illinois v. Caballes*] [51]

2. **Touch:** Similarly, there's probably a ***"plain touch"*** doctrine. For instance, if an officer is conducting a legal pat-down of a suspect under the "stop and frisk" doctrine (see below), and touches something that feels like contraband, the officer may probably seize it under a "plain touch" analog to the plain view doctrine. [50]

   a. **Police must have a right to touch:** But this "plain touch" doctrine applies only if the police have the ***right to do the touching in the first place*** (just as the "plain view" doctrine applies only where the police have the right in the first place to be in the position from which they get the view). [50]

      Example: A U.S. Border Guard gets on a bus (as he has a statutory right to do), then squeezes the luggage of every passenger that's located on the overhead storage rack. When he squeezes a soft suitcase owned by D, he feels a brick-like substance. That causes him to suspect illegal drugs, so he opens the suitcase and indeed finds narcotics. *Held*, for D: because the agent didn't have the right to squeeze D's luggage in the first place (the squeezing violated D's reasonable expectation of privacy), the agent wasn't entitled to act on the suspicions that he developed from the squeezing, and therefore didn't have probable cause to open the suitcase. [*Bond v. U.S.*]

F. Police on defendant's property: The plain view doctrine applies not only where the police obtain a view from public property, but also where they are ***lawfully on the owner's property***. [52]

Example: The police come to D's house to make a lawful arrest of him. Any observation they make while in the ordinary process of arresting him does not constitute a Fourth Amendment search. (But this does not allow the police to open closed containers or packages while they are making the arrest, or even move items to get a better view — this would not fall within the plain view doctrine, and would be a Fourth Amendment search.)

V. PROBABLE CAUSE GENERALLY

A. Where requirement of probable cause applies: The requirement of "probable cause" applies to two different situations: (1) before a judge or magistrate may issue a ***warrant*** for a search or arrest, she must be satisfied that probable cause to do so exists; and (2) before the police may make a ***warrantless*** search or arrest (permissible only in special circumstances described below), the officer must have probable cause for that search or arrest. [53-54]

1. **Source of requirement:** Only case (1) above — the requirement of probable cause prior to issuance of a warrant — is expressly covered in the Fourth Amendment. But the Supreme Court has, as a matter of constitutional interpretation, held that probable cause must exist before a warrantless search or arrest as well, to avoid giving the police an incentive to avoid seeking a warrant.

B. Requirement for probable cause: The meaning of the term "probable cause" is not exactly the same in the search context as in the arrest context.

1. **Probable cause to arrest:** For there to be probable cause to ***arrest*** a person it must be ***reasonably likely*** that:

   a. a ***violation of the law*** has been committed; and

   b. the ***person*** to be arrested ***committed*** the violation. [54]

2. **Probable cause to search:** For there to be probable cause to ***search*** particular premises, it must be reasonably likely that:

   a. the specific items to be searched for are ***connected*** with ***criminal*** activities; and

   b. these items will be ***found in the place to be searched***. [54]

3. **Less than 50-50 chance:** It appears that as long as the police have "particularized suspicion" regarding the existence of fact X, they need ***not*** reasonably believe that fact X exists ***more likely than not*** in order to have "probable cause" to believe it. For example, a ***1/3 chance*** of fact X apparently *can* constitute probable cause.

   Example: The police properly stop a car containing three occupants, and during a legal search find cocaine in the backseat. When none of the three makes any explanation, the officer arrests all three. One of the three, D (who was the front-seat passenger) confesses at the stationhouse to owning the cocaine; he then tries to have this admission suppressed as the fruit of an arrest made without probable cause. *Held*, even though D was only one of three occupants of the car, and he was no more likely than the other two to be the cocaine's owner, the police had probable cause to believe that he was the owner, and thus probable cause to arrest him. [*Maryland v. Pringle*] [56]

C. No admissibility limitation: Any trustworthy information may be considered in determining whether probable cause to search or arrest exists, ***even if the information would not be admissible at trial***. [54]

D. Only evidence heard by magistrate used: Probable cause for the issuance of a warrant must be judged only by reference to the ***facts presented to the magistrate*** who is to issue the warrant.

(Usually, information for a warrant will be in the form of a police officer's affidavit, not oral testimony.) [54]

> **Example:** Officer asks for a warrant to search Dwight's apartment for the fruits of a recent specified burglary. Officer's supporting affidavit does not mention to Magistrate the basis for Officer's belief that such fruits will be found there. Magistrate grants the warrant, the search takes place, fruits of the burglary are found, and Dwight is tried for the burglary. At Dwight's trial, Dwight probably can successfully move to have the fruits of the search excluded, because the Magistrate was not presented with specific facts that would have given Magistrate probable cause to believe that the fruits would be found at Dwight's premises.

1. **Perjured affidavit:** If D can show, by a preponderance of the evidence, that affidavits used to obtain the warrant contained ***perjury*** by the affiant, or a ***"reckless disregard for the truth"*** by the affiant, the warrant will be ***invalidated*** (assuming that the rest of the affidavit does not contain materials sufficient to constitute probable cause). [*Franks v. Delaware*] But D can't knock out the warrant merely because it contains ***inaccurate*** material; he must show actual perjury or reckless disregard of the truth by the affiant himself (not merely by the affiant's sources, such as informers). [55]

    a. **Honest police error:** So if the police make an ***honest error*** — they honestly and reasonably, but erroneously, believe certain information and use it in affidavits to get a warrant — the warrant will not be rendered invalid when the error later comes to light. [*Maryland v. Garrison*] [55]

VI. PARTICULAR INFORMATION ESTABLISHING PROBABLE CAUSE

A. **Information from informants:** When the information on which probable cause is based comes from ***informants*** who are themselves engaged in criminal activity, courts closely scrutinize the information. Whether the informant's information creates probable cause for a search or arrest is to be determined by the ***"totality of the circumstances."*** [*Illinois v. Gates*] [57]

1. **Two factors:** The magistrate should consider two factors in evaluating the informant's information: (1) whether the informant is a generally ***reliable witness***; and (2) whether facts are set forth showing the informant's ***"basis of knowledge,"*** that is, the particular means by which the informant came upon the information that he supplied to the police. [57-59]

    a. **Strong factor can buttress weak factor:** But a strong showing on one of these factors can make up for a weak showing on the other one. (*Example:* If a particular informant is known for being unusually reliable, his failure to set forth the basis of his knowledge in a particular case will not be a bar to a finding of probable cause based on his tip.) [58]

    b. **Prediction of future events:** Also, if later events help ***corroborate*** the informant's story, these events can be combined with the informant's story to establish probable cause, even though neither by itself would suffice. [58]

B. **Non-criminal sources:** Where the police procure information from ***non-criminal sources*** (e.g., ordinary citizens, victims of crime, etc.), the courts are more ***lenient*** concerning the information than where it comes from, say, informants who are themselves criminals. [60]

1. **Other police officers:** But where an officer making an affidavit for a warrant (or making a warrantless search or arrest) acts in response to statements made by ***other police officers***, probably the arrest or search is valid only if the ***maker*** of the original statement acted with probable cause.

   Example: The County Sheriff broadcasts a bulletin stating that D1 and D2 are wanted for breaking and entering. Officer, a city police officer, hears the bulletin, and without knowing anything else, arrests D1 and D2, who happen to live on his beat. Probably, probable cause for the arrest will be found only if the County Sheriff himself had probable cause to make the arrest.) [60]

2. **Trained sniffer dog as reliable informant:** A ***dog*** that is trained to ***sniff the odor*** of drugs or other contraband, and to alert his handlers to the contraband, can be the source of probable cause. The ***reliability*** of the dog as an "informant" is to be determined by the same ***"totality of the circumstances"*** rule that applies to humans under *Gates*, *supra*. This standard means that if the dog has satisfactorily performed in an odor-detection ***training course***, that fact alone will typically allow the dog's "I smell drugs here" alert to constitute probable cause. [*Florida v. Harris*] [61]

VII. SEARCH WARRANTS — ISSUANCE AND EXECUTION

A. **Who may issue:** A search warrant must be issued by some sort of ***judicial officer***, usually either a judge or a magistrate. (We'll use the term "magistrate" here.)

   1. **Neutrality:** The magistrate must be a ***neutral party***, detached from the law-enforcement side of government. [62]

B. **Affidavit:** Normally, the police officer seeking a search warrant must put the facts establishing probable cause into a ***written, signed affidavit***. [63]

C. ***Ex parte*** **nature of warrant:** The proceeding for issuing a warrant is ***ex parte***. That is, the suspect whose premises are to be searched ***does not have the opportunity to contest the issuance of the warrant***; only the police officer's side of the story is heard by the magistrate. (However, the suspect, if he becomes a criminal defendant, will eventually have a chance to show, at a suppression hearing, that the warrant was issued without probable cause.) [63]

D. **Requirement of particular description:** The Fourth Amendment requires that a warrant contain a ***particular description of the premises to be searched, and the things to be seized***. This means that the warrant must be specific enough that a police officer executing it, even if she had no initial connection with the case, would know where to search and what items to seize. [63-65]

   1. **Description of place:** The description of the ***place*** to be searched must be precise enough that the officer executing the warrant can figure out where to search. For instance, if the search is to be in an apartment building, the warrant must probably contain the name of the occupant, or the number of the particular apartment, not merely the address of the entire building. [63]

   2. **Things to be seized:** The ***things to be seized*** must also be specifically identified in the warrant. [64]

      a. **Not such a strict requirement:** However, this requirement is not very strictly interpreted today. (*Example:* The warrant refers to a particular alleged crime of selling real estate by false pretenses. The warrant then authorizes a search for various types of documents, "together with other fruits, instrumentalities and evidence of [this particular] crime" but does not specify anything about these other fruits or instrumentalities. *Held*, the warrant is not fatally vague. [*Andresen v. Maryland*]) [64]

b. Contraband: ***Contraband*** (property the possession of which is a crime, such as illegal drugs or outlawed firearms) does not have to be described as particularly as material that is innocuous on its face — the officer executing the search is presumed to be able to identify contraband by its very nature. [64]

E. What may be seized: Any item that is the subject of a valid search warrant may be ***seized*** by the police executing the warrant. [65]

1. Incriminating evidence: In particular, this rule means that even items whose only interest to the police is that they ***incriminate*** the defendant may be seized. [*Warden v. Hayden*] [65-66]

2. No Fifth Amendment interest: Even items, such as documents, that contain ***incriminating statements*** made by the defendant may be seized — this does not violate the defendant's Fifth Amendment privilege against self-incrimination. (*Example:* Police, executing a valid warrant, seize business records from D's office. These records contain incriminating statements made by D. *Held*, seizure of these records did not violate the Fifth Amendment, even though it might have been a violation of D's Fifth Amendment rights to have required him to produce these records under a subpoena. [*Andresen v. Maryland*]) [66]

F. Warrants against non-suspects: The Fourth Amendment permits searches to be made of the premises of persons who are ***not criminal suspects***, if there is probable cause to believe that the search will produce evidence of someone else's crime. [66]

1. Subpoena not necessary: Such a search of a non-suspect's premises may be made ***even if a subpoena would be equally effective***. [*Zurcher v. The Stanford Daily*] [66]

G. Execution of warrants: The Fourth Amendment requires that the ***procedures*** which the police use in carrying out a search not be ***"unreasonable."*** Thus in general, the police may not behave in an unduly intrusive manner. [67]

1. Entry without notice: As a general rule, the officer executing the warrant must knock on the door and ***announce*** that he is a law enforcement officer, that he possesses a warrant, and that he is there to execute it. Thus usually, the police may not forcibly break into the premises to be searched unless they have first announced their presence and waited a reasonable time for a response. This is known as the ***"knock and announce"*** requirement. [67]

a. Preventing the destruction of evidence: However, the Supreme Court has recognized at least one exception: Officers may constitutionally enter without first identifying themselves if the circumstances pose a threat of ***immediate destruction of evidence***. (*Example:* D is a narcotics suspect, believed to be carrying a small amount of narcotics. He eludes police shortly before they come to arrest him at his house. *Held*, the officers' suspicion that D would probably destroy the narcotics by, for instance, flushing them down the toilet, justified the police in breaking into the house without first identifying themselves or ringing the doorbell. [*Ker v. California*]) [68]

b. Physical danger to police: Similarly, lower courts have held that the possibility of ***physical danger to the police*** sometimes justifies unannounced entry. (*Example:* The police have reason to think that D has a gun, and won't be "taken alive." They can probably break in without first knocking or announcing themselves.) [68]

2. **Where no response or entry refused:** If the officer identifies himself, and is then refused entry (or gets no response), he may use ***force*** to break into the premises. [69]

   a. **Need not wait for answer:** Similarly, if the officer identifies himself but there's a risk of ***immediate destruction of evidence,*** the officer may break in ***without giving the occupant enough time to get to the door.***

3. **Search of persons on premises:** Assuming that the police have only a search warrant, and not an arrest warrant (or probable cause to arrest anyone), the police may ***not*** automatically search everyone found on the premises. [70]

   a. **Named items on person:** If the police have probable cause to believe that an individual has ***on his person*** items that are named in the search warrant, they may search him.

   b. **Person attempting to leave:** Similarly, if a person attempts to ***leave*** during a premises search, and the items being sought are of a type which might be easily carried away, the police may probably temporarily detain the person to make sure he is not carrying the items away. [70]

   c. **Persons unrelated to search:** But where a person simply happens to be on the premises to be searched, and appears not to have any connection with the criminal activity giving rise to the search warrant or with items mentioned in the warrant, that person may not be searched or detained. [*Ybarra v. Illinois*] [70]

4. **Restricted area of search:** In executing a search pursuant to a warrant, the police must confine their search to the ***area specified*** in the warrant, and they must look only in those places where the items sought might possibly be concealed. (*Example:* If the police are looking for a full-size rifle, they may not look into drawers that are too small to contain such a rifle.) [70]

5. **Seizure of unnamed items in "plain view":** If the police are properly conducting a search, and come across items that are ***not listed in the warrant*** (but that appear relevant to a crime), the police may generally ***seize*** the unlisted items. This right is an aspect of the ***"plain view"*** doctrine. [71-71]

   a. **Incriminating evidence:** The evidence must be sufficiently connected with criminal activity that a warrant could have been procured for it.

      i. **Unrelated items:** The items discovered in plain view don't have to relate to the same criminal activity that gave rise to the warrant, as long as there is probable cause for the seizure of these new items. (*Example:* If the police are executing a warrant naming stolen property and they come upon illegal narcotics, they may seize the narcotics even though they have nothing to do with the stolen property charge.)

   b. **Inadvertence not required:** It is ***not*** required, for application of the plain view doctrine, that the police's discovery of an item in plain view be ***"inadvertent."*** [*Horton v. California*] (*Example:* When police apply for a warrant to search D's home in connection with a robbery, they have a description of the weapons used. But they get a warrant authorizing the search only for robbery proceeds. While executing the warrant, they come across the weapons. *Held,* the police could constitutionally seize the weapons under the plain view doctrine, even though the discovery of the weapons was not "inadvertent." [*Horton, supra*]) [71]

6. **Bodily intrusions:** A search warrant can be issued for search of a ***person***, rather than a place. Such a bodily search (whether done pursuant to a search warrant or not) must of course

be "reasonable." In general, courts measure reasonableness by weighing the individual's interest in privacy against society's interest in conducting the search. [72-73]

a. **Allowable procedures:** Thus the forcible ***taking of blood*** from a drunk-driving suspect, and the use of x-rays to obtain evidence that D is concealing drugs in his stomach, have been held to be "reasonable" and therefore allowable.

b. **Surgery:** On the other hand, it is ***not*** reasonable to place D under a general anesthetic and to remove a bullet lodged deep in his chest, in order to show that D was involved in a particular robbery. [*Winston v. Lee*]

H. **"Good faith" exception:** Normally, if a search warrant is ***invalid*** (e.g., it is not supported by probable cause), any search done pursuant to it will be unconstitutional, and the evidence will be excluded at trial. However, if the police ***reasonably (but erroneously) believe*** that the warrant which they have been issued is valid, the exclusionary rule will ***not apply***. (See *U.S. v. Leon*, discussed in the treatment of the exclusionary rule below.) [73]

CHAPTER 3

WARRANTLESS ARRESTS AND SEARCHES

I. INTRODUCTION

A. **Warrant not always required:** The Fourth Amendment mentions warrants specifically, but does not actually ***require*** warrants — the amendment merely says that "no warrants shall issue, but upon probable cause, supported by Oath or affirmation, and particularly describing the place to be searched, and the persons or things to be seized." So going by the literal text of this amendment, a warrant might ***never*** be constitutionally required.

1. **Judicial interpretations sometimes requires:** But the Supreme Court has ***interpreted*** the Fourth Amendment to sometimes require a warrant. In very general terms, the rules for when a warrant is required may be summarized as follows:

a. **Arrest warrants:** An ***arrest*** warrant will ***rarely*** be required. Only when the police need to ***enter a private home*** to make the arrest, and there are ***no exigent circumstances***, does the Fourth Amendment require the police to procure an arrest warrant before they make the arrest. [93]

b. **Search warrant:** But just the converse is true in the case of a ***search***: the ***general rule*** is that a warrant is ***required***. Only if some special exception applies will the requirement of a search warrant be dispensed with. Some of the more common exceptions are:

i. A search ***incident to a valid arrest***;

ii. A search motivated by ***exigent circumstances*** (e.g., to avoid destruction of evidence);

iii. Certain types of ***automobile*** searches (e.g., a search of a car when the driver is arrested and both driver and car are taken to the police station);

iv. Searches done after the person to be searched or the owner of the property to be searched ***consents***;

v. Partial searches done pursuant to the ***"stop and frisk"*** doctrine; and

vi. Certain ***inspections*** and ***regulatory searches*** (e.g., immigration searches at U.S. borders, sobriety checkpoints on highways, etc.).

Note: The fact that in a particular situation no search warrant is required does ***not*** necessarily mean that ***probable cause*** is not required. In some but not all of the above listed situations (e.g., exigent circumstances), the police must have probable cause to believe that a search will furnish evidence of crime, even though they are not required to get a warrant. In others of the above situations, something less than probable cause, and perhaps no real suspicion at all, will be needed. (*Example*: Less than probable cause, but some suspicion, is required for "stop and frisk," whereas no suspicion is required for a consent search.)

II. WARRANTLESS ARRESTS

A. **Not generally required:** An ***arrest*** warrant is ***not*** generally required by the Constitution. This is true even where the police have sufficient advance notice that procurement of a warrant would not jeopardize the arrest. [*U.S. v. Watson*] [94]

B. **Entry of dwelling:** The only situation in which an arrest warrant *is* likely to be constitutionally required is where the police wish to enter ***private premises*** to arrest a suspect. In that instance, the requirement for a warrant will depend on whether exigent circumstances exist. [94]

1. **No exigent circumstances:** If there are no exigent circumstances, the police ***may not enter a private home*** to make a warrantless arrest. [*Payton v. New York*] [94]

   a. **Result of invalid arrest:** A warrantless arrest made in violation of *Payton* will not prevent D from being brought to trial (since he can always be re-arrested after a warrant has been issued). However, if the police make an in-house arrest that required a warrant because there were no exigent circumstances, then any evidence seized as a result of a ***search*** incident to the arrest will be excluded.

2. **Exigent circumstances:** If there ***are*** exigent circumstances, so that it is impractical for the police to delay the entry and arrest until they can obtain an arrest warrant, no warrant is necessary (at least if the crime is a serious one, such as a felony — as to minor crimes, see *Atwater*, below). [95]

   a. **Destruction of evidence:** For instance, if the police reasonably believe that the suspect will ***destroy evidence*** if they delay their entry until they can get a warrant, the requisite exigent circumstances exist.

   b. **Hot pursuit:** Similarly, if the police are pursuing a felony suspect, and he runs into his own or another's dwelling, a warrantless entry and arrest may be permitted under the "hot pursuit" doctrine.

C. **No exception for fine-only or other minor crimes:** A warrantless arrest for a crime committed in an officer's presence is permissible even where the crime is ***so minor*** that the only potential punishment is a ***fine*** rather than imprisonment. (This assumes that the arrest is not made inside a private dwelling, the situation discussed above.) [95]

Example: Officer stops D, a driver, for not wearing a seat belt. This offense is punishable under state law only by a $25 fine, not imprisonment. Officer decides to arrest D, handcuffs her in front of her young children (who are in the car with her), books her in the station house, and causes her to be held in a cell until she can post bail.

Held, Officer's arrest of D without a warrant was not "unreasonable," and thus not a violation of the Fourth Amendment. As long as an officer has reasonable cause to believe that an offense has been committed in his presence, he may make an arrest no matter how minor the offense is, and regardless of the fact that only a fine rather than imprisonment is the maximum punishment for it. [*Atwater v. Lago Vista*]

D. Probable cause need not be for offense stated at time of arrest: Suppose that at the time of the warrantless arrest the officer specifies to the suspect that the arrest is being made for ***Offense A***; if it finally turns out that there was not probable cause for Offense *A*, but that there *was* probable cause for ***Offense B*** (never mentioned by the arresting officer), there is no problem for the police: Even if Offense *B* is ***not closely related*** to Offense *A*, the arrest is still ***valid***. [*Devenpeck v. Alford*] [97-97]

1. **Significance:** This rule is of special significance when the police conduct a ***search incident to the warrantless arrest*** (see *infra*, p. C-23). Even if there's no probable cause for the offense on which the police purport to make the arrest, as long as it turns out that there was *some* offense as to which the police knew facts amounting to probable cause, the search incident to the arrest will be valid even though the police never mention (or even think about) that offense at the time of the arrest.

E. Statutory requirements: In addition to the constitutional requirements regarding arrest warrants described above, many states impose some ***statutory*** requirements concerning such warrants. (*Example:* Many states allow an officer to make a warrantless misdemeanor arrest only if the misdemeanor was committed in the officer's presence.) [97]

F. Use of deadly force to make arrest: The Fourth Amendment also places limits on ***how*** an arrest may be made. The main rule is that the police may ***not*** use ***deadly force*** to make an arrest, if the suspect poses ***no immediate threat*** to the officer and no threat to others. [*Tennessee v. Garner*] [98]

1. **No need to abandon chase:** On the other hand, if the suspect *does* pose a serious threat to the police or to others, the police may use deadly force to stop or arrest him. And they may do so instead of reducing the threat by abandoning the chase. [*Scott v. Harris*] [98]

CAPSULE SUMMARY

III. SEARCH INCIDENT TO ARREST

A. Search incident to arrest generally allowed: In general, when the police are making a lawful arrest, they may ***search*** the area within the arrestee's ***control***. This is known as a ***"search incident to arrest."*** Search-incident-to-arrest is the most important exception to the general rule that a search warrant is required before a search takes place. [99]

> **Example:** Officer watches D run out of a coin shop at night, while the shop's alarm is ringing. Assuming that these facts give Officer probable cause to arrest D (which they almost certainly do), Officer may conduct a fairly full search of D's person after the arrest. For instance, Officer can require D to empty his pockets to show that there are no weapons, contraband, or stolen property from the coin shop on his person. If on these facts Officer had arrested D while D was driving a car, Officer would also be permitted, under the search-incident-to-arrest doctrine, to search the passenger compartment of the car for weapons, contraband, etc.

1. **Limited area around defendant:** Only the area that is at least theoretically within D's ***immediate control*** may be searched incident to arrest. (The basic idea is that only the area

that D might get to in order to destroy evidence or gain possession of a weapon may be searched.)

Example: Officers come to arrest D at his house for a recent robbery. They have an arrest warrant but no search warrant. After arresting D, the police conduct a full-scale search of D's three-bedroom house. They discover some of the stolen property in one of the bedrooms, not the room in which they arrested D. *Held*, the property may not be admitted against D because it was found pursuant to a search that was unnecessarily widespread. Only the area within D's immediate control could be searched incident to the arrest. [*Chimel v. California*] [99-100]

B. Protective sweep: The Supreme Court also upholds ***"protective sweeps"*** under the search-incident-to-arrest doctrine. That is, where the arrest takes place in the suspect's ***home***, the officers may conduct a protective sweep of ***all or part of the premises***, if they have a "reasonable belief" based on "specific and articulable facts" that ***another person*** who might be dangerous to the officer may be present in the areas to be swept. [*Maryland v. Buie*] [105]

1. **Adjoining spaces:** But "specific and articulable facts" are ***not*** needed for the officers to search in ***closets*** and other spaces ***immediately adjoining*** the place of an arrest, to make sure that no possible attacker lurks there.

C. Automobile searches incident to arrest: The basic rule that a warrantless search incident to arrest must be limited to areas within the arrestee's "immediate control" applies to ***searches of vehicles*** after the arrest of the driver. So in most driver arrests for ***traffic violations***, the police will ***not*** be entitled to ***search the passenger compartment*** incident to the arrest. [*Arizona v. Gant*] [101]

1. **Two-part rule:** More precisely, the search-incident-to-arrest rationale allows a warrantless search of the passenger compartment ***only*** if ***one of two things*** is true:

   [1] the arrestee has ***access to the passenger compartment*** at the moment of the search (which will virtually never be the case if the standard police practice of placing the driver ***securely in a patrol car*** is followed prior to the search); *or*

   [2] the police reasonably believe that the passenger compartment might contain ***evidence of the offense for which the arrest is being made.***

   [*Gant, supra*] [101]

2. **Traffic arrest where driver is handcuffed:** In the most common driver-arrest scenario — the police make an arrest for a ***traffic violation***, handcuff the driver and put him in the patrol car, and then find evidence of some other crime when they search the passenger compartment — *Gant* means that the search ***cannot be justified by the incident-to-arrest doctrine.*** [101]

   Example: The police reasonably (and correctly, as it turns out) believe that D's driver's license has been suspended and that there is an outstanding warrant for his arrest for driving with a suspended license. They wait for D at his residence and, when he drives into the driveway, arrest him on the warrant. They then handcuff him, lock him in the back seat of the patrol car, and search the passenger compartment of his car. There, they find cocaine in the pocket of a jacket on the back seat.

   Held, for D: the search of the passenger compartment was not a proper search incident to arrest because by the time of the search, the compartment was not even theoretically within D's immediate control, as is required for a search incident to arrest. [*Gant, supra*]

a. **Search for evidence of offense that led to arrest:** But even if the driver has been secured so that he has no possible access to the passenger compartment, rationale [2] of *Gant* (see immediately *supra*) may apply: if the police "reasonably believe" that the passenger compartment might contain ***evidence of the offense for which the arrest is being made, they may search that compartment.*** This rationale will almost never apply to a traffic arrest, but will often apply to arrests on outstanding warrants for, say, ***drug offenses***. [103]

Example: The police learn that a warrant has been issued for the arrest of D on charges of smuggling heroin from Mexico into Arizona in his black Ford Explorer with license plate "XYZ123." Officer Brown, while patrolling in Arizona near the Mexican border, spots a black Explorer with that plate. He pulls the vehicle over, sees that D is the driver, arrests D on the warrant, and handcuffs him to the inside of the patrol car. Brown then conducts a search of the passenger compartment, and finds heroin in the glove compartment.

The search will likely be *valid* under the "search for evidence of the offense for which the arrest is being made" rationale. Even if Brown didn't have "probable cause" to believe that the vehicle was currently being used to smuggle drugs, the fact that D was driving that vehicle in Arizona near the Mexican border probably gave Brown "reason to believe" that the vehicle "might" contain evidence relevant to the drug-smuggling charges. ("Reason to believe" that evidence "might" be found is clearly a much-easier-to-satisfy standard than "probable cause" to believe such evidence "will" be found, the usual standard for a proper search.) If the court agrees that Brown had such "reason to believe," then the search of the vehicle for evidence relating to the "offense of arrest" (the drug smuggling) will be valid as a special form of search incident to arrest. [Cf. *Gant*]

3. **Other opportunities for vehicle search:** Keep in mind that in passenger-compartment search cases, *Gant only* wipes out the search-incident-to-arrest doctrine, not ***other long-established doctrines*** that may independently permit a warrantless search of the compartment.

a. **Driver possibly dangerous:** For instance, suppose the police have stopped the car, asked the driver to exit, and are interrogating him, but have ***not arrested*** him. If the police reasonably conclude that the driver may be ***dangerous and might gain access to a weapon*** inside the car once he's permitted to return to the car post-interrogation, under a form of the ***stop-and-frisk*** doctrine, the police may conduct a ***brief protective search of the passenger compartment*** for weapons. Then, if they find some contraband item (e.g., drugs), they can seize the item. This scenario does not rely on the search-incident-to-arrest doctrine, and is therefore not affected by the new rule of *Arizona v. Gant*. [See *Michigan v. Long*, *infra*, p. C-43.]

b. **Probable cause to search:** Similarly, when the police properly stop a car, then whether they make an arrest of the driver or not, if they have ***probable cause*** to believe that the vehicle contains ***contraband or evidence of crime***, they can search ***any part*** of the vehicle where the evidence ***might plausibly be found.*** [*U.S. v. Ross, infra,* p. C-33.] Again, this exception to the warrant requirement does not depend on the search-incident-to-arrest doctrine, and is therefore unaffected by *Gant*. And this exception applies even though the stop (and/or the arrest) is ***not for the same crime*** to which the probable-cause-for-search relates.

D. Contemporaneity of search: For the search to be incident to arrest, it need ***not*** be exactly ***contemporaneous*** with the arrest — a search that takes place some time before, or sometime after, the arrest, will still be held "incident" to that arrest as long as it is closely connected to it logically speaking. [106-107]

1. **Search prior to arrest:** Thus the police may make a search before they arrest D, as long as they already have probable cause to make the arrest and are doing the search in order to protect themselves. Generally, the arrest must follow quite quickly on the heels of the protective search. [*Rawlings v. Kentucky*] [106]

2. **Search long after arrest:** Similarly, the search-incident-to-arrest exception is applicable even to searches that do not occur until sometime ***after*** the arrest, at least where the search is made of objects in the suspect's possession at the time of arrest. [107]

   a. **Search of person:** Most commonly, the police may arrest D, take control of the objects in D's possession at the time of the arrest, and examine those objects at a later time.

E. Legality of arrest: The search-incident-to-arrest exception to the search warrant requirement applies only where the arrest is ***legal***. Thus if the arrest turns out to have been made without probable cause, the search incident to it cannot be justified on the search-incident-to-arrest rationale, and the arrest must be suppressed unless some other exception to the warrant requirement (e.g., prevention of destruction of evidence) justifies it. [108]

F. Applicable even to minor crimes: The search-incident-to-arrest exception seems to apply to arrests even for ***minor*** crimes. For instance, if D is arrested for a ***traffic violation***, he may be searched incident to the arrest even though the crime is not an especially "serious" one. [*U.S. v. Robinson*] [108]

1. **Must be custodial arrest:** However, for the search-incident-to-arrest doctrine to apply, the arrest must be a ***"custodial"*** one. That is, the officer must be planning to take D to the stationhouse for booking. (*Example:* Suppose that Officer stops D, a driver, for driving with an expired registration sticker. Suppose further that this is a misdemeanor, and that under local police department procedures, a driver stopped for such an offense is virtually never arrested, but is instead given a summons to be answered at a later date. On these facts, D is not really being "arrested," and his body, or his car, may not be searched incident to arrest.) [109]

   a. **D may be required to step out of car:** However, even in the case of such a non-custodial stop, D may be required to ***step out of the car***. Once he has stepped out of the car, presumably he may be subjected to at least a cursory frisk under the stop-and-frisk doctrine, discussed below. [109]

G. Search of items carried on person of arrestee: When a search is properly made incident to a lawful arrest, the police may examine ***items of personal property found on the person of the arrestee.*** [109]

1. **Items that are not suspected of being weapons or evidence:** Furthermore, this right to examine items found on the arrestee's person is ***not limited*** to items that the officer reasonably fears may be ***weapons*** or may constitute ***evidence of crime*** — putting aside the issue of digital devices (discussed below), the Supreme Court's incident-to-arrest cases indicate that *any* physical item found on the arrestee's person (or within his immediate control) can be searched.

Example: A police officer properly makes a traffic-related arrest of D. The officer pats D down, feels a soft package in his pocket, removes the package, and discovers that it is a crumpled cigarette package containing what turns out to be heroin. The officer concedes that when he patted D down, he had no reason to fear that the crumpled package he was feeling might be a weapon or might constitute evidence of crime.

Held (by the Supreme Court), the package containing the heroin was properly searched and seized incident to D's lawful arrest. It's true that the need to protect arresting officers from weapons, and helping them prevent destruction of evidence being carried by the arrestee, were the reasons for which the incident-to-arrest doctrine was originally adopted. The arresting officer's right to search for and examine items on the arrestee's person does not depend on what a court may later decide was the probability that in the particular arrest situation at issue now, ***weapons or evidence would in fact be found*** on the arrestee's person or within his control. [*U.S. v. Robinson*] [110]

a. **Purses, contents of pockets:** Lower courts interpreting *Robinson* have reasoned that the right of search incident to arrest covers ***any items found on or in the control of the arrested person,*** such as ***purses, billfolds, address books,*** and anything ***found in the arrestee's pockets.***

2. **Cellphones and their digital contents:** But the Court has held (unanimously) that when the police properly make a custodial arrest of a person who happens to be carrying a ***cell phone***, the incident-to-arrest doctrine does ***not*** permit the police to perform a ***warrantless search of the digital contents of the phone.*** [***Riley v. California*** (2014)] [110]

a. **Rationale:** The Court in *Riley* reasoned that "modern cell phones, as a category, ***implicate privacy concerns far beyond*** those implicated by the search of a cigarette pack, a wallet, or a purse." For instance, the Court said, "the ***sum of an individual's private life can be reconstructed*** through a ***thousand photographs*** labeled with dates, locations, and descriptions [on a cell phone]; the same cannot be said of a photograph or two of loved ones tucked into a wallet."

b. **Warrant now required before search:** Here's the rule set out in *Riley* that now governs searches of data on cell phones found incident to arrest: "Our answer to the question of ***what police must do before searching a cell phone seized incident to an arrest*** is . . . ***simple — get a warrant."***

i. **Illustration from *Riley*:** *Riley* was based on two separate cases that were consolidated before the Supreme Court. The following Example shows the facts of one of those cases, and illustrates how the Court's rule disallowing cellphone data searches incident to arrest limits the way the police may proceed.

Example: Police see D make a drug sale from a car, arrest him, and seize a "flip phone" (a phone with fewer features than a smart phone) from his person. At the station house, the police notice that the phone is ringing with calls from a source listed on the phone's display as "my house." The police access the call log to find the phone number associated with "my house." They then use an online phone directory to trace that phone number to an address at an apartment building. At that building, the police see D's name on a mailbox, obtain a search warrant for the apartment, and while executing the warrant find narcotics that become the basis for prosecuting D.

Held, the police violated D's Fourth Amendment rights when, without first getting a search warrant, they retrieved data from the phone, including accessing the call log. Therefore, D's conviction is reversed as deriving from unconstitutionally-obtained evidence. [*Riley v. California*] [110-114]

c. **Broad reading likely:** It seems fair to read *Riley* as holding that whenever ***any*** modern device containing ***significant amounts of digital data*** is found on or near an arrestee, the police may not search (i.e., read or examine) the digital data without first getting a search warrant. Presumably this logic applies not only to small handheld digital devices, but even to somewhat ***larger*** ones — ***tablets and laptops,*** for instance — found on or near the arrestee. [114]

H. **Breath and blood tests incident to arrest:** Suppose the police arrest a ***driver*** based on probable cause to suspect ***drunk driving***; can the police then rely on the search-incident-to-arrest doctrine to perform a warrantless test of the driver's ***breath*** or ***blood*** in order to confirm the driver's blood alcohol content (***"BAC"***)? As the result of a trio of 2016 cases decided under the name ***Birchfield v. North Dakota***, a warrantless test of the driver's ***breath*** is ***permissible***, but such a test of the driver's ***blood*** is ***not***. [115]

1. **Breath test:** *Birchfield* establishes that when the police make a *legal* drunk-driving arrest (i.e., when they have probable cause to believe that D was driving while drunk), they may ***conduct a breath test (a "breathalyzer") without first getting a search warrant.*** Furthermore, the states may make it a ***crime*** for the driver to ***refuse to consent to a breathalyzer*** after his legal arrest for drunk driving. [118]

2. **No warrantless blood tests:** But now, suppose the driver refuses to consent to the warrantless breath test (making him vulnerable to a criminal conviction for doing so); that refusal does ***not entitle*** the police to take him to the hospital and forcibly subject him to a ***blood test.*** The police ***must get a search warrant*** before doing this (assuming there are no exigent circumstances at play). [*Birchfield, supra*]

   a. **Blood test of unconscious suspect:** What happens if the driver is ***unconscious***, so that it's not possible for the police to use a breathalyzer test in the field. In this special situation, the Court has held that exigent circumstances for a warrantless BAC blood test will ***almost always be found to exist.*** [*Mitchell v. Wisconsin*] [121]

      i. **Result in *Mitchell*:** In *Mitchell*, the Court reasoned that if the driver is unconscious, he will normally be ***taken to an emergency room*** where his ***blood would be drawn for diagnostic purposes anyway,*** even if the police were not seeking BAC information. Therefore, Court said, allowing a warrantless BAC ***does not increase the invasion of the driver's privacy.*** [121]

IV. EXIGENT CIRCUMSTANCES

A. **Exigent circumstances generally:** Even where the search-incident-to-arrest exception to the search warrant requirement does not apply, there may be ***exigent circumstances*** that justify dispensing with the warrant requirement. The most common exigent circumstances are: (1) preventing the imminent ***destruction of evidence***; (2) preventing ***harm to persons***; and (3) searching in ***"hot pursuit"*** for a suspect. [120-126]

B. Destruction of evidence: The police may conduct a search or seizure without a warrant, provided that they have probable cause, and provided that the search or seizure is necessary to prevent the possible ***imminent destruction of evidence***. [123]

1. **Blood alcohol concentration (BAC) test:** One scenario that often calls for use of the "exigent circumstances" rationale for a warrantless search is where the police have probable cause to believe that a person (call him D) has been driving drunk, but there is a risk that D's ***blood-alcohol concentration*** or ***BAC*** (see *supra*, p. C-28, Par. H) ***will drop*** significantly before the police can get a warrant authorizing them to ***seize a blood sample***. If it's indeed the case that getting a warrant will delay the BAC breath test to the point where the results will likely be unusable, the police may proceed without a warrant. [*Schmerber v. California*] [120-121]

   a. **Not a categorical rule:** But the Supreme Court has ***refused*** government requests to establish a ***categorical*** (automatic) rule that the risk of destruction of BAC evidence necessarily allows the police to take a driver's blood sample without a warrant if they have probable cause to suspect him of drunk driving. (The Court's main rationale is that BAC dissipates over time in a ***predictable way***, so the passage of a certain amount of time while a warrant is obtained will not prevent prosecutors from using even the results of a delayed test to establish the suspect's BAC as of an earlier pre-test moment.) [*Missouri v. McNeely*] [121]

      i. **Result:** So in drunk-driving cases and any other case where a suspect's BAC is at issue, the police may not use the destruction-of-evidence rationale to avoid getting a warrant unless they can show that taking the time to get a warrant would likely have significantly ***undermined the value*** of the eventual BAC test.

      ii. **Breath test distinguished:** But keep in mind that the police ***never need*** a warrant to require a driver whom they properly arrest for drunk-driving to take a roadside ***breath*** test. Therefore, the presence or absence of exigent circumstances won't even matter if that's the only sort of test the arresting officer wants to perform; see *Birchfield v. No. Dakota, supra*, p. C- 28. [116]

2. **Easily-destroyed contraband:** Another common "destruction of evidence" scenario occurs when the police have probable cause to believe that particular ***premises contain contraband or evidence of crime***, but fear that if they leave the premises unguarded while obtaining a search warrant, an occupant will destroy the evidence before the warrant can be obtained. Most commonly, the police have reasonable cause to believe that there are ***narcotics*** in the premises, and wish to search for and seize the drugs before they can be destroyed (e.g., ***flushed down the toilet***) or moved to another location.

   a. **Sealing off premises:** Often, the police can and should deal with this disposal-of-evidence problem by ***sealing off the premises*** (a "seizure" under the Fourth Amendment) until a search warrant can be obtained. That is, the police can ***require the occupants to leave the premises*** (or remain under police observation); police officers are then ***posted outside the premises*** to make sure that no one else enters for the purpose of destroying the evidence. Once a search warrant for the premises has been obtained, the police conduct the search.

      i. **Generally successful:** This warrantless and searchless "seizure to preserve evidence" will generally ***comply*** with the Fourth Amendment, as long as the police have a reasonable belief that without a seizure of the premises, the occupants will learn of the danger and destroy the evidence before the police can get a search warrant. [*Illinois v. McArthur*] [122]

3. **The "police-created exigency" exception:** Courts recognize an "exception to the exception" in this destruction-of-evidence scenario: the ***"police-created exigency"*** doctrine. Under this doctrine, if the police's own conduct ***"created"*** or ***"manufactured"*** the exigency (the threat of evidence-destruction), then the main evidence-destruction exception to the warrant requirement will not apply, and the police will need to get a warrant before they conduct a search. [122]

   a. **Narrowly interpreted:** But the police-created-exigency doctrine is narrowly interpreted; it will nullify the police's right to enter warrantlessly only when the police "gain entry to premises by means of an ***actual or threatened violation of the Fourth Amendment.***" [*Kentucky v. King*] [122]

      Example: The police are chasing X, a drug suspect. They know he went into an apartment seconds ago, but don't know whether it was the left-hand one or the right-hand one. They smell marijuana coming from the one on the left. They knock, hear sounds suggesting that the occupants are destroying narcotics, break down the door, and find D and others smoking marijuana. They arrest D and search incident to that arrest, finding additional contraband. It turns out that X went into the right-hand apartment, and D had nothing to do with X. At trial, D claims that the police "manufactured" the emergency (when they picked the wrong apartment, and then without a warrant broke down the door), so that the police-created-exigency doctrine makes the entry unlawful.

      Held, for the prosecution. It's true that the police-created-exigency exception to the right to enter warrantlessly to stop the threatened destruction of evidence will sometimes invalidate the search. But that will happen only if the police committed or threatened to commit a Fourth Amendment violation in order to gain entry. That didn't happen here (they made a reasonable and honest mistake), so the entry and search were lawful. [*Kentucky v. King*] [122-123]

C A P S U L E S U M M A R Y

C. **Danger to life:** A warrantless search may be allowed where ***danger to life*** is likely if the police cannot act fast. [123]

   Example: At 3 a.m., police respond to a call that a loud party is taking place at a house. When they arrive, they hear shouting and see, through a screen door, a fight taking place in the kitchen. They open the screen door, enter, announce themselves, and arrest several people for fighting.

   Held, the police entry, though warrantless, did not violate the Fourth Amendment, because the entry was justified by the exigent circumstances. The police may make a warrantless entry into a home to assist an injured occupant or prevent imminent injury. [*Brigham City v. Stuart.*] [124]

D. **Hot pursuit:** If the police are pursuing a felony suspect, and have reason to believe that he has entered particular premises, they may enter those premises to search for him. While they are searching for him, they may also search for weapons which, since he is still at large, he might seize. This is called the ***"hot pursuit"*** exception to the search warrant requirement. [125]

   1. **Other items:** The "hot pursuit" exception is often combined with the "plain view" exception (discussed in detail below). That is, while the police are engaged in a hot pursuit of a sus-

pect and any weapons he might have, they may seize any other evidence of criminal behavior that they stumble upon in plain view.

E. **Entry to arrest non-resident:** One commonly occurring situation does ***not*** automatically constitute "exigent circumstances": Where the police are not in hot pursuit, and there are no specific exigent circumstances, the police ***may not enter one person's private dwelling to arrest another***, even if they are acting pursuant to an arrest warrant. [125-126] [*Steagald v. U.S.*]

> **Note:** But this rule does not apply where the suspect is to be arrested at his *own* premises. That is, a warrant for D's arrest, even without a search warrant, will be enough to allow the police to enter D's house to make the arrest; while there, they may make a search incident to an arrest, and also seize any evidence they find in plain view. It is only where the police have a warrant for *A's* arrest, and use it to enter *B's* residence, that the special *Steagald* rule summarized above applies to prevent a warrantless search of *B's* premises.

V. THE "PLAIN VIEW" DOCTRINE AND SEIZURE OF EVIDENCE

A. **The doctrine generally:** The ***"plain view"*** doctrine is often applied to allow police who are on premises for lawful purposes to make a warrantless seizure of evidence that they come across. [127]

B. **Requirements for doctrine:** For the plain view doctrine to be applied so that a warrantless seizure of evidence is allowable, three requirements must be met [127]:

> The officers must ***not have violated the Fourth Amendment in arriving at the place*** from which the items are plainly viewed;
>
> The incriminating nature of the items must be ***immediately apparent***;
>
> The officers must have a ***lawful right of access*** to the ***object itself***.

Let's look at these three requirements in more detail.

1. **Legally on premises:** First, the officers must ***not have violated the Fourth Amendment*** in arriving at the place from which the items were plainly viewed.

> **Example:** Officer trespasses on D's front lawn to look into D's front window, where Officer gets the plain view. The doctrine does not apply, because Officer has violated the Fourth Amendment by getting into the position from which he has the view. [127]

2. **Incriminating nature must be apparent:** Second, the incriminating nature of the items seized must be ***"immediately apparent."*** To put it another way, the police must, at the time they first see the item in plain view, have ***probable cause*** to believe that the object is incriminating.

> **Example:** Officer is legally in D's apartment. Officer notices an expensive stereo. He picks the stereo up, reads the serial number on the bottom, and learns by phone that a unit with that number has recently been stolen. *Held*, the plain view doctrine does not apply, because at the moment Officer picked up the stereo, he did not have probable cause for the search he performed by moving it. [*Arizona v. Hicks*] [127]

3. **Lawful right of access:** Finally, the officer must have a lawful ***right of access*** to the ***object itself***.

Example: Officer, standing on the public sidewalk, can see through the window of D's house and can view marijuana growing in D's living room. Officer may not make a warrantless entry into D's house to seize the marijuana, because she doesn't have lawful access to the inside of the house. [128]

C. **No requirement of inadvertence:** The plain view doctrine applies even where the police discovery of a piece of evidence that they want to seize is ***not inadvertent***. [128]

VI. THE "AUTOMOBILE EXCEPTION" TO THE REQUIREMENT OF A SEARCH WARRANT

A. **Relation of car searches to other kinds of searches:** All of the exceptions to the requirement of a search warrant that we've discussed above may apply to the search of an automobile as well as to the search of persons and premises.

1. **Exigent circumstances:** For instance, ***exigent circumstances*** will often cause the warrant requirement to be suspended when a car search is involved. Thus the police may search a vehicle without a warrant if such a search is necessary to ***preserve evidence***, as will be the case where the car can be quickly ***driven out of the jurisdiction***. [128]

2. **Incident to arrest:** Similarly, if the police arrest the driver, and have "reason to believe" that the vehicle may contain evidence of the crime for which they made the arrest, they may search the car under a form of search incident to arrest. [128]

B. **The "automobile exception" to the warrant requirement – generally:** Even apart from the above situations in which the *general* exceptions to the requirement of a search warrant apply to the automobile context, the Supreme Court has long recognized a specific auto-related exception, which is usually called the ***"automobile exception"*** to the warrant requirement. [128]

1. **Main statement of rule:** Here's a general statement of the automobile exception: A police officer may ***search a motor vehicle without first getting a search warrant, as long as she has probable cause to believe that evidence or contraband is located in the vehicle.*** [*California v. Carney*] [129]

2. **Rationales for the exception:** There are two distinct rationales for the automobile exception:

[1] **"Ready mobility":** The first rationale is based on the ***inherent mobility*** of motor vehicles. Even though a person has a constitutionally-protected privacy interest in her vehicle, the ***"ready mobility"*** of vehicles justifies giving the vehicle a lesser degree of protection than in the case of a fixed structure. Why? Because when the police arrive at probable cause to believe that evidence or contraband is located in the vehicle, it is usually ***not practicable for them*** to obtain and execute a search warrant before the vehicle is moved.

[2] **Lesser expectation of privacy:** The second rationale is that a person should be ***deemed to have a lesser expectation of privacy*** with respect to a vehicle she owns than with respect to, say, her home or workplace, because of the ***"pervasive regulation" of vehicles***.

[*California v. Carney*] [129]

C. The "automobile exception" – special contexts: Here are some contexts in which the "automobile exception" to the search-warrant requirement has (or hasn't) been applied.

1. **Search at station house after arrest:** Where the police arrest the driver, take him and his car ***to the station***, and search the car there, no search warrant is generally required.

   Example: The police, hearing a description of the getaway car used in a robbery, stop a car meeting that description, driven by D. They arrest D, and take D and the car to the station house. There, they search the car without a warrant, and find incriminating evidence. *Held*, the search was valid, despite the fact that once the car was at the station house the police could easily have gotten a search warrant. [*Chambers v. Maroney*] [130]

2. **Search at place where vehicle is stopped:** If the police properly stop a vehicle and have probable cause to believe that the vehicle contains contraband or evidence of crime, they may use the automobile exception to conduct an immediate warrantless search at the ***scene of the stop.*** (That is, they don't need to drive the car to the police station and search it there, as in *Chambers, supra.*) [*California v. Carney*] [131]

3. **Search of vehicle parked in the driveway of a home:** The automobile exception may also apply to dispense with the need for a warrant where the vehicle to be searched is located not on a public street, but on ***private residential property***, such as on the ***driveway*** of a home.

   a. **Vehicle not in curtilage:** If vehicle is on a portion of a homeowner's property that is ***not*** part of the property's "curtilage," then the automobile exception will ***apply***, assuming the police have probable cause to believe the vehicle contains contraband or evidence of crime.

   b. **Vehicle in curtilage:** But where the vehicle ***is*** located within the curtilage of a person's dwelling, the automobile exception will ***not apply*** to allow the warrantless search of the vehicle, even if the police have probable cause for a search. That's because the automobile exception ***does not "override"*** the special Fourth Amendment protections given to the "home" (and a home's curtilage is deemed part of the home, just as, say, any room inside the home would be). [*Collins v. Virginia* (2018)] [133]

4. **Extends to search of closed containers in the vehicle:** When the automobile exception applies to allow a warrantless search of a vehicle, the exception also allows the police to ***search any closed container inside the vehicle.*** (This assumes that the container might plausibly hold evidence or contraband relating to whatever it was that gave the police probable cause to stop and search the vehicle.) [*U.S. v. Ross*] [136]

   a. **Passenger's belongings:** Once the police have probable cause to believe that the car contains contraband or evidence of crime, they may search closed containers inside it that could hold that type of contraband or evidence, even if those containers belong to a ***passenger***, and even if there is no probable cause to believe that the passenger has been involved in carrying the contraband or any other illegality. [*Wyoming v. Houghton*] [136]

5. **Traffic stop followed by ticket:** Where the police make a routine stop to issue a ***traffic ticket***, and don't make an "arrest," they ***don't thereby get the right to search the car.*** [*Knowles v. Iowa*] [139]

D. Actions directed at passengers: If the driver's conduct leads the police to make a proper stop and/or arrest, this does not mean that the officer has the right to search the person of any ***passenger*** who happens to be in the car. No matter what the driver has done, the officer may search a passenger only if the officer has has either: (1) probable cause to believe that the passenger possesses evidence of a crime, or (2) probable cause to arrest the passenger (in which case the search is justified as being incident to arrest). [138]

However, the officer does have several other rights regarding passengers [139]:

As a method of protecting officer safety, the officer may demand that the passenger ***step out of the vehicle.***

Also as a matter of protection, if the officer has a reasonable fear that the passenger may be armed or dangerous, he may ***frisk and pat down*** the passenger, to make sure that the passenger is not carrying a weapon.

Finally, if the officer has the right to search the vehicle, he may as noted above also ***search any container*** in the car that might contain the thing being looked for, even if the officer knows that the container ***belongs to a passenger***, and even if the officer has no probable cause to believe that the container contains that thing.

E. Lack of probable cause: Of the various automobile scenarios that present an exception to the requirement of a search warrant, in most of them ***probable cause*** to make the search is required, but in a few it is not:

1. **Needed if searched on scene:** Where the driver is stopped and the police want to search the car ***on the scene***, they ***will*** normally need probable cause to conduct that search: belief that they will find either incriminating evidence or contraband. [131] (Remember that they may perform a search incident to the arrest of the driver, but this right extends only to the passenger compartment. If they want to search, say, the trunk, they will need probable cause to believe that it contains contraband or evidence of crime.)

2. **Plain view:** If the police find evidence in ***plain view*** in a vehicle as they are impounding it, they may seize the evidence even though they did not previously have probable cause to search or seize. [138]

3. **Impoundment:** If the car has been ***impounded*** by the police pursuant to standardized procedures, the police may usually conduct a search at the station house even though they do ***not*** have probable cause. For instance, where a police department routinely tows cars for ***illegal parking***, the police may unlock and search each such towed car in the impoundment lot. [*South Dakota v. Opperman*] [138]

   a. **Containers in car:** Similarly, once the impounded vehicle is searched, even ***closed containers*** inside it may be subjected to a warrantless and probable-cause-less inventory search. [138]

   b. **Standardized procedures and good faith:** But such warrantless inventory searches must satisfy two conditions: (1) the police must follow ***standardized procedures***, so that the person searching does not have unbridled discretion to determine the scope of the search; and (2) the police must not have acted in ***bad faith*** or for the ***sole purpose of investigation***. (*Example:* If the arrest or impoundment took place just to furnish an excuse for a warrantless search, the inventory-search exception will not apply.) [*Colorado v. Bertine*]

VII. CONSENT SEARCHES GENERALLY

A. Consent generally: The police may make a warrantless search if they receive the ***consent*** of the individual whose premises, effects, or person are to be searched. [139-143]

B. D need not know he can refuse consent: A person's consent will be ***effective*** even if the person ***did not know she had a right to refuse to consent*** to the search. [*Schneckloth v. Bustamonte*] [140]

1. **Must be voluntary:** The consent, to be effective, must be ***"voluntary,"*** rather than the product of duress or coercion. But the Court measures voluntariness by a ***"totality of the circumstances"*** test, and the fact that the consenter did or did not know she had a right to refuse consent is merely ***one factor*** in measuring voluntariness.

2. **Consent given in custody:** Even where the consent is given while the person is in ***custody***, the fact that the person is not told that he may refuse consent appears not to render the consent involuntary. [*U.S. v. Watson*] In other words, nothing like the *Miranda* rule — where the suspect *must* be warned that he has the right to remain silent — applies to a custodial suspect's consent to search his person or premises. [141]

C. Claims of authority to search: Suppose the consent to search is procured after the officer states that she has, or will get, ***authority to search*** if the person does not give consent. Courts generally distinguish between ***false claims of present authority***, and ***threats of future action*** — a false claim of present authority is much more likely to negate the voluntariness of the consent than is a threat of future action.

1. **False claim of present authority:** Where an officer ***falsely asserts that he has a search warrant***, and then procures "consent," the consent is ***invalid***. [*Bumper v. North Carolina*] [141]

2. **Consent induced by reference to invalid warrant:** Similarly, if the police ***truthfully*** state that they have a search warrant, but the warrant is in fact ***invalid*** (e.g., because rendered with a lack of probable cause), the consent of the person whose premises are to be searched is ***invalid***. [142]

3. **Threat to obtain warrant:** But where the police merely ***threaten to obtain a warrant*** if consent is not given (and the consent is given), the result depends on whether the police ***in fact have grounds*** to get a warrant. If they do, the consent is usually found valid; if they don't, the consent is likely to be nullified. (However, the Supreme Court has not yet decided this issue explicitly.) [142]

D. Misrepresentation of identity: Where the police ***misrepresent their identity*** by acting ***undercover***, this deception does ***not*** vitiate any "consent." (*Example:* Officer, wearing plain clothes, comes to D's house pretending to be the meter reader for the local electric company. D, believing Officer's cover story, lets Officer into D's basement. While purporting to read the meter, Officer spots incriminating evidence in the basement in plain view. D will almost certainly be found to have consented to Officer's entry, notwithstanding the deception.) [143]

E. Physical scope of search: Where D's consent is reasonably interpreted to apply only to a ***particular physical area***, a search that extends ***beyond*** that area will not be covered by the consent, and will be invalid unless it falls within some other exception to the warrant requirement. (*Example:* Officer asks D for permission to search D's living room for certain evidence. D responds, "O.K." Officer then goes into the kitchen and basement, and finds incriminating evidence. Since

Officer went beyond the scope of the consented-to search, the evidence will be suppressed if no other exception to the search warrant requirement applies.) [143]

1. **Plain view exception:** But always keep in mind the ***"plain view"*** exception to the warrant requirement — if while the searching officer is standing within part of the consented-to area, she spots evidence in another part of the premises, she can seize that evidence under the plain view doctrine.

VIII. CONSENT BY THIRD PERSONS

A. **The problem generally:** Be careful of consent issues raised when the police seek the consent of ***one person*** for the search of the ***property of another***, or for the search of an area as to which another has an expectation of privacy — the mere fact that the first person has voluntarily consented does not mean that the police may conduct the search and introduce evidence against the second person. In general, *A* may not consent to a search that would invade *B's* expectation of privacy — only if special circumstances exist (e.g., both *A* and *B* have authority over the premises) will *A's* consent be in effect binding on *B*.

B. **Joint authority:** In cases in which the defendant and a ***third person*** have ***joint authority*** over the premises, that third party's consent will often be binding on the defendant. We will consider two separate scenarios: (1) where D is ***absent*** at the time the third person consents; and (2) where D is ***present***, and ***refuses to consent***, while the third person consents. [144-146]

By "joint authority," we mean a situation in which D and the third party have some sort of ***joint access to***, and some sort of ***joint expectation of privacy in***, the place to be searched. Common examples of joint authority are:

roommates, as to the common areas of the dwelling or any shared bedroom;

husband and wife, as to the marital dwelling;

a homeowner (or tenant) and his ***social guest***, where the homeowner gives the consent and the evidence is then used against the guest.

All of these scenarios are evaluated according to the same basic set of rules.

1. **D is absent when third person consents:** Where D is ***absent***, and the police ask for and receive consent of the third person to search the jointly-controlled premises, the basic rule is that the third party's consent is ***effective***, if that third party either (a) ***actually*** has or (b) is ***reasonably believed*** by the police to have, joint authority over the premises.

   Example: G cohabits in a house together with D. The police show up at this house one day, arrest D in the front yard, and put him in a squad car nearby. They then knock on the front door, and G answers. They explain that they are looking for money and a gun from a recent bank robbery, and ask if they can search the house. G gives consent to the police to search the house, including her and D's bedroom. In the bedroom, the police find money and the gun from the robbery.

   Held, G's consent was valid as against D. G had joint authority over the bedroom. In such a joint-authority scenario, "it is reasonable to recognize that *any of the co-inhabitants* has the right to permit the inspection in his own right and that the others have *assumed the risk* that one of their number might permit the common area to be searched." [*U.S. v. Matlock*] [144]

a. **Reasonable mistake:** The third-party consent will be binding on the absent defendant even if the police were ***mistaken*** about whether the consenter in fact had joint authority over the premises, as long as the ***mistake was a reasonable one.*** For instance, if the consenting third person falsely tells the police that she lives in the premises to be searched, and the police reasonably believe her, the lie will not invalidate the consent. [*Illinois v. Rodriguez*]

2. **D is present and objecting when third person consents:** Now, let's consider the second scenario: D is ***present*** when the third party consents to a search of the premises over which the two have joint authority, and D makes it clear that he, D, is ***not consenting.*** Here, the third party's consent is ***not binding on D***, at least where it appears to the police that the third person and D have equal claim to the premises. [145]

Example: W, who is estranged from her husband D, returns to the former marital residence. There, she calls the police. They arrive without a warrant and meet W. D then arrives back at the house. W tells the police that there are items showing D's drug use in the house. The police ask D for his consent to a search of the house, and he refuses. The police then ask W for consent and she gives it. In D's bedroom, the police find cocaine.

Held, W's consent was not effective as against D. Where as here the two parties are not living within some "recognized hierarchy" (like a household with parent and child), the co-tenant who wishes to open the door to a third person "has no recognized authority in law or social practice to prevail over a present and objecting co-tenant." Consequently, even though W may have had joint authority with D over the house, the police's warrantless entry in the face of D's express refusal to consent made this an unreasonable search. [*Georgia v. Randolph*] [145]

C. **Other theories:** Even where the person doing the consenting does not have joint authority over the premises, some other theory may apply to justify a search that would otherwise violate D's rights:

1. **Agency:** First, it may be the case, as a factual matter, that D has ***authorized*** a third person to consent, even though the third person does not have direct ownership or control. (*Example:* D gives X, his trusted valet, complete run of the premises, and the authority to decide who will be admitted. If X consents to a police search, this will be binding on D under the doctrine of agency.) [146]

2. **Property of consenter:** If the person doing the consenting is the ***owner of the particular item*** to be searched or seized, this will be binding even if the search or seizure violates D's property interests. (*Example:* X owns a rifle, and consents to have the police seize it and test it. The rifle turns out, as the police suspect, to have been used by D, X's grandson, in a crime. This evidence can be used against D, because X as the owner of the item seized had the right to consent to the seizure.) [146]

3. **Assumption of risk:** Finally, the relationship between the third party and D may be such that D will be found to have ***"assumed the risk"*** that the third party might see or scrutinize D's property, in which case the third party may also consent to a search. (*Example:* D shares a duffle bag with X, his cousin. X consents to a police search of the bag. *Held*, this consent was binding on D, because D assumed the risk that X or others would look in the bag, and thus D had no expectation of privacy in the bag's contents. [*Frazier v. Cupp*]) [146]

D. Relatives: Consent issues often arise where one person consents to a search that implicates the privacy interests of the consenter's ***relative***.

1. **Husbands, wives, and lovers:** Where one ***spouse*** consents to the search of the property of the absent other, the search will usually be ***upheld***. (See, e.g., *Matlock, supra*, p. C-36). [146]

    a. **Personal effects:** One of the rare exceptions is that if one spouse permits the search of the other's ***personal effects*** stored in a separate drawer or closet used only by the other, the consent may be invalid.

2. **Parent/child:** Most courts have held that when a ***child*** is living at home with his parents, the parents may consent to a search of the ***child's room***. [147]

    a. **Consent by child:** The child, on the other hand, may ***not*** normally consent to a full-scale search of the parents' house. (But if the child merely lets the police into the front area of the house and the child is generally allowed to admit strangers to that front area, the limited consent will probably be valid and anything the police can see from there will fall under the plain view doctrine.)

E. Other situations: Here are some other situations that frequently arise regarding third-party consent:

1. **Landlords:** Generally, a ***landlord*** may not consent to a search of his tenants' rooms, even though the landlord has the right to enter them for cleaning. But the landlord may consent to a search of the areas of "common usage," such as hallways and common dining areas. [147]

2. **Employer:** An ***employer*** probably may consent to a search of his employee's work area if the search is for items ***related to the job***. But probably the employer cannot consent to a search of areas where the employee is, by the terms of the job, permitted to store personal effects (e.g., a locker given to the employee to store his street clothes at a factory). [148]

F. Ignorance of consenter: It is irrelevant that the consenter does not know the purpose of the search, or mistakenly believes that the person for whom she is consenting is innocent and has nothing to hide. [148]

IX. STOP-AND-FRISK AND OTHER BRIEF DETENTION

A. Problem generally: Sometimes the police, when they encounter a suspect, do not want to make a full arrest, but merely want to ***briefly detain*** the person. This happens most typically when the police are not investigating any particular crime, and are simply performing routine patrolling functions. The two questions which the "stop-and-frisk" doctrine deals with are: (1) When may the police ***briefly detain*** a person even though they ***do not have probable cause*** to arrest him or to search him, and (2) to what extent may the police conduct a protective, limited ***search*** for weapons on the suspect's person? [148-170]

B. General rule: In general, the stop-and-frisk doctrine lets the police do both of the above things in appropriate circumstances:

1. **Right to stop:** Where a police officer ***observes unusual conduct*** which leads him reasonably to conclude that criminal activity is afoot, he may briefly detain the suspect in order to make inquiries. Probable cause is not required — ***reasonable suspicion***, based on ***objective facts***, that the individual is involved in criminal activity, will suffice. (The stop is a seizure under the Fourth Amendment, but it does not require probable cause, merely reasonable suspicion.)

2. **Protective frisk:** Once the officer conducts a stop as described above, then assuming nothing in the initial encounter dispels his reasonable fear for his or others' safety, the officer may conduct a ***carefully limited search*** of the ***outer clothing*** of the suspect in an attempt to discover ***weapons***. This limited ***"frisk"*** or ***"pat-down"*** is a Fourth Amendment search, but is deemed "reasonable." Consequently, any weapons seized may be introduced against the suspect. [***Terry v. Ohio***; *Brown v. Texas*] [148-150]

C. **Stop of vehicle:** The "stop and frisk" doctrine also may apply to allow an officer to order the stop of a ***vehicle***. (*Example:* Officer, while in his patrol car, is approached by an informant he knows, who says that D, in a parked car nearby, possesses a gun and narcotics. Officer detains the car and driver, waits for D to roll down his window, then puts his head in, discovers a weapon in D's waistband, and removes it. *Held*, the informant's tip had sufficient indicia of reliability to allow Officer to forcibly stop D's car; given that the stop was reasonable, the pat-down of D's waistband and removal of the gun were justified to protect Officer. [*Adams v. Williams*]) [150-152]

1. **Suspect and passengers required to leave car:** Once the officer conducts a justified "stop" of a vehicle, the officer may also require the stopped motorist and even the ***passengers*** in the vehicle to ***leave the car***, as a legitimate safety measure. [*Pennsylvania v. Mimms*; *Maryland v. Wilson*] [151]

a. **Pat-down of non-suspect passenger:** Similarly, if the car has been properly stopped and the occupants temporarily detained, the police are entitled to do a ***pat-down*** of any ***passenger — even if the police have no reason to suspect the passenger of wrongdoing*** — as long as the police have a reasonable suspicion that the passenger may be ***armed and dangerous***. [*Arizona v. Johnson*] [152]

D. **Degree of probability required:** Something ***less than probable cause*** to arrest or search is required in order for the officer to make a "stop."

1. **Vague suspicion not enough:** ***Vague suspicion*** is not enough. The officer may "stop" the suspect only if he has a "***reasonable suspicion***, based on ***objective facts***, that the individual is involved in criminal activity." (*Example:* D is stopped because: (1) he is walking in an area having a high incidence of drug traffic; (2) he "looks suspicious" to Officer; and (3) he has not been seen in that area previously by Officer. *Held*, these facts don't meet the "reasonable suspicion based on objective facts" test. Therefore, the stop was an unreasonable seizure in violation of the Fourth Amendment. [*Brown v. Texas*]) [153]

2. **"Modest suspicion" enough:** But a fairly modest amount of suspicion ***will*** be enough for a brief stop.

a. **Innocent acts taken together:** For instance, suppose D engages in a number of acts in sequence, each of which is ***innocent in itself***; if, viewed under a ***"totality of circumstances"*** approach, the acts together would create reasonable suspicion that D is engaged in wrongdoing, that will suffice for a *Terry* stop. [154]

3. **Flight as a cause for suspicion:** The fact that an individual has ***attempted to flee*** when seen by the police will normally raise the police's suspicion, and may even without more justify the police in making a *Terry*-style stop. [154]

Example: D flees when he sees police officers patrolling the high-crime area where he is walking. They therefore stop him and pat him down. *Held*, the officers were justified in stopping D, because the combination of his fleeing from the police and his presence in a high-crime area created a reasonable suspicion that D was engaged in some sort of wrongdoing. [*Illinois v. Wardlow*]

4. **Informant's tip:** A *Terry*-like "stop" may be justified not only based on the officer's own observations, but also based on an ***informant's tip***. Again, all that is required is "reasonable suspicion," and in the case of an informant's tip this is to be determined by the "totality of the circumstances." [154]

   a. **Prediction of future events:** A key factor is whether the informant has ***predicted future events*** that someone without inside information would have been unlikely to know. [109]

   b. **Knowledge of hidden criminality:** Also, where the informant is ***anonymous***, the police must have reason to believe that the ***informant's knowledge about the suspect's criminal conduct*** is ***reliable***. It's not enough that the informant merely knows something non-criminal about the suspect that anyone could know (e.g., the suspect's physical appearance and present location). [155]

      Example: The police get an anonymous phone tip that a black male wearing a plaid shirt is standing on a particular street corner and carrying a concealed illegal weapon. The police stop D (who meets that description), pat him down, and find an illegal weapon on him. *Held*, the police didn't have enough suspicion from the tip to make the stop. That's because the anonymous informant didn't give the police any reason to believe that his information about D's *criminal conduct* (hidden weapon) was reliable — the mere fact that the informant knew something non-criminal and publicly-visible about D (what D was wearing and where he was standing) was not an indicator of the informant's reliability as to the criminal conduct. [*Florida v. J.L.*]

5. **Common-sense may be relied on (*Kansas v. Glover*):** As we've noted (p. 000), a fairly modest amount of suspicion will suffice for a *Terry* stop. Often, whatever level of suspicion an officer has, that suspicion will be based on the officer's law enforcement training. But an officer may have sufficient suspicion based instead on the sort of ***"common sense"*** that a non-lawyer might also have. If so, that common-sense suspicion can constitute the required suspicion That's what happened in the case described in the following Example.

   Example: A police officer (O) observes an individual (Glover) driving a pickup truck. O does not observe any violations of traffic laws. Without approaching the truck, O runs a license-plate search, which reveals that Glover is the registered owner of the truck and that Glover's driver's license has been revoked. O then makes the common-sense inference that any given vehicle has a more-than-trivial chance of being driven by its registered owner. This causes O to suspect that Glover is the driver, and is driving with a revoked license. O therefore makes a *Terry* stop of the truck. Once O verifies that the driver of the truck is indeed Glover, O arrests him for driving with a revoked driver's license.

   In a suppression hearing, Glover asserts that in determining whether reasonable suspicion (needed for a *Terry* stop) existed, O's inference that the driver was the registered owner had to be based ***solely on O's law enforcement training or experience.*** Consequently, he claims, the stop did not qualify under *Terry*, and violated his Fourth Amendment rights.

   Held, for the government. When an officer is making inferences to determine whether there is reasonable suspicion adequate for a *Terry* stop, the officer is ***not limited to***

"knowledge gained only through law enforcement training and experience." To the contrary, the officer may make ***common-sense inferences.*** So here, the inference that the driver of a car is its registered owner "does not require any specialized training; rather, it is a ***reasonable inference made by ordinary people*** on a daily basis." Therefore, prior to the stop O had the required level of suspicion sufficient for a *Terry* stop. [*Kansas v. Glover*] [156]

E. What constitutes a "stop": Not every brief encounter between a police officer and a person on the street or in a car constitutes a ***"stop"*** within the meaning of the Fourth Amendment (i.e., a detention of such severity that it rises to the level of a Fourth Amendment seizure and must therefore be "reasonable"). [157-161]

1. The "reasonable person" test: Here is the test for determining whether an encounter constitutes a Fourth Amendment "seizure": "A person has been 'seized' within the meaning of the Fourth Amendment only if, in view of all of the circumstances surrounding the incident, a ***reasonable person*** would have believed that he was ***not free to leave***." [*U.S. v. Mendenhall*]) [157]

a. Illustrations showing lack of freedom to leave: Here are examples (cited by the Court in *Mendenhall*, *supra*) of circumstances that might indicate to a reasonable person that he is not free to leave: (1) the ***threatening presence*** of several officers; (2) the ***display of a weapon*** by an officer; (3) some ***physical touching*** of the person; or (4) the use of ***language*** or ***tone of voice*** indicating that compliance with the officer's request might be compelled.

Example: Suppose Officer, upon passing D in the street, says, "Could I ask you a question, sir?" At this point, probably no Fourth Amendment seizure has occurred, because a reasonable person in D's situation would probably think he was free to refuse to answer the question and continue walking. If so, Officer would not need any "reasonable suspicion, based on objective facts...," and even in the absence of such suspicion any incriminating statement made by D would be admissible against him. (That is, D could not have his statement excluded as the fruit of the poisonous tree, because no illegal Fourth Amendment seizure would have occurred.)

2. Chase by police: If the police are ***chasing*** a suspect, the chase itself does ***not*** constitute a "seizure" — until the suspect ***submits*** to the chase (by stopping), there is no seizure. [157]

a. Exception for police shooting and other forcible "touchings": Now, suppose that the officer doesn't just chase the suspect, but instead ***applies force to the suspect's body,*** and the suspect then ***breaks away*** from that force. Here, a seizure occurs ***at the moment the officer applies force to the body of D*** (though the stop ends if and when if D then breaks away from that force). [158]

Example: Two police officers approach Torres while she sits in her parked car. They are trying to serve an arrest warrant, but they don't realize that Torres is not the person mentioned in the warrant. When the officers attempt to speak to Torres, she doesn't realize the men are police officers (she thinks they're carjackers trying to steal her car). She starts to drive off, and the officers fire their pistols to stop her; two of their bullets hit and injure her. She nonetheless continues driving for 75 miles until she is hospitalized and arrested.

After the arrest is dismissed (because Torres wasn't the person named in the arrest warrant), Torres brings a suit against the officers under 42 U.S.C. §1983, which allows for a civil suit for damages by a person whose constitutional rights have been violated by persons acting under color of state law.[2] (She claims that the shooting was a use of excessive force, constituting a violation of her constitutional rights.) The government defends by claiming that the shooting of Torres was not a "seizure," and that therefore, a pre-requisite for a §1983 recovery (existence of a seizure) was not satisfied.

Held, for Torres. A seizure occurs ***at the moment the officer applies force to the body of D, even if D then breaks away*** from that force. It's true that (as the government claims), once Torres continued driving after being shot, she was no longer "seized." But the moment Torres was shot was nonetheless a seizure, no matter how brief. Therefore, Torres is ***eligible*** to raise her §1983 claim of excessive force, because she was seized "for the instant that the bullets struck her." [*Torres v. Madrid*] [159]

F. "Stop" vs. arrest: At some point, the stop is sufficiently long and intrusive that it turns into a ***full-scale arrest***. Remember the significance of the distinction between stop and arrest: for a stop, only "reasonable suspicion" is required, whereas for an arrest, probable cause is required. Here are the factors the Court looks to in determining whether a detention has remained a "stop":

1. **No longer than reasonably necessary:** The detention must not be ***longer*** than the circumstances justifying it require. Typically, this will not be more than a few minutes, but in unique situations (e.g., waiting for a suspected "alimentary canal" drug smuggler to void), longer may be allowed. [161]

2. **No more intrusive than reasonably necessary:** The stop must also be ***no more intrusive than needed*** to verify or dispel the officer's suspicions. [161]

   a. **May demand identification:** The police may demand that D orally ***identify himself***. [*Hiibel v. Sixth Judicial Dist. Ct.*] But we don't yet know whether the police may demand to see an identification document like a ***driver's license***. [162]

3. **Transporting D to somewhere else:** Finally, if the police ***transport*** the suspect to another place, especially the ***station house***, this is likely to turn the stop into an arrest. Thus even if ***no formal arrest*** is made, the police cannot transport a suspect to the police station without probable cause. [*Dunaway v. New York*]

G. Scope of permissible frisk: When the police perform a ***frisk*** after making a stop, the frisk must be limited to a search for ***weapons***, or other sources of ***danger***. That is, the purpose of the frisk may not be to search for ***contraband*** or ***incriminating evidence***. (*Example:* Officer temporarily stops D, a patron in a bar, and frisks him. Officer feels, through D's clothing, what appears to be a cigarette pack with some objects in it. Officer then removes the pack, and discovers heroin packets inside it. *Held*, the search went beyond the permissible scope of a frisk pursuant to a stop-and-frisk: Officer had no reasonable belief that D was armed or dangerous, so Officer was not entitled to even start the frisk. [*Ybarra v. Illinois*]) [163-164]

1. **Armed or dangerous:** The frisk may take place only if the officer has a reasonable belief that D may be ***armed or dangerous***. Thus if D's hands are empty, he gives no indication of possessing a weapon, he makes no gestures indicating an intent to commit assault, and he acts generally in a non-threatening manner, the officer probably may not conduct even the basic outside-the-clothes pat-down. [See *Ybarra v. Illinois*, *supra*] [164]

---

2. For more about §1983, see *infra*, p. 357. Civil suits using this provision are often brought by plaintiffs who say they have been the victims of ***police brutality*** (i.e., excessive use of force) during an arrest.

H. Search of automobile: When the police make a "stop" of a person in a car, the police may then search for weapons in the car's ***passenger compartment***, even though the suspect is no longer inside the car. [*Michigan v. Long*] Just as the police may frisk the body of a suspect who has merely been stopped rather than arrested if the officers reasonably believe the suspect may be armed, so the police may search the passenger compartment if: (1) the officers reasonably believe that the driver is dangerous and may gain control of weapons that may be in the car; and (2) they look only in those parts of the passenger compartment where weapons might be placed or hidden. [164-166]

1. **Limited application:** In the typical situation of a stop for a ***traffic violation***, there probably will be no right to search the passenger compartment for weapons, because the police would not have a "reasonable belief based on specific and articulable facts" that weapons may be found in the car. But if the police find weapons on the suspect's ***person***, or they see a weapon in plain view in the car, then presumably they become entitled to conduct a weapons search throughout the passenger compartment. [166]

I. Detention during house search: When the police are ***searching a residence*** for contraband, pursuant to a ***search warrant***, they may ***detain the occupants*** while the search continues. [*Michigan v. Summers*] [166]

1. **Use of force, including handcuffs:** When the police exercise this right to detain the occupants while executing a search warrant, they may use ***reasonable force*** to carry out the detention. If they're searching for ***weapons***, reasonable force includes the ***handcuffing*** of all occupants of the house. [*Muehler v. Mena*] [167-169]

2. **Applies only to immediate vicinity of arrest:** The holding of *Michigan v. Summers, supra* — that while police are executing a search warrant, they may temporarily detain any persons present on the searched premises — applies only to persons who are detained while they are either ***on*** the premises or ***in the immediate vicinity of*** those premises. Once a person is permitted to ***leave*** the immediate vicinity of the premises being searched, the automatic "police may detain" rule of *Summers* no longer applies, ***no matter how "reasonable" it may be*** for the police to then detain that person. Instead, the usual Fourth Amendment procedures (including the rules on "stop and frisk") apply. [*Bailey v. U.S.*] [167]

   Example: The police have a valid search warrant for 103 Lake Drive, to search for a .380 caliber handgun. While they are outside the building and about to start their search, they see someone (D) drive away from number 103. They follow him for a mile, then stop and detain him. When they question him about his connection to number 103, he tells inconsistent stories, which lead the police to disbelieve him and search him (which results in incriminating evidence). D claims that the police had no right to detain him merely because he had just left the place they had a warrant to search.

   Held, for D. The fact that the police were about to execute a search warrant at number 103 did not give them the right to detain anyone who was no longer in the "immediate vicinity of the premises to be searched." Since D was not stopped until he was nearly 1 mile away from number 103, the right of the police to detain him under *Summers* had passed, no matter how reasonable the police behavior was. Therefore, the stop of D will have to be justified on some other principle (e.g., stop-and-frisk). [*Bailey v. U.S., supra.*]

X. REGULATORY AND OTHER "SPECIAL NEEDS" SEARCHES

A. Summary: So far, we've looked at the Fourth Amendment only in the context of the investigation of specific crimes. In that context, as we've seen, probable cause to search is usually necessary, and a search warrant is necessary unless there is a specific exception to the warrant requirement.

Now, we turn to certain kinds of law enforcement activities that may invade areas protected by the Fourth Amendment, but whose ***special nature*** may justify dispensing with either ***probable cause***, or a ***search warrant***, or both. These activities are commonly said to be ones presenting ***"special needs."*** Most of these activities have a ***"regulatory"*** rather than "investigation of crime" flavor. [171-190]

The "special needs" activities that we'll examine here are:

[1] ***health, fire*** and other ***safety-related inspections*** of ***physical premises*** by government inspectors who are ***not investigating suspected crimes***;

[2] ***border*** and other ***immigration-related*** searches;

[3] routine ***traffic stops*** (including ***sobriety checkpoints***);

[4] capturing the ***DNA*** of arrestees;

[5] searches of ***parolees and probationers***; and

[6] ***school searches.***

B. Health and safety inspections of physical premises: The Supreme Court has laid down special rules governing how the Fourth Amendment restricts the circumstances under which government ***inspectors*** may perform inspections of physical premises to ensure that ***health, fire and other safety regulations*** are being complied with. We'll refer to this sort of premises inspection as a ***"building search."*** [3]

1. Summary of rules: Here is a summary of these special rules governing building searches:

[1] Most importantly, the inspector ***does not need to have any suspicion at all*** that there are health or safety violations at the particular premises to be inspected. Thus ***"area-wide building inspections"*** are possible.

[2] On the other hand, the inspector is ***not*** free to demand an inspection of premises ***without some sort of warrant.*** As shown in rule [3] below, the warrant can be of a special and easy-to-obtain sort, but the inspector cannot simply demand to inspect a particular building "empty handed," assuming there is no emergency.

[3] The required warrant is quite different from a standard "search warrant" as described in the warrant clause of the Fourth Amendment for use in criminal investigations. In the building-search context, the warrant requirement (essentially a ***judge-made rule*** created by the Supreme Court in interpreting the Fourth Amendment's general "no unreasonable

---

3. The inspector is always free to arrive at premises without any warrant or grounds for suspicion and to ask the owner or occupant to ***consent*** to a building search; if the latter agrees, then the search is lawful regardless of whether the inspector had any grounds for suspicion, and regardless of whether she had any kind of search warrant. Our discussion here focuses on the rules that apply if the owner/occupant *refuses consent*.

searches" clause, ***not*** the warrant clause) works this way:

[a] The official seeking the warrant does ***not*** have to show ***probable cause*** that the particular building to be inspected ***violates*** any health or safety regulation.

[b] Instead, the official merely has to show that government is proposing to conduct an ***"area inspection"*** that is ***reasonably tailored to making sure that the relevant health or safety codes are being observed.***

[c] The main function of the warrant requirement in this building-inspection context is to make sure that government inspectors are ***not given undue discretion*** that they can use to harass particular owners or occupants for non-safety-related purposes.

Example: The need for an area-wide warrant would help prevent a corrupt building inspector from "shaking down" a particular restaurant owner — if the inspector wasn't required to have such a warrant, the inspector could threaten to conduct a bogus "for harassment only" health inspection of the restaurant premises twice a day for months if the owner didn't pay her a bribe.

[4] The inspector doesn't necessarily have to be in possession of the warrant at the time she ***first seeks to enter the premises.*** Instead, the inspector can ask the owner to consent to the search, and if he refuses, hand him an administrative subpoena. The owner can then delay the search while seeking to having the subpoena quashed by a judge.

[Cf. *Camara v. Municipal Court of San Francisco*]

2. **Houses and businesses, generally:** The above rules, requiring an administrative "area-wide" warrant, apply to both ***housing inspections*** and to ***safety-related inspections of businesses generally***.

Example: A federal occupational-safety statute, OSHA, purports to let federal inspectors search any workplace covered by OSHA during regular working hours, in order to inspect for violation of federal job-safety standards. The statute says that the inspector does not need any sort of search warrant before demanding the inspection. P, an owner of an ordinary, non-closely-regulated business, contends that such warrantless inspections violate his Fourth Amendment rights.

Held, for P. Warrantless inspections of certain types of *closely-regulated* businesses (discussed below) may be permissible. But the Fourth Amendment requires some sort of a warrant before a compulsory regulatory inspection of an ordinary, non-closely-regulated, business, such as the one here. [*Marshall v. Barlow's, Inc.*] [173]

3. **Special rule for closely-regulated businesses:** But the Supreme Court has ***allowed*** governments to make warrantless regulatory inspections of certain types of ***closely-regulated businesses.*** The Court has not given a consistent explanation of when this "closely-regulated business" exception applies. But a 2015 case says that the exception applies only to businesses that "pose[] a clear and significant ***risk to the public welfare."*** [*Los Angeles v. Patel, infra*] [173]

a. **What businesses are deemed "closely-regulated":** The Supreme Court has, over many decades, identified only ***four types*** of businesses as falling within this "closely-regulated" category for which no prior inspection warrant is required:

[1] businesses that ***sell liquor*** on the premises (e.g., liquor stores and catering halls);

[2] ***firearms dealers***;

[3] ***mining*** businesses; and

[4] ***automobile junkyards***.

b. Hotels are not closely-regulated: One category of business that the Court has held ***not*** to be "closely regulated" is ***hotels***. Therefore, inspectors who are not equipped with at least an administrative search warrant may not demand to make a regulatory inspection of a hotel's registry of guests. [*City of Los Angeles v. Patel* (2015)] [174]

Example: D (the City of Los Angeles) enacts an ordinance requiring every hotel operator to keep a registry of information about each guest including name, address, license plate number, etc. The ordinance also requires every operator to make this registry available for inspection by any L.A. police officer on demand. The Ps, a group of motel operators, claim that by requiring them to furnish such information to the police without a warrant and without any provision for pre-compliance judicial review, the ordinance violates their Fourth Amendment rights.

Held (by a 5-4 vote), for the Ps. Even administrative search schemes — allowing searches whose primary purpose is regulatory, not crime control — must normally give the person whose property is being searched the opportunity to have a neutral decision maker (not the officer seeking to do the search) review the reasonableness of the search before the property owner is required to comply.

It's true that owners of businesses in a few types of "closely-regulated" industries, ones posing a "clear and significant risk to the public welfare." may be subjected to warrantless searches. But hotels as a category do not pose such a risk. Therefore, the Ps have the right to insist on not being searched unless and until a magistrate first reviews the propriety of the inspector's administrative subpoena. [*City of Los Angeles v. Patel, supra*] [174]

C. Immigration searches: Certain types of ***immigration***-related searches may be carried out without a warrant and without probable cause. [175-176]

1. Border searches: At the ***border***, immigration and customs officials may search baggage and vehicles (and to a limited extent, the traveler's own person) ***without probable cause*** to believe that there is an immigration violation or smuggling, and ***without a warrant***. [*Almeida-Sanchez v. U.S.*] [175]

2. Interior patrols and checkpoints: Where a search does not occur at the border or its "functional equivalent," however, a stronger showing of reasonable suspicion is required. A vehicle inside the border and ***not known to have recently crossed the border*** may be stopped and searched only if there is probable cause to believe that aliens or smuggled objects are present. [*Almeida-Sanchez, supra*] [175-176] But there are two exceptions to this tougher rule:

a. Roving patrol: Where immigration officials, as part of a ***"roving patrol,"*** stop a car in the interior not to make a search, but to briefly question the occupants, probable cause is not required. The officials must, however, point to ***specific factors*** giving rise to some ***significant suspicion*** that a violation has occurred. (*Example:* The Mexican appearance of the car's inhabitants is not by itself sufficient to allow even a brief stop for questioning, even in, say, southern Texas.)

b. **Fixed check-point:** Where a ***fixed checkpoint*** is set up in the interior, ***all*** cars may be stopped for brief immigration-related questioning. Then, if the questioning gives rise to additional suspicion, motorists may be referred to a second place where they can be questioned and if necessary searched. [*U.S. v. Martinez-Fuerte*]

D. **Routine traffic stops:** Apart from the border-search and immigration issues, the police may wish to stop cars for regulatory purposes (e.g., to make sure that the driver is ***licensed*** and the car is ***registered)***.

1. **Random stops:** If the police ***randomly*** stop cars to do this checking, they may not make a particular stop unless they have a ***suspicion*** of wrongdoing based upon an "objective standard." That is, a practice of making ***totally random*** stops, where a stop is made even though the officer has no objective grounds for suspicion, violates the Fourth Amendment. [*Delaware v. Prouse*] [179]

2. **Check-point:** However, the police may set up a ***fixed checkpoint*** on the highway to test for compliance related to driver-safety. Thus they can stop to check for ***drunkenness*** [*Mich. Dept. of State Police v. Sitz*], and can probably check to see that the ***driver is licensed*** and the vehicle is registered. [Dictum in *Delaware v. Prouse*] [179]

a. **Seeking of eyewitnesses to crime:** Similarly, the police may set up a fixed roadblock or checkpoint to ***find witnesses*** to a recent crime, if that's a reasonable method of finding such witnesses.

Example: V is killed in a hit-and-run accident on a highway late on a Saturday night. One week later, at the same place and time, the police stop each car and hand the driver a flier seeking witnesses to the crime. D, who is stopped but has nothing to do with the hit-and-run, is arrested when the police smell alcohol on his breath. *Held*, the stop here was reasonable, because it searched for witnesses, not suspects, and did so in a minimally-intrusive way. [*Illinois v. Lidster*] [178]

3. **No general crime-fighting:** But police may ***not*** set up a fixed checkpoint to pursue ***general crime-fighting objectives***, such as ***narcotics detection***. [177]

Example: Police set up a fixed checkpoint and stop a pre-determined number of cars. When each car is stopped, police walk around it to see if they can spot (in plain view) any evidence that the car contains narcotics. They also use a drug dog to sniff for narcotics. *Held*, these warrantless stops are unreasonable and thus a violation of the Fourth Amendment, because they are being done for general crime-fighting purposes, not administrative concerns relating to road safety. [*Indianapolis v. Edmond*]

E. **Capturing the DNA of arrested persons:** The police may, without a search warrant, ***take a DNA sample*** from ***anyone arrested for a serious crime***. Consequently, federal, state and local police may all ***build databases of the DNA of anyone they arrest*** for a "serious offense," and use that data to match suspects with prior or future unsolved crimes. [*Maryland v. King* (2013)] [181]

Example: D is arrested in Maryland in 2009 on assault charges. A Maryland statute permits police to collect DNA samples from any individual who has been ***charged*** with an actual or attempted ***crime of violence***, even if the person hadn't yet been convicted. Since the assault charge against D involves a crime of violence, the police — as part of their ***routine booking procedures*** — collect D's DNA sample by swabbing the inside of his cheek. D's sample, when checked against an FBI database, matches the DNA taken from a victim in an unsolved 2003 rape case. D is charged with the 2003 rape and convicted. D argues that the Maryland statute, by authorizing the taking of a DNA sample from him based on ***mere arrest*** — not yet followed by conviction — gave rise to an "unreasonable" search, and thus violated his Fourth Amendment rights.

Held, for the prosecution: D's conviction is valid, and the Maryland statute does not violate an arrestee's Fourth Amendment rights. It's true that the taking of a DNA swab from an arrestee without consent constitutes a Fourth Amendment search. But such searches serve the government's legitimate interest in identifying the person taken into custody. Therefore, the taking of a DNA swab is, "***like fingerprinting and photographing***, a legitimate police ***booking procedure*** that is ***reasonable under the Fourth Amendment.***" [*Maryland v. King, supra*] [181-187]

F. Other contexts: Here are some other contexts in which the government's right to make inspections and regulatory searches has arisen:

1. **Supervision of parolees and probationers:** ***Parolees*** and ***probationers*** may be subjected to warrantless searches by officials responsible for them, even if probable cause is lacking. [*Griffin v. Wisconsin*] Instead of probable cause and a warrant, all that is required for the search of a probationer or a parolee is that it be conducted pursuant to a ***valid regulation***. [187]

   a. **Search on street:** In fact, the police may subject parolees to a warrantless stop and search at any time ***even if the officer has no grounds to suspect wrongdoing at all,*** so long as this condition is disclosed to the prisoner prior to his release on parole. That's because parolees have "severely diminished expectations of privacy by virtue of their status alone." [*Samson v. California*] (It's not clear whether this "no suspicion required" rule also applies to *probationers*, who seem to have greater constitutional rights than parolees.) [187]

   b. **Pre-trial detainee:** Similarly, ***pre-trial detainees*** may be subjected to cell searches and in some cases searches of body cavities, without probable cause or a warrant. Such a detainee, even though he has not been convicted of any crime, has a ***"diminished"*** reasonable expectation of privacy. [*Bell v. Wolfish*] [188]

2. **Searches in schools:** The rules regarding when searches of ***students*** and their possessions may take place without a warrant and without probable cause are still uncertain. We do know that the schools have substantial power to take these actions if they don't act in connection with the police.

   a. **Warrantless search for violation of school rules:** Thus a ***school official*** acting alone (not acting in concert with law enforcement authorities) may search the person and premises of a student ***without a warrant***. All that is required is that the official have "***reasonable grounds*** for ***suspecting*** that the search will turn up evidence that the student has violated or is violating either the law or the ***rules of the school***." [*New Jersey v. T.L.O.*] [188]

      Note: It's not clear whether the same "suspicion of violating school rules" standard applies where the search of the student is actually carried out by law enforcement officials as opposed to school officials. Probably the Supreme Court would say that the Fourth Amendment applies once the police get involved.

   b. **Drug tests for participants in competitive extracurricular activities:** Similarly, a school district may require that all students who want to participate in ***"competitive extra-***

curricular activities" (e.g., interscholastic sports) submit to a ***drug test*** (urinalysis), at least where the results are not shared with the police, and the testing is conducted in a relatively unintrusive manner. This is true even if the school district does not yet have a significant drug problem. [*Bd. of Ed. v. Earls*] [189]

CHAPTER 4

ELECTRONIC SURVEILLANCE AND SECRET AGENTS

I. ELECTRONIC SURVEILLANCE

A. Wiretapping and bugging generally: There are two main techniques of "electronic surveillance" often used by law enforcement officials, on which the Fourth Amendment places strict limits. These two techniques are ***"wiretapping"*** and ***"bugging."***

1. **Wiretap:** In a wiretap, the listener (in our context, the government) places electronic equipment on the ***telephone wires***, and uses this equipment to listen to conversations that take place on the telephone.

2. **Bugging:** In "bugging" (also known as "electronic eavesdropping"), the listener puts a microphone in or near the place where a conversation is to occur, and uses this equipment to listen directly to the conversation. (An example of bugging would be the placement of a microphone inside a lamp inside the suspect's bedroom, where the microphone is used to pick up and transmit conversations taking place in that room.)

B. Requires warrant and probable cause: Both wiretapping and bugging normally constitute ***Fourth Amendment searches***, and must therefore satisfy the requirements of ***probable cause*** and a ***warrant***. That is, so long as the conversation that is intercepted is one as to which both participants had a ***reasonable expectation of privacy***, the fact that the microphone or wiretapping equipment is located outside the suspect's premises makes no difference. The famous case of *Katz v. U.S.*, in which the Supreme Court first articulated its "justifiable expectation of privacy" test for determining when the Fourth Amendment applies, was in fact a bugging case. [218]

1. **Participant monitoring:** But where the wire-tapping or eavesdropping occurs with the ***consent*** of one of the parties to the conversation, then there is ***no Fourth Amendment problem***. (*Example:* The FBI learns that D and X will be having a conversation in which D is likely to implicate himself in a crime. They ask X for permission to place a wiretap on X's phone; X agrees. The conversation takes place, and the agents record it. This wiretapping is not a violation of the Fourth Amendment, because it occurred with the permission of one of the participants. Therefore, the recording can be introduced against D at his criminal trial.) [219]

C. Federal statutory regulation: The use of wiretapping and electronic eavesdropping by government is now tightly regulated by a federal statute, Title III of the Omnibus Crime Control and Safe Streets Act of 1968. [219-222]

1. **Regulates state and federal law enforcement:** No ***federal or state*** law enforcement official may conduct electronic surveillance except by following the strict procedural requirements of Title III. (Also, a state official may not do so unless her state has passed enabling legislation, which fewer than half the states have done.)

2. **Requirements:** Under Title III, electronic surveillance may not take place except under a special ***judicial order*** authorizing the surveillance ***in advance***. The judge may authorize an intercept only if he finds that (*inter alia*): (1) there is ***probable cause*** to believe that a ***specific individual*** has committed one of certain crimes listed in the statute; (2) there is probable cause to believe that the intercept will ***furnish evidence*** about the crime; (3) normal investigative procedures have been tried and have failed, or reasonably appear likely to fail or be dangerous; and (4) there is probable cause to believe that the facilities where the intercept is to be made are being used in conjunction with the offense or are linked to the suspected individual.

3. **Covert entry allowed:** Once officials get a Title III judicial order authorizing bugging, they may make a ***covert entry*** even into private premises to install the bug. [*Dalia v. U.S.*] [221]

4. **Consenting party exception:** Title III does not apply where an interception takes place with the ***consent*** of one of the parties to a communication; in this situation, no warrant is needed (because, as noted above, the Fourth Amendment itself is never triggered). [221-222]

II. SECRET AGENTS

A. **Secret agents generally:** Fourth Amendment questions can also arise where the police make use of ***"secret agents."*** A secret agent is, in essence, a person who has ***direct contact*** with a suspect, under circumstances in which the suspect ***does not realize*** that he is dealing with someone who is helping the government. A secret agent can either be "bugged" (i.e., equipped with an electronic device that records and/or transmits conversations) or "unbugged."

1. **Summary of law:** In brief, ***neither "bugged" nor "unbugged" secret agents pose Fourth Amendment problems*** — so long as the target is aware that a person (the agent) is present, the fact that the target is unaware that the agent is indeed a secret agent or informer (as opposed to being the suspect's friend, for instance) does not turn the mission into a "search" or "seizure" under the Fourth Amendment.

B. **Bugged agents:** Thus the Supreme Court has held several times that "bugged agents" — secret agents equipped with electronic surveillance equipment — are not eavesdropping and thus cannot possibly violate the Fourth Amendment. [*On Lee v. U.S.*; *U.S. v. White*] [226-227]

> **Example:** Informer is wired to transmit to narcotics agents conversations that he hears or is a part of. Informer then has conversations with D in a restaurant, in D's home, and in Informer's car. Tapes of these transmitted conversations are introduced at D's criminal trial.
>
> *Held*, no Fourth Amendment right has been triggered. When a person misplaces his trust and makes incriminating statements to an informer, he does not have any justifiable expectation of privacy which has been violated — there is no Fourth Amendment protection given to "a wrongdoer's misplaced belief that a person to whom he voluntarily confides his wrongdoing will not reveal it." This is true whether the informer is bugged or not. [*U.S. v. White*, *supra*]

C. **Unbugged agents:** Since the use of bugged agents does not implicate the Fourth Amendment, it is not surprising that the use of ***unbugged*** agents does not violate that amendment either.

Example: A Teamster-turned-informant visits Jimmy Hoffa's hotel room and overhears conversations concerning Hoffa's plan to bribe jurors. The informant testifies about these conversations in Hoffa's later jury-tampering trial.

Held, Hoffa's Fourth Amendment rights were not even implicated, let alone violated, by introduction of these statements. Hoffa's "misplaced trust" was his own fault, and did not vitiate his consent to the informant's entry into the hotel suite. [*Hoffa v. U.S.*] [227]

Note on the right to counsel: But the use of a bugged or unbugged informer against a suspect who has already been ***indicted*** may violate the suspect's ***Sixth Amendment right to counsel***, discussed below. Once a suspect has been indicted and has counsel, it is a violation of that right to counsel for the secret agent to "deliberately elicit" incriminating statements from the suspect in the absence of counsel, and to pass these on to the prosecution for use in the case involving the indictment. For instance, in *Hoffa*, *supra*, if Hoffa had already been indicted by the time the informant came to Hoffa's hotel room — which he had not — the statements could not have been used against Hoffa in the trial on that indictment.

D. Entrapment: Very occasionally, a secret agent may be so active that his role constitutes ***"entrapment"*** of the defendant. In most jurisdictions, entrapment occurs if a law enforcement official, or someone cooperating with him, has ***induced*** D to commit a crime which D was not otherwise ***predisposed*** to commit. (*Example:* X, a secret government agent, repeatedly says to D over many months, "Why don't we rob the local 7-11?" D resists each time. Finally, D agrees to drive a car and wait while X does the robbery. As they arrive at the 7-11, police arrest D and charge him with attempted robbery. D may be able to establish that he was not predisposed to commit robbery and did so only because X induced him; if so, D may succeed with an entrapment defense.) [228]

1. **Not a constitutional defense:** The Supreme Court has never recognized any ***constitutional basis*** for the entrapment defense. Thus it is up to each state legislature (and, in the federal system, up to the Supreme Court in the exercise of its supervisory powers over the administration of justice in the federal court system) to decide under what facts the entrapment defense should be allowed. So in an exam question that is focusing on constitutional criminal procedure, you can probably ignore the possibility that the secret agent's conduct amounted to entrapment. [229]

CHAPTER 5

CONFESSIONS AND POLICE INTERROGATION

I. INTRODUCTION

A. Two requirements for confessions: In both state and federal courts, a ***confession*** may be introduced against the person who made it only if the confession satisfies ***each*** of the following two requirements:

1. **Voluntary:** The confession must have been ***voluntary***, i.e., not the product of ***coercion*** by the police; and

2. ***Miranda* warnings:** The confession must have been obtained in ***conformity*** with the ***Miranda*** decision — in brief, if the confession was given by the suspect while he was in custody and under interrogation by the authorities, the suspect must have been warned that he had the right to remain silent, that anything he said could be used against him, and that he had the right to have an attorney present.

II. VOLUNTARINESS

A. Voluntariness generally: Regardless of whether *Miranda* warnings are given to the suspect, his confession will only be admissible against him if it was given ***voluntarily***. [235]

1. **Must be police coercion:** But the test for determining the "voluntariness" of a confession is one that is fairly easy to satisfy. Apparently the only thing that can now prevent a confession from being found to be "voluntary" is ***police coercion***. Thus neither coercion by non-government personnel, nor serious ***mental illness*** on the suspect's part, is relevant to this question.

   Example 1: Victim says to Suspect, "Because you shot me, I will take revenge on you by shooting your sister unless you turn yourself into the police and confess." Suspect goes to the police and confesses. It appears that this confession would be treated as "voluntary," and admitted against Suspect at his criminal trial, even though it was in a sense the product of coercion by Victim — so long as there was no police coercion, nothing else matters in deciding the question of voluntariness.

   Example 2: Suspect is in a psychotic schizophrenic state. He confesses to a crime because the "voice of God" tells him he should do so. *Held*, this confession is admissible against Suspect, because there was no police or other governmental wrongdoing. [*Colorado v. Connelly*]

2. **Collateral use:** If a confession ***is*** obtained by police coercion (and is thus "involuntary"), it must be excluded not only from the prosecution's case in chief, but also from use to ***impeach*** D's testimony. (This makes involuntary confessions quite different from confessions given in violation of *Miranda*, which may be admitted to impeach D's testimony on the stand.)

III. *MIRANDA* GENERALLY

A. *Miranda:* The main set of rules governing confessions in both state and federal courts derive from ***Miranda v. Arizona***. In general, *Miranda* holds that when a suspect is questioned in custody by the police, his confession will be admissible against him only if he has received the "*Miranda* warnings." [239]

B. Three requirements for application: Before *Miranda* will be found to apply, ***three requirements*** must be satisfied:

1. **Custody:** First, *Miranda* warnings are necessary only where the suspect is taken into ***custody***. (Thus if the police ask a question to someone they meet on the street, without formally detaining him, *Miranda* is not triggered.) [239]

2. **Questioning:** Second, the *Miranda* rule applies only where the confession comes as the result of ***questioning***. (Thus statements that are truly ***"volunteered"*** by the suspect are not covered.)

3. **Authorities:** Finally, *Miranda* applies only where both the questioning and the custody are by the ***police*** or other ***law enforcement authorities***. (Thus if a private citizen, acting independently of law enforcement officials, detains a suspect and questions him, any resulting confession is not covered.)

C. **Warnings required:** There are ***four warnings*** that are required once *Miranda* applies at all. The suspect must be warned that [239]:

1. He has the right to ***remain silent***;
2. Anything he says can be ***used against him*** in a court of law;
3. He has the right to the ***presence*** of an ***attorney***; and
4. If he cannot ***afford*** an attorney, one will be ***appointed for him*** prior to any questioning if he desires.

D. **Inadmissibility:** Any statement obtained in violation of the *Miranda* rules will be ***inadmissible*** as prosecution evidence, even if the statement is in a sense "voluntary." [240]

1. **Impeachment use:** But a confession given in violation of *Miranda*, although not admissible as part of the prosecution's case in chief, may generally be introduced for purposes of ***impeaching*** testimony that the defendant has given. This "impeachment exception" to *Miranda* is discussed further below.

E. **Rights may be exercised at any time:** The suspect may exercise his right to remain silent, or to have a lawyer present, at ***any time*** during the questioning. Thus even if the suspect at first indicates that he waives his right to silence and to a lawyer, if he ***changes his mind*** the interrogation must ***cease***. [240]

F. **Waiver:** The suspect may ***waive*** his right to remain silent and to have a lawyer. However, this waiver is effective only if it is ***knowingly and intelligently made***. The suspect's ***silence*** may not be taken as a waiver. [240]

1. **Suspect already aware of rights:** The police must give the *Miranda* warnings even if they have reason to believe that the suspect is already ***aware*** of his rights.

G. **Right to counsel:**

1. **Right to appoint counsel applies only where questioning occurs:** If the suspect says that he wants his own lawyer present, or that he cannot afford a lawyer and wants one appointed for him, the police do ***not*** have an absolute duty to provide the previously-retained lawyer or a new appointed one — the rule is merely that the police ***must not question the suspect*** until they get him a lawyer. So the police can avoid the need for procuring counsel by simply not conducting the interrogation. [240]

2. **Right to have lawyer present during questioning:** The right to counsel imposed by *Miranda* is not merely the right to ***consult*** a lawyer prior to the questioning, but the right to ***have the lawyer present*** while the questioning occurs. [240]

H. **Fifth Amendment basis for:** The basis for *Miranda* is the ***Fifth Amendment's*** privilege against ***self-incrimination***, ***not*** the Sixth Amendment's right to counsel. The basic idea is that when a suspect is questioned while in custody, this questioning is likely to induce confessions made in violation of the Fifth Amendment. [241]

1. **Constitutional status unclear (*Dickerson*):** It's not clear whether a violation of a suspect's *Miranda* rights is *necessarily* a violation of the Fifth Amendment. In [*Dickerson v. U.S.*],

Congress tried to "repeal" the requirement of *Miranda* warnings in federal prosecutions. But the Court said that Congress didn't have the power to do this, because *Miranda* was at least indirectly ***based upon the Constitution***.

a. ***Not necessarily constitutionally required*:** However, in a post-*Dickerson* case, *Vega v. Tekoh*, the Court seemed to ***back away*** from the idea that a *Miranda* violation is necessarily a violation of the suspect's constitutional rights. There, the Court held that *Miranda* constitutes the Court's use of a "***prophylactic***" power to avoid constitutional violations, by setting out a ***"bright-line" rule*** requiring warnings in all cases to prevent constitutional violations in some. Therefore, *Vega* says, when D's un-*Mirandized* confession is used against him at trial but he is nonetheless acquitted, D may not recover damages under §1983 for this violation of his *Miranda* rights because D's constitutional rights were not directly violated. [*Vega v. Tekoh* (2022].[4] [243]

IV. WHAT IS A "CUSTODIAL" INTERROGATION

A. **"Custody" required:** *Miranda* warnings must be given only when police questioning occurs while the suspect is in ***"custody."*** [243]

1. **"Focus of investigation" irrelevant:** In deciding whether the suspect is in "custody," the fact that the police investigation has (or has not) ***"focused"*** on that suspect is ***irrelevant.*** [243]

2. **Objective "reasonable suspect" test:** Whether a suspect is or is not in "custody" as of a particular moment is to be determined by an objective ***"reasonable suspect"*** test: the issue is ***whether a reasonable person in the suspect's position would believe that he was (or was not) in custody at that moment.*** [244-245]

a. **Officer's unexpressed intent irrelevant:** This "reasonable suspect" standard means that the ***unexpressed intent of the interrogating officer*** to hold (or not hold) the suspect is ***irrelevant.***

Example: D, a motorist, is stopped by Officer and required to get out of his car. Officer asks D a question, to which D gives an incriminating response. At the moment Officer asked the question, Officer had decided to arrest D, but had not yet told D of this fact.

Held, D was not necessarily in custody from the moment he was required to get out of the car — the issue is "how a reasonable person in the suspect's position would have understood his situation," and a reasonable person on these facts might have believed he was free to go. [*Berkemer v. McCarty*] [247]

b. **Suspect is minor:** Suppose that the suspect is a ***child.*** When the objective "reasonable suspect" test is being applied, the child's ***age will be taken into account*** in determining whether a reasonable person in the suspect's position would believe he was in custody. So the younger the child, the quicker the court will be to conclude that a reasonable person of that child's age would have believed that he was in custody and not free to leave. [*J.D.B. v. North Carolina*] [246]

3. **Undercover agent:** One consequence of the "reasonable suspect" rule is that if D talks to an ***undercover agent*** or to a government ***informant***, and D does not know he is talking to a law

4. *Vega* is discussed more extensively *infra*, p. C-78.

enforcement officer, no "custodial interrogation" has taken place. This is true even if D is ***in jail***. [*Illinois v. Perkins*] [244]

Note: However, the use of undercover agents, although it will never cause a *Miranda* violation, may lead to a violation of the suspect's ***Sixth Amendment*** right to ***counsel*** — once a suspect has been indicted or otherwise charged, it violates his right to counsel for a secret agent to deliberately obtain incriminating statements from him in the absence of counsel.

B. **Place of interrogation:** The ***place*** in which the interrogation takes place will often have an important bearing on whether "custody" exists. The test is always whether a reasonable person in D's position would believe he was free to leave, and this will depend in part on the locale. [246-249]

1. **Station-house:** Thus interrogations that take place in a ***station house*** are more likely to be found "custodial" than those in, say, the defendant's home. [246]

   a. **Arrest:** If D has been told that he is ***"under arrest"*** and is escorted to the police station, that's virtually dispositive — D is clearly in custody, because a person under arrest is not free to leave (at least until further steps, such as arraignment, have taken place).

   b. **Placed in patrol car:** Similarly, if D has been placed in a ***patrol car*** under circumstances suggesting that D has been arrested, he is clearly in "custody."

   c. **Voluntary station house questioning:** A suspect who ***"voluntarily"*** comes to the police station in response to a police request is normally ***not*** in custody, and is therefore not entitled to *Miranda* warnings. [*Oregon v. Mathiason*]

      i. **Lack of formal arrest not dispositive:** However, the mere fact that there has been ***no formal arrest*** will ***not*** by itself suffice to prevent station house questioning from being custodial. If the surrounding circumstances would indicate to a reasonable person in D's situation that he was not free to leave the station house, then the questioning is "custodial" however voluntary D's initial decision to come to the station may have been. (*Example:* During the course of "voluntary" questioning, the police let D know that they now consider him the key suspect in the crime. This is likely to be enough to convince a reasonable person in D's position that the police are about to arrest him; if so, D is already in custody.)

2. **Street encounters:** The issue of whether D is in custody often arises where the encounter takes place on the ***street***.

   a. **Scene-of-the-crime questioning:** The police may engage in a general questioning of persons ***near the scene of a crime*** without giving *Miranda* warnings. [247]

      i. **Focus on suspect:** But if the police seize one particular suspect fleeing the scene of the crime, the warnings presumably have to be given.

   b. **D acts suspiciously:** The police may sometimes detain a person not as part of a general "scene of the crime" investigation for a specific known crime, but because the person is ***acting suspiciously***. (*Example:* A brief "stop and frisk" detention.) Such encounters are usually not custodial, even where the suspect is frisked for the policeman's safety. [247]

3. **Traffic stops:** Stops of ***motorists*** for ***minor traffic violations*** will normally ***not*** be "custodial." Here, as in other contexts, the test is whether one in the motorist's position would

believe that he was or was not free to leave. Usually a driver in this position would reasonably believe that he was free to leave after a ticket had been issued to him. [248]

a. **Arrest:** Of course, if the police notify the motorist that he is ***under arrest***, he is immediately deemed to be in custody.

4. **Interview at home:** If the encounter takes place at D's ***home***, while he has not been placed under arrest, D is probably ***not*** in custody. [248]

V. MINOR CRIMES

A. **No "minor crimes" exception:** There is ***no "minor crimes" exception*** to the *Miranda* requirement. That is, if an interrogation meets all of the standard requirements for *Miranda* warnings (especially the requirement that the suspect be "in custody"), these warnings must be given ***no matter how minor the crime***, and regardless of the fact that ***no jail sentence*** may be imposed for it. [*Berkemer v. McCarty, supra*] [249]

1. **Traffic stops:** This means that if the suspect is charged with a ***minor traffic violation***, but is then taken into custody, he is entitled to *Miranda* warnings. [249]

VI. WHAT CONSTITUTES INTERROGATION

A. **Volunteered statements:** A ***"volunteered statement"*** is not covered by *Miranda*. That is, if a suspect, without being questioned, ***spontaneously*** makes an incriminating statement, that statement may be introduced against him, despite the absence of *Miranda* warnings. [250]

1. **Voluntary custodial statements:** This is true even if the statement comes from a suspect who is ***in custody***. So long as the statement is not induced by police questioning, the fact that the suspect is in custody is not enough to trigger *Miranda*.

B. **Indirect questioning:** But "interrogation" for *Miranda* purposes includes more than just direct questioning by the police. Interrogation will be deemed to occur whenever a person in custody is subjected to either express questioning, or to words or actions on the part of the police that the police "should know are ***reasonably likely*** to ***elicit*** an ***incriminating response*** from the suspect." [*Rhode Island v. Innis*] [250]

1. **No interrogation found:** Application of this "should know are reasonably likely to elicit an incriminating response" test will often mean that even though the police make comments that lead directly to an incriminating result, no "interrogation" is found.

Example: D is arrested for a murder committed by use of a sawed-off shotgun, which has not been found. While D is being transported near the crime scene, Officer comments to his colleagues in front of D that there is a school for handicapped children nearby, and that "God forbid one of the children might find a weapon with shells and they might hurt themselves." D then directs the officers to the place where the gun can be found. *Held*, Officer's comment did not constitute interrogation of D, so D was not entitled to *Miranda* warnings. [*Rhode Island v. Innis, supra*] [250]

C. **Police allow situation to develop:** The requirement of "interrogation" means that even if the police allow a situation to develop that is likely to induce the suspect to volunteer an incriminating remark, no *Miranda* warnings will be given if the police do not directly interact with the suspect. For instance, where the police allow a meeting between D and his spouse in which D is likely to incriminate himself while under covert observation, probably no "interrogation" occurs. [*Arizona v. Mauro*] [251]

1. **Police set up situation:** But if the police intentionally set up a compromising situation for the ***purpose*** of inducing D to incriminate himself, interrogation is much more likely to be found.

D. **Identification questions:** Routine questions asked to a suspect for ***identification only*** probably do not require *Miranda* warnings. (*Example:* Routine questions asked during the booking of a suspect, such as questions about D's name, address, height, weight, etc., do not require *Miranda* warnings.) [252]

E. **Questions by non-police:** Where questions are asked by people other than the police, these will invoke *Miranda* only if asked by other ***law enforcement*** officials. [253]

1. **Investigator or victims:** Thus questions asked of a suspect by a ***private investigator***, or by a victim of the crime, will not be covered by *Miranda*.
2. **Government officials:** But questions by ***probation officers***, ***IRS agents*** conducting tax investigations, or a court-ordered psychiatrist evaluating D's sanity for purposes of penalties, are all likely to be found to trigger a requirement of *Miranda* warnings.

VII. THE "PUBLIC SAFETY" EXCEPTION TO *MIRANDA*

A. **The public safety exception generally:** *Miranda* warnings are ***unnecessary*** where the questioning is "reasonably prompted by a concern for the ***public safety***." [*New York v. Quarles*] [254-256]

> **Example:** Officer and three colleagues accost D, a suspected rapist, in a grocery store. When he sees the officers, D runs towards the back of the store, where he is caught and handcuffed. Officer, without giving D *Miranda* warnings, asks him whether he has a gun and where it is. D answers, "Over there." The gun is found, and D's statement — plus the gun — are introduced against him at his trial.
>
> *Held*, even though D was in custody and was under interrogation at the time of his statement, he was not entitled to *Miranda* warnings because the police questioning was motivated by a need to protect the public safety. [*Quarles*, *supra*]

1. **Objective standard:** The existence of a threat to the public safety is to be determined by an ***objective***, not subjective, standard. That is, the questioning officer's subjective belief that there is or is not a significant threat to the public safety is ***irrelevant***, and the test is whether a ***reasonable officer*** in that position would conclude that there was such a threat.
2. **May still show compulsion:** Despite the "public safety" exception to *Miranda*, the defendant is always allowed to show that his answers were ***actually coerced***. If he can make this showing, he will still be entitled to have those answers excluded — this exclusion will be based on lack of voluntariness, not on the police failure to give *Miranda* warnings.

VIII. WAIVERS AND INVOCATIONS OF *MIRANDA* RIGHTS

A. **Waivers and invocations generally:** After being read the *Miranda* warnings, a suspect may ***waive*** his right to a lawyer and his right to remain silent. Conversely, the suspect may ***invoke*** his *Miranda* rights.

1. **Two different rights:** Keep in mind that there are ***two distinct Miranda rights*** that may be the subject of a waiver or invocation: the right to have ***questioning cease*** until the suspect can ***consult a lawyer***, and the right to ***remain silent***. The rules on waiver and invocation are similar, but not identical, as between the two contexts. [259]

B. **Determining whether a waiver occurred:** Here are the rules for determining ***whether a suspect has waived*** one or both of his *Miranda* rights.

1. **"Knowing and voluntary":** For the suspect to be deemed to have waived either *Miranda* right (silence or counsel), the prosecution will have to show that the waiver was ***"knowing and voluntary."*** [260]

   a. **Fact of confession not enough:** The mere fact that the suspect ***answered questions*** after being given his *Miranda* warnings will not, without more, constitute the required proof of knowing and voluntary waiver. There must in addition be affirmative evidence of both the voluntary element (i.e., lack of coercion) and the knowing element (understanding of at least some of the consequences of waiving).

   Example: At a hearing on whether D in fact waived his *Miranda* rights before speaking to the police, the arresting officer O testifies that he read D his *Miranda* warnings from a printed card, and that D then confessed when asked whether he was involved in the crime in question. O testifies that he cannot remember whether he asked D if he understood the rights, or whether O made an effort to determine if D was capable of understanding these warnings.

   Held, this testimony is not enough to demonstrate waiver, because it does not satisfy the "knowing" element. The mere fact that warnings were read to the suspect, and that the suspect thereafter immediately confessed, does not establish that he understood the nature of the rights he was waiving. [*Tague v. Louisiana*] [260]

2. **Express waivers:** Waivers can, of course, be "***express***." For instance, if a suspect signs a standard waiver form, that's an express waiver. Express waivers can be oral, too; if the suspect says to the police, "I understand these rights but I'm willing to talk to you," that's an express waiver. Express waivers will be ***valid*** as long as there is no indication of ***coercion*** or of basic ***lack of understanding*** by the suspect. [261]

3. **Implied waivers:** But ***"implied"*** waivers are also possible, and, indeed, common. That is, in some cases waiver can be clearly "***inferred*** from the ***actions and words*** of the person interrogated." [*North Carolina v. Butler*] [261]

   a. **Answering of questions:** The most common form of implied waiver comes after the suspect is read his warnings, indicates that he understands them, never expressly says that he is waving his rights, and then ***answers one or more questions***. This will certainly be a waiver of the right to silence, and will probably be a waiver of the right to counsel.

   b. **Additional factors:** Here are two additional factors that will make it more likely that an implied waiver will be found to have occurred:

      D was ***familiar with the criminal justice system*** by virtue of his having been arrested and interrogated on multiple recent occasions. This familiarity makes it more likely that D understood his rights and understood the consequences of waiving them.

      D answers ***some*** questions but refuses to answer others. This selective response

C A P S U L E S U M M A R Y

makes it more likely that D understood his rights and intended to waive them. [262]

4. **Information about scope of questioning:** For a waiver to be valid, the suspect does not need to be told much if anything about the ***scope*** of the proposed questioning, as long as the police do not intentionally mislead the subject on this point. [262]

   Example: Suppose the suspect believes that the upcoming interrogation will focus only upon the ***minor crime*** for which he has been arrested, and waives his rights to permit the interrogation. If the police suddenly change the questioning to cover a different, much more major crime (e.g., a murder committed years ago), this does not make the waiver invalid. [*Colorado v. Spring*]

5. **Knowledge that D's lawyer is trying to contact him:** Suppose the suspect is ***represented by an attorney who is trying to see him,*** and this fact is known to the police but not to the suspect. (For instance, perhaps the lawyer has been retained ***on the suspect's behalf*** not by the suspect himself but by a ***friend or family member***). The suspect's waiver of his *Miranda* rights will be ***effective*** even though the police: (1) ***decline to tell*** the suspect that a lawyer has been retained for him or is trying to see him; and (2) ***prevent***, or by use of trickery discourage, the lawyer from seeing his client. [*Moran v. Burbine*] [263-264]

6. **Mentally ill defendant:** Suppose that a suspect who waives his *Miranda* rights is ***mentally ill***, and his illness in some sense causes him to waive his *Miranda* rights and confess. Assuming that there is no police coercion, does the fact that the suspect's decision to waive his rights is not fully rational make the waiver invalid? The answer is "no" — ***no matter how irrational the suspect's decision to waive his Miranda rights, the waiver will stand so long as there was no police coercion***. [*Colorado v. Connelly*] [264]

   Example: D is a chronic schizophrenic, and is in a psychotic state when he walks up to Officer, waives his *Miranda* rights, and confesses. D, in confessing, thinks he is following the "voice of God." There is no evidence that Officer knew of D's mental state, or used any coercion.

   Held, the confession is admissible. "*Miranda* protects defendants against ***government coercion*** leading them to surrender rights protected by the Fifth Amendment; it goes ***no further*** than that." [*Colorado v. Connelly*] [264]

   a. **Significance:** As *Connelly* and other cases show, the Court refuses to ***consider anything but police coercion*** in determining whether a waiver of *Miranda* rights is "voluntary."

C. **Invocation must be "clear and unequivocal":** Just as a *waiver* of either *Miranda* right must be ***"clear and unequivocal,"*** so an ***invocation*** of either right must be clear and unequivocal. [265]

   1. **Police can keep trying:** Consequently, until a clear and unequivocal invocation of either right has occurred, the police may ***continue to question the suspect*** and/or to ***repeatedly request a waiver.***

      Example: D is interrogated by Detective Helgert and another detective in connection with a fatal shooting one year earlier. They read D *Miranda* warnings from a document, and then ask him to sign the waiver clause at the bottom. D makes an ambiguous indication about whether he understands the rights listed on the document, and refuses to sign the form. The police interrogate him for two and three-quarter hours, during which he mostly remains silent but occasionally gives a one-word non-incriminating answer. Then,

Helgert asks D, "Do you pray to God?", to which D answers yes. Helgert next asks, "Do you pray to God to forgive you for shooting that boy down?" D answers yes, and looks away. D later tries to have this last remark suppressed from his trial, arguing that when he gave an ambiguous statement about whether he understood his right to remain silent and intended to invoke it, the police were required to clarify his intent before they resumed questioning.

Held, the incriminating remark is admissible. An invocation of the *Miranda* right to remain silent must be unambiguous. D's conduct was ambiguous as to whether he was asserting his right of silence, so he will be deemed not to have asserted that right. Since there is no evidence that he was coerced, the police were entitled to continue questioning him up until the incriminating remark. [*Berguis v. Thompkins*] [266]

2. **Mere answering of questions:** So the prosecution must demonstrate only three things in order to establish an implied waiver of the right to silence:

   [1] that the police gave the suspect *Miranda* warnings;

   [2] that the suspect ***understood*** the warnings; and

   [3] that the suspect ***answered*** one or more questions following the warnings.

   If they can show these three things, then the fact that the police ***continued to interrogate*** the suspect at length after he made an ambiguous indication about whether he was invoking his right to silence will not matter. [267]

CAPSULE SUMMARY

D. **Waiver after successful invocation of the right:** Let's turn now to the rules governing what happens when the suspect *does* invoke with sufficient clarity either his right to remain silent or his right to counsel. The suspect's later words or conduct can sometimes be deemed to be an ***undoing*** of that invocation. The rules for undoing an invocation of the right to counsel are somewhat stricter than those for undoing an invocation of the right to remain silent. [267]

1. **Right to counsel:** Where the defendant asserts in the first session that he ***wants a lawyer***, the Supreme Court has made it ***very hard*** for the prosecution to establish that this demand has subsequently been waived. The bright-line rule is that once the suspect says he wants to deal with the police only through counsel, he "is ***not subject to further interrogation*** by the authorities ***until counsel has been made available to him***, unless the ***accused himself initiates*** further communication, exchanges or conversations with the police." [*Edwards v. Arizona*] [267]

   a. **Response to questioning:** Waiver will not be established by the mere fact that the suspect ***responded*** to later ***police-initiated*** interrogation (even if that interrogation was preceded by a new reading of the *Miranda* warnings). [*Edwards*]

   b. **"Initiating the conversation" test:** So once a suspect indicates a desire to have a lawyer, any subsequent ***waiver*** of that right will not be measured by the usual tests for waiver (the "knowing and voluntary" standard; see *supra*, p. C-58). Instead, the only way the suspect may waive a previously-asserted desire to have a lawyer present at interrogation is by ***initiating the conversation*** with the police.

   c. **Questioning after a suspect has consulted lawyer:** Suppose the suspect asks for a lawyer, ***consults*** with this lawyer, and is subsequently interrogated by the police outside the lawyer's presence. In this situation, the rule that a suspect who asks for a lawyer may not then be subject to police-initiated interrogation will be deemed to be ***violated***. In other words, the lawyer must be present ***during the subsequent questioning***, and a mere consultation before the questioning will be no substitute for this. [*Minnick v. Mississippi*] [270]

d. Break in custody: The "no police-initiated questioning after invocation of the right to counsel" rule ***ceases to apply*** once there has been a substantial ***break in custody.*** In this narrow situation, the Supreme Court has laid down a very bright-line rule: once the suspect has been ***out of custody for at least 14 days***, the police may initiate questioning even though they never furnished counsel in response to the suspect's initial request for it. [*Maryland v. Shatzer*] [271]

Example: In August 2003, while D is already in prison on an unrelated crime, a detective tries to question him about allegations that he sexually assaulted his son. D invokes his right to counsel; questioning ceases, and D is returned to the general prison population, without being given counsel. Then, in March, 2006, a different detective learns new information about the assault incident, and decides to question D again. D, who is still in prison, signs a written waiver of his *Miranda* rights, and then undergoes several questioning sessions during which he incriminates himself. He argues that the 2006 questioning was invalid because it was initiated by the police, after D had previously requested counsel and not been given it.

Held, for the prosecution. The break in custody (2 1/2 years) was sufficiently long that the ***coercive effect*** of the initial interrogation, which had led D to invoke his right to counsel, should be deemed to have ***dissipated***. In fact, any break in custody longer than ***14 days*** would have sufficed to dissipate this coercive effect. And even though D remained in prison for the 2 1/2 years, this doesn't count as "custody," because D was part of the general prison population and was not subjected to coercion of the sort that *Miranda* was designed to prevent. [*Maryland v. Shatzer*] [271]

2. Right to silence: When may the police initiate a new interrogation after the suspect has invoked his ***right to silence***? In the right-to-silence scenario there is no equivalent of the bright-line "police may not initiate questioning" rule that applies after the suspect requests counsel.

a. "Scrupulously honored" standard: Instead, the Court applies a much-weaker standard: ***"scrupulously honored."*** That is, "the admissibility of statements obtained after the person in custody has decided to remain silent depends [on] whether his 'right to cut off questioning' was 'scrupulously honored.'" [*Michigan v. Mosley*] [272]

Example: D is interrogated about two robberies after receiving his *Miranda* warnings. He says he does not want to answer police questions. Questioning is then immediately terminated. Several hours later, D is taken to a different floor of the building where he is being held, and, after again being given his *Miranda* warnings, is questioned by a different officer about a fatal shooting which had occurred in a third robbery. Williams implicated himself. At trial, he moves to strike his statements on the ground that they were procured in violation of his right not to be questioned after he initially exercised his *Miranda* rights.

Held, for the prosecution. D's right not to be questioned was ***not violated*** by the resumption of questioning. The issue is whether D's right was "scrupulously honored." The police here "***immediately ceased*** the interrogation, resumed questioning only after the passage of a ***significant period of time*** and the provision of a ***fresh set of warnings***." That was enough to constitute a scrupulous honoring of D's right of silence. [*Michigan v. Mosley*]

i. **Significance:** According to subsequent lower-court cases, the police must satisfy ***three requirements*** in order to be deemed to have "scrupulously honored" the suspect's invocation of his right to remain silent:

The police must have ***immediately ceased the interrogation*** once the suspect invoked his right;

The ***gap*** between the cessation of questioning and the initiation of the new session must represent a ***significant passage of time*** (a ***"cooling off"*** period); and

Prior to the second interrogation, the police must give a ***second set*** of *Miranda* warnings.

(1) **No ban on re-initiating questioning:** Unlike the situation in which the suspect invokes the right to *counsel*, the police are permitted to ***re-initiate*** questioning in the right-to-silence scenario. In other words, the bright-line rule for right-to-counsel cases (that when a suspect has invoked the right to counsel, any new questioning session must be initiated by the suspect, not the police) does *not apply* where the right being invoked is the right to silence. [274]

b. **Ambiguous invocation of right:** If the police give the *Miranda* warnings and the suspect gives an ***ambiguous*** response as to whether he means to assert his right to silence, two things happen:

The ambiguous response does ***not*** constitute an invocation of the right (because only unambiguous invocations count; see *supra*, p. C-59); and

The police may ***continue asking questions*** to the suspect, rather than either stopping the interrogation or even trying to clarify the suspect's intent.

Taken together, these two facts mean that until the police receive an unambiguous indication that the suspect wants to remain silent and not be further questioned, the police have an ***incentive to continue asking questions***. [275]

CAPSULE SUMMARY

IX. OTHER *MIRANDA* ISSUES

A. **Grand jury witnesses:** A witness who is subpoenaed to appear before a ***grand jury*** probably does ***not*** have to be given *Miranda* warnings. [276]

B. **Impeachment:** A confession obtained in violation of *Miranda* may not be introduced as part of the prosecution's case-in-chief. But the prosecution ***may*** use such statements to ***impeach*** D's testimony at trial. [*Harris v. New York*]

Example: D is charged with selling heroin on two occasions. At his trial, he takes the stand and denies making one of these sales. The prosecution then reads a statement, obtained in violation of *Miranda*, in which D admits making both sales. *Held*, even though the statement was made without benefit of *Miranda* warnings, it may be used to impeach D's trial testimony. [*Harris*, *supra*] [277]

1. **Coercion:** Although a statement obtained in violation of *Miranda* may be admissible for impeachment purposes, it may ***not*** be used even for this limited purpose if it was the product of ***coercion***, or was ***involuntary*** for some other reason. [*Mincey v. Arizona*] [278]

C. Use of D's silence:

A key issue is whether and when the prosecution may call to the jury's attention at trial the fact that the defendant has ***remained silent at some prior point,*** thus raising a reasonable ***inference of guilt.*** The answer depends heavily on the situation in which the silence occurred.

1. **Comment on D's failure to take the stand:** Where D exercises his Fifth Amendment right ***not to take the stand at his trial***, the Fifth Amendment itself ***prevents the prosecution from pointing out to the jury*** that D ***could have taken the stand*** to "tell his story" and elected not to do so. [*Griffin v. California*] Similarly, the trial judge ***may not instruct the jury*** that D's silence (his failure to take the stand) constitutes evidence of guilt. [*Id.*] [279]

2. **Impeachment by showing D's silence during custodial interrogation:** Suppose D raises a particular defense at trial (e.g., an alibi defense), and the prosecution would like to disprove that defense and/or impeach D's credibility as a witness, by showing that while D was ***being subjected to custodial interrogation***, he ***remained silent***, in a way that is inconsistent with his story at trial. [279]

   a. **D does not take the stand:** Where D does ***not even take the stand***, the prosecution ***may not comment*** on the fact that D invoked his right to remain silent during questioning. And that's true even if D is asserting at trial (through third-party witnesses) an ***alibi*** that an innocent suspect would be likely to have explained to police during the interrogation.

   b. **Impeachment of D's credibility:** Now, let's suppose that D *does* elect to take the stand, and recites his present version of the facts (e.g., an ***alibi***). On cross-examination, may the prosecution attempt to impeach D's credibility by saying, in effect, "If your story is true, ***why didn't you tell that story to the police*** when they had you in custody and gave you your *Miranda* warnings"? Here, too, the prosecution ***may not refer, directly or indirectly, to D's silence under custodial questioning,*** even if that silence is inconsistent with D's present trial testimony. [*Doyle v. Ohio*] [280]

3. **Silence under non-custodial questioning:** Now, suppose that at a time when the police have ***begun to suspect D*** of a particular crime, but ***before*** they have ***arrested*** him, they ask him to ***undergo voluntary questioning*** and he agrees. If D then refuses to answer a particular question or to discuss a particular topic, may the prosecution comment on that refusal at trial? The answer seems to depend on whether D is found to have ***formally invoked*** his ***Fifth Amendment*** rights during the questioning:

   [1] If D *has* formally invoked those rights, it's not yet clear as of this writing whether the prosecution may comment on his silence (though the odds are good that the Court will ultimately decide that the prosecution may not comment). But ...

   [2] If D has ***not*** explained why he is remaining silent (so that he is ***not found to have invoked*** his Fifth Amendment rights), it's clear that the prosecution ***may comment*** on that silence. [*Salinas v. Texas* (2013)] [280]

   Example of [2]: In a double-shotgun-murder case, the police have come to suspect D, so they visit him at his home. During the home visit, D agrees to hand over his shotgun for ballistic testing. The police then ask D if he will voluntarily accompany them to police headquarters for questioning; D agrees. At the station, the officers do not arrest or charge D, and do not read him his *Miranda* warnings. D initially answers the officers' questions. But when the police ask him whether his shotgun will match the shells recovered at the scene of the murder, D declines to answer (without giving a reason), and behaves with evasive body language. At trial, D does not take the stand. The prosecution introduces testimony by the officers about D's silence (and physical reactions) during the questioning about shell-matching. D claims that this testimony violates his Fifth Amendment privilege against self-incrimination.

Held, for the prosecution. Five Justices believe either that (1) where a suspect is engaged in a ***"voluntary"*** rather than custodial interrogation, the suspect must ***explicitly*** tell the police that his silence is due to his reliance on his Fifth Amendment privilege, or else the prosecution may comment on his silence (three votes) or (2) it doesn't *matter* whether a suspect undergoing voluntary (non-custodial) interrogation expressly invokes his Fifth Amendment rights, because prosecutors may comment on a defendant's pre-custody silence even if he *did* make such an invocation (two votes). So a majority holds that here, the prosecution may comment, since D volunteed for the questioning, and then merely cut off his answers without citing his privilege against self-incrimination. [*Salinas v. Texas, supra*] [280-282]

4. **D's silence without interrogation:** Finally, suppose D was never subjected to questioning (voluntary or custodial), but simply ***failed to come forward*** to tell the police his "story," under circumstances in which an innocent and truthful person would likely have done so. In this situation, like the "voluntary questioning" situation addressed in *Salinas*, *supra*, the prosecution ***may comment*** on the defendant's initial silence. [*Jenkins v. Anderson*]

   Example: D raises a self-defense claim at his murder trial. The prosecution impeaches this claim by pointing out that for two weeks after the murder, D failed to go to the authorities to surrender himself or explain the self-defense incident. *Held*, D's pre-arrest silence *may* be used to impeach his trial testimony, because D was not in custody at the time of his silence, *and* no governmental action induced him to remain silent before his arrest. [*Jenkins v. Anderson*] [283]

CHAPTER 6

LINEUPS AND OTHER PRE-TRIAL IDENTIFICATION PROCEDURES

I. I.D. PROCEDURES GENERALLY

A. Various procedures: There are a number of methods by which the police may get an ***identification*** of a suspect to link him with a crime: ***lineups***, ***fingerprints***, ***blood samples***, ***voice prints***, the use of ***photographs***, etc.

B. Possible constitutional problems: There are four plausible constitutional objections that D may be able to make to the use of one of these procedures against him: (1) that it violates D's privilege against ***self-incrimination***; (2) that it constituted an ***unreasonable search or seizure*** in violation of the Fourth Amendment; (3) that if D did not have a lawyer present, the use of the procedure violated his ***Sixth Amendment right to counsel***; and (4) that the procedure was so suggestive that it violated D's Fifth/Fourteenth Amendment right to ***due process***. [297]

C. Right to counsel as main weapon: The objection that is most likely to succeed is that use of one of these procedures (especially a lineup or show-up) without D's lawyer present violated his right to counsel; the next most likely to succeed is the argument that the procedure was so suggestive that it violated due process (most likely to work where the procedure was a lineup, show-up, or photo I.D.). The self-incrimination argument will almost never work, and the search and seizure argument has a chance of working only if the police lacked a warrant and/or probable cause.

II. THE PRIVILEGE AGAINST SELF-INCRIMINATION

A. General rule: ***Physical identification procedures*** — fingerprints, blood samples, voice prints, etc. — will generally ***not*** trigger the Fifth Amendment privilege against ***self-incrimination***. That privilege protects only against compulsion to give ***"testimony or communicative*** evidence," and these physical procedures have been found not to be "testimony or communicative." [*Schmerber v. California*]

> **Example:** D is arrested for drunk driving. A blood sample is forcibly taken from him over his objection, by a physician acting under the direction of the police. *Held*, D's privilege against self-incrimination was not violated by the forcible test, because the privilege protects only against being compelled to give testimony or communicative evidence, not being forced to give real or physical evidence. [*Schmerber, supra*] [298]

1. **Other procedures:** This principle has been broadly applied, so that D has no self-incrimination privilege against being forced to: (1) appear in a ***lineup***; (2) ***speak*** for identification; (3) give ***fingerprints***; (4) be ***photographed***; (5) be ***measured***; (6) be required to make ***physical movements***; (7) give a ***handwriting*** sample; or (8) be examined by ultraviolet light. [299]

2. **Non-cooperation:** If the suspect refuses to cooperate with a request to provide one of these sources of physical identification, the court may order him to do so. If he still refuses, the court may hold him in contempt and jail him. [299]

   a. **Prosecution's right to comment:** Furthermore, if D refuses to cooperate with such a request, the prosecution may ***comment*** on that fact at D's later trial.

III. THE RIGHT TO COUNSEL AT PRE-TRIAL CONFRONTATIONS

A. Rule generally: A suspect against whom formal criminal proceedings have been commenced has an ***absolute right*** to have ***counsel present*** at any pre-trial ***confrontation*** procedure. Such confrontations include both ***lineups*** (in which a witness picks the suspect out of a group of persons) and ***show-ups*** (in which the witness is shown only the suspect and asked whether the suspect is the perpetrator). [*U.S. v. Wade*; *Gilbert v. California*] [299]

> **Example:** D is indicted for robbery, arrested, and brought to the police station. He is placed in a lineup with other men of similar appearance. V, the robbery victim, is asked to identify the perpetrator. V picks D out of the lineup. Unless the police offered D the chance to have counsel present at the lineup, the results of the lineup will not be admissible against D at his criminal trial.

1. **Effect on in-court I.D.:** Furthermore, if the confrontation is conducted in violation of the right of counsel, the prosecution will not only be barred from introducing at trial the fact that D was picked out of the lineup, but may even be barred from having the witness who made the identification (V in the above example) ***testify in court*** that the person sitting in the dock is the person observed by the witness at the scene of the crime. Once the lineup is shown to have been improper, the prosecution will have to come up with ***"clear and convincing evi-***

dence" that the in-court identification is not the "fruit of the poisonous tree" (i.e., the product of the improper lineup identification). [301]

B. Waiver: The right to have counsel at the pre-trial confrontation proceeding may be ***waived***. But the waiver must be an "intelligent" one; probably, the police must inform D of his right to counsel, and D must be capable of understanding that right and must voluntarily choose to give it up. [302]

C. Exceptions to the right:

1. **Before formal proceedings against D:** The right to have counsel at the pre-trial confrontation probably applies only to confrontations occurring after the institution of ***formal proceedings*** against the suspect. [*Kirby v. Illinois*] The right will be triggered by the fact that D has been formally charged, given a preliminary hearing, indicted, arraigned, or otherwise subjected to formal judiciary proceedings. Probably the right is triggered if an ***arrest warrant*** is issued; but the right is probably ***not*** triggered if D has merely been ***arrested without a warrant*** and then put in the lineup or show-up. Certainly the right seems not to be triggered where the police have not even arrested D yet, but have asked him to voluntarily appear in a lineup, and D agrees. [303]

2. **Photo I.D.:** The right to counsel does ***not*** apply where a witness views ***still or moving pictures*** of the suspect for identification purposes. [303]

   Example: D is not present when the police bring photos of D, together with photos of innocent people, to V, and ask V to pull the photo of the perpetrator from the group. The fact that D has not been given a chance to have a lawyer present during this procedure makes no difference, because D has no Sixth Amendment right to counsel in this non–face-to-face situation. [*U.S. v. Ash*]

   Note: But the due process right not to be subjected to "unduly suggestive" procedures may be triggered in this photo I.D. situation, as discussed below.

3. **Scientific I.D. procedures:** No Sixth Amendment right to counsel attaches where ***scientific methods***, as opposed to eye witness identification procedures, are used to identify D as the perpetrator. Thus if the police extract or analyze D's fingerprints, blood samples, clothing, hair, voice, handwriting samples, etc., D does not have a right to have counsel present during these extractions or examinations. [304]

IV. DUE PROCESS LIMITS ON I.D. PROCEDURES

A. Suggestive procedures: Even where the right to counsel is never triggered by an identification procedure (or has been triggered but complied with), D may be able to exclude the resulting identification on the grounds that it violated his ***due process*** rights. To do this, D will have to show that, viewed by the "totality of the circumstances," the identification procedure was so ***"unnecessarily suggestive"*** and so conducive to mistaken identification, as to be deeply unfair to D. [305]

   Example: D is suspected of robbery. D is lined up with men several inches shorter than he. Only D wears a jacket similar to that known to have been used by the robber. After V is unable to positively identify anyone, the police then use a one-man show-up of D. When V is still uncertain, the police put on, several days later, a second lineup, in which D is the only repeater from the previous lineup.

Held, the procedures used here were so suggestive that an identification of D as the perpetrator was "all but inevitable." Therefore, the fact that V picked D out of the second lineup must be excluded from D's trial, as a violation of his due process rights. (This is true regardless of whether D had, or used, any right to have counsel present.) [*Foster v. California*]

B. Suggestive procedures allowed if reliable: But an identification procedure is not violative of due process if the court finds that it is ***reliable*** (i.e., not likely to cause error), even if it is somewhat suggestive. [305]

Example: If V has a long time to view the perpetrator during the crime, under adequate light, up close, these facts will make it more likely that the resulting identification procedures are fair to D, even if there is some suggestiveness during the procedures themselves. Similarly, the fact that V is very certain of the identification, or that V has given an extremely thorough description of the perpetrator before the identification procedure, will make the court more likely to uphold it. [*Neil v. Biggers*]

C. Photo I.D.s: Where a witness identifies the suspect through the use of ***photographs***, the "totality of the circumstances" test is used to determine whether D's due process rights have been violated, just as this test is used in the lineup or show-up situation. [*Simmons v. U.S.*; *Manson v. Brathwaite*] [305]

Example: The photo I.D. is more likely to be upheld if the police show V photographs of numerous people — without hinting to V which photo they believe to be of the prime suspect — than if the police show one photo to V, and say, "Is this the guy?"

1. **Must be very likely to be mistaken:** As with the lineup and show-up situation, a due process violation will be found only if the photo I.D. session is ***very likely*** to have produced a misidentification. The fact that the procedure is somewhat "suggestive" will not be enough. Thus if the victim had an usually good opportunity to view the perpetrator, or was unusually experienced at identifying perpetrators, this will probably overcome some suggestiveness in the procedure (e.g., the use of only a single photo). [See *Manson, supra.*]

CHAPTER 7

THE EXCLUSIONARY RULE

I. THE RULE GENERALLY

A. Statement of rule: The "exclusionary rule" provides that evidence obtained by violating D's constitutional rights ***may not be introduced by the prosecution*** at D's criminal trial, at least for purposes of providing direct proof of D's guilt. [315]

Example: A car driven by D is randomly stopped by Officer, who has no reasonable grounds for suspecting D of any wrongdoing. Officer requires D to leave the car, and then searches the car. In the car's trunk, Officer finds heroin. At D's trial for possession of heroin, the prosecution will not be permitted to introduce the heroin itself (or the fact that the heroin was found in D's car) against D. The reason is that the discovery and seizure of the heroin was a direct result of the illegal stop and search, and any evidence directly derived from violation of D's constitutional rights is prevented by the exclusionary rule from being introduced against D as part of the prosecution's case in chief.

B. Judge-made rule: The exclusionary rule is a ***judge-made***, not statutory, rule. Over the years, the rule has been shaped by a long series of Supreme Court decisions. The rule is binding on both ***state*** and ***federal*** courts. [317]

1. **Not constitutionally required:** The Supreme Court has held that the exclusionary rule is ***not required by the Constitution***. [*U.S. v. Leon*] Instead, the rule has been created by the Supreme Court as a means of ***deterring*** the police from violating the Fourth, Fifth, and other Amendments.

C. Dwindling application: In general, the scope of the exclusionary rule has been steadily ***cut back*** during the Burger and Rehnquist years.

II. STANDING TO ASSERT THE EXCLUSIONARY RULE

A. Standing rule generally: In general, D may assert the exclusionary rule only to bar evidence obtained through violation of ***his own*** constitutional rights. That is, D may not keep out evidence obtained through police action that was a violation of X's rights but not a violation of D's own rights. [317]

> **Example:** The police illegally wire-tap a conversation between D1 and X (without the knowledge of either). Statements made in this conversation are used at a trial of D2. D2 argues that since the evidence was obtained by a violation of constitutional rights (the rights of D1), the evidence should not be usable against anyone, including D2. *Held*, for the prosecution. Evidence obtained by violation of the Fourth Amendment or any other constitutional provision may only be excluded by a person whose own rights were violated. [*Alderman v. U.S.*]

B. Confession cases: The standing requirement means that in the case of an illegally-obtained confession, only the person who ***makes*** the confession may have it barred by the exclusionary rule.

> **Example:** Suspect A confesses without being given the required *Miranda* warnings. In his confession, A implicates B. The confession may still be introduced in evidence against B (though not against A), because B's constitutional rights were not violated by the obtaining of the confession from A.) [319]

C. Search and seizure cases: In search and seizure cases, the standing requirement means that D may seek to exclude evidence derived from a search and seizure only if his ***own*** "legitimate expectation of privacy" was violated by the search. [*Rakas v. Illinois*] [319-322]

1. **Possessory interest in items seized:** This means that the mere fact that D has a ***possessory interest*** in the ***items seized*** is ***not*** by itself automatically enough to allow D to challenge the constitutionality of the seizure. Only if D had a legitimate expectation of privacy with respect to the items seized, may D exclude those items.

> **Example:** D and his friend Cox are both searched by the police. In Cox's handbag, the police find 1,800 tablets of LSD and other drugs. D claims ownership of these drugs, and can prove that he owns them. The search and seizure occurred without probable cause. D tries to have the drugs suppressed from his drug possession trial.
>
> *Held*, for the prosecution. Even though D owned the drugs, D's own rights were not violated by the search of Cox's handbag, because once D placed the drugs in Cox's handbag, he had no further legitimate expectation of privacy with respect to those drugs. [*Rawlings v. Kentucky*] [320]

2. **Presence at scene of search:** Similarly, the fact that D is ***legitimately on the premises*** where a search takes place does ***not*** automatically mean that D can exclude the fruits of the search if the search was illegal. Again, only if D had a legitimate expectation of privacy with respect to the ***areas*** where the incriminating materials were found, may D benefit from the exclusionary rule.

   Example: D is riding as a passenger in a car that is illegally searched by the police. The police find a sawed-off rifle under the passenger seat occupied by D.

   Held, the mere fact that D was on the scene during the search did not give him standing to assert the exclusionary rule. Since D did not have a legitimate expectation of privacy as to the area under his seat, he could not assert the exclusionary rule and the rifle could be admitted against him. [*Rakas v. Illinois*] [321-322]

3. **Vehicle searches:** When the police stop a ***vehicle***, both the ***driver*** and ***all passengers*** will normally ***have standing*** to challenge the constitutionality of the vehicle stop.

   a. **Passengers:** Any ***passengers*** will have standing: "When a police officer makes a traffic stop, the driver of the car is seized within the meaning of the Fourth Amendment [and any] ***passenger*** is ***seized as well*** and so may challenge the constitutionality of the stop." [*Brendlin v. California*] [322]

   b. **Driver:** The ***driver***, too, will almost always have standing to challenge the constitutionality of the vehicle stop.

      i. **Where D is driver but not owner, and owner is absent:** The driver will normally have standing to challenge the stop even if the ***owner*** of the vehicle is ***absent***. At least where the driver is ***driving with the consent*** of the absentee owner, the driver will normally be found to have ***a reasonable expectation of privacy*** with respect to the vehicle, and consequently will have standing to assert a Fourth Amendment claim. (We discuss the topic further *supra*, C-9.)

4. **Co-conspirators:** Where one member of a ***conspiracy*** is stopped or searched, the ***other members*** of the conspiracy do ***not*** automatically get standing to object to the stop or search merely by virtue of their membership. [*U.S. v. Padilla*]

   Example: Suppose D1 is driving a car as part of a drug-dealing conspiracy of which D2 is a part, and the car is stopped by police and searched. D2 does not get standing to object to the search merely because he and D1 are part of a single conspiracy and the car is being used in that conspiracy — D2 must show that he has a privacy interest in the car or its contents, just as if there were no conspiracy. [322]

III. DERIVATIVE EVIDENCE GENERALLY, AND THE "INDEPENDENT SOURCE" AND "INEVITABLE DISCOVERY" EXCEPTIONS

A. **Derivative evidence generally:** The exclusionary rule clearly applies to evidence that is the ***direct*** result of a violation of D's rights (e.g., evidence is seized from D's premises during an illegal search). But the exclusionary rule also applies to some ***"derivative evidence,"*** that is, evidence that is only ***indirectly*** obtained via a violation of D's rights. In general, if police wrongdoing leads in a relatively short, unbroken, chain to evidence, that evidence will be barred by the exclusionary rule, even though the evidence was not the direct and immediate fruit of the illegality.

1. **"Poisonous-tree" doctrine:** The idea that evidence deriving indirectly from a violation of D's constitutional rights should normally be excluded from use against D is often referred to as the ***"poisonous-tree doctrine."*** That is, once the original evidence (the ***"tree"***) is shown to have been unlawfully obtained, ***all evidence stemming from that illegality (the "fruit" of the poisonous tree) is equally unusable***. [324]

   Example: Federal agents, acting without probable cause, break into Toy's apartment and handcuff him. Toy makes a statement accusing Yee of selling narcotics. The agents go to Yee, from whom they seize heroin.

   Held, the drugs seized from Yee are "fruits of the poisonous tree," since they were seized as the direct result of the agents' illegal entry into Toy's apartment. Therefore, the drugs from Yee cannot be introduced against Toy, under the exclusionary rule. [*Wong Sun v. U.S.*]

B. **The independent source exception:** The "fruits of the poisonous tree" doctrine has a couple of major ***exceptions***, one of which is known as the ***"independent source"*** exception. When the police have ***two paths*** leading to information, and only one of these paths begins with illegality, the evidence is not deemed fruit of the poisonous tree, and is not barred by the exclusionary rule. [325-327]

C A P S U L E   S U M M A R Y

1. **Use for warrantless arrests or seizures:** The main utility of the "independent source" exception arises where the police have probable cause to obtain a search warrant, which would have led them to certain evidence; instead, the police make an illegal search, discover evidence, then go back and get a warrant. The law now seems to be that since the police ***could have*** lawfully obtained a warrant, they are deemed to have had an "independent source" for the evidence, so the evidence will not be barred by the exclusionary rule even though it was illegally obtained. [325-327]

   a. **Scope:** More precisely, evidence will be admissible under this branch of the "independent source" exception when three requirements are satisfied:

      i. **Illegally on premises:** First, the method by which the police discovered or seized the evidence or contraband in question must have been a violation of the Fourth Amendment (e.g., a warrantless search of the premises when a warrant was required).

      ii. **Probable cause for search warrant:** Second, although the police did not have a search warrant, at the moment of entry they must have had knowledge that would have ***entitled*** them to ***procure*** a search warrant. That is, they must have had ***probable cause*** to believe that contraband, or evidence of crime, would be found on the premises. (This theoretical availability of a warrant is the "independent source" that justifies the admission of the evidence even though the police were acting illegally at the moment they seized the evidence.)

      iii. **Would have gotten warrant anyway:** Third, the police must show that they would probably have ***eventually applied for a search warrant*** even had they not engaged in the illegality.

      Example: The police have probable cause to arrest D for narcotics violations, and probable cause to search his apartment for evidence. The police arrest D outside his apartment. They do not get a search warrant, even though warrantless entry is not allowed without one. They then enter the apartment, where they see narcotics paraphernalia. They post agents to prevent destruction of evidence, and 20 hours later get a warrant; they then conduct a search which turns up narcotics that they had not previously observed.

Held, the seized narcotics are not the fruit of the poisonous tree, and thus not excludable in D's trial, because the police had an independent source for discovery those narcotics — since the police were already, prior to the illegal entry, entitled to get a search warrant, they could have staked out the apartment from the outside, gotten the warrant and seized the very same evidence. [*Segura v. U.S.*] [325]

C. Inevitable discovery: There is a second exception related to the "independent source" exception, called the ***"inevitable discovery"*** exception. Evidence may be admitted if it would ***"inevitably"*** have been discovered by ***other police techniques*** had it not first been obtained through the illegal discovery. [327-329]

1. **Discovery of weapon or body:** The "inevitable discovery" rule is most often applied where the evidence illegally obtained is a ***weapon*** or ***body***, which the police would eventually have discovered anyway, even without the illegality.

Example: The police, in violation of *Miranda*, induce D to reveal the location of the body of his murder victim. The police are then able to find the body, and evidence near the body that relates to the manner of death. D seeks to suppress this evidence at trial, on the theory that it was procured by violation of his *Miranda* rights.

Held, because the facts were such that the police would inevitably have discovered the location of the body eventually anyway, even without D's statement, the evidence need not be excluded. This is true even though the police may have used bad faith in tricking D into revealing the location — there is no "good faith" requirement for application of the inevitable discovery exception. [*Nix v. Williams*] [327]

IV. "PURGING THE TAINT" OF POLICE ILLEGALITY — THE SIGNIFICANCE OF SUBSEQUENT INTERVENING EVENTS

A. The "purged taint" exception in general: Suppose that the police obtain a piece of evidence indirectly through a constitutional violation, and that neither the independent source nor the inevitable discovery exceptions seem to apply. In such a situation, it may nonetheless be the case that the exclusionary rule does not apply, due to a long-recognized judicial exception known as the ***"purged taint"*** doctrine.

1. **Doctrine defined:** The principle of the purged taint doctrine is that if enough ***additional factors intervene*** between the original illegality and the final discovery of evidence, the link between the two is so tenuous that the exclusionary rule should not be applied. In this situation, the intervening factors are said to be enough to have ***"purged the taint" of the original illegal police conduct.*** [330]

Example: Wong Sun is arrested without probable cause, arraigned, and released on his own recognizance. Several days later, he voluntarily comes to the police station, where he receives *Miranda* warnings and makes an incriminating statement.

Held, the statement may be introduced against Wong Sun, despite the exclusionary rule. It is true that Wong Sun's statement in some sense "derived" from his original illegal arrest. But the fact that Wong Sun had been released for several days between arrest and statement, and the voluntariness of his return to make the statement, so attenuated the connection between arrest and statement as to purge the taint of the illegality. [*Wong Sun v. U.S.*] [330]

B. Standards for determining if intervening events "have purged the taint": The Supreme Court considers ***three factors*** in deciding whether an event (or even the passage of time) occurring between the illegal conduct and the police's acquisition of the possibly-tainted fruit is sufficient to ***"purge the taint"*** of the illegality. [*Brown v. Illinois* (1975)] [331]

1. **Types of "fruit" covered:** In *Brown,* the illegality was an arrest that violated the Fourth Amendment, and the possibly-tainted "fruit" was a *confession* by the arrestee. But the Court has since indicated that these factors are to be applied in other types of derivative-evidence scenarios as well.

2. **Three factors listed:** According to *Brown,* here are the three factors the Court will take into account in deciding whether the taint from the illegality has been "purged":

   [1] The ***"temporal proximity"*** of the illegality to the fruit (in *Brown,* the proximity of the illegal arrest to the confession by the arrestee);

   [2] The "presence of ***intervening circumstances***" between the illegality and the fruit; and

   [3] Of "particular" importance, "the ***purpose and flagrancy*** of the ***official misconduct."***

C A P S U L E S U M M A R Y

3. **Illegal stop is followed by discovery of outstanding arrest warrant:** The main case in which the Court has applied the *Brown* three-factor test is a 2016 case posing the issue of whether the taint of an illegal stop will be purged by the officer's discovery that there is an ***outstanding arrest warrant*** for the suspect. The case holds that discovery of the warrant will normally be such an important intervening event that it will ***purge the taint*** of the stop, thereby permitting the police to ***make an arrest*** on account of the warrant and then a ***search incident to that arrest.*** [***Utah v. Strieff*** (2016)] [333]

   a. **Facts:** In *Strieff,* a police detective, Fackrell, stopped D, a pedestrian, in what was later stipulated to be an unlawful stop due to Fackrell's lack of reasonable grounds to suspect D of wrongdoing. Fackrell demanded D's ID, then called in D's name to a police dispatcher. The dispatcher reported that D had an outstanding arrest warrant for a traffic violation. Fackrell then arrested D on the warrant, searched him incident to the arrest, and discovered narcotics on D's person.

   b. **Holding:** The Supreme Court ***agreed with the prosecution*** that discovery of the outstanding warrant was ***enough to purge the taint*** of the illegal stop, based on the three-factor test of *Brown, supra.* The Court applied the three *Brown* factors this way:

      [1] **Temporal proximity: *"Temporal proximity"*** between the stop and the search cut in favor of suppression. The proximity factor will favor suppression unless "substantial time" elapses, and here, the search took place ***"only minutes"*** after the illegal stop, which was *not* a substantial amount of time.

      [2] **Intervening circumstances:** On the other hand, "the presence of ***intervening circumstances"*** factor cut strongly against suppression. The outstanding warrant predated Fackrell's investigation and was "entirely ***unconnected with the stop."***

      [3] **"Purpose and flagrancy of misconduct":** Finally, the "***purpose and flagrancy*** of the official misconduct" also cut strongly against suppression. Fackrell was ***"at most negligent,"*** and his main error — making the stop without having adequate grounds

to suspect D of any wrongdoing — was a ***"good-faith mistake."*** Furthermore, there was no indication that this unlawful stop was part of any ***"systemic or recurrent police misconduct."***

Since two of the three *Brown* factors cut strongly in favor of a finding that the taint from the unlawful stop was "sufficiently attenuated" by the preexisting arrest warrant, the fruits of the search incident to the arrest on the warrant were ***not required to be excluded.*** [334]

c. Significance: Here's what *Strieff* seems to allow the police to do: After every stop (even an illegal one, so long as the illegality is a good-faith mistake), the police can detain the person for long enough to determine whether he or she has an outstanding arrest warrant. And once the existence of the outstanding warrant is confirmed (no matter how old or minor the offense or the warrant), the officer is free to arrest the suspect. At that point, the officer can do a search incident to the arrest, and any contraband or evidence of criminality she finds can serve as admissible evidence in a prosecution predicated on that evidence. The prosecution can treat the original stop, and the reasons for it, as irrelevant to the crime being charged. [335]

C. Illegality leads police to focus on particular suspect: If the illegality (an illegal search, arrest, lineup, etc.) leads the police to ***focus on a particular suspect*** they were not previously focusing on, usually the final arrest of the suspect will ***not*** be found to be tainted by the original illegality: the full-scale investigation that the police conduct between the time they first focus on the suspect and the time they arrest him is usually enough to purge this taint. [336]

D. Lead to different crime: Suppose the police are investigating one crime, and an illegal action they commit leads them to evidence of a ***completely different crime***. Here, too, probably the evidence of the new crime may be introduced despite the earlier illegality.

Example: D is illegally arrested for burglarizing an empty house, and is immediately photographed. Weeks later, the police show the photo to a witness, who identifies the person in the photo as having been one of three men who robbed a bank recently during the daytime. Probably this later-robbery I.D. would not be deemed tainted by the original illegal arrest and photograph. [336]

E. Lead to witness: One of the fruits of police illegality may be the discovery of the ***existence of witnesses*** who can give testimony against D. In general, D will rarely be successful in arguing that the testimony of the live witness should be suppressed because the witness would not have been found but for the illegality — it is far easier to suppress an "inanimate" fruit of illegality (e.g., contraband, or evidence of crime) than it is to suppress "animate" fruits such as witnesses who testify. [See *U.S. v. Ceccolini*] [337]

Example: The police, acting without probable cause, arrest D on suspicion of being one of two men who burglarized a particular premises. They interrogate D without giving him his *Miranda* warnings. D implicates X, who he says was the other person who took part in the burglary. The police, who had no previous reason to suspect X, accost X, and convince him to turn state's evidence against D. X's evidence will probably be admissible against D, even though it is in a sense the fruit of the original illegal arrest and interrogation of D — the courts hesitate to apply the "fruits of the poisonous tree" doctrine to a fruit consisting of a witness' live testimony.

F. Confession as tainted fruit: A ***confession*** may also be found to be tainted fruit. This is especially likely to be the case where the confession stems directly from the ***illegal arrest*** of the suspect who gives the confession. In general, where the confession comes in the period of ***custody immediately following*** the arrest, the court is likely to find that the confession is tainted fruit, and must therefore be excluded from the trial of the confessor. [337]

> **Example:** Acting without probable cause, the police arrest D on suspicion of robbery. While D is in custody, the police give him his *Miranda* warnings, and he waives his rights, then confesses. A court would almost certainly hold that D's confession must be excluded as a fruit of the illegal arrest.

1. ***Mirandizing* of D not sufficient:** It is clear that the mere fact that D was given his ***Miranda warnings*** before confessing is ***not*** sufficient to purge the taint of the earlier illegality. [*Brown v. Illinois*] [338]

2. **Other factors:** But the fact that the police gave *Miranda* warnings is a ***factor*** that the court will consider, in addition to other factors, in determining whether the confession was sufficiently distinct from the earlier illegality that it should be deemed untainted. Other factors that the courts consider are the three listed in *Brown v. Illinois, supra*, p. C-72:

   a. **Time delay:** How long a ***time*** elapsed between the illegality and the confession (the longer the time, the more likely the taint is to have been purged);

   b. **Police intent:** The police ***intent*** in carrying out the illegal arrest or other illegal act (so that if the police knowingly arrest D illegally, for the purpose of being able to interrogate him, the taint will almost certainly not be purged); and

   c. **Intervening factors:** Whether ***intervening events*** have occurred that weaken the causal link between the illegality and the confession.

   Example: If D is illegally arrested, then released from custody for several days, during which he consults with friends and relatives, a voluntary confession by D thereafter is much less likely to be found to be tainted than if D confessed without ever having left custody and without consulting with anyone.

3. **Second confession as fruit of prior confession:** Suppose D makes an ***inadmissible confession***, and shortly thereafter makes a ***second, otherwise-admissible, confession***. Does the illegality surrounding the first confession taint the second confession? Here are the general rules governing this two-confession scenario:

   The second confession will not be deemed tainted as long as it was ***"voluntarily made,"*** and the Court will ordinarily ***presume*** that the second confession is indeed voluntary if made after warnings, even though that confession followed an earlier unwarned confession. (That is, the voluntariness of the second confession normally ***won't*** be impaired by the fact that the suspect feels that since he has already ***"let the cat out of the bag,"*** there is little to be gained by remaining silent the second time.) [*Oregon v. Elstad*] [339]

   The second confession is ***more likely*** to be deemed to be ***voluntarily*** made if the underlying circumstances do not make that second confession a ***mere continuation*** of the first. (So, for instance, the second is more likely to be found voluntary if the two were meaningfully ***separated*** by ***time, place, or interrogator***, or if it was made clear to the suspect that the first, unwarned, confession would not be admissible.) [*Elstad*]

   The second confession is less likely to be deemed tainted if the failure to warn prior to the first confession was the result of an ***inadvertent mistake*** by the police. [*Elstad*]

By contrast, where the police follow an ***intentional "two-step" practice*** of eliciting an unwarned confession, then immediately giving a warning under circumstances that lead the suspect to believe that ***even the already-made confession can be used against him*** (so that the suspect sees no reason not to repeat the confession after the warning), the second confession *will* probably be deemed involuntary and thus ***tainted.*** [*Missouri v. Seibert*] [339]

G. Confession as "poisonous tree": Suppose the police illegally obtain a confession, and this confession furnishes them with ***leads*** to other evidence (e.g., ***inanimate objects*** or ***witnesses*** who can testify). May this ***confession*** itself be a ***"poisonous tree"*** that taints the leads to other evidence? The answer is "***no***," at least where the confession is illegally obtained only because of a lack of *Miranda* warnings, rather than because it is made following a no-probable-cause arrest.

Example: D is arrested for domestic violence. He's questioned without *Miranda* warnings, and reveals that he's in possession of an unregistered pistol, whose location he shows the police. The gun will be admissible against D — the fact that the police would never have found the gun had D not confessed to its location during unwarned custodial questioning is irrelevant, because an unwarned confession won't ever be a "poisonous tree" with respect to physical fruits derived from that confession. [*U.S. v. Patane*] [342]

1. **Leads to witnesses:** The same result is almost certainly true of ***leads to third-party witnesses.***

Example: The police, as the result of questioning D in a way that doesn't comply with *Miranda*, learn that W was a witness to a crime committed by D. Although the Supreme Court hasn't yet directly discussed the matter, it seems almost certain that *Patane*, *supra*, will be interpreted so that W's testimony can be used against D — the fact that the police would probably never have learned of W's existence had it not been for the non-Mirandized questioning of D will be irrelevant. [343]

V. COLLATERAL USE EXCEPTIONS

A. Collateral use generally: The exclusionary rule basically applies only to evidence presented by the prosecution as part of its ***case in chief*** at D's trial. In other contexts, the rule is much less likely to apply, as described below.

B. Impeachment at trial: Thus illegally-obtained evidence may be used to ***impeach the defendant's trial testimony***, even though it cannot be used in the prosecution's direct case. [*Harris v. N.Y.*] [344]

1. **Statements made in direct testimony:** Most obviously, illegally-obtained evidence may be used to impeach statements made by D ***during his direct testimony***.

Example: D is arrested on suspicion of burglarizing a particular premises. The police do not give him the required *Miranda* warnings. They ask him where he was on a particular evening, and he replies that he was at his girlfriend's house. At trial, during D's direct testimony after taking the stand, D says that at the time in question, he was at home. The prosecutor may bring out on cross-examination the fact that D told a different story in his non-*Mirandized* confession. [344]

2. **Statements made during cross-examination:** Furthermore, illegally-obtained evidence may be used by the prosecution to impeach even statements that are made by D on ***cross-examination***. So the prosecution can ***elicit*** one story from D during cross-examination, then impeach D by showing he told a different story while making his otherwise-inadmissible confession. [344-345]

3. **Impeachment of defense witnesses:** But illegally-obtained evidence may ***not*** be used to impeach the testimony of ***defense witnesses*** other than the defendant himself. [*James v. Illinois*] [346]

    Example: While D is under arrest for burglary, and without receiving *Miranda* warnings, D states that he was at home at the time of a burglary under investigation. At trial, D presents as a witness W, D's girlfriend, who says that at the time in question, D was with W at W's house. The prosecution may not impeach W's testimony by introducing D's contrary statment made during the un-*Mirandized* confession.

C. **Impeachment in grand jury proceedings:** A ***grand jury witness*** cannot prevent illegally-obtained evidence from being introduced against him during the grand jury proceeding. [*U.S. v. Calandra*] [346]

VI. THE "GOOD FAITH WARRANT" AND "KNOCK-AND-ANNOUNCE VIOLATION" EXCEPTIONS

A. **The "good faith warrant" exception:** The exclusionary rule does ***not*** bar evidence that was obtained by officers acting in ***reasonable reliance*** on a ***search warrant*** issued by a proper magistrate but ultimately found to be ***unsupported by probable cause***. [*U.S. v. Leon*] [348-356]

    Example: The police, relying on information from an informant as well as their own investigations, obtain a search warrant that is valid on its face. They search several premises under the warrant, obtaining evidence of narcotics violations. Later, a judge holds that the information presented to the magistrate did not establish probable cause for the search. Now, the issue is whether the illegally-seized evidence may be admitted against D.

    Held, the evidence may be admitted against D, because the exclusionary rule should not be applied where officers have a good-faith, objectively reasonable belief that they have probable cause, and the warrant is issued according to proper procedures. [*Leon, supra*]

1. **Reliance on non-existent arrest warrant:** The "good faith" exception has been extended to one additional situation: If the police reasonably (but mistakenly) believe that there is an ***arrest warrant outstanding*** for a particular suspect and arrest him, evidence found during a ***search incident to this wrongful arrest*** will be ***admissible***, at least where any police misconduct consists of ***"nonrecurring and attenuated negligence."*** [*Herring v. U.S.*] [352]

    a. **Source of error irrelevant:** This is true whether the mistake is due to police error, or to error by some other part of government (e.g., the ***judicial*** system).

    Example: D drives to the Sheriff's Department to retrieve something from his impounded truck. A Sheriff's officer checks with his own county and a nearby one to see whether there are any outstanding warrants for D's arrest. A clerk in neighboring Dale County reports to the officer that her database shows that there is an active arrest warrant out for D. The officer therefore stops D as he drives out of the impound lot, arrests him on that warrant, searches his body, and finds contraband on him. But it turns out that there *is* no outstanding warrant — the warrant was recalled five months earlier, but this fact was never entered by the Dale County Sherriff's Department into its database.

Held, the search is still valid as one properly made incident to arrest. The officer acted in good-faith reliance on the existence of the apparent warrant. When an arrest and incident search arises from "nonrecurring and attenuated negligence" by the police department, rather than from "systemic error or reckless disregard of constitutional requirements," the error will not invalidate the search incident to the (invalid) arrest. [*Herring v. U.S.* (2009)] [353-356]

2. **Reliance on later-overruled legal principle:** The prosecution may also make use of the *Leon* good-faith-error exception in the case of a reasonable error about ***what the appropriate legal rule is.*** More precisely, when the police conduct a search that is legal under a binding legal precedent that is later ***overruled***, the police and prosecution get the benefit of *Leon*, so that the exclusionary rule will not be applied to keep out the results of the search. [*Davis v. U.S.*] [355]

   a. **Broader significance:** In fact, *Leon* will be applied (preventing application of the exclusionary rule) whenever the police obtain evidence "as a result of ***non-culpable, innocent police conduct.***" [*Davis v. U.S.*] [355]

   Example: The police make a routine traffic stop of a car in which D is a passenger and X is the driver. Both are handcuffed and placed in the back of separate patrol cars. The police then search the passenger compartment of the vehicle, and find a revolver inside the pocket of a jacket belonging to D. The incident happens in Alabama, which is part of the Eleventh Circuit. At the time of the search, the Eleventh Circuit (like most federal courts) interprets the prior Supreme Court case of *New York v. Belton* as holding that such a passenger-compartment search is legal regardless of whether the arrestee was within reaching distance of the vehicle.

   Then, after D is convicted but while his appeal is still pending in front of the Eleventh Circuit, the Supreme Court in *Arizona v. Gant* overrules this reading of *Belton*, by validating searches incident to the arrest of a vehicle's occupants *only* if the arrestee was within reaching distance of the vehicle during the arrest (which D wasn't). D argues that since his case is not yet final, he should get the benefit of the new decision (*Gant*), and that the search should be ruled illegal.

   Held, for the prosecution. The police and prosecution ***get the benefit of the precedent on which they reasonably relied***, even though the precedent turned out while the case was still pending to be bad law. Police reliance on what turns out to be an erroneous — but at the time, binding — appellate decision falls within the general rule that the good-faith exception applies to all ***"nonculpable, innocent police conduct."*** [*Davis v. U.S.*] [355-356]

3. **Fourth Amendment only:** So far, the "good faith exception" summarized above applies only to evidence obtained in violation of the ***Fourth*** Amendment (search/seizure and arrest), not evidence obtained in violation of other amendments (e.g., the Fifth or Sixth Amendments, each of which can be violated by, say, interrogation without benefit of *Miranda* warnings).

4. **Police must behave with objective reasonableness:** The exception applies only where the police behave in ***good faith*** and in an ***objectively reasonable*** manner. So, for instance, in cases where a search warrant is based on an incorrect affidavit, the exception does not apply if the police officer who prepares the affidavit for the warrant ***knows*** that the information in it is false, or recklessly disregards its truth or falsity. Also, the affidavit must on its face seem to be valid, and to be based on probable cause.

B. **Exception for "knock and announce" violations:** Under most circumstances, when the police wish to enter a private dwelling — for instance, to execute a search warrant — they are required by the Fourth Amendment to ***"knock and announce."*** That is, they are required to knock first, announce that they are the police, and give the occupant a chance to answer the door — only if the occupant does not answer may the police enter forcefully. (See *supra*, C-19.) But even if the police violate this knock-and-announce rule, ***the exclusionary rule will not apply.*** [*Hudson v. Michigan.*]

1. **Consequence:** Therefore, even if D can show that certain evidence would not have been acquired by the police but for their failure to wait for the door to be answered (e.g., that if they had waited a reasonable time before entering with their warrant, D might have had time to destroy the evidence), the evidence will still be admissible against him.

C
A
P
S
U
L
E

S
U
M
M
A
R
Y

VII. THE RIGHT TO SUE FOR CIVIL DAMAGES (§1983)

A. **Right to sue officers:** As we've just seen, many exclusionary-rule cases have involved the defendant's Fourth Amendment right to be free of unreasonable searches and seizures; the exclusionary rule will often give the defendant the remedy of having any evidence deriving from the unreasonable (and thus illegal) search or seizure ***excluded*** from the criminal case against him.

But another important consequence of a Fourth Amendment violation is that the violation may entitle the suspect to bring a ***civil suit for money damages against the officer(s) who committed the illegal action.*** [357]

B. **§1983:** An important federal statute, ***42 U.S.C. §1983***, allows a person to bring a civil tort action against any person who, ***"under color of" state law,*** deprives the plaintiff of "any ***rights***, privileges, or immunities" ***secured by the federal Constitution or a federal statute.*** So the basic effect of §1983 is to permit a ***tort suit*** by anyone who is injured when a ***state or local official violates the plaintiff's federal rights,*** typically her constitutionally-guaranteed civil rights. [358]

1. **Fourth Amendment violations:** Many §1983 actions successfully allege that state or local officials have violated the ***Fourth Amendment's*** prohibition of ***unreasonable searches and seizures.***

2. **No remedy for *Miranda* violations (*Vega v. Tekoh*):** But suppose that the claim raised by a plaintiff in a §1983 suit is based not on a state official's violation of the plaintiff's Fourth Amendment's protection against unreasonable searches and seizures, but instead on the official's violation of ***plaintiff's Miranda rights.*** That is, suppose P's un*Mirandized* confession is improperly used against him at his criminal trial, but P is nonetheless ***acquitted***; may P then recover damages under §1983 for this violation of his *Miranda* rights? The Supreme Court answered ***"no"*** in *Vega v. Tekoh*, 142 S.Ct. 2095 (2022). [000]

a. **Holding:** In *Vega,* the Court said that the requirement of *Miranda* warnings is ***merely "prophylactic,"*** not required by the Fifth Amendment.

i. **Cost/benefit:** Therefore, *Vega* says, since a violation of *Miranda* is not necessarily a violation of the Fifth Amendment, people whose *Miranda* rights have been violated ought to be allowed to recover under §1983 only if the ***"benefits*** [of allowing such a recovery] ***outweigh the costs."*** And, the case says, the benefits of allowing a §1983 recovery for *Miranda* violations "would be ***slight,***" whereas "the costs would be ***substantial.***"

Consequently, *Vega* means that no §1983 recovery will be allowed to people who suffer *Miranda* violations. [358]

3. **Implied right of action against federal officials:** Section 1983 by its terms allows only actions against ***state and local*** government officials, ***not federal ones.*** However, when a federal official violates a citizen's constitutional rights, the citizen is often permitted to bring a ***federal tort-like suit*** against the official. This occurs because the court finds that the citizen has an ***"implied private right of action"*** for violation of those constitutional rights. [359]

   a. **Fourth Amendment violation:** For example, suppose that a federal law-enforcement official violates P's Fourth Amendment right to be free from unreasonable searches and seizures. The Supreme Court has held that P may then bring a federal civil damages suit against the official for this violation. See [*Bivens v. Six Unknown Named Agents of FBI*] (civil suit for money damages allowed against FBI agents for search and arrest made without probable cause). [359]

4. **Qualified immunity:** Even if a police officer violates a suspect's Fourth or Fifth Amendment rights, any §1983 suit by the suspect must overcome a significant obstacle: the defendant officer's ***"qualified immunity."*** [358]

   a. **Nature of immunity:** The Supreme Court has described qualified immunity this way: "The doctrine of qualified immunity shields officers from civil liability so long as their conduct does not violate ***clearly established*** statutory or constitutional rights of which a ***reasonable person would have known."*** [*City of Tahlequah v. Bond*] [359]

      i. **Consequence:** Qualified immunity thus protects "all but the ***plainly incompetent*** or those who ***knowingly violate the law.***" *Id.* This gives the officer lots of protection. [359]

CAPSULE SUMMARY

CHAPTER 8

THE RIGHT TO COUNSEL

I. THE INDIGENT'S RIGHT TO COUNSEL

A. **Introduction:** The Sixth Amendment says that "In all criminal prosecutions, the accused shall enjoy the right . . . to have the Assistance of Counsel for his defense." [375]

1. **Right to appointed counsel where jail is at stake:** The Sixth Amendment right means that an ***indigent*** defendant has the right to have counsel ***appointed for him by the government*** in any prosecution where the accused can be sent to jail. Thus in any felony prosecution, and in any misdemeanor prosecution for which the sentence will be a jail term, the indigent has the right to appointed counsel.

2. **Right to retained counsel:** The Sixth Amendment also means that the government cannot materially interfere with a non-indigent defendant's right to ***retain*** (i.e., pay for) his own private lawyer.

B. Right to retained counsel, generally: The Sixth Amendment guarantees the right of a criminal defendant who does not need appointed counsel to ***hire private counsel of her own choosing*** to represent her. [*Caplin & Dysdale v. U.S.*] [376]

1. ***Per se*** **right:** If the private counsel chosen by defendant is qualified, the court's denial of permission for the lawyer to conduct the defense is ***automatically reversible error*** — the defendant does not even need to demonstrate on appeal that denial of counsel of choice is likely to have ***affected the outcome***. [*U.S. v. Gonzalez-Lopez*]

2. **Federal or state:** This right to a counsel of one's own choosing, imposed by the Sixth Amendment, applies to ***both state and federal*** trials.

3. **Limitations:** But the theoretically "unqualified" right to be represented by one's own retained attorney is ***not absolute***. [376-377]

   a. **Ability to pay may be blocked:** For instance, the government may place limits on the mechanism by which the defendant ***pays*** his retained lawyer. For example, federal "civil ***forfeiture***" statutes allow the government to seize and keep any property used in, or money earned from, violations of drug or other laws. Such forfeiture statutes may be enforced even where the forfeited property is the only property with which the defendant could pay his retained lawyer, and even if the effect of enforcement is that the lawyer refuses to represent the defendant because of the difficulty in obtaining payment. [*Caplin & Drysdale v. U.S.*].

   b. **Conflict:** Similarly, a defendant's right to a lawyer of his own choosing does not give him the right to choose a lawyer where this would result in a ***conflict*** between the lawyer's representation of the defendant and his representation of some other co-defendant. This is true even where all defendants are willing to "waive" the conflict.

C. The right to appointed counsel, generally: The most important aspect of the Sixth Amendment is that it guarantees ***indigent*** defendants the right to have counsel ***appointed for them*** by the government in felonies and in some misdemeanors.

1. **Applicable to states:** The Sixth Amendment right to counsel applies to the ***states***, not just the federal government. [*Gideon v. Wainwright*] [378]

2. **Various stages:** The right to appointed counsel does not mean merely that the accused has the right to have a lawyer *at trial*; other parts of the prosecution that are found to represent a "critical stage" in the proceedings (e.g., the arraignment) also trigger the right to appointed counsel. This is discussed more extensively below.

3. **Right to effective assistance:** The right to counsel includes the right to ***effective*** assistance — thus if the appointed counsel does not meet a certain minimal standard of competence, the Sixth Amendment has been violated. This aspect, too, is discussed below. [379]

D. Proceedings where the right applies:

1. **Felonies:** The right to appointed counsel clearly applies where the defendant is charged with a ***felony*** (i.e., a crime for which a prison sentence of more than a year is authorized).

2. **Misdemeanors with potential jail sentence:** Additionally, the right applies in a ***misdemeanor*** prosecution, if the defendant is going to be sentenced to even a ***brief*** jail term. [*Argersinger v. Hamlin*] [380]

   a. **Jail sentence possible but not imposed:** But if an indigent D is not ***sentenced*** to incarceration, the state is not required to appoint counsel for him, even if the offense is one which is ***punishable*** by imprisonment. [*Scott v. Illinois*] [381]

   b. **Conviction used to increase sentence for later crime:** Also, a misdemeanor conviction ***may*** be used to increase the permissible prison sentence for a ***subsequent*** conviction, even though D was not offered appointed counsel during the first proceeding. [*Nichols v. U.S.*] [381]

3. **Juvenile deliquency proceedings:** The right to appointed counsel applies in a ***juvenile delinquency*** proceeding, if the youthful defendant may be committed to an ***institution*** (even a "youth facility" or "reform school" rather than a prison) upon conviction. [*In re Gault*] [382]

E. **Stages at which the right to counsel applies:** In addition to the trial itself, the right to counsel applies at various other stages of the proceedings:

1. **Police investigation:** A suspect will frequently have the right to counsel during the period in which the police are conducting their ***investigation***. But this right generally does not derive from the Sixth Amendment; instead, it stems from the Fifth Amendment's right against self-incrimination. (*Example:* Although a defendant in custody has the right to an appointed lawyer before being questioned by the police, under *Miranda*, this right derives from the Fifth Amendment, not the Sixth.) [382]

2. **The "critical stage" doctrine:** The Sixth Amendment is triggered wherever there is a ***"critical stage"*** of the proceedings. In brief, a stage will be "critical" if D is compelled to make a decision which may later be formally ***used against him***.

   a. **Initial appearance:** Thus the ***initial appearance***, the ***preliminary hearing***, and the ***arraignment*** are all likely to be found, in a particular case, to be critical stages. (But if local procedures make it clear that nothing done by D at a particular stage binds him, then presumably counsel does not have to be appointed.) [383]

   b. **Post-trial stages:** Stages occurring ***after*** the trial may also be found "critical," thus triggering the right to counsel.

      i. **Sentencing:** For instance, a post-trial ***sentencing*** will normally be a "critical stage," requiring that D be furnished with an attorney. [*Mempa v. Rhay*]

         (1) **Suspended sentence:** Suppose D is convicted of a crime, and is given a ***suspended sentence***, under which he is ***placed on probation*** and will be imprisoned if and only if he later violates the terms of the probation. Here, too, D has the right to appointed counsel *before* trial and imposition of the suspended sentence.

         Example: The state charges D with a minor misdemeanor. The state intends that if D is convicted, the state will recommend, in return for a plea bargain, that the judge give D a suspended sentence plus probation. If the state wants to preserve the ability to have D sent to jail for one year should he violate the probation, the state will have to supply counsel during trial and sentencing. (In other words, the state can't meet its appointed-counsel obligation by saying, "We won't supply counsel unless/until there's a probation-revocation proceeding.") [*Alabama v. Shelton*] [382]

ii. **Psychiatric exam:** Similarly, where the court orders a ***psychiatric examination*** to determine whether a murder convict deserves the death penalty, the convict is entitled to consult a lawyer before submitting to the exam. [*Estelle v. Smith*] [385]

iii. **Probation revocation not covered:** But there is ***no*** right of counsel in a proceeding to ***revoke*** the defendant's ***probation***. [*Gagnon v. Scarpelli*] [386]

c. **Appeals:** A convicted defendant's right to appointed counsel during his ***appeals*** depends on the nature of the appeal. A defendant has the right to appointed counsel for his ***first appeal as of right***, i.e., the appeal made available to all convicted defendants. [*Douglas v. California*] [386]

i. **Discretionary review:** But D has ***no*** right to appointed counsel to assist with his applications for ***discretionary review***. That is, once D's conviction has been affirmed by the first appellate court, and the government provides a second discretionary review (e.g., discretionary review by the state supreme court, or petition for certiorari to the U.S. Supreme Court), D is on his own. [*Ross v. Moffitt*]

d. **Habeas corpus:** A defendant does ***not*** have a right to appointed counsel for pursuing ***federal habeas corpus*** relief after he has exhausted state remedies. But he does have a limited Sixth Amendment right to legal assistance: prison authorities are required to ***assist the inmate*** in filing *habeas corpus* papers. The prison must give at least one of the following forms of assistance: (1) an adequate law library; (2) the training of some inmates as paralegal assistants; (3) the use of non-prisoner paralegals and law students; or (4) the use of lawyers, perhaps on a part-time volunteer basis. [*Bounds v. Smith*] [386]

II. ENTITLEMENTS OF THE RIGHT TO COUNSEL

A. **Effectiveness of counsel:** The Sixth Amendment entitles D not only to have a lawyer, but to have the ***"effective assistance"*** of counsel.

1. **Standard:** Where a lawyer has actually participated in D's trial, D has a hard burden to show that he did not receive "effective assistance." D must show *both* that:

[1] counsel's performance was ***"deficient,"*** in the sense that counsel was not a ***"reasonably competent attorney"***; *and*

[2] the deficiencies were ***prejudicial*** to the defense, in the sense that there is a "reasonable probability that, but for counsel's errors, the ***result*** of the proceeding ***would have been different."***

[*Strickland v. Washington*] [386] (These two requirements are frequently called the ***"two prongs"*** of *Strickland*.)

B. **Advice as to plea-bargaining:** The right to effective assistance of counsel applies during the ***plea-bargaining*** process. There are two distinct scenarios, in either of which counsel might be found to have failed to furnish effective assistance:

[1] Due to poor advice from counsel, the defendant ***agrees to accept a plea bargain***, when going to trial would likely have led to a better outcome;

[2] Due to poor (or no) advice from counsel, the defendant ***fails to accept a plea bargain***

offered by the prosecution, ***goes to trial***, gets convicted, and receives a ***longer sentence*** than the one offered under the plea bargain.

In each scenario, the two-pronged test of *Strickland*, *supra*, applies. [387]

1. **D accepts a bad plea-bargain offer:** Suppose that due to bad legal advice, D unwisely ***takes*** the ***"bad" plea bargain.*** If D can show that (1) his lawyer's "take the plea" advice was deficient, and (2) this advice caused him "prejudice," D can succeed on his effective-assistance claim. [387]

   Example: D is a non-citizen who has resided lawfully in the U.S. for 40 years. He is charged with marijuana smuggling. His lawyer fails to tell him that if he pleads guilty to the charge, he will be automatically *deported* under federal immigration law. D pleads guilty, and then discovers that he is automatically and immediately deportable. D, claiming ineffective assistance, tries to withdraw the plea and get a trial.

   Held, by the Supreme Court, for D (at least in part). The automatic-deportation consequences of a guilty plea here were so great that the lawyer's failure to mention those consequences caused his performance to fall below the level of competence (the first *Strickland* prong). However, to fully succeed with his ineffective assistance claim (i.e., to be entitled to withdraw his plea and go to trial), D will have to show on remand that he has suffered "prejudice." (Case remanded to the state courts to determine whether D can make this showing of prejudice.) [*Padilla v. Kentucky*] [388]

   a. **"Prejudice" standard for bad-plea-bargain cases:** Whenever a defendant makes an ineffective-assistance claim, as we noted, he has to show that the poor representation caused him "prejudice." Where D's claim is that he was not accurately advised about the potential ***negative consequences*** of a plea bargain, the requirement to show prejudice means that D has to show "a reasonable probability that, but for counsel's unprofessional errors, ***the result of the proceeding would have been different"*** (the second prong of the *Strickland* formulation, *supra*, p. C-82). But in the case where D takes a bad plea bargain, what does it *mean* to say that but for counsel's poor advice, "the result of the proceeding would have been different"? "Different" how?

      i. **The "I would have insisted on going to trial" standard:** Here's the Supreme Court's answer: The defendant does ***not*** have to make the difficult showing that had he not taken the bad plea-bargain, he would probably have been *acquitted* at trial. Instead, he ***merely*** has to make a much easier showing: a ***"reasonable probability that,*** but for counsel's errors, he ***would not have pleaded guilty and would have insisted on going to trial."*** [*Hill v. Lockhart*] [389]

         Example: D is a non-U.S. citizen who pleads guilty to a narcotics crime in order to get a somewhat shorter sentence (the difference between an 18-year sentence and one of 16 or 17 years) than he would get if convicted at trial. Before D takes the plea, his lawyer erroneously assures him that he will not be deported if he pleads guilty. (In reality, deportation is not just possible but *mandatory*, whether he pleads guilty or is found guilty at trial.) After taking the plea, D discovers the error and unsuccessfully tries to withdraw his plea. He claims that the lawyer's advice deprived him of effective assistance of counsel.

         Held, for D. The issue is whether D can show a "reasonable probability that, but for counsel's errors, he would not have pleaded guilty and would have insisted on going

CAPSULE SUMMARY

to trial." Even though D would have had no "viable defense" at trial, he can still meet this "reasonable probability" test if there is substantial evidence that because of his circumstances he would have found it attractive to pursue "even the smallest chance of success at trial." Here, before he took the plea, D made it clear that his main objective was to ensure that he would not be deported; therefore, it was not irrational for him to prefer taking a small chance at acquittal rather bargaining for a slightly shorter prison sentence. Therefore, he has shown the required "prejudice" — that without the incorrect advice he would probably have gone to trial. Consequently, D is entitled to a new trial. [*Lee v. U.S.*] [389]

2. **D rejects a good plea-bargain offer:** Now, let's look at the opposite situation: the prosecution offers the defendant a particular plea bargain, and due to counsel's bad advice (or total lack of advice), the defendant ***doesn't take the offer***, goes to trial, gets convicted, and gets a longer prison term than the one originally offered under the plea-bargain. There can be a violation of the Sixth Amendment right to effective assistance in this situation, too. Here are the main rules:

   [1] Defense counsel has the ***duty to communicate*** to D ***any formal plea offer*** from the prosecution, if these may be favorable to D (so that failure to pass along the offer can be deficient assistance under the first prong of *Strickland*). [392]

   [2] Whether D does or doesn't learn about the offered plea bargain, if D fails to ***accept*** the bargain due to incompetent advice, D must still show all of the following to win any practical relief on ineffective-assistance grounds:

   [a] a ***"reasonable probability"*** that D ***would have accepted*** the earlier plea offer had he been given competent legal advice;

   [b] a "reasonable probability" that the plea would have been ***entered without the prosecution canceling it*** (if the prosecution had the power under state law to make such a cancellation); and

   [c] a "reasonable probability" that the plea would have been entered ***without the trial court refusing to accept it*** (again assuming the judge had the power under state law to refuse to accept the plea).

   [*Missouri v. Frye*; *Lafler v. Cooper*] [393]

3. **Other causes of ineffectiveness:** Apart from actual blunders made by the lawyer at trial or in plea bargaining, some other events may be found to amount to a denial of effective assistance. These include a showing that:

   [1] the court refused to grant a ***postponement*** to allow a newly-appointed lawyer ***adequate time to prepare*** for trial;

   [2] the lawyer was not given a ***reasonable right of access*** to his client before or during the trial; or

   [3] the lawyer represented ***multiple defendants***, and the interests of those defendants conflicted to the detriment of D.

   [395-398]

C. Other aspects of the Sixth Amendment:

1. **Expert assistance:** The defendant may have a Sixth Amendment right to have the state pay for an ***expert*** to be retained on his behalf. (*Example:* If D raises the insanity defense, he is entitled to have the state pay for a psychiatrist to examine him, and to have that psychiatrist give testimony as to D's sanity.) [398]

2. **Fees and transcripts:** The defendant is entitled to have the state pay for any ***transcripts and records*** necessary to present an effective appeal, and any related ***fees***. [399]

D. **Secret agents:** Once a suspect has been ***indicted*** and has counsel, it is a violation of the right of counsel for a ***secret agent*** to deliberately obtain incriminating statements from D in the absence of counsel, and to pass these on to the prosecution. [*Massiah v. U.S.*] [399]

1. **Must be "deliberately elicited":** But this ban on secret agents applies only where the agent ***"deliberately elicits"*** the incriminating testimony, not where the agent merely "keeps his ears open." [*Kuhlmann v. Wilson*] [401]

   a. **Does not cover pre-indictment situations:** Even the ban on the deliberate eliciting of confidences by secret agents applies only ***after formal proceedings*** (e.g., an indictment) have begun against D. So during the pre-indictment investigation stage, the police may use a secret agent to entrap D even if the police or agent know that D has a regular lawyer, and even though the agent passes the confidences on to the police or prosecutors.

2. **Presence at attorney-client conference:** The presence of an undercover agent at a ***conference*** between a suspect and his ***lawyer*** will also be a violation of the suspect's right to counsel, if materials from this conference are used by the prosecution, at least if the agent goes to the meeting for the purpose of spying (as opposed to going there for the purpose of maintaining his own cover). [401]

3. **May be used for impeachment of D's testimony:** Even where the police or prosecution violate D's Sixth Amendment rights by deliberately having an undercover informant elicit incriminating statements from D outside the presence of D's counsel, the prosecution may ***use*** these statements to ***impeach D's trial testimony.*** [*Kansas v. Ventris*] [402] In other words, just as statements elicited in violation of D's Fifth Amendment *Miranda* rights may be used to impeach the defendant's trial testimony (see *Harris v. N.Y.*, *supra*, p. C-75), so statements elicited by informants in violation of D's Sixth Amendment rights may be used for this same purpose. [402]

III. THE CLIENT'S RIGHT TO CONTROL THE DEFENSE

A. **The right generally:** There are some decisions about the defense that are the province of the lawyer, and others that are ***reserved to the defendant.***

   Note on self-representation: A defendant's right to ***represent himself*** does not really fall into either of the two categories. We consider this right separately *infra*, C-88.

B. **Rights reserved to lawyer:** Assuming the defendant chooses to have a lawyer manage and present her case, then many of the decisions about how the case should be defended – typically decisions that can be described as matters of ***"trial strategy"*** – are ***reserved to the lawyer,*** not the client.

1. **Consequence:** If a decision falls within this "trial strategy" category, two important Sixth Amendment consequences follow:

[1] the ***lawyer*** is entitled to ***make the decision on her own***, and need not follow the wishes of the client; and

[2] the fact that the lawyer has made her own decision rather than following the client's wishes ***will not constitute ineffective assistance of counsel***.[5]

2. Decisions falling into the "lawyer's prerogative" category: Decisions will be found to fall within this "province of the lawyer" category if the decision is primarily about the ***tactics and strategy to be used by the defense,*** rather than about what the ***objectives*** of the defense should be. As the Court has said, "***Trial management*** is the ***lawyer's province.***" [*McCoy v. Louisiana* (2018)]

a. Examples: Therefore, counsel – not the client – is empowered to make decisions about the following issues, all of which are deemed to be matters of "trial management":

[1] whether to move to ***suppress prosecution evidence*** obtained by a constitutional violation (e.g., evidence from searches that violated D's Fourth Amendment rights);

[2] whether to have D ***wear civilian clothing*** rather than prison garb during the trial;

[3] whether to ***object*** to an improper ***jury instruction***;

[4] whether to ***forgo cross-examination*** of a witness;

[5] whether to ***call a witness*** (other than D himself) at trial.

[407]

b. No obligation to argue all issues on appeal: Here is another situation in which the lawyer, not the client, gets to make the decision: An ***appellate*** lawyer is ***not required*** by the Sixth Amendment to ***raise all issues which his client would like him to argue***. Rather, the lawyer is permitted to ***use his own professional judgment*** about what issues have the best probability of success on appeal. Consequently, even if one or more appellate arguments urged by the client and rejected by the lawyer are non-frivolous, the client has not been deprived the effective assistance of counsel. [*Jones v. Barnes*] [407]

CAPSULE SUMMARY

C. Decisions that belong solely to the client: In contrast to the above category of "trial management" decisions, as to which the lawyer has control, there is a category of decisions that are so ***"fundamental"*** that the Supreme Court confers the decision-making power on the ***client***, not the lawyer. [*McCoy v. Louisiana*, (2018)] [405-407] According to *McCoy*:

[1] if the decision consists of "***strategic choices*** about ***how best to achieve a client's objective***," the decision belongs to the ***lawyer***; *but …*

[2] if the decision concerns "***what the client's objectives in fact are***" (emphasis in original), then it's the ***client***, not the lawyer, who holds the right to make the decision.

1. Examples where client has the decision-making power: *McCoy, supra*, gives this list of choices that are sufficiently "***fundamental***" that they belong to the client:

[1] whether to ***"self-represent"***;

---

5. Of course, the lawyer's decision may be ***so ill-advised*** that it constitutes ineffective assistance. But when a reviewing court is later trying to decide whether the decision amounted to ineffective assistance, that court will essentially ignore the fact that the client objected to the decision.

[2] whether to ***plead guilty***;

[3] whether to ***waive a jury***;

[4] whether to ***testify in one's own behalf***;

[5] whether to ***take an appeal***; and …

[6] whether to ***concede guilt*** in the context of a capital-murder proceeding (the issue posed by *McCoy* itself).

Example of [6]: D is charged with the capital murder of three members of his estranged wife's family. He hires English to be his trial lawyer. English wants to concede D's guilt in the guilt phase (he thinks the evidence that D did the killings is overwhelming), so that D will be less likely to be sentenced to death. But D demands that English not concede guilt, and instead assert an alibi-plus-"corrupt cops did the killings" defense. English disobeys, telling the jury during the guilt phase that D did the killings. The jury convicts. In the penalty phase, English begs the jury to sentence D to life on account of his serious mental-and-emotional issues. However, the jury sentences D to death. On appeal, represented by new lawyers, D claims that English's refusal to follow D's instructions not to concede guilt deprived him of effective assistance of counsel.

Held (by the U.S. Supreme Court), for D. Certain decisions are "reserved for the client." This category consists *not* of "strategic choices about how best to *achieve* a client's objectives" but rather, "choices about ***what the client's objectives in fact are***." Whether to concede guilt is one of these reserved-to-the-client choices, since one in D's position might well "wish to avoid, above all else, the ***opprobrium*** that comes with ***admitting he killed family members.***"

Furthermore, the error here, since it "block[ed] the defendant's right to make the fundamental choices about his own defense," was ***"structural"*** in nature. When an error is structural, it is ***not subject to "harmless-error" review.*** Thus D is automatically entitled to a new trial, with no need to show how the error caused him prejudice. [*McCoy v. Louisiana*] [405-407]

C A P S U L E S U M M A R Y

IV. WAIVER OF THE RIGHT TO COUNSEL

A. Appointed vs. retained: In both the appointed-counsel and retained-counsel situations, the defendant may be found to have ***waived*** his Sixth Amendment right to counsel. Essentially the same standards apply for both situations. [407]

B. The "knowingly and intelligently" standard: D will be found to have waived his right to counsel only if he acted ***"knowingly and intelligently."*** However, the government must prove merely by a "preponderance of the evidence" that D acted knowingly and intelligently, a relatively easy-to-satisfy standard. [408]

1. ***Miranda* warnings suffice:** If D is given his ***Miranda*** warnings, and does not ask for counsel, this will be found to be a valid waiver of his Sixth Amendment right to counsel.

C. Waiver after pre-trial appointment of counsel: Suppose a suspect has been formally charged, and is represented by counsel (retained or appointed); trial has not yet begun, and the police want to ***question the suspect outside of the presence of his counsel.*** In this scenario, as a matter of Sixth Amendment law the police ***may*** ask the suspect whether he is willing to answer their questions, and treat his willingness to answer as constituting a waiver of his right to have his counsel present at any questioning. This principle is set forth in *Montejo v. Louisiana* (2009). [410]

1. **Non-custodial interrogations:** If the police interrogation takes place ***in custody***, the police's freedom from Sixth Amendment problems won't help them very much. That's because the police still have to worry about *Edwards v. Arizona* (*supra*, C-60), under which once a suspect has asked for counsel after being given *Miranda* warnings, any later custodial confession outside the presence of counsel will automatically be deemed a *Miranda* (Fifth Amendment) violation unless the conversation was ***initiated by the suspect.***

   But in the case of a ***non-custodial police-initiated interrogation*** (to which *Edwards* doesn't apply because *Miranda* doesn't apply to non-custodial questioning), *Montejo* means that the police ***don't have to worry about the suspect's Sixth Amendment right to counsel***. (The court has to find that the suspect's willingness to speak to them outside the presence of his lawyer constituted a "knowing and intelligent" waiver of those Sixth Amendment rights; but there's no bright-line rule, as there is in the *Edwards/Miranda* context, that there can be no waiver if the police initiate the conversation.)

   Example: D is charged with murder, and is arraigned before a magistrate. At D's request, the magistrate appoints counsel for him. D is then released on bail. The next day, the police visit D at his house and, without referring to the fact that D has had counsel appointed for him, ask him if he is willing to talk to them about the crime. D (having never consulted with his newly-appointed counsel) agrees to talk, and confesses. At trial, D tries to get the confession suppressed on the grounds that the court should impose a bright-line rule that any waiver of the right to counsel induced by police-initiated questioning outside the presence of counsel should be deemed invalid.

   D will lose with this argument. As long as the court finds that D's willingness to speak to the police constituted a "knowing and intelligent" waiver of the right to have counsel present (which the court will probably find), the confession will come in. In cases involving suspects in *custody*, the bright-line rule of *Edwards v. Arizona* (*supra*, p. C-60) says that once a suspect has asked for counsel after being given *Miranda* warnings, any later custodial confession outside the presence of counsel must automatically be deemed invalid unless the conversation was initiated by the suspect. But no such rule applies in the case of the Sixth Amendment and non-custodial police-initiated conversations: the suspect's willingness to speak without having consulted his lawyer will be deemed to be an implied waiver of his Sixth Amendment rights, as long as the facts indicate that waiver was "knowing and intelligent." [Cf. *Montejo v. Louisiana*, *supra*]

D. Entry of guilty plea: If a purported waiver of the right to counsel is followed by entry of a ***guilty plea,*** courts are especially skeptical of whether the waiver was "knowingly and intelligently" made, which it is required to be.

1. **Minimum requirements:** Thus courts generally hold that at the least, the defendant must be ***aware of the charges against him*** and must ***understand the full significance of his decision*** to waive counsel.

E. Right to defend oneself: The Sixth Amendment guarantees the right of a defendant to proceed ***pro se***, i.e., to ***represent himself without counsel***. [*Faretta v. California*] (By choosing to represent himself, D waives any later claim that he was denied the effective assistance of counsel.) [411]

1. **Mentally incompetent defendant:** But if the defendant has a ***severe mental illness*** that prevents her from being competent to conduct her own defense, the state may ***insist on appointing counsel.*** [412]

CHAPTER 9

FORMAL PROCEEDINGS

Introductory note: In this last chapter, we cover aspects of the criminal procedure system once formal proceedings have begun against the defendant (as opposed to the investigative phase, covered above).

I. GRAND JURY PROCEEDINGS

A. **Grand jury indictment generally:** Defendants accused of federal felonies, and some state-court defendants, are "entitled" to a grand jury indictment. [423]

1. **Federal practice:** The Fifth Amendment provides that "no person shall be held to answer for a capital, or otherwise infamous crime, unless on a presentment or indictment of a Grand Jury." This provision means that anyone charged with a ***federal felony*** (i.e., a federal crime punishable by more than one year of imprisonment) may only be tried following issuance of a grand jury indictment.

2. **State courts:** The Fifth Amendment's right to a grand jury indictment is one of the two Bill of Rights guarantees that is ***not*** binding on the states by means of the Fourteenth Amendment. So each individual state decides whether to require a grand jury indictment. Today, about 19 states require indictment for all felonies, with the remaining states dispensing with the requirement in at least some kinds of felonies.

B. **Self-incrimination and immunity:** The Fifth Amendment privilege against ***self-incrimination*** will frequently entitle a witness who is subpoenaed by a grand jury to refuse to testify. However, this refusal may be overcome by a grant of immunity. [425-426]

1. **The privilege:** The privilege against self-incrimination applies in grand jury proceedings — if the witness believes that the testimony she is being asked to give might incriminate her in a subsequent criminal case (whether in the jurisdiction that is conducting the grand jury investigation, or a different one), she may decline to testify on Fifth Amendment grounds. [*Counselman v. Hitchcock*] (The Fifth Amendment does ***not*** allow the witness to refuse to appear at all — the witness must appear in response to the subpoena, and must then state for the record the Fifth Amendment claim.) [425]

2. **Grant of immunity:** The grand jury, acting under the prosecutor's direction, may combat Fifth Amendment claims by granting ***immunity*** to the witness. There are two types of immunity: ***transactional*** immunity (which protects the witness against any prosecution for the entire transactions about which the witness has testified), and ***use*** immunity (a much narrower protection, which protects only against the direct or indirect use of the testimony in a subsequent prosecution). [425]

   a. **Use immunity sufficient:** ***Use immunity is sufficient*** to nullify the witness' Fifth Amendment privilege. [*Kastigar v. U.S.*] [425] But use immunity is interpreted in a way that is favorable to the defendant — usually, use immunity requires that any eventual prosecution of the witness be conducted by someone who did not witness or read the transcript of the grand jury testimony.

CAPSULE SUMMARY

II. BAIL AND PREVENTIVE DETENTION

A. Bail: The system of ***bail*** is the way courts have traditionally dealt with the problem of making sure that D shows up for trial. D is required to post an amount of money known as a "bail bond"; if he does not show up for trial, he forfeits this amount. [426-427]

1. **Right to non-excessive bail:** The Eighth Amendment (applicable in both state and federal proceedings) provides that ***"excessive bail shall not be required."*** However, the Bail Clause does ***not*** give D a right to affordable bail in all situations — it merely means that when the court does set bail, it must not do so in an ***unduly high*** amount, judged on factors such as the seriousness of the offense, the weight of the evidence against D, D's financial abilities and his character. (*Example:* If a judge were to set bail of $1 million for an indigent D accused of the non-violent crime of marijuana possession, this might be found to be "excessive" bail, in violation of the Eighth Amendment.) [427]

   a. **Individualized consideration:** The guarantee against excessive bail means that the judge must consider D's ***individual circumstances*** in fixing bail. The court may not consider the seriousness of the offense as the ***sole*** criterion (so that ability to pay, weight of the evidence, character of D, etc. must all be considered). [427]

   b. **Defendant's ability to pay:** The fact that the defendant ***cannot afford*** the bail set in the particular case does ***not*** automatically make the bail "excessive" — D's financial resources are merely one factor to be considered. [427]

B. Preventive detention: A jurisdiction may decide that bail will simply ***not be allowed*** at all for certain types of offenses. That is, the state or federal government may set up a ***"preventive detention"*** scheme, whereby certain types of defendants are automatically held without bail until trial. But a preventive detention scheme will violate the Eighth Amendment if its procedures do not ensure that only those defendants who are genuinely dangerous or likely to flee are denied release. [427-428]

1. **Factors to be considered:** The jurisdiction may, of course, consider D's likelihood of ***flight*** before trial as a factor in whether to deny bail entirely. But the jurisdiction may consider other factors as well, most notably the likelihood that D will, if released before trial, commit ***additional crimes***.

2. **Individualized circumstances of defendant:** A preventive detention scheme probably must give D the opportunity for a ***hearing***, at which D's ***individual circumstances*** (e.g., his dangerous past tendencies, his community ties, his past convictions, etc.) may be considered. (*Example:* If a state were to provide that bail should automatically be denied without a hearing, and preventive detention ordered, for any defendant charged with any act of murder, this mandatory scheme would almost certainly violate the Bail Clause.) [428]

III. PLEA BARGAINING

A. Plea bargaining generally: Most criminal cases are resolved by ***plea bargain*** rather than by trial. To give D an incentive to "settle" the case rather than insist on a trial, the prosecutor normally gives D an inducement of a ***lighter sentence*** than what he would get if he were convicted at trial. The three common types of plea bargains are: (1) the plea to a ***less serious charge*** (*Example:* D is allowed to plead guilty to second-degree sexual assault rather than to the rape charge that is supported by the evidence); (2) D pleads guilty to the crime charged, but the prosecutor agrees to recommend a ***lighter sentence*** to the judge (but the judge will not necessarily follow the recommendation, though she usually does so); and (3) D pleads to one charge in return for the prosecution's promise to ***drop other charges*** that might also have been brought. [428-429]

1. **Generally enforceable:** Plea bargains are generally ***enforceable***. For instance, if D pleads guilty to a charge, is sentenced, and then has a change of heart, he is almost always stuck with his bargain. [429]

2. **Prosecutor may refuse to bargain:** The prosecutor has ***no obligation*** to bargain. Even if the prosecutor routinely offers a plea bargain in other, similar, circumstances, she has a right in a particular case to decide to go to trial without offering a plea bargain. [*Weatherford v. Bursey* ("There is no constitutional right to plea bargain...")] [429]

B. Promises by prosecutor:

1. **Threats by prosecutor:** There are relatively few constraints on the prosecutor's right to use ***threats*** during the negotiation. For instance, the prosecutor may charge one crime, and then tell D, "If you don't plead guilty to this charge, I'll file more serious charges." So long as the threatened extra charges are reasonably supported by the evidence, D will not be able to plead guilty, then attack the plea on the grounds that he was coerced. This is true even if D shows that the prosecutor has treated him more harshly than the prosecutor treats others accused of the same crime. [429]

   a. **Threats about third person:** But if the prosecutor tries to induce D to plead guilty by offering leniency to a ***third person*** (or, conversely, threatens to prosecute the third person if D does not plead guilty), D has a somewhat greater chance of getting the plea bargain overturned on the grounds of duress. This is especially true where the third person is D's ***spouse, sibling, or child*** — but even here, D usually cannot succeed in getting a plea bargain overturned on grounds of duress.

2. **Broken promises:** The plea bargain is essentially a contract, and the rules of contract law apply. Consequently, if the prosecution fails to ***honor its part of the bargain***, D may usually either "terminate the contract" (i.e., elect to go to trial) or seek "specific performance" (i.e., insist that the terms as originally agreed upon be carried out). [430]

   a. **Judge disagrees:** But D only has the right to receive what the prosecution has promised, and no more. For instance, if the plea bargain is a "lesser sentence" arrangement, in which the prosecutor has promised to ***recommend*** a particular lighter sentence, D's constitutional rights are not violated where the prosecutor keeps this part of the bargain but the trial judge unexpectedly ***imposes a more serious sentence***. (But many states, and the federal system, although not constitutionally required to do so, would allow D to ***withdraw*** his guilty plea at that moment and go to trial.) [430]

   b. **Breach by defendant:** If *D* fails to live up to the plea bargain, then the *prosecution* has the right to elect to terminate the agreement and try D on the originally-charged offense. This is true even if a judgment of conviction has already been entered as the result of the plea bargain. (*Example:* D agrees to testify against his confederates in return for a lesser charge or lesser sentence. He receives the reduced charge or sentence, then refuses to testify. The prosecution has the right to withdraw the conviction and try D on the original charge.) [*Ricketts v. Adamson*]. [431]

C. **Receipt of plea:** The trial judge will not "receive" (i.e., accept) the plea until she has assured herself that certain requirements, designed to protect D, have been complied with. Thus the judge must be satisfied that: (1) D is ***competent*** to enter into the plea, and the plea is truly voluntary; (2) D ***understands the charge***; and (3) D understands the ***consequences*** of the plea, such as the minimum and maximum possible sentences. [431]

   1. **Factual basis:** Some states, and the federal system, also require that the judge not take the guilty plea unless the judge is convinced that there is a ***factual basis*** for the plea. Thus if D continues to protest his innocence, and says that he is pleading guilty only to avoid the risk that the judge or jury may disbelieve his truthful professions of innocence, the judge will normally ***not accept*** the guilty plea. In this scenario, it is ***constitutional*** for the trial judge to refuse to take the guilty plea — there is no absolute constitutional right to have one's guilty plea accepted by the court. [*North Carolina v. Alford*]

D. **Withdrawal of plea by defendant:** Under some circumstances, D may have the right to ***withdraw*** his guilty plea. [432]

   1. **Before sentencing:** ***Before sentencing*** has taken place, most jurisdictions give D a broad right to withdraw the plea.

   2. **After sentencing:** But ***after sentencing***, it is far ***harder*** for D to withdraw the plea. Courts normally don't let D get two bites of the apple (i.e., they don't let D plead guilty, see what sentence will be imposed, and then rescind the arrangement if he is disappointed).

      a. **Trial judge ignores recommendation:** But in one situation courts usually ***do*** allow a post-sentencing withdrawal of the plea: where the prosecution agrees to recommend a certain sentence, and the trial judge ignores the recommendation and sentences more severely, most jurisdictions allow D to withdraw and go to trial (though it is probably ***not*** a violation of D's constitutional right for the court to refuse to allow withdrawal in this situation).

E. **Rights waived by plea:** Normally, a defendant who enters a guilty plea and undergoes sentencing is deemed to have ***waived*** any rights, including constitutional ones, that he could have asserted at trial. With rare exceptions, therefore, D may not ***appeal*** the pleaded-to conviction or the sentence under it. This is true even where D now asserts constitutional rights that were not recognized until ***after*** the plea was entered. [*McMann v. Richardson]* [433]

IV. SELECTIVE PROSECUTION

A. **Background:** Suppose a prosecutor decides that in cases where the potential charge is distribution of crack cocaine (with a 10-year minimum sentence), (1) she will charge all ***Black*** defendants with that offense, but (2) she will charge all ***white*** defendants with the ***lesser*** misdemeanor charge of small-scale cocaine possession. When that prosecutor charges a particular Black defendant, D, with crack distribution, may D seek to have the charges dismissed on the grounds that Black defendants including himself are the victim of ***"selective prosecution"?***

   In theory, the answer may in some cases be yes, because D can plausibly argue that his Equal Protection rights have been violated. But the Supreme Court has placed such huge procedural obstacles to such a defense that it will be ***exceedingly rare*** for a defendant to succeed with it. [434]

1. **Racial discrimination:** In most cases where defendants have raised claims of unconstitutional selective prosecution, their claim is that the prosecutor's decision to prosecute was ***based on the defendant's race.*** Typically, D is Black, and his argument is that prosecutors either don't prosecute white people at all for the offense in question, or bring lesser charges against whites than against Blacks. [434]

B. **Requirements for selective prosecution claim:** The Supreme Court has made defense claims that the prosecutor has engaged in unconstitutional selective prosecution ***virtually impossible to establish.*** Indeed, ***no defendant*** in any court seems to have succeeded with a selective-prosecution claim going back to the late nineteenth century.

1. **Two requirements:** The Court has held that to bring a successful selective-prosecution claim, the defendant has to show ***"clear evidence" of two things:***

   [1] **"Discriminatory effect":** First, D must show that the prosecutor's policy "had a ***discriminatory effect***."

   [2] **"Discriminatory purpose":** Second, D must show that that policy was "motivated by a ***discriminatory purpose.***"

   [*U.S. v. Armstrong*] [434]

2. **Hard to establish:** Each of these elements tends to be ***virtually impossible to prove*** by the required clear evidence. [435]

   a. **Discriminatory effect:** To meet the ***"discriminatory effect"*** requirement requirement, the Court has said, D must "show that ***similarly situated individuals of a different race*** were not prosecuted." [*U.S. v. Armstrong, supra*] [435]

      i. **Very high bar:** Lower courts interpreting *Armstrong* have said that to satisfy this "similarly situated individuals" requirement, D must point to ***particular white persons*** who, faced with potential charges based on the same type of offense, were not charged by the same prosecutor or office. This is generally an insurmountable obstacle, since as one commentator has noted, "it is impossible for a person of color to point to ***similarly situated white individuals*** who were not arrested because ***there is no record of such people."*** [435]

   b. **Discriminatory purpose:** Similarly, it is nearly impossible for D to satisfy the second requirement for a selective prosecution claim: proving that the prosecution's charging policies were motivated by a ***"discriminatory purpose."*** This is true because, as the same commentator has said, "In the era of colorblindness … officials in the criminal justice system ***are unlikely to explicitly voice any discriminatory sentiments[.]"*** [435]

C. **Obtaining discovery to show bias:** In most cases involving claims of selective prosecution, the defendant does not even *try* to have the case dismissed on that grounds. Instead, defendants typically ask for the right to ***conduct discovery of the prosecution's files,*** to help them find evidence that the requirements for a selective prosecution claim have been met.

1. **Same requirements apply:** But the Supreme Court has held that the ***same requirements*** (clear evidence of discriminatory purpose and effect) have to be satisfied before the defendant will even have the right to do such discovery. [*Armstrong*, *supra.*] As one observer has noted, "[T]he requirement that defendants moving for discovery present evidence showing the ***same data*** whose existence they are seeking to prove has created a ***'Catch-22' situation.'"*** [435]

Example: The Ds, who are Black, have been charged with the federal crime of distributing crack cocaine. They assert that they were selected for federal prosecution because they are Black, and they move to be allowed to conduct discovery into the prosecution's files, in the hopes of finding find evidence supporting their claim. In their motion, they supply an affidavit from the public defender's office that during the year in question, every one of the crack-distribution charges filed by the relevant federal prosecutor's office was against a Black defendant.

Held, the Ds are not entitled to discovery. To obtain discovery, the Ds would have to first satisfy the ***same requirements*** (clear evidence of discriminatory purpose and effect) as would be imposed on a defendant seeking outright dismissal for selective prosecution. The Ds would thus need to "***identify individuals*** who were ***not black***, ***could have been prosecuted*** for the [same] offenses for which [the Ds] were charged, but were ***not*** so prosecuted." Since the affidavit submitted by the Ds did not identify any such similarly-situated non-Black potential defendants, the Ds are not entitled to discovery. [*U.S. v. Armstrong, supra*] [436]

V. RIGHT TO SPEEDY TRIAL

A. The right generally: The Sixth Amendment provides that "In all criminal prosecutions, the accused shall enjoy the right to a ***speedy . . . trial***." This right applies to both federal and state prosecutions. [436]

1. **Factors:** There is no bright-line rule setting forth exactly how speedy a trial must be. Instead, the Supreme Court uses a "balancing test," in which both the prosecution's and the defendant's conduct are weighed. There are four factors which courts are to consider in deciding whether the trial has been unreasonably delayed: (1) the ***length of the delay*** (with most delays of eight months or longer found "presumptively prejudicial"); (2) the ***reason*** for the delay (the more culpable the government's conduct regarding the delay, the better D's speedy trial claim); (3) whether D ***asserted*** the speedy trial right ***before*** a trial began (as opposed to an assertion of the right after the trial was conducted and D lost); and (4) what ***prejudice*** D has suffered by the delay (with the most weight given to any impairment of D's ability to defend himself, such as by the death or unavailability of witnesses).

B. Federal Speedy Trial Act: In federal prosecutions, speedy trial problems are covered by the Speedy Trial Act, which as a very general rule provides that the time between indictment and commencement of trial must normally be no more than 70 days (but which allows various "periods of delay" that do not count in the 70-day limit). [437]

VI. PRE-TRIAL DISCOVERY

A. Discovery for the defense: The defense may be entitled to advance ***disclosure*** by the prosecution of evidence relevant to the case.

1. **Prosecutor's constitutional duty to disclose:** There is no ***general*** constitutional duty on the part of the prosecutor to disclose material evidence to the defense. But there is one constitutional rule: the prosecution must disclose to the defense ***exculpatory evidence within the prosecution's possession***. [*Brady v. Maryland*] (A defense request for exculpatory material is called a "*Brady* request.") [439-440]

a. **Good faith irrelevant:** Even if the prosecution's failure to disclose exculpatory evidence is ***not*** motivated by a desire to hamper the defense, and is truly the result of ***negligence*** or even circumstances beyond the prosecution's control, this makes no difference. (But if the prosecution is ***unable*** to disclose exculpatory evidence because the evidence has been ***lost*** or ***destroyed***, the *Brady* doctrine does ***not apply*** unless the defense shows ***bad faith*** on the part of the police. [*Arizona v. Youngblood*])

2. **Practice:** Apart from constitutional requirements, most states, and the federal system, have enacted elaborate ***statutory*** pre-trial disclosure schemes. For instance, nearly all states and the federal system require the prosecution upon request to give the defense copies of ***prior recorded statements*** by the defendant. Similarly, many states also require the prosecution to disclose to D any recorded statements made by a ***co-defendant***, as well as copies of scientific tests, physical examinations, and a list of witnesses whom the prosecution intends to call at trial. (But the defense usually may ***not*** get ahold of ***police reports***.) [440]

B. **Discovery for the prosecution:** Most states and the federal system give the ***prosecution*** some discovery rights. These are usually less broad than those given to the defense. For instance, most states, and the federal system, require D to give advance notice of his intent to raise an ***alibi*** defense. [441]

C A P S U L E S U M M A R Y

VII. THE RIGHT TO A JURY TRIAL

A. **The right generally:** Criminal defendants have a right to a ***jury trial***. This right is conferred by the Sixth Amendment, which says that "The accused shall enjoy the right to a ... public trial, by an ***impartial jury*** of the State and district wherein the crime shall have been committed[.]" [442]

1. **Applicable to state trials:** This right applies to both ***federal*** and ***state*** trials.

2. **Serious criminal prosecutions only:** The Sixth Amendment right to jury trial applies only to ***criminal prosecutions*** for ***serious*** crimes. That is, the right does not apply where what is charged is a ***petty*** rather than serious crime.

a. **Six months as dividing line:** As a general rule, the dividing line between a "serious" crime and a "petty" one is a ***potential sentence of greater than six months***. Thus there is automatically a right to jury trial for any crime punish*able* by more than six months in prison, regardless of whether a more-than-six-month sentence is ***actually*** imposed. [442]

i. **Multiple offenses:** Where D is charged with ***multiple offenses*** that are to be tried together, the Court will ***not "aggregate"*** these offenses together for purposes of the six-month test — each is evaluated on its own.

B. **Waiver:** The defendant may ***waive*** the right to jury trial, provided that the waiver is ***voluntary***, ***knowing*** and ***intelligent***.

1. **Prosecution's right to veto:** But most states, and the federal system, allow the judge or the prosecutor to ***"veto"*** the defendant's waiver of a jury. That is, the judge or the prosecution may ***insist on a jury trial*** even though the defendant does not want one. [*Singer v. U.S.*] [451]

C. **Issues to which the right applies:** Once the right to jury trial applies to an offense, D has the right to have the jury, rather than the judge, decide ***every element*** of the offense. Furthermore, the jury must find each element to exist ***"beyond a reasonable doubt."*** [443]

1. **No jury right as to sentencing:** On the other hand, the right to a jury trial does not extend to the area of ***sentencing***. For instance, the determination of whether particular ***"sentencing factors"*** specified by the legislature (e.g., existence of a prior conviction) do or do not exist in the particular case can be made by the judge. [443]

2. **Fact increases the maximum sentence:** But if the existence of a particular fact ***increases the maximum punishment*** to which D is subjected, the existence of that fact will be treated as an element of the offense, as to which the jury must make the decision. [444]

   a. **New "elements" added to the crime:** So whenever a legislature says that the ***maximum*** statutorily-authorized sentence for ***a given set of elements*** is *X*, but that the maximum-authorized sentence becomes ***higher*** than *X* if a particular ***extra fact*** is found to exist, that extra fact must be found by the jury, not the judge. [*Apprendi v. N.J.*] [444]

   Example: New Jersey defines the crime of possession of a firearm for an unlawful purpose as a "second degree" offense. The punishment for a second-degree offense is imprisonment for between ***5 and 10 years.*** A separate statute, however, says that if a second-degree offense is committed "with a purpose to ***intimidate*** an individual or group ... because of ***race, color*** [or] ***gender[,]***" the crime is punishable by an ***"enhanced sentence"*** of between ***10 and 20 years***. D is charged with possessing a firearm for an unlawful purpose, and pleads guilty. During the sentencing phase the trial judge (not a jury) conducts a hearing on the basis of which the judge concludes that D's unlawful purpose included racial bias. Therefore, the judge sentences D to an enhanced (more-than-10-year) sentence. D claims that his Sixth Amendment right to have a jury decide each "element of the offense" means that he had a right to have a jury, not the judge, decide whether D's use of the firearm was motivated by racial bias.

   Held, for D. "Other than the fact of a prior conviction, any ***fact*** that increases the ***penalty*** for a crime beyond the [otherwise-applicable] ***prescribed statutory maximum*** must be submitted to a jury, and proved beyond a reasonable doubt." Since D's possession of a race-based motive increased the penalty beyond the 5-10 year maximum that would otherwise apply, the existence of such a motive was required to be determined by a jury. [*Apprendi v. N.J.*] [444]

      i. **Death penalty cases:** This principle that any fact that increases the maximum statutory punishment must be found by a jury has important applications to ***death-penalty*** cases. If the legislature says that the maximum penalty for a crime is something ***less than death*** in the absence of some statutorily-specified ***"aggravating factor,"*** then the existence of that aggravating factor must be determined by the jury (beyond a reasonable doubt) rather than by a judge. [*Ring v. Arizona*] [444]

   b. **Sentence within range:** If, by contrast, the existence of a particular fact merely bears on ***where within the range of possible sentences*** the defendant's sentence should fall, the existence of that fact will merely be a ***sentencing factor*** (on which the judge may constitutionally make the decision). [*Apprendi v. N.J., supra*] [444]

   c. **Increase in mandatory minimum:** A fact whose existence increases the ***mandatory minimum*** sentence that the court is ***required*** to impose must be decided by the jury, just as a fact that increases the maximum allowable sentence must be. [450]

   Example: D is charged with the federal crime of carrying a firearm in relation to a crime of violence (in this case, a robbery). The statute says that if the firearm is "use[d] or carrie[d,]" the mandatory minimum sentence is five years; but if the firearm is ***"brandished"*** during the crime, the mandatory minimum becomes seven years. The jury convicts D, and indicates on the verdict form that D "used or carried" a firearm during the crime. But the jury does not put on the form any finding about whether D "brandished" a firearm. The judge finds that D "brandished" that firearm, and therefore sentences D to a mandatory minimum of seven years. D argues that he had a right to have a jury decide (under a "reasonable doubt" standard) whether he did or did not "brandish" the firearm.

Held, for D. The rule that every "element" of a crime must be found by the jury applies not only to facts that ***increase the "ceiling"*** of permissible sentences (i.e., facts that increase the statutory ***maximum***) but also to facts that increase the ***"floor"*** (i.e., facts that increase the statutory ***minimum***). Therefore, D was entitled to have the jury, rather than the judge, decide whether he "brandished" the weapon. [*Alleyne v. U.S.* (2013)] [450]

3. **Sentencing guidelines:** The principle that punishment-increasing facts must be found by a jury also means that schemes involving mandatory ***"sentencing guidelines"*** will typically be ***invalid***. In such schemes, the legislature establishes both a maximum sentence for a particular offense (say 10 years), and a standard sentence ***range*** for that offense (say 3-5 years). The legislature then orders trial judges to add to or subtract time from the standard range according to various aggravating or mitigating factors found to exist by the judge, with the result never exceeding the maximum.

The Court has held that ***any increase*** in the sentence given to a defendant — beyond the standard range — by virtue of the judge's finding on a guideline-mandated factor ***violates*** the defendant's right to a jury trial. [*Blakely v. Washington*] [444]

Example: D is convicted of kidnapping, a Class B felony. The maximum penalty for Class B penalties is 10 years. But state sentencing guidelines prescribe a standard range of 49 to 53 months for kidnapping. However, the guidelines instruct the judge to consider various aggravating (or mitigating) factors that if present can move the sentence out of the standard range. The judge finds that D acted with "deliberate cruelty," an aggravating factor that under the guidelines can add 37 months to the standard range; therefore, the judge sentences D to a term of 90 months (37 months more than the top of the standard range).

Held, for D: the application of the guidelines to increase D's sentence beyond the maximum that it could otherwise have been (i.e., beyond 53 months), based on a fact (deliberate cruelty) found by a judge, violated D's right to a jury trial on all punishment-increasing elements. [*Blakely v. Washington, supra*]

a. **Federal Guidelines are invalid as written:** This principle means that the ***Federal Sentencing Guidelines are unconstitutional as written***. The Guidelines ***cannot require*** (as they purport to do) a federal judge to impose a heavier sentence based solely on a fact found by the judge. Instead, the Guidelines are merely ***"advisory,"*** and it's essentially up to the judge whether to follow them or not. [*U.S. v. Booker*] [447-449]

Example: D is found by the jury to have possessed "500 or more grams" of cocaine. For this offense, the maximum sentence authorized by the Federal Sentencing Guidelines is 78 months. The judge finds, in a post-conviction proceeding, that D actually possessed much more than 500 grams (and also that D was the leader of a drug-dealing enterprise). The Guidelines require the judge, if he finds these "aggravating facts," to sentence D to an "upward departure," namely a term of 188 to 235 months.

Held, insofar as the Guidelines require this upward departure beyond the longest sentence that could have been based on the jury's 500-gram finding (i.e., beyond 78 months), the Guidelines violate D's Sixth Amendment rights. Because of this unconstitutionality, the Guidelines cannot be mandatory. Instead, it is left to the judge's reasonable discretion what sentence to impose (though the judge must "consult" the Guidelines). [*U.S. v. Booker, supra*] [448-449]

i. **Right to appeal judge's actual sentence:** Given that the Federal Sentencing Guidelines are merely advisory, what happens if the trial judge seems to ***disregard*** them by imposing a sentence ***outside the Guidelines' range?*** If that happens, the prosecution (or the defense) may ***appeal*** the sentence as being too low (or high), and point to the judge's departure from the Guidelines' range in support.

(1) **Abuse-of-discretion standard:** But the federal appeals court may ***reverse*** the outside-of-Guidelines-range sentence (assuming the actual sentence fell within the ***statutory*** minimum and maximum) ***only*** for "***abuse of discretion***." And the abuse-of-discretion standard is a very ***deferential*** one. So even where the trial judge imposes a sentence well outside of the Guidelines' range, the appeals court will rarely find "abuse of discretion," and thus rarely reverse on that ground. [*Gall v. U.S.*] [450]

D. **Size and unanimity of the jury:** The Sixth Amendment places limits on states' ability to restrict the ***size*** of juries, and forbids ***less-than-unanimous*** verdicts in federal and state felony trials.

1. **Size:** Historically, juries have of course been composed of 12 persons. However, the Court has held that ***juries of six or more satisfy the Sixth Amendment***. [*Williams v. Florida*] On the other hand, juries of ***five or fewer violate*** the Sixth Amendment. [*Ballew v. Georgia*] [451]

2. **Unanimity:** The Sixth Amendment is now interpreted to require that the jury's verdict in ***both state and federal felony*** trials be ***unanimous***. [*Ramos v. Louisiana* (2020)] [452]

E. **Selection of jurors:** There are constitutional limits on the procedures by which jurors are ***selected***.

1. **The venire, and the requirement of a "cross-section of the community":** The Sixth Amendment guarantees the accused the right to a trial by "an ***impartial jury.***" This requirement of has been interpreted to mean that the venire (jury pool) from which petit juries are selected must ***represent a fair cross-section of the community***. [*Taylor v. Louisiana*] Thus if a state or federal venire systematically excludes or underrepresents, say, African-Americans or women, the Sixth and Fourteenth Amendments are violated. [452]

2. **Peremptory challenges:** With respect to the selection of the "petit jury" (the jury that actually decides a case) the main area of constitutional concern involves ***peremptory challenges.*** In nearly all jurisdictions, both the prosecution and defense are given a certain number of peremptory challenges, i.e., the right to have prospective jurors ***excused without cause***.

a. **Race- or gender-based challenges:** The most important rule regarding peremptory challenges is that in both federal and state trials, it is a violation of equal protection for the prosecution to exercise its peremptory challenges for the purpose of excluding jurors ***on account of their race or gender***. [*Batson v. Kentucky; J.E.B. v. Alabama ex rel. T.B.*] [454]

Such a claim that the prosecution has used its peremptory challenges in an illegal race- or gender-based way is known as a ***"Batson claim."*** [454-456]

i. Procedure for *Batson* claim: The procedure by which D may make a *Batson* claim is as follows:

(1) Prima facie case: First, D must, while jury selection is still proceeding, establish a *prima facie* case of intentional racial (or gender) discrimination. He must do this by showing that: (a) at least some members of a ***particular cognizable racial group*** (or gender) have been ***eliminated*** from D's jury; and (b) the circumstances of the case raise an ***inference*** that this exclusion was ***based on race*** (or gender). In demonstrating (b), D can rely on any relevant circumstances, but especially probative are (i) a ***pattern*** of strikes (either as to this particular petit jury, or as to other juries drawn from the same venire) and (ii) ***questions asked by the prosecution*** during voir dire that tend to show race- (or gender-) consciousness. [000]

(2) Rebuttal by prosecution: If D makes this *prima facie* showing, the ***burden then shifts*** to the prosecution to ***come forward with a "neutral explanation"*** for challenging jurors of a particular race (or gender). This requires more than a conclusory denial of a discriminatory motive. Nor does the prosecution's belief that jurors of that race would be partial to the defense suffice.

(3) Decision by court: If the prosecution comes up with a race-neutral explanation, it is up to the trial court to decide ***whether the defendant has borne his burden*** of establishing that the real reason for the strikes was racial (or gender) discrimination. For a successful *Batson* claim, the court must conclude, as a finding of fact, that the race-neutral explanation proffered by the prosecution was a ***pretext***, rather than the real reason, and that the real reason was some sort of intent to make strikes on race- or gender-conscious grounds. In that case, the trial court must order the struck juror to be ***reinstated*** absent a successful for-cause challenge. The trial court's ruling will be reversed on appeal only if it is clearly erroneous. [455]

VIII. THE TRIAL

A. The right to a "public" trial: The Sixth Amendment provides that "In all criminal prosecutions, the accused shall enjoy the right to a . . . ***public*** trial." This right means that there must be ***some access*** by members of the public. Thus it would be a violation of D's public trial right for the trial to be held against his wishes in a closed judge's chambers, or in a prison. [456]

1. D does not have right to closed trial: D does ***not*** have the right to insist on a ***private*** trial — the court may, without violating D's constitutional rights, order that the trial be conducted publicly over D's objection.

2. Partial closure: Occasionally, D's right to a public trial may be ***outweighed*** by a competing interest, on the part of the public or a witness, in having ***part*** of the trial ***closed***. In general, the party (usually the prosecution) seeking to close part of a trial must show: (1) that there is a ***compelling state interest*** in favor of closure; (2) that the closure will be ***no broader than necessary*** to protect that state interest; and (3) that there are no ***reasonable alternatives*** to closing the proceeding. [*Waller v. Georgia*] [456]

Examples: If D is being tried for raping V, a minor, the court probably can order the trial closed during the testimony of V, to protect her interest in confidentiality; but it probably cannot close the entire trial — the judge should instead consider ordering the parties not to refer to V by name. Similarly, if the case involves testimony by W, an undercover informant, it would probably be constitutional to close just the portion of the trial involving W's testimony, but probably not to close the entire trial.

B. D's right to be present: The defendant has a constitutional right to be ***present*** at his trial. This right derives from the Sixth Amendment's right of the accused "to be confronted with the witnesses against him." (However, this right can be lost by D's disruptive behavior which persists after a warning.) [458]

C. D's Confrontation Clause rights: The Sixth Amendment gives any criminal defendant "the right . . . to be ***confronted with the witnesses against him***." This is the Confrontation Clause. It applies to the states as well as the federal government. The Confrontation Clause has two main components:

[1] the right to compulsory ***process***; and

[2] the right to ***cross-examine*** hostile witnesses.

1. **Compulsory process:** The compulsory-process branch of the Confrontation Clause means that D has the right to have the court ***issue a subpoena*** to compel the testimony of any witness who may have information that would be useful to the defense. [458]

   a. **Assistance by the prosecution:** Sometimes, the compulsory-process right means that the prosecution must ***assist*** the defense in finding witnesses. Thus if the prosecution knows the whereabouts or identity of a witness who would be useful to the defense, the prosecution may be constitutionally compelled to disclose that information. [*Roviaro v. U.S.*] (But in the case of an undercover ***informant***, D's Confrontation Clause right to learn the informer's identity may be outweighed by the interest of the state, or the informer, in confidentiality to protect ongoing investigations or the informer's safety.) [458]

2. **Right of cross-examination:** The Confrontation Clause puts limits on the government's ability to restrict D's right of ***cross-examination***. (*Example:* A rule preventing D from cross-examining juvenile witnesses based upon their juvenile court records violates the Confrontation Clause. [*Davis v. Alaska*])

   a. **Limits on hearsay:** Similarly, the Confrontation Clause places some limits on the state's right to use ***hearsay*** evidence against D. For instance, hearsay may not be admitted unless it was obtained under circumstances providing reasonable ***"indicia of reliability."*** [*Ohio v. Roberts*] (But hearsay admitted under long-standing ***common law exceptions*** to the hearsay rule, such as the dying declaration exception, will almost always be found to have sufficient "indicia of reliability.")

3. **D1's confession used against D2:** The Confrontation Clause also prevents, in some circumstances, the use of ***one person's out-of-court confession against another.*** The Supreme Court has held that *A*'s Confrontation Clause rights are violated if the confession of *B*, his non-testifying co-defendant, naming *A* as a co-participant in the crime, is introduced without redaction at their joint trial. This is true even if the jury is instructed to consider the confession only against *B*, not *A*. ***Bruton v. U.S.*** [460]

Example: D1 and D2 are jointly tried for robbery. Before trial, D1 orally confesses that he and D2 committed the robbery together. At the joint trial, D1's full, unredacted, confession is admitted into evidence. The judge instructs the jury that the confession is to be considered only as evidence against D1, not against D2. D1 never takes the stand, so D2 never gets a chance to cross examine him about the confession.

Held, D2's Confrontation Clause rights were violated as soon as the jury heard D1's out-of-court confession implicating D2. This is true even though the confession was never admitted into evidence against D2, and even though the jury was instructed to ignore the confession in assessing D2's guilt. In this situation, the risk that the jury would not or could not follow the judge's limiting instruction was so great, and the consequences of failure so enormous, that the limiting instruction was not sufficient to protect D2. [*Bruton v. U.S., supra*] [460]

a. **Confessor takes the stand:** The *Bruton* principle probably applies only where the defendant who allegedly confessed ***declines to take the stand.*** If the confessor takes the stand and denies having made a confession, there is probably ***no*** Confrontation Clause problem. See, e.g, [*Nelson v. O'Neil*] (no Confrontation Clause problem where co-defendant took the stand, denied making an out-of-court statement implicating D, and testified favorably to D about the underlying events). [460]

b. **Full or partial redaction of D1's confession:** In *Bruton* itself, the part of D1's confession implicating D2 was read to the jury word-for-word, leaving the jury in no doubt about whether D1 had implicated D2. Suppose, however, that in an attempt to avoid a *Bruton* problem, the prosecution ***redacts*** (edits) D1's confession so that ***D2 is not mentioned.***

   i. **Confession "directly accuses" other defendant:** This prosecution technique may or may not work; if the redacted confession ***"directly accuses"*** D2, it's inadmissible under the *Bruton* principle. But if D1's confession does *not* "directly accuse" D2, it's admissible against D1. [*Samia v. U.S.*, also discussed *infra*, p. C-101]

   ii. **Complete redacting:** Where the editing of the confession is ***extensive,*** so that nothing as the jury hears it mentions or even alludes to the involvement of a third person, there is ***no Confrontation Clause problem***, and *Bruton* does not apply.

   iii. **"Deleted and I" violates *Bruton*:** Now suppose that D1's confession, when it's read to the jury, is ***redacted only slightly,*** so that the names of any co-defendants mentioned in the original confession are replaced with the word ***"deleted."*** In this scenario, the Court held in 1998 that *Bruton* was violated. [*Gray v. Maryland*] [461]

   iv. **References to "the other person" allowable:** But since *Gray*, the Court has ***dramatically narrowed the protection*** given to defendants by the *Bruton* rule. In a 2023 decision the Court held that when D1's confession indirectly refers to D2, *Bruton* applies ***only*** if what's read to the jury contains incriminating statements that are ***"directly accusatory"*** of D2. And the Court found that the redaction there was ***not*** "***directly accusatory of D2,*** even though the redaction seemed highly similar to the "deleted" redaction ruled insufficient in *Gray*. [*Samia v. U.S.* (2023)]

   Example: Stillwell and Samia are arrested for the murder-for-hire of Lee, which occurred in a van that Stillwell was driving. After his arrest, Stillwell gives a confession in which he admits to participating in the plot, but says that he was only the driver and that Samia was the one who actually shot and killed Lee while Stillwell and Samia rode in a van together. Stillwater and Samia are both charged with the murder. The prosecution says in its opening statement that the murder occurred when Stillwell and Samia rode in a van together. Stillwell invokes his Fifth Amendment right not to testify (see Par. D below).

The prosecution then ***redacts*** Stillwell's confession before presenting it to the jury; a police officer tells the jury that Stillwell in his confession "described a time when ***the other person he was with*** pulled the trigger on [Lee] in a van that he [the other person] and Mr. Stillwell were driving." Samia asserts that Stillwell's confession as described to the jury was so lightly redacted that its admission violated *Bruton* and *Gray, supra*, because any rational juror would infer, from the opening statement and the confession taken together, that the "other person" who pulled the trigger while in the van was Samia.

Held, for the prosecution: there was no *Bruton* violation. The *Bruton* rule ***"applies only to 'directly accusatory' incriminating statements,*** as distinct from those that '[do] ***'not refer directly to the defendant'*** and 'bec[o]me incriminating only when ***linked with evidence introduced later at trial.***' " Stillwell's redacted confession is not covered by *Bruton*'s ***"narrow exception,"*** because the confession did not "directly accuse" Samia and became incriminating only when linked with other evidence. [*Samia v. U.S., supra*] [461]

Note: So as the result of *Samia*, *Bruton* is easily skirted. To see how, suppose that as in *Samia*, D1's confession implicates D2, and D1 declines to testify. When the prosecutors present D1's redacted confession, they merely need to replace the name of D2 with a reference to ***"the other person"*** who participated in the crime, and the *Bruton* problem goes away. That's so even if any rational juror, when considering not just the confession but all the evidence taken together, would infer that the "other person" must be D2. [462]

D. Defendant's right to remain silent: The Fifth Amendment provides that no person "shall be ***compelled*** in any criminal case to be a witness ***against himself***." [463]

1. **Right not to take the stand:** The privilege does not mean merely that D may refuse to answer questions asked of him by the prosecution. Instead, it means that D has the right to ***not even take the witness stand***. (Most criminal defendants take advantage of this right.)

   a. **Waiver:** But the privilege may be ***waived***. A defendant who ***does*** take the witness stand has waived his privilege as to ***any matters*** within the fair scope of cross-examination. (*Example:* Once D takes the stand at all, he may be cross-examined about any prior convictions that shed light on his propensity to tell the truth, such as convictions for any crime involving dishonesty or false statement. See FRE 609(a).)

2. **Comment by prosecution:** The privilege against self-incrimination means that the prosecution may not ***comment*** on the fact that the defendant has declined to take the witness stand. [*Griffin v. California*] [463]

IX. DOUBLE JEOPARDY

A. The guarantee generally: The Fifth Amendment provides that no person shall "be subject for the same offence to be twice put in jeopardy of life or limb." This is the guarantee against "double jeopardy." The most classic application of the doctrine is to prevent D from being retried after he has been ***acquitted*** by a jury. But it occasionally applies in other contexts as well (e.g., if D's conviction is reversed on appeal on the grounds that the evidence at trial was insufficient to support a conviction, no reprosecution is allowed). [464]

1. **Applicable to states:** The double jeopardy guarantee applies to ***state*** as well as federal trials. [*Benton v. Maryland*] [464]

B. When jeopardy attaches: The protection against double jeopardy does not apply until jeopardy has ***"attached."*** [465]

1. **Jury trial:** In a case to be tried by a jury, jeopardy is deemed to "attach" when the jury has been ***impaneled and sworn***, i.e., when the whole jury has been selected and taken the oath. [*Crist v. Bretz*]

2. **Bench trial:** If the case is to be tried by a judge sitting without a jury, jeopardy attaches when the ***first witness has been sworn***.

C. Reprosecution after mistrial: If the trial begins and is then terminated by a ***mistrial***, the prosecution is usually ***not barred*** from retrying the defendant. [465]

1. **With D's consent:** If the mistrial has been brought about by the request of, or the acquiescence of, the defendant, reprosecution is ***always allowed***. This is true even though D's motion for a mistrial is required because of the prosecution's intentional misconduct.

2. **Without D's consent:** Even where the defendant has ***not*** consented, the mistrial will frequently not bar reprosecution. If the court finds that the mistrial is required by ***"manifest necessity,"*** reprosecution will be allowed. [465]

   a. **Hung jury:** Most commonly, the retrial issue arises in cases where there is a ***hung jury***. As long as the court is reasonably satisfied that the jury is truly deadlocked, and that additional deliberations will be fruitless, the situation meets the manifest-necessity standard, and the court can declare a mistrial over the defendant's objection. The decision of the trial judge that the jury is hopelessly deadlocked is given ***"great deference"*** by the appellate courts. [*Arizona v. Washington*] [465-466]

      i. **Time spent in deliberation:** One factor to which trial courts give a lot of weight is whether the jury has ***deliberated*** for a ***significant period of time*** before reaching the apparent deadlock — the longer the deliberation, the more likely the court is to conclude that the disagreement cannot be overcome. Consequently, if the jury reports a deadlock after a relatively brief deliberation period, the trial court is likely to (and should) instruct the jury to ***continue further deliberation***. [466]

         (1) **Deference to trial court:** But because of the large deference given by appeals courts to trial court judgments on the issue of deadlock, a trial judge will typically ***not be reversed*** even if she orders a mistrial following a very brief period of deliberation by the jury, and even if she does not order the jury to make another attempt to break the deadlock.

D. Reprosecution after acquittal: The classic application of the Double Jeopardy Clause is to prevent reprosecution after the defendant has been ***acquitted***. [467]

1. **Acquittal by jury:** Where the case has been tried to a ***jury*** and the jury has come in with a verdict of ***not guilty***, the clause always prevents D from being retried. This is true even though the acquittal was brought about by the admission of what should have been inadmissi-

ble evidence, and even if it was brought about by what can later be proved to have been ***perjured testimony*** offered by the defense. For this reason, the prosecution is ***never*** permitted to ***appeal*** a jury acquittal.

2. **Acquittal by judge:** Similarly, an acquittal by the judge sitting alone is final, and cannot be appealed.

E. **Reprosecution after conviction:** Occasionally, the fact that D has been ***convicted*** may bar a later prosecution. [467-468]

1. **Verdict set aside on appeal:** If D is convicted at trial, and then gets the verdict ***set aside on appeal***, the double jeopardy rule usually does ***not*** bar a retrial. [000]

a. **Insufficiency of evidence:** But there is one big exception: if the appellate court reverses because the evidence at trial was ***insufficient*** to support a conviction (i.e., no reasonable jury could have found D guilty on the evidence presented), a reprosecution is ***not*** allowed.

2. **Resentencing:** Where D is convicted, then appeals and receives a new trial, the Double Jeopardy Clause places some limits on the ***length of imprisonment*** that may be imposed on the new conviction. [468]

a. **Credit for time served:** The Constitution requires that D be given ***credit*** for the time he served under the first charge before it was overturned. [*North Carolina v. Pearce*]

b. **Longer sentence:** On the other hand, the judge hearing the second trial is ***not*** prevented from giving D a ***longer sentence*** than was imposed following the first conviction. [*North Carolina v. Pearce, supra*] (But if D in a death penalty case is sentenced to something less than death in the first trial, he may not be sentenced to death upon retrial.)

F. **Reprosecution by a different sovereign:** A conviction or acquittal by ***one jurisdiction*** does ***not*** bar a reprosecution by ***another jurisdiction***. This is the so-called ***"dual sovereignty"*** doctrine. [468]

1. **Rationale:** The dual sovereignty doctrine is based on the idea that even if two jurisdictions prosecute a person for the same conduct, the two prosecutions are ***by definition not for the "same offense."*** As the Supreme Court has put it, "a crime under ***one*** sovereign's laws is not 'the same offence' as a crime under the laws of ***another*** sovereign." [*Gamble v. U.S.* (2019)] [468]

Example: Suppose that D, a police officer, is charged in a state trial with aggravated assault upon X, a suspect in custody. D is acquitted. D is then charged with the federal crime of violating X's civil rights; all of the facts making up this offense are the same as they were in the earlier, state, trial.

The federal prosecution would be held not to violate D's double jeopardy rights, because it is being brought by a different jurisdiction than brought the first case. The same would be true if the federal case came before the state case.

2. **Non-constitutional limits:** But many states have state-constitutional or statutory provisions protecting D against reprosecution after conviction by some other jurisdiction. Similarly, federal guidelines bar a federal trial where a comparable state prosecution has already occurred, unless an Assistant Attorney General has approved the reprosecution.

G. **Overlapping offenses:** Occasionally, two different offenses involve the same set of facts to such an extent that the two offenses are deemed the "same" for double jeopardy purposes. You probably need to worry about this "overlapping offenses" problem only where one charge is a ***lesser included offense*** of the other. [470-470]

1. **Lesser included offense tried first:** Suppose the lesser included offense is ***tried first***. Here, whether the first trial results in an acquittal or conviction, the prosecution cannot bring a later prosecution for the greater offense. [*Brown v. Ohio*])
2. **Lesser included offense tried second:** Conversely, the Double Jeopardy Clause also bars prosecution for the lesser included crime ***after*** conviction of the greater one.
3. **Unable to try both at once:** But the rule barring serial prosecutions on the greater and lesser included offenses does ***not apply*** where the prosecution is ***unable*** to try both cases at once for reasons that are not the government's fault. (*Example:* If facts needed for proving the second crime had not yet been discovered at the time of the first trial, despite the prosecutor's due diligence, the second trial will not be barred.)

CHAPTER 1

CONSTITUTIONAL CRIMINAL PROCEDURE GENERALLY

I. INTRODUCTION

A. Meaning of "criminal procedure": The term ***"criminal procedure"*** refers to the methods by which the criminal justice system functions. The term encompasses the arresting of suspects, the searching of premises and persons, the interrogation of suspects, the use of police lineups, the introduction of evidence at trial, etc. Criminal procedure must be distinguished from the ***substantive criminal law***, which is the body of law defining crimes. Thus the cases and statutes that describe the state of mind necessary for first-degree murder, for instance, are part of the substantive criminal law, not of criminal procedure.

B. Function of the U.S. Constitution: Many aspects of criminal procedure are regulated by the U.S. Constitution, particularly the Bill of Rights (the first 10 Amendments). In fact, of the 23 separate rights set forth in the first eight Amendments to the Constitution, 12 concern criminal procedure. (Nutshell, p. 2.) When the U.S. Constitution speaks to an issue of procedure, its provisions are, of course, binding on the federal courts; furthermore, in most, but not all, instances, ***the state courts must also comply***. The extent to which state courts must comply with the constitutional provisions concerning criminal procedure is discussed *infra*, p. 2.

C. Not all procedure is constitutionally regulated: While the Constitution regulates many aspects of criminal procedure, it is of course not a complete code of criminal procedure. Therefore, both state and federal legislatures are free to enact statutes and rules setting forth procedures for administering criminal justice, as long as those procedures do not violate constitutional provisions.

> **Example:** The Fourth Amendment prohibits "unreasonable searches and seizures," but the Amendment's applicability to wiretaps is unclear. Congress has enacted a federal wiretapping statute that prohibits wiretaps in most law enforcement situations. As long as the act does not authorize conduct which is constitutionally prohibited, the act must be respected by federal and state law enforcement officials, even if it prohibits procedures that would otherwise be constitutionally permissible.

1. **Federal Rules:** Perhaps the best thought-out set of codified regulations concerning criminal procedure is the ***Federal Rules of Criminal Procedure***. These Rules are applicable only to federal crimes (i.e., crimes prohibited by Acts of Congress and triable in federal court.)

> **Note:** This outline concerns principally the ***constitutional*** aspects of criminal procedure. It therefore relies mainly on case law (principally U.S. Supreme Court decisions), and contains few references to statutes or court rules. There are a number of references, however, to the American Law Institute's *Model Code of Pre-Arraignment Procedure* (1974), which is not word-for-word the law in any jurisdiction, but which represents the most significant attempt to codify criminal procedure on the state level.

2. **State constitutions:** State constitutions are another important source of criminal procedure regulations. Even if a state constitutional provision is identical to a provision of the federal constitution, the state courts are free to interpret it as they wish, without regard to how the U.S. Supreme Court interprets the federal provision.

   Example: The U.S. Supreme Court overruled the South Dakota Supreme Court's holding that a particular search of an automobile was a violation of the U.S. Constitution's Fourth Amendment ban on "unreasonable" searches and seizures. See *infra*, p. 13. On remand, the South Dakota Supreme Court held that the search was a violation of a nearly identical provision in the South Dakota Constitution. *South Dakota v. Opperman*, 428 U.S. 364 (1976); *State v. Opperman*, 247 N.W.2d 673 (S.D. 1976).

II. STATE PROCEDURES AND THE FEDERAL CONSTITUTION

A. **Nature of the Bill of Rights:** The Bill of Rights was originally enacted solely for the purpose of limiting the federal government, not the states. (See Nutshell, p. 4.) The Fourteenth Amendment, however, enacted in 1868, specifically applies to ***state action***. That Amendment provides, in part, that no state may ***"deprive any person of life, liberty, or property, without due process of law. . . . "*** Since the acts of state law enforcement officials are clearly state actions for Fourteenth Amendment purposes, state criminal procedures are to a certain extent governed by the Constitution.

B. **Applicability of Bill of Rights to states:** It does not follow, however, from the fact that the Fourteenth Amendment regulates state criminal procedure, that the guarantees of the ***Bill of Rights*** apply to state proceedings. In fact, the extent to which the Fourteenth Amendment makes the Bill of Rights applicable to the states has been the subject of great dispute both within the Supreme Court and among commentators. Three principal views have at one time or other been espoused by members of the Supreme Court:

   1. **Fundamental rights approach:** The ***"fundamental rights"*** approach holds that the fact that a particular criminal procedure is prohibited by the Bill of Rights does not necessarily mean that the Fourteenth Amendment prohibits its use by the states. This approach views the Fourteenth Amendment as requiring only that the states apply those procedures that are ***"implicit in the concept of ordered liberty"*** (Cardozo, in *Palko v. Connecticut*, 302 U.S. 319 (1937)) or which are ***"fundamental to the American scheme of justice"*** (White, in *Duncan v. Louisiana*, 391 U.S. 145 (1968)). If a procedure is inconsistent with "the concept of ordered liberty" or with "the American scheme of justice," it cannot be used by the states, whether or not it is prohibited by the Bill of Rights. All other procedures, even those prohibited by the Bill of Rights, can be applied by the states. The fundamental rights approach examines each case on its facts, rather than applying a particular right to all situations. Thus double jeopardy might violate the Fourteenth Amendment in some situations, but not others, even though it would always violate the Fifth Amendment in federal cases.

   2. **Total incorporation approach:** The ***"total incorporation"*** approach argues that all of the guarantees given in the Bill of Rights are "incorporated" into the Fourteenth Amendment, and are thus applicable to the states. Proponents of the total incorporation approach are divided as to whether "fundamental rights" which are not specifically covered by the

Bill of Rights, but which in federal cases are required by the general Fifth Amendment due process clause, are binding on the states. (See Nutshell, p. 10). For an example of a total incorporation view that does not include fundamental rights not enumerated in the Bill of Rights, see Justice Black's dissent in *In re Winship*, 397 U.S. 358 (1970). For an example of a total incorporation theory that requires the states to respect every procedural right that the federal government must respect, whether or not that right is specifically enumerated in the Bill of Rights (sometimes called the ***"total incorporation plus"*** theory — Nutshell, p. 10), see Justice Murphy's dissent in *Adamson v. California*, 332 U.S. 46 (1947).

3. **Selective incorporation approach:** The ***"selective incorporation"*** approach holds that not all rights enumerated in the Bill of Rights are applicable to the states, but that ***if any aspect of a right*** is so necessary to fundamental fairness that it applies to the states, then ***all aspects*** of that right apply. By the selective incorporation approach, if the right is applicable at all in state courts, its scope is the same as in federal courts.

    Example: Suppose the question arose whether the prosecution in a state trial may comment on the accused's failure to take the stand. A proponent of the ***fundamental rights*** approach would ask whether the prosecution's silence is necessary to "the concept of ordered liberty" (and would probably answer this question in the negative, as in *Adamson*, above.) A ***total incorporation*** proponent would determine whether the prosecution's comment violates the Fifth Amendment self-incrimination privilege, and if so, would hold that the Fourteenth Amendment incorporated that privilege. If not, a ***"total incorporation plus"*** theory might still hold that the prosecution's comment was barred in state court because a fundamental right falling within the Fifth Amendment's due process requirement was at stake. A ***selective incorporationist*** would determine whether any aspect of the right against self-incrimination was so important that it should apply to the states, and if so, would conclude that every part of that right, including the right not to have the prosecution comment on the defendant's silence, applied to the states. Furthermore, the selective incorporationist would define the privilege against self-incrimination as broadly as in federal trials.

C. **Pre-1960s use of fundamental fairness doctrine:** Prior to the 1960s, only rights which were found to be "fundamental" were held applicable to the states. Before 1930, almost no rights were found to be "fundamental"; from 1930 to 1960, a few rights, including the right of an indigent defendant in certain felony cases to court-appointed counsel, were held to be binding on the states.

1. **Rise of selective incorporation:** In the 1960s, however, the fundamental rights approach lost its majority in the Supreme Court, and the ***selective incorporation*** approach gained control. By the end of the Warren Court, every criminal procedural guarantee in the Bill of Rights except the Eighth Amendment's prohibition against excessive bail and the Fifth Amendment's requirement of grand jury indictments in felony cases had been applied to the states. Furthermore, as each new right was applied to the states, the application of that right became ***exactly the same as in federal cases***.

    a. **Rationale:** As Justice Brennan put it in *Malloy v. Hogan*, 378 U.S. 1 (1964), "the prohibition of unreasonable searches and seizures of the Fourth Amendment . . . and the right to counsel guaranteed by the Sixth Amendment . . . are all to be enforced against the States under the Fourteenth Amendment according to the same standards that protect those personal rights against federal encroachment. . . . The Court has ***rejected*** the notion that the Fourteenth Amendment applies to the States only a ***'watered-down'*** subjective version of the individual guarantees of the Bill of Rights."

2. The following list gives the particular Bill of Rights guarantees that have been held ***applicable*** to the states:

a. The Fourth Amendment right to be free from ***unreasonable searches and seizures*** and to have any ***illegally seized evidence excluded from criminal trials***. See *Mapp v. Ohio*, 367 U.S. 643 (1961).

b. The Fifth Amendment ***privilege*** against self-incrimination. See *Malloy v. Hogan*, 378 U.S. 1 (1964).

c. The Sixth Amendment ***right to counsel.*** *Gideon v. Wainwright*, 372 U.S. 335 (1963).

d. The Sixth Amendment rights to a ***speedy*** (*Klopfer v. N.C.*, 386 U.S. 213, (1967)) and ***public*** (*In re Oliver*, 330 U.S. 257 (1942)) trial.

e. The Sixth Amendment right to ***confront*** opposing witnesses. See *Pointer v. Texas*, 380 U.S. 400 (1965).

f. The Sixth Amendment ***right to an impartial*** jury. See *Duncan v. La.*, 391 U.S. 145 (1968).

g. The Fifth Amendment guarantee against ***double*** jeopardy. *Benton v. Md.*, 95 U.S. 784 (1969).

Note: Of course, the precise boundaries of the various Bill of Rights guarantees are constantly being re-interpreted. For instance, in *Williams v. Florida*, 399 U.S. 78 (1970), the Court held that the Fifth Amendment right to jury trial did not mean a right to a twelve-person jury, and a state's use of a six-person jury in a non-capital case was therefore allowed. Then, a ***five-person jury*** was held to be a violation of the Fifth Amendment, in *Ballew v. Georgia*, 435 U.S. 223 (1978). (The Court in *Ballew* held that its ruling applied to all state trials of "non-petty" criminal cases, which the Court defined as cases in which the maximum potential penalty was more than six months in prison.) Still later, a provision allowing a conviction based on a vote of ***five out of six jurors***, was struck down in *Burch v. Louisiana*, 441 U.S. 130 (1979).

3. Guarantees not yet applicable to states: Only two Bill of Rights guarantees, the guarantee against ***excessive bail*** and the right to a ***grand jury indictment in felony cases***, have ***not*** been extended to the states.

D. Bill of Rights applies only to governmental conduct: Keep in mind that all of the Bill of Rights guarantees protect ***only against governmental, not private, conduct.*** Therefore, if a private person (e.g., a company security guard) takes an action that seems to violate the privacy of a person who later becomes a criminal defendant, the Bill of Rights ***won't*** be involved as long as the government didn't sponsor that private person's act in some way.

Example: Dave works at Big Brother Corp., a private company. As Dave is leaving work one day, Guard, a private security guard posted by Big Brother at the plant gates, insists on searching Dave. Guard finds cocaine on Dave's person, and turns that cocaine over to the police. The Fourth Amendment's prohibition on unreasonable searches and seizures does not apply to Guard's conduct, because that was private conduct not instigated by the government. Therefore, the cocaine can be introduced against Dave at his trial for drug possession. (But if the local police had asked Guard to perform the search, then the Fourth Amendment *would* apply to Guard's conduct.)

E. **Raising of constitutional claims in federal court:** A defendant in a state criminal proceeding is of course free to raise in the proceeding itself the claim that his federal constitutional rights have been violated (e.g., by a coerced confession, an illegal search and seizure, etc.). He may also have the chance to make these constitutional contentions in the U.S. Supreme Court, if the Court accepts *certiorari* on the case, as it sometimes does in cases of great interest or legal significance.

1. **Federal *habeas corpus:*** But the state criminal defendant has another forum in which he may be able to argue that the state trial violated his federal constitutional rights. This is in the form of a petition for a ***writ of habeas corpus***. He can petition for a writ of *habeas corpus* only after he has been convicted, and has exhausted his state appellate remedies.

   a. **Heard by federal district court:** The petition for writ of *habeas corpus is made to a **federal district court judge***. If the judge finds that the conviction was obtained through a violation of the defendant's constitutional rights, she can order the defendant released (usually subject to a new trial). The prosecution can then appeal this decision to the Court of Appeals and/or the Supreme Court.

   b. **Limitations on *habeas* arguments:** The full subject of *habeas corpus* is complex, and is beyond the scope of this outline. However, you should understand that there are some major ***limitations*** on the extent to which a convicted state-court defendant can make use of *habeas* to have his conviction reviewed by the federal courts. Here are two of the most important limitations:

      i. **Search and seizure cases:** The federal courts will generally ***not*** consider *habeas* claims that the conviction was due in part to the admission of ***search and seizure evidence*** obtained in violation of the Fourth Amendment. The Supreme Court held in *Stone v. Powell*, 428 U.S. 465 (1976), that so long as a state prisoner got a fair chance at his trial to argue that the evidence should not be introduced because it was the fruit of an illegal search or seizure, the prisoner cannot make this argument in a later *habeas* petition, even if the federal court is convinced that the state court reached a constitutionally-indefensible conclusion.

      ii. **Antiterrorism Act:** More broadly, a statute enacted by Congress in response to the 1995 Oklahoma City bombing, the Antiterrorism and Effective Death Penalty Act of 1996 (AEDPA), contains several provisions that significantly restrict the federal courts' *habeas* powers. To cite only one of these, 28 U.S.C. §2254(d)(1) provides that *habeas* relief shall not be granted on any claim that was adjudicated on the merits in the state court proceeding unless the state court reached a "decision that was ***contrary to***, or involved an ***unreasonable application of***, ***clearly established*** Federal law, as ***determined by the Supreme Court*** of the United States[.]"

(1) **Consequence:** So to paraphrase this section, a federal district court does not have the power to correct what it believes is a "mistaken" state-court legal conclusion, unless the federal judge also finds that the decision was either "contrary to" or an "unreasonable application of" a "clearly established" federal principle, as determined by the Supreme Court. This leaves the federal court ***unable to correct*** what it believes is a mistake of law in several major categories of cases, such as where:

the issue has ***never reached the Supreme Court***, but all or most federal courts of appeal agree on an interpretation of federal law that is at odds with the state court's interpretation; or

the issue has been resolved by the Supreme Court, but although the federal judge believes that the state court has incorrectly applied Supreme Court law, the judge cannot say that the state court opinion was so wrong as to be an "***unreasonable*** application" of that Supreme Court law. (In other words, not all "incorrect" applications of law to fact are "unreasonable" ones, and the incorrect ones that aren't unreasonable can't be disturbed by the federal court on *habeas*).

In summary, there are a number of important procedural limits on federal judges' powers to use *habeas corpus* to correct what they believe are federal-law (including constitutional) mistakes in state-court criminal proceedings.

F. **Independent state grounds:** The selective incorporation doctrine, as noted, requires that state courts apply nearly all the guarantees of the federal Bill of Rights in trials on state criminal charges. But the states are, of course, free to place additional criminal safeguards in their ***own state constitutions***. Furthermore, if a state constitution contains a guarantee that is phrased in the same way as a federal one, the state courts are nonetheless free to ***interpret*** that state guarantee as giving the individual ***more protection*** than the comparable federal guarantee.

1. **Review by Supreme Court:** The Supreme Court will ***not review*** the reversal by a state court of a conviction, where that reversal relies on the greater protection given by the state constitution than would be given by the federal constitution. This state ground must be ***"independent and adequate"*** — independent of the federal constitution or statute, and adequate to result by itself in the reversal.

2. **Judging existence of state ground:** But it is not always clear from a state court's opinion whether there was such an "independent and adequate state ground" supporting the reversal. For instance, the state court may talk mostly about a federal guarantee, conclude that that guarantee warrants a reversal, and then note that the state constitution provides the same protection. If the Supreme Court believes that the state court's interpretation of the federal guarantee is wrong, what should it do about the reference to the state constitution? Two solutions are possible: (1) the Court can assume that the state court would have repeated its original conclusion about the meaning of the state constitution, notwithstanding that this would make that constitution mean something different from what the federal guarantee means; or (2) the Court can assume that the state court meant for the state and federal guarantees to be co-extensive, so that the state court would now revise its view of

the state constitution. The Supreme Court will review the case if it uses solution (1), but not if it uses (2).

a. **Lack of independent state grounds presumed:** In *Michigan v. Long*, 463 U.S. 1032 (1983), the Supreme Court formulated a new standard for dealing with such ambiguities. When a state court decision appears to rest ***primarily on federal law***, or seems to be ***interwoven with federal law***, and the adequacy and independence of any possible state law ground is ***not clear*** from the face of the opinion, the Supreme Court will "accept as the most reasonable explanation that the state court decided the case the way it did because it believed that federal law required it to do so."

b. **Significance:** Thus in ambiguous situations, the Supreme Court will ***presume that there is no independent and adequate state ground***, and that federal law presents the sole issue. In such a situation, the Supreme Court will decide the federal issue, which may lead to a reinstatement of the conviction. (If it is apparent from the face of the state court opinion that there is an independent and adequate state ground justifying a reversal of the conviction, the Supreme Court will not hear the prosecution's appeal, since a decision on the federal issue would not make any difference to the result — the conviction would still be invalid.)

III. STEPS IN A CRIMINAL PROCEEDING

A. **Many steps:** There are many distinct steps in a criminal proceeding. At each of these steps, some defendants "drop out," typically by either not being prosecuted or by choosing to plead guilty.

1. **Arrest:** Where a police officer has probable cause to believe a suspect has committed a crime, the officer makes an ***arrest***. An arrest is generally deemed to take place when the officer takes the suspect into ***custody*** in order to transport him to the police station so that he can be charged with a crime. K,L,I&K, p. 8. (In most states, where the charge is a ***misdemeanor***, the officer may, instead of taking the suspect into custody, write a "citation" — what we commonly call, in traffic cases, a "ticket." The suspect is then released on his own recognizance and ordered to appear before a judge at some later date.)

   a. **Mostly without warrants:** An arrest may occur either with or without a warrant. The vast majority of arrests are made without a warrant. K,L,I&K p. 8, n. g. See *infra*, p. 73.

2. **Booking:** The arresting officer then transports the suspect to the police station for ***"booking."*** In the booking procedure, the suspect's name, offense, and other information are entered into a police blotter. The suspect is usually photographed and fingerprinted. He is usually allowed to make one telephone call. For minor offenses, the suspect is usually given the right to pay a cash "stationhouse bail," and ordered to report before a magistrate. For more serious crimes (or if the suspect cannot make the stationhouse bail), he is kept in some kind of a cell until he can be taken before a magistrate (see paragraph 4, below).

3. **Filing complaint:** A prosecutor is now typically brought into the case. The prosecutor reviews the facts, and decides whether charges should be brought, based mostly on the

sufficiency of the evidence. If the suspect is to be charged, the prosecutor prepares a ***"complaint."***

4. **First appearance:** After the complaint has been filed, the suspect (who is now a "defendant") is brought before a ***magistrate***. The step of bringing the defendant before the magistrate for the first time is typically called the ***"first appearance."*** If the defendant received stationhouse bail, the first appearance is usually several days after the arrest. But in the usual case where there is no stationhouse bail, the suspect is still in custody and must be brought for the first appearance ***"without unnecessary delay."*** There will usually be a few hours between arrest and first appearance, and there may be an intervening weekend (e.g., D is arrested on Friday night, and not brought for the first appearance until Monday morning). The magistrate does not evaluate the sufficiency of the evidence in any way during the first appearance. Instead, she typically does the following:

   a. **Notice of charges:** She ***informs*** D of the ***charges***; and

   b. **Right to counsel:** She notifies D that he has the ***right to counsel***. If D is indigent and desires appointed counsel, the magistrate usually begins the process of appointment.

   c. **Bail:** Where D did not previously post stationhouse bail, the magistrate will ***set bail***. Alternatively, the magistrate may release D without bail, on his own recognizance. Finally, a preventive detention statute (see *infra*, p. 426) may allow the magistrate to deny bail altogether, typically if she finds that there is no bail amount that ensures that D will show up for trial and also guarantees the safety of the community in the interim.

5. **Preliminary hearing:** The next proceeding, in felony cases, is usually the ***"preliminary hearing."*** This, like the first appearance, takes place before a magistrate. The purpose of the preliminary hearing is for the magistrate to make a neutral determination of whether there is probable cause to believe that D committed the crime charged. Typically, live witnesses are presented, and both the prosecution and the defendant are represented by counsel. If the magistrate finds probable cause, he will "bind over" for the next stage (either sending it to the grand jury if an indictment is required, or sending it directly to the trial court if an indictment is not needed).

6. **Filing of indictment or information:** Recall that the Constitution does not require the states to proceed by means of a grand jury indictment. (See *supra*, p. 4.) Thus it is up to the states whether to require an indictment or not. In about half the states, an indictment is required for at least some, if not all, felony prosecutions. (In the federal system, an indictment is always required for a felony prosecution, unless the defendant waives that right.)

   a. **Nature of grand jury proceeding:** The grand jury proceeding is a closed proceeding, at which the grand jurors decide, by majority vote, whether to issue an indictment. Grand jury procedure is discussed further *infra*, p. 423.

   b. **Information:** If the state does not require an indictment for the particular crime in question, an ***"information"*** issued by the prosecutor is used instead. The information recites the charges, and is filed with the trial court.

7. **Arraignment:** Once an indictment or information has been filed, D is ***"arraigned"*** on the information or indictment. In the arraignment, D is brought before the trial court, informed of the charges against him, and asked whether he pleads innocent or guilty.

Note: The above steps do not have the same names or order in all jurisdictions. In New York, for instance, there is nothing called a "preliminary hearing"; there is an "arraignment" shortly after arrest, followed by an indictment, followed by a "first appearance." The states are basically free to decide how to order their pre-trial proceedings, so long as they provide for a prompt neutral review (typically by a magistrate) of whether probable cause exists to believe that D committed the crime charged.

8. **Pretrial motions:** Next, defense counsel has the opportunity to make various ***pretrial motions***. Most common are motions to: (1) obtain discovery of the prosecution's evidence; and (2) have some of the prosecution's evidence suppressed (e.g., to have a confession ruled inadmissible because *Miranda* procedures were not followed).

9. **Trial:** Next comes the ***trial.***[1] If the charge is a felony, or a misdemeanor punishable by more than six months in prison, all states give D the right to have the case tried before a ***jury***. Most states give D the right to a jury trial for a lesser misdemeanor as well, although they are not constitutionally required to do so. Most felony cases (probably 60-65%) are tried before a jury. L&I, v. 1, p. 28.

10. **Sentencing:** If D pleads guilty or is found guilty during the trial, he is then ***sentenced***. Sentencing is usually done by the judge, not the jury.

11. **Appeals:** All convicted defendants are entitled to an ***appeal***. Most appeals are by defendants who were convicted at trial and sentenced to imprisonment. However, in most states even defendants who have plead guilty are usually allowed to challenge the plea bargain on appeal (e.g., by asserting that the prosecution did not live up to the terms of the deal). L&I, v. 2, p. 662. The most frequently-asserted ground for appeal, and the most commonly successful one, is that the evidence admitted against D at trial was the result of an unconstitutional search.

12. **Post-conviction remedies:** Even after D has exhausted all "direct" appeals, certain ***"post-conviction remedies"*** will be theoretically available to him. Most importantly, both state and federal prisoners may challenge their convictions through federal-court ***habeas corpus*** procedures. In a habeas corpus proceeding (see *supra*, p. 5), D asserts that his conviction violated the federal constitution. For instance, D might assert that his conviction rested in part upon a confession whose admission violated the *Miranda* doctrine. Recall that the basis for federal habeas corpus review of state court convictions has been steadily narrowed by the Supreme Court over the last two decades.

Quiz Yourself on
CONSTITUTIONAL CRIMINAL PROCEDURE GENERALLY *(ENTIRE CHAPTER)*

1. Until 2012, there had been no definitive answer to the "second interrogation" problem. This issue arises in the following kind of situation: the suspect is in custody, is given his *Miranda* warnings, and states that he does not want to talk to the police unless he can speak to his lawyer first. He is allowed to speak to his lawyer. The police then want to conduct another interrogation; they start asking questions, and the suspect does not ask to speak to his lawyer at that time. The issue is whether this "second interrogation" — done

---

1. This step assumes that the defendant does not make a ***"plea bargain"*** as an alternative to exercising his right to a trial. Over 90% of cases end in a plea bargain. See *infra*, p. 392.

without the presence of counsel — violates *Miranda.*

In 2012, the Supreme Court, deciding a case involving a federal prosecution and interrogation by FBI agents, held that this "second interrogation" violates *Miranda*, and that in federal prosecutions, the authorities may not initiate, without a lawyer present, a conversation with a suspect who has previously asked to have his lawyer present for questioning. *Smith v. U.S* (not a real case). The Supreme Court, in *Smith*, referred to general *Miranda* principles and to cases decided under *Miranda*, but gave no indication of whether this principle would be binding on the states. In 2020, the Supreme Court of the State of Ames had to decide, on appeal, a case presenting precisely the same "second interrogation" issue, but this time one involving a state prosecution and state police officers. Assuming that the Supreme Court's 2012 *Smith* decision was based solely on the Fifth and Sixth Amendments, is the Ames Supreme Court constitutionally required to follow the decision in that case? ________________

2. Until 2012, the State of Langdell instituted all felony prosecutions by having a prosecutor present his case to a grand jury, which then issued an indictment. In 2012, the Langdell legislature passed a statute setting out a new procedure, to be applicable to all crimes committed after the date of the statute. Under this new procedure, a prosecutor, when he wished to bring charges, would issue something called an "information," setting forth the charges. The information would serve as the basis for an arrest warrant. Immediately after the defendant was arrested, a "preliminary hearing" would be held before a judge, to determine whether there was probable cause to believe that the defendant had committed the crime charged. No involvement of the grand jury, and thus no indictment, would be needed.

   Applicable U.S. Supreme Court decisions make it clear that as a constitutional matter, no federal prosecution for a felony (that is, no prosecution for a crime punishable by more than one year in prison) may commence except by a grand jury indictment. Smith, charged by Langdell with the crime of murder committed in 2013, has challenged the proceedings against him; he asserts that it violates his federal constitutional right to a grand jury indictment for him to be prosecuted for a felony based on a method other than a grand jury indictment. Should the Langdell Supreme Court order that the proceedings be dismissed until Smith is indicted by a grand jury? ________________

Answers

1. **Yes.** The Fifth Amendment privilege against self-incrimination and the Sixth Amendment right to counsel have both been held binding on the states (via the Fourteenth Amendment's Due Process Clause) just as they are applicable to the federal government. The prosecution here might try to argue that merely because these guarantees are in a general sense binding on the states, this does not mean that the precise ***contours*** of each are binding on the states in the same way as on the federal government. But the Supreme Court has consistently rejected this argument — the Court has always held that once a particular Bill of Rights guarantee is binding on the states, it is binding in ***precisely the same way*** as on the federal government. See, e.g., *Malloy v. Hogan*. Since the 2012 *Smith v. U.S.* decision held that the interrogation there violates the suspect's Fifth and Sixth Amendment rights, and since the facts here are virtually indistinguishable, the Ames Supreme Court is constitutionally bound to find in favor of the defense.

2. **No.** It is true that in the vast majority of situations where the Supreme Court has found that a particular Bill of Rights guarantee exists as against the federal government, the Court has also found that guarantee binding on the states via the Fourteenth Amendment's Due Process Clause (the ***"selective incorporation"*** doctrine). But there is one notable exception to this general rule: The right to a grand jury indictment has never been held by the Supreme Court to be binding upon the states. Therefore, any state may (and indeed most states do) commence a felony prosecution against the defendant based on some method other than a

grand jury indictment, even though a defendant would have the right not to have a ***federal*** felony prosecution commenced against him without a grand jury indictment.

Exam Tips on *CONSTITUTIONAL CRIMINAL PROCEDURE GENERALLY*

Here are the most frequently tested areas on criminal procedure generally:

Always consider that a state criminal defendant with a constitutional challenge may be able to rely on ***both*** the U.S. Constitution and the constitution of the ***state*** prosecuting him. States are free to ***give greater procedural protection*** to criminal defendants than that conferred by the U.S. Constitution, but ***may not give less.***

Example: Bob grows marijuana in a fenced-in area of land 50 feet from his home. Although he may not have an expectation of privacy in the area as interpreted under the U.S. Constitution, the state constitution may grant him a privacy interest in the area that would give him protection against warrantless searches and seizures.

Exam questions frequently test your knowledge of the fact that the Bill of Rights only protects against ***governmental*** conduct. It does ***not*** restrict the conduct of ***private entities,*** unless they are acting at the express direction of a government agent.

Example: Defendant goes to a bus terminal run by a private bus company. The gun in his pocket triggers the metal detector. Bus company officials require him to submit to a search, find the gun, then turn it over to the police. At Defendant's trial for carrying a gun without a license, the gun will be admissible no matter how unreasonable the search; Defendant has no basis in the Fourth Amendment to challenge the bus company's conduct, because that conduct was private, not governmental.

CHAPTER 2

ARREST; PROBABLE CAUSE; SEARCH WARRANTS

ChapterScope

This chapter examines the circumstances under which search warrants and arrest warrants are required by the Fourth Amendment. The Fourth Amendment applies both to searches and seizures of property and to arrests of persons. The important concepts in this chapter are:

Probable cause: The Fourth Amendment requires that a search or arrest warrant be issued only based on ***"probable cause."***

Probable cause to arrest: For there to be probable cause to ***arrest*** a person, it must be ***more likely than not that a violation of the law has been committed*** and that the person to be arrested ***committed the violation.***

Probable cause to search: For there to be probable cause to ***search***, it must be ***more likely than not*** that the specific items to be searched for are ***connected with criminal activities*** and that these items will be ***found in the place to be searched.***

Places protected: Police must generally ***obtain a search warrant*** in order to search areas in which the suspect has a ***reasonable expectation of privacy.*** A person has a reasonable expectation of privacy in a place if two tests are met:

the person must show an ***actual***, ***subjective*** expectation of privacy in the area; *and*

the expectation must be one which society recognizes as ***reasonable.***

Plain view doctrine: Police do not violate the Fourth Amendment when they see an object in ***plain view*** from a position in which they have a right to be.

Search warrants: A search warrant must be issued by a ***neutral judicial officer***, and must contain a ***description*** of the premises to be searched and the things to be seized. Any item that is the subject of a valid search warrant may be seized by the police executing the warrant. Execution of the search warrant must be done in a reasonable manner.

"Good faith" exception: Normally, if a search warrant is invalid (e.g., it is not supported by probable cause), any search done pursuant to it will violate the Fourth Amendment, and the evidence will be excluded at trial. However, if the police ***reasonably but erroneously believe*** that the warrant which they have been issued is valid, the seized evidence may be used at trial.

I. GENERAL PRINCIPLES

A. Fourth Amendment: The Fourth Amendment to the U.S. Constitution provides, "The right of the people to be secure in their persons, houses, papers, and effects, ***against unreasonable searches and seizures***, shall not be violated, and ***no Warrants shall issue, but upon probable***

cause, supported by Oath or affirmation, and ***particularly describing*** the place to be searched, and the persons or things to be seized."

B. Applicable to both searches and arrests: As the language of the Fourth Amendment makes clear, that Amendment applies both to searches and seizures of property, and to arrests of persons. Most Fourth Amendment problems relate to the constitutional legality of searches, not arrests.

1. **Way in which litigation arises:** Most litigation about the Fourth Amendment validity of a particular search and seizure arises in the following manner: a search is conducted, and evidence is seized. After the suspect is arrested, he seeks to show, at a ***suppression hearing***, that the search was conducted in violation of the Fourth Amendment. If he can show this, then the evidence which was obtained as a result of the search will ***not be admissible at trial***, in either the federal or state courts. *Mapp v. Ohio*, 367 U.S. 643 (1961).

2. **Invalid arrest no defense:** The unconstitutionality of an arrest, unlike that of a search, is in itself of little use to a defendant, since it cannot serve as a defense. Except in a very few cases of shocking and violent police conduct, a defendant may be ***tried and convicted regardless of the fact that his arrest was made in violation of the Fourth Amendment***. See *Frisbie v. Collins*, 342 U.S. 519 (1952).

   a. **Abduction from foreign country:** The ultimate illustration of this principle is the case of *U.S. v. Alvarez-Machain*, 504 U.S. 655 (1992).

      i. **Facts:** D, a Mexican citizen and resident, was forcibly kidnapped in Mexico and brought to the U.S. to answer charges of murdering a Drug Enforcement Administration agent. The abduction of D was apparently arranged by DEA officials, who offered to pay a reward to anyone who brought D to the U.S. This method of getting D to the U.S. was used instead of the procedures provided in the U.S.-Mexico extradition treaty. Mexico strongly protested the abduction.

      ii. **Holding:** The Supreme Court held that even though D's abduction may have been "shocking" and may have been in violation of "general international law principles," D could still be tried in the U.S. courts. (The Court found that although the extradition procedure specified in the extradition treaty was not used, the use of the alternative abduction method was not actually a violation of the treaty. The Court implied that had there been a treaty violation, then the trial in the U.S. might have violated due process.)

   b. **Importance of valid arrest:** There is, however, one situation in which the constitutional validity of an arrest may become an important issue: although a search is not usually valid unless a search warrant has been obtained, no warrant is required for a search made ***"incident"*** to a valid arrest. When evidence is seized as part of a warrantless search conducted incident to an arrest, the defendant will therefore frequently argue that the arrest itself violated the Fourth Amendment, that the search was thus invalid, and that the evidence obtained from it is inadmissible under *Mapp v. Ohio*.

C. Two clauses of Fourth Amendment: The Fourth Amendment applies both to situations in which a warrant is used, and to those in which no warrant is procured. If a warrant is used, the

Amendment requires that it not be issued unless there is ***"probable cause"***; whether or not there is a warrant, the Amendment requires that the arrest or search ***not be "unreasonable."***

II. THE "REASONABLE EXPECTATION OF PRIVACY"; THE INTERESTS THAT ARE PROTECTED BY THE FOURTH AMENDMENT

A. Generally: The Fourth Amendment guarantees "the right of the people to be secure in their persons, houses, papers and effects, against unreasonable searches and seizures. . . . " But the Supreme Court has not been consistent as to exactly what constitutes a Fourth Amendment search.

1. **Two different types:** The Supreme Court recognizes ***two different ways*** in which a Fourth Amendment search may occur:

   [1] First, a search of a defendant will be deemed to occur if the government (a) ***physically intrudes*** on the defendant's property; *and* (b) does so in "an attempt to ***find something*** or to ***obtain information***." *U.S. v. Jones*, 132 S.Ct. 945 (2012). This concept of searches as being a form of ***trespass*** on the defendant's property dates back to the original enactment of the Fourth Amendment in 1791.

   [2] Second, a search will be deemed to occur if the government (a) infringes on the defendant's ***"reasonable expectation of privacy"***; *and* (b) does so in an attempt to find something or obtain information. This "reasonable expectation of privacy" approach is much more ***recent***; it dates from the Supreme Court's 1967 holding in *Katz v. U.S.*, 389 U.S. 347 (1967), which we discuss extensively below.

   So there are two distinct means — one involving physical intrusion on the defendant's property, and the other an interference with his reasonable expectation of privacy (even without a physical intrusion) — by either of which government will be deemed to have conducted a search for Fourth Amendment purposes.

   a. **Consequence of "search":** Why does it matter whether government conduct is or isn't a search?

      If government officials *are* going to do something that constitutes a Fourth Amendment search, the officials must either ***procure a search warrant in advance*** (which itself requires a showing of ***probable cause***), or show after the fact that some specific ***exception*** to the requirement of a search warrant applied. (See Chapter 3, *infra*, p. 93, a long chapter that consists mostly of a discussion of these exceptions to the warrant requirement apply.)

      On the other hand, if the officials' proposed action will *not* be a Fourth Amendment search, they can act ***without either probable cause or a search warrant*** (and they therefore don't even have to *think about* whether an exception to the warrant requirement applies).

B. Pre-*Katz* "protected places" approach: Until the 1967 decision in *Katz v. U.S.*, which we'll be discussing in a moment, courts viewed the Fourth Amendment as applying only in the first of the two situations described in Par. 1 above. That is, the Amendment was viewed as protecting only certain ***places***, almost always limited to ***private property owned by the subject of the search***. So a Fourth Amendment search would not be deemed to exist unless the government committed some sort of physical intrusion onto the defendant's person, real estate or possessions. In this pre-1967 world, determining whether a Fourth Amendment search had occurred did not involve any subjective concept of "privacy."

1. **Discussed later:** This property-based type of Fourth Amendment search still exists. However, we defer our discussion of it until after we discuss the more modern, and more prevalent, expectation-of-privacy approach of *Katz*. For our property-oriented discussion, see *infra*, p. 18.

C. ***Katz*** **and the "reasonable expectation of privacy" doctrine:** In 1967, the Supreme Court abruptly ***rejected the traditional notion that only private property could be protected*** by the Fourth Amendment, in a seminal decision, ***Katz v. U.S.***, 389 U.S. 347 (1967). There, the Court held that the Fourth Amendment applies to any government search or seizure that interferes with a person's ***"reasonable expectation of privacy,"*** even if there was no interference with that person's property.

1. **Facts of *Katz:*** In *Katz*, FBI agents placed electronic eavesdropping equipment on the outside of a public telephone booth from which Katz, a bookmaker, conducted his business.

2. **Traditional result rejected:** The traditional private-property-based concept of what constitutes a "search" would, if applied, have meant that no Fourth Amendment search had occurred in *Katz* — Katz made his phone calls on public property, and the FBI agents did not commit trespass in installing their devices. The Supreme Court, however, ***rejected*** the notion that the Fourth Amendment protects only private property.

   a. **Protection of people:** The Court stated, in a now famous passage, "***the Fourth Amendment protects people, not places***. What a person knowingly exposes to the public, even in his own home or office, is not a subject of Fourth Amendment protection . . . But what he seeks to preserve as private, even in an area accessible to the public, may be constitutionally protected."

   b. **Privacy approach:** Justice Harlan, in a concurrence that has become almost as well known as the majority opinion, stated a ***two-pronged test*** for determining whether a person is entitled to Fourth Amendment protection in a particular situation. Harlan's test would require:

      i. "first, that a person have exhibited an ***actual (subjective) expectation of privacy*** and, . . . "

      ii. "second, that the expectation be ***one that society is prepared to recognize as 'reasonable.'*** "

   The entire Supreme Court eventually adopted both of these rules to determine when a person has a privacy interest that's protected by the Fourth Amendment.

3. **Criticism of subjective approach:** It's not completely obvious why Harlan's test should include the first requirement above, that the person have a subjective expectation of privacy. As one commentator noted in 1974, "the government could diminish each person's

subjective expectation of privacy merely by ***announcing*** half-hourly on television that [Orwell's] 1984 was being advanced by a decade and that we were all forthwith being placed under comprehensive electronic surveillance." 56 MINN. L. REV. 349 (1974).

D. Digital databases of personal information: We live in an age in which vast amounts of sensitive personal data about each American are compiled into huge ***electronic databases*** maintained by private companies. Typically, an individual who wishes to make use of modern technology – by talking on a cell phone, making online purchases, sending emails, etc. – has essentially no choice but to allow service providers to amass this sensitive information. If government then demands or requests this information from the company that has collected it, does the individual have a reasonable expectation of privacy as to the compiled data?

1. **Why the answer matters:** The answer matters a lot. If we conclude that the individual does *not* have a reasonable expectation of privacy in the company-held data pertaining to him, then law enforcement will be free to subpoena the information from the company without worrying about the Fourth Amendment and without first obtaining a search warrant.

   a. **Effect if there is such an expectation:** If, on the other hand, the individual *does* have a reasonable expectation of privacy in the data about him, then the government's demand for the information ***will constitute a Fourth Amendment search***, at least if we assume that the fact that the data has been compiled by a private third party doesn't somehow prevent the Fourth Amendment from applying.

2. **Impact of *Carpenter* case:** As we'll see in detail (*infra*, p. 34), a major 2018 case, ***Carpenter v. U.S.***, 138 S.Ct. 2206 (2018), holds that when government wants to access at least one important type of electronic database of personal information, the person whose information is being sought *does* have a reasonable expectation of privacy in the data, so that government must obtain a search warrant supported by probable cause.

   a. **"CSLI":** The type of personal data found in *Carpenter* to be protected by the Fourth Amendment is so-called ***"CSLI"*** or ***"cell site location information,"*** which specifies, for any particular cell phone at a particular time, the precise location of the phone, and thus of the person carrying the phone.

3. **Rationale for the holding in *Carpenter*:** Here's a summary of the factors the majority in *Carpenter* relied on in reaching this conclusion that a person has a reasonable expectation of privacy in his CSLI information:[1]

   [1] Individuals "have a reasonable expectation of privacy in the ***whole of their physical movements***";

   [2] Prior to the digital age, "society's expectation" was that law enforcement ***would not,*** and in fact could not, "secretly monitor and catalogue ***every single movement of an individual's car*** for a ***very long period***."

   [3] Allowing government access to CSLI contravenes the expectation in [2]. The "time-

---

1. More precisely, *Carpenter* holds that a person has a reasonable expectation that government will not access ***seven days or more*** worth of the individual's CSLI. See *infra*, p. 37, for more about how the decision came to apply only to requests covering seven days or more of data.

stamped" data furnished by CSLI is highly revealing; it "provides an ***intimate window into a person***'s life, revealing not only his particular movements, but through them his '***familial, political, professional, religious, and sexual associations.***'"

[4] Cell phone tracking via CLSI is "***remarkably easy, cheap, and efficient*** compared to traditional investigative tools."

[5] Unlike pre-digital-age location-tracking methods, CSLI gives government access to ***historical information.*** Thus government "can now ***travel back in time*** to retrace a person's whereabouts, subject only to the retention polices of the wireless carriers[.]"

[6] In sum, while an individual might not have a reasonable expectation that his public movements at a particular moment won't be tracked, the individual *is* entitled to expect that government will not ***cheaply and easily track his every movement, both prospectively and retrospectively, over long periods of time.*** Permitting warrantless access to CSLI would contravene that expectation.

a. **Extension of *Carpenter* to other types of digital databases:** As we'll also see when we discuss *Carpenter*, the rationale of the case seems to mean that an individual similarly has a reasonable expectation of privacy as to a wide variety of other types of electronically stored data about the person – data about ***credit card usage***, ***online searches***, the substance of ***emails or texts*** sent or received by a person, etc. – that government may want to obtain. See *infra*, p. 34.

E. **The property-based "trespass" approach to searches:** Recall (p. 15) that apart from government intrusions that infringe on a person's reasonable expectation of privacy, a Fourth Amendment search can occur if government ***physically intrudes*** on a person's property, and does so for the purpose of finding evidence or other information. This is truly an ***alternative*** path by which a defendant can show that a Fourth Amendment search occurred — in other words, if there is a ***physical intrusion by government on a person's property*** coupled with an investigative purpose, a search has occurred ***even if the individual had no reasonable expectation of privacy*** as to the type of information the police end up learning.

Three modern-era cases, from 2012, 2013 and 2018, illustrate that this age-old principle is alive and well.

1. **Installation of GPS:** The first of these three cases involved the government's secret installation of a GPS tracking device on the defendant's vehicle. The case demonstrated that a physical intrusion can suffice for a search regardless of whether the defendant had a reasonable expectation of privacy. The case is ***U.S. v. Jones***, 132 S.Ct. 945 (2012).

a. **Facts:** The FBI and local law enforcement officials had reason to suspect that D was engaged in cocaine trafficking. They obtained a search warrant to put a GPS tracking device on a Jeep belonging to D's wife. They secretly installed the tracker underneath the Jeep while it was parked in a public parking lot. However, the agents failed to honor the terms the warrant specified for when the tracker must be installed and how it would be used.[2] For 28 days, the tracker sent the government constant wireless signals

2. For instance, the police installed the GPS tracker after the time specified for doing so in the warrant had expired.

showing the vehicle's movements over public roads. When D was tried for narcotics trafficking, the government used the locational evidence from the tracker to show that D had visited the "stash house" where large amounts of cocaine were found.

b. Issue: The issue before the Supreme Court was whether the installation and use of the tracker was a Fourth Amendment search at all. (If it was not a search, then the agents' failure to honor the warrant didn't matter; if it *was* a search, then the government's failure to follow the warrant would make the use of the evidence inadmissible under the exclusionary rule.) The court below (the D.C. Circuit Court of Appeals) held that a search had occurred, and that D's conviction must be reversed because that search occurred without a valid warrant.

i. Government's argument: The government argued that no search had occurred, because D ***did not have any reasonable expectation of privacy*** either in the area under the Jeep where the device was placed, or in the movements of the Jeep on the public roads. The government's theory was that both the Jeep's undercarriage and the vehicle's movements ***would have been visible to any member of the public***. It was (and still is) clear from prior Supreme Court case law that a person can't have a reasonable expectation of privacy with respect to something that's visible to a member of the public. So if only violations of a person's reasonable expectations of privacy can constitute a Fourth Amendment search, the government would win.

c. Search found: But the Supreme Court unanimously agreed that a Fourth Amendment search *had* occurred here, and that D's conviction must therefore be reversed. However, what's interesting for our present purposes is that five members of the Court, in an opinion by Justice Scalia (joined by Roberts, Kennedy, Thomas and Sotomayor), believed that the ***mere conducting of a physical intrusion*** by the government — the placing the GPS tracker on D's vehicle — was itself ***enough*** to constitute a Fourth Amendment search, ***regardless*** of whether D's reasonable expectation of privacy was ever violated.

i. Rationale: Scalia reasoned that the government had "physically occupied private property for the purpose of obtaining information." Such a physical intrusion, he said, "would have been considered a 'search' within the meaning of the Fourth Amendment ***when it was adopted***." It's true, he agreed, that *Katz* (*supra*, p. 16) established that the existence of a search would no longer be determined solely by use of this "exclusively property-based approach." But, Scalia said, *Katz* merely established an ***alternative*** non-property-based method by which a search could occur. *Katz* "did not erode the principle that 'when the government *does* engage in ***physical intrusion of a constitutionally protected area*** in order to obtain information, that intrusion may constitute a violation of the Fourth Amendment.'"

ii. Dissent from this rationale: But four justices, although they concurred in the *result* in *Jones* (i.e., that a Fourth Amendment search had occurred), disagreed with the majority's holding that physical intrusion should suffice. These justices (Alito, joined by Ginsburg, Breyer and Kagan) believed that issues about whether a search had occurred should ***all*** be decided by "asking ***whether [D's] reasonable expectations of privacy were violated***[.]"

iii. **Five votes for physical-intrusion as sufficient:** So in *Jones*, a majority believed that when government commits a ***physical trespass*** on D's property (e.g., by attaching a monitoring device onto D's car) in an attempt to obtain information, that's enough to constitute a Fourth Amendment search, even if D had no reasonable expectation of privacy with regard to information that the monitoring device would disclose.

2. **Use of drug-sniffing dog on D's porch:** The second recent case showing that physical intrusion will suffice for a search is ***Florida v. Jardines***, 133 S.Ct. 1409 (2013). There, the Court held that when police brought a trained ***drug-sniffing dog onto a homeowner's front porch*** to investigate whether the house contained narcotics, a Fourth Amendment search occurred, regardless of whether the owner had a reasonable expectation of privacy as to the porch or as to the odors perceived by the dog.

   a. **Facts:** In *Jardines*, local police got an unverified tip that marijuana was being grown in D's house. (Since the tip was unverified, it did not furnish the police with probable cause from which they could have gotten a search warrant.) A "trained canine handler" who worked for the police brought his trained drug-sniffing dog, Franky, onto D's front porch. Franky sniffed the base of the front door, and then indicated (by sitting) that one of the odors he was trained to detect was strongest at that point. Since Franky was trained only to detect narcotics, the police concluded that his signaling gave them probable cause to believe that the inside of D's house contained narcotics. They used that information to procure a search warrant, did the search, and indeed found marijuana inside.

      i. **The issue:** The issue was whether the police, by bringing Franky onto D's porch and letting him sniff, conducted a Fourth Amendment search. If the answer was "yes," then the resulting search warrant — based on the probable cause that the police got by conducting the front-porch search — would have been invalid, because the police would have had no right to perform that porch-search in the first place.[3]

   b. **Majority finds a search:** By a 5-4 vote, the Court determined that the police conduct in bringing Franky onto the porch for purposes of doing the sniff-test ***was a search***. As in *Jones*, *supra*, the majority opinion was, perhaps surprisingly, by Justice Scalia. (He was joined by the unusual alignment of Thomas, Ginsburg, Sotomayor and Kagan.)

      i. **Rationale:** Scalia quoted the conclusion in *Jones*, *supra*, that when "the Government obtains information by physically intruding" on persons, houses, papers, or effects, "a 'search' within the original meaning of the Fourth Amendment" has "undoubtedly occurred." This principle made the present case "a straightforward one." That's because the officers were gathering information in an area owned by D and "immediately surrounding his house" — that immediately-surrounding area (called the "curtilage"; see *infra*, p. 22) "enjoys protection as part of the home itself."

---

3. Then, if the warrant was invalid, the evidence the police got by performing the in-house search based on the warrant would have been illegally-obtained evidence, inadmissible under the exclusionary rule.

ii. **No implied consent:** Scalia agreed that there would not have been a Fourth Amendment search if the police had acted with D's ***express or implied consent.*** But, Scalia said, there was ***no*** such implied or express consent by D here. It's true that D had hung a knocker on the door, which by custom implicitly gives a visitor the right to (as Scalia put it) "approach the home by the front path, knock promptly, wait briefly to be received, and then (absent invitation to linger longer) leave." So, for instance, "a police officer not armed with a warrant may ***approach a home and knock***, precisely because that is ***no more than any private citizen might do***."

(1) **Beyond scope of license:** But, Scalia said, the police here had ***gone beyond this implied license***. "[I]ntroducing a ***trained police dog*** to explore the area around the home in hopes of ***discovering incriminating evidence*** is something else. There is ***no customary invitation*** to do *that*. An invitation to engage in canine forensic investigation assuredly does not inhere in the very act of hanging a knocker."

(2) **Privacy expectations irrelevant:** Because the police had made a physical intrusion onto the curtilage (here, the porch) of D's home, whether the search violated any ***legitimate expectation of privacy*** on D's part was ***irrelevant***. "We need not decide whether the officer's investigation of [D's] home violated his expectation of privacy under *Katz*. ... That the officers learned what they learned only by ***physically intruding on [D's] property to gather evidence*** is ***enough*** to establish that a search occurred."

c. **Concurrence based on reasonable expectations of privacy:** The three liberals who joined Scalia's majority opinion (Kagan, Ginsburg and Sotomayor) thought there was a ***second theory*** on which the dog-sniff could and should also have been found to be a search. In a concurrence by Kagan, these three justices thought that under the Court's precedents, the use of a highly-trained drug-sniffing dog ***violated D's reasonable expectation of privacy.***

i. **Rationale:** Kagan pointed to a prior case (*Kyllo v. U.S.*, *infra*, p. 46), in which the Court held that officers conducted a Fourth Amendment search when, without committing any trespass, they used a ***thermal-imaging device*** to detect heat emanating from inside a private home. There, the Court had said that a search occurs "where ... the government uses a device that is not in general public use, to explore details of the home that would previously have been unknowable without physical intrusion[.]" For Kagan, the same rule applied here: "The police officers here conducted a search because they used a ***'device ... not in general public use'*** (a trained drug-detection dog) to 'explore details of the home' (the presence of certain substances) that they would not otherwise have discovered without entering the premises[.]"

d. **Dissent:** The four dissenters in *Jardines* (Alito, joined by Roberts, Kennedy and Breyer) agreed that if there had been an unconsented-to physical intrusion on D's home or curtilage, that would have been a search. But they ***disagreed*** with the majority's conclusion that the police conduct here ***went beyond the implied license*** that D granted the public by ***hanging a knocker*** on his door.

i. **Rationale:** Alito argued that members of the public may lawfully proceed along the walkway leading to the front door of a house because "custom grants them a license to do so." And under state laws of trespass, that license applies even to ***probably-unwelcome categories,*** like "solicitors, hawkers and peddlers" (not to mention the police themselves). To Alito, as long as the person approaching the house ***limits himself*** to the ***amount of time that it would take to approach the door and see if someone is home***, the person "is not necessarily required to ring the doorbell, knock on the door, or attempt to speak with an occupant."

ii. **Expectation of privacy:** Alito also argued that the police conduct here did ***not*** violate D's ***reasonable expectation of privacy***: "the occupant of a house has no reasonable expectation of privacy with respect to ***odors that can be smelled by human beings who are standing in ... places*** [where members of the public may ***lawfully stand***]. And I would not draw the line between odors that can be smelled by ***humans*** and those that are detectable ***only by dogs***[.]"

3. **Significance of a home's "curtilage":** The most recent of our trio of modern-era cases demonstrating that government's physical intrusion onto defendant's property can constitute a search regardless of expectation-of-privacy considerations involved the concept of a home's "***curtilage***." The case is ***Collins v. Virginia***, 138 S.Ct. 1663 (2018). But before we can sensibly discuss *Collins* (which we do beginning on p. 23), we need to understand what curtilage means, and why the concept matters if we're deciding whether a government intrusion onto a person's residential property constitutes a Fourth Amendment search requiring a warrant.

   a. **The original property-oriented concept behind the Fourth Amendment:** As we noted (*supra*, pp. 15 and 18), the significance of a ***physical intrusion*** by government into a person's dwelling dates back to the original property-oriented (as opposed to privacy-oriented) view of the Framers about when the Fourth Amendment would apply.

   b. **Why "curtilage" matters:** But this original property-oriented approach has always been — and still is — subject to an important ***limitation***. The Fourth Amendment covers intrusions into a person's "***house***" (as well as into someone's "person ... papers and effects"). But a person's "house" does ***not include*** all of a person's residential real estate, merely the actual house and what the Supreme Court calls the house's ***"curtilage."*** In brief, the curtilage is ***"the area 'immediately surrounding and associated with the home'."*** *Jardines*, *supra*.

   c. **Outbuildings and open fields:** So, for instance, on a ***farm or ranch***, the curtilage will typically include the farmhouse and ***immediately-surrounding*** structures used for ***primarily-family purposes*** (e.g., a garage). But the curtilage will ***not*** include ***open fields*** or ***distant "outbuildings"*** that are used for non-residential purposes, even though these are part of the same piece of land.

   d. **Test:** The main Supreme Court case on how to determine whether a particular building or area falls within the curtilage of the main dwelling is ***U.S. v. Dunn***, 480 U.S. 294 (1987). There, the Court held that four factors should be looked to in making this determination:

[1] the ***proximity*** of the home to the area claimed to be curtilage;

[2] whether the area is included within an ***enclosure*** that surrounds the home;

[3] the nature of the ***uses*** (domestic vs. non-domestic) to which the area is put; and

[4] the ***steps taken*** by the resident to ***protect*** the area from ***observation*** by people passing it.

Example: D owns a 190-acre ranch, enclosed by an outer fence. D's farmhouse is surrounded by an interior fence that does not include any other structures. The police, acting without a warrant, search a barn on the property, which is located about 60 yards from the farmhouse (and outside the interior fence). The issue is whether the barn is within the farmhouse's curtilage: the police required a search warrant if (but only if) the barn is within the curtilage.

Held (by applying the above four factors), the barn was not within the curtilage. For instance, as to factor (3), the barn was not (as the police knew prior to the start of the episode) being used for any activities related to the home — the police had evidence that drugs were being manufactured in the barn. *U.S. v. Dunn, supra.*

e. **Open fields:** ***Open fields*** beyond the curtilage are ***not protected by the Fourth Amendment.*** The Court so held in *Oliver v. U.S.*, 466 U.S. 170 (1984).

i. **Rationale:** The majority in *Oliver* reached this result on two separate grounds. First, it concluded that the Fourth Amendment's protection of individuals' "persons, houses, papers, and effects" simply does not cover "open fields," so that governmental intrusion upon the open field is therefore simply not an "unreasonable search" proscribed by that Amendment. Secondly, the majority concluded that an individual cannot have a "reasonable expectation of privacy" (the *Katz* standard) with respect to an open field he owns.

f. **Front porch:** On the other hand, the Court has held that the ***front porch*** of a house ***is*** within the curtilage. That finding was necessary to the result in *Jardines*, *supra*, where the majority found that under the property-oriented approach to defining what is a search, the police intruded upon the curtilage of D's house when they used a drug-sniffing dog on D's front porch.

g. **Driveway:** We now come to the third and most-recent of our trio of modern-era Supreme Court cases applying the traditional property-oriented approach to the Fourth Amendment. That case, ***Collins v. Virginia***, 138 S.Ct. 1663 (2018), involved the question of whether or when the ***driveway*** of a house should be deemed part of the curtilage. *Collins* tells us that at least the portion of the driveway that ***immediately abuts the house*** *is* usually part of the curtilage.

i. **Facts:** In *Collins*, a police officer, Rhodes, had probable cause to believe that a particular orange-and-black motorcycle had been stolen and was now in the possession of Collins. Rhodes saw on Collins' Facebook page a photo of such a motorcycle, parked in the driveway of what seemed to be Collins' girlfriend's house. Rhodes drove to the street in front of the house to investigate.

(1) **What Rhodes could see:** From that position on the street, Rhodes could see that the house had a driveway that ran from the street up alongside the property's front lawn, and then alongside the house to a point a bit past the house's front perimeter. From his position on the street, Rhodes could also see that at the top of the driveway, next to the house and partly visible from under a tarpaulin, there was a parked motorcycle.

(2) **Officer walks up the driveway:** Believing that the partially-visible motorcycle was probably the stolen one, Rhodes took a photo of it from the street. He then walked up the driveway to where the motorcycle was parked under the tarp, lifted the tarp, and saw that the motorcycle resembled the stolen orange-and-black one. He used his hands to examine the cycle, uncovered the vehicle's license plate and VIN, verified by cellphone that these matched the details of the stolen motorcycle, and replaced the tarp. Rhodes then went to the front door of the house, where he eventually arrested Collins for receiving stolen property.

ii. **Collins' motion to suppress:** Before trial, Collins moved to suppress the evidence that Officer Rhodes had obtained from inspecting the motorcycle. Collins argued that when Rhodes walked up to the cycle, he was trespassing on the curtilage of the house; that trespass, Collins said, made the warrantless search a violation of Collins' Fourth Amendment rights.

(1) **Motion denied:** The trial court denied the suppression motion. That court did so by reasoning that even if the vehicle being searched was within the curtilage, the "automobile exception" to the search warrant requirement (see *infra*, p. 128) applied. The fruits of the search were then used against Collins, and he was convicted.

iii. **Issue presented:** When the case got to the Supreme Court, a threshold issue was whether the part of the driveway on which the motorcycle was parked should be considered part of the curtilage of the house. If it wasn't, Collins would automatically lose, because no Fourth Amendment search would have occurred – the Court had previously held that a homeowner has no reasonable expectation of privacy in those parts of a residential parcel that are not within the curtilage, even if those parts are not visible from the street. (See *supra*, p. 23.)

iv. **Motorcyle was within the curtilage, making search illegal:** By an 8-1 vote, the Court ***agreed with Collins*** that Rhodes had committed ***an illegal warrantless search***. In reaching that conclusion, the majority agreed with Collins' argument on the threshold issue: the part of the driveway where the motorcycle was parked ***was indeed part of the curtilage.*** The Court's opinion was written by Justice Sotomayor.

(1) **Definition of "curtilage":** Sotomayer began by quoting the opinion in *Jardines*, *supra*, according to which "curtilage" is defined as "the area ***'immediately surrounding and associated with the home.'*** " When defined this way, she said, curtilage was " ***'part of the home itself*** for Fourth Amendment purposes' " (still quoting *Jardines*).

(2) **Description of the driveway:** Sotomayor then gave a highly detailed description of the layout of the driveway; we quote this description in full here because the detail is needed in order to understand her legal conclusion:

> According to photographs in the record, the driveway runs alongside the front lawn and up a few yards past the front perimeter of the house. The top portion of the driveway that sits behind the front perimeter of the house is enclosed on two sides by a brick wall about the height of a car and on a third side by the house. A side door provides direct access between this partially enclosed section of the driveway and the house. A visitor endeavoring to reach the front door of the house would have to walk partway up the driveway, but would turn off before entering the enclosure and instead proceed up a set of steps leading to the front porch. When Officer Rhodes searched the motorcycle, it was parked inside this partially enclosed top portion of the driveway that abuts the house.

(3) **Conclusion as to the curtilage:** This "partially enclosed top portion of the driveway" in which the motorcycle was parked was, Sotomayor concluded, part of the curtilage of the house. Just like the front porch, side garden, or area 'outside the front window' [in] *Jardines*," she said, the "driveway enclosure" in which Rhodes did his search of the motorcycle was "an area adjacent to the home and 'to which the activity of home life extends,' " and so was "properly considered curtilage,"

(4) **Auto exception doesn't apply:** The fact that the search took place in the curtilage was by itself enough to make the search a Fourth Amendment one for which a warrant was required, Sotomayor concluded. That was so because – as she said in a part of her opinion discussed *infra*, p. 133 – the "automobile exception" to the search warrant requirement does not apply to the search of a vehicle located within the home or its curtilage.

v. **What *Collins* says about how "curtilage" applies to driveways:** So *Collins* tells us something – but unfortunately not very much – about when a driveway will be deemed part of the "curtilage" of a home.

(1) **What we know for sure:** Here are the three features of the "driveway enclosure" (the majority's term) that seem to have led the Court to conclude that the enclosure was part of the curtilage:

[1] This part of the driveway was indeed an ***"enclosure,"*** because three sides of it were each enclosed, either by the house or by a wall "about the height of a car";

[2] The enclosure was ***adjacent to the house***; and

[3] There was an ***entrance to the house*** from within the enclosure.

h. **Effect of *Katz* expectation-of-privacy rule:** How does the concept of a house's curtilage interact with *Katz*'s concept of reasonable expectation of privacy? Well, it's pretty clear that the curtilage of a house is ***protected*** against unconsented-to intrusions by the police, *even if* the area is one as to which the homeowner might ***not otherwise have a reasonable expectation of privacy.***

i. ***Jardines* as illustration:** That's what happened in *Jardines*, *supra* p. 20 — because D's front porch (where Franky the dog did his sniffing) was part of the curtilage of D's house, it ***didn't matter*** whether D did or did not have a reasonable expectation of privacy in the odors that may have escaped from inside the house onto the front porch. Either way, the use of the sniffing dog on the porch/curtilage was a Fourth Amendment search.

F. **Third party's prior knowledge limits privacy interest:** The Fourth Amendment, like the other constitutional principles discussed in this book, applies only to ***governmental action***; if a search is performed by a ***private individual*** who is not acting as an agent of or with the participation of the government, there can be no Fourth Amendment violation no matter how "unreasonable" the search is. See, e.g., *U.S. v. Jacobsen*, 466 U.S. 109 (1984).

The Supreme Court has developed a significant corollary to this well-established principle: if a government agent performs a search or seizure of the same material that has ***already been subjected to a private search or seizure***, the government will be deemed to have intruded upon the owner's privacy interests ***only to the extent that the governmental search or seizure exceeds the scope of the private one***. *U.S. v. Jacobsen, supra*.

1. **Rationale:** The rationale behind this rule is that once the private search or seizure takes place (even if it is unauthorized), the owner of the property no longer has a justifiable expectation as to any information that was already disclosed by that private examination.

2. **Illustration:** The application of this rule is illustrated by the facts of *Jacobsen*. A package addressed to D was sent via Federal Express and was damaged by FedEx in handling. Employees of FedEx opened the package, saw that it contained a tube, cut open the tube, and found plastic bags containing white powder. The employees notified the federal Drug Enforcement Administration, and replaced the plastic bags in the tube and the tube in the box before the DEA agents arrived. The first DEA agent to arrive saw that the end of the tube had been slit open, removed the plastic bags from the tube, saw the white powder, opened the bags, removed a trace of the white substance, and performed a field test that identified the substance as cocaine.

3. **Holding:** The Court concluded in *Jacobsen* that there had been ***no Fourth Amendment search or seizure at all***, because D at the time no longer had any legitimate expectation of privacy that was infringed by the DEA agent's actions. He had no such expectation, in turn, because the Federal Express employees had ***already performed the same search***, and had authorized the DEA agents to view the contents of the box. "The ***additional invasions*** of [D's] privacy by the government agent must be tested by the ***degree to which they exceeded the scope of the private search***."

G. **"Yes/no" test for contraband:** A party who possesses ***contraband*** (i.e., an illegal substance or object) has no legitimate expectation of privacy with respect to that possession. The Supreme Court has relied on this concept to hold that a ***chemical test*** that merely discloses ***whether or not a particular substance is contraband*** (and that does not disclose what the substance is if it is not contraband) does ***not violate any legitimate interest in privacy***. Therefore, such a test may be performed without probable cause and without a warrant. *U.S. v. Jacobsen*, 466 U.S. 109 (1984).

1. **Application:** In *Jacobsen* (another aspect of which is discussed *supra*, p. 24), drug agents took a small sample of white powder from a package addressed to D, and performed a chemical test on it. The test merely disclosed whether or not the substance was cocaine. The Court reasoned that "Congress has decided . . . to treat the interest in 'privately' possessing cocaine as illegitimate; thus governmental conduct that can reveal whether a substance is cocaine, and no other arguably 'private' fact, compromises no legitimate privacy interest." (In the Court's view, if the substance is not cocaine, the negative result "reveals nothing of special interest.")

   a. **Analogy to canine "sniff test":** The Court analogized to the use of dogs to perform canine "sniff tests" to discover drugs; such sniff tests were held not to constitute Fourth Amendment searches in *U.S. v. Place*, *infra*, p. 51.

   b. **Taking custody of package:** But two other aspects of the drug test in *Jacobsen* ***did*** implicate the Fourth Amendment interests of the package's owner. First, the government agents' conduct in ***taking custody*** of the package from a private freight company was a Fourth Amendment "seizure." However, that seizure was not "unreasonable" — by the time of the seizure (just prior to the drug test, but after the agents had already seen that what was being shipped was white powder packed suspiciously in plastic bags enclosed in a tube), the government agents had reasonable cause to believe that the package contained contraband, so the seizure for further testing was reasonable.

   c. **Destruction of drug by test:** The ***destruction*** of a small amount of the drug as an inevitable part of the test was, the Court held, a further "seizure" (since it transformed what had been a brief deprivation of D's possessory interest into a permanent one). However, this "seizure," too, was not an "unreasonable" one, since it was already highly probable that the substance was contraband, and since only a very small amount of the substance was destroyed.

H. **Trash and other abandoned property:** ***Trash*** or other ***abandoned*** property will normally ***not*** be material as to which the owner has an objectively reasonable expectation of privacy. Therefore, the Supreme Court has held, when a person puts trash out on the curb to be picked up by the garbage collector, the police may ***search that trash without a warrant***. ***California v. Greenwood***, 486 U.S. 35 (1988).

1. **Rationale:** The Court in *Greenwood* reasoned that regardless of whether the particular trash owner subjectively believes that his trash will remain private and unexamined, society should not and does not recognize that belief as "objectively reasonable." Trash left at curbside is readily accessible to "animals, children, scavengers, snoops, and other members of the public," so the owner cannot reasonably expect that it will remain private. Furthermore, the Court observed, when the owner puts the trash on the street for pickup, he is intentionally and voluntarily conveying it to a third party (the trash collector), who may himself sort through the trash.

   a. **Dissent:** Two dissenters (Brennan, joined by Marshall) contended in *Greenwood* that a person's privacy interest in his trash, when the trash is wrapped in sealed opaque bags, *is* objectively reasonable. "Most of us, I believe, would be incensed to discover a meddler — whether a neighbor, reporter, or detective — scrutinizing our sealed trash containers to discover some detail of our personal lives." The mere possibility that someone might snoop in this way did not so weaken the reasonable expectation of privacy that the police should be allowed to inspect trash as a routine investigative measure, the dissenters argued, "any more than the possibility of a burglary negates an expectation of privacy in the home."

b. **Result:** The practical result of *Greenwood* is that the police have a standard investigatory technique: if they suspect (even without probable cause) that a person may have committed a crime evidence of which might be contained in his trash, they can simply inspect the trash themselves, or request the trash collector to turn that person's trash over to them. In *Greenwood*, they did this legally for two months. Even if the police conduct is totally irrational, highly discriminatory, or the result of some personal vendetta, and continues over months or years as to a particular person, the resulting evidence will be fully admissible.

c. **Trash still on property:** Suppose the owner puts his trash out for collection, but places it not on the public street or sidewalk (as in *Greenwood*), but rather on a portion of his ***own property***, and under local custom the trash collector comes onto the property to retrieve it. The Court in *Greenwood* seemed to be relying on the fact that the garbage there was left "on or at the side of the street" or "in an area accessible to the public." Where the trash is left on the owner's property and only the trash collector is permitted to come on that property to retrieve it, the result may be different — the Court might hold that a property owner still has an objectively reasonable expectation of privacy that others will not illegally trespass upon his property to inspect his (admittedly abandoned) trash. This might be enough to prevent the police themselves from coming onto the property to inspect the trash.

2. **Abandoned houses and hotel rooms:** Similarly, a person probably has no reasonable expectation of privacy in ***houses, hotel rooms, vehicles***, etc. that he has abandoned. The police must bear the burden, however, of demonstrating that the owner ***intended*** to abandon the property. Thus where the defendant's absence from his apartment was due to his arrest and imprisonment, a court held that the prosecution had not met its especially heavy burden of showing that he intended to abandon it. *U.S. v. Robinson*, 430 F.2d 1141 (6th Cir. 1970).

   a. **Building destroyed by fire:** A property owner's reasonable expectation of privacy is not vitiated merely because of the property's ***destruction by fire***. See *Michigan v. Tyler*, 436 U.S. 498 (1978); *Michigan v. Clifford*, 464 U.S. 287 (1984).

3. **Abandonment at time of arrest:** In some cases, particularly narcotics cases, the owner of property will ***drop it on the ground*** when approached by a policeman. Most courts have held that such property is ***not abandoned***. Of course, if the police at the time they approach have probable cause to make an arrest, they can make a search incident to arrest even without a warrant (see *infra*, p. 99), and the question of whether a Fourth Amendment search has occurred is not important. But where the police approach or stop a person without probable cause (and without even the lesser degree of probable cause required for a "stop and frisk" — see *infra*, p. 148), the issue of the Fourth Amendment's applicability to property hurriedly disposed of by the defendant will be important, and in most situations the "abandoned property" doctrine will not apply.

I. Jail cells: A prisoner has no "legitimate expectation of privacy" in his ***prison cell***. *Hudson v. Palmer*, 468 U.S. 517 (1984). "[S]ociety is not prepared to recognize as legitimate any subjective expectation of privacy that a prisoner might have in his prison cell. . . . " Therefore, there are no Fourth Amendment limitations on prison officials' right to conduct searches of such cells, and seizures of their contents. *Id.*

1. **Consequence:** Thus, even if an inmate shows that a guard has searched his personal possessions that are highly unlikely to relate to security issues (e.g., letters or snapshots), that these items have been seized without justification, and that the guard's only motive was to ***harass***, the inmate has still not made out a Fourth Amendment claim.

J. Social guests: A ***guest*** in another person's house or place of business may or may not have a legitimate expectation of privacy in the premises being visited. Where the person is a ***social guest*** at a private home, she generally ***has a legitimate expectation of privacy*** in that home, the Court has indicated. But where a person's visit is solely for a ***business purpose***, the Court is likely to find that the visitor had no such legitimate expectation of privacy regarding the premises, especially where the visit is a brief one.

1. **Overnight guest:** At one end of the spectrum of guests, an ***overnight social guest*** clearly has a legitimate expectation of privacy in the home where she is staying. The Court so held in ***Minnesota v. Olson***, 495 U.S. 91 (1990). Consequently the police may not normally make a warrantless arrest or warrantless search of the premises where the defendant is staying. (If the owner of the premises consents to a search, the guest is out of luck; see *infra*, p. 147. But if the owner is not home, as was the situation in *Olson*, the police may not enter the premises to arrest the guest or to search for evidence against him, unless the police have a warrant or an exception to the warrant requirement applies.)

2. **Brief business purpose:** At the other end of the spectrum of guests, where a person visits a house only ***briefly***, and does so for a ***purely business purpose***, the Court has held that ***no legitimate expectation of privacy exists***. Thus in ***Minnesota v. Carter***, 525 U.S. 83 (1998), the Court held that the Ds, two men who spent 2 1/2 hours in a third person's apartment bagging cocaine for resale, did not have a legitimate expectation of privacy in the apartment. Consequently, no Fourth Amendment search took place when a police officer standing outside the building peered into the apartment through half-drawn blinds.[4]

   a. **Rationale:** *Carter* was a close decision — on the issue of whether the Ds had a legitimate expectation of privacy, the vote was 5-4. Chief Justice Rehnquist, writing for the majority, said that the "purely commercial nature of the transaction," coupled with the "relatively short period of time on the premises, and the lack of any previous connection" between the Ds and the tenant, were dispositive.

   b. **Different majority would protect almost all "social guests":** But a different majority of the *Carter* Court said that ***nearly all "social guests" do*** have Fourth Amendment protection as to the visited premises. It was only the briefness of the visit in *Carter*,

---

4. More precisely, the Ds' Fourth Amendment rights were not violated by the search, because the Ds' lack of a privacy interest in the apartment prevented them from having standing to protest the police's conduct, even though the owner of the apartment would have had such standing. As to the standing issues, see *infra*, p. 322.

coupled with the business-rather-than-social aspect of the Ds' presence, that prevented the Ds from having a reasonable expectation of privacy.

3. **Limited to area to which guest has access:** Keep in mind that even where a person is a guest who is found to have a legitimate expectation of privacy in the visited premises, that expectation will extend only to those ***portions*** of the premises to which the host has given the guest ***access***.

    Example: Suppose that D visits the house of his ex-wife, W, a house in which D used to live while the two were married. W then goes out for an errand, but allows D to remain. While W is out, the police conduct a warrantless search of W's basement, and find there evidence implicating D in a crime which he committed while he lived in the house. If the prosecution shows that W's invitation to D to stay in the house did not encompass the right to be in the basement, D would be found to have had no legitimate expectation of privacy as to the basement, and therefore no right to complain about the police's search of that basement.

K. **Searches of passengers in, or non-owner drivers of, a vehicle:** Just as a social guest in another person's home may well have a legitimate expectation of privacy in that home (see *Minn. v. Olson*, *supra*, p. 29), so a ***passenger*** in a ***vehicle***, or a ***driver who does not own the vehicle,*** will ordinarily have a reasonable expectation of privacy in the vehicle (and thus have standing to assert a Fourth Amendment violation) if the police stop the vehicle or search it.

1. **Passengers:** First, let's analyze the Fourth Amendment rights of a ***passenger*** in a vehicle that's stopped ("seized") and/or searched. Even if the passenger has ***no ownership or possessory interest*** in the vehicle, her mere ***presence*** in the vehicle at the time of the stop or search will almost always be sufficient to give her a reasonable expectation of privacy in the vehicle. Consequently, if the stop or search occurs without probable cause (and no exception to the requirement of probable cause applies), the passenger will be able to assert that her Fourth Amendment rights have been violated.

    Example: Assume that police officer O, acting without probable cause or even a reasonable suspicion of wrongdoing, stops a car that's owned and driven by X, and in which D is a passenger. O then (1) recognizes D as a parole violator for whom there is an outstanding arrest warrant; (2) arrests D; (3) searches D's person and the passenger compartment incident to the arrest; and (4) finds contraband in D's possession. Given that D has no ownership interest in the car, does he nonetheless have a reasonable expectation of privacy in the vehicle so that he has standing to assert that the initial stop violated his Fourth Amendment rights?

    On essentially these facts, the Supreme Court has held that the answer is ***"yes."*** "When a police officer makes a traffic stop, the driver of the car is seized within the meaning of the Fourth Amendment. [Any] passenger is seized as well and so may challenge the constitutionality of the stop." *Brendlin v. California*, 551 U.S. 249 (2007).

2. **Driver is not the owner:** Now, let's consider the status of a person (call her D) who is ***not the owner of a vehicle***, but who is ***driving the vehicle*** at the time it is stopped by the police. Does D's lack of an ownership interest in the vehicle prevent her from having a reasonable expectation of privacy in the vehicle, and thereby deprive her of standing to

assert that the stop violated her Fourth Amendment rights? Let's assume that the owner of the vehicle is not present. And let's begin our analysis by distinguishing between (1) the scenario in which D, the driver, ***was authorized*** by the owner to drive the vehicle; and (2) the scenario in which D was ***not*** so authorized.

a. **Authorized use of vehicle:** Scenario 1 (the driver D is authorized by the owner to drive the vehicle) is quite easy to analyze. Just as a social guest in a home normally has a reasonable expectation of privacy (REP) with respect to the portion of the home where the owner has authorized the guest to be present (see, e.g., *Minnesota v. Olson*, *supra*, p. 29), so the authorized-driver D normally has an REP with respect to the car, and therefore has standing to raise the Fourth Amendment argument.

b. **Unauthorized use – the rental car scenario:** Now, let's analyze Scenario 2 (the non-owner driver D is driving the vehicle ***without authorization*** by the owner). This scenario is most likely to arise when the vehicle is a ***rental car***, and the rental agreement lists someone other than D as the sole person authorized to drive the vehicle. In this scenario, D's standing to assert the Fourth Amendment if the vehicle is improperly stopped is a closer question than in Scenario 1. But here, too, the Court has held that the fact that the rental agreement prohibits D from driving the vehicle will ***not*** normally deprive D from asserting that the stop violated his Fourth Amendment rights. See ***Byrd v. U.S.***, 138 S.Ct. 1518 (2018).

   i. **Facts of *Byrd*:** In *Byrd*, Latasha Reed rented a car and then gave the keys to D (Byrd), even though D was not listed on the rental agreement as an authorized driver. (The agreement also specified that Reed, as the sole authorized driver, would be financially responsible for any loss caused by an unauthorized driver.) While D was driving the car — and Reed was absent — D was stopped for a traffic violation; a search of the car produced evidence that D had committed a crime. The prosecution asserted that because D was an unauthorized driver, he did not have a reasonable expectation of privacy as to the vehicle and its contents, and therefore did not have standing to raise a Fourth Amendment claim about the search.

   ii. **Holding in D's favor:** But the Court held – *unanimously* in fact – that ***D had a reasonable expectation of privacy in the car***, and thus had standing to raise the Fourth Amendment claim. The Court had previously held that a social guest in a friend's apartment "had a reasonable expectation of privacy in [the] apartment because he [had] 'complete dominion and control over the apartment and could exclude others from it.' " Now, in *Byrd*, the Court said that a similar rule should apply in the rental car context; there was "no reason why the expectation of privacy that comes from lawful possession and ***control*** and the ***attendant right to exclude*** would differ depending on whether the car in question is rented or privately owned by ***someone other*** than the person in current possession of it[.]"

   iii. **"Responsibility for loss" provision:** The prosecution in *Byrd* pointed out that the rental agreement there not only prohibited anyone not listed on the agreement from driving, but also made the authorized driver ***"fully responsible for all loss or damage"*** caused by an unauthorized driver. This clause was sufficient, the prosecution argued, to deprive D of any reasonable expectation of privacy in the car.

(1) **Court rejects:** But the Court ***rejected*** this argument. The rental contract contained a long list of prohibited activities (e.g., driving on unpaved roads) that even the government conceded should not be treated as nullifying the expectation of privacy. The clause making the authorized driver financially liable for damage caused by an unauthorized one – what the Court dismissed as a ***"risk allocation"*** provision – had "little to do with whether one would have a ***reasonable expectation of privacy*** in the rental car if, for example, he or she otherwise had lawful possession of and control over the car."

iv. **Illegality:** The prosecution made one other argument about why D should be found not to have a legitimate expectation of privacy in the vehicle. There was evidence, the prosecution said, that D had ***defrauded*** the rental company from the beginning, by "intentionally us[ing] a third party as a strawman in a calculated plan to mislead the rental company from the very outset, all to aid him in committing a crime."[5]

(1) **The contention:** The prosecution contended that if D had simply ***stolen*** the vehicle, he would have had no reasonable expectation of privacy as to it. (The Court seemed to accept this contention.) The Court then conceded that "it may be that there is no reason that the law should distinguish between one who obtains a vehicle through subterfuge of the type the Government alleges occurred here and one who steals the car outright."

(2) **To be decided on remand:** But the Court ***didn't decide*** what the consequences of such fraud – if it was demonstrated – should be. Rather, it remanded the case to the Court of Appeals, with instructions to determine (1) whether the government's allegation of fraud was correct, and (2) if so, whether such a fraud would indeed make D "no better situated than a car thief," such that he would not have a reasonable expectation of privacy in the vehicle.

L. **Foreign nationals and foreign territories:** Where a search or arrest takes place on ***foreign territory***, or involves a ***foreign national***, special problems arise.

1. **Foreign national in U.S.:** It appears to be the case that a ***foreign national*** who is present in the U.S. ***has*** Fourth Amendment rights. The Supreme Court assumed that this was the case (though it did not expressly so hold) in *INS v. Lopez-Mendoza*, 468 U.S. 1032 (1984).

2. **Foreign national, foreign country:** On the other hand, the Fourth Amendment does ***not*** apply to actions by U.S. officials that take place in a ***foreign country*** and involve a foreign national. For instance, property owned abroad by a foreign national may be searched for and seized by U.S. officials without probable cause and without a warrant. *U.S. v. Verdugo-Urquidez*, 495 U.S. 259 (1990).

3. **U.S. citizen, foreign country:** Where a search or arrest is directed at a ***U.S. citizen***, but takes place in a foreign country, the Court has never decided whether the Fourth Amendment applies.

---

5. D had a criminal record and, the prosecution claimed, knew that if he put his own name on the agreement, the rental company would have learned of the record and refused to rent to him.

III. THE "THIRD-PARTY" DOCTRINE: VOLUNTARY DISCLOSURE TO OTHERS AS VOIDING THE EXPECTATION OF PRIVACY

A. **Transfer to third person:** Suppose a person has ***transferred information to a third person***; that transfer may well indicate that the transferor no longer has a reasonable expectation of privacy with respect to the information. This idea has important Fourth Amendment implications: under the so-called ***"third-party" doctrine*** long recognized by the Supreme Court, when an individual voluntarily transfers information to a third party, the transferor enjoys no further Fourth Amendment protection as to that information. Where the doctrine applies, government may ***demand that the third party turn the information over,*** even if government not only ***lacks probable cause or a warrant,*** but doesn't even have reasonable grounds for suspecting that the information may be relevant to a criminal investigation.

1. **The third-party doctrine, generally:** Here is the Supreme Court's most-concise statement of the third-party doctrine: "The Fourth Amendment does not prohibit the obtaining of information ***revealed to a third party*** and ***conveyed by him to government authorities***, even if that information is revealed on the assumption that it will be used only for a ***limited purpose*** and the confidence placed in the third party will not be betrayed." *U.S. v. Miller*, 425 U.S. 435 (1976) (further discussed below).

2. **Cutting back of the doctrine:** But as we'll see, the use of the third-party doctrine has been dramatically ***curtailed*** as a result of a 2018 decision, *Carpenter v. U.S.*, discussed extensively *infra*, pp. 34-43. For many kinds of ***digital-era databases***, *Carpenter* means that the fact that an individual has allowed a third-party non-government actor to collect the data in question ***no longer automatically means*** that the individual is deemed to have surrendered any reasonable expectation of privacy in the information.

B. **Two key Supreme Court cases:** There are two main cases, both from the 1970s, in which the Supreme Court applied the third-party transfer doctrine. One involved a defendant's ***banking records*** held by his bank, and the other involved lists of ***phone numbers dialed*** by the defendant and kept in the phone company's records.

1. **Bank records (*U.S. v. Miller*):** The bank records case was ***U.S. v. Miller***, 425 U.S. 435 (1976). There, the Court held that when the customer of a bank gives banking-related information to the bank in furtherance of the relationship, the customer will be found to have no reasonable expectation of privacy in the material. Consequently, the government was permitted to ***subpoena that material from the bank*** without showing probable cause that the material is evidence of crime. Indeed, according to *Miller*, the subpoena (culminating in the bank's turning over the records) ***did not even constitute a "search"*** for purposes of the account-holder's Fourth Amendment rights. The facts of *Miller*, recited in the following example, show how this works.

   Example: D, in his dealings with Bank (his own bank), gives Bank access to his checks, deposits, and financial statements. The federal government, acting without a warrant, subpoenas Bank's microfilm copies of these records, and uses the copies to prosecute D. D claims that the government's seizure of these records was a Fourth Amendment search, requiring probable cause and a search warrant.

Held, for the government. D had no reasonable expectation of privacy with respect to these documents. "The depositor takes the risk, in revealing his affairs to another, that the information will be conveyed by that person to the government." *U.S. v. Miller, supra*.

2. **Outbound telephone numbers called by D (*Smith v. Maryland*):** The case involving a ***phone company's records*** of ***numbers dialed*** by its subscriber was ***Smith v. Maryland***, 442 U.S. 735 (1979). As in *Miller*, the Court held that the person who "turns over" data to a third person — in this case, the phone subscriber who supplies to his phone company the numbers he wishes to call — has no Fourth Amendment right to object when the government warrantlessly subpoenas the relevant records (the numbers called) from the phone company.

   a. **Facts:** In *Smith*, the police, with the assistance of the phone company, installed a ***"pen register"*** device in the phone company offices, to track all calls made by D, a robbery suspect, from his home phone. The police did not get a warrant before requesting the phone company's help. The register recorded all numbers called by D, but did not monitor the conversations. The numbers were introduced at D's criminal trial to show that a phone registered to him had been used to place calls to the robbery victim. D claimed that the government's retrieval of the phone numbers from the pen register was a search, for which a warrant was required.

   b. **Holding:** The Court held that D had no legitimate expectation of privacy with regard to the numbers he dialed (as distinguished from the *contents* of the calls to those numbers). Individuals ***"voluntarily convey[] numerical information to the telephone company*** and ***'expose[]' that information*** ... in the ordinary course of business." Therefore, no Fourth Amendment "search" or "seizure" of the numbers occurred, which meant that no warrant was required.

C. **Modern digital databases and the third-party doctrine (*Carpenter v. U.S.*)** The two key cases on the third-party doctrine we've just discussed – *Miller* (p. 33) and *Smith* (p. 34) – were both decided in the 1970s. These cases thus pre-date the ***rise of smart phones, the Internet,*** and other technological advances that allow ***non-governmental third-parties to amass huge amounts of potentially-intimate data about a person.*** During the decades following the two cases, it became clear that if the third-party doctrine was applied broadly so as to encompass all privately-operated databases fed by these emerging communications technologies, the Fourth Amendment would be no barrier to a vast enlargement of government's surveillance powers.

1. **Enlargement of government's access to private information:** Yet until 2018, the broad third-party doctrine relied on in *Smith* and *Miller* – that a person has no reasonable expectation of privacy in data she has voluntarily placed into the custody of a third party, so that such data will be deemed free from Fourth Amendment protection – tacitly remained the law.

2. ***Carpenter* changes the rules:** But the continued viability of the third-party doctrine has been dramatically ***weakened*** by a seminal 2018 Supreme Court decision involving government access to ***"cell-site location information" ("CSLI").*** CSLI refers to information — typically held by phone companies — showing the ***location of a person's cell phone***

from moment to moment. In the 2018 case, ***Carpenter v. U.S.***, 138 S.Ct. 2206 (2018), a 5-4 decision, the majority held that because CSLI exposes far more private information than the limited bank records in *Miller* or the phone-numbers-dialed data in *Smith*, a person ***maintains a reasonable expectation of privacy*** in her own CSLI ***even though the information is held by a third-party.***

a. **Significance of *Carpenter*:** *Carpenter* means that when police officers request a person's CSLI from a wireless carrier, the officers are ***conducting a Fourth Amendment search.*** As we'll see, this fact means that before the police may even request — let alone demand — CSLI from the carrier, the police must:

[1] ***demonstrate*** to a judge or magistrate ***probable cause*** to believe that the information sought will reveal evidence of crime or contraband (i.e., they must have probable cause for a search warrant); and

[2] ***obtain the search warrant.***

3. **Facts of *Carpenter*:** In *Carpenter*, local police arrested four men in connection with several robberies of Radio Shack and T-Mobile stores in Detroit. One of the men confessed that he and a group of 15 accomplices had robbed nine different stores over the previous four months. The FBI was brought in, and the suspect gave the Bureau the cell phone numbers of some of the accomplices. The FBI then reviewed the suspect's call records to identify additional numbers he had called around the time of the robberies. Based on this review, federal prosecutors applied for and received court orders compelling two wireless carriers to produce CSLI showing the locations, over various time periods relevant to the robberies, of the various suspects' cell phones, including the phone of D (Timothy Carpenter).

a. **What the prosecutors asked for:** In *Carpenter*, the federal prosecutors made a showing, based on less-than-probable-cause, of their need to know D's cellphone movements near the robberies at the various times over the four-month period when the robberies occurred. Two federal judges responded, each issuing an orders directing one of D's wireless carriers – MetroPCS in one instance and Sprint in the other – to disclose the CSLI for D's phone during this four-month period. One order demanded ***152 days of CSLI*** from MetroPCS, and resulted in the production of records spanning ***127 days.*** The other demanded ***seven days of CSLI*** from Sprint, and resulted in the production of two days of records (which overlapped with the 127 days). Between the two orders, the government ended up obtaining nearly 13,000 location points covering D's movements, an average of about ***101 data points*** for ***each*** of the 127 days.

b. **D moves to suppress the CSLI:** D was charged with the various robberies and with the related federal crime of carrying a firearm in connection with a crime of violence. Before trial, he moved to suppress the CSLI data; he contended that the government had violated his Fourth Amendment rights, on the theory that the court-ordered production of the data should be considered a "search" requiring a warrant issued upon probable cause.

c. **Use against D:** The trial court denied D's motion to suppress. The government then used the CSLI in its case against him. It did so by putting on expert testimony from an FBI agent showing that at the exact time of each of four of the robberies charged, D's phone (and thus D himself) was "right where the robbery was." D was convicted on nearly all of the charges.

d. **Issue at the Supreme Court:** In D's appeal to the Supreme Court, the core issue was whether the two court orders compelling the carriers to produce the CSLI records to the government indeed violated D's Fourth Amendment rights. As we'll see, a 5-Justice majority of the Court ***agreed*** with D's contention.

4. **The majority opinion in *Carpenter*:** The majority opinion in *Carpenter* was written by Chief Justice Roberts. The opinion was joined by the four liberal members of the Court (Ginsburg, Breyer, Sotomayor and Kagan). The four conservatives dissented. Roberts' decision in *Carpenter* to align himself with the Court's liberals resulted in a major ***expansion of individuals' justifiable privacy expectations.***

a. **Outcome of the case:** The actual holding in *Carpenter* was fairly narrow: each order compelling production of the CSLI ***amounted to a Fourth Amendment search***, and each search was invalid because no warrant supported by probable cause was issued. The majority reached this outcome in two steps, by concluding that:

[1] If one ignores the third-party doctrine, D had a ***reasonable expectation of privacy*** (REP) in the CSLI data; and

[2] The fact that the data was ***held by a third-party*** when the police asked for it ***should not be treated as preventing D from having this REP***, because the third-party doctrine should not be applied to such highly-intimate and detailed information.

i. **Two separate discussions:** Step [1] (above) of the *Carpenter* decision – that D had an REP in the CSLI data at issue here – is discussed *supra*, p. 17, as part of our general treatment of *Katz* and the reasonable expectation of privacy. Step [2] of the decision – that the third-party doctrine should not be applied to the CSLI – is the more important aspect of *Carpenter*, and that's the aspect we'll discuss here.

b. ***Smith* and *Miller* not "extended" to cover CSLI:** Roberts' opinion for the Court ***did not overturn*** the third-party doctrine as that doctrine had been articulated and applied in *Smith* and *Miller*. Rather, the majority said it "***declines to extend***" the doctrine to cover these novel circumstances," for two reasons.

i. **Technological change:** First, Roberts said that CSLI constituted a ***"qualitatively different category"*** from the telephone numbers and bank records at issue in *Smith* and *Miller*. The primary difference was that the technology on which CSLI was built was ***far more advanced*** than the technology that served as the basis for the pen register and check-storage mechanisms involved in the two earlier cases:

(1) **CSLI is different:** In contrast to the relatively unrevealing nature of the check records and call lists in the two earlier cases, CSLI can furnish ***"a detailed chronicle of a person's physical presence compiled every day, every moment, over several years."*** As Roberts memorably put it, "When the government tracks the location of a cell phone it ***achieves near perfect surveillance,*** as if it had ***attached an ankle monitor to the phone's user***."

ii. **CSLI data not truly "voluntary":** As to the second rationale for distinguishing CSLI from the pen register and check-storage data in the earlier cases, the third-party doctrine supporting those holdings, Roberts said, was that a person sharing her data with the third-party business has ***voluntarily chosen to expose that data***, again justifying a reduced expectation of privacy in the data. But, Roberts said, CSLI was different on this score as well. Cell phone location information "is ***not truly 'shared'*** as one normally understands the term." ***Cell phone service*** is "***indispensable to participation in modern society***," so a person's decision to share the resulting location data with the carrier ***can't accurately be said to be "voluntary."***

iii. **The "seven days of CSLI" aspect:** By the way, the majority's opinion does ***not*** say that *any* order or request for CSLI data made to a carrier is a Fourth Amendment search requiring a search warrant supported by probable cause. Rather, the opinion only establishes that *if* government ***accesses seven days or more of CSLI,*** that's enough of an intrusion to constitute a Fourth Amendment search, thereby requiring a warrant.

c. **The *Carpenter* multi-factor test:** Roberts listed ***the factors*** that led to his conclusion that the court orders for the CSLI there constituted a Fourth Amendment search. Although he spoke only about CSLI, not other forms of data-gathering by government, he indicated that when a post-*Carpenter* lower court has to decide whether government access to *any* third-party-maintained digital database filled with personal information constitutes a Fourth Amendment search, the court will need to look to these three factors:

[1] whether the information is ***"deeply revealing"***;

[2] whether the information's ***"reach"*** is "***deep,***" ***"broad,"*** and ***"comprehensive"***; and

[3] whether the ***process*** by which the information is collected is ***"inescapable and automatic."***

d. **Consequence of not applying third-party doctrine:** Roberts' decision in *Carpenter* not to apply the third-party doctrine to the CSLI there led to the ultimate outcome in the case:

[1] First, the inapplicability of the third-party doctrine meant that whether the FBI's receipt of the CSLI constituted a Fourth Amendment search turned ***solely*** on whether D had a reasonable expectation of privacy ***(REP)*** as to the material, a determination to be made by the same criteria as if the data had been directly extracted from D by the government, or created by the government acting without the involvement of any third party.

Example of [1]: Thus the test for whether D had an REP as to the CSLI data held by the carrier would be applied the same way as if, say, the police had (legally) ***found the same CSLI data physically on D's phone*** when he was arrested. In other words, the fact that the data was in the ***possession of a third party*** (the cellular carrier), not on D's person, was ***constitutionally irrelevant***.

[2] Given consequence [1] (no third-party doctrine used), the Court was left to use fairly-conventional REP analysis to decide that, given the great ***intimacy and breadth*** of the CSLI – a continuous record of D's movements over many days – D had a reasonable expectation that these details would remain private.

[3] Putting consequences [1] and [2] together, when the FBI obtained and scrutinized the CSLI data it ***conducted a "search" for Fourth Amendment purposes.***

[4] Given consequence [3] (that this was a Fourth Amendment search), and given that ***no exception*** to the usual requirement of a search warrant applied, the FBI was ***required to apply for a search warrant,*** rather than simply obtaining an SCA order as it actually did.

[5] As a final consequence, in order to properly obtain a search warrant in step [4], the FBI would have had to show in its warrant application ***probable cause*** (not just some lesser level of suspicion) to believe that the particular data being sought would furnish evidence of specified crimes.

5. **The dissents in *Carpenter*:** Each of the four ***dissenters*** in *Carpenter* wrote separately. Two of the dissents – those by Kennedy and Alito – had a lot to say about two main issues: (a) when and whether the third-party doctrine should apply to CSLI; and (b) whether the fact that the government was not using its ***own*** agents to search through the third-party-held records – but was instead compelling the carrier to do the searching of its own records – should make a constitutional difference. We'll concentrate on these two dissents.

   a. **Kennedy's dissent:** Justice ***Kennedy's*** dissent contained a long discussion of each of these issues.

      i. **Not D's records:** As to the first of these issues – why the majority was wrong not to apply the traditional third-party doctrine to CSLI – Kennedy noted that the CSLI in question ***did not belong to Carpenter***, but rather, to the cell phone carriers. The Fourth Amendment protects "[t]he right of the people to be secure in *their* [emphasis by Kennedy] … persons, houses, papers, and effects," he said, not the "persons, houses, papers, and effects" of ***others***. The records here were "the ***business entities'*** [i.e., the carriers'] records, plain and simply." Because Carpenter "had no reason to believe the records were owned or controlled by [him]," that fact alone should prevent him from having a reasonable expectation of privacy in those records.

      ii. **Government's use of compulsory process:** As to the second of the issues – whether the fact that government was not itself going to do the searching should make a constitutional difference – Kennedy believed that it should. The government received the records ***by obtaining what was in effect a court-ordered subpoena.*** The Court had long held that government may, without getting a warrant, use ***"compulsory process"*** (typically, a subpoena) to obtain a ***"wide variety of business records,"*** such as the financial records in *Miller* and the telephone records in *Smith*. Now, Kennedy contended, the majority opinion was making an

illogical distinction between two types of information subpoenaed from third parties.

iii. **Handicapping law enforcement:** Furthermore, Kennedy said, disfavoring law enforcement's ability to obtain cell-site records would place a major and unnecessary ***handicap on law enforcement.***

b. **Alito's dissent:** Justice ***Alito's*** dissent warned that the majority's approach ***"guarantees a blizzard of litigation*** while threatening many legitimate and valuable investigative practices upon which law enforcement has rightfully come to rely." Alito agreed with the two central points of Kennedy's dissent (see above).

i. **Significance of the court order:** The majority, Alito said, "ignores the basic ***distinction*** between ***an actual search*** (dispatching law enforcement officers to enter private premises and root through private papers and effects) and an order merely ***requiring a party to look through its own records*** and produce specified documents." The former "***intrudes on personal privacy far more deeply***, [and thus] requires probable cause [while] [t]he latter does not."

6. **D gets no benefit from ruling:** Ironically, D ended up ***getting no personal benefit*** from his "victory" in the Supreme Court, because after the Court remanded the case, the lower courts ultimately ruled that the government had ***relied in good faith*** on the orders to produce the CSLI.[6]

D. **Post-*Carpenter* case law:** The Supreme Court has not heard any cases interpreting *Carpenter* since that case was decided. However, lower courts have had occasion to decide whether *Carpenter* applies to various fact patterns. Here's an overview of some of the scenarios raised by *Carpenter*, and how some courts have decided (or in one scenario, how I think they might decide in the future) the applicability of *Carpenter* to those scenarios.

1. **Length of CSLI surveillance period:** A key issue left unresolved in *Carpenter* is the ***maximum length of time CSLI surveillance can last*** before becoming a search that requires a warrant.

a. **Seven days or more:** ***If the surveillance continues for seven days or more***, *Carpenter* itself supplies the answer: that surveillance is ***sufficiently lengthy and intrusive*** that it ***automatically*** constitutes a Fourth Amendment search for which a warrant is required.

b. **Less than seven days:** But *Carpenter* does not decide whether ***shorter-than-seven-day*** surveillance periods will also be Fourth Amendment searches. A few lower courts have had to decide, post-*Carpenter,* whether obtaining CSLI data ***covering just a few hours*** constitute a search. The courts have ***split*** on this question.

i. **Not a search:** Some courts have held that tracking for a ***few hour***s is ***not*** a search. For instance, in *U.S. v. Hammond*, 996 F.3d 373 (7th Cir. 2021), investigators received reports about D's whereabouts from D's carrier (AT&T) in real time every 15 minutes for ***6 hours.*** The court held that the surveillance there ***was much***

6. For the doctrine that protects the police if they rely in good faith on an erroneously-issued search warrant, see *infra*, p. 348.

less intrusive than in *Carpenter*, because law enforcement only ***followed D on public roads,*** and just for the duration of ***one car trip.*** This made the case more like obtaining the beeper data in *Knotts* (see p. 45; not a search) than like the much-longer seven-day surveillance in *Carpenter* (a search). See K,K&P, pp. 264-65.

ii. **A search:** But another case has ruled that a similar tracking of a cell phone for a few hours ***does*** constitute a search. In *Commonwealth v. Reed*, 647 S.W.3d 237 (Ky. 2022), the police asked D's cell phone provider to ping D's phone continually for ***1 ½ hours,*** thus giving the police D's location throughout that period. The court held that this *was* a search, because it was ***like "a technological trespass"*** of the sort that "we find the ***average citizen unwilling to accept.***" The court said that "individuals have an ***objectively reasonable expectation*** that their cell phones will not be used as ***real-time tracking devices*** through the direct and active interference of law enforcement." Cf. K,K&P, p. 265.

2. **Real-time CSLI:** The CSLI in *Carpenter* was ***"historical"*** data – the government was asking the wireless carriers to supply location data for a designated time ***in the past.*** But CSLI can also be tracked on a ***"real time"*** basis – that is, law enforcement can and does send a request to a carrier in the form: "Track the location of whatever cell phone is associated with the phone number (xxx) xxx-xxxx for one week starting tomorrow at noon." Is such a seven-days-or-more ***real-time*** (or ***"forward-looking")*** gathering of CSLI necessarily a Fourth Amendment search?

   a. **Affirmative answer:** The answer is almost certainly "***yes.***" Applying the multi-factor test of *Carpenter* (*supra,* p. 37), the real-time CSLI is just as ***"revealing"*** as the historical CSLI, and is "***deep,***" "inescapable" and "automatic" once the monitoring is put in motion. True, the data is not as "***broad***" as historical CSLI (since the government's ability to "time travel" to any point in the past is not relevant), but this is a minor difference. And the Court said in *Carpenter* that "when government tracks the location of a cell phone it ***achieves near-perfect surveillance***, as if it had ***attached an ankle monitor*** to the phone's user"; that comment is just as applicable to real-time monitoring as it is to historical CSLI. Therefore, when the police requisition a seven-day-or-more batch of real-time CSLI data, this seems almost certain to ***be a search.***

      i. **Few hours of tracking:** Whether real-time tracking for, say, a ***few hours*** is a search is a different matter, on which, as we've seen, the few lower courts to consider the issue have split.

3. **Pole camera surveillance of D's home:** Another issue is whether *Carpenter* applies (i.e., whether the police commit a search) when officers install a ***"pole camera"*** to ***monitor the front door of a suspect's house***, in order to track comings and goings there. Typically, the camera is mounted on a ***pole or a tree, usually on public property.*** Since the camera is small and readily hidden, often the suspect does not ***realize*** she is being surveilled, even if the camera operates for multiple months. Here, as in the case of less-than-seven-day CSLI surveillance, courts have ***split*** about whether a lengthy observation by the pole camera constitutes a search. K,K&P, pp. 265-66.

a. **Split court in *Moore-Bush*:** For instance, in one recent case, *U.S. v. Moore-Bush*, 36 F.4th 320 (1st Cir. 2022), a 6-judge panel of the First Circuit ***split 3-3*** about whether pole camera surveillance for ***8 months*** was a search.

   i. **3 say it's a search:** Three judges argued that this *was* a search, because its degree of intrusiveness was comparable to that of the seven-day on-the-road surveillance of the defendant in *Carpenter*. "[T]he sum total of ***all visible activities that take place in a location*** that by its nature is associated with the ***sanctity of a man's home*** and the ***privacies of life*** can be even more revealing than the sum total of one's movements while out and about [as in *Carpenter*], given the nature of ***what transpires in front of the home."***

   ii. **3 say it's not a search:** But the other three judges in *Moore-Bush* decided that ***no search had occurred.*** They pointed out that the pole camera merely captured D's (and his co-conspirators) movements ***"in one place in the public view,"*** and did not track their movements once they left the home. Therefore, these judges said "there can be no expectation of privacy in the ***aggregate of these movements*** because they ***occur in one place where a person expects to encounter and be seen by people again and again."***

4. **Automatic License Plate Readers:** Many jurisdictions use ***Automated License Plate Readers (ALPRs)***, which ***take a picture of every license plate*** that passes by a fixed location on the roadway. Does the use of ALPRs to track the movements of D's vehicle constitute a search under *Carpenter*?

   a. **Not a search (*McCarthy*):** At least one case has answered ***"no,"*** given the relatively non-intrusive nature of the ALPR data collection there. In *Commonwealth v. McCarthy*, 142 N.E.3d 1090 (Mass. 2020), police suspected that D was transporting narcotics by car to a co-conspirator on Cape Cod. They knew that for D to get there, he would have to cross over one of two bridges, both of which had an ALPR at each end. The police tracked, for ***2 ½ months,*** the time, direction and even lane each time D crossed either bridge.

      i. **"Mosaic" theory:** The court in *McCarthy* concluded that intensive use of ALPR surveillance of a suspect's vehicle might in *some* cases constitute a search. The court applied the ***"mosaic theory."*** Under that theory, the court said, a small number of sightings might reveal little, like seeing the color of a single stone; but with enough sightings, the government could develop a ***"complete mosaic,"*** creating a ***"highly detailed profile"*** of not just a person's movements, but also of their ***"associations*** … and of the pattern of [their] ***professional and avocational pursuits."*** Therefore, the court said "With ***enough cameras and enough locations***, the historic location data from an ALPR system in Massachusetts would invade a ***reasonable expectation of privacy*** and ***would constitute a search***" under *Carpenter*.

      ii. **Not enough surveillance here:** But the court held that the surveillance there was ***too limited to constitute a search.*** The police were not "monitor[ing] the ***whole*** of the defendant's public movements, or ***track[ing] enough*** of his comings and goings so as to reveal the ***privacies of life."*** Whatever the dividing line is between a search and a non-search, the court said, ***no search occurs*** where the data is "produced by ***4 cameras at fixed locations on the ends of two bridges."***

5. **Tracking IP addresses:** One common investigative technique is the ***tracking of Internet Protocol (IP) addresses.*** Any computer used to browse a website has an IP address, which is the equivalent of a phone number. Suppose the police learn that some unidentified person has committed a crime by accessing a particular Internet application (which we'll assume here is a messaging app) at a particular time. The authorities submit a subpoena to the operators of the messaging app, asking them to disclose which IP addresses were used (by anyone) to access the messaging app during that period of time. That way, the user/criminal can be identified based on their IP address. Do the police commit a search under *Carpenter* when they ask the messaging-app operator to furnish such a list of incoming IP addresses?

   a. **Limited information:** At least one case has answered ***"no"*** on the facts there. See *U.S. v. Hood*, 920 F.3d 87 (1st Cir. 2019). There, the police requested from the application operator all IP addresses that had accessed the application during a ***4-day window*** when the crime occurred. Based on this data, the police learned that the relevant addresses belonged to P, whom they arrested. P argued that the request to the app operator amounted to a search under *Carpenter,* for which a warrant was required. But the court held that the ***degree of intrusiveness*** was so much less than that in *Carpenter* that ***no search should be found to have occurred,*** for two reasons:

      [1] The IP address information was only generated when the user made the ***"affirmative decision"*** to access a website or application. In *Carpenter*, by contrast, a cell phone passes cell-tower-location information to the CSLI system whenever a call, text, email, etc. occurs on a phone, ***without the user lifting a finger.***

      [2] Also, the IP addresses didn't convey any ***location information,*** unlike the CSLI information in *Carpenter*. Therefore, the surveillance here ***did not pose the invasion-of-privacy concerns*** that the Supreme Court raised in *Carpenter*, under which if CSLI information was monitored for, say, months, "only the few without cell phones could escape tireless and absolute surveillance."

      i. **Result:** Since the court in *Hood* ruled that no Fourth Amendment search occurred there, the police did not need a search warrant, and the IP address information could be used against D at trial.

6. **Does not apply to the contents of emails:** There's one final category of electronic data as to which the rationale of *Carpenter* might conceivably apply. That data consists of the actual ***contents*** of a person's ***emails or instant messages***, when maintained on a third party's computer (say the server of an ISP who handled the message).

   a. **Analogy to a mailed letter:** Even before *Carpenter*, most of the federal cases to consider the issue held that a user who sends an email – even if she knows a copy is going to reside on some third-party computer system – should not be viewed as having thereby surrendered any expectation of privacy in the email's contents. See, e.g., *U.S. v. Warshak*, 631 F.3d 266 (6th Cir. 2010). That's because the Supreme Court has long held that the Fourth Amendment protects mailed ***letters***, as well as sealed packages sent with postage, from being warrantlessly inspected by postal authorities; see *U.S. v.*

Van Leeuwen, 397 U.S. 249 (1970). Since an email is analogous to a letter, "agents of the government cannot compel a commercial ISP to turn over the contents of an email without triggering the Fourth Amendment." *Warshak*, supra.

b. ***Carpenter* doesn't change this:** Furthermore, nothing in *Carpenter* should change this result. Emails are, if anything, *more* likely to be deeply revealing of intimate thoughts than was the CSLI data at issue in *Carpenter*. And most of the other factors mentioned in the *Carpenter* multi-factor test similarly cut in favor of treating email content the same way as CSLI data. So the Court would likely hold that the rationale of *Carpenter* dictates that the third-party doctrine not be applied to the contents of email communications or text messages.

IV. THE "PLAIN VIEW" DOCTRINE

A. **Plain view doctrine, generally:** The courts have long recognized, even before the *Katz* "privacy" approach, that where objects on private property can be seen from public places, observation by the police ***does not constitute a Fourth Amendment search***. As the Supreme Court reiterated this doctrine in a post-*Katz* case, "it has long been settled that objects falling in the ***plain view*** of an officer who has a ***right to be in the position to have that view*** are subject to seizure and may be introduced in evidence." *Harris v. U.S.*, 390 U.S. 234 (1968).

1. **Effect of *Katz:*** The *Katz* holding reinforces this "plain view" doctrine, at least in those instances where the view is obtained from a ***public place***, since generally one does not reasonably expect to keep private what can be seen by the public.

   Example: A policeman standing on a public right-of-way looks into defendant's window, and sees and hears criminal activity. Because the defendant should have expected that people standing on the street could see inside, he had no reasonable expectation of privacy, and no Fourth Amendment search occurred. *People v. Wright*, 242 N.E.2d 180 (Ill. 1968).

2. **Warrantless seizure of evidence:** It is important to distinguish between ***observation*** of an object in "plain view," and ***seizure*** of that object. Mere observation of an object which is in "plain view" will never constitute a Fourth Amendment "search." But the fact that an object, say contraband or evidence of a crime, is in "plain view" does not automatically give the police the right to ***seize*** that object without a warrant. For seizure to be proper, there must either be a generally-applicable ***warrant*** in force, or some exception to the warrant requirement. (Warrant requirements, and exceptions to them, form a major part of this book.) That is, the "plain view" doctrine itself is ***not an exception to the warrant requirement***, when seizure of an object is concerned.

   a. **Explanation:** The Supreme Court has explained the nature of the "plain view" doctrine this way: " 'Plain view' provides grounds for seizure of an item when an officer's 'access to the object' has ***some prior justification*** under the Fourth Amendment. 'Plain view' is perhaps better understood, therefore, not as an independent 'exception' to the warrant clause, but simply as an extension of whatever the prior justification for an officer's 'access to an object' may be." *Texas v. Brown*, 460 U.S. 730 (1983).

b. **Search with warrant:** Where the police have obtained a ***valid search warrant*** describing particular items, and during the course of their search they discover an object which is ***not covered by the warrant***, but which is obviously contraband or evidence of a crime, they may seize that object ***without getting a new warrant*** specially covering it. Similarly, if the police are already on private premises pursuant to some exception to the warrant requirement (e.g., exigent circumstances), they may seize contraband or incriminating evidence.

c. **No entry without warrant:** But if the police, while standing on public property, see in "plain view" an object on private property, this does ***not*** entitle them to enter the private property and seize it. For instance, if a policeman standing on the sidewalk looks through the living room window of a house and sees drugs inside, he is not entitled to make a warrantless entry and seize the evidence. He must instead get a warrant.

d. **Items for sale don't lose privacy expectation:** Even in a ***public*** place, the circumstances may be such that there is a reasonable expectation of privacy against ***government intrusion***, rendering the "plain view" doctrine inapplicable. For instance, the fact that a merchant has placed ***items on display*** in order to sell them to the public does not mean that he has no legitimate expectation of privacy against government intrusion. Thus where a merchant displays pornographic books and films, he has not lost his right to object to an unreasonable search and seizure of them. *Lo-Ji Sales, Inc. v. New York*, 442 U.S. 319 (1979). (But if the police in *Lo-Ji Sales* had merely looked at the covers of the books and films and concluded that they were obscene, this probably would have fallen within the "plain view" doctrine, since the store customers were free to do the same.)

B. **Use of mechanical devices, generally:** Where police stand on public property, but use ***mechanical devices*** to obtain the view of defendant or his property, the "plain view" doctrine will often nonetheless apply.

1. **Flashlights:** The use of a ***flashlight*** by a policeman in the nighttime does not prevent an observation from falling within the "plain view" doctrine. Thus in *Texas v. Brown*, 460 U.S. 730 (1983), an officer stopped D's car as part of a routine driver's license checkpoint, and shone his flashlight into the car, where he saw a balloon which he believed (correctly) to contain narcotics. The Court held that the balloon could then be seized pursuant to the "plain view" doctrine; "The use of artificial means to eliminate a darkened area simply does not constitute a search, and thus triggers no Fourth Amendment protection."

a. **Binoculars:** Similarly, lower courts have held that the use of ***binoculars*** to see an object does not prevent the observation from coming within the "plain view" doctrine. See, e.g., *Johnson v. State*, 234 A.2d 464 (Md. Ct. Spec. App. 1967).

2. **More sophisticated devices:** Even where the devices used to gain a view of the defendant's property are somewhat more sophisticated than a flashlight or binoculars, the Supreme Court will often uphold their use under the "plain view" doctrine, if two conditions are met:

[1] the view takes place from a ***location*** where the police ***have a right to be*** (e.g., public property); and

[2] the information obtained ***could have been gotten*** from "plain view" surveillance executed ***without*** the special device.

a. **Electronic "beeper" on car:** This principle is illustrated by a 1983 case involving the use of a now-outmoded ***electronic "beeper."*** In the pre-Internet age, when the police desired to trail a vehicle, they sometimes put such a "beeper" on the vehicle, which sent out a local radio signal that enabled a nearby human observer to follow the vehicle. In ***U.S. v. Knotts***, 460 U.S. 276 (1983), the police, acting with the consent of a seller of chemicals, put a beeper into a can of chemicals that was about to be sold. After the purchase, the police then used the beeper to follow (by helicopter) the beeper-equipped can, and thus the purchaser's movements in a car that contained the can.

   i. **Holding:** The Court held that this use of the beeper did ***not violate*** the driver's reasonable expectation of privacy in his movements over the roads.

   ii. **Rationale:** The Court reasoned that a driver ***voluntarily conveys to anyone who watches him*** the fact that he is traveling over particular roads in a particular direction to a particular destination. Since the beeper merely supplied the same information that could have been amassed through ordinary plain view surveillance of such no-expectation-of-privacy movements, no Fourth Amendment violation could have occurred.

   iii. **Where beeper supplies data on interior locations:** There was no constitutional violation in *Knotts* because the beeper only enabled the police to learn information about the defendant's ***public movements***, information that could have been learned through ordinary "plain view" surveillance. But suppose a beeper or other electronic device is used to elicit information about a person's location or movements ***in the interior of a structure***, information that could *not* be obtained by an officer using his own eyes from a public place. Here, ***a Fourth Amendment search has taken place***, so probable cause and a search warrant *are* required.

   Example: One year after *Knotts*, police place a beeper in a can of ether, and then track the beeper in a way that allows them to learn that the beeper is in a particular house. They use this knowledge to obtain a search warrant for the house.

   Held, the monitoring of the beeper to show its location within the house is a Fourth Amendment search. Use of the beeper "reveal[ed] a critical fact about the interior of the premises that the Government [was] extremely interested in knowing and that it could not have otherwise obtained without a warrant." The case is thus distinguishable from *Knotts*, where the beeper merely conveyed the same information as was available to any member of the public who wanted to observe the driver's movements over the public roads. *U.S. v. Karo*, 468 U.S. 705 (1984).

   iv. **GPS or other extended tracking:** *Knotts* involved a standard beeper of 1983 vintage, which was not advanced technology even then. Suppose, however, that the police in a post-*Carpenter* era use a modern-era ***location-tracking device*** such as a "cell site simulator" that enables them to track, cheaply and easily, the movements of a cell phone over long periods of time. Such a device enables far deeper and longer surveillance than a police officer can perform by visual observation. Therefore, it's likely that police use of the device *will* be a Fourth Amendment search for which probable cause and a warrant are required. Thus the situation will need to be analyzed not by the easy-to-satisfy standard used in *Knotts*, but as in the "thermal imager" case of *Kyllo v. U.S.*, *infra*, p. 46, or even by use of the multi-factor test applied to CSLI in *Carpenter v. U.S.*, *supra*, p. 37.

b. **Aerial camera:** Just as short-term use of a primitive beeper was not a search in the 1983 *Knotts* decision, even the use of a sophisticated ***aerial camera*** did not prevent the "plain view" doctrine from applying in 1986's *Dow Chemical Co. supra,* p. 15. The camera in *Dow* was used from a plane overflying D's commercial property, cost $22,000, and the photographs from it could be enlarged to such a degree that objects of one-half inch in diameter were visible. But the Court held that "the mere fact that human vision is enhanced somewhat, at least to the degree here, does not give rise to constitutional problems."

   i. **Not publicly available:** The Court in *Dow* indicated that had the equipment been of a type that was ***not generally available to the public***, the result might have been otherwise. For instance, "an electronic device to ***penetrate walls or windows*** so as to hear and record confidential discussions . . . would raise very different and far more serious questions . . . " But the aerial camera here, although it was a "precise" one, was still merely a "conventional . . . commercial camera commonly used in map-making."[7]

C. **Mechanical devices "not in general public use":** So far, the mechanical devices we have been considering are ones that are in use not just by government but by fairly broad segments of the ***general population***.[8] What happens, however, when government obtains special ***high-tech devices, not in general civilian use***, and employs them from public places to gain "views" that could ***not*** be had by the naked eye. As a result of a 2001 case, the use of such devices will be ***considered a search***. ***Kyllo v. U.S.***, 533 U.S. 27 (2001).

   1. **Thermal imager:** The device in *Kyllo* was a ***thermal imager***, which could be used to produce an image showing the relative amounts of heat escaping from various places in a structure.

   2. **Use of device:** D was a homeowner whom DEA officials suspected of growing marijuana in his home. The officials knew that indoor marijuana cultivation typically requires high-intensity lamps. They therefore set up a thermal imager from the street outside D's house, and pointed it at D's outside walls. The imager detected invisible infrared radiation — heat — and converted it to a visible image showing relative warmth, with cool areas shown as black and hot areas as white. The scan indicated that D's garage was warmer than any part of any adjacent houses; this convinced officers that D was using heat lamps

---

7. A later case, *Kyllo v. U.S.*, immediately *infra*, confirms that the use of high-tech devices that are not generally available to the public, to perceive data that could not be perceived with the naked eye, *won't* qualify for the plain view doctrine and will be a search.

8. For instance, even as long ago as 2013, when *U.S. v. Jones (supra*, p. 18) was decided, it was probably true that the general public could and did use the type of GPS tracker at issue there, one that could wirelessly broadcast the device's location to device's owner. So *Jones* did not raise the issue, which we're exploring here, of government's use of a special high-tech device not available to the general public.

to grow marijuana there. This information, coupled with other data, was enough to convince a judge to issue a search warrant for the house. D indeed turned out to be using heat lamps to grow marijuana.

3. **Contentions of parties:** D contended that the use of the high-tech thermal imager was a "search," which therefore could not be performed without a warrant. But the government argued that the infrared radiation was being released into the outside atmosphere, so that the police's perception of it from a public place should not be deemed to be a search but rather, a plain view.

4. **Court finds a search:** By 5-4 vote, the Court agreed with D that the use of the thermal imager here constituted a search. In a very surprising lineup of the justices, the usually-conservative Justice Scalia wrote the majority opinion (joined by Justices Souter, Thomas, Ginsburg and Breyer), and the usually-liberal Stevens wrote the dissent (joined by Justices Rehnquist, O'Connor and Kennedy).

   a. **Rationale:** The majority began by acknowledging that the degree of privacy afforded to citizens by the Fourth Amendment has shrunk at least somewhat due to the advance of technology. (For instance, the invention of flight has enabled the government to perform aerial observations that were found in *Ciraolo*, *infra*, p. 49, to fall within the plain view doctrine). But, the majority wrote, there was a ***"minimum expectation"*** of privacy that must be maintained; "[t]o withdraw protection of this minimum expectation would be to ***permit police technology to erode the privacy guaranteed by the Fourth Amendment."***

   b. **Test:** The majority then articulated the following test for when use of technology would constitute a search: "we think that obtaining by ***sense-enhancing technology*** any information regarding the ***interior of the home*** that could not otherwise have been obtained without ***physical 'intrusion*** into a constitutionally protected area' . . . ***constitutes a search*** — at least where (as here) the technology in question is ***not in general public use***." This standard would ensure "preservation of that degree of privacy against government that ***existed when the Fourth Amendment was adopted.***"

   c. **Application:** By this standard, the use of the thermal imager here constituted a search. The fact that the device only picked up heat radiating from the "external surface" of the house — a point emphasized by the dissent — was irrelevant to the majority. For "just as a thermal imager captures only heat emanating from a house, so also a powerful ***directional microphone*** picks up only sound emanating from a house — and a satellite capable of scanning from many miles away would pick up only visible light emanating from a house." Using the dissent's "external surface" test "would leave the homeowner ***at the mercy of advancing technology*** — including imaging technology that could discern all human activity in the home."

   d. **Bright-line rule:** The majority said that it was adopting a ***bright-line rule***, clearly specifying those devices that would require a warrant. The court, Scalia said, "must take the long view," and "must take account of the ***more sophisticated systems*** that are already in use or in development."

   e. **No limitation to "intimate details":** Scalia also rejected the government's argument that no search should be found because the imager here was not reporting ***"intimate***

***details.*"** The Fourth Amendment's protection of the home, he said, had never been "tied to measurement of the quality or quantity of information obtained." Also, he concluded, a distinction based upon the degree of intimacy would be unworkable — "[N]o police officer would be able to know in advance whether his through-the-wall surveillance picks up 'intimate' details — and thus would be unable to know in advance whether it is constitutional."

5. **Dissent:** The dissent, by Justice Stevens, relied on the distinction between ***"through-the-wall"*** surveillance and ***"off-the-wall"*** surveillance. In the former, the surveillance gives the observer "direct access to information in a private area," and should therefore be classified as a search. But in the latter case, the surveillance merely takes information "in the public domain," and applies "thought processes" to "draw inferences" from that information; this process should, he said, be treated as falling within the plain view doctrine and thus not be classified as a search.

   a. **Application:** Under this distinction, Stevens said, the thermal imager fell on the public-domain side of the line. "[O]rdinary use of the senses" might enable a neighbor to notice that one part of a building was hotter than another, if, for instance, rainwater evaporated or snow melted at different rates across the building's surfaces. The thermal imager was merely doing the same thing. "Heat waves, like aromas that are generated in a kitchen, or in a laboratory or opium den, ***enter the public domain*** if and when they leave a building." D could not have had a reasonable expectation that these heat waves would remain private.

   b. **Criticism of majority's rule:** Stevens criticized the majority's new rule as "far too broad." That rule covers what the majority called "sense-enhancing technology." It would therefore, Stevens said, cover "potential mechanical substitutes for dogs trained to react when they sniff narcotics," as well as "other new devices that might detect the odor of deadly bacteria or chemicals for making a new type of high explosive."

6. **Limitations on the *Kyllo* approach:** The majority approach in *Kyllo* is not as broad as it might at first appear. Here are some of its important limitations:

   [1] **Interior of home only:** The rule applies only to information "regarding the ***interior of the home.***" Therefore, the Court may well give less protection where sense-enhancing technology is used in a non-residential context, such as in the ***workplace*** or in ***public spaces*** like airports and train stations.

   [2] **Resident or owner:** Because of the court's rules on ***standing*** (see *infra*, p. 321), the *Kyllo* rule probably applies only where the device is used against a ***resident or owner*** of the home in question. For instance, if the police point the device at *A*'s home, and discover evidence implicating *B*, a friend of *A* who does not live at the house, the evidence can presumably be used against *B* even though not against *A*.

   [3] **Not in general public use:** The rule applies only to the extent that the technology "is ***not in general public use***." So as a particular type of technology becomes more broadly used by the civilian population, individuals' privacy interest in being shielded from the technology diminishes.

Example: Suppose that at some point in the future, two percent of American households own a thermal imaging toy, which works essentially the same way as the imager in *Kyllo*. In that event, perhaps use of such a device by police, even when directed to homes, will no longer constitute a Fourth Amendment search.

[4] Police can get warrant: Finally, remember that the rule does not say that the police can't *use* the sense-enhancing device, merely that the device's use constitutes a search, requiring a ***warrant***. In the situation of *Kyllo*, as long as the police had probable cause to suspect that D was growing marijuana in the house, they could have gotten a search warrant either to use the thermal imager or to conduct a search directly.

D. Contorted positions: The fact that the police officer who obtains the "plain view" does so from a ***contorted*** or otherwise unusual ***position*** does not prevent the "plain view" doctrine from applying, assuming that the policeman is in a place where he has a prior right to be (e.g., on public property). For instance, in *Texas v. Brown*, 460 U.S. 730 (1983), a police officer who had legally stopped an automobile "changed [his] position" and "bent down at an angle so [he] could see what was inside" the car. But the fact that the officer got into the unusual position solely for the purpose of observing the contents did not prevent the "plain view" doctrine from applying (and the officer's subsequent warrantless seizure of a balloon containing narcotics inside the car was upheld).

E. Aerial observation: Suppose the police use an ***aircraft*** to view the defendant's property from the air. Assuming that the aircraft is in public, navigable, airspace, ***anything the police can see with the naked eye*** from that airspace falls within the "plain view" doctrine.

1. **Marijuana in backyard:** Thus in ***California v. Ciraolo***, 476 U.S. 227 (1986), police got a tip that D was growing marijuana in his backyard. They rented a private plane, flew over his house at an altitude of 1,000 feet (within navigable airspace), spotted marijuana plants growing in the backyard, and photographed them. Even though D had placed a 10 foot wall around his backyard, thus clearly showing an intent to shield it from passers-by, the overflight did not violate any expectation of privacy "that society is prepared to honor." "The mere fact that an individual has taken measures to restrict some views of his activities [does not] preclude an officer's observations from a public vantage point where he has a right to be and which renders the activities clearly visible. . . . Any member of the public flying in this airspace who glanced down could have seen everything that these officers observed."

   a. **Dissent:** Four dissenters in *Ciraolo*, in an opinion by Justice Powell, thought that the "plain view" doctrine should not be applied here. It was simply not the case that the police were doing no more than a private flier would do, since such fliers "normally obtain at most a fleeting, anonymous, and nondiscriminating glimpse of the landscape and buildings over which they pass," and since members of the public use the airspace for "travel, business, or pleasure, not for the purpose of observing activities taking place within residential yards." The dissenters believed that as a result of the majority's view, "families can expect to be free of official surveillance only when they retreat behind the walls of their homes."

2. **Helicopters:** In *Ciraolo*, the aircraft was a fixed-wing plane that flew at 1,000 feet. Suppose the police use a ***helicopter***, and because of the unusual features of helicopters (as dis-

tinguished from fixed-wing aircraft) the police are able to fly much ***lower***. In *Florida v. Riley*, 488 U.S. 445 (1989), a five-Justice majority held that even a view taken by the police from a helicopter flying only ***400 feet*** above the ground still fell within the "plain view" doctrine, and was therefore not a search.

F. Use of other senses: The "plain view" doctrine can apply where items are discovered through the use of ***senses other than sight*** (e.g., touch, hearing or smell). If a police officer who is in a place where he has a right to be can discover the probable existence of contraband, evidence of crime, etc. through one of these other senses, the "plain view" doctrine apparently applies, permitting immediate seizure of the item.

1. **"Plain touch":** In the one case in which the Supreme Court has applied the use of a sense other than sight by analogy to the "plain view" doctrine, the Court upheld a ***"plain touch"*** or ***"plain feel"*** corollary to the plain-view doctrine. In *Minnesota v. Dickerson*, 508 U.S. 366 (1993), the Court held that where an officer is conducting a ***frisk*** or ***pat-down*** pursuant to *Terry v. Ohio* (see *infra*, p. 148), the officer may seize any object which his sense of touch gives him probable cause to believe is contraband, a weapon, or some other form of evidence. (But on the actual facts of *Dickerson* itself, the Court held that the officer doing the frisk, during the time he was still within the legitimate bounds of that frisk, did not yet have probable cause to believe that he was feeling contraband, so that the officer's seizure of a lump was not justified. The case is further discussed *infra*, p. 164.)

   a. **Must have right to do the touching:** But the "plain touch" corollary to plain view will apply only if the officer in fact ***had the right to do the touching*** or feeling in the first place. If the officer's act of touching was itself a violation of the person's reasonable expectation of privacy, then the officer is ***not*** entitled to use what he has learned from the touching as the basis for probable cause to continue with the search. Thus what made the officer's touching legal in *Dickerson* was that the officer was at that moment already entitled, under *Terry*, to conduct the frisk.

      Example: A member of the U.S. Border Patrol boards a Greyhound bus as part of a legal border search. The agent walks up and down the bus and squeezes each piece of soft luggage stored in the overhead luggage racks. When he squeezes D's bag, he feels a brick-like substance inside that seems like contraband. He opens the bag, and finds that the brick-like thing is indeed illegal methamphetamine. *Held*, for D: when the agent first squeezed D's bag, the squeezing violated D's reasonable expectation of privacy. Therefore, his perception of the brick-like object did not furnish him with properly-obtained probable cause to then open the bag. *Bond v. U.S.*, 529 U.S. 334 (2000).

2. **"Plain odor":** The Supreme Court has also implicitly indicated that the "plain view" doctrine may sometimes apply to ***smell***. In *U.S. v. Johns*, 469 U.S. 478 (1985) (discussed more fully *infra*, p. 137), drug enforcement officials stopped a truck, and seized from it parcels that smelled of marijuana. The Court did not decide whether there should be a ***"plain odor"*** doctrine, but it did note that "whether [Ds] ever had a privacy interest in the packages reeking of marijuana is debatable. We have previously observed that certain containers may not support a reasonable expectation of privacy because their contents can be inferred from their outward appearance. . . . "

a. **Summary:** Thus the matter of "plain odor" seizures must be viewed as open, but with the probability being that the Court will approve a "plain odor" analog to the "plain view" and "plain touch" doctrines.

b. **Canine "sniff test":** Another hint that the Supreme Court effectively recognizes a "plain odor" doctrine in at least some instances stems from a pair of holdings by the Court that the use of dogs to perform a ***canine "sniff test"*** to detect illegal drugs did not constitute a Fourth Amendment "search" at all. One of these upheld a sniffing of the outside of a person's ***luggage*** at an airport (*U.S. v. Place*, 462 U.S. 696 (1983)); the other upheld the sniffing of the outside of a person's ***car*** during a proper traffic-ticket stop (*Illinois v. Caballes*, 543 U.S. 405 (2005)).

   In *Place*, the Court reasoned that since a sniff test by a well-trained dog "discloses only the presence or absence of narcotics, a ***contraband*** item," the sniff test ***does not compromise any legitimate privacy interest*** of the person whose possessions are being sniffed (because no one has the right to possess contraband, and thus no right to object to the disclosure that she is in possession of contraband). Then in *Caballes*, the Court relied on *Place* to hold that since D's car was properly stopped for a traffic violation, the use of a dog to sniff around the exterior of his car for contraband did not amount to an extra Fourth Amendment intrusion (and thus could legally occur even in the absence of any suspicion of drug activity).

   i. **Test for odor of contraband:** So *Place* and *Caballes*, *supra*, clearly mean that if the police, while standing in a place they have a right to be, use a dog to perform an odor test that merely determines whether ***contraband*** is present or not, ***no search takes place,*** because no information about a legally-possessable substance is being revealed. However, these two canine-sniff cases do ***not*** answer the more general question of whether government may rely on a "plain odor" doctrine to run canine sniff tests in public places to find the existence of substances that may be ***legally possessed***.

      Example: Suppose that a particular type of explosive, PETN, emits a characteristic odor whose presence a dog (but not a human) can be trained to detect. Suppose further that while PETN is often possessed by criminals and terrorists, it is also frequently possessed perfectly legally by private citizens. If government were to run canine PETN tests on cars stopped for traffic violations or parked in public parking lots — i.e., in situations where there is no articulable basis for suspecting criminal activity — it's not clear whether the use of the dogs to detect the telltale odor would constitute a Fourth Amendment search. A strong case can be made that this *would* be a Fourth Amendment search, because a person has a legitimate expectation of privacy as to a legally-possessable substance in his car that cannot be detected from the street by human senses.

   ii. **Sniff gives probable cause:** If a trained dog, standing in a public place, signals that he has detected the odor of drugs coming from inside a private place (e.g., a car), the dog's signal can give officers ***probable cause*** to believe that drugs are present inside that place. See, e.g., yet another "canine sniff" case, *Florida v. Harris*, 133 S.Ct. 1050 (2013) (*infra*, p. 61), where the Court unanimously held that a signal by a properly-trained drug-sniffing dog indicating that the car outside which he was standing contained marijuana gave the dog's police handler probable cause to search the car's interior.

iii. **Police must have a right to be where the sniff occurs:** However, keep in mind that police use of a sniffer dog even to determine solely whether contraband is present can avoid being a Fourth Amendment search only if the police and the dog are ***standing in a place where they have a legal right to be.*** So, for instance, if the police acting without a warrant or permission enter the ***"curtilage" of D's house*** and then conduct a canine odor test, they have clearly performed a Fourth Amendment search, even if the dog has been trained to detect only the odor of drugs and other contraband. That's the direct consequence of *Florida v. Jardines*, 133 S.Ct. 1409 (2013) (*supra*, p. 20), where five justices agreed that police use of a dog to sniff for the odor of drugs on D's front porch (part of the curtilage) was a search, regardless of whether D had a legitimate expectation of privacy as to non-human-smellable odors escaping from his house onto the porch.

c. **Sense-enhancing technology:** In any event, any "plain odor" doctrine would probably ***not apply*** where the police are employing ***high-tech "sense enhancing" technology.*** *Kyllo v. U.S.* (*supra*, p. 46), the thermal-imaging case, suggests that if the police were to use a machine to detect odors, this *would* constitute a search, at least if it were directed at a home, and if the device were not one generally used by the public. See Justice Steven's remark in his dissent in *Kyllo*, criticizing the majority's opinion in part because the majority's requirement of a warrant would also apply to "the use of other new devices that might detect the odor of deadly bacteria or chemicals for making a new type of high explosive[.]"

Example: On the above example of government tests for PETN explosive, suppose the government uses a high-tech machine, rather than a dog, to test for PETN in the air in public places. The Court's logic in *Kyllo* suggests that this *would* be a Fourth Amendment search or seizure if directed at a home, car, or other place whose owner had a legitimate expectation of privacy. (However, the search or seizure might well be found to be a *reasonable* one — and permissible as a regulatory search [*infra*, p. 171] — given the minimal nature of the intrusion and the severity of the risk of, say, terrorist car bombings.)

G. **Plain view where police on defendant's property:** The plain view doctrine may apply not only where the police obtain the view from public property, but also where they are ***lawfully on the owner's property***. Thus where the police come to a person's house to lawfully arrest him, any observation they make while in the process of arresting him does not constitute a Fourth Amendment search.

1. **Degree of scrutiny:** Most courts have extended the plain-view-while-lawfully-on-defendant's-property rule far enough to allow even fairly close scrutiny of the defendant's possessions.

Example: A postal inspector is in D's apartment by consent. He sees a rifle on a wall rack, and picks it up to read its serial number.

Held, there was "no intrusion into [D's] privacy beyond that to which he had expressly consented." *U.S. v. Catanzaro*, 282 F. Supp. 68 (S.D.N.Y. 1968).

2. **Inspection of contents of container:** However, if a ***package*** or ***container*** is in plain view, its ***contents*** cannot normally be inspected under the plain view doctrine. For instance, in *Walter v. U.S.*, 447 U.S. 649 (1980), FBI agents came into legitimate possession of a previously-opened box of obscene movies. The Supreme Court held that this did not entitle the agents to ***screen*** the films; "an officer's authority to possess a package is distinct from his authority to examine its contents." See also *U.S. v. Chadwick* (discussed *infra*, p. 100) (right of police to seize foot locker does not imply right to open and inspect foot locker's contents).

   a. **Inspection of contents of container in car:** But if a closed container is found during a valid warrantless search of an ***automobile***, it may usually be opened and its contents searched. This is ***not*** done pursuant to the "plain view" doctrine, but rather as an extension of the automobile-search exception to the warrant requirement. See *U.S. v. Ross*, 456 U.S. 798 (1982), discussed *infra*, p. 136.

3. **Police illegally on defendant's property:** Suppose that the police are ***illegally on the defendant's property***, and then have the plain view into a building. Even here, the plain view doctrine may apply so that there is no Fourth Amendment search. This will be the case, for instance, if the police were trespassing on defendant's ***open fields*** — anything outside the "curtilage" — at the time they had the plain view. See, e.g., *U.S. v. Dunn*, discussed *supra*, p. 22, where the police trespassed onto D's fields and then looked into his barn; because the police were not standing within the curtilage, the plain view doctrine applied and there was no search, even assuming that D had a justifiable expectation of privacy as to the contents of the barn.

V. PROBABLE CAUSE GENERALLY

A. **Applicability of probable cause:** The Fourth Amendment provides that no warrant, whether for search or arrest, be issued unless there is ***"probable cause."*** The term "probable cause" is an abstract one. Basically, it means that the law enforcement officials in question must have trustworthy evidence that would make a reasonable person think it ***more likely than not that the proposed arrest or search is justified***.

   1. **Also required in warrantless cases:** Although the Fourth Amendment does not explicitly require the existence of probable cause prior to a ***warrantless*** arrest or search (permitted in situations described below), the case law requires that such probable cause nonetheless be present. If this were not the case, the requirements for arrest and search would be less stringent in the warrantless case than in the situation where a warrant is sought, and the policy of encouraging warrants would be thwarted. See *Wong Sun v. U.S.*, 371 U.S. 471 (1963).

      Note: The means by which the existence of probable cause is determined prior to search or arrest is not the same in the warrantless situation as in the warrant case. In the former, it is the police themselves who make the determination whether probable cause exists. In the latter, it is a neutral magistrate (described *infra*, p. 62) who judges the existence of probable cause. In either case, the existence of probable cause can later be reviewed by the trial judge at a *suppression hearing* (i.e., a hearing to determine whether particular evidence was obtained in violation of the Fourth Amendment and therefore inadmissible).

Note: Most of the material in this section concerns the means by which probable cause is determined when a warrant is applied for. In most cases, a set of facts which would establish probable cause for purposes of procuring a warrant would also supply probable cause for acting without a warrant in those situations where warrantless arrests or searches are permitted. The Supreme Court has indicated that in a very close case, a slightly lower standard for probable cause might be applied where a warrant was sought than where the search or arrest occurred without warrant, but generally the test is the same for both cases.

B. Basic requirements for probable cause: Although probable cause is required for both searches and arrests, the meaning of the term is not exactly the same in the two situations.

1. **Probable cause to arrest:** For probable cause to ***arrest*** a person to exist, two conclusions must be justified by substantial, trustworthy, evidence:

   a. that a ***violation of the law has been committed***; and

   b. that the ***person to be arrested committed the violation***.

2. **Probable cause to search:** For there to be probable cause to ***search*** particular premises, the conclusions which must be supported by the evidence are:

   a. that the specific items to be searched for are ***connected with criminal activity***; and

   b. that these items will be ***found in the place to be searched.***

   Note: Observe that a given state of evidence might establish probable cause for arrest but not for search, or vice versa. For instance, the police might have reliable evidence that a particular individual had committed a certain crime, but no reason at all to believe that evidence of the crime could be discovered at the suspect's home. There would, in this situation, be probable cause for arrest but not for search.

C. No admissibility limitation: Any trustworthy information may be considered in determining whether probable cause to search or arrest exists, ***even if the information would not be admissible at trial.***

1. **Non-admissible items used:** Thus the police may use ***hearsay*** information as part of their showing of probable cause, or even a ***prior criminal record*** of the suspect. (Nutshell, p. 101.) The reliability of the information will, of course, depend in part on its source, and certain kinds of information (e.g., a prior criminal record) will never by themselves be enough to establish probable cause; but the magistrate may consider any evidence, no matter where it comes from, in making his decision on probable cause.

D. Only evidence heard by magistrate used: Probable cause for the issuance of a warrant must be judged only by reference to the ***facts presented to the magistrate*** who is to issue the warrant. Thus if the police do not present to the magistrate evidence sufficient to establish probable cause, but the warrant is issued anyway and is later challenged in a suppression hearing, the warrant cannot be retroactively validated by police testimony that they had other facts not presented to the magistrate. "The question is whether the magistrate acted properly, not whether the police officer did." (Nutshell, p. 99.)

1. **Rationale:** The requirement that a warrant's validity be tested only by reference to facts presented to the magistrate forces the police to ***put on record the state of their information before the search or arrest***. They are thus prevented from conducting a search without probable cause, discovering new evidence during the search, and asserting at the suppression hearing that they knew these new facts all along. In fact, the major justification for the requirement that warrants be (in most situations) obtained is to establish a written record by which probable cause may later be judged. As the Supreme Court said with reference to the rule requiring affidavits to be judged only by information presented to the magistrate, "a contrary rule would, of course, render the warrant requirements of the Fourth Amendment meaningless." *Whiteley v. Warden*, 401 U.S. 560 (1971).

2. **Perjured affidavit:** The defendant may sometimes have a search warrant invalidated on the grounds that ***perjured police testimony*** was used to get it. In *Franks v. Delaware*, 438 U.S. 154 (1978), the Supreme Court held that where the defendant can show, by a preponderance of the evidence, that affidavits used to obtain the warrant contain ***perjury*** by the affiant, or a ***"reckless disregard for the truth"*** by him, and the rest of the affidavit does not contain materials sufficient to constitute probable cause, the warrant will be invalidated. (The fruits of the search will then be excluded just as if the affidavit did not contain allegations sufficient to constitute probable cause.)

   a. **Right to hearing:** The Court in *Franks* further held that once the defendant makes a "substantial preliminary showing" that the affidavit contains such perjured or reckless testimony by the affiant, he is entitled to a ***hearing*** on the issue, at which he may cross-examine the police officer who applied for the warrant, and any other witnesses, in his attempt to suppress the warrant. But *Franks* does not allow the defendant to knock out the warrant merely because it contains inaccurate material; a showing of actual perjury or reckless disregard of the truth, by the affiant himself (not merely by the affiant's sources, such as informers) must be made.

E. **Facts as reasonably believed by police:** As noted above, information not disclosed to the magistrate cannot be used to retroactively validate a warrant. Conversely, a warrant will not be rendered ***invalid*** if it later turns out that the police erroneously (but reasonably and honestly) believed the information they gave the magistrate.

F. **Required degree of probability:** Exactly ***how probable*** must an event be before there is "probable cause" to believe it?

1. **"More than likely":** A number of earlier cases suggested — although they did not expressly state — that for the police to have probable cause to believe that fact X existed, they would have to reasonably believe that fact X was ***more likely than not.***

   Example: The police have information that a rape has been committed by a masked black man. They arrest all three of the blacks who had access to the cellar where the rape took place. *Held*, probable cause was lacking for each arrest: "Presumably, whomever the police arrest they must arrest on 'probable cause.' It is not the function of the police to arrest, as it were, at large, and to use an interrogating process at police headquarters in order to determine whom they should charge before a committing magistrate on 'probable cause.' " *Mallory v. U.S.*, 354 U.S. 449 (1957).

2. **Less than 50-50 chance:** But at least one much more recent case suggests that as long as the police have "particularized suspicion" regarding the existence of fact X, they need ***not*** reasonably believe that fact X exists more likely than not. For example, that case seems to mean that a ***1/3 chance*** of fact X *can* constitute probable cause.

   Example: The police properly stop a car for speeding. There are three occupants: the driver; D (who is the front-seat passenger); and a rear-seat passenger. The officer asks the driver for his license and registration; when the driver opens the glove compartment, the officer sees a bundle of rolled-up money in the glove compartment. The driver then gives consent for the vehicle to be searched, and during that search the officer finds (1) $763 cash in the glove compartment; and (2) five baggies of cocaine behind the rear-seat armrest. The officer questions all three men about the ownership of the drugs and money, and none of them says anything. The officer therefore arrests all three. At the station house, D confesses that the cocaine belonged to him. At trial, D tries to get the confession suppressed as the fruit of an arrest that was illegal because the officer had no probable cause to arrest D (since he was only one of three people in the car, and there was nothing to tie him to the drugs at the moment of arrest).

   Held, for the prosecution: Probable cause to arrest D existed. The cash was in the glove compartment directly in front of D, and the cocaine was behind the back-seat armrest accessible to all three men. None of the three gave the officer any information with respect to the ownership of the either the money or the cocaine. Therefore, "We think it an entirely reasonable inference from these facts that *any or all three* of the occupants had knowledge of, and exercised dominion and control over, the cocaine. Thus a reasonable officer could conclude that there was probable cause to believe [D] committed the crime of possession of cocaine, either *solely or jointly*." (emphasis added.) *Maryland v. Pringle*, 540 U.S. 366 (2003).

   Note: It's the Court's use of the phrases "any or all three" and "solely or jointly" that would lead a careful reader to believe that *Pringle* stands for the proposition that a 1/3 chance of fact X's existence can be enough for probable cause. The words "any" and "solely" certainly seem to mean that for the *Pringle* Court, even apart from the possibility that the three men were *jointly* in possession of the cocaine, there was probable cause to believe that *D alone* was in possession. Cf. K,L,I&K, nn. 1 and 2. Since there was nothing to suggest that D, the front-seat passenger, was more likely to be the sole owner of the cocaine in the back seat than were either of the other two occupants, the Court must have been satisfied that a probability no higher than 1/3 that D was the possessor sufficed for probable cause to arrest him.

3. **Random searches of groups:** But even for today's Court, clearly there is some minimum possibility of fact X's existence — even if we can't pinpoint it numerically — that is required before there is probable cause to believe that X exists. For instance, suppose the police properly search a bar, and find cocaine on a seat, when there are 10 people in the bar and there's no way to determine who was sitting at that seat before the search got under way. It's unlikely that even the present Court would conclude that the police had probable cause to arrest all 10 occupants of the bar. Cf. *Ybarra v. Illinois*, discussed *infra*,

p. 70 (not exactly on point, but saying that when the police are properly searching a bar and its bartender for drugs, they do not thereby have probable cause to search each patron on the premises, because the probable cause to search a person must be "particularized with respect to that person").

VI. PARTICULAR INFORMATION ESTABLISHING PROBABLE CAUSE

A. **Evidence from officer's own observation:** In some situations, probable cause for a search or arrest can be established from the police officer's own personal knowledge. In the case of an arrest, for instance, some of the kinds of evidence which a police officer might acquire first-hand and which could contribute to probable cause, are:

1. the ***flight*** of a suspect when approached by the policeman;
2. ***physical clues*** (e.g., footprints or fingerprints linked to a particular person);
3. ***voluntary admissions*** by a suspect;
4. ***suspicious or surreptitious conduct***;
5. a suspect's ***previous criminal record***;
6. a suspect's presence in a ***high-crime area***.

B. **Information from informants:** Frequently, the information on which probable cause is based comes from ***informants*** who are themselves engaged in criminal activity. Because police informants often have an incentive to gain the police's good graces by furnishing information of dubious veracity, the courts have generally applied stringent tests for determining whether an informant's testimony establishes probable cause.

1. **"Totality of the circumstances" test:** The Supreme Court has decided that the issue of whether an informant's information creates probable cause for a search or arrest is to be determined by the ***"totality of the circumstances." Illinois v. Gates***, 462 U.S. 213 (1983). In essence, this means that in a case involving an informant's information, the probable cause issue will be resolved in essentially the same manner as in cases where the facts come from other sources (e.g., direct observation by police officers).

   a. **Prior doctrine:** *Gates* overruled prior doctrine, under which material from an informant had to meet ***two separate tests*** ("prongs") before it would constitute probable cause for a warrant:

      i. **First prong:** First, there had to be evidence (usually in the form of an affidavit from the officer seeking the warrant) that the informant was a ***reliable witness*** (either because he had been reliable in the past, or because there were special reasons to believe that his information in ***this particular case*** was reliable); and

      ii. **Second prong:** Second, there had to be facts showing the ***"basis of knowledge"*** of the informant, that is, the particular means by which he came upon the information which he supplied to the police.

2. **Overruled in *Gates:*** *Gates* directly ***overruled*** this two-prong test. As the result of *Gates*, so long as a neutral magistrate can reasonably determine that, based on the informant's information and all other available facts, there is probable cause to believe that a search or arrest is justified, he may issue the warrant.

   a. **Facts:** In *Gates*, the Bloomington, Ill. police received an anonymous letter stating that a couple named Susan and Lance Gates were drug dealers, that Susan would drive their car to Florida on May 3, and that Lance would fly down shortly thereafter, and drive the car back with $100,000 worth of drugs in the trunk. The police confirmed that a Lance Gates lived in Bloomington, and that a reservation in his name had been made to fly to West Palm Beach on May 5. Cooperative federal drug officials put Lance under surveillance when he arrived in West Palm Beach, followed him to a hotel room registered in Susan's name, and saw Gates and a woman (presumably Susan) drive northbound on the highway early the next morning, in a car registered to Lance. The Bloomington police, citing these facts, obtained a search warrant for the Gates' residence and car. When the Gates arrived in Bloomington, the police were waiting, and searched their car and house, finding drugs in both places.

   b. **Holding:** The Supreme Court concluded that there was probable cause for issuance of the search warrant. In reaching this conclusion, the Court abandoned the requirement of two independent prongs; instead, it held that the two prongs should be treated as "relevant considerations in the totality of circumstances analysis that traditionally has guided probable cause determinations."

   c. **Strong factor makes up for weak one:** The direct consequence of the holding in *Gates* is that a ***strong showing*** on one of the prongs can in effect make up for an inadequate showing on the other one. For instance, as the Court said in *Gates* itself, if a particular informant is known for being unusually reliable, his failure to set forth the basis of his knowledge in a particular case will not be an absolute bar to a finding of probable cause based on his tip. Similarly, even if there is reason to be suspicious of the informant's motives (thus reducing his general reliability), his detailed description of wrongdoing, along with a statement that he observed the event first-hand (satisfying the "basis of knowledge" prong) may be enough to make his tip rise to the level of probable cause.

   d. **Corroboration:** Also, ***corroboration*** of aspects of the informant's story may be combined with the story itself, in determining whether there is probable cause. This is especially likely to be the case where (as in *Gates*): (1) the informant's identity is not known to the police; and (2) the corroboration is of the ***future actions*** of third parties that are ordinarily not easily predicted. Thus in *Gates*, the fact that the informant correctly predicted that Lance Gates would fly to Florida sometime shortly after May 3, and that he would drive the family car back again immediately thereafter, justified a magistrate in concluding that it was "not unlikely" that the informant also had access to reliable information about the Gates' alleged illegal activities. (The tip by itself was clearly not sufficient to establish probable cause, the Court noted, since it established ***neither*** the informant's reliability nor how he came about his information.)

3. **Criticism:** Many commentators believe that the biggest danger in permitting liberal use of anonymous informants' tips is that the police will ***invent*** fictitious informants in order

to procure a warrant for which they would not otherwise have probable cause (at least probable cause obtained through legal means), or in order to establish probable cause retroactively for a warrantless search or arrest. The *Gates* Court's abandonment of the two-prong *Aguilar* test makes these dangers even more real. For instance, suppose the Bloomington police in *Gates* had learned about the Gates' plans for a particular Florida drug trip not through an informant, but through an ***illegal wiretap*** on the Gates' phone. It would have been an easy matter for an officer to write an "anonymous" letter solely for the purpose of obtaining a warrant (even including a "prediction" of Gates' flight, which might already have been known to have occurred by the time such a letter was written). Even the two-prong test is no guarantee that such a thing could not happen, but abandonment of that test gives the magistrate less cause to scrutinize such a letter to determine its genuineness.

4. **Identity of informer:** Nothing in the Fourth Amendment requires the police to divulge the ***identity*** of their informant either to the magistrate, or in the subsequent suppression hearing. As long as the magistrate is persuaded, and reasonably so, that the affiant policeman is truthfully describing what the informant told him, the informant does not have to be produced, or his identity disclosed. Similarly, at the suppression hearing, the informant does not have to be produced or identified, as long as the police officers testify in detail as to what the informer told them, and why they had reason to believe his information was trustworthy. The police officers must, however, be subjected at the suppression hearing to any ***cross-examination*** which the defense attorney wishes to make concerning the reliability or existence of their informant; only the latter's identity is privileged. See *McCray v. Illinois*, 386 U.S. 300 (1967).

   a. **Criticism:** The Supreme Court in *McCray*, in justifying its refusal to require the divulging of an informant's identity, stated "Nothing in the Due Process Clause of the Fourteenth Amendment requires a state court judge in every [suppression] hearing to assume that the arresting officers are committing perjury." Many commentators have criticized this statement, and the holding of *McCray* generally, on the grounds that it actually induces police perjury.

5. **Lesser suspicion needed for stop:** Just as the "totality of the circumstances" test is now used to determine whether an informant's information creates probable cause for a search or arrest (*Gates*, *supra*, p. 57), that "totality" test is also used to determine whether an informant's information is sufficiently reliable that although it does not furnish probable cause, it provides the ***"reasonable suspicion"*** needed to make an ***"investigatory stop."*** *Alabama v. White*, 496 U.S. 325 (1990). *White* is discussed further in the context of "stop and frisk" law, *infra*, p. 154.

C. **Suspect's criminal reputation:** A suspect's ***reputation*** for past criminal activity may be considered in determining probable cause, if supporting facts indicating past criminality are also present. ***U.S. v. Harris***, 403 U.S. 573 (1971).

   1. **Facts of *Harris:*** *Harris* involved the existence of probable cause for a search of the premises of a suspect thought to be running an illegal still. The affidavit supporting the request for a search warrant included the statement that "[The suspect] has had a reputation with me for over four years as being a trafficker of non-tax-paid distilled spirits, and over this period I have received numerous information from all types of persons as to his activities." The affidavit also stated that a colleague of the affiant officer had "located a

sizeable stash of illicit whiskey in an abandoned house under [the suspect's] control during this period of time." Finally, the affidavit stated that an informant had himself purchased illegal whiskey from the suspect.

2. **Reputation evidence allowed:** The Supreme Court concluded that the affiant's statement that the suspect had a criminal reputation could be considered by the magistrate as part of the determination of whether probable cause to search existed. The Court appeared to hold that while a suspect's reputation for criminality can never by itself be enough to demonstrate probable cause, that reputation can be combined with ***factual statements*** about the suspect's past criminal activity, such as the statement that Harris had been found to have whiskey on his premises before.

3. **Declaration against interest:** The Court in *Harris* attached great importance to the fact that the informant's information constituted an admission that the informant had ***violated the law***. "Admissions of crime, like admissions against proprietary interests, carry their own indicia of credibility — sufficient at least to support a finding of probable cause to search." The Court asserted that the fact that the informant might have been paid or promised a "break" "does not eliminate the residual risk and opprobrium of having admitted criminal conduct."

D. **Information from non-criminal sources:** The informants discussed in the preceding section were generally ones who were themselves engaged in criminal activity, often the same activity as was the suspect. Sometimes, however, the police will procure information from ***non-criminal sources*** (e.g., ordinary citizens, victims of crime, other police officers, etc.) In such cases, the courts have been ***more lenient*** concerning the information which must be presented to demonstrate the informant's reliability.

1. **Ordinary citizen:** Most courts have presumed that the ***ordinary citizen*** who is either a victim of crime or an eyewitness to crime is a reliable informant, even though his reliability has not been previously tested. See, e.g., *U.S. v. Lewis*, 738 F.2d 916 (8th Cir. 1984). The Supreme Court's "totality of the circumstances" test (see *Illinois v. Gates*, *supra*, p. 57) presumably means that the usual reliability of law-abiding citizens will be a factor which the magistrate may take into account in determining whether probable cause exists. But some evidence of how the citizen informant came by his information will probably also be needed in such situations, even though it is not flatly required as a matter of law, as it was before *Gates*.

2. **Other police officers:** Sometimes the police officer making an affidavit for a warrant (or making a warrantless search or arrest) will act in response to ***statements made by other police officers***. A police officer may, for instance, respond to a radio alert, or to orders from his superior, or to a post office poster. A Supreme Court decision, ***Whiteley v. Warden***, 401 U.S. 560 (1971) implies that in such circumstances, the arrest or search is valid only if the ***maker*** of the original alert, order, or poster acted with probable cause.

   a. ***Whiteley* case:** In *Whiteley*, the Laramie, Wyoming police arrested two men who fit a description given in a bulletin issued by the Carbon County Sheriff, and transmitted over the state police radio network. The bulletin stated that the men were wanted for breaking and entering, and that a warrant had been issued for their arrest. The warrant turned out to have been issued without probable cause, but the arresting officers claimed that the arrest was nonetheless legal, because "they reasonably assumed that whoever authorized the bulletin had probable cause to direct [the suspects'] arrest."

b. **Probable cause lacking in *Whiteley:*** The Supreme Court disagreed with this assertion. The Court held that if it turned out that the original warrant had been issued without probable cause, "an otherwise illegal arrest cannot be insulated from challenge by the decision of the instigating officer to rely on fellow officers to make the arrest."

3. **Police informant's reliability:** Where one police officer acts on information relayed to her by a fellow officer, the courts have generally presumed that the latter is a credible informant, just as a similar presumption is made with respect to a noncriminal citizen informant. Again, however, there will usually need to be an explanation of how the informant came by his information.

4. **Trained sniffer dog as reliable informant:** A ***dog*** that is trained to ***sniff the odor*** of drugs or other contraband, and to alert his handlers to the contraband, can be the source of probable cause, the Supreme Court has held. The ***reliability*** of the dog as an "informant" is to be determined by the same ***"totality of the circumstances"*** rule that applies to humans under *Gates*, *supra*. This standard means that if the dog has satisfactorily performed in an odor-detection ***training course***, that fact alone will typically allow the dog's "I smell drugs here" alert to constitute probable cause. ***Florida v. Harris***, 133 S.Ct. 1050 (2013).

Example: O, a police officer, properly makes a routine traffic stop of D's truck. O has with him Aldo, a trained drug-detecting dog. Aldo stands by the driver's-side door handle, and indicates (in the manner he has been trained to do) that he smells marijuana. O treats Aldo's signal as giving O probable cause to search the interior of the truck. O does the search, does not find marijuana, but does find methamphetamine, for the possession of which D is prosecuted. The Florida Supreme Court rules that Aldo's signal could constitute probable cause to believe the truck contained contraband only if the prosecution establishes Aldo's reliability by presenting extensive evidence of the dog's record of "hits" and "misses" in the field (which the prosecution didn't do here).

Held (by the Supreme Court in a unanimous opinion), for the prosecution — the Florida court's rule of evidence is reversed. It's true that for an alert by a drug-sniffing dog to constitute probable cause, the dog must be shown to be a reliable source of information, just as with a human informer. But the decision of whether an informer (dog or human) is reliable enough to give rise to probable cause is to be determined under the *Gates* "totality of the circumstances" test. And evidence that the dog has had a "satisfactory performance in a ***certification or training program*** can itself provide sufficient reason to trust his alert." (But the defendant must be given the opportunity in a suppression hearing to challenge this evidence of the dog's reliability, such as by cross-examining the handler about the dog's in-field performance.) Here, since Aldo was shown to have completed two drug-detection courses and to have maintained his proficiency through weekly training exercises, that was enough to establish that his alert outside of D's truck constituted probable cause for O's vehicle search. *Florida v. Harris*, *supra*.

VII. SEARCH WARRANTS — ISSUANCE AND EXECUTION

A. Who may issue: A search warrant is a document authorizing a law enforcement official to make a search, and is issued by a "judicial officer" or "magistrate." We shall use the term ***"magistrate"*** here.

1. Neutrality: The magistrate must be a ***neutral party*** detached from the law enforcement side of government. The magistrate's neutrality increases the probability that a correct decision as to the existence of probable cause will be reached before an arrest or search is made, and that unconstitutional arrests and searches will be kept to a minimum.

Example: New Hampshire state law authorizes the state Attorney General to issue search warrants. The Attorney General issues such a warrant in a case the investigation of which he is directing. Because the Attorney General is not "the neutral and detached magistrate required by the Constitution," the warrant is invalid. *Coolidge v. New Hampshire*, 403 U.S. 443 (1971).

a. Pecuniary interest: If the official issuing the warrant has a ***pecuniary interest*** affecting his judgment about whether to issue a warrant, he may fail to be a "neutral and detached magistrate," in which case the warrant is ineffective.

Example: A Justice of the Peace in Georgia receives no salary, and is compensated principally by the $5 fee he receives every time he issues a warrant. He receives nothing if he rejects a warrant application. Therefore, he is not a "neutral and detached magistrate," the search warrant issued by him is invalid, and the search conducted pursuant to it is a violation of the Fourth Amendment. *Connally v. Georgia*, 429 U.S. 245 (1977).

b. Magistrate who leads search: Similarly, a magistrate who not only accompanies the police to the scene of a search, but ***actively participates in the search***, is not "neutral and detached." *Lo-Ji Sales, Inc. v. New York*, 442 U.S. 319 (1979). In *Lo-Ji Sales*, the magistrate in a pornography investigation signed a search warrant listing two items, then accompanied the police to the suspect's store, where he examined dozens of items, making a decision about which ones should be seized as obscene. The Court invalidated the search and its fruit because of the magistrate's lack of neutrality.

2. Statutory authorization: The magistrate must be authorized by statute to issue warrants.

a. Federal courts: In the federal courts, "magistrate judges" are special-purpose judges who handle pre-trial matters, including issuance of warrants, under the direction of district judges. See 18 U.S.C. §3060.

b. State courts: In state courts, clerks of the state court, justices of the peace, and even municipal court clerks may constitutionally be authorized by statute to issue warrants.

Example: In *Shadwick v. City of Tampa*, 407 U.S. 345 (1972), the Supreme Court held that a statutorily-authorized municipal court clerk could constitutionally issue arrest warrants for municipal ordinance violations.

B. Affidavit: In virtually all jurisdictions, the policeman seeking a search warrant must put the facts establishing probable cause into a ***written, signed, affidavit***. The submission of an affidavit may even be a constitutional requirement, although as noted above (*supra*, p. 55), the courts are split as to whether the police may show at the suppression hearing that facts not contained in the affidavit were presented orally to the magistrate.

1. **Particular description:** Because the Fourth Amendment requires that the warrant itself "particularly describe . . . the place to be searched, and the . . . things to be seized," the affidavit should contain this information. The requirement of particularity of description in the warrant is discussed *infra*, p. 63.

2. **Stale information:** Since the affidavit must establish probable cause to believe that the requested search will reveal the particular items sought, the information in the affidavit must be sufficiently ***recent*** to allow the magistrate to reasonably believe that the items have not yet been removed from the premises to be searched. The required degree of recentness will depend in part on whether the crime pursuant to which the search is sought is an ongoing violation, or a "one-shot" offense.

C. *Ex parte* nature of warrant: The proceeding for issuing a warrant is ***ex parte***. That is, the suspect whose premises are to be searched ***does not have the opportunity to contest the issuance of the warrant***; only the policeman's side of the story is heard by the magistrate. However, the suspect will have the chance to show, at a suppression hearing, that the warrant was issued without probable cause.

D. Requirement of particular description: The Fourth Amendment requires that a warrant contain a ***particular description of the premises to be searched, and the things to be seized***. The courts have interpreted this language to require that the warrant be specific enough that a police officer executing it, even if he had no initial connection with the case, would know where to search and what items to seize.

1. **Place to be searched:** The courts have not required absolute, technical accuracy in the description of the premises. The description must merely be precise enough that the officer executing the warrant can ascertain, perhaps even by asking questions of people in the neighborhood, where he should search.

   Example: A warrant describes the premises to be searched as "325 Adkinson Street." The house intended to be searched is at the corner of Adkinson and Short Streets, but its true address is "325 Short Street." The officer executing the warrant goes to the correct house and searches it.

   Held, the warrant was valid. The two-part test is: (1) whether the warrant enables the officer to "locate and identify the premises with reasonable effort"; and (2) whether there is "any reasonable probability that another premises might be mistakenly searched." Here, these two standards were satisfied. *Lyons v. Robinson*, 783 F.2d 737 (8th Cir. 1985).

   a. **Apartment buildings:** Where the search is to be of an apartment building or other multi-family dwelling, the warrant must contain the name of the occupant, or the number of the particular apartment, so that other inhabitants of the structure will not be needlessly searched.

   b. **Search of person:** A warrant may be issued for the search of a ***person***, rather than a place. If this occurs, the warrant should state the person's name, or at least a description of him so complete that it is unlikely to apply to anyone except the suspect.

2. **Things to be seized:** The ***things to be seized*** must, like the premises to be searched, be specifically identified in the warrant. One old Supreme Court case, never explicitly overruled, stated that "nothing is [to be] left to the discretion of the officer executing the warrant." *Marron v. U.S.*, 275 U.S. 192 (1927).

   a. **A more liberal view:** The modern Court has allowed greater generality in warrants than is indicated by this statement from *Marron*. The Court has, for instance, approved a search warrant which contained a long list of types of documents that, in the warrant's language, would "tend . . . to show . . . elements of the crime of false pretenses" with respect to sales of a particular real estate lot, and which concluded with the phrase "together with other fruits, instrumentalities and evidence of crime at this [time] unknown." The Court read the phrase "evidence of crime" as referring to the particular crime and real estate lot previously mentioned in the warrant, and held that interpreted this way, the warrant was not fatally vague. *Andresen v. Maryland*, 427 U.S. 463 (1976).

      i. **Evidence of other crimes:** The Court in *Andresen* even allowed the seizure and introduction of evidence of false pretenses in connection with ***other lots*** than the one mentioned in the warrant. The Court concluded that " . . . the trained special investigators reasonably could have believed that the evidence specifically dealing with another lot in the . . . subdivision could be used to show petitioner's intent with respect to the lot [mentioned in the warrant]." This other evidence was thus permitted to be introduced at trial, even for the purpose of showing the defendant's guilt on additional charges not referred to in the warrant.

   b. **Contraband:** ***Contraband*** (property the possession of which is a crime, such as illegal drugs or outlawed firearms) does not have to be described as particularly as material which is innocuous on its face and sought only because of its connection with a particular crime. The reason for this distinction is that the officer executing the search will be able to identify contraband by its very nature; non-contraband connected with a crime, on the other hand, may be very similar to other items on the premises that have no connection with the crime (e.g., a few stolen furs in a warehouse with hundreds of legitimate furs).

   c. **First Amendment implications:** Where a seizure has First Amendment implications, the description of the goods seized must be extremely specific. Thus where ***obscene materials*** are sought, they must be very accurately described. *Marcus v. Search Warrants*, 367 U.S. 717 (1961). Furthermore, only a few copies may be seized until the owner has a chance to litigate the issue of obscenity. *A Quantity of Copies of Books v. Kansas*, 378 U.S. 205 (1964).

   d. **Automobile search:** A warrant may sometimes be required for the search of an ***automobile*** (e.g., where the car is parked on private property, and there are no exigent circumstances). Where this is the car, the warrant should contain either the car's license number, or its make and the name of its owner. (Nutshell, p. 112.)

E. What may be seized: It has always been the case that certain classes of items may be constitutionally seized if they are described in a search warrant issued with probable cause. Thus the instrumentality (e.g., a gun) used to commit a crime, the fruits of a crime (e.g. stolen money) and contraband (i.e., materials, like narcotics, whose very possession is prohibited by law) have always been subject to seizure. Items whose only interest to the police is that they may be introduced in court to ***incriminate*** the defendant, however, have only since 1967 been subject to seizure. Prior to that, a doctrine known as the ***"mere evidence"*** rule prevented the seizure of such items, largely on the grounds that the government had no valid property interest in them.

1. ***Gouled:*** The rule disallowing seizure of material whose only interest is its incriminating nature was formulated in *Gouled v. U.S.*, 255 U.S. 298 (1921), where the Court said that seizures could constitutionally be made only "when the property is an instrumentality or fruit of crime, or contraband." The rule of *Gouled*, that items which are only of evidentiary value cannot be seized, became known as the "mere evidence" rule.

2. ***Warden v. Hayden:*** The "mere evidence" rule was abruptly overturned by the Supreme Court in ***Warden v. Hayden***, 387 U.S. 294 (1967). There, the items seized were clothing belonging to an armed robbery suspect. The clothing matched an eyewitness' description, and was introduced at the trial. The Supreme Court held that although the clothing was "mere evidence" by the *Gouled* test, its seizure was constitutional.

   a. **Rationale:** The Court's decision was based mainly on a rejection of the principle that the government could seize only those items as to which it had a common-law property interest: "The requirement that the Government assert . . . some property interest in material it seizes has long been a fiction, obscuring the reality that government has an interest in solving crime." The Court noted that "the principal object of the Fourth Amendment is the protection of privacy rather than property, and [we] have increasingly discarded fictional and procedural barriers rested on property concepts."

   b. **"Limited search" argument rejected:** The Court then discarded the idea that the "mere evidence" rule helps protect privacy. Proponents of the rule had argued that "limitations upon the fruit to be gathered tend to limit the quest itself." (Learned Hand, quoted in *Warden*). The Court retorted that "privacy would be just as well served by a restriction on search to the even-numbered days of the month. . . . And it would have the extra advantage of avoiding hair-splitting questions."

   c. **Fifth Amendment:** In rejecting the "mere evidence" rule, the Court did, however, recognize the possibility that some seizures might violate the Fifth Amendment privilege against ***self-incrimination***. The Court stated, "the items of clothing involved in this case are not 'testimonial' or 'communicative' in nature, and their introduction therefore did not compel respondent to become a witness against himself in violation of the Fifth Amendment. . . . This case thus does not require that we consider whether there are items of evidential value whose very nature precludes them from being the object of a reasonable search and seizure." (But see *Andresen v. Maryland*, discussed *infra*.)

   d. **Douglas' dissent:** Justice Douglas, in a dissent, asserted that "The personal effects and possessions of the individual (all contraband and the like excepted) are sacrosanct from prying eyes, from the long arm of the law, from any rummaging by police. . . .

There is a zone that no police can enter—whether in 'hot pursuit' or armed with a meticulously proper warrant. . . . "

Note: After *Warden*, federal law was revised so as to allow the issuance of a search warrant for "mere evidence" of a crime. Federal Rule of Crim. Pro. 41(b), for instance, provides that "A warrant may be issued . . . to search for and seize any . . . property that constitutes evidence of the commission of a criminal offense. . . . " See also 18 U.S.C. 3103(a).

3. **Fifth Amendment now irrelevant to search issue:** The Supreme Court has since foreclosed the possibility, left open by *Warden*, that a search and seizure might violate the Fifth Amendment, and thus be "unreasonable" under the Fourth Amendment as well. In ***Andresen v. Maryland***, 427 U.S. 463 (1976), the Court upheld the search, with warrant, of the defendant's law office and of the office of a real estate firm which he controlled, and the seizure of ***business records*** at each of the two offices. These business records contained, *inter alia,* ***incriminating statements*** made by the defendant.

   a. **Holding:** The Court acknowledged that it would have been a violation of the defendant's Fifth Amendment rights to have required him to *produce* these business records (as by a subpoena). But the seizure of these records by law officers was not a violation of the Fifth Amendment. "[T]he protection afforded by the self-incrimination clause of the Fifth Amendment 'adheres basically to the person, not to information that may incriminate him.' Thus, although the Fifth Amendment may protect an individual from complying with a subpoena for the production of his personal records in his possession because the very act of production may constitute a compulsory authentication of incriminating information . . . a seizure of the same materials by law enforcement officers differs in a crucial respect — the individual against whom the search is directed is not required to aid in the discovery, production, or authentication of incriminating evidence."

F. **Warrants against non-suspects:** The Fourth Amendment permits searches to be made of the premises of persons who are ***not criminal suspects***, if there is probable cause to believe that the search will produce evidence of someone else's crime.

1. **Subpoena not necessary:** The Supreme Court has held that such a search of a non-suspect's premises may be made ***even if a subpoena would be equally effective***. *Zurcher v. The Stanford Daily*, 436 U.S. 547 (1978). The Court held that the probable cause required for issuance of a search warrant (i.e., that it be probable that evidence of crime will be discovered on the premises) is the same for non-suspects as for suspects, and that there need be no indication that the owner is himself connected with the crime. Nor do the police have to show that there is a particular danger that evidence will be destroyed if a subpoena, rather than a warrant, is used.

   a. **No special free-press protection:** The Court also held in *Stanford Daily* that ***newspapers***, despite their First Amendment protection, are ***not entitled to special treatment***, and that the requirements for obtaining a warrant for search of newspaper premises are no stricter than for other kinds of premises.

   b. **Dissent:** A dissent by Justice Stewart, joined by Justice Marshall, stressed that permitting a newspaper's confidential files to be searched without advance warning would "prevent a newsman from being able to promise confidentiality to his potential sources," leading to impairment of the flow of information to the public.

c. **Stevens' dissent:** Justice Stevens dissented on the broader ground that where the premises to be searched belong to a non-suspect, a warrant should issue only if there is particular danger that he will "conceal or destroy the object of the search." He pointed out that the scope of searches was already drastically expanded by the holding in *Warden v. Hayden* (*supra*, p. 65) that "mere evidence" could be seized in a search; allowing the seizure of mere evidence in the premises of non-suspects is an even greater intrusion.

G. **Execution of warrants:** Most jurisdictions, including the federal system, have statutes prescribing the ***manner*** in which search warrants are to be executed. These statutes set forth the time period within which the search must be executed, the hours of the day during which search is permissible, the way in which the officer executing the warrant must identify himself, etc. In addition to these statutes, the case law indicates, in a general way, the procedures that must be followed for the search not to be an ***"unreasonable"*** one violative of the Fourth Amendment.

1. **Period within which warrant must be executed:** Many statutes and court rules fix a period of days within which the search warrant must be executed. Fed. R. Crim. Pro. 41(d), for instance, requires that the search be conducted within 10 days after issuance of the warrant.

2. **Time of day:** About half of the states have statutes restricting the execution of search warrants to the ***daytime*** hours, unless there are special circumstances. Similarly, Fed. R. Crim. Pro. 41(c) provides that "The warrant shall be served in the daytime, unless the issuing authority, by appropriate provision in the warrant, and for reasonable cause shown, authorizes its execution at times other than daytime."

3. **Entry without notice vs. "knock and announce":** As a general rule, the officer executing the warrant must ***announce*** that he is a law enforcement officer, that he possesses a warrant, and that he is there to execute it. This is called the ***"knock and announce"*** requirement. Thus 18 U.S.C. § 3109 provides that a federal officer may break into a place to be searched only "if, after notice of his authority and purpose, he is refused admittance." This requirement of an announcement derives from the Fourth Amendment's ban on "unreasonable" searches: in many situations, an unannounced, forcible entry will be so disruptive and frightening to the inhabitants that it will for that reason alone be unreasonable.

a. **Preventing the destruction of evidence:** However, the Supreme Court has recognized at least one situation, the threat of ***immediate destruction of evidence***, that *does* allow the officers to constitutionally enter without identifying themselves. See *Ker v. California*, 374 U.S. 23 (1963).

i. **Facts of *Ker*:** In *Ker*, a narcotics suspect eluded police shortly before they came to arrest him at his house. The Court held that the officers' knowledge that the suspect would probably be expecting them, coupled with the knowledge that the suspect possessed a small, easily disposable amount of narcotics, was enough to prevent their unidentified entry from being an "unreasonable" search and arrest violative of the Fourth Amendment.

ii. Dissent in *Ker:* Four dissenters in *Ker* asserted that there are only two situations, neither of them present in *Ker*, in which a police officer may make an unannounced entry:

(1) "where such circumstances as an escape and hot pursuit by the arresting officer leave no doubt that the fleeing felon is aware of the officer's presence and purpose"; and

(2) "possibly where the officers are justified in the belief that someone within is in immediate danger of bodily harm."

Note: *Ker* was a warrantless arrest case. However, its language about when an unidentified entry may be made presumably applies both to search and to arrest situations, and to both situations involving a warrant and those in which an exception to the warrant requirement exists.

b. Entry by stealth: The principle that the officers must identify themselves, absent exigent circumstances, applies ***even where force is not used*** for the entry. Thus in *Ker*, a landlord's passkey was used, but the test for reasonableness of the unidentified entry was the same as if the door had been broken down. The Court subsequently held, in *Sabbath v. U.S.*, 391 U.S. 585 (1968), that the requirement of identification applied even where a closed, but unlocked, door is opened. The Court has not yet passed on whether an entry by ***ruse*** (e.g., misrepresentation of the officer's identity) must similarly be justified by exigent circumstances, but several states have so held.

c. Specific danger of destruction of evidence: Most courts, relying on *Ker*, have held that where the facts of the particular situation indicate the likelihood that identification by the officers would lead to the ***destruction of evidence***, unannounced entry to execute a search warrant may be made. However, the officers may not rely merely on the fact that the case involves narcotics, betting slips, or some other easily disposed-of evidence. Rather, there must be ***specific indications*** that the destruction of evidence in the particular case at hand is imminent. Circumstances in which a police officer might enter without fully identifying himself include the following:

i. the officer starts to identify himself, and then hears running footsteps, whispers, or flushing toilets;

ii. the officer knows he has been seen from a window, and knows that the inhabitants are in possession of easily disposable amounts of narcotics;

iii. a reliable informant tells the police that the narcotics to be seized are always kept near the toilet.

For more about destruction of evidence, from the perspective of when a warrant is required, see p. 120.

d. Physical danger to police: Just as the possibility of destruction of evidence will sometimes justify unannounced entry, so the possibility of ***physical danger to the police*** may sometimes justify such entry. For instance, if the police have reason to believe that the suspect has a gun and is inclined to use it, the police are probably justified in breaking in without pre-announcement, in order to minimize the likelihood that the suspect will fire on them. This is especially true where the suspect has previously said that he'd "never be taken alive," or given some similar indication of dangerousness.

e. **Considered in determining "reasonableness":** *Ker* and the cases decided under it make it clear that in many instances, the police don't need to knock or announce themselves before making entry. But the Supreme Court has held, post-*Ker*, that the fact that the police didn't knock or announce before entering is nonetheless a ***factor to be considered*** when the court decides whether the entry was "reasonable" (as the Fourth Amendment requires it to be). See *Wilson v. Arkansas*, 514 U.S. 927 (1995).

   i. **Consequence:** So if the police enter without knocking or announcing themselves, and none of the special circumstances (physical danger to the police; likelihood that evidence will be destroyed, etc.) applies, there's a good chance the court will find that the unannounced break-in to arrest or conduct a search was "unreasonable," and thus a violation of the Fourth Amendment.

   ii. **Exclusionary rule does not apply:** On the other hand, even if on particular facts the Fourth Amendment requires the police to knock and announce themselves, their failure to do so will ***not*** require that any evidence they end up seizing be ***excluded*** from the defendant's criminal trial. See *Hudson v. Michigan*, 547 U.S. 586 (2006), discussed further *infra*, p. 356. The "exclusionary rule" (discussed beginning *infra*, p. 315) usually requires that the "fruits" of an illegal search or seizure of D be excluded from D's criminal trial; but as the result of *Hudson* this general principle does not apply in the case of evidence seized following a knock-and-announce violation.

4. **Where no response from inhabitants:** If the officer identifies himself, and is then refused entry, he may use ***force*** to break into the premises.

   a. **Silence:** If the occupant is known to be home, and makes no answer, the officer may break in. He must, however, give the occupant an adequate time in which to respond.

      i. **Exception where evidence may be destroyed:** But under *Richards v. Wisconsin*, 520 U.S. 385 (1997), the ordinary duty to give the occupant an adequate time to answer the door will ***not apply*** under circumstances in which this would be ***dangerous*** (e.g., the occupant is believed to be armed and violent) or would likely lead to the ***destruction of evidence.*** And, in the case of evidence, the ***more easily disposed-of the evidence is***, the ***less time the police must wait.*** So, for instance, a very quick entry will usually be allowed where the police are planning to search for easily-disposed-of evidence like ***small quantities of drugs.*** See, e.g., *U.S. v. Banks*, 540 U.S. 31 (2003).

   b. **Absent:** If there is no one home, the officer may also break in — searches have not been held "unreasonable" solely because they were executed by forcible entry in the absence of the inhabitants.

5. **Search of persons on premises:** As part of their search of premises, the police sometimes want to search ***persons*** who are on the premises. If there is probable cause to ***arrest*** a person who is on the premises, the police may do so and then conduct a ***search incident to arrest***. But if probable cause is lacking, it is only in some circumstances that the police may search persons present.

   a. **Named items on person:** If the police have probable cause to believe that an individual has on his person items which are named in the search warrant, they may search him, since if they could not, they would not have time to procure an additional warrant and he might leave with the items.

   b. **Person attempting to leave:** If a person attempts to leave during a search, and the items being sought are of a kind which might easily be carried away, it is probably proper for the police to temporarily detain him to ensure that he is not carrying them off. This could be justified by analogy to *Terry v. Ohio*, which permitted certain temporary "stops" and "frisks" even when probable cause for full arrest is lacking.

   c. **Frisk:** Similarly, the police can probably frisk a person on the scene if they have reason to fear that he may be dangerous. But as *Terry* indicates, they may not make a full-scale body search, but may only pat down the suspect to determine whether hard objects which could be weapons are on his person.

   d. **Persons unrelated to search:** But where a person simply happens to be on the premises to be searched, and appears not to have any connection with the criminal activity which gave rise to issuance of the warrant, that person may ***not be searched***. Thus in ***Ybarra v. Illinois***, 444 U.S. 85 (1979), the police obtained a warrant to search the Aurora Tap Tavern and its bartender, "Greg," for heroin. While executing the warrant, the police frisked D, one of the patrons in the bar. The frisk led them to believe that D had heroin, so they conducted a fuller search which did indeed turn up the drug on D's person.

      i. **Frisk invalidated:** The U.S. Supreme Court held that the initial frisk could not be justified as part of the execution of the warrant, since the warrant mentioned only the bar itself and the bartender. "A person's mere propinquity to others independently suspected of criminal activity does not, without more, give rise to probable cause to search that person. . . . Where the standard is probable cause, a search or seizure of a person must be supported by probable cause ***particularized with respect to that person***." (Nor was the frisk justified under *Terry v. Ohio*, since the police could not reasonably have believed that D was armed; this aspect of the case is discussed *infra*, p. 164.)

      ii. **Dissent in *Ybarra:*** Three dissenters (Rehnquist, Burger and Blackmun) in *Ybarra* would have allowed the initial frisk. They argued that where the police have already procured a valid warrant, their acts in executing it should be judged merely by a general standard of "reasonableness," not by whether there is probable cause to frisk each person in the premises.

6. **Restricted area of search:** In executing a search pursuant to a warrant, the police must confine their search to the area specified in the warrant, and they must look only in those

places where the items sought might possibly be concealed. Thus if the police are looking for a full-size rifle, they may not look into drawers which are too small to contain it.

7. **Seizure of unnamed items:** As the police are conducting a search, they may sometimes come across items which they would like to seize, but which are ***not listed in the warrant.*** The courts have generally been liberal in allowing such seizure as long as the search was conducted in the proper area and the unnamed item was in ***"plain view"*** at some point during the lawful search.

   a. **Requirement that evidence be incriminating:** The police may not, of course, seize just any item they come across during the search. They must seize only items which are ***sufficiently connected with criminal activity that a warrant could have been procured for them.*** Thus a seizure of objects which turn out to have been stolen is not valid, if at the time of seizure the police did not have probable cause to believe that they were stolen.

      i. **Unrelated items:** The items inadvertently discovered do not have to relate to the same criminal activity which gave rise to the warrant, as long as there is probable cause for the seizure of these new items. Thus if the police are executing a warrant naming stolen property, and they come upon narcotics whose possession is illegal, they may seize the narcotics even though there is no reason to believe that they are stolen.

   b. **Degree of examination permissible:** Because the rule permitting the seizure of unnamed items is built upon the "plain view" doctrine, there are limits on the ***degree of scrutiny*** which the police can give to a discovered object to see whether it is incriminating.

      Example: While executing a warrant for seizure of certain items of stolen property, the police find a television set which is not one of the named items. One officer recalls that such a set had been taken in a recent robbery, and calls a TV repairman to remove the back of the set so that the serial number can be compared with the number of the stolen set. The numbers match. *Held*, the search and seizure of the set were in violation of the Fourth Amendment since the serial number (which was what gave rise to the existence of probable cause to seize) was not in plain view. *Commonwealth v. Bowers*, 274 A.2d 546 (Pa. Super. Ct. 1970).

   c. **No requirement of inadvertence:** It is ***not*** required, for application of the plain view doctrine, that the police's discovery of an item in plain view be ***"inadvertent."*** In other words, if the police know that they are likely to find items 1, 2, and 3 in a search of D's premises, and they get a warrant listing items 1 and 2, they may seize item 3 if they encounter it in plain view while executing the search warrant, even though their spotting of number 3 was not "inadvertent." The Court so held in *Horton v. California*, 496 U.S. 128 (1990).

      i. **Illustration:** This lack of an "inadvertence" requirement is illustrated by the facts of *Horton*. At the time police applied for a warrant to search D's home in connection with a robbery, the police had a description of the weapons used. But they obtained a warrant authorizing a search only for robbery proceeds, including three specific rings. While the police were properly executing the warrant to search for the rings, they came across the weapons, as they suspected they might. The *Horton* Court allowed the seizure and subsequent introduction into evidence of the weapons under the plain view doctrine, even though the police discovery of the weapons was not inadvertent and could easily have been covered by the warrant. So as the result of *Horton*, the police have very little incentive to conscientiously list all items for which they have probable cause to search — they can instead list one or a few, and then pick up anything else they happen across while searching for the listed items.

8. **Intrusions into body:** A search warrant will occasionally be issued for a search of a ***person***, rather than a place. This is most likely to be the case where the search will involve some degree of ***intrusion*** into the body of the person (almost always a suspect) to be searched. Since the Fourth Amendment protects the "right of the people to be secure in their persons . . . against unreasonable searches and seizures," such intrusions, whether done pursuant to a search warrant or not, must be ***"reasonable."***

   a. **Examples of intrusions:** This reasonableness issue can arise in a number of contexts: the taking of blood samples, the pumping of a suspect's stomach, the use of surgery to remove evidence of a crime, etc.

   b. **Balancing test:** In general, the reasonableness of any such intrusion is to be determined by a use of a ***balancing test***. "The individual's interests in privacy and security are weighed against society's interests in conducting the procedure." *Winston v. Lee*, 470 U.S. 753 (1985).

      i. **Removal of bullet:** Thus in *Winston*, the Court used its balancing formula to determine that it was *not* reasonable to allow the state to place D under a general anesthetic and then to remove a bullet lodged an inch deep in his chest. A robbery victim had shot the perpetrator in the chest; the state sought to remove the bullet from D to show that it had been fired from the victim's gun. Because the surgical procedure was a non-trivial one that might last over two hours and injure D's nerves, blood vessels and other tissue, the intrusion on D was "substantial." On the other side of the scale, the state's need for the evidence was not "compelling," since there was other evidence tying D to the crime.

   c. **Local anesthetic:** But the use of a balancing test does not mean that all surgical interventions will be found to be "unreasonable" as the one in *Winston* was. For instance, had the bullet in *Winston* been more superficially lodged, so that it could have been removed with only a local anesthetic and less probing of tissue, the Court in *Winston* might well have allowed the procedure.

   d. **Taking of blood:** Similarly, the Court has held that the forcible ***taking of blood*** from a suspect to determine whether he has been driving while intoxicated is not unreasonable. *Schmerber v. California*, 384 U.S. 757 (1966) (discussed *infra*, p. 107 and p. 298).

   e. **DNA sample of arrestee:** Likewise, if D is arrested for a "serious crime," the forcible and warrantless taking of a ***DNA sample*** by means of a swab of the inside of D's cheek — done as part of a standard post-arrest police booking procedure — is not unreasonable for Fourth Amendment purposes. The police may then enter the sample in a local or national DNA ***database***, to determine whether the sample matches any unsolved crimes. *Maryland v. King*, 133 S.Ct. 1958 (2013) (discussed *infra*, p. 181).

f. **X-rays:** Finally, the use of ***x-rays*** to obtain evidence that the defendant is concealing drugs within his alimentary canal may, at least under some circumstances, not be "unreasonable." See, e.g., Justice Stevens' concurrence in *U.S. v. Montoya de Hernandez*, 473 U.S. 531 (1985) (discussed *infra*, p. 163), indicating that a person suspected of this type of smuggling can be compelled to submit to an x-ray examination. However, in many if not most instances, such intrusive procedures will only be allowed when there is a warrant issued upon probable cause.

g. **Self-incrimination:** Where the defendant is forced to undergo a bodily intrusion so that the state may extract evidence that he has committed a crime, it could be plausibly argued that entirely apart from the reasonableness of the search, there is a violation of the Fifth Amendment's bar to compulsory self-incrimination. However, the Supreme Court has held that the Fifth Amendment bars only the compulsion of "testimonial" evidence, and that evidence procured by intrusion on the body is not testimonial. See *infra*, p. 298 (discussing this issue as it arose in the context of *Schmerber*, *supra*, p. 72).

H. **"Good faith" exception:** Normally, if a search warrant is ***invalid*** for any of the reasons summarized above (e.g., it is not supported by probable cause), any search done pursuant to it will be ***unconstitutional***. Furthermore, the ***exclusionary rule*** will generally be applicable, so that the evidence so seized may not be introduced at the trial of the person whose Fourth Amendment rights were violated by the search. However, the Supreme Court has held that if the police ***reasonably believe*** that the warrant which they have been issued is valid, the exclusionary rule will ***not apply*** to bar the items seized from being introduced at the trial of the person whose rights were violated by the search. See *U.S. v. Leon*, *infra*, p. 348.

VIII. ARREST WARRANTS

A. **General unimportance:** The above sections have been concerned chiefly with search warrants. Arrest warrants, although they exist in all jurisdictions, are much less frequently used, largely because there are few circumstances in which the courts have held their use to be a constitutional requirement. (See *infra*, p. 94.)

B. **Similarity to search warrant:** Most of the analysis of search warrants given above applies equally to arrest warrants. For instance, the time of day in which the warrant must be executed, and the identification which the officer must give, are similar in the two situations. A few of the more important differences between the two kinds of warrants are as follows:

1. **Probable cause:** Although the arrest warrant, like the search warrant, can constitutionally be issued only on probable cause, the meaning of probable cause in the arrest case is slightly different. See p. 54, *supra*.

2. **Time within which warrant must be executed:** Whereas a search warrant must be issued within a period of time short enough so that there is still probable cause to believe that the items to be seized are still on the premises, the execution of an arrest warrant is not subject to such strict limitations. Once there is probable cause to believe that a particular

person committed a particular crime, probable cause for his arrest continues indefinitely, unless new evidence is found which removes that probable cause.

3. **Plain view:** When, in executing an arrest, the police come across an incriminating object, they may seize it just as when they come across such an object while executing a search. But since the police will have less occasion to move around the premises when making an arrest than when searching, the physical area in which the plain view doctrine will apply will typically be smaller.

4. **Particularity of description:** The Fourth Amendment requires that an arrest warrant particularly describe "the person to be seized." But this requirement of particular description is obviously less burdensome than the requirement that objects to be seized be particularly described in a search warrant.

   a. **Other contents of warrant:** Other than the name of the person to be arrested, the warrant need contain only the crime with which he is charged, and the name of the court issuing it. Arrest warrants are generally good only in the state of their issuance, and extradition proceedings must be used to gain custody of a suspect who is in a different state from the state which wishes to try him.

Quiz Yourself on
ARREST; PROBABLE CAUSE; SEARCH WARRANTS *(ENTIRE CHAPTER)*

3. The Empire Police Department received an anonymous and unsubstantiated "tip" that Dexter, an Empire resident, was buying and selling unlicensed handguns in violation of an Empire statute. This information did not, under applicable U.S. Supreme Court decisions, give the Empire Police probable cause to arrest Dexter for any crime. However, the police arrested Dexter anyway, and charged him with violating the state's handgun statute. Shortly after the arrest (before it had been at all publicized) Wendy, Dexter's ex-wife, came of her own volition to the Empire police station and furnished compelling evidence that Dexter had indeed been buying and selling unlicensed handguns. Wendy turned out to be the anonymous informant — she had not wanted to be deeply involved, but then had changed her mind.

Dexter is now being tried for the crime of buying and selling unlicensed handguns. He argues that because his arrest was made without probable cause and was thus a violation of his Fourth Amendment rights, he may not be tried for this crime. Assuming that Dexter is correct in asserting that his arrest was in violation of his federally-guaranteed Fourth Amendment rights, must the prosecution against him be dismissed? _______________

4. Law enforcement officials working for the Jefferson State Organized Crime Task Force suspected Johnny ("The Cigar") Jordan of being the boss of a local organized-crime family. However, they had never been able to get any evidence of criminal activity conducted by Johnny. Johnny was known for never conducting business at his apartment, and for not maintaining any office. Instead, at nine o'clock every evening, under cover of darkness, Johnny would take a walk through Central Park, accompanied by two or three people who police thought were his henchmen. Johnny and his companions would walk through the park, and only when no one was nearby would they say anything.

However, unbeknownst to Johnny, a new invention just acquired by the Task Force was about to change the equation. The invention was an infrared telescope. From high up in an office building next to the park, the Task Force set up this device, which looked like an ordinary telescope. However, it was a telescope that worked on infrared light given out by human bodies. Therefore, even though it was dark, officials could spot Johnny in their telescope, focus in tightly on his face, and have an experienced lip reader interpret what Johnny and his companion were saying. By the use of this method, they were able to learn that Johnny's organization was processing raw cocaine into crack at a "still" in downtown Jefferson City. (The police did not have a search warrant or probable cause to search or eavesdrop on Johnny.) Using the telescopically-obtained information, they procured a search warrant, raided the still, and charged Johnny with various violations of state drug laws.

Johnny now argues that his initial words describing the drug operation were intended to be private, that the infrared operation was an illegal Fourth Amendment search of him, and that the search warrant thus obtained was illegal. Should the court accept Johnny's argument and rule that the search warrant was invalid? (For this question, assume that the answer is "yes" if by using the infrared device to read Johnny's lips the police were carrying out a Fourth Amendment search.) ________________

5. The police heard rumors that Darwin had carried out a murder for hire of Victor at the behest of Victor's estranged wife Delia, and that Darwin would soon be picking up his payment from Delia's house. The police knew that because of the unsubstantiated nature of these rumors, they did not have probable cause to believe that Darwin was the hit-man in the Victor killing. Therefore, they did not try to procure a search or arrest warrant. Instead, the police followed Darwin from his home to a local fast-food restaurant. Darwin left his briefcase on the table while he went to the bathroom. The police quickly attached a small flat electronic device to the outside of the briefcase, hoping that Darwin wouldn't notice the device. The device was a GPS tracker that wirelessly broadcast, to a police-controlled Internet address, the tracker's location. The device remained undiscovered by Darwin for 60 days. On the 58th day, the website showed that Darwin had visited Delia's house. Darwin and Delia were charged with murdering Victor. At the start of the trial, the police sought to introduce the Internet record showing Darwin's visit to Delia's house. Darwin objected that the evidence had been obtained by a violation of his Fourth Amendment rights. The prosecution answered this objection solely on the grounds that no Fourth Amendment search had ever occurred, thereby relieving the police of either the requirement to have probable cause before tracking Darwin's movements or a search warrant to do so.

(a) Should the court conclude that a Fourth Amendment search occurred? ________________

(b) Based on your answer to (a), what consequences will flow with respect to the admissibility of the record showing Darwin's visit, and why? ________________

6. Elaine came to the police station to report that her car had been stolen from a mall parking lot one hour earlier. She described the vehicle as a cobalt-blue, 2019 Jaguar F-Type convertible with a vanity plate on the front with the words "sweet ride." The detective who took the information immediately transmitted it to all officers on patrol within a ten-mile radius of the mall. As he was driving down Magnolia Avenue, Officer Pete saw a cobalt-blue sports car that he thought was a Jaguar pull into the garage that was attached to the side of a private home, # 123 Magnolia. As Pete watched from the street, the driver exited through the garage door (leaving it open), then entered the house through its front door. Since the open garage door was only about 20 feet from the street, Pete entered the garage through that door and looked closely at the front of the car. He confirmed that it was a Jaguar F-Type with a front vanity plate saying "sweet ride." Pete used this information to secure an arrest warrant for the driver, Matt, who lived at # 123 Magnolia. Now, Matt has moved to quash the arrest warrant, claiming that Pete's conduct violated Matt's Fourth Amendment rights. Should the motion be granted? ________________

7. Police Officer Baker was walking her beat one day when she discovered a small cocker spaniel which appeared to be lost. The dog was wearing a collar saying, "My name is Rex. If I'm found, please return me to my home at 123 Maple Street." Baker decided to do just that. She took the dog to 123 Maple, and rang the doorbell. The door was answered by a white-haired grandmotherly-looking woman, who identified herself as Mrs. Jones, owner of Rex. While the door was open, Baker happened to look past Jones into the center hall of the house, where she spotted what she instantly recognized (from reading *Soldier of Fortune* magazine) to be an Uzi submachine gun. Since Uzi submachine guns are illegal in every state, Baker knew that somebody was committing a felony. She kept her cool, did not give any hint about what she had seen, got a search warrant, and seized the submachine gun. Jones was prosecuted for illegal possession of the gun, and defended on the grounds that Baker's act of spotting the gun, which began the whole episode, occurred without probable cause or a warrant, and that the gun must therefore be suppressed.

(a) If you were the prosecutor, what doctrine or rule should you cite in opposition to Jones' suppression motion? ________________

(b) Should the judge grant Jones' suppression motion? ________________

8. Same basic facts as the prior question. Now, however, assume that Officer Baker did not see any submachine gun, or anything unusual, while she stood in the hallway returning the dog. Mrs. Jones invited her in to her living room to give her a cup of tea. When she went out of the room to prepare the tea, Officer Baker noticed a long, narrow case in the living room, which she knew to be of a type that often contains a gun; she had never seen such a container used for anything but a gun. She flipped open the top (which was not secured in any way), and discovered an Uzi submachine gun inside. Since Uzis are not permitted in private dwellings in the state under any circumstances, Officer Baker immediately confiscated the box and the weapon. At Jones' trial, if Jones moves to suppress the Uzi and the box, should her motion be granted? ________________

9. Same facts as prior two questions. Now, however, assume that at the start of the whole episode, Baker had had an unsubstantiated and anonymous tip that there might be some sort of illegal weapon stored at 123 Maple Street. Baker didn't know how she would get probable cause for a search warrant. She hung around the outskirts of Jones' house at 123 Maple for some time, hoping to catch some sort of break. Then, the dog (see Question 6) emerged from a small dog-sized door at the side of the house, and ran out to the sidewalk. Baker knew perfectly well that the dog was not lost. She seized upon this as a pretext, gathered up the dog, and rang the doorbell, hoping to get a glimpse into the house. Events later transpired as in Question 7. Should the judge grant Jones' suppression motion? ________________

10. Officer White was patrolling her beat one day. While she was standing on the sidewalk, she happened to look over into the big picture window on the first floor of a house owned by Desmond. White could see through the window what appeared to be two large marijuana plants. She went up to the window (standing on Desmond's property to do so), opened the window, which was not locked, and stepped inside. There, she confiscated the two plants, which turned out to indeed be marijuana. Desmond was charged with violating state anti-drug laws. He has moved to suppress the plants as the fruits of an illegal search.

(a) If you were the prosecutor, what doctrine would you cite, as your best chance to defeat Desmond's motion? ________________

(b) Would the argument you make in (a) succeed? ________________

11. Police had probable cause to believe that evidence of a recent armed robbery might be found in the master bedroom of a house owned by Dubinski. They procured (using proper procedures) a warrant to search that room in Dubinski's house. Officer Piston rang Dubinski's bell, showed him the warrant, and immediately went to the bedroom. While in the bedroom, Piston (who had an unusually strong sense of smell) detected an odor which he believed was that of rotting meat or flesh. Since the kitchen was in an entirely different part of the house, Piston believed (assume reasonably) that this smell must belong to some fairly large organism that was dead, either a large pet or, perhaps, a human being. Piston followed his nose into the basement, where he discovered the partially decomposed body of a woman who turned out to be Dubinski's wife. The officer immediately impounded the body as evidence, and Dubinski was ultimately charged with murdering his wife. Dubinski has moved to suppress the body as evidence, arguing that Piston only found the body by going into a part of the house (the basement) where his warrant did not authorize him to be.

(a) If you were the prosecutor, what argument or doctrine might you cite to help defeat Dubinski's motion? ________________

(b) Should Dubinski's suppression motion be granted? ________________

12. Oscar was a police officer who had for several months worked as the handler of a trained drug-sniffing dog, Rover. Oscar was standing at an intersection of public streets, while wearing his police uniform, and accompanied by Rover on a leash. Gina, wearing a backpack, approached Oscar and asked for directions to a nearby location. Oscar, who had no suspicion that Gina was engaged in any sort of wrongdoing, began to answer. During the ensuing brief conversation, Gina put her backpack on the pavement. Rover circled around the backpack, sniffed it several times, and gave a special signal (sitting and raising his paw). As Oscar knew, this signal meant "I smell narcotics here." Oscar therefore, without asking Gina's permission, picked up the backpack and opened it; when he did so, he immediately spotted a large packet of marijuana, and arrested Gina for marijuana possession. At a suppression hearing, Gina argued that unless the prosecution could show that, based on recent statistics about Rover's record of "hits" and "misses" in the field, a positive drug signal by Rover was generally reliable, the marijuana must be excluded as a Fourth Amendment search made without probable cause. The prosecution did not have any evidence available to show how frequently Rover's in-the-field positive drug signals had recently proved accurate or inaccurate. However, the prosecution produced evidence that Rover had, three years before, completed a standard canine-drug-sniffing training program, and that at least monthly, the police department put him through "workouts" to keep his drug-detection skills up-to-date. Should the court grant Gina's suppression motion? ________________

13. Federal Treasury officials believed, without probable cause, that George was counterfeiting U.S. currency in his basement. They realized that it is almost impossible to counterfeit bills without producing some unsuccessful ones that must be burned or otherwise discarded. They therefore decided to stake out George's garbage. Twice a week, George put several sealed opaque large garbage bags out on the curb in front of his house, to be picked up by Urban Carting (UC), the private sanitation company that supplied garbage-pickup service to George's neighborhood. Each morning, shortly before the UC truck came, the Treasury agents (acting without a search warrant) would open George's trash bags and see whether there was any evidence of counterfeiting inside. Eventually, they discovered a sheet of uncut $20 bills, which turned out to be counterfeit. They arrested George and charged him with counterfeiting. He moved to suppress the evidence found in his trash as a violation of the Fourth Amendment. Should George's suppression motion be granted? ________________

14. Same facts as the prior question. Now, however, assume that George did not put his trash out at curbside every day. Instead, he put the trash out in his back yard inside two garbage cans. Twice a week, the UC workers would (with George's implied consent), go into George's back yard, bring the bags out to the street, and put them into the garbage truck. One day, the Treasury officials snuck into George's back yard shortly after he had put out the trash, took the bags out to the street, and viewed their contents. They then gave all the contents except the counterfeit bills to the UC collectors to put into the garbage truck. May the counterfeit bills be suppressed? ________________

15. Joe had been staying for several days in an apartment owned by his brother Bob, while Bob was away. While in the apartment, Joe periodically smoked marijuana. Occupants of neighboring apartments had called the police to complain about the suspicious smells. The police could have obtained a search warrant, but they lazily declined to do so. Instead, they rang the doorbell of the apartment, ascertained that Joe was not the owner of the apartment, forced their way in, and looked over the apartment. They spotted marijuana in an open pouch on a coffee table, and arrested Joe for possessing it. At Joe's trial for drug possession, can he have the marijuana suppressed on the grounds that it is the fruit of an unlawful search and/or seizure? ________________

16. After Mimi missed the final commuter-train-ride home, she asked her co-worker Eric for a ride home, since they lived down the street from one another. Eric was happy to help her out but told Mimi that they needed to drop co-worker Jerry at Jerry's home first. When they arrived at Jerry's house, Eric wanted to visit with Jerry, and asked Mimi if she would be willing to drive his, Eric's, car to her house and park it out front; he would then take an Uber to her place to retrieve the car after he finished his visit with Jerry. Mimi agreed. Mimi always carried an unlicensed firearm for protection, and she placed it in the glove compartment of Eric's car before she started driving home. Thirty minutes later, as Mimi neared her residence, Officer Zohra pulled her over for speeding. Zohra thought Mimi seemed nervous and ordered Mimi out of the car. Zohra then searched the vehicle, finding the firearm in the glove compartment and cocaine in the center console. Eric was charged with possession of cocaine and Mimi with possession of an unlicensed firearm. Eric now moves to suppress the cocaine, and Mimi moves to suppress the firearm. Which of them has a sufficient Fourth Amendment interest to challenge Officer Zohra's conduct? ________________

17. On October 1, after neighbors complained about a persistent foul odor coming from an apartment in Capital City, Ohio, rented by Justin, the landlord contacted the police. Officer Luke found Justin dead in his bedroom from a gunshot wound, which appeared to have been inflicted in that room. The coroner estimated that the victim had been killed sometime in August. Police suspicion centered on Marcus, with whom Justin had been heard arguing during the summer about a failed business venture in which Marcus had invested at Justin's recommendation. Marcus claimed that during August he was never within 50 miles of Justin's apartment. Acting without a search warrant, the prosecutor subpoenaed Marcus' cell phone carrier, requesting that the company review their records of Marcus' "cell site location information" ("CSLI") to determine whether he was within 50 miles of Justin's apartment at any time during August. If he was, the subpoena required the carrier to provide those dates and locations to the prosecutor's office. The carrier complied with the subpoena, providing the prosecutor's office with data showing that Marcus was in the 50-mile radius of the apartment on two separate occasions during August, each for no more than two hours. The company also provided the corresponding location coordinates on those dates for those time periods. Did the subpoena and the carrier's response violate Marcus' Fourth Amendment rights? ________________

18. Police were investigating a sexual assault. Surveillance footage of the small apartment building where the assault took place showed an individual wearing a mask entering the building with a key just prior to the attack. Detectives focused their attention on the occupants of one unit, Terence and his fiancée Sally. They interviewed Terence and Sally at the apartment, and Terence gave conflicting accounts of his whereabouts at the time of the crime. While the detectives found Terence's answers suspicious, they lacked probable cause to arrest him at that point. However, as the officers were leaving, Detective Yasmin noticed an envelope addressed to Terence from 23andme.com on the kitchen table. When Yasmin commented that she had sent a DNA sample to that company to learn more about her own heritage, Sally volunteered that Terence had done the same and that the envelope probably contained the results.

As soon as the prosecutor's office learned this, they sent (without obtaining a search warrant) a package to 23andme containing (1) a printout of the DNA made from semen taken from the sexual assault victim; and (2) a subpoena demanding the identity of anyone who ever submitted a sample to 23andme matching that DNA printout. The company complied, and notified the prosecutor that Terence was a match. Terence has now moved to suppress the identification on grounds that the demand for it constituted a Fourth Amendment search of his private information, and therefore required a search warrant. Terence points out (correctly) that he never authorized 23andme to share any information about him with any other entity. Moreover, Terence points out that 23andme's website promises confidentiality from all inquiries, including those from law enforcement. Should the court grant Terence's motion? ________________

19. The Olmstead Police Department found a bullet-riddled body at an outdoor rural location, and were able to determine that the murder had taken place sometime between 6 PM and 11 PM the day before, at the location where the body was found (the "Murder Site"). Officers found an abandoned laptop computer at the Murder Site that had been used to send encrypted messages to three other unidentified computers during the 5 hours surrounding the murder (the "Time Period"). The police knew that every computer has a particular "IP address," and that the Internet Service Provider (ISP) who supplies service to any given computer (a "Target Computer") has records of the IP address and owner of any other computer that was in contact with the Target Computer at any specific time. Therefore, the police demanded (without a search warrant) that the main ISPs covering that rural area search their records for communications between the Target Computer and each of the three IP addresses during the Time Period, and report to the police the identity of the owner of each of those three computers.

One such ISP, NetCarrier Co., compiled a list that included the identity of the owner of one of these three computers during the Time Period. That owner was Swenson. Other evidence also pointed to Swenson as one of the murderers, so prosecutors charged him with the murder. At the start of trial, the prosecutors proposed to present the IP address of Swenson's computer as part of their case, to show that the communication between the Target Computer and Swenson's computer indicated he was likely part of the group involved with the murder. Swenson moved to suppress the ISP information, arguing that before the police were entitled to demand subscriber information from NetCarrier, the Fourth Amendment required that they get a search warrant based on probable cause.

Should the court grant Swenson's motion to exclude the IP address information? ________________

20. The police in a small town are trying to solve a recent burglary. They know from local probation records that Robert, the most prominent and active burglar in the town over the last two years, was released from prison on parole just two days before the burglary they are now investigating. The police want to search Robert's apartment. They have presented themselves to a neutral and detached magistrate, and have asked for a warrant to search Robert's house, based on the information summarized above. Assume that the above information, taken in its entirety, would justify a reasonable magistrate in concluding that proceeds of the recent burglary probably would be found at Robert's apartment. Assume furthermore that if Robert were to be charged with and tried for the burglary, evidence of his prior burglaries, and his recent release from prison (i.e., the items on which the request for the warrant is based), could not be admitted against Robert under the local rules of evidence. May the magistrate properly issue a search warrant? ________________

21. Officer Brady submitted to a neutral and detached magistrate a request to search the home of Kaplan for evidence of drug possession. In support of the request, Brady submitted an affidavit written by him, stating that according to one Longo, a confidential informant who had previously been reliable, Kaplan was a drug user who kept large quantities of cocaine at his home. It was true that Longo did in fact give this information to Brady, and Brady honestly believed the information. However, in reality, the information was false — Kaplan was not a drug user, and (unbeknownst to Brady) Longo was Kaplan's archenemy and was merely trying to harass Kaplan. Brady was negligent in not quizzing Longo further about his information, but Brady did not behave recklessly in believing Longo's story or in submitting the affidavit.

The magistrate issued the warrant. Brady executed the warrant. He did not find any drugs, but he did find an illegal gun. At Kaplan's trial for unlawful possession of the gun, he has moved to suppress all the fruits of the search on the grounds that the warrant was improperly procured. Assuming that he demonstrates all of the above facts (including particularly that had the true facts been as stated in Brady's affidavit, there would not have been probable cause to search his premises for drugs), should the judge order the fruits of the search suppressed? ________________

22. Authorities suspected that Desmond, an insurance broker, was defrauding his clients by taking premiums from them and then not paying the money to the insurance companies. An affidavit from a police officer described with adequate particularity why the police believed that Desmond was doing this. The principal reason for suspicion of Desmond was a complaint by Edward, a client of Desmond's, that Edward's coverage had been cancelled by the insurer for non-receipt of premiums. The police officer requested, and the magistrate issued, a warrant authorizing a search of Desmond's office and the seizure of "all business books and records relating to Desmond's insurance business." Authorities raided Desmond's office and seized virtually every piece of paper in it, including a diary in which he wrote statements making Desmond seem to be guilty of tax fraud in a transaction unrelated to Desmond's dealings with Edward. In Desmond's tax fraud trial, may he have the diary suppressed on the grounds that the warrant was issued in violation of the Fourth Amendment? ________________

23. The police had probable cause to believe that a particular small convenience store was also used as a numbers betting operation. The police obtained a warrant entitling them to search the premises, and to seize any evidence of illegal betting. The officers went to the store to execute the warrant. First, however, they frisked all persons present, including the owner of the store and Doug, a customer who was standing with a dollar bill and a quart of milk at the counter. When they frisked Doug, they found drugs. May Doug have the drugs suppressed on the grounds that they are the fruits of an unlawful search? ________________

24. Armand Chisel, noted tycoon and art collector, suffered a terrible burglary in his collection. Chisel explained to the police that two valuable Van Gogh paintings had been stolen from him, one entitled "Irises" and the other entitled "Lilies." He showed them colored photographs of each. Later, the police developed probable cause to believe that both of these paintings might be found in the home of a notorious local fence, Frank. Due to their desire to do the least possible work, the police prepared an affidavit that listed these facts, but that requested a warrant to search for and seize only "Irises," without mentioning that "Lilies" might also be found at Frank's premises. The warrant was issued. The officers went into

Frank's one-room studio apartment, saw (and seized) "Irises" right away, and then noticed "Lilies" on the wall right near where "Irises" had been. They seized "Lilies" as well. At Frank's trial for receiving stolen goods, may he have "Lilies" suppressed as the fruits of an unlawful seizure? ________________

25. Same basic fact pattern as the prior question. Now, assume that the police found "Irises" as soon as they walked into Frank's studio. They nonetheless continued looking in other areas of the apartment to see if there was anything else they might find that was incriminating. In a closet, they found "Lilies." May Frank have "Lilies" suppressed from his trial for receiving stolen goods? ________________

Answers

3. No. In all but the most unusual and shocking cases of violent police misconduct, the unconstitutionality of an arrest does not itself serve as a defense to charges. That is, a defendant may be tried and convicted regardless of the fact that his arrest was made in violation of the Fourth Amendment. (The legality of the arrest is, however, important in determining whether evidence obtained pursuant to a search that was incident to the arrest must be suppressed, an issue not present on these facts.) So the fact that Dexter was illegally arrested is of absolutely no value to him here — the prosecutor may proceed anyway, without even having to re-arrest Dexter or re-charge him.

4. Yes, probably. *Katz v. U.S.* establishes that even communications which in some sense occur in "public" may be protected under the Fourth Amendment. Basically, if (1) the defendant had an actual (subjective) expectation of privacy about the communication, and (2) that expectation was one which society recognizes as reasonable, then the communication will be protected by the Fourth Amendment, even if it occurred outside of a private home or office. Here, Johnny's communication probably satisfied this test — (1) he certainly showed an actual or subjective expectation that his words were not being overheard, and (2) in private everyday life one's words are not overheard by such specialized devices, so that society ought to regard an expectation of privacy in these circumstances as being "reasonable."

Therefore, even though the communication occurred in a public place, it was probably protected by the Fourth Amendment. Since the police did not have a warrant or probable cause to monitor the conversation, Johnny will probably be entitled to have the conversation suppressed, and the search warrant therefore thrown out. (The facts are roughly analogous to those of *Katz* itself, where eavesdropping done from the outside of a public phone booth was found to violate the Fourth Amendment rights of the defendant who used the booth to make calls.)

If the police had merely been using a conventional device, such as an ordinary telescope, to get the information, then there would not have been a Fourth Amendment violation, because the ***"plain view"*** doctrine would have been applicable. But because the information here was attainable only by use of equipment that was not generally available, plain view probably does not apply, and Johnny's Fourth Amendment rights are probably violated. (See, e.g., *Dow Chemical Co. v. U.S.*, stating that "an electronic device to penetrate walls or windows so as to hear and record confidential discussions...would raise very different and far more serious questions" than would the ordinary generally-available aerial camera used in *Dow*.)

By the way, *U.S. v. Leon* might save the prosecution here — that case holds that if a search warrant is issued by a detached and neutral magistrate but is ultimately found to be unsupported by probable cause, the search and its fruits are nonetheless valid and admissible; so even if the Task Force relied on improperly-obtained materials (the conversation) to get their search warrant, they might be able to get the fruits of the warrant admitted under *Leon*. That is why the facts tell you to ignore all issues except whether the conversation in the park was protected by the Fourth Amendment.

5. **(a) Yes.** There are two different scenarios in which a Fourth Amendment search may be deemed to have occurred: (1) where the police infringe on a person's "reasonable expectation of privacy" in an attempt to find information; and (2) where the police ***physically intrude*** on (to use the Fourth Amendment's language) someone's "person, house, papers [or] effects" Here, whether or not the placement and use of the GPS qualifies under (1), it clearly qualifies under (2). We know this because, in *U.S. v. Jones*, the Court held that the attachment of a GPS tracking device to the underside of D's car while the car was parked in a public place constituted a Fourth Amendment search, without regard to whether the attachment or use violated D's reasonable expectation of privacy. *Jones* is indistinguishable from the situation here — the briefcase was an "effect" belonging to Darwin (just as the car belonged to the defendant in *Jones*), and attaching the tracker was a physical intrusion on that effect. So whether or not tracking Darwin's movements over the public roads for 60 days violated Darwin's reasonable expectation of privacy (which it probably did), the physical intrusion was enough to give rise to a Fourth Amendment search.

(b) The record must be excluded. Since there was a search, the police needed probable cause to believe that the search would likely lead to evidence of Darwin's involvement in the murder. But the facts tell us that the police did not have such probable cause at the time they attached the device. Furthermore, the police ordinarily need a ***search warrant*** before conducting a search; there are numerous exceptions to the search warrant requirement (covered in the next chapter), but none of those exceptions applies here.

6. **Yes**. Under the ***"automobile exception"*** to the requirement of a search warrant, a vehicle may be searched without a warrant where there is probable cause to believe it contains contraband or evidence of a crime. *However*, absent exigent circumstances, an officer cannot enter a ***home or its curtilage*** to access the vehicle without a search warrant, even if the conditions for the automobile exception otherwise apply. *Collins v. Virginia*. Here, it's true that Officer Pete had probable cause for a search of the vehicle, since the vehicle matched the description provided by Elaine, and was spotted relatively close to the mall from where it was stolen. However, the garage was part of the curtilage of the home at # 123 Magnolia (since the garage was an enclosure attached to the home, and was part of "the area immediately surrounding and associated with the home," the definition of "curtilage.") Given that the garage was part of the curtilage, the automobile exception was irrelevant — Pete was required to get a search warrant before entering the garage and/or inspecting the car inside the garage, unless some other exception to the usual requirement of a search warrant applied. (But if Matt had parked the car on the *street*, Pete *would* have been entitled to do a warrantless search of the car (even its insides) there, in reliance on the automobile exception).

It's conceivable that the "exigent circumstances" exception might apply. But since Pete could have just remained in front of the house to ensure that no one drove the Jaguar away (while radioing for someone else to obtain the search warrant), it's unlikely that a court would find that these facts qualified for this exemption. There are no other exceptions to the search warrant requirement that might plausibly apply here, so a warrant was required before the search began.

7. **(a) The "plain view" doctrine.** Under this doctrine, "objects falling in the plain view of an officer who has a right to be in the position to have that view are subject to seizure and may be introduced in evidence." *Harris v. U.S.* More precisely, where an officer standing where she has a right to be spots something in plain view, no "search" is deemed to have taken place. Therefore, even if the officer got to that spot without having probable cause, there has been no Fourth Amendment violation. (The view does not necessarily entitle the officer to go in and seize the item, it merely assures that the view will not be deemed an unreasonable and thus illegal search.)

(b) No. The plain view doctrine is applicable on these facts. Baker obviously did not violate any law by gathering up the dog and returning it home. Baker was certainly standing where she had a right to be when she stood at the door and looked in after it was opened. Therefore, her spotting of the weapon was not a Fourth Amendment search at all, so her lack of probable cause before the moment where she spotted it is irrelevant. The view itself then supplied probable cause to obtain the warrant, thus making the seizure legal as well.

8. **Yes.** It is true that Officer Baker was lawfully in the living room, which was where the gun was located. But the "plain view" doctrine does not apply here. Jones did not consent to Officer Baker's opening of the closed container, so the contents of that container will not be deemed to have been in plain view — the question is whether one in Jones' position would reasonably have expected a casual social guest to open closed containers, and the answer is almost certainly "no." Since Jones will thus not be found to have consented to Officer Baker's opening of the container, Baker will be deemed to have overstepped her invitation, and the plain view doctrine will not apply. See, e.g., *Walter v. U.S.* (the fact that police were legitimately in possession of a closed package did not mean that they were entitled to open it to see that it contained obscene films).

9. **No.** As long as the officer did not violate any laws or engage in shocking conduct, the fact that she was standing in a place where she had a right to be at the time she got the view is dispositive. So the fact that Baker used a ***pretext*** to ring the bell and get her glimpse will not prevent the plain view doctrine from applying.

10. **(a) The "plain view" doctrine.** According to the plain view doctrine, a defendant has no reasonable expectation of privacy, and thus no Fourth Amendment interest, in anything that is seen by a police officer "in plain view" while the officer is standing in a place where he has a right to be. When Officer White, standing on the public sidewalk where she had a right to be, saw the marijuana plant, no search occurred.

    (b) No. As noted above, White did not commit a Fourth Amendment search by standing on the sidewalk and spotting the marijuana plant, since at the time she did so she was standing in a place where she had the right to be. But spotting the plant did ***not*** automatically give her the right to ***seize*** the plant without a warrant. Once she went onto Desmond's property, entered his house without a warrant, and confiscated the plant, she was then committing a seizure. This seizure, because it was warrantless and did not occur under exigent circumstances, was a violation of the Fourth Amendment's ban on unreasonable seizures. Therefore, Desmond is entitled to get the plants excluded from evidence against him. (Obviously, White should have gone to get a search warrant once she spotted the plants from the sidewalk. If she was worried about the plants being destroyed, she should have had a colleague stand on the sidewalk looking in the window while she went to get the warrant.)

11. **(a) The "plain odor" doctrine.** The Supreme Court has at least implied that just as viewing objects that are in "plain view" does not constitute a search, so perceiving the nature of an object by the smell it emits does not constitute a search. See, e.g., *U.S. v. Place* (use of dogs to perform a canine "sniff test" on luggage in an airport does not constitute a Fourth Amendment search of the luggage).

    (b) No, probably. The "plain odor" analogy to the "plain view" doctrine, which is pretty clearly valid, probably applies here. If "plain view" were being relied upon, the fact that the officer followed his line of sight into a place where he was not previously authorized to be would probably not be fatal — thus an officer who is entitled to stand in the foyer (perhaps because the owner of the house has consented to his being there), and who then sees an item in plain view in the living room, almost certainly has the right to go into the living room to inspect it more closely. By analogy, one who smells an odor while standing in a place where he has the right to be (the bedroom), probably has the right to "follow his nose" to get to the source. (The right to smell and thus find the body does not by itself automatically give the officer the right to seize the body; but since Officer Piston was already on the premises with a validly-issued warrant, he probably had the right to impound the body as yet another piece of evidence of crime.)

12. No. The facts here are very similar to those in *Florida v. Harris*. There, the Supreme Court held that a positive signal from a police dog trained in narcotics-sniffing creates probable cause for a drug search, as long as there is evidence that the dog has been properly trained. According to *Harris*, the defendant is entitled to try to show that the dog's in-the-field performance is so inaccurate that a positive signal does not constitute probable cause; but the prosecution does not have the burden to come forward with in-the-field performance statistics (proof of adequate training suffices). So here, the prosecution's evidence that Rover was properly trained, and his skills were kept up-to-date, was enough to establish that his signal gave Oscar probable cause to search the backpack for narcotics. Now, if the episode had begun by Oscar's making an illegal stop of Gina (e.g., stopping her on the street on a random suspicionless hunch that she might be involved in illegality), then the fruit of the search would be excludable no matter how reliable Rover's post-stop signal was, since the police opportunity to get the signal would have derived directly from the illegal stop. But here, it's clear that the encounter was initiated by Gina, not Oscar, so there is no issue about whether police illegality proceeded Rover's sniff and positive signal. Therefore, the marijuana is admissible.

13. No. In *California v. Greenwood*, the Court held that trash (as well as other abandoned property) will normally not be material as to which the owner has an objectively reasonable expectation of privacy. Therefore, when a person puts trash out on the curb to be picked up by the garbage collector, the police may search that trash without a warrant.

14. Yes, probably. The Court in *California v. Greenwood* (see prior answer) seemed to be limiting its holding to trash left at curb-side, or picked up by the actual garbage collector and brought to curb-side. Probably the Court would hold that George, by consenting to have the UC workers come into his back yard, was not thereby consenting to have government agents come onto his property to inspect his (admittedly abandoned) trash. After all, suppose that George's arrangement for trash disposal was that his day maid would come inside the house each morning, and take the trash out to the street — this would almost certainly not constitute consent by George to have government agents come into his house and take the trash away. The area right outside George's house in his back yard is within the "curtilage," and thus has a legitimate expectation of privacy associated with it, so the agents were presumably unlawfully infringing George's privacy by going there even if the ultimate result of their actions was to look at trash which they could have legally looked at had it been in the street.

15. Yes. The Supreme Court has held that an overnight guest normally has a legitimate expectation of privacy in the home where he is staying. *Minnesota v. Olson*. Therefore, the police were required to get a search warrant, just as if the apartment had been owned by Joe. When they did not do so, they violated the warrant requirement, and the marijuana will be deemed the fruits of an illegal search.

16. Both Eric *and* Mimi. As the owner of the car, Eric has the authority to challenge a search of it; the fact that he was not present in the vehicle at the time of the search does not diminish his privacy interest in it. Mimi, too, can challenge the search of the car. Although she was not the owner, she was alone in the vehicle under circumstances in which she had dominion and control over it, including the right to exclude others. This dominion was enough to give her a legitimate expectation of privacy in the vehicle at the time of the search. *Byrd v. U.S.* (By contrast, if Eric had been present in, and driving, the vehicle at the time of the search, Mimi would have been considered a "mere passenger" and, as such, would likely have been found to lack a privacy expectation sufficient to allow her to challenge a search of glove compartment.)

17. Probably not, though it's a very close question. In *Carpenter v. U.S.* (2018), the Supreme Court held that a warrant was necessary to secure from cell phone carriers the CSLI at issue there. In that case, the government received data spanning 127 days, and showing every move of Carpenter's phone during that period. The Court held that this cell site location information ("CSLI") was deep enough, broad enough, and revealing enough that just seven days of it triggered the need for a warrant, because that much CSLI provided such "an intimate window into [Carpenter's] life" as to make the third-party doctrine inapplicable; this data was therefore distinguishable from the data from the far less-revealing data collections in *Smith* and *Miller* (bank records and telephone numbers dialed), where the Court had applied the third-party doctrine. Here, the government requested CSLI data covering one month, a far longer period than the seven days found sufficient to trigger the need for a warrant in *Carpenter* itself. So based solely on this fact, the subpoena here would be so invasive of Marcus' reasonable expectation of privacy that Carpenter suggests that the third-party doctrine would not apply, and that a warrant was required.

However, the above analysis is not sufficient. The *Carpenter* majority emphasized that the privacy interest being infringed by the CSLI demand there was the defendant's privacy interest "in the whole of his physical movements" throughout the full 127-day period. In this problem, by contrast, the subpoena only required the cell phone carrier to give a yes/no answer to whether CSLI indicated that Marcus was within 50 miles of the crime scene at any time during the one-month period and, if the answer was yes, to tell the police where he was, within that radius, and during exactly what time periods. Thus the subpoena did not request a detailed report of the totality of Marcus' movements during this period; in fact, if the CSLI had failed to disclose any presence within the 50-mile radius, the carrier would have reported nothing at all about Marcus' whereabouts. Furthermore, no more than four hours of total CSLI was furnished here. Based on the foregoing, the government would argue that its subpoena did not constitute the sort of pervasive privacy infringement that caused the Court in *Carpenter* to refuse to apply the third-party doctrine. In response, Marcus could claim that responding to the subpoena required the cell phone carrier to conduct an invasive review of the totality of his movements for one month, even though the carrier ended up disclosing to law enforcement only a few locations, over two two-hour time periods.

All in all, this is a close question, on which the Supreme Court would be likely to be split, just as it was in *Carpenter* itself. But the much smaller volume of data furnished to the government here, compared with that in *Carpenter,* would likely be decisive. That is, the volume would probably be just small enough to convince a majority of the Court that the privacy invasion here was enough smaller than in *Carpenter* as to justify treating the situation as being more like the scenario in *Smith/Miller* (third-party doctrine applied) than like that in *Carpenter* (third-party doctrine not applied).

18. Probably not. Terence probably has a reasonable expectation of privacy in the contents of his DNA. So the real question is whether the fact that he surrendered a sample of that DNA to a third party — 23-and-me — makes a constitutional difference. Until the 2018 decision in *Carpenter v. U.S.*, the answer would have been a clear "no" — the Court had held in a pair of cases from the 1970s (*Smith v. Maryland* and *U.S. v. Miller*) that when a person voluntarily discloses data to a third party, the person is deemed to surrender any reasonable expectation of privacy as to that data. But in *Carpenter*, the Court refused to extend the third-party doctrine to cell site location information ("CSLI"), so the issue is whether the DNA here is similar enough to the CSLI in *Carpenter* as to justify a similar treatment.

In *Carpenter*, the Court expressly noted that its decision was narrow and did not apply in a number of other contexts, such as "tower dumps" or "conventional surveillance techniques and tools, such as security cameras." In refusing to apply the third-party doctrine to the CSLI in *Carpenter*, the majority emphasized that the CSLI there provided "a detailed and comprehensive record" of the defendant's movements for 127 days and profoundly invaded the "privacies of life," including the cell phone user's "familial, political, professional, religious and sexual associations." Here, the genetic profile generated by 23-and-me arguably has less wide-ranging implications, in that the profile identifies nothing about an individual's political, professional or religious affiliations. However, by providing a blueprint of Terence's genetic make-up, the profile undoubtedly intrudes upon his deeply private and personal information. So based on privacy concerns alone, it's hard to say whether *Carpenter* dictates treating the DNA identification here in the same (protected) way as the CSLI in *Carpenter*.

Here is an additional consideration: in the two pre-*Carpenter* third-party doctrine cases mentioned above, the Court noted that information an individual ***voluntarily discloses*** to a third party loses privacy protection even if, as with the bank records at issue in *Miller,* the disclosing party assumes the information will be "used only for a limited purpose." Here, Terence voluntarily decided to disclose his DNA to 23andme, and the fact that the website promised confidentiality would not by itself prevent the third-party doctrine from operating. So this factor cuts in favor of applying the third-party doctrine even after *Carpenter*.

One further consideration: the *Carpenter* majority underscored that CSLI is not "voluntarily disclosed" in the conventional sense, since the carrying and use of cell phones is a "pervasive and insistent part of daily life" and thus "indispensable to participation in modern society." By contrast, providing a DNA sample to learn more about one's racial and ethnic heritage *is* truly voluntary in the conventional sense. (Nor is obtaining this knowledge "indispensable to participation in modern society"). In fact, providing such a sample is *more* voluntary than creating the bank records at issue in *U.S. v. Miller* or the phone-numbers-dialed at issue in *Smith v. Maryland,* since those items were linked to core services integral to daily life.

So, all in all, a court is likely to conclude that notwithstanding *Carpenter*, the third-party doctrine should *apply* here so as to free the police from the need to procure a search warrant prior to issuing their subpoena.

19. No, probably. Under normal circumstances, a person has no expectation of privacy regarding information he has entrusted to a third-party; therefore, under the "third-party doctrine," law enforcement can subpoena that information from its holder without the need for either probable cause or a search warrant. However, the Court significantly limited the third-party doctrine in *Carpenter v. U.S.* (2018). In *Carpenter*, the police received by subpoena *C*'s cellphone carrier's records showing all locations of *C*'s cellphone (so-called Cell Site Location Information or "CSLI"), minute-by-minute during a 7-day period. The Court held that minute-by-minute CSLI information about a person's cellphone movements for 7 days is so intrusive, and so personally revealing, that the person *does* have a reasonable expectation of privacy in this data held by a third party; therefore, the Court said in *Carpenter*, the police were required to have probable cause and a search warrant before subpoenaing the information.

Here, the information subpoenaed consisted solely of the movements of a computer (Swenson's) over a 5-hour period, and was limited to messages from or to a single computer at a tightly-defined location (the Murder Site). So the question is whether this information is sufficiently similar in its intrusiveness to the 7-day CSLI data at issue in *Carpenter* that its owner should be deemed to have a reasonable expectation of privacy in it, in which case the police would be barred from demanding the information without probable cause and a warrant. The Supreme Court has not yet issued any opinions examining the scope of *Carpenter*; therefore, answering this question requires us to predict, on limited information, whether the Court would apply *Carpenter* to these facts. It seems ***unlikely*** that the Court would find these facts to be sufficiently similar to those of *Carpenter* that *Carpenter* would apply. The information here is much less voluminous and intrusive than that in *Carpenter*: First, the time period covered is much shorter here (7 days in *Carpenter* versus 5 hours here). Second, the geographical scope of the location information is much narrower here (in *Carpenter*, everywhere the defendant's phone went on a minute-by-minute basis, whereas here, only the location of a computer that communicated with another specific computer located at a tightly-fixed location, the Murder Site). These differences suggest that Swenson, as the owner of the computer here, did *not* have a reasonable expectation of privacy in this much-more limited information. One court concluded, on facts similar to the scenario here, that the information was too limited for *Carpenter* to apply; therefore, the police did not need a warrant or probable cause. See *U.S. v. Hood*, 920 F.3d 87 (1st Cir. 2019).

20. Yes. Any trustworthy information may be considered in determining whether probable cause to search or arrest exists, even if the information would ***not be admissible*** at trial. Thus the police may use hearsay information, or even a prior criminal record of the suspect, as part of their showing of probable cause.

21. No. In general, the issue is whether the *magistrate* acted properly — that is, whether detailed assertions making out probable cause are presented to the magistrate — not whether the officer acted properly. So it will normally not matter that false information is supplied to the magistrate. This is true even where the officer acted negligently in not catching the error. (But if the officer intentionally perjured himself in the affidavit, or acted recklessly in not catching the error, the result will probably be different.)

22. Yes, probably. The Fourth Amendment provides that no warrant shall issue except one "***particularly describing*** the…things to be seized." Probably the warrant here was so broad as to violate this requirement. Clearly the warrant could have been limited to records relating to Desmond's dealings with Edward, or in the worst case, records dealing with payments remitted to insurance companies on behalf of customers. The warrant here was utterly unparticular — it asked for all books and records, yet there is very little in an insurance office except books and records. Also, where the items seized have First Amendment value (like the diary here), the requirement of specificity is usually enforced somewhat more strictly.

23. Yes, probably. The police may protect themselves while performing a search, in the sense that they may check any person in control of the premises who is likely to be dangerous. But where a person simply happens to be on the premises to be searched, and appears not to have any connection with the criminal activity that gave rise to the warrant, that person may not be searched or frisked. Since Doug, here, seemed to be an ordinary patron unconnected to any illegal betting that may have been going on on the premises, the police probably did not have the right to stop him and frisk him. See *Ybarra v. Illinois* (warrant to search a bar and its bartender did not allow the police to frisk each patron).

24. No. Even though "Lilies" was not mentioned in the warrant, the police were entitled to seize it because it was in plain view while they were carrying out their lawfully-issued warrant for "Irises." It is not required, for application of the plain view doctrine, that the police's discovery of an item in plain view be "inadvertent," so the fact that the police knew in advance that they were just as likely to find "Lilies," which was not named in the warrant, does not matter. See *Horton v. California*.

25. Yes. The police are not permitted to go beyond the scope of the warrant. They may seize items that they find in plain view while they are properly executing the warrant (as happened in the prior question). But once they have found what they came for, they must stop. Similarly, if they are looking for something large, like a human body, they may not look in places that could not possibly hold the item they are looking for (e.g., small closed containers).

Exam Tips on ***ARREST; PROBABLE CAUSE; SEARCH WARRANTS***

Here are the things to remember about arrests, probable cause and search warrants:

Remember that the Fourth Amendment prohibition against unreasonable searches and seizures can be triggered in ***only two types of situations***:

Where the police ***physically intrude*** on D's property (in essence, a ***trespass***), in an attempt to find evidence or information; or

Where the police infringe on D's ***"reasonable expectation of privacy,*** in an attempt to find evidence or information.

Therefore, unless the police have intruded on D's property (e.g., by attaching a tracking device to D's car), there cannot be a Fourth Amendment "search" unless the defendant had a ***"reasonable expectation of privacy"*** in the area that was searched.

For instance, there is no reasonable expectation of privacy from ***aerial surveillance*** of an area over which there is an ***established aerial route.*** This is true regardless of the owner's clear intent and efforts to maintain his privacy in the area, because such attempts are unreasonable.

Example: Defendant owns a home with a yard, around which he puts a very tall privacy fence. The police fly over his yard and use binoculars to take aerial photographs of the marijuana growing in Defendant's yard. This does not violate the Fourth Amendment, because Defendant is deemed not have had a reasonable expectation of privacy with regard to those parts of his yard that can be seen from a legal over-flight.

Similarly, visual ***surveillance*** by the police from the ground will usually ***not*** constitute a search of him — assuming no physical intrusion on D's property, surveillance will only constitute a search where the conduct violates a defendant's reasonable expectation of privacy. So if police watch D from a ***public vantage point,*** their conduct is not a search, and no warrant is required.

Example: Police suspect Defendant of drug activity. Detective maintains visual non-contact surveillance of Defendant by stationing himself in the lobby of Defendant's apartment building and watching Defendant's movements as he enters and leaves the building. This is not a search, because Defendant has no expectation of privacy in the lobby. Therefore, the Fourth Amendment is not implicated (and no search warrant is needed).

Remember that a homeowner has a reasonable expectation of privacy not just in the inside of her house, but also in the ***"curtilage,"*** i.e., the area ***immediately surrounding the house***, typically including things like ***garages, porches*** and ***backyards***.

Example: The police climb the stairs onto the front porch of D's house, accompanied by a trained drug-sniffing dog. The dog sniffs the outside of D's front door and signals that drugs are present. The front porch is a part of the curtilage of D's house. Therefore, D is deemed to have a reasonable expectation of privacy in that front porch. By bringing the dog onto the porch without D's consent to drug-sniffing activities, the police have carried out a Fourth Amendment search (which was probably illegal unless they had both probable cause and a search warrant). [Cite to *Florida v. Jardines.*]

Curtilage may also include ***part of a driveway***. That is, the part of the driveway that immediately abuts the house is usually part of the curtilage. [Cite to *Collins v. Virginia.*]

Remember that search warrants must be ***based on probable cause*** and must ***specifically identify the premises or persons*** to be searched.

Probable cause for a search warrant exists if it is ***reasonably likely*** that ***incriminating evidence will be found*** at the time and place the search is made. (But the likelihood probably ***doesn't*** need to be ***greater than 50%*** — a 1/3 chance might well be enough. Cite to *Maryland v. Pringle* on this point.)

Probable cause is a very ***fact-intensive*** determination, so your professor will have to give you lots of facts if probable cause is an issue. The conclusion you come to will probably be a judgment call; at least recognize that probable cause is an issue, and explain which facts are relevant to the determination of whether it is more likely than not that evidence of criminal activity will be found.

Remember that an ***illegal search cannot form the basis of probable cause*** to obtain a search warrant. (*Example:* Police can't make an illegal warrantless search of D's apartment, find cocaine, then seek a search warrant for that apartment based on their knowledge of the cocaine.)

Look out for scenarios in which D ***turns over data to a third person***: that turnover may mean that D ***no longer has an expectation of privacy*** in the data, so the police can demand that the third party turn over a copy to it, even though the police ***don't have a warrant or probable cause.***

Example: D opens a checking account with Bank. As D knows, every time D writes a check, Bank keeps a digital copy of it in a database. Even without a warrant or probable cause, the police can demand that Bank supply copies of all checks written by D during, say, a particular time period. Because D "voluntarily" turned over the check copies to a third party (Bank), he is deemed to have surrendered any reasonable expectation of privacy with regard to those copies. [Cite to *U.S. v. Miller*.]

But keep in mind that the third-party doctrine probably ***won't*** apply in the case of most ***modern-era digital databases*** kept by companies, if the database captures large numbers of details of individuals' electronically-recorded transactions. Government requests that a company supply significant chunks of data about a suspect from such a database will probably be ***considered to be Fourth Amendment searches***, if

[1] the information is ***"deeply revealing"*** about the suspect;

[2] the information's ***"reach"*** is "***deep,"*** ***"broad,"*** and ***"comprehensive"***; and

[3] the ***process*** by which the information has been collected is ***"inescapable and automatic."***

Example: Police arrest D in connection with 10 robberies of local Radio Shack stores over a 2-month period. Suspicion — not amounting to probable cause — focuses on D, who the police know owned a cellphone serviced by Sprint Wireless at the time of each of the robberies. The police — without a search warrant — send a subpoena to Sprint, asking the company to supply "CSLI" ("cell-site location information") showing where D's phone was at the time of each of the robberies. Sprint does so, supplying CSLI that shows, on each of 10 days, where D's phone was at the time of each robbery. D moves to suppress the CSLI from his trial, arguing that when the police demanded the data from Sprint, this was a Fourth Amendment search, which should not have been performed except pursuant to a search warrant issued upon probable cause.

You should say that D's argument is correct, and that the CSLI should be suppressed. The CSLI data requested by the police is highly revealing of D's intimate details, and is "broad" and "comprehensive." Also, the collection of the data was "inescapable and automatic" (since anyone needing a cellphone, a virtually indispensable product for modern life, would have to allow such data to be automatically collected). Therefore, the police committed a Fourth Amendment search when they subpoenaed the data. That subpoena should have been issued only by a "neutral magistrate," after the police showed probable cause to believe that the CSLI would constitute evidence of crime. [Cite to *Carpenter v. U.S.*]

Keep your eyes peeled for applications of the ***"plain view"*** doctrine: if authorities view an item of evidence from a ***vantage point where they have a right to be,*** that item is ***admissible*** even though the police don't have a warrant.

A variant of the "plain view" doctrine applies to ***senses other than sight,*** such as hearing and smell.

Example: Officer goes to Defendant's hotel room to execute what turns out to be an invalid search warrant. While standing in the hallway, he hears the sounds of a struggle taking place within the hotel room. At Defendant's murder trial, Officer can testify about the sounds he heard. This is so because Officer had the right to be in the hall at the time he heard the struggle (an Officer has the right to execute what turns out to be an invalid search warrant so long as the Officer is acting in good faith without reasonable grounds to suspect the invalidity.) Therefore, Officer's discovery of the sounds fell within the plain view exception.

Confidential informers are a rich source of exam questions. If the warrant is based on the hearsay of a police informer, the sufficiency of the information is determined based on the ***"totality of the circumstances."*** There must be corroboration of the facts, or other means of determining that the informer is credible.

Example: An arrest warrant is issued based on an affidavit that states merely that a confidential informant "knows" Defendant and knows that stolen merchandise is now in Defendant's apartment. This is probably insufficient, because there is no reason given for believing that the informant is reliable, and no way to tell what the basis of the information is (e.g., personal observation, versus mere hearsay from another party).

A ***misidentification*** of the premises to be searched will invalidate the warrant unless officers executing it could not mistake the place to be searched.

A search warrant gives the police executing it the right to ***scan the entire premises*** if they have reasonable suspicion that ***other armed persons*** may be present (based on a concern for officer safety.)

Example: Officer goes to a home to confiscate contraband. He knows that the contraband will be located in the bedroom, but he opens a door in the hall which he correctly assumes to be a closet and finds a different item of contraband. He also knows that the Homeowner/Defendant has a violence-prone boyfriend. The discovery of the second item is legal, because Officer reasonably feared that an armed person, the boyfriend, might be hiding in the closet.

Police may not, however, search places where the item they are looking for ***cannot possibly be concealed*** and where no armed person could possibly be hiding. (*Example:* Officer executing a search warrant for a counterfeiting machine may not look inside a jewelry box, since neither the machine nor an armed person could possibly fit inside it.)

Remember that the ***"good faith"*** exception to the warrant requirement will save a search even though the warrant is invalid, if the officers are acting in the objective, good faith belief that the warrant is valid.

The requirement of an ***arrest warrant*** is the perfect example of exceptions swallowing the rule. There are, however, some limited circumstances when a warrant is still required to make an arrest. Generally, arrest warrants are ***not required*** even when the police have time to obtain them — there is no exigent-circumstances requirement. However:

If the offense is a ***misdemeanor*** and wasn't committed in the ***officer's presence***, an arrest warrant is required.

Police need a warrant to arrest a defendant ***inside his own home,*** if there's no emergency.

Don't assume that because officers don't need a warrant to make an arrest that they also don't need probable cause. Even without a warrant, officers ***still have to have probable cause*** to make a legal arrest.

CHAPTER 3

WARRANTLESS ARRESTS AND SEARCHES

ChapterScope

We looked earlier at the requirements and scope of search and arrest warrants. This chapter examines the many situations in which police are ***not required*** to obtain a search or arrest warrant.

Arrest warrants: ***Arrest*** warrants are required only when the police ***enter a private home*** to make an arrest and ***no exigent circumstances*** exist.

Search warrants: Police ***ordinarily need a search warrant to conduct a search or seizure of property.*** There are, however, several common ***exceptions***:

Search incident to a valid arrest: When the police are making a ***lawful arrest,*** they may search the ***area within the arrestee's control***.

Search under exigent circumstances: Exigent circumstances, such as ***"hot pursuit"*** or preventing the ***destruction of evidence*** or harm to persons, may justify dispensing with the warrant requirement.

"Plain view": Police who are lawfully in a particular place may make a warrantless seizure of evidence that they come across in ***"plain view."***

Automobile searches: When the driver of a ***car*** is arrested, the car may be searched at the station-house without a warrant (an "inventory search.") Also, if the police reasonably believe that a car is carrying ***contraband***, it may be subjected to a full warrantless search in the ***field***, including a search of any closed containers.

Consent searches: No warrant is needed if the person whose premises, person, or effects are to be searched ***consents*** to the search.

"Stop and frisk" searches: An officer may briefly ***detain*** a suspect to make inquiries if he has ***reasonable suspicion*** (a lower standard than probable cause) that criminal activity is afoot. In doing so, he may make a ***"frisk"*** or ***"pat-down"*** of the suspect's ***outer clothing*** in an attempt to discover weapons.

Inspections and regulatory searches: For most types of inspections, a warrant is required. But certain types of regulatory searches, such as immigration-related ones, may be carried out without a warrant.

I. INTRODUCTION

A. **Necessity for warrants generally:** The previous chapter considered the requirements of probable cause for search and arrest, and also treated the formal requisites of warrants. But although probable cause is necessary for all arrests and searches, a warrant does not always have to be procured before an arrest or search is made. This chapter concerns the various exceptions to the warrant requirement.

1. **Stops and inspections:** Although probable cause is always necessary for a full-scale search or arrest, the Supreme Court has held that certain types of less severe intrusions, such as on-the-street "stop and frisks," and ***regulatory searches***, do not require probable cause. Because these more limited intrusions do not require a warrant either, they are considered in this chapter.

II. WARRANTLESS ARRESTS

A. **Constitutional requirement:** Arrest warrants are seldom used, and have as a general rule been held ***not to be constitutionally required***. See ***U.S. v. Watson***, 423 U.S. 411 (1976). This is true even where the police have sufficient advance notice so that procurement of a warrant would not jeopardize the arrest. *Id.*

   1. **Constitutional requirement for entry of dwelling:** The only situation in which an arrest warrant may be constitutionally required is where the police wish to enter ***private premises*** to arrest a suspect.

      a. **Non-exigent circumstances:** If there are ***no exigent circumstances***, the police ***may not enter a private home*** to make a warrantless arrest. ***Payton v. New York***, 445 U.S. 573 (1980). The Court in *Payton* noted that entry into a private home is an extreme intrusion, and that an entry for the purpose of making an arrest is nearly as intrusive as an entry for a search. Therefore, the Fourth Amendment requires that a neutral and detached official certify that there is probable cause to make the arrest before this intrusion may take place. The Court conceded that 24 states now have statutes permitting such warrantless entry for routine felony arrests, but noted that most state courts that have passed on such statutes have held them to be unconstitutional where applied in the absence of exigent circumstances.

         i. **Result of invalid arrest:** A warrantless arrest made in violation of *Payton* will not prevent the defendant from being brought to trial. (He can always be re-arrested, after a warrant has been issued.) The principal consequence of an invalid arrest is likely to be that ***evidence seized*** during the arrest will not be admissible. Thus in *Payton* itself, the police entered Payton's residence to arrest him, and found a shell casing in plain view, which was later admitted against Payton at his trial. As a result of the Supreme Court's ruling that the warrantless entry was impermissible, the shell became inadmissible and a new trial necessary.

         ii. **Confession stemming from arrest:** Suppose that the defendant is arrested without a warrant, in violation of *Payton*, and then gives a ***confession*** at the stationhouse. The confession seems to derive from the illegal arrest in this situation, so that you might expect it to be inadmissible at trial under the "fruit of the poisonous tree" doctrine (see *infra*, p. 324). But the Rehnquist Court appears to view *Payton* violations as being in some way less serious than, say, arrests made without probable cause — a confession that follows a warrantless arrest in violation of *Payton* will ***not*** be excluded, even though a confession made following an arrest lacking probable cause will be. See *N.Y. v. Harris, infra*, p. 338.

b. **Exigent circumstances:** If there are ***exigent circumstances***, so that it is impractical for the police to delay the entry and arrest until they can obtain a warrant, no warrant is necessary, assuming that the crime is a serious one.

   i. **Destruction of evidence:** For instance, if the police have reasonable cause to believe that the suspect will ***destroy evidence*** if they delay their entry until they can get a warrant, the requisite exigent circumstances exist. See *Illinois v. McArthur, infra*, p. 122.

   ii. **"Hot pursuit":** Similarly, if the police are pursuing a felony suspect, and he runs into either his own or another's dwelling, a warrantless entry may be permitted under the ***"hot pursuit"*** doctrine. See, e.g., *U.S. v. Santana*, 427 U.S. 38 (1976).

2. **No exception for fine-only or other minor crimes:** A warrantless arrest for a crime committed in an officer's presence is permissible even where the crime is ***so minor*** that the only potential punishment is a ***fine*** rather than imprisonment. As the result of a controversial case involving a motorist who did not wear a seat belt, it is now clear that the Fourth Amendment does not prevent an officer from making a full custodial arrest for any ***traffic violation*** or other ***minor misdemeanor*** committed in the officer's presence, no matter how slight are the law-enforcement interests favoring such an arrest. ***Atwater v. City of Lago Vista***, 532 U.S. 318 (2001).

   a. **Facts:** In *Atwater*, a Texas woman, Gail Atwater, was stopped while driving with her three-year-old son and five-year-old daughter. None of the three was wearing a seat belt, a misdemeanor punishable under Texas law by a fine of not more than $50. Bart Turek, a local police officer, observed the violation, pulled Atwater over, and yelled, "We've met before" and "You're going to jail." Turek then handcuffed Atwater, put her in his squad car, and drove her to the local police station, where she was booked, had her mug shot taken, and was kept in a cell for about an hour before being released on a $310 bond. She ultimately paid a $50 fine. Atwater brought a civil suit against the city for which Turek worked, alleging that the arrest for such a minor crime was unreasonable and thus a violation of her Fourth Amendment rights. (A federal statute allows recovery where a governmental entity violates a person's constitutional rights "under color of law.")

   b. **Majority find no violation:** By 5-4 vote, the Court found that the arrest was ***not a violation of the Fourth Amendment*** even though the offense was extremely minor and ***punishable only by a fine***. The lineup of the judges was somewhat unusual, with the usually-liberal Justice Souter writing the majority opinion, and the usually-conservative Justice O'Connor writing the dissent.

      i. **No clear historical rule:** Souter's opinion began by considering what the framers of the Fourth Amendment had believed about the circumstances in which an arrest was permissible for a minor non-jailable offense. He concluded that the historical record was ambiguous, and thus not dispositive on whether such an arrest should be considered "unreasonable" today.

ii. **Case-specific facts don't control:** Souter then turned to the modern policy issues at stake. He conceded that if the court were to "to write a rule exclusively to address the uncontested facts of this case," Atwater "might well prevail," because as a local resident she was an unlikely flight risk, and the circumstances of her arrest "were merely gratuitous humiliations imposed by a police officer who was (at best) exercising extremely poor judgment." Therefore, Atwater's "claim to live free of pointless indignity and confinement clearly outweighs anything the City can raise against it specific to her case." But, Souter said, the case-specific facts should not control. Instead, the Court should follow a less fact-bound, more bright-line rule, by adopting "standards sufficiently clear and simple to be applied with a fair prospect of surviving judicial second-guessing months and years after an arrest or search is made."

iii. **Proposed rule rejected:** Souter rejected Atwater's proposed bright-line rule, under which arrest would be allowed only for "jailable," not "fine-only," offenses. The problem with this rule, he said, was that an officer on the street would sometimes ***not be able to tell*** which category an offense fell into — some offenses, for instance, prescribe jail only for repeat offenders, or only for drug possession if more than a certain weight is involved, and the officer won't know whether the condition is satisfied.

iv. **Souter's bright-line rule:** Instead, Souter concluded, the only suitable bright-line rule was the one implied by the Court's prior decisions: "If an officer has ***probable cause*** to believe that individual has committed even a ***very minor criminal offense*** in his presence, he may, without violating the Fourth Amendment, ***arrest the offender.***"

c. **Dissent:** The dissent by Justice O'Connor (joined by Justices Stevens, Ginsburg and Breyer) argued that the arrest here was an "unreasonable . . . seizure," and thus violated the Fourth Amendment. O'Connor agreed with Atwater's assertion that arrest ***should not normally be permitted for fine-only offenses:*** "I would require that when there is probable cause to believe that a fine-only offense has been committed, the police officer should issue a citation unless the officer is 'able to point to ***specific and articulable facts*** which, taken together with rational inferences from those facts, reasonably warrant [the additional] intrusion' of a full custodial arrest." For instance, a large risk that the suspect would fail to report for trial if given just a ticket might justify an arrest even for a minor offense. But, she said, here no such facts existed to warrant the intrusion of a full-scale arrest, since Atwater, as a local resident with deep roots, was very unlikely to fail to show up for trial if given a citation.

i. **Risk of harassment:** O'Connor warned that the majority's approach would heighten the ***risk of harassment***, especially of ***racial minorities***. "[A]s the recent debate over ***racial profiling*** demonstrates all too clearly, a relatively minor traffic contraction may often serve as an excuse for stopping and harassing an individual. After today, the arsenal available to any officer extends to a full arrest and the searches permissible concomitant to that arrest."

d. **Significance:** It's unlikely that police officers after *Atwater* will frequently make full-scale custodial arrest for fine-only offenses. The principal significance of the case is that it furnishes the police with an opportunity to ***make a search*** of a stopped vehicle incident to the arrest of the driver in circumstances where they otherwise would not have been able to do so.

Example: Suppose that Officer has a belief, not based on facts, that many young black males driving expensive cars are drug dealers. Officer spots X, a 22-year-old black male, driving a Mercedes-Benz. He follows the Mercedes for two blocks, and sees X change lanes without signaling, a very minor traffic violation punishable solely by a $25 fine. Officer's sole desire is to have a pretext for searching X's car. He therefore pulls X over, makes him exit the car, and arrests him for the failure to signal (as *Atwater* says he can). Officer then conducts a full-scale search of the car's interior, incident to this valid arrest. (*Whren v. U.S., infra*, p. 135, says that such a pretextual stop-and-search is nonetheless valid, if there really was a violation.) Officer finds marijuana hidden under the seat. X can be convicted of drug possession, even though the entire episode came about through a pretextual stop based upon Officer's gross and inaccurate racial profiling.

e. **Right of states to modify law:** Of course the states are free to modify their laws to prohibit, as a statutory matter, the making of arrests for all or certain types of fine-only offenses. If a state did so, *Atwater* would have no application (since the case assumes that the arrest is valid under state law). Statutory requirements for warrantless arrest are discussed *infra*, p. 97.

3. **Probable cause need not be for offense stated at time of arrest:** Suppose that at the time of the warrantless arrest the officer specifies to the suspect that the arrest is being made for ***Offense A***; if it finally turns out that there was not probable cause for Offense *A*, but that there *was* probable cause for ***Offense B*** (never mentioned by the arresting officer), does this make any difference to the validity of the arrest? The Supreme Court has answered ***"no"*** — even if Offense *B* is ***not closely related*** to Offense *A*, the arrest is still ***valid*** so long as the arresting officer was in possession of facts that created probable cause regarding Offense *B* (the unmentioned, and perhaps unthought-about, offense). *Devenpeck v. Alford*, 543 U.S. 146 (2004).

   a. **Significance:** *Devenpeck* is of special significance when the police conduct a ***search incident to the warrantless arrest*** (see *infra*, p. 99). Even if there's no probable cause for the offense on which the police purport to make the arrest, as long as it turns out that there was *some* offense as to which the police knew facts amounting to probable cause, the search incident to the arrest will be valid even though the police never mentioned (or even thought about) that offense pre-arrest.

B. **Statutory requirements:** In addition to the rules described above for when an arrest warrant is constitutionally required, many states have ***statutes*** requiring arrest warrants in some circumstances, even where the warrant is not constitutionally required.

   1. **Felonies:** All states allow an officer to make an arrest for a ***felony*** without a warrant, even if the felony was committed outside of the officer's presence.

   2. **Misdemeanors:** Many states allow an officer to make a warrantless ***misdemeanor*** arrest only if the misdemeanor was ***committed in the officer's presence***. (Nutshell, p. 119). In states with such statutes, the requirement is often interpreted to mean merely that the offi-

cer must have reasonable grounds to believe that a misdemeanor was committed in his presence; if it turns out that the misdemeanor was committed elsewhere, evidence found pursuant to any search of the arrestee is not thereby suppressible.

a. **More liberal test:** Some states, finding the "presence of the officer" test too stringent even in misdemeanor cases, allow a warrantless arrest to be made simply on ***"reasonable grounds."***

C. **Post-arrest probable cause hearing:** If a suspect is arrested without a warrant (even if the situation is one in which such a warrantless arrest is permissible), he is entitled to a ***prompt post-arrest determination*** of whether there was probable cause for his arrest. *Gerstein v. Pugh*, 420 U.S. 103 (1975). In *Gerstein*, the Court specifically held that a suspect arrested on the basis of a ***prosecutor's information*** (i.e., a prosecutor's decision that there is probable cause for arrest, permitted in many states in lieu of a grand jury indictment) is entitled to a prompt post-arrest probable cause hearing. But the Court's rationale clearly applies to any other warrantless arrest, including one made under exigent circumstances.

1. **No adversary rights:** However, the Court in *Gerstein* held that the probable cause finding could be made by a magistrate rather than a judge, and that such aspects of the adversary system as cross-examination and a right to appointed counsel do not apply. That is, all that is required is the same kind of proceeding that would be used to issue an arrest warrant. (But four Justices concurring in the result in *Gerstein* argued that these adversary safeguards should not be ruled out.)

2. **48-hour rule:** When *Gerstein* says that the post-arrest determination of probable cause must be "prompt" what does "prompt" mean? In the later case of *County of Riverside v. McLaughlin*, 500 U.S. 44 (1991), the Court held that ordinarily this determination must be made within ***48 hours*** of the arrest. The 48-hour rule is not hard and fast, but controls the burden of proof— if the hearing is held within 48 hours, the burden is on the defendant to show undue delay, whereas if it occurs after this time, the burden is on the government to show that some extraordinary circumstance prevented a prompter hearing.

D. **Use of deadly force to make arrest:** Even where an officer has probable cause to arrest a suspect, the Fourth Amendment places limits on ***how*** the arrest may be made. In particular, use of ***deadly force*** to arrest a fleeing suspect is sometimes an unreasonable seizure under the Fourth Amendment. As a constitutional matter, "where the suspect poses ***no immediate threat*** to the officer and ***no threat to others***, the harm resulting from failure to apprehend him ***does not justify the use of deadly force*** to do so." *Tennessee v. Garner*, 471 U.S. 1 (1985).

1. **Threat to others:** *Garner* was a case in which the police had no reason to believe that the fleeing suspect was a danger to them or to others. Where the police *do* have reason to think the suspect is dangerous to them or others, then as a Fourth Amendment matter the police are ***entitled to use deadly force*** if they reasonably believe that lesser force will not or may not suffice. And at least where the suspect is fleeing by driving recklessly, the police are ***not*** required to ***call off the chase even if this would reduce the danger.*** *Scott v. Harris*, 550 U.S. 372 (2007).

III. SEARCH INCIDENT TO ARREST

A. **Pre-1969 law on search incident to arrest:** Before 1969, most courts held that when the police validly arrested a person, they could constitutionally search the ***entire premises*** where he was arrested, even though they did not have a search warrant. *U.S. v. Rabinowitz*, 339 U.S. 56 (1950). Such a search was known as a ***search incident to arrest.***

1. **Control:** While a few courts restricted the search incident to arrest to the physical area within the suspect's "control," even these courts interpreted the term in a loose manner, so that often several rooms of a house were subjected to warrantless search.

B. ***Chimel:*** But in 1969, the Supreme Court radically restricted the scope of the search incident to arrest. This occurred in ***Chimel v. California***, 395 U.S. 752 (1969). Although *Chimel* did not reduce the number of situations in which a search incident to arrest could be conducted (these circumstances are discussed below), it drastically restricted the ***physical area in which the search could be performed.***

1. **Facts of *Chimel:*** In *Chimel*, police officers came to the home of the defendant, who was suspected of having robbed a coin shop. The police had an arrest warrant, but no search warrant. After arresting the defendant, the police conducted a full-scale search of the defendant's three-bedroom house and discovered some of the stolen coins. During the entire search-and-arrest, the defendant's wife was present.

2. **Holding:** The Court found the search to have been invalid, because it was ***unnecessarily widespread***. The Court recognized the police's right to search the area within the defendant's ***immediate control***, but held that the portion of the premises ***outside of that control*** could ***not*** be warrantlessly searched incident to arrest.

   a. **Rationale:** The Court, in an opinion by Justice Stewart, explained its holding in the following language: "When an arrest is made, it is reasonable for the arresting officer to search the person arrested in order to ***remove any weapons*** that the latter might seek to use in order to resist arrest or effect his escape. Otherwise, the officer's ***safety might well be endangered,*** and the arrest itself frustrated. In addition, it is entirely reasonable for the arresting officer to search for and seize any ***evidence on the arrestee's person*** in order to prevent its ***concealment or destruction***. And the ***area into which an arrestee might reach*** in order to ***grab a weapon or evidentiary items*** must, of course, be governed by a like rule. A ***gun on a table or in a drawer in front of one who is arrested*** can be as dangerous to the arresting officer as one concealed in the clothing of the person arrested. There is ample justification, therefore, for a search of the arrestee's person and the area ***'within his immediate control'*** — construing that phrase to mean ***the area from within which he might gain possession of a weapon or destructible evidence***."

      i. **Limited scope:** But Stewart emphasized that the right to search incident to arrest applied ***only*** to this area within the arrestee's "immediate control." "There is ***no comparable justification***, however, for routinely searching ***rooms other than that in which an arrest occurs*** — or, for that matter, for searching through ***all the desk drawers or other closed or concealed areas in that room itself***. Such searches, in the absence of well-recognized exceptions, may be made ***only under the authority of a search warrant."***

3. **Dissent:** A dissent, by Justice White (joined by Justice Black), argued that "assuming that there is probable cause to search premises at the spot where a suspect is arrested, it seems to me unreasonable to require the police to leave the scene in order to obtain a search warrant when they are already legally there to make a valid arrest, and when there must almost always be a strong possibility that confederates of the arrested man will in the meanwhile remove the items for which the police have probable cause to search." In *Chimel* itself, for instance, argued the dissent, if the police had left the defendant's house to procure a warrant after the arrest, "it seems very likely that petitioner's wife, who in view of petitioner's generally garrulous nature must have known of the robbery, would have removed the coins."

   a. **Arrest as exigent circumstance:** The dissent agreed with the majority that as a general rule, search warrants are required. But the dissent contended that an arrest in a case where evidence might be destroyed constituted an "exigent circumstance."

C. **Distance and time limits on search under *Chimel:*** The Supreme Court has never given much guidance about ***how wide an area*** will be deemed within the arrestee's ***"immediate control"*** (the phrase used in *Chimel*), and thus subject to search incident to arrest. Nor has the Court given much help on ***how long after the arrest*** the search can take place. (For more about the "remote in time" problem, see *infra*, p. 106.)

1. **Can't be "remote in time or place":** In the one major post-*Chimel* Supreme Court case on these issues, the Court made it clear that there must be ***some real possibility*** that the suspect can ***reach the area*** being searched. In ***U.S. v. Chadwick***, 433 U.S. 1 (1977), the police arrested several suspected smugglers, and seized the footlocker in which they were thought to be transporting marijuana. After the suspects were safely incarcerated, and more than an hour after the arrest, the officers opened and searched the footlocker, without a warrant. The Court held the search ***invalid***, saying that a search is not incident to arrest if it is ***"remote in time or place from the arrest."***

   a. **Dissent:** Justice Blackmun, joined by Justice Rehnquist, dissented in *Chadwick*, saying that he would "adopt a clear-cut rule permitting property seized in conjunction with a valid arrest in a public place to be searched without a warrant."

2. **Different room:** It's probably safe to assume that, as the *Chimel* Court seemed to say, the arrestee does ***not*** have "immediate control" of items that are in a ***different room*** than where the arrestee is being held. (But the Supreme Court has never addressed the "separate room" scenario post-*Chimel*.)

   Example: The police properly arrest and handcuff D while in the kitchen of D's house. The police probably cannot then search the living room on an incident-to-arrest rationale, because it's unlikely that objects in the living room would be found to be within D's "immediate control" while he remains in the kitchen. (But if the police reasonably feared that a *confederate* might be present in the house, then they might use the "protective sweep" rationale, *infra*, p. 105, to look throughout the house in order to ensure their own safety.)

   a. **Substantial area within same room:** But many post-*Chimel* lower-court cases have held that the defendant, even after his arrest, maintains "immediate control" over a

substantial area within the ***room when he is being held***, even if he is handcuffed and/or numerous officers surround him.

Example: A female defendant is arrested by five officers for forgery. While she is standing in the doorway between her kitchen and her living room, several of the officers search a kitchen shelf six feet from her. *Held*, the warrantless search is "incident to arrest" because it was made within an area in the defendant's "control," despite the fact that one of the officers stood between her and the shelf at all times. *U.S. v. Patterson*, 447 F.2d 424 (10th Cir. 1971).

3. **Scope of automobile search:** If the arrest is of a ***driver***, the car's ***passenger compartment*** can no longer be searched incident to the arrest, if the driver has been physically restrained from accessing the compartment. See *Arizona v. Gant*, discussed immediately *infra*.

D. **Automobile searches incident to arrest:** The basic theory of *Chimel* — that a warrantless search incident to arrest must be limited to areas within the arrestee's ***"immediate control"*** — now essentially applies to ***searches of vehicles*** after the arrest of the driver. So in the usual case in which a driver is arrested for a traffic violation and placed securely in the patrol car, the *Chimel* rationale will normally ***not permit the police to search the passenger compartment*** incident to the arrest. That's the consequence of ***Arizona v. Gant***, 129 S.Ct. 1710 (2009), an important case that effectively overruled a prior Supreme Court case that had governed the issue of passenger-compartment-searches for the previous 28 years.

1. **Prior law (*New York v. Belton*):** From 1981 until early 2009, lower courts and commentators almost universally believed that when the police made a proper custodial arrest of a driver, the police could use the incident-to-arrest rationale to conduct a warrantless search of the ***entire passenger compartment*** (including a search of any ***containers***, even closed ones, found inside the compartment). And it was believed that the police could do this even if the driver had been handcuffed and, as per standard police procedure, placed in the arresting officer's patrol car. This belief stemmed from ***New York v. Belton***, 453 U.S. 454 (1981), where the majority stated, "[W]e hold that when a policeman has made a lawful custodial arrest of the occupant of an automobile, he may as the contemporaneous incident of that arrest, search the passenger compartment of that automobile."

   a. **Not limited to area within arrestee's control:** Nothing in the language of *Belton* seemed to limit the police's right to search the passenger compartment to those situations in which the compartment was ***still within the arrestee's reach.*** So the vast majority of lower courts, both federal and state, interpreted *Belton* as allowing a search of the passenger compartment even though the arrestee had been ***handcuffed, or removed from the scene.*** But many courts and commentators ***criticized*** this broad rule, on the grounds that the reason for the *Chimel* search-incident-to-arrest exception to the warrant requirement was to ***protect the officer's safety*** (hence the "immediate control of the arrestee" limitation), a reason that did not apply where the arrestee could not possibly gain access to the passenger compartment.

2. ***Arizona v. Gant* overrules *Belton*:** Finally, in the 2009 *Gant* decision, the Court by a 5-4 vote agreed with these critics, and essentially ***overruled Belton*** (though the majority claimed that it was merely clarifying and limiting *Belton*, not overruling it). *Gant* estab-

lishes that the search-incident-to-arrest rationale allows a warrantless search of the passenger compartment ***only*** if ***one of two things*** is true:

(1) the arrestee has ***access to the passenger compartment*** at the moment of the search (which will virtually never be the case if standard police practice is followed); or

(2) the police reasonably believe that the passenger compartment may contain ***evidence of the offense for which the arrest is being made.***

In the most common scenario to which *Belton* applied — the police make an arrest for a ***traffic violation***, handcuff the driver and put him in the patrol car, and then find evidence of some other crime when they search the passenger compartment — the search will now ***no longer be justified by the incident-to-arrest doctrine.***

a. **Facts of *Gant*:** The facts of *Gant* illustrate the core situation in which the incident-to-arrest rationale will no longer permit a search of the passenger compartment. The police reasonably (and correctly, as it turned out) believed that Gant's driver's license had been suspended, and that there was an outstanding warrant for his arrest for driving with a suspended license. They waited for Gant at his residence and, when he drove into the driveway, arrested him on the warrant. They then handcuffed him, locked him in the back seat of the patrol car, and searched his car. There, they found cocaine in the pocket of a jacket on the back seat. Gant was charged with drug possession, and moved to suppress the cocaine; he argued that the search-incident-to-arrest rationale of *Chimel* should not be applied to situations where the arrestee could not possibly have gained access to the passenger compartment.

b. **Majority agrees with Gant:** By a 5-4 vote, the Court ***agreed with Gant***: the search-incident-to-arrest rationale did not apply to the search here because of Gant's ***lack of access*** to the passenger compartment at the time of the search. Therefore no exception to the warrant requirement applied, making the search "unreasonable" under the Fourth Amendment. The majority opinion was by Justice Stevens; in a somewhat surprising lineup, Stevens was joined by Souter, Thomas, Ginsburg and (in a somewhat grudging concurrence) Scalia.

   i. **Holding:** Stevens conceded that lower courts had "widely understood" *Belton* to "allow a vehicle search incident to the arrest of a recent occupant even if there is no possibility the arrestee could gain access to the vehicle at the time of the search." But such a reading of *Belton*, he said, would "untether the rule [governing vehicle searches] from the justifications underlying the *Chimel* [incident-to-arrest] exception[.]" Therefore, Stevens said, "we ***reject this reading*** of *Belton* and hold that the *Chimel* rationale authorizes police to search a vehicle incident to a recent occupant's arrest ***only*** when the arrestee is ***unsecured and within reaching distance of the passenger compartment at the time of the search."***

      (1) **Rare event:** Stevens then noted in a footnote that "Because officers have many means of ensuring the safe arrest of vehicle occupants, it will be the ***rare case*** in which an officer is unable to fully effectuate an arrest so that a real possibility of access to the arrestee's vehicle remains." In other words, the new rule of *Gant* will in the vast majority of cases ***take away the police's right to make a passenger-compartment search incident to a traffic arrest.***

(2) **Search for evidence of offense that led to arrest:** Stevens then eased slightly the impact on the police of the Court's ruling. He did this by adding a ***second way*** in which the police could gain the right to search the passenger compartment incident to arrest: "We also conclude that circumstances unique to the vehicle context justify a search incident to a lawful arrest when it is 'reasonable to believe that ***evidence relevant to the crime of arrest might be found*** in the vehicle.' " In other words, if the arrest was for the sort of offense evidence of which would likely be found in the car — a ***drug possession offense***, for instance — the police could still search the passenger compartment (and any containers therein) for evidence of that offense. But Stevens conceded that in the core case of an arrest for a ***traffic violation***, this rationale would ***not*** apply, since evidence of a traffic violation will rarely be expected to be found inside the passenger compartment.

ii. **Bright-line benefits outweighed:** Stevens then turned to a discussion of the ***costs and benefits*** of the Court's new approach to vehicle searches incident to arrest. He conceded that the Court was taking away the benefits of the ***bright-line rule*** that *Belton* had seemed to confer: the police had known, since *Belton*, that if they made a proper custodial arrest of a driver, they could automatically search the passenger compartment without worrying about whether the arrestee had access to the passenger compartment or whether there was reasonable ground to believe that evidence of the offense of arrest would be found.

(1) **Large privacy impact:** But, Stevens said, the benefits of the former bright-line rule were far ***outweighed*** by the large negative impact that rule had on individuals' ***privacy*** rights. "*Belton* searches authorize police officers to search not just the passenger compartment but ***every purse, briefcase, or other container within that space.*** A rule that gives police the power to conduct such a search whenever an individual is caught committing a traffic offense, when there is no basis for believing evidence of the offense might be found in the vehicle, creates a serious and recurring threat to the ***privacy of countless individuals.*** Indeed, the character of that threat implicates the central concern underlying the Fourth Amendment — the concern about giving police officers ***unbridled discretion to rummage at will*** among a person's private effects."

iii. ***Stare decisis*:** Finally, Stevens rejected the dissent's contention that ***stare decisis*** required the Court to keep in force the broad version of *Belton*. The Court had "never relied on *stare decisis* to justify the continuance of an ***unconstitutional police practice***." Stevens conceded that law enforcement officers had, during the 28 years after *Belton*, ***relied*** on the automatic right to search the passenger compartment incident to arrest. But, he said, "If it is clear that a practice is unlawful, individuals' interest in its discontinuance clearly outweighs any law enforcement 'entitlement' to its persistence."

c. **Fifth vote from Scalia:** Only three other justices (Souter, Thomas and Ginsburg) fully joined the reasoning of Stevens' opinion. The necessary fifth vote was supplied by Scalia, who concurred in the result but would have actually gone further than Stevens in limiting the police's right to search the passenger compartment incident to arrest. Whereas Stevens would still allow a search if "the arrestee is within reaching distance of the passenger compartment at the time of the search," Scalia would not, left to his own devices, have recognized even that narrow exception. He reasoned that "this standard fails to provide the needed guidance to arresting officers and also leaves much room for manipulation, inviting officers to leave the scene unsecured ... in order to conduct a vehicle search." But, since no other member of the Court shared his view, Scalia decided that joining the Stevens opinion was better than joining the four dissenters, a result that would "open the field to what I think are plainly unconstitutional searches — which is the greater evil."

d. **Dissent:** Four justices ***dissented*** in *Gant*. The main dissent was by Alito, who was joined by Roberts, Kennedy and in part Breyer. Alito contended that the majority was flatly ***overruling*** *Belton* even though it claimed to be merely clarifying that case's holding. And, Alito said, there was no good reason why *stare decisis* should not be followed, so as to maintain *Belton*'s clear rule allowing a search of the passenger compartment in all custodial arrests.

   i. **Reliance interest:** Alito stressed that police departments had a strong ***reliance interest*** in maintenance of the rule permitting an automatic search of the passenger compartment. And, he said, circumstances had not changed in any material way since *Belton* had announced this automatic right 28 years earlier.

   ii. **Workable rule:** Alito also believed that the *Belton* rule was quite ***workable***. It had the merit of supplying a bright-line rule, by "providing a test that would be ***relatively easy for police officers and judges to apply***." By contrast, the majority's new two-part rule would introduce hard-to-apply "case-by-case fact-specific decision-making[.]" For instance, officers would have to decide on a case-by-case basis whether the passenger compartment was within the arrestee's reach at the time of the arrest. More significantly, there would be great case-by-case uncertainty in the application of the second part of the Court's new test, i.e., whether the police had "reason to believe that the vehicle contains evidence of the crime of arrest."

3. **Other opportunities for vehicle search:** Keep in mind that in passenger-compartment search cases, Gant *only* wipes out the search-incident-to-arrest doctrine, not ***other long-established doctrines*** that may independently permit a warrantless search of the compartment.

   a. **Driver possibly dangerous (*Michigan v. Long*):** For instance, suppose the police have stopped a car, have asked the driver to exit, and are now interrogating him, but have ***not arrested*** him. If the police reasonably conclude that the driver may be ***dangerous and might gain access to a weapon*** inside the car once he's permitted to return to the car post-interrogation, *Michigan v. Long* (*infra*, p. 164) says that under a form of the ***stop-and-frisk*** doctrine, the police may conduct a ***brief protective search of the passenger compartment*** for weapons. Then, if they find some contraband item (e.g., drugs), they can seize the item. This scenario does not rely on search-incident-to-arrest, and is therefore not affected by the new rule of *Arizona v. Gant*. (Justice Scalia's concurrence in *Gant* makes this point.)

b. **Probable cause to search:** Similarly, when the police properly stop a car, then whether they make an arrest of the driver or not, if they have ***probable cause*** to believe that the vehicle contains ***contraband or evidence of crime***, they can search ***any part*** of the vehicle where the evidence ***might plausibly be found.*** See *U.S. v. Ross*, 456 U.S. 798 (1982), discussed *infra*, p. 136. Again, this exception to the warrant requirement does not depend on the search-incident-to-arrest doctrine, and is therefore unaffected by the holding in *Gant*. And this exception applies even though the stop (and/or the arrest) is ***not for the same crime*** to which the probable-cause-for-search relates. Therefore, if the police stop a car on suspicion of Crime A, and then during the stop learn additional information that makes them suspect that the car may contain evidence of Crime B, they can search those areas of the car where that evidence might be, without relying on the search-incident-to-arrest doctrine (or *Gant*) at all.

Example: A police officer sees a red Ford make a left turn without signaling, a minor traffic offense. The officer pulls over X, the driver. The officer has no intention of arresting X for this failure to signal, and intends merely to issue X a ticket. During the course of their interaction, X tells the officer that the reason she failed to signal was because she was upset at having just smelled the odor of marijuana coming from the trunk, which she thinks is due to her boyfriend's recent marijuana smuggling. The officer still does not arrest X, but, without asking X's consent, opens the trunk to see if there's marijuana there. He doesn't find any marijuana, but instead finds a knapsack that turns out to belong to X, and that contains vials of heroin.

The heroin may be introduced against X. Since the officer never arrested X at all, the officer never had the right to search any part of the car incident to arrest, a result that would have been true under pre-*Gant Belton* law just as under *Gant*. But the officer's conversation with X gave him probable cause to suspect that the trunk contained marijuana. Therefore, under the doctrine of *U.S. v. Ross* (*infra*, p. 136) — a doctrine providing that warrantless field searches of properly-stopped automobiles may be made as long as there is probable cause for the search and the search is limited to places where the evidence being sought might plausibly be found — the officer was entitled to search the trunk without a warrant. Being entitled to make that search, he was then entitled to seize any contraband or evidence of crime that he found during the course of the properly-conducted search.

c. **Significance:** So whenever you are analyzing a police search of a stopped car, ***don't assume*** that the fact that the search-incident-to-arrest rationale happens not to apply means that the search is invalid. You have to examine *all possible exceptions* to the search warrant requirement, including the stop-and-frisk (*Michigan v. Long*) and probable-cause-to-search-the-vehicle (*U.S. v. Ross*) exceptions just discussed.

E. **Protective sweeps:** A development that cuts back on the effect of *Chimel* is the Court's willingness to uphold ***"protective sweeps."*** *Chimel* holds that a warrantless search incident to arrest must be limited to areas within the arrestee's "immediate control." But post-*Chimel*, the Court has held that where the arrest takes place in the suspect's ***home***, the officers may conduct a protective sweep of ***all or part of the premises***, if they have a "reasonable belief" based on "specific and articulable facts" that ***another person*** who might be dangerous to the officer may be present in the areas to be swept. ***Maryland v. Buie***, 494 U.S. 325 (1990).

1. **Nature of protective sweep:** A "protective sweep" is a quick and limited search of premises incident to arrest, and is conducted to protect the safety of the arresting officers. According to the Court in *Buie*, it is ***not*** a full search of the premises, but may extend "only to a cursory inspection of those spaces where a person may be found."

2. **Facts:** The Court in *Buie* did not say whether the facts there satisfied the Court's requirement that there be "specific and articulable facts" making it reasonable for the arresting officers to believe that there was a danger that someone else on the premises might attack them. (The Court remanded on this point.) But the facts of *Buie* are suggestive of the type of situation where the "protective sweep" rationale will apply. The arresting officers, by a phone call to D's house before the arrest, knew that at least one other person (a woman) was present there apart from D. The officers went to the house, and then "fanned out through the first and second floors." One of the officers shouted down into the basement that anyone there should come out; D emerged from the basement. After D was arrested and handcuffed, another officer went into the basement "in case there was someone else" there; while in the basement, he found evidence that implicated D. The prosecution sought to use this evidence — fruits of a "protective sweep" — against D.

   a. **Application to facts:** It is not clear whether these facts satisfy *Buie's* standard for a protective sweep: "articulable facts supporting a reasonable suspicion." The officers could say, in support of their decision to protectively sweep the basement, "We knew from our prior phone call that at least one person other than D was in the house, and the fact that D was hiding in the basement suggested that D had advance notice that we were coming. Anyone else in the house would therefore also probably have had advance notice, and would be likely to hide in the basement, if they wanted to attack us." Probably even this limited hunch would meet the Court's "articulable facts" standard.

   b. **Adjacent spaces:** "Specific and articulable facts" are ***not*** needed for the officers to search in ***closets*** and other spaces ***immediately adjoining*** the place of an arrest, to make sure that no possible attacker lurks there. This may be done as a "precautionary measure," even where there are no specific facts suggesting a risk of attack, and does not count as a "protective sweep."

3. **Dissent:** Two dissenters in *Buie* (Brennan, joined by Marshall) argued that "in light of the special sanctity of a private residence and the highly intrusive nature of a protective sweep, . . . police officers must have ***probable cause*** to fear that their personal safety is threatened by a hidden confederate of an arrestee before they may sweep through the entire home."

F. **Contemporaneity of search:** Although a few decisions have held the search-incident-to-arrest exception applicable only where the search immediately follows the arrest, the Court seems to be ***lenient*** with respect to the ***time which may elapse*** between arrest and search.

   1. **Search prior to arrest:** The Supreme Court has approved a search as being incident to arrest even though it occurred immediately ***before*** the arrest. In *Rawlings v. Kentucky*, 448 U.S. 98 (1980), the Court noted that "Where the formal arrest followed quickly on the heels of the challenged search of [D's] person, we do not believe it particularly important

that the search preceded the arrest rather than vice versa." (But the Court took pains to observe that probable cause for the arrest existed independently of the fruits of the search.)

a. **Rationale approved:** Israel and LaFave agree with allowing such searches, noting that "a search before arrest when there are grounds to arrest involves no greater invasion of the person's security and privacy, and has the advantage that if the search is not productive the individual may not be arrested at all." (Nutshell, p. 123).

b. **Where arrest never made:** If the arrest is not made at all following the search, or is made illegally (as where there is no probable cause for it), the warrantless search may nonetheless fall within one of the other exceptions to the search warrant requirement, e.g., the exception for preventing the destruction by the suspect of "highly evanescent evidence" (discussed below).

2. **Search after long post-arrest delay:** The search-incident-to-arrest exception is applicable even to searches which do not occur until ***some time after the arrest***, at least where the search is made of ***objects in the suspect's possession*** at the time of arrest.

a. **Search of person:** Thus searches of an arrestee's person which are made on the way to the police station, or after the suspect is in custody, have been upheld despite the absence of a warrant. Such searches are generally justified on the grounds that the police have the right to ***inventory*** the suspect's property before incarcerating him.

i. ***Edwards:*** Such post-arrest personal searches without warrant were recognized by the Supreme Court in ***U.S. v. Edwards***, 415 U.S. 800 (1974). There, the Court stated that "once the defendant is lawfully arrested and is in custody, the effects in his possession at the place of detention that were subject to search at the time and place of his arrest may lawfully be searched and seized without a warrant even though a substantial period of time has elapsed between the arrest and subsequent administrative processing on the one hand and the taking of the property for use as evidence on the other. . . . " But the Court limited such searches to those which are ***not unreasonable*** "either because of their number or their manner of perpetration."

ii. **Intrusion into the body:** The *Edwards* Court's caveat that searches which are "unreasonable" in their "manner of perpetration" are not covered by the search-incident-to-arrest exception indicates that ***intrusions*** into the suspect's body will require a warrant, unless delay would threaten the loss or destruction of the evidence. Thus in *Schmerber v. California*, 384 U.S. 757 (1966), the Court indicated that the incident-to-arrest exception would not have applied to a drawing of a ***blood sample*** pursuant to a drunken-driving arrest, except for the fact that the blood-alcohol content of the defendant would have dropped so much in the time necessary to procure a warrant that the test would no longer have been useful. *Schmerber's* statement that bodily intrusions will not normally be permitted by the search-incident-to-arrest exception does not seem to be overruled by *Edwards.* See also *supra*, p. 72.

b. **Return to premises:** Where the police ***return to the scene of the arrest*** after incarcerating the arrestee, the courts have been much less willing to permit a warrantless search of the premises than where the prisoner himself is to be searched.

G. Legality of arrest: The search-incident-to-arrest exception to the requirement of a search warrant applies only where the arrest is ***legal***. Thus if the arrest turns out to have been made ***without probable cause***, the search incident to it ***cannot be justified on the incident-to-arrest rationale***, and the evidence must be ***suppressed*** unless some other exception to the warrant requirement (e.g., prevention of destruction of evidence by the suspect) justifies it.

H. Application to minor crimes: *Chimel* stated that the only purpose of allowing a search incident to arrest was to prevent the suspect from getting hold of a weapon and from destroying evidence. In view of this statement, it might be expected that the Court would not allow the incident-to-arrest exception to apply to ***minor crimes***, such as traffic violations, where the likelihood that the arrestee will have either weapons or evidence of the crime is very slim. But in ***U.S. v. Robinson***, 414 U.S. 218 (1973), the Court ***allowed*** the incident-to-arrest exception to apply to the search of the person of a driver who was stopped on suspicion of ***driving with a revoked license***, a relatively minor crime.

1. **Facts of *Robinson*:** The defendant in *Robinson* had been stopped by a policeman, Jenks, several days previously, and his license examined. After letting Robinson go, Jenks ran a check on his license number, and determined that it had been revoked. He then recognized Robinson's car being driven down the street, stopped it, and informed Robinson that he was being arrested for driving after revocation. He then had Robinson get out of the car, and patted him down in a general frisk. Feeling a soft package in Robinson's pocket, he removed it, and discovered that it was a crumpled cigarette package. He looked inside the package, and discovered capsules of white powder which turned out to be heroin.

   a. **Search according to regulations:** The body search of Robinson was conducted according to police department regulations, which required that any time a person is stopped for a "full-custody arrest" (i.e., an arrest where he is to be taken to the police station for booking), a full-body search should be conducted.

2. **Holding:** The Supreme Court held that the body search was ***valid*** under the search-incident-to-arrest exception. The Court stated that such a body search would be allowable ***in any situation in which a "full-custody" arrest occurs***. "In the case of a lawful custodial arrest a full search of the person is not only an exception to the warrant requirement of the Fourth Amendment, but is also a 'reasonable' search under that Amendment."

   a. **Rationale:** The Court based its holding largely on the right of the police to ***protect themselves*** by looking for weapons concealed on the person of the arrestee. The majority rejected the contention that because the arrest was for a minor traffic violation, the suspect was very unlikely to have dangerous weapons on him; the Court cited the fact that "approximately 30% of the shootings of police officers occur when the officer approaches a person seated in a car."

      i. **Later judicial second-guessing undesirable:** The majority also relied on the fact that the officer's decision to check for concealed weapons is a "quick *ad hoc* judgment." The Court stated that "The authority to search the person incident to a lawful custodial arrest, while based upon the need to disarm and to discover evidence, does not depend on what a court may later decide was the probability in a particular arrest situation that weapons or evidence would in fact be found upon the person of the suspect."

b. **Car not searched:** The ***vehicle*** in *Robinson* was not searched. The Court implied that a search of the vehicle would not, even in the custodial arrest case, be justified by the incident-to-arrest exception, presumably since the driver is usually made to get out of the vehicle before being searched, and is then taken to the police station without returning to the car.

3. **Dissent:** Marshall (joined by Douglas and Brennan) dissented in *Robinson*. The dissent argued that the majority's holding perverted the previous rationale for the search-incident-to-arrest exception, which was to allow a search for weapons. The dissent conceded that the officer in *Robinson* had the right to frisk for hard objects that might be weapons, but asserted that once it was clear that there were no hard objects that could be weapons, the officer had no reason to inspect a soft package. The dissent suggested that the officer could in any case have held on to the package, without opening it, and obtained a warrant for opening it later.

4. **Effect of *Robinson*:** *Robinson* seems to stand for the proposition that any time a traffic or other arrest is made, ***no matter how minor the crime is*** for which the arrest is being made, a full bodily search may be conducted incident to that arrest, as long as the arrest is "custodial," i.e., as long as the arrestee will be taken to the station house for booking.

   a. **No subjective fear required:** The search does not have to be made specifically for weapons, nor does the officer have to have a "subjective fear" that the suspect is armed. (The arresting officer in *Robinson* testified that he did not have such fears, and was merely looking for evidence.)

5. **Other minor crimes:** *Robinson* apparently applies not only to custodial traffic arrests, but also to custodial arrests for other minor crimes, such as ***loitering*** or ***vagrancy.***

6. **Non-custodial stops:** Since the arrest in *Robinson* was custodial (i.e., the officer intended to take the defendant to the station and hold him), the Court did not have occasion to discuss the kind of search which could be made pursuant to a ***routine, non-custodial, traffic stop,*** where only the ***writing of a ticket*** is contemplated. But a later case holds that an officer who makes a stop and issues a ticket may not ***search the vehicle*** of the driver incident to the stop. See *Knowles v. Iowa*, 525 U.S. 113 (1998), discussed more extensively *infra*, p. 139. The result in *Knowles* strongly suggests that the officer ***may not do a full body search of the driver*** either, in this traffic-ticket scenario.

   a. **May be required to get out of car:** However, even in the case of such a routine stop for issuance of a traffic ticket, the police may order the driver to ***step out of the car***. See *Pennsylvania v. Mimms,* 434 U.S. 106 (1977). At that point, if the officer has reasonable fears for his safety, he may probably conduct a limited "pat down" of the driver and of any passengers. See *Terry v. Ohio* and the "stop-and-frisk" doctrine, discussed beginning *infra*, p. 148.

I. **Search of items carried on person of arrestee:** The Court has long held that when a search is properly made incident to a lawful arrest, the police may examine ***items of personal property found on the person of the arrestee.***

   1. **Items that are not suspected of being weapons or evidence:** Furthermore, this right to examine items found on the arrestee's person is ***not limited*** to items that the officer reason-

ably fears may be ***weapons*** or may constitute ***evidence of crime*** — rather, the Court's incident-to-arrest cases (at least prior to 2016) have suggested that *any* physical item found on the person could be searched.

a. **Cigarette package in *Robinson*:** For instance, in *U.S. v. Robinson*, the 1973 case discussed *supra*, p. 108, recall that when the police officer properly made a traffic-related arrest of Robinson, the officer patted Robinson down, felt a soft package in his pocket, and discovered that the item was a crumpled cigarette package containing capsules that turned out to contain heroin.

   i. **Search upheld:** Even though the officer testified that he had had no reason to fear that this particular crumpled package he was feeling might be a weapon, or might constitute evidence of crime, the Court held that the search-incident-to-arrest doctrine entitled the officer to examine the package (the examination being a "search" for Fourth Amendment purposes).

   ii. **Rationale:** The *Robinson* Court reasoned that while protecting the officer from weapons and facilitating the discovery of evidence might be the reason for which the incident-to-arrest doctrine was originally adopted, the arresting officer's right to search for and examine items on the arrestee's person "does not depend on what a court may later decide was the ***probability in [that] particular arrest situation*** that ***weapons or evidence would in fact be found*** upon the person of the suspect."

b. **Purses, contents of pockets:** In the first four decades after the 1973 decision in *Robinson*, the Supreme Court never again directly confronted the issue of whether some items found on the arrestee's person might be immune from search incident to the arrest. But during this period, lower courts assumed that the right of search incident to arrest would cover ***any items found on or in the control of the arrested person,*** such as ***purses*** and things ***found in the arrestee's pockets.***[1]

2. **Cellphones and their digital contents:** But then, in an important 2014 case, the Court held (unanimously on this point) that when the police properly make a custodial arrest of a person who happens to be carrying a ***cell phone***, the incident-to-arrest doctrine does ***not*** permit the police to perform a ***warrantless search of the digital contents of the phone.*** The case so holding is ***Riley v. California***, 134 S.Ct. 2473 (2014).

   a. **Facts:** The *Riley* decision disposed of two separate lower-court cases.

      i. **David Riley's case:** In one case, the police stopped a driver (David Riley) on a minor traffic offense, arrested him when it turned out his license was expired, and seized a "smart phone" from his pocket. Both the arresting officer at the site, as well as a detective later at the police station, made a warrantless examination of the phone under the incident-to-arrest doctrine. The police discovered various text messages, photos and videos that suggested Riley was a member of the Crip Killers gang; one photo showed Riley standing in front of a car that the police suspected had been involved in a prior gang-related shooting. Riley was prosecuted

1. In the 2014 Supreme Court case of *Calif. v. Riley*, discussed immediately below, the Court listed various types of items that lower courts had permitted to be examined incident to arrest when found on or near the arrestee's person; the list included ***billfolds, address books, wallets,*** and ***purses.***

on various California state charges related to that prior shooting, and evidence of the photos and videos was admitted as part of the case.

ii. **Brima Wurie's case:** In the other case, police saw Brima Wurie make a drug sale from a car, arrested him, and seized a "flip phone" (a phone with fewer features than a smart phone) from his person. At the station house, the police noticed that the phone was ringing with calls from a source listed on the phone's display as "my house." The police accessed the call log to find the phone number associated with "my house," then used an online phone directory to trace that phone number to an address at an apartment building. At that building, the police saw Wurie's name on a mailbox, obtained a search warrant for the apartment, and while executing the warrant found narcotics that became the basis of a federal prosecution of Wurie.

b. **Claims by Ds:** Both Riley and Wurie claimed that although the search-incident-to-arrest doctrine might have justified the police in *seizing* the cell phone each was carrying, that doctrine did not authorize them to *search* the phones' digital contents without first getting a search warrant. Therefore, each sought to have any of those contents excluded under the fruits-of-the-poisonous-tree (see *infra*, p. 324) doctrine.

c. **Supreme Court agrees with Ds:** The Supreme Court ***unanimously agreed*** with both Ds: the search-incident-to-arrest doctrine ***did not entitle the police to examine the digital contents of the cell phones without a warrant.***[2]

i. **Basis for the incident-to-arrest exception:** The opinion for the Court, by Chief Justice Roberts, began by examining the reasons the Court had recognized the search-incident-to-arrest exception to the warrant requirement in the first place (in *Chimel*, *supra*, p. 99). *Chimel* had relied on two justifications for allowing such warrantless searches (as Roberts described these justifications):

[1] First, allowing the officer to search the arrested person would let the officer take the reasonable step of "***remov[ing]*** any ***weapon*** that the [arrested person] might seek to use in order to ***resist arrest or effect his escape.***"

[2] Second, it was "entirely reasonable" for the arresting officer to "search for and seize any ***evidence on the arrestee's person*** in order to prevent its ***concealment or destruction***."

ii. **"Whole category at a time" approach:** Roberts emphasized that under post-*Chimel* cases, the availability of the exception would ***not*** depend on "the probability in a ***particular arrest situation*** that weapons or evidence would in fact be found." Instead, the exception's availability would be decided ***a whole "category" at a time.*** So if application of the exception to that category would ***"untether the rule*** from the ***justifications underlying the ... exception"*** (quoting *Robinson*, *supra*, p. 99), the exception would be ***denied for that entire category.***

---

2. Chief Justice Roberts' opinion for the Court was joined by seven other justices. Justice Alito wrote a separate concurrence, but even he agreed with Roberts' conclusion that where a lawful search-incident-to-arrest results in the seizure of a cell phone, the police must normally obtain a search warrant before they can examine the phone's digital contents.

iii. **Category-wide approach to cell phone data:** Roberts then turned to deciding whether the search-incident-to-arrest exception should apply to the ***whole category of digital data on cell phones.*** It was clear to him that neither of the two *Chimel* rationales supported allowing seizure of such digital data.

iv. **Cell data can't be used as weapon:** As to the first rationale, Roberts wrote, "digital data stored on a cell phone ***cannot itself be used as a weapon*** to harm an arresting officer or to effectuate the arrestee's escape." (He noted that the officer could check the phone's *physical* aspects for safety issues, such as to "determine whether there is a razor blade hidden between the phone and its case"; but the officer could not examine the digital data itself, since that data could not be a dangerous or escape-facilitating weapon.)

v. **Anti-evidence-destruction rationale:** Roberts took the second rationale — preventing destruction of evidence — more seriously. The two governments that were arguing in favor of allowing the warrantless searches here (California and the U.S.) conceded that as soon as the arresting officer physically seized the cell phone incident to the arrest, the ***arrestee would not himself*** be able to destroy the digital data. But the governments claimed that if the police did not have the right to immediately retrieve the data, there were two other possible sources of data destruction: ***"remote wiping"*** (by which a confederate might cause a signal to be sent by a signal via the wireless network, causing the data to be destroyed) and ***"data encryption"*** (by which the phone might be ***remotely "locked" by a confederate,*** which would cause the data to become encrypted and readable only with a password that the police would not have).

However, Roberts rejected both of these possible types of destruction as justifications for allowing warrantless search of the digital data. He cited two reasons.

(1) **Not "prevalent":** First, neither danger had been shown by the governments to be ***"prevalent."***

(2) **Immediate search wouldn't make a difference:** Second, allowing the arresting officer to start an immediate warrantless examination of the data (as opposed to requiring him to wait for a warrant) would probably ***not make much of a difference***, since both remote wiping and remotely-triggered encryption/locking might be carried out almost immediately following the arrest. And in any event, he pointed out, if the police in a given situation had a particular reason to fear remote wiping or encryption, they could act based on the doctrine of "exigent circumstances" — they didn't need a general category-wide rule allowing an immediate warrantless search regardless of whether the facts suggested a real danger of remotely-triggered destruction.

vi. **Large privacy implication:** Roberts also pointed out that the cases approving the incident-to-arrest doctrine relied on the concept that when a person is being taken into custody he has ***"reduced privacy interests"***; for instance, in *Robinson* (*supra*, p. 108) when the officer patted down the arrestee's clothing and examined the cigarette pack in his pocket, that conduct caused "only minor additional intrusions compared to the substantial government authority exercised in taking [him] into custody."

(1) **Large privacy implications:** By contrast, he said, "modern cell phones, as a category, ***implicate privacy concerns far beyond*** those implicated by the search of a cigarette pack, a wallet, or a purse." Cell phones have an immense storage capacity, and can store many distinctive types of information "that ***reveal much more in combination than any isolated record.*** . . . The ***sum of an individual's private life can be reconstructed*** through a thousand photographs labeled with dates, locations, and descriptions; the same cannot be said of a photograph or two of loved ones tucked into a wallet."

vii. **Government's fallback options rejected:** Having rejected the governments' arguments in favor of a wholesale right to warrantlessly inspect all digital data on a cell phone incident to arrest, Roberts then rejected a slew of "fallback options" offered by them, under which at least *certain types* of digital searches would be allowed as incident to arrest.

(1) **Two arguments discussed:** Since none of these fallback options came even close to convincing the Court, we won't review them all here. But two are worth mentioning.

(2) **Access call logs by analogy to pen register case:** One fallback the Court rejected was that at least a phone's ***call log*** should be warrantlessly searchable, by analogy to the Court's prior "pen register" case law. The governments pointed out that in an earlier case (*Smith v. Maryland, supra*, p. 34), the Court had held that no warrant was required (because no "search" occurred) when the police demand that a ***phone company use a "pen register" to identify numbers dialed by a particular caller***. The governments argued in *Riley* that a similar rationale should permit the police at least to search ***the phone's "call log" to identify callers to and from the phone.*** But Roberts quickly rejected this argument, by pointing out that cell phone call logs typically contain ***more than just phone numbers;*** for instance, they usually contain ***labels*** to each number added by the phone owner, such as "my house" in Wurie's case. Therefore, examination of call-log data was invariably intrusive enough that it constituted a Fourth Amendment "search," unlike the pen-register situation.

(3) **"Pre-digital analogue" argument:** A second fallback position that the Court rejected might be called the ***"pre-digital analogue"*** argument, by which officers should be able to search particular cell phone data "if they could have obtained the same information from a pre-digital counterpart." Under this approach, since the police in the pre-digital age would have been able to examine, say, a hard-copy photograph or two in the arrestee's wallet, they should now be entitled to examine photographs found on a cell phone retrieved from arrestee's pocket. But the Court quickly rejected this argument, too. For one thing, the ***sheer quantity*** of digital items that could be carried on a cell phone dwarfed the number of items that might be carried in a pocket in physical form; thus "In Riley's case, for example, it is implausible that he would have strolled around with ***video tapes, photo albums, and an address***

book all crammed into his pockets. But because each of those items has a pre-digital analogue, police under California's proposal would be able to search a phone for all of those items — a ***significant diminution of privacy."*** Furthermore, Roberts wrote, the analogue test "would launch courts on a ***difficult line-drawing expedition*** to determine which digital files are comparable to physical records. [It] would 'keep defendants and judges guessing for years to come.' "

viii. **Special nature of cell phones:** Roberts closed by emphasizing how modern cell phones, because of the vast volume of personal data they can carry, present special Fourth Amendment issues: "Modern cell phones are not just another technological convenience. With all they contain and all they may reveal, they hold for many Americans ***'the privacies of life'.*** The fact that technology now allows an individual to carry such information in his hand does not make the information ***any less worthy of the protection*** for which the Founders fought."

(1) **The Court's new rule:** He then gave a crisp ***black-letter summary*** of what the Court had just decided in *Riley*: "Our answer to the question of ***what police must do before searching a cell phone seized incident to an arrest*** is accordingly ***simple — get a warrant."***

3. **Significance of *Riley* for other types of digital data:** So how does *Riley* change the rules governing when the police may search digital data found incident to a valid arrest?

a. **Cell phones:** *Riley* by its facts involved ***only cell phones***, not other types of digital storage devices. And in the cell-phone situation, *Riley* yields an easy-to-interpret bright-line rule that limits police who make an arrest: even if the arrest is perfectly proper, and even if a cell phone is found directly on the arrestee's person (e.g., in a pocket), the police ***may not examine any digital content on the phone without first getting a search warrant.***[3]

b. **Other types of digital devices:** Although *Riley* dealt specifically only with cell phones, the Court's rationale applies equally to ***any*** devices found on or near an arrestee's person that contain significant amounts of digital data. Roberts' opinion, from the start, takes a broad view of what devices should be covered by the opinion's logic, when he says, "The term 'cell phone' is itself ***misleading shorthand***; many of these devices are in fact ***minicomputers*** that also happen to have the capacity to be used as a telephone. They could just as easily be called ***cameras, video players, rolodexes, calendars, tape recorders,*** libraries, diaries, albums, televisions, maps, or newspapers. One of the most notable distinguishing features of modern cell phones is their ***immense storage capacity."***

---

3. This bright-line rule assumes that the police do not face any ***"exigent circumstances."*** So, for instance, if the police happen to learn that the phone is set up so that a confederate can send a remote signal to erase or encrypt the contents (*and* the police have reason to believe that such a confederate may be aware of the arrest and is about to trigger the erase-or-encrypt signal), these exigent circumstances would permit the police to make an immediate search of the digital contents without taking the time to procure a warrant. But in the cell phone situation, it should rarely be the case that the police have such knowledge of impending data-destruction, so exigent circumstances entitling the police to dispense with a warrant ought to be quite unusual.

i. **Broad reading likely:** Given this inclusive language, it seems fair to read *Riley* as holding that whenever ***any*** modern device containing ***significant amounts of digital data*** is found on or near an arrestee, the police may not search (i.e., read or examine) the digital data without first getting a search warrant. Presumably this logic applies not only to small handheld digital devices, but even to somewhat ***larger*** ones — ***tablets and laptops,*** for instance — found on or near the arrestee.

c. **"Digital info is different":** *Riley* means that, in the case of searches incident to arrest, the police seem to have to follow one rule for ***physical*** evidence and a quite different rule for ***digital*** evidence.[4]

Example: Suppose Suspect 1 is arrested, and a pocket diary found in his pocket contains a page with photo of person X, and some handwritten information giving X's name, address and occupation. Suspect 2 is arrested at the same time, and is carrying a cell phone whose "Contacts" section contains an entry with X's name; that entry then displays that same photo of X and the same identifying information about X as in Suspect 1's diary.

The police can "search" (i.e., examine) the entire contents of Suspect 1*'s* diary, and learn whatever it shows or says about X, without getting a warrant. But Riley says that the police have to *get a warrant* before they can even open up the digital entry for X in Suspect 2's phone. So entirely different rules now apply for physical versus digital data in the search-incident-to-arrest area.

J. **Breath and blood tests incident to arrest:** Suppose the police arrest a ***driver*** based on probable cause to suspect drunk driving; can the police then rely on the search-incident-to-arrest doctrine to perform a warrantless test of the driver's ***breath*** or ***blood***, to confirm the driver's blood alcohol content (***"BAC"***)? As the result of a trio of cases decided under the name ***Birchfield v. North Dakota***, 579 U.S. __ (June 23, 2016), there is a "split decision": a warrantless test of the driver's ***breath*** is ***permissible***, but such a test of the driver's ***blood*** is ***not***.

1. **Why issue is important:** The issue is of great practical importance, because the difficulty of deterring drunk driving has caused an increasing number of states to impose criminal penalties on a driver who, after a proper arrest for drunk driving, refuses to ***consent*** to a warrantless breath or blood test.

a. **How issue developed in *Birchfield*:** At the time *Birchfield* was decided, most states still made the driver's consent to a breath or blood test following a drunk driving arrest "voluntary," with the only sanction for refusal being a suspension of one's driver's license. But as the criminal penalties for a conviction of drunk driving increased over the decades, more and more drivers (more than 20% in 2011) began to ***refuse to consent*** — even at a cost of losing their driver's license — rather than undergoing a test that might show a BAC high enough to trigger not just a drunk driving conviction but a jail term for that conviction. Consequently, a number of states — including the two states whose statutes were at issue in *Birchfield*, North Dakota and Minnesota — made

---

4. Cf. Kerr, "The Significance of *Riley*" (in The Volokh Conspiracy), Washington Post, June 25, 2014.

it a ***crime to refuse to consent*** to a blood or breath test incident to a proper arrest for drunk driving.

b. **Nature of "breathalyzer" breath test:** The type of ***"breath" test at*** issue in *Birchfield* was what is commonly called a ***"breathalyzer"*** test: the arrestee is required to ***blow continuously*** for 4-15 seconds into a straw-like mouthpiece that is connected by a tube to a portable test machine. The machine then promptly reports back the suspect's BAC. Often, the breath test is performed by the ***police at roadside*** immediately following the arrest, using a machine the police carry in the patrol car. Nationally, most tests of drunk-driving suspects are now done by this method.

c. **Nature of blood test:** When a ***blood test***, rather than a breath test, is used to measure BAC, the procedure is ***more invasive:*** a medical technician uses a ***syringe to draw a blood sample from the arrestee's veins***, and the sample is shipped to a laboratory. Blood tests are almost never done at roadside — they are typically performed in a ***hospital*** (as was the blood test at issue in *Birchfield*).

2. **Facts of the 3 cases in *Birchfield*:** All three of the defendants whose cases were combined in *Birchfield* were properly arrested by police officers who had probable cause to believe they were driving while intoxicated.

[1] Danny Birchfield was convicted under a North Dakota statute for refusing to consent to a ***blood*** test.

[2] William Bernard was convicted under a Minnesota statute for refusing to consent to a ***breath*** test.

[3] Steve Beylund, after his drunk-driving arrest, was told that under a North Dakota statute (the same one at issue in Danny Birchfield's case), refusing to consent to a blood test would itself be a crime. He then agreed to the test, which was performed by a nurse in a hospital. Based on the test results, Beylund's license was administratively suspended. He argued in litigation that criminalizing his refusal to consent to a blood test would have violated his Fourth Amendment rights; therefore, he contended, his consent to be tested under a ***threat*** of criminal conviction was coerced and invalid.

3. **Supreme Court upholds breath tests, strikes blood tests:** Of the 8 members of the Court deciding *Birchfield*,[5] 6 reasoned that (1) the Fourth Amendment was ***not violated*** by a state's requiring a drunk-driving arrestee to undergo a warrantless ***breath test,*** but (2) the Amendment ***was*** violated by requiring a ***blood test*** under the same circumstances. The main difference between the two situations was the much ***greater intrusiveness of blood tests.***

a. **Court's opinion by Alito:** The opinion for the Court was by Justice Alito (joined by Chief Justice Roberts, and Justices Kennedy, Breyer and Kagan). Justices Thomas and Sotomayor both dissented in part, but in opposite ways.[6]

---

5. The case was decided after Justice Scalia's death and before the appointment of his replacement.

6. As we'll see, Thomas thought that *both* the blood and the breath tests were constitutional, and Sotomayor thought that *neither* was.

i. **Balancing test:** As to each type of test, Alito applied the same ***balancing test*** — weighing the degree of interference with the arrestee's privacy interests against the size of the state's law-enforcement interest in not being required to get a search warrant — as the court had applied in the *Riley* cell-phone-search case (*supra*, p. 110).

ii. **Breath tests:** Alito concluded that as to ***breath tests,*** the intrusion on an arrestee's privacy was ***minimal***, and was outweighed by the benefits to the state's strong interest in combating drunk driving. In a breath test, he said, "the ***physical intrusion is almost negligible.*** ... The effort is ***no more demanding than blowing up a party balloon."***

(1) **"Only one bit of information":** Furthermore, he said, the ***information*** revealed by the police from a breath test is extremely minimal, disclosing ***"only one bit of information,*** the amount of alcohol in the subject's breath." And ***"no sample*** of anything is ***left in the possession of the police."*** This made breath tests vastly less revealing than, say, DNA tests, which the Court had previously permitted to be taken warrantlessly from arrestees (see *Maryland v. King*, *infra*, p. 181), and in which the sample itself could be stored by the government and perhaps used eventually to disclose "a wealth of ... highly personal information."

(2) **Strong governmental interest:** On the other side of the balance, Alito said, government had a ***strong interest*** in not being required to get a search warrant before performing any breath test incident to arrest in non-exigent circumstances. If warrants were routinely required, "the ***courts would be swamped*** ... Particularly in sparsely populated areas, it would be no small task for courts to field a large new influx of warrant applications that could come on any day of the year and at any hour."

iii. **Blood tests:** But the balance was quite different in the case of ***blood tests,*** Alito said.

(1) **Strong privacy interest in avoiding:** Compared with breath tests, he said, "Blood tests are a different matter." They ***"require piercing the skin"*** and ***"extract a part of the subject's body."*** They are thus ***"significantly more intrusive than blowing into a tube."*** Furthermore, a blood test "places in the hands of law enforcement authorities a ***sample that can be preserved*** and from which it is ***possible to extract information beyond a simple BAC reading"*** of the sort that results from a breath test. Even if the police are forbidden from testing the blood for any purpose other than measuring BAC,"the potential [for abuse] remains and may result in ***anxiety for the person tested."***

(2) **Weak governmental interest:** On the other end of the balance, the governmental need for blood tests was quite ***weak***, Alito wrote. Since breath tests were already in common use, the states needed to show why they needed warrantless access to the ***more intrusive*** blood-test method, and they had not done so here. In the few cases involving special law-enforcement needs (e.g., the need to test for ***other substances*** that may have impaired the driver), the police

could get a warrant, or rely on the exigent-circumstances exception to the warrant requirement.

(3) **Conclusion:** Therefore, Alito concluded, allowing the incident-to-arrest exception to cover warrantless use of blood tests in non-exigent circumstances would be ***unreasonable***, and was ***not permitted*** by the Fourth Amendment.

iv. **Result in the 3 cases:** So the result in the three actual cases was that:

[1] Birchfield's conviction was reversed (since the warrantless blood test violated his Fourth Amendment rights);

[2] Bernard's conviction was affirmed (since it's constitutional for the police to conduct a warrantless breath test incident to a proper trunk-driving arrest, and therefore constitutional to make it a crime to refuse to consent or cooperate when the police demand such a test in those circumstances); and

[3] Beylund's case was remanded to the lower court, to decide whether his being incorrectly informed that he could be convicted if he refused to consent to the warrantless blood test vitiated his consent to that test.

v. **Significance:** *Birchfield* establishes that when the police make a legal drunk-driving arrest (i.e., they have probable cause to believe that D was driving while under the influence), they may ***conduct a breath test without first getting a search warrant.*** Furthermore, the states may make it a crime for the driver to refuse to consent to a breath test in the event he is legally arrested for drunk driving.

(1) **No warrantless blood tests:** But even if the driver refuses to consent to the warrantless breath test (making him vulnerable to a criminal conviction for doing so), that does ***not entitle*** the police to take him to the hospital and forcibly subject him to a ***blood test*** — the police ***must get a search warrant*** before doing this (assuming there are no exigent circumstances at play, such as the need to test for non-alcohol substances that are suspected, and that if they are present would likely be rapidly disappearing from the bloodstream).

vi. **Tactics by lawmakers:** *Birchfield* gives state legislatures a strong incentive to follow North Dakota and Minnesota, and ***criminalize*** a refusal to consent to a ***breath test*** when a person is properly arrested for drunk driving.

K. Arrest on probable cause but in violation of state law: Suppose a search is made incident to an arrest that was supported by probable cause, but that was made ***in violation of state law*** (e.g., because the crime is considered so minor by the state that only a summons is to be issued). Does the fact that state law did not authorize the offense mean that the search incident to it is a violation of the Fourth Amendment? The answer is ***"no."*** *Virginia v. Moore*, 128 S.Ct. 1598 (2008).

1. **Facts:** In *Moore*, the police arrested D for the misdemeanor of driving on a suspended license. During a search of D's body incident to that arrest, the police found crack cocaine. It turned out that although D had in fact been driving with a suspended license, state law required that the officer in such misdemeanor cases merely give the offender a summons, rather than arresting him. D claimed that because the arrest was unauthorized under state law, the search incident to it was automatically a violation of the Fourth Amendment.

2. **D loses:** But the Supreme Court unanimously ***disagreed*** with D's argument. The Court held that "[W]arrantless arrests for crimes committed in the presence of an arresting officer are reasonable under the Constitution, and ... while States are free to regulate such arrests however they desire, state restrictions do not alter the Fourth Amendment protections."

3. **Significance:** So just as *Robinson* (*supra*, p. 108) holds that there is no "minor crimes" exception to the rule permitting a search incident to any valid arrest, so *Moore* holds that there is no "crimes that are not arrestable under state law" exception to the rule. No matter how minor the crime or offense, and no matter how strong the state policy against allowing arrests for it, as long as the officer has probable cause to believe that the suspect committed the crime/offense, he may search the offender incident to the arrest. (But remember that the officer must indeed *make* a custodial arrest. If he merely issues a summons or traffic ticket, he may not make the search-incident-to-arrest; see, e.g., *Knowles v. Iowa*, *infra*, p. 139.)

L. Subterfuge arrests: The search-incident-to-arrest exception in general, and *Robinson* (*supra*, p. 108) in particular, have given rise to the likelihood that ***"trumped up"*** or ***"pretext"*** arrests will often be made simply to afford the police an opportunity to conduct a search. This has been particularly true of arrests for minor crimes, such as illegal parking, loitering, and the like.

1. **Probably allowable:** The Supreme Court has never said whether the fact that the arrest was pretexual renders the search incident to it a Fourth Amendment violation. However, the Court has said that the fact that a ***stop*** of a motorist for a ***traffic violation*** is made for pretextual reasons does not mean that any evidence garnered as the result of that stop was unlawfully obtained, or inadmissible. See *Whren v. U.S.*, 517 U.S. 806 (1996) (also discussed *infra*, p. 135). Although *Whren* applied only to stops rather than custodial arrests, the rationale of *Whren* probably extends to pretextual arrests as well. If so, a search incident to a pretextual arrest is nonetheless lawful, as long as the police in fact had probable cause to believe that the person arrested had committed a crime for which arrest was allowed under local law.

M. Right of police to accompany arrestee: Just as the police may conduct a search incident to a valid arrest, they may also ***physically accompany*** the arrestee at all times following the arrest, even if no exigent circumstances require such accompaniment. *Washington v. Chrisman*, 455 U.S. 1 (1982).

1. **Facts:** In *Washington*, Overdahl, a student, was observed by a policeman to be carrying liquor while leaving a dormitory. State law forbade persons under 21 to possess liquor; also, university regulations prohibited anyone from possessing liquor while on university property. The policeman arrested Overdahl, and asked for his I.D.; Overdahl said that he would have to retrieve it from his dormitory room. The officer accompanied him to the dormitory room, and waited in the doorway. While waiting at the doorway, the policeman noted seeds and a small pipe on a desk 10 feet away. Believing these to be marijuana seeds and a marijuana pipe, he entered the room, confirmed that the seeds were marijuana, and arrested D (Overdahl's roommate), who consented to a search which uncovered more illicit drugs. At trial, D moved to suppress the evidence, on the grounds that the officer's

entry into the room was not justified by exigent circumstances, and that he was therefore not permitted to make a warrantless seizure of the seeds or pipe.

2. **Holding:** The Supreme Court held that the policeman, having made a valid arrest of Overdahl, was permitted to ***remain with him at all times following the arrest***. This was true even though there were no "exigent circumstances" which required the policeman to stay at Overdahl's side.

   a. **Rationale:** The Court reasoned that the mere possibility that Overdahl might escape or gain access to a weapon in the room was enough to permit the policeman to stay with Overdahl. Since the officer had a right to be in the room, anything ***within his plain view*** (see *infra*, p. 127) could lawfully be seized even without a warrant, and used as evidence.

IV. EXIGENT CIRCUMSTANCES

A. **Exigent circumstances generally:** Even where the "search-incident-to-arrest" exception to the search warrant requirement does not apply, there may be ***exigent circumstances*** which justify dispensing with the warrant requirement. These circumstances may include ***preventing the imminent destruction of evidence, preventing harm to persons***, and ***searching in "hot pursuit" for a suspect***.

   1. **Statement of rule:** As one casebook puts it, "The basic idea of exigent circumstances is easy: ***officers should not be required to get a warrant when they can't feasibly do so***." A,S,H,L&L, p. 453.

B. **Destruction of evidence:** Probably the most common scenario calling for use of the exigent circumstances exception is where the police reasonably fear that ***evidence*** of a crime will be ***destroyed or dissipated*** before a search warrant can be procured.

   1. **Blood alcohol concentration (BAC) test:** One scenario that often calls for use of the "exigent circumstances" rationale for a warrantless search is where the police have probable cause to believe that a person (call him D) has been driving drunk, but there is a risk that D's ***blood-alcohol concentration (BAC) will drop*** significantly before the police can get a warrant authorizing them to seize a blood sample. If it's indeed the case that getting a warrant will delay the BAC test to the point where the results will likely be unusable, the police may proceed without a warrant.

      Example: D is injured in a collision involving a car he has been driving. D is arrested on drunk-driving charges, then taken to the hospital for treatment. The police, fearing that any further delay in testing D's BAC will cause that BAC to diminish, don't want to take the time to get a search warrant (for which they clearly have probable cause). Therefore, without asking for D's consent, the police request that a hospital official take a sample of D's blood. The evidence from the sample is used against D in a later prosecution for drunk driving; he contends that the evidence is inadmissible because it was obtained without a search warrant.

      Held, for the prosecution. The taking of D's blood was clearly a Fourth Amendment search and seizure. A search warrant would normally be required for something as invasive as a blood test. But because of the time the police had already used to bring D to the hospital and to investigate the scene of the accident, there was "no time to seek out a magistrate and secure a warrant." Given these "special facts," the police's warrantless taking of evidence of D's BAC was not unreasonable, and therefore did not violate the Fourth Amendment. ***Schmerber v. California***, 384 U.S. 757 (1966) (other aspects of which are discussed *infra*, p. 298).

a. **Not a categorical rule:** But the Supreme Court has ***refused*** government requests to establish a ***categorical*** (automatic) rule that the risk of destruction of BAC evidence always allows the police to take a driver's blood sample without a warrant if they have probable cause to suspect him of drunk driving. *Missouri v. McNeely*, 133 S.Ct. 1552 (2013).

   i. **Case-by-case analysis required:** The Court in *McNeely* said that courts must make a "careful ***case-by-case assessment*** of exigency," not use a categorical rule that always allows warrantless blood samples in drunk-driving cases. "In those drunk-driving investigations where police officers can reasonably obtain a warrant before a blood sample can be drawn ***without significantly undermining the efficacy of the search***, the Fourth Amendment ***mandates*** that they do so."

   ii. **Breath test distinguished:** But keep in mind that the police ***never need*** a warrant to require a driver whom they properly arrest for drunk-driving to take a roadside ***breath*** test (i.e., to use a ***"breathalyzer"***). Therefore, the presence or absence of exigent circumstances won't even matter if a breathalyzer is the only sort of test the arresting officer wants to perform; see *Birchfield v. No. Dakota, supra*, p. 118.

b. **Blood test of unconscious suspect:** Suppose the driver is ***unconscious***, so that it's not possible for the police to use a breathalyzer test in the field. In this special situation, the Court has held that exigent circumstances for a warrantless BAC blood test will ***almost always be found to exist.*** See *Mitchell v. Wisconsin*, 139. S.Ct. 2525 (2019).

   i. **Result in *Mitchell*:** In *Mitchell*, a four-Justice plurality said that "the exigent-circumstances rule almost always permits a blood test without a warrant" following a drunk driving arrest, if the driver is unconscious. The plurality reasoned that if the driver is unconscious, he will normally be ***taken to an emergency room*** where his ***blood would be drawn for diagnostic purposes anyway,*** even if the police were not seeking BAC information. Therefore, the plurality said, allowing a warrantless BAC ***does not increase the invasion of the driver's privacy.***

      (1) **Fifth vote:** A fifth Justice in *Mitchell*, Thomas, agreed, but urged an even ***broader*** rule. He argued that a warrantless BAC blood test after a drunk driving arrest should ***automatically*** be allowed — due to the rapid metabolization of alcohol in the bloodstream — even if the driver is ***conscious***. So *Mitchell* means that five members of the Court believe that at least where a person arrested for drunk driving is unconscious, that fact will virtually *always* mean that the police may take the blood sample without a warrant.

2. **Easily-destroyed contraband:** Another common "destruction of evidence" scenario occurs when the police have probable cause to believe that particular ***premises contain***

contraband or evidence of crime, but fear that if they leave the premises unguarded while obtaining a search warrant, an occupant will destroy the evidence before the warrant can be obtained. Most commonly, the police have reasonable cause to believe that there are ***narcotics*** in the premises, and wish to search for and seize the drugs before they can be destroyed (e.g., flushed down the toilet) or moved to another location.

a. **Sealing off premises:** Often, the police can and should deal with this disposal-of-evidence problem by ***sealing off the premises*** (a "seizure" under the Fourth Amendment) until a search warrant can be obtained. That is, the police can ***require the occupants to leave the premises*** (or remain under police observation); police officers are then ***posted outside the premises*** to make sure that no one else enters for the purpose of destroying the evidence. Once a search warrant for the premises has been obtained, the police conduct the search.

   i. **Generally successful:** This "searchless seizure to preserve evidence" will generally comply with the Fourth Amendment, as long as the police have a reasonable belief that without a seizure of the premises, the occupants will learn of the danger and destroy the evidence before the police can get a search warrant. *Illinois v. McArthur*, 531 U.S. 326 (2001).

b. **Immediate search:** But sometimes, the police may reasonably believe that destruction of the evidence is ***so imminent*** that merely sealing off the premises will not work, and that an ***immediate entry*** into the premises to conduct a search for and seizure of the evidence is the only reliable method. If the prosecution can convince the court that this was indeed the situation, then the search and seizure of the evidence itself — without any attempt to first seal the premises and obtain a search warrant — will fall within the "destruction of evidence" exception to the general Fourth Amendment requirement of a search warrant.

3. **The "police-created exigency" exception:** Courts recognize an exception to the general rule that if there is a serious threat of destruction of evidence, a search warrant is not needed. Under the ***"police-created exigency"*** doctrine, if the police's own conduct ***"created"*** or ***"manufactured"*** the exigency (the threat of evidence-destruction), then the main evidence-destruction exception to the warrant requirement will not apply, and the police will need to get a warrant before they conduct a search.

   a. **Narrowly interpreted:** But the police-created-exigency doctrine is ***narrowly interpreted***; it will nullify the police's right to enter warrantlessly only when the police "gain entry to premises by means of an ***actual or threatened violation of the Fourth Amendment***." The Supreme Court so held in ***Kentucky v. King***, 131 S.Ct. 1849 (2011).

      i. **Facts:** In *King*, an undercover police officer radioed to uniformed officers that the subject of a surveillance operation had just completed a drug deal and was moving quickly towards the breezeway of a nearby apartment building. The undercover officer instructed the uniformed officers to get to the breezeway quickly, before the suspect could enter an apartment. The officers got there too late — they heard a door slam, and they smelled a strong odor of burnt marijuana in the area.

(1) **The police pick an apartment:** There were only two apartments that the suspect could have gone into, one on the left of the breezeway and one on the right. Because the one on the left was where the marijuana odor was coming from, the police presumed that that was where the suspect had gone, so they approached that door. They knocked loudly and announced "this is the police." They heard things being moved around in the apartment, and concluded that what they were hearing was an attempt to destroy evidence. They then announced they were going to enter the apartment, and kicked in the door.

(2) **The police arrest D:** After entering, the police found D (the resident of the apartment), his girlfriend, and a guest, all smoking marijuana. The police then found additional drugs in a protective sweep (see *supra*, p. 105) of the apartment, and arrested D. It later turned out that D was not the original suspect that they had been chasing, and that this suspect had entered the other apartment, the one on the right.

ii. **Issue:** So the issue in *King* boiled down to this: assuming that the police just before they entered the apartment had reasonable grounds to believe that evidence was being destroyed inside, and assuming that this created exigent circumstances, should the police be deemed to have "manufactured" the emergency by their own conduct, so as to trigger "police-created exigency" doctrine? If so, this would prevent the general exigent-circumstances exception to the warrant requirement from applying.

iii. **Holding:** By an 8-1 vote, the Court held that the police-created-exigency doctrine should apply *only* when the police created the exigency by "engaging or threatening to engage in ***conduct that violates the Fourth Amendment***[.]" This principle means that as long as the police behavior is "reasonable" in Fourth Amendment terms, that behavior will not deprive the police of the ability to enter without a warrant in order to prevent the imminent destruction of evidence.

(1) **Outcome:** The Court in *King* did not decide whether the facts there actually represented exigent circumstances, and thus qualified for the destruction-of-evidence exception to the warrant requirement — the Court ***remanded*** to the Kentucky Supreme Court on this issue. But the Court's opinion establishes that if there *are* exigent circumstances that would ordinarily relieve the police of the obligation to get a warrant, the police forfeit that right on account of the police-created-exigency doctrine *only* if they were in fact ***violating***, or ***threatening to violate***, the ***Fourth Amendment.*** And, the Court concluded, there was no such violation or threat on the facts in *King*.

C. **Need for fast action:** Some cases have allowed warrantless searches or seizures whose motivation is not that evidence may be destroyed, but that ***danger to life*** may occur if the police cannot act fast.

1. **Political crimes:** Political assassination cases have sometimes given rise to such warrantless searches.

Example: A few hours after the shooting of Robert Kennedy, police conducted a warrantless search of Sirhan Sirhan's house. The search was upheld: "Although the officers did not have reasonable cause to believe that the house contained evidence of a conspiracy to assassinate prominent political leaders, we believe that the mere possibility that there might be such evidence in the house fully warranted the officer's actions. . . . Today when assassinations of persons of prominence have repeatedly been committed in this country, it is essential that law enforcement officers be allowed to take fast action in their endeavors to combat such crimes." *People v. Sirhan*, 497 P.2d 1121 (Cal. 1972).

2. People may need assistance: Indications that a person may be in danger ***inside the premises*** may constitute exigent circumstances justifying a warrantless search. As the Supreme Court has put it, "One exigency obviating the requirement of a warrant is the need to assist persons who are seriously injured or threatened with such injury ... Accordingly, law enforcement officers may ***enter a home without a warrant*** to render ***emergency assistance to an injured occupant*** or to ***protect an occupant*** from imminent injury." *Brigham City v. Stuart*, 547 U.S. 398 (2006).

Example: At 3 a.m., acting without a warrant, police respond to a call that a loud party is taking place at a house. When they arrive, they hear shouting, and they then see, through a screen door, an altercation taking place in the kitchen, in which four adults are trying to restrain a juvenile. They see the juvenile break free and hit one of the adults in the face, who spits blood into a sink. At that moment, the police open the screen door, enter, announce themselves, and arrest several adults present on various charges such as contributing to the delinquency of a minor. The adults claim that the warrantless entry violated their Fourth Amendment rights, rendering their subsequent arrest invalid.

Held, the police entry, though warrantless, did not violate the Fourth Amendment, because the entry was justified by the exigent circumstances. The police may make a warrantless entry into a home to assist an injured occupant or prevent imminent injury; this is what the police did here. *Brigham City*, *supra*.

a. "Objectively reasonable" test, not actual motive: By the way, in this exigent-circumstances scenario, the reasonableness of the police action will be judged *not* by considering whether the police's ***motive*** in making the entry was to respond to the exigency, but rather by whether the circumstances, viewed ***objectively***, were exigent.

Example: In *Brigham City*, *supra*, the Ds argued that the warrantless entry violated the Fourth Amendment because the police were actually motivated by law-enforcement purposes (to make an arrest or to collect evidence) rather than by a desire to assist injured persons or to prevent further injury. The Court *rejected* this defense without even considering what the officers' real motives were: "An action is 'reasonable' under the Fourth Amendment, regardless of the individual officer's state of mind, as long as the circumstances, viewed *objectively*, justify [the] action." Therefore, it "does not matter here ... whether the officers entered the kitchen to arrest [the Ds] and gather evidence against them or to assist the injured and prevent further violence."

3. Weapons: The "need for immediate action" rationale has also been applied to allow warrantless searches of premises where the police have a reasonable suspicion that dangerous

weapons will be on the premises to be searched. But it is only in the unusually frightening case, such as a political assassination or major terrorist plot, that the requirement of ***probable cause to believe the weapons will be found*** is likely to be dispensed with.

D. Hot pursuit: If the police are pursuing a felony suspect, and have reason to believe that he has entered particular premises, they may enter those premises to search for him. While they are searching for him, they may also search for weapons which, since he is still at large, he might seize. This is sometimes called the ***"hot pursuit"*** exception to the search warrant requirement.

1. **Other items:** While the police are engaged in such a "hot pursuit" for a suspect and any weapons he might have, they may come across other evidence of criminal behavior. This evidence may be seized and admitted, at least if it is discovered at a place where the police were reasonably searching for the suspect or his weapons.

   Example: Police get word that D, an armed robbery suspect, has just entered a particular house. (The house later turns out to be his own.) The police ring the doorbell, and D's wife answers. The police ask for and receive permission to search for what they describe as "a burglar." During their search, they look for weapons that D might have concealed, and find incriminating clothing in a washing machine.

   Held, the warrantless search was justified by the police's "hot pursuit," regardless of the validity of D's wife's consent to the search: "The police were informed that an armed robbery had taken place, and that the suspect had entered a certain house less than five minutes before they reached it. They acted reasonably when they entered the house and began to search for a man of the description they had been given and for weapons which he had used in the robbery or might use against them." *Warden v. Hayden*, 387 U.S. 294 (1967) (also discussed *supra*, p. 65)

E. Entry to arrest non-resident: The mere fact that the police are attempting to make an arrest does not by itself permit them to enter a private dwelling in search of the suspect. Thus where the police are not in hot pursuit, and there are no other exigent circumstances, ***they may not enter one person's private dwelling to arrest another, even if they are acting pursuant to an arrest warrant. Steagald v. U.S.***, 451 U.S. 204 (1981).

1. **Facts of *Steagald:*** In *Steagald*, federal agents learned from an informer that one Lyons, a federal fugitive, could probably be found at a certain address. They procured a warrant for his arrest (although the warrant did not mention the address); they entered the premises, and while searching for Lyons there, came upon drugs belonging to Steagald, a resident of the house. (They did not find Lyons at all).

2. **Holding:** The Court held that the arrest warrant could not be used as legal authority to enter the home of a person other than the person named in the warrant. The Court's principal objection was that no neutral magistrate ever evaluated the police officers' probable cause to believe that Lyons would be found ***at Steagald's home***. (The Court's opinion indicated that had the magistrate who issued the arrest warrant found that there was probable cause to believe that Lyons would be found at Steagald's house, there would have been no constitutional difficulty with searching for Lyons in that house.)

a. **Potential for abuse:** The Court observed that "A contrary conclusion — that the police, acting alone and in the absence of exigent circumstances, may decide when there is sufficient justification for searching the home of a third party for the subject of an arrest warrant — would create a significant potential for abuse. Armed solely with an arrest warrant for a single person, the person could search all the homes of that individual's friends and acquaintances. . . . Moreover, an arrest warrant may serve as the pretext for entering a home in which the police have a suspicion, but not probable cause to believe, that illegal activity is taking place."

3. **Dissent:** Justice Rehnquist, in a dissent joined by Justice White, argued that no separate search warrant should be necessary where there is an arrest warrant, so long as there is in fact probable cause to believe that the suspect will be found in the third party's house. The dissent pointed out that the need to procure a separate search warrant in this situation will often increase the probability that the fugitive will have time to escape.

4. **Limited application:** The opinion in *Steagald* is limited to a fairly narrow set of facts. As the Court noted there, the prior decision in *Payton v. New York* (*supra*, p. 94) holds that an arrest warrant alone will suffice to allow the police to enter a ***suspect's own residence*** to arrest him. So *Steagald* applies only where the police attempt to arrest a suspect by entering a house ***other than the suspect's own house***.

a. **Additional limitations:** Furthermore, no arrest warrant at all is required to arrest a suspect in a ***public place***, assuming that there is probable cause, so that the subject of an arrest warrant may be arrested before entering or after leaving the home of a third party. In addition, where exigent circumstances are present (e.g., where the police are in "hot pursuit" of a suspect who runs into a third party's house), *Steagald* will not apply, and even a third person's home may be entered without a search warrant.

F. **Search of scene of murder:** The fact that the place being searched is the ***scene of a recent murder*** is ***not*** by itself an "exigent circumstance" automatically justifying warrantless search. In *Mincey v. Arizona*, 437 U.S. 385 (1978), the defendant, in his own apartment, shot an undercover police officer, and was shortly thereafter arrested by other officers. Homicide detectives then began an extensive warrantless search of the entire apartment, a search which lasted four days.

1. **Holding:** The Supreme Court rejected an Arizona rule that a warrantless search of the scene of a homicide is automatically valid, as long as its scope is reasonable and the police have a right to be on the premises in the first instance (as they did here, when they arrested the defendant). The Court stressed that this was not really an emergency situation, since there was no indication that evidence would be lost, destroyed or removed during the time required to obtain a search warrant, and the police in fact ***posted a guard*** on the premises during the entire four-day search anyway.

V. THE "PLAIN VIEW" DOCTRINE AND SEIZURES OF EVIDENCE

A. General applicability: The ***"plain view"*** doctrine (discussed *supra*, p. 43, in the context of what constitutes an expectation of privacy) is often applied to allow police who are on premises for lawful purposes to make a warrantless seizure of evidence which they come across.

1. **Incident to arrest:** The "plain view" doctrine has become of increasing importance since *Chimel* limited the scope of a search incident to arrest. If the police are within the permissible area of a search incident to arrest (i.e., the area of "control" of the defendant), they may seize evidence which falls into their view, even if the item itself is outside of the control area.

B. Requirements for doctrine: For the plain view doctrine to be applied so that a warrantless seizure of evidence is allowable, ***three requirements*** must be met:

The officers must ***not have violated the Fourth Amendment in arriving at the place*** from which the items are plainly viewed;

The incriminating nature of the iterms must be ***immediately apparent***; and

The officers must have a ***lawful right of access*** to the ***object itself***.

These three requirements were listed by the Court in *Horton v. California*, 496 U.S. 128 (1990). Let's discuss them one at a time.

1. **Legally on premises:** First, the officers must ***not have violated the Fourth Amendment*** in arriving at the place from which the items were plainly viewed. So, for instance, if they trespassed on D's front lawn to look into his front window to get the plain view, the doctrine would not apply.

2. **Incriminating nature must be apparent:** Second, the incriminating nature of the items seized must be ***"immediately apparent."*** For instance, if the item plainly viewed is an automobile, but the incriminating evidence is fingerprints that are found on the windshield only after microscopic analysis, the incriminating nature of the evidence is not "immediately apparent" and the plain view doctrine does not apply.

   a. **Probable cause:** The requirement that the incriminating nature of the item be "immediately apparent" seems to be another way of saying that the police must, at the moment they first see the item in plain view, have ***probable cause*** to believe that the object is incriminating (i.e., that it is contraband or stolen property, or that it is useful as evidence of a crime).

   Example: A bullet comes through D's apartment and injures a man in the apartment below. Police enter D's apartment to locate the shooter, other victims, and any weapons. While doing so, one officer notices an expensive stereo, which seems out of place in the squalid apartment. Suspecting it to be stolen, he picks up one of the components, records its serial number, reports it by phone to his headquarters, learns that the turntable had been taken in a robbery, and seizes it. The prosecution wants to introduce the stereo as evidence against D, by use of the plain view doctrine.

Held, the plain view doctrine does not apply, because at the moment the officer picked up the stereo, he did not have probable cause for the search he performed by moving it, merely a "reasonable suspicion." (By the time he seized it, he did have probable cause, but he got that probable cause — by learning that the serial number had been reported stolen — via the illegal search.) *Arizona v. Hicks*, 480 U.S. 321 (1987).

3. **Lawful right of access to object:** Third and last, the officers must have a lawful ***right of access*** to the ***object itself***.

Example: Suppose the police, standing on the public sidewalk, can see through the window of D's house and can view marijuana growing there. The police may not make a warrantless entry into D's house to seize the marijuana, because they don't have lawful access to the inside of the house. On the other hand, if they were already lawfully in the house, say to arrest D with a warrant, they could seize the marijuana plant under the plain view doctrine.

C. **No requirement of inadvertence:** The "plain view" doctrine applies even where the police's discovery of a piece of evidence they want to seize is ***not inadvertent***. Thus if the police know that they are likely to find, say, both the gun used in a robbery as well as proceeds of the robbery, they may procure a warrant for the proceeds, and they may then seize the gun if they happen upon it in plain view while they are searching for the proceeds. See *Horton v. California*, 496 U.S. 128 (1990), also discussed *supra*, p. 71.

VI. THE "AUTOMOBILE EXCEPTION" TO THE REQUIREMENT OF A SEARCH WARRANT

A. **Relation of car searches to other kinds of searches:** All of the exceptions to the requirement of a search warrant that we've discussed so far may apply to the search of an automobile as well as to the search of persons and premises.

1. **Exigent circumstances:** For instance, ***exigent circumstances*** will often cause the warrant requirement to be suspended when a car search is involved. Thus the police may search a vehicle without a warrant if such a search is necessary to ***preserve evidence***, as will be the case where the car can be quickly ***driven out of the jurisdiction***. ***Carroll v. U.S.***, 267 U.S. 132 (1925).

2. **Incident to arrest:** Similarly, if the police arrest the driver, and have "reason to believe" that the vehicle may contain evidence of the crime for which they made the arrest, they may search the car under a form of search incident to arrest. See *Arizona v. Gant*, *supra*, p. 103.

B. **The "automobile exception" to the warrant requirement – generally:** Even apart from the above situations in which the *general* exceptions to the requirement of a search warrant can apply in the automobile context, the Supreme Court has long recognized a specific auto-related exception, which is usually called the ***"automobile exception"*** to the warrant requirement.[7]

1. **Main statement of rule:** Here's a general statement of the automobile exception: A police officer may search a motor vehicle without first getting a search warrant, ***as long as she has probable cause to believe that evidence or contraband is located in the vehicle.*** Cf. *California v. Carney*, 471 U.S. 386 (1985) (discussed in more depth *infra*, p. 131).

2. **Rationales for the exception:** The Supreme Court has relied on two distinct rationales for the automobile exception:

   [1] **"Ready mobility":** The first (and original) rationale is based on the ***inherent mobility*** of motor vehicles. Even though a person has a constitutionally-protected privacy interest in her vehicle, the "ready mobility" of vehicles justifies giving the vehicle a lesser degree of protection than in the case of a fixed structure.

   Where it is a *structure* that is to be searched, there is generally time to obtain a search warrant, so we should require the police to get the warrant, assuming circumstances allow. But in the case of a motor vehicle, when the police arrive at probable cause to believe that evidence or contraband is located in the vehicle, it is usually ***"not practicable*** to secure a warrant because the vehicle ***can be quickly moved*** out of the locality or jurisdiction in which the warrant must be sought." *Carroll v. U.S.*, 267 U.S. 132 (1925).

   [2] **Lesser expectation of privacy:** A second rationale is that a person should be ***deemed to have a lesser expectation of privacy*** with respect to a vehicle she owns than with respect to, say, her home or workplace. The expectation of privacy with respect to vehicles is reduced because of the ***"pervasive regulation of vehicles*** capable of traveling on the public highways." *California v. Carney, supra.*

   The Court has explained the significance of this pervasive regulation as follows:

   > As an ***everyday occurrence***, police stop and examine vehicles when ***license plates or inspection stickers*** have ***expired***, or if other violations, such as exhaust fumes or excessive noise, are noted, or if headlights or other ***safety equipment*** are not in proper working order. ... [T]he ***pervasive schemes of regulation***, which ***necessarily lead to reduced expectations of privacy*** ... justify [warrantless] searches ... so long as the overriding standard of probable cause is met.
   >
   > *California v. Carney, supra.*

3. **Examples of the exception:** As we'll see below (*infra*, pp. 130-139), the Supreme Court has gradually extended the vehicle exception in a variety of ways. Here are some examples of contexts in which the Court has concluded that the vehicle exception applies:

   [1] Where an officer looking through the ***window of a car*** sees an item of evidence or contraband in ***plain view*** in the passenger compartment, the officer is entitled to open the car door, and seize and inspect the item.

   [2] Where the police have probable cause to ***open a car's locked trunk*** to see whether it contains a particular piece of expected evidence, the officer is then entitled to ***seize***

---

7. The exception can also be described as the "vehicle exception," since it applies to trucks, vans, mobile homes, motorcycles, and other vehicles beyond "automobiles." But we'll use the traditional label "automobile exception" here.

additional unexpected items of evidence he finds in plain view inside the trunk. Cf. *Cady v. Dombrowki*, 413 U.S. 433 (1973).

[3] Where the police arrest (on probable cause) a driver for selling narcotics from his car, they are entitled to open the car's trunk, open a ***closed paper bag they find there***, and seize any contraband or evidence of crime they find inside the bag. *U.S. v. Ross*, 456 U.S. 798 (1982) (further discussed *infra*, p. 136).

[4] Where the police arrest (on probable cause) the driver of a getaway car after a robbery, and seize the car and ***drive it to the police station***, they are entitled to immediately search the car's interior without a search warrant, even though no injury to law-enforcement interests would occur if they were instead to hold the car and wait until they could get a warrant. *Chambers v. Maroney*, 399 U.S. 42 (1970) (further discussed *infra*, p. 130).

[5] When DEA agents (acting on probable cause for a search in a narcotics case) enter and search a ***"motor home"*** whose windows are covered, the search is proper even though the vehicle is capable of serving as a residence. *Cal. v. Carney*, 471 U.S. 386 (1985).

4. **Guide to sub-topics:** In Paragraphs C through M below, we'll examine various aspects of the automobile exception. These will include:

   Vehicle searches ***at the station house***, after the police have driven or towed the vehicle there following an arrest elsewhere. (Pars. C, *infra*, p. 130 and K, p. 138.)

   Immediate searches at the ***place where the vehicle stop has just occurred***. (Par. D, *infra*, p. 131.)

   Search of a vehicle parked in a ***driveway*** that's part of a home's curtilage. (Par. E, *infra*, p. 131.)

   Police use of a ***pretext*** to make a vehicle stop, done for the purpose of triggering the auto exception. (Par. F, *infra*, p. 134.)

   The non-vehicle-search powers of the police when they make the stop ***solely to issue a traffic ticket***. (Par. G, *infra*, p. 135.)

   Use of the exception to justify warrantless search of a ***closed container*** inside the vehicle. (Par. H, *infra*, p. 136.)

   Use of the exception where the only ***probable cause*** the police have relates to a ***closed container*** inside the vehicle. (Par. I, *infra*, p. 137.)

   Search for the vehicle's ***Vehicle Identification Number***. (Par. J, *infra*, p. 138.)

   Searches directed at the vehicle's ***passengers***. (Par. L, *infra*, p. 138.)

   Vehicle searches when the stop was made solely to ***issue a traffic ticket***. (Par. M, *infra*, p. 139.)

C. **Search at station after arrest:** Several kinds of exceptional circumstances have been recognized by the Supreme Court as applying particularly to vehicle searches. One such circumstance is where the police arrest a driver, take him and his car ***to the station***, and search the car there. Such a search was allowed in ***Chambers v. Maroney***, 399 U.S. 42 (1970).

1. **Holding of *Chambers:*** In *Chambers*, the defendant was an armed robbery suspect whose getaway car was stopped by the police shortly after the robbery, based on a description of the vehicle furnished by the victim. The car was driven to the station, where it was warrantlessly searched, and incriminating evidence found. The Court held that the search was ***valid***, despite the fact that, since the car was in police possession, a warrant could have been procured without endangering the preservation of evidence.

   a. **Rationale:** The Court's holding rested chiefly on the following two-part syllogism: (1) the destruction-or-removal-of-evidence exception at least permitted the arresting officers to seize the car and deny its use to anyone; and (2) that being the case, "there is little to choose in terms of practical consequences between an immediate search [at the station] without a warrant and the car's immobilization until a warrant is obtained."

   b. **Probable cause:** The *Chambers* Court emphasized that the police had ***probable cause*** to search the car at the police station, since such probable cause had arisen from the description of the car by the victim. It was apparently a *sine qua non* of the Court's validation of the *Chambers* search that probable cause for search existed. However, the Court has subsequently held, as discussed below, that ***inventory*** of an impounded car's contents may sometimes be taken, even if there is no probable cause to search. See *South Dakota v. Opperman*, discussed *infra*, p. 138.

D. **Search at place where vehicle is stopped:** *Chambers* was a case in which the police stopped the vehicle without a search warrant and towed it to the police station; they did not conduct the search until this "impoundment." But the police also generally have a right to conduct a warrantless search of a vehicle ***immediately*** at the place where they have stopped it (assuming that they had ***probable cause*** to make the stop).

   Example: DEA agents, based on word from an informant and their own observations, have probable cause to believe that a motor home parked in a parking lot is being used for distribution of marijuana. The agents and the informant knock on the motor home's door. When D steps out, the agents identify themselves, and one steps into the motor home without a warrant, finds marijuana, and arrests D.

   Held, the warrantless search here was valid, and fell within the automobile exception to the requirement of a search warrant, recognized by *Carroll v. U.S.* (*supra*, p. 128). ***California v. Carney***, 471 U.S. 386 (1985).

   Note: *Carney* also establishes that a mobile home will be treated as a "vehicle" (with its lesser expectation of privacy), rather than a fixed dwelling, at least where the home is parked in a parking lot. (But the Court indicated that a different rule might apply where the home is located in a way or place suggesting that it is actually ***used as a residence***.)

E. **Search of vehicle parked in curtilage portion of driveway (*Collins v. Virginia*):** Can the automobile exception apply to dispense with the need for a warrant where the vehicle to be searched is located not on a public street, but on ***private residential property***, such as on the ***driveway*** of a home?

   To focus the question more tightly, let's assume that (1) the police ***have probable cause*** to make the vehicle search, so that if the car were on the street, the automobile exception would apply; and (2) the vehicle is ***visible from the street***. Does the automobile exception entitle the police to enter the property without a warrant, walk up to the vehicle, and search it? The answer depends mostly on whether the portion of the driveway or other private property where the vehicle is located is or is not within the home's "***curtilage.***"[8]

1. **Vehicle not in curtilage:** First, let's examine the situation in which the vehicle is on a portion of a homeowner's property that is ***not*** part of the property's curtilage.

   a. **"Open fields" not protected by the Fourth Amendment:** Recall (*supra*, p. 22) that the Fourth Amendment ***simply doesn't apply*** to searches or seizures that occur in ***"open fields."*** And you'll also recall that the Supreme Court has defined "open fields" quite ***broadly***, so that the term includes all portions of a homeowner's property that are not contained within either the actual dwelling or the dwelling's curtilage.[9]

      Example: Suppose that D, a homeowner, has built a 10-foot-tall opaque fence around a field located on the back portion of D's residential lot, to the rear of the actual house. D is growing marijuana in that fenced-in field. Let's assume that no part of the field is part of the house's "curtilage," because no part is "immediately surrounding and associated with the home" (the definition of curtilage, as given in the prior footnote).

      The fact that no one on the ground can see through the fence to observe the marijuana is *irrelevant* to whether the field (and things growing in it) are protected by the Fourth Amendment – since the field is not part of the curtilage, D's interest in it is not protected by the Fourth Amendment. Therefore, it follows that even though the police do not have probable cause to suspect that the field contains evidence of criminality, they are entitled to fly a helicopter over the field, observe the marijuana, and use that observation as the basis for an immediate warrantless entry into the field to seize the marijuana plants. See *California v. Ciraolo*, *supra*, p. 49, based on similar facts.

   b. **Consequence for vehicle outside of curtilage:** Now then, let's consider the automobile exception's availability when the vehicle is located on the ***non-curtilage portion*** of a homeowner's property. Because the non-curtilage portion of a residential property is treated the same for Fourth Amendment purposes as a public place (e.g., a street), it follows that when a vehicle is located in the non-curtilage portion, the automobile exception to the search warrant requirement ***relieves the police of the need to procure a warrant*** before they enter the property and search and/or seize the vehicle, just as if the vehicle were parked on the street.

      Example: On the facts of the above example, suppose D has parked his truck in the middle of the fenced-in field behind his house, so that the truck is obscured from public view by the fence. Let's assume that the police acquire probable cause (e.g., via a tip from an informant known to be reliable) to believe that the truck's passenger compartment contains a pistol used in a homicide. Even though the police don't have a search warrant, the open-fields doctrine entitles them to climb the fence, walk up to

---

8. Recall from our earlier discussion (p. 22), that the curtilage of a house is "the area 'immediately surrounding and associated with the home'."

9. See *supra*, p. 23.

the truck, open it, and search its contents to find and seize the pistol. In other words, the automobile exception to the warrant requirement applies to the truck parked in this enclosed area near — but not part of the curtilage of — D's house, just as it would apply if the truck was parked on the public street.

2. **Vehicle is within the curtilage (*Collins v. Virginia*):** But now, let's analyze the automobile exception where the vehicle ***is*** located within the curtilage of a person's dwelling. As the result of the 2018 decision in *Collins v. Virginia* (*supra*, p. 23), we know that the vehicle exception ***does not apply*** to allow the warrantless search of a vehicle located within the curtilage. Therefore, the police must procure a search warrant before searching or seizing the vehicle, unless some other exception to the warrant requirement applies.

   a. **Facts of *Collins*:** As you'll recall (*supra*, p. 25), the core issue in *Collins* was whether police officer Rhodes, who spotted what appeared to be a stolen motorcycle parked on D's girlfriend's driveway, was entitled to use the automobile exception to conduct a warrantless search of the motorcycle, which was parked within the house's curtilage.

   b. **Exception not applicable:** In an 8-1 ruling, Justice Sotomayor gave an unequivocal answer: the automobile exception ***does not apply to vehicles located within the curtilage of a person's home.*** And that's so even if the vehicle can be seen by the police from a street or other public vantage point.

      i. **Rationale:** Sotomayor called this "an easy case," and posed a hypothetical variation on the facts of the case to explain why. Suppose, she asked, a motorcycle was "parked ***inside the living room of a house,*** visible through a window to a passerby on the street." Assume further that a police officer, seeing the motorcycle from the street, had probable cause to believe that the vehicle had been involved in a traffic accident. Could the officer, acting without a warrant, ***enter the house*** to search the motorcycle to confirm that it was the right one? Her answer: "surely not."

      ii. **Explanation:** Continuing her analysis of this hypo, Sotomayor noted that "[T]he scope of the automobile exception ***extends no further than the automobile itself.***" That is, the Court's cases on the automobile exception furnished no reason to believe that in the hypo, the exception would give the police "the ***right to enter a home*** ... to access a vehicle without a warrant."

      iii. **Tie-in to search in the curtilage:** Since in the hypo the officer couldn't use the automobile exception to enter the house, it followed that on the real facts of *Collins* the officer couldn't use the exception to enter the curtilage, either. That was so because the Court had consistently held that the curtilage of a home is entitled to the ***same constitutional protection*** as the home's interior.

      iv. **"Visibility" not a significant factor:** In litigating *Collins*, the state of Virginia claimed that the fact that the motorcycle was not only outside the house, but ***visible from the street,*** should trigger the automobile exception even if that exception would not apply to an automobile parked in, say, a fully enclosed garage. But Sotomayor rejected this argument, saying that the visibility or invisibility of the vehicle was constitutionally irrelevant. "So long as it is curtilage, a parking patio or carport into which an officer can see from the street is ***no less entitled to protection*** from trespass and a warrantless search than a fully enclosed garage."

c. **Consequence:** The Court's refusal in *Collins* to extend the automobile exception to cover vehicles located in a home's curtilage meant that Officer Rhodes' warrantless search of the motorcycle (even if supported by probable cause) violated D's Fourth Amendment rights, unless some other exception to the warrant requirement applied.

d. **Other exception might apply:** But as Sotomayor's opinion carefully noted, the warrantless intrusion into the curtilage might still be constitutional if ***some other (non-automobile-specific) exception*** to the warrant requirement applied. The Court therefore remanded the case for a "resolution [of] whether the … warrantless intrusion on the curtilage of [D's] house may have been reasonable on a different basis[.]"

   i. **Exceptions that might apply:** Since the search in *Collins* was a search of a "home" (because the curtilage is deemed part of the home), there were only a few exceptions to the warrant requirement that could possibly apply.[10]

   ii. **Exigent-circumstances exception:** The exception that would most plausibly apply here is the one based on ***exigent circumstances.*** (See *supra*, p. 120.) Indeed, the majority opinion in *Collins* mentioned this exception – and no others – as a potential reason that might justify a finding on remand that the search was reasonable despite the unavailability of the automobile exception.

   Example: Consider the following variation on the facts of *Collins*: This time, assume that Officer Rhodes saw a motorcycle ridden by D collide with a pedestrian and then drive off, constituting the crime of leaving the scene of an accident. Let's further assume that Rhodes was able to follow D to a house, but was far enough behind D that by the time Rhodes got there, all she saw in the curtilage portion of the driveway was a tarpaulin covering something that might or might not have been motorcycle.

   On these facts, there is of course a risk that unless Rhodes can make an immediate search, D will be able to destroy evidence that the object under the tarpaulin was indeed the motorcycle used in the hit-and-run. (For instance, D might be able to wash any blood off the front of the cycle.) Therefore, the prosecution can make a strong argument that the exigent-circumstances exception to the warrant requirement should apply. If the prosecution succeeds with that theory, the search will not be deemed a violation of D's Fourth Amendment rights, and the evidence produced by the search will have been properly admitted at trial.

F. **Use of pretext to make stop:** Suppose the police have a vague suspicion that a particular motorist is engaged in some illegal activity (e.g., drug smuggling), but this suspicion does not rise even to the level permitting a warrantless "stop" (see *infra*, p. 148), let alone a warrantless

---

10. A warrantless search is less likely to be "reasonable," and thus constitutional, when it is a search of a home than when it is a search of any other type of location. Thus searches of a workplace, of an automobile, of a place of public accommodation (e.g., a store or a restaurant), or even of a person incident to an arrest, are all more likely to be considered "reasonable" because of some exception to the warrant requirement than are searches of a home.

search or arrest. But suppose further that the police, after further observing the motorist, notice him ***violate some minor traffic regulation*** not related to the suspected illegality. May the police seize upon this violation as a ***pretext*** for stopping the motorist? The short answer is ***"yes."*** The Court so held in *Whren v. U.S.*, 517 U.S. 806 (1996).

1. **Significance:** In other words, *Whren* illustrates that the fact that the police's "real" reason for the stop is something other than the traffic violation is irrelevant — once the police have probable cause to believe that even a minor traffic (or other) violation has occurred, they may stop the vehicle. Then, if the stop in turn gives them probable cause to believe that contraband is inside, they may perform a warrantless search.

   Example: Washington D.C. police are patrolling a "high drug area" in an unmarked car. Their suspicions are aroused when they see a truck with temporary license plates and youthful occupants waiting at a stop sign, with the driver looking into the passenger's lap. The truck remains stopped at the intersection for 20 seconds, an unusually long time. The patrol car does a U-turn to head back toward the truck. The truck then turns suddenly towards its right (without signaling), and drives off at excessive speed. The officers stop the driver on account of traffic violations (failure to signal, failure to pay attention to operation of the vehicle, and speeding). After they make the stop, they look into the truck's window and see what appears to be crack in the hands of D (the passenger). They arrest D, and retrieve drugs from the vehicle. D claims that because the stop was "pretextual" (i.e., the police weren't really motivated by the minor traffic offenses, but instead by their hunch of drug trafficking), the stop should be ruled a violation of the Sixth Amendment.

   Held, for the prosecution. If the police have probable cause to believe that a traffic (or other) law has been broken, they may stop the perpetrator, even if their motive in doing so is to seek evidence of some other crime for which they do not have probable cause or even reasonable suspicion. In other words, there's no "pretext" exception to the general rule that police may make a warrantless stop of a vehicle when they have probable cause to believe that an offense has been committed. *Whren*, *supra*.

G. **Traffic tickets:** Where the police stop a car and merely write a ***traffic ticket*** instead of making an arrest, their search-and-seizure powers are ***more limited*** than where they make an arrest. In the traffic-ticket case, the officer may ***not*** search the vehicle (or the driver's person), unless there is probable cause to believe that evidence of something other than the traffic violation will be found. See *Knowles v. Iowa*, 525 U.S. 113 (1998), discussed more extensively *infra*, p. 139.

1. **Some powers remain:** On the other hand, even in the traffic-ticket situation, the officer who conducts the vehicle stop has some limited search-and-seizure powers. For instance:

   The officer may order the driver and/or passenger to ***step out of the car*** (see *Pennsylvania v. Mimms*, *infra*, p. 151 and *Maryland v. Wilson*, *infra*, p. 152), as a means of protecting the officer's safety.

   If there is reason to believe that an occupant of the vehicle may be armed and dangerous, the officer may conduct a ***"pat down"*** of the occupant's person, and also of the vehicle's interior (see *Michigan v. Long*, *infra*, p. 164).

H. Extended to closed containers: The Court has extended its liberal rules for automobile searches to ***closed containers*** (including ***luggage***) carried by car or other form of transport. Such items, when found in an automobile, may normally be searched without a warrant, if the car itself is being subjected to a valid *Carroll* or *Chambers*-type warrantless search based on probable cause. ***U.S. v. Ross***, 456 U.S. 798 (1982).

1. **Facts of *Ross:*** In *Ross*, the police acted on a tip received from an informant that defendant was selling narcotics kept in the trunk of his car. The informant gave a description of both the seller and the car; the police spotted an auto and driver matching the description. They did not obtain either a search or arrest warrant but arrested the driver. One of the officers then opened the trunk of the car and found a closed paper bag. He opened the bag and discovered several glassine bags containing a white powder (which turned out to be heroin). Another warrantless search of the car took place at the police station several minutes later, which turned up a zippered leather pouch containing cash.

2. **Holding:** Since the police legitimately stopped the automobile and had ***probable cause*** to believe that ***contraband*** was contained in it, the Court in *Ross* allowed them to conduct a warrantless search of the vehicle. Such a search could be ***as thorough as one authorized by a warrant issued by a magistrate***. Thus every part of the vehicle where the contraband might be stored could be inspected, the Court held. This included ***all receptacles and packages that could possibly contain the object of the search***. "The scope of the search is not defined by the nature of the container in which the contraband is secreted. Rather, it is defined by the object of the search and the places in which there is probable cause to believe that it may be found."

3. **Container belonging to passenger:** Where the police have probable cause to believe a stopped vehicle contains contraband or evidence of crime (i.e., probable cause to do a *Ross*-type warrantless search of the vehicle and its contents), they may also search any container that they know belongs to a ***passenger*** rather than to the driver, ***even if the police have no grounds whatever to suspect the passenger of any wrongdoing. Wyoming v. Houghton***, 526 U.S. 295 (1999).

   a. **Facts:** In *Houghton*, an officer stopped a car for speeding. The officer noticed that the driver had a syringe in his pocket, which the driver admitted he used for drugs. The officer then ordered the other two occupants of the car, both women, out of the car. The officer began to search the car for contraband in light of the driver's admission, and found a purse on the rear seat. One of the women, D, said that the purse was hers. (At that moment, the officer had no reason to suspect D of any wrongdoing.) The officer opened the purse and found drugs and drug paraphernalia in it. The officer then arrested D for drug possession.

   b. **Court upholds search:** The Court, by a 6-3 vote, held that the search of the purse did ***not*** violate D's Fourth Amendment rights: "We hold that ***police officers with probable cause to search a car may inspect passengers' belongings found in the car*** that are capable of concealing the object of the search."

   c. **No effect from *Gant*:** The decision in *Arizona v. Gant* (*supra*, p. 101), holding that the police may no longer automatically search the passenger compartment incident to the arrest of the driver, does not affect the validity of *Houghton*. The police's right under *Houghton* — to make a warrantless search of a vehicle's contents where they have probable cause to believe the vehicle contains contraband or evidence of crime — does not rely on the search-incident-to-arrest doctrine (which is the doctrine to which *Gant* relates).

4. **Time delay before container search:** A *Ross*-style warrantless search of a car's containers will be valid even though there is a ***significant delay*** between the time the police stop the vehicle and the time they perform the search of the container. Thus in *U.S. v. Johns*, 469 U.S. 478 (1985), customs officers stopped two trucks they suspected of carrying marijuana. They removed several sealed packages they believed to contain marijuana, and put them in a government warehouse. ***Three days*** after they removed the packages from the trucks, other officials opened them without a warrant, and found them to contain marijuana. By a 7-2 vote, the Court held that this warrantless search was valid under *Ross*.

5. **Consent to search:** Suppose that the warrantless search takes place not because the police have probable cause to search the car, but because the suspect ***consents*** to an auto search. In this event, the driver's consent to the search will be deemed to ***extend*** to any closed containers inside the vehicle, if the container might reasonably contain the object of the search. So, for instance, if a suspect allows the officer to search the car and the search turns up cocaine in a folded paper bag, the cocaine will be admissible as the fruit of a consent search. See *Florida v. Jimeno*, 500 U.S. 248 (1991), discussed further *infra*, p. 143.

I. **Probable cause for container only:** *Ross* was a case in which the police's probable cause related to the automobile, not to the closed container by itself; until 1991, the rationale of the case was never applied to situations where the police's probable cause focused on the container. But then, the Court held that the same principle applies to this latter situation: ***if the police have probable cause to believe that a container contains contraband, they may wait until the container is in the car, stop the car, and seize and open the container, all without a warrant***. *California v. Acevedo*, 500 U.S. 565 (1991).

1. **Facts of *Acevedo*:** In *Acevedo*, police saw D leaving a house with a paper bag similar to one they had seen earlier containing marijuana. D put the bag in his car's trunk, and drove away. The officers then stopped D and searched the trunk for the bag, even though they lacked probable cause with respect to the car itself, and lacked a warrant.

2. **Holding:** By a 6-3 vote, the Court held that the police conduct here was proper. The police's right to conduct a warrantless search of containers in a car should apply not only where their probable cause relates to the car as a whole (the situation in *Ross*), but also where their probable cause extends only to the container itself. The majority believed that the intrusion in this situation was no more severe than in the *Ross* "probable cause as to the whole car" situation.

3. **Criticism:** Observe that *Acevedo* gives the police a powerful incentive to postpone getting a warrant. If they see a person carry a container that they believe contains contraband, the police will normally need a warrant to make a seizure on the street. But if they follow the suspect and wait long enough, he may eventually put the container in his car — at that point, they can stop the car, seize the container and search it without bothering to get a warrant.

J. Search for Vehicle Identification Number: All cars are required by federal law to have a ***Vehicle Identification Number*** (***"VIN"***), a kind of serial number widely used by law enforcement agencies. The federal law requires that the VIN be placed on the dashboard so that it can be seen by someone outside the car. The Court has held that where a traffic stop is made and the driver exits the vehicle, the officer may reach into the car to clear away anything that obscures the VIN. If in so doing he finds weapons, contraband, etc., these will then be treated as having been in "plain view." *New York v. Class*, 475 U.S. 106 (1986).

K. Impoundment search where no probable cause: In many cases, the police will ***impound a vehicle*** pursuant to an arrest. Where the police would have been justified in conducting a warrantless search of the vehicle prior to impoundment, *Chambers* indicates that a search after impoundment is permissible. But in *Chambers*, there was ***probable cause*** to search the vehicle either before or after impoundment, and the only issue was the requirement of a warrant. Where ***probable cause to search is lacking***, may the police nonetheless make a ***post-impoundment search***? As a general rule, ***"yes."***

1. **Plain view:** It is well settled that if the police find evidence in ***plain view*** in a vehicle as they are impounding it, they may seize the evidence. *Harris v. U.S.*, 390 U.S. 234 (1968).

2. **Forfeiture:** Similarly, if the police have impounded a vehicle for purposes of conducting ***forfeiture*** proceedings, the Supreme Court has allowed a search. In *Cooper v. California*, 386 U.S. 58 (1967), where the police had to hold the car for forfeiture proceedings because state law required such proceedings for vehicles involved in narcotics violations, the Court held that it "would be unreasonable to hold that the police, having to retain the car in their garage [until the forfeiture proceedings] had no right, even for their own protection, to search it."

3. **Towed cars:** If the car is impounded because it has been ***towed*** for illegal parking, the Court has held, it may similarly be subjected to a warrantless ***"inventory search,"*** even though the police have never had probable cause to believe it contains contraband or evidence of crime. *South Dakota v. Opperman*, 428 U.S. 364 (1976).

4. **Containers in car:** The warrantless inventory search of an impounded vehicle may include the ***entire vehicle***, including a search of the contents of ***closed containers*** found inside the vehicle. *Colorado v. Bertine*, 479 U.S. 367 (1987).

   a. **Rationale:** In so holding, the Court in *Bertine* reasoned that such inventory searches protect the property from being stolen or damaged, protect the police from false claims of theft or vandalism, and may protect the police's safety.

   b. **Conditions:** The majority in *Bertine* imposed ***two conditions*** that must be met before an inventory search of an impounded vehicle may be made: (1) that the police follow ***standardized procedures***, so that the individual searching officer does not have unbridled discretion to determine the scope of the search; and (2) that the police not have acted ***in bad faith*** or for the ***sole purpose of investigation*** (so that if the arrest or the impoundment took place just to furnish an excuse for a warrantless search, the *South Dakota v. Opperman* exception would not apply).

L. Actions directed at passengers: If the driver's conduct leads the police to make a proper stop and/or arrest, this does ***not*** mean that the officer has the right to search the person of any

passenger who happens to be in the car. No matter what the driver has done, the officer may search a passenger only if the officer has either: (1) probable cause to believe that the passenger possesses evidence of a crime, or (2) probable cause to arrest the passenger (in which case the search is justified as being incident to arrest). See *Knowles v. Iowa*, *infra*, p. 139.

However, the officer does have several other rights regarding passengers:

As a method of protecting officer safety, the officer may demand that the passenger ***step out of the vehicle***. See *Maryland v. Wilson*, *infra*, p. 152.

Also as a matter of protection, if the officer has a reasonable fear that the passenger may be armed or dangerous, he may ***frisk and pat-down*** the passenger, to make sure that the passenger is not carrying a weapon. See *Arizona v. Johnson*, *infra*, p. 152.

Finally, if the officer has the right to search the vehicle (e.g., because he is arresting the driver, or because he has reasonable cause to believe the vehicle contains contraband or evidence of crime), the officer may also ***search any container*** in the car that might contain the thing being looked for, even if the officer knows that the container ***belongs to a passenger***, and even if the officer has no probable cause to believe that the container contains that thing. See *Wyoming v. Houghton*, *supra*, p. 136.

M. Traffic stop followed by ticket: Where the police make a routine stop to issue a ***traffic ticket***, and don't make an "arrest," they ***don't thereby get the right to search the car.*** The Court so held (by a unanimous vote, in fact) in ***Knowles v. Iowa***, 525 U.S. 113 (1998).

1. **Rationale:** The Court observed that cases allowing searches incident to arrest (e.g., *U.S. v. Robinson*, *supra*, p. 108) have been premised on the need to: (1) protect officer safety; and (2) avoid the hiding or destruction of evidence. But, the Court said, neither of these rationales applies with anywhere near the same strength to the traffic-ticket situation:

   a. **Officer's safety:** The officer's safety can adequately be protected by several techniques that the Court had previously approved. For instance, the Court had previously held that the officer may order the driver to step out of the car (see *Pennsylvania v. Mimms*, *infra*, p. 151 and *Maryland v. Wilson*, *infra*, p. 152). Also, if there is reason to believe that an occupant of the vehicle may be armed and dangerous, the officer can do a "pat-down" not just of the occupant's person but of the vehicle compartment. (See *Michigan v. Long*, *infra*, p. 164). Therefore, in the ordinary traffic-ticket scenario, protecting the safety of officers does not require an automatic right to search the vehicle.

   b. **Destruction of evidence:** The danger that ***evidence*** will be ***hidden or destroyed*** is also less pressing in the traffic-ticket situation than in the arrest situation, the Court said. In the typical traffic stop, all the needed evidence has already been gathered by the time the car has been stopped.

VII. CONSENT SEARCHES GENERALLY

A. Consent generally: Even if none of the above exceptions to the requirement of a search warrant is present, the police may nonetheless make a constitutional warrantless search if they receive the ***consent*** of the individual whose premises, effects, or person are to be searched. Because of the ease of gaining consent to search in many (perhaps most) cases, a substantial portion of all searches are conducted by consent.

B. *Schneckloth:* Although before 1973 many courts had thought that "consent" to a search was only valid if the consenter ***knew that he had a right to refuse to consent***, the Court ***rejected*** this view in ***Schneckloth v. Bustamonte***, 412 U.S. 218 (1973).

1. **Facts:** In *Schneckloth*, a police officer stopped a car with six men in it, after observing that a headlight was burned out. He asked one of the men, Alcala, for permission to search the car, and Alcala replied "Sure, go ahead." Stolen checks were found in the trunk, and one of the other passengers, Bustamonte (not Alcala) was tried for the theft.

2. **Issue in case:** Although *Schneckloth* involved the validity of a "third-party consent" (i.e., a consent by one other than the person incriminated by the evidence discovered in the search), the third-party aspects of the search were not of particular interest to the Court. (The special problems of a third-party consent have been treated by the Court in a number of other cases, and will be discussed below.) Instead, the Court discussed the factors which may be considered in determining whether any consent to search (whether given by the eventual defendant or by a third person) is valid. In particular, the Court discussed whether a consent could be valid if the consenter was not aware that he had a legal right to refuse consent.

3. **Holding:** The Court concluded that the consenter's ignorance of his right to refuse consent was ***only one factor to be considered*** in ascertaining the validity of the consent. "While knowledge of the right to refuse consent is one factor to be taken into account, the government need not establish such knowledge as the *sine qua non* of an effective consent."

   a. **Totality of the circumstances:** The Court thus applied a ***"totality of the circumstances"*** test to the determination of a consent's validity. The Court explicitly referred to the pre-*Miranda* "totality of the circumstances" test for the voluntariness of confessions, and held that it applied to consents to searches. The Court stressed that the issue was whether the consent was "voluntary"; the Court appears to have felt that a consent is "voluntary" as long as it is not "the product of duress or coercion, express or implied."

   b. **Warning of rights rejected:** The Court rejected the suggestion that the police should, when they solicit consent to search, ***tell the consenter that he has a right to refuse***. The opinion contended that "it would be thoroughly impractical to impose on the normal consent search the detailed requirements of an effective warning," because of the informality of such searches, and the suddenness with which the need to conduct them may arise.

      i. ***Miranda* distinguished:** In rejecting the view that a warning of the right to refuse consent should be required, the Court took great pains to distinguish *Miranda*, and its requirement that a suspect be warned of his right to remain silent. The Court stressed two major differences between consent searches and confessions: (1) consent searches are typically "non-custodial," and the atmosphere of coercion characteristic of custodial interrogation is thus lacking; and (2) the

Fourth Amendment right to be free of unreasonable searches is not related to the guarantee of a fair trial, whereas the right to remain silent and have a lawyer at interrogation is closely tied to the fair trial right; this being the case, the concept of "knowing waiver" applies to confessions but not to searches.

4. **Dissent:** Justices Brennan, Douglas, and Marshall, dissenting in three separate opinions, all stressed that it is nonsense to say that someone had "voluntarily" consented to a search if he did not know he had the right to refuse. As Brennan put it, "It wholly escapes me how our citizens can meaningfully be said to have waived something as precious as a constitutional guarantee without ever being aware of its existence."

5. **Subjective vs. objective test:** *Schneckloth* does not explicitly state whether the test for voluntary consent is an ***"objective"*** or ***"subjective"*** one. For instance, suppose that unbeknownst to the police, the suspect is an unusually timid person, and believes that he is being coerced into submitting to a search or seizure; if the policeman reasonably believes that the suspect is giving his voluntary consent, is that consent nonetheless invalid because of the suspect's state of mind?

   a. **Subjective test applied:** *U.S. v. Mendenhall*, 446 U.S. 544 (1980) (discussed more extensively *infra*, p. 157), indicates that the suspect's ***subjective mental state*** is what is relevant. The Court held that on the issue of valid consent, the question was whether the consent was "***in fact*** voluntary." (But a majority of the Court held that the prosecution had met its burden of proving that D's consent to a search had in fact been voluntary; the Court relied heavily on the fact that the officers twice told D that she was free to withhold her consent. This was true even though D did not make any verbal expression of consent, but merely complied with the request that she undress to facilitate the search.)

C. **Importance of probable cause:** In determining whether the consent was voluntary, it might be sensible to take into account whether probable cause to search was present. For if probable cause was present, and a warrant could have been obtained, the consent merely speeds up a search which could otherwise take place anyway. If probable cause to search is lacking (as it appears to have been in *Schneckloth*), however, the consent enables the police to perform a search that they could otherwise not have performed. Therefore, a good argument can be made that the validity of a consent should be tested by a more strict standard where probable cause is not present.

D. **Claims of authority to search:** Suppose the consent to search is procured after the officer states that he has, or will get, ***authority to search***, regardless of whether the consent is given. The courts have often distinguished between ***false claims of present authority*** and ***threats of future action.***

1. **False claim of present authority:** The Supreme Court has explicitly held that where an officer ***falsely asserts that he has a search warrant***, and then procures "consent," the consent is invalid. This was the holding of ***Bumper v. North Carolina***, 391 U.S. 543 (1968).

   a. ***Bumper:*** In *Bumper*, four white North Carolina police came to the house of an African American widow, as part of the investigation of a rape to which her grandson had been linked. The officers asserted that they had a search warrant, and the widow responded that in that case, they could search. The officers did not tell her anything about the crime they were investigating, or that her grandson had anything to do with it. At the subsequent suppression hearing the prosecution did not rely on any warrant (although the State later contended that a valid warrant had been issued). When the case reached the Supreme Court, only the validity of the consent, and not the existence or validity of any warrant, was considered.

b. **Holding:** The Supreme Court held that the consent was ***not voluntary***, because it had been procured through a ***claim of lawful authority***. The Court noted that the prosecution bears the burden of showing the voluntariness of consent to search, and that "this burden cannot be discharged by showing no more than acquiescence to a claim of lawful authority. A search conducted in reliance upon a warrant cannot later be justified on the basis of consent if it turns out that the warrant was invalid. The result can be no different when it turns out that the State does not even attempt to rely on the validity of the warrant, or fails to show that there was, in fact, any warrant at all."

i. **Rationale:** The Court's holding was based on the ***coercion*** inherent in an announcement by a police officer that he has the authority to search: "When a law enforcement officer claims that he has the authority to search a home under a warrant, he announces in effect that the occupant has no right to resist the search. The situation is instinct with coercion — albeit colorably lawful coercion. Where there is coercion there cannot be consent."

2. **Consent induced by reference to invalid warrant:** If the police state that they have a search warrant, and the warrant is in fact ***invalid*** (either because of insufficient definiteness, lack of probable cause, etc.), the consent of the person whose premises are to be searched is similarly ***invalid***. This is particularly true where the person himself is placed under arrest. Such consent is given in the face of "colorably lawful coercion," and cannot be regarded as voluntary. *Lo-Ji Sales, Inc. v. New York*, 442 U.S. 319 (1979).

3. **Threats to obtain warrant:** Where the police do not state that they presently have a warrant, but ***threaten to obtain one*** if consent is not given, the result seems to depend mostly on whether the police ***in fact have grounds*** to get a warrant.

a. **Police have grounds:** Where the police have grounds, their threat to obtain a warrant does not vitiate the consent of the person whose premises are to be searched.

b. **No grounds:** But where the police do not have grounds, then their threat to get a warrant — which amounts to deception on the issue of whether they have grounds — usually ***will*** nullify the consent.

i. **Illegal stop:** Similarly, if it is only because of ***illegal police conduct*** that the police have the opportunity to ask the defendant to choose between consenting or awaiting a search warrant, the police illegality is likely to cause the Court to hold that the consent was not "voluntary."

E. **Other kinds of deception:** In addition to the deception involved in falsely stating that they have a warrant, the police will sometimes use other kinds of deception to procure consent to a search. Such deceptions include misrepresentation of the officer's identity, and misrepresentation of his intentions.

1. **Misrepresentation of identity:** Where the police make use of an ***undercover agent*** (i.e., an agent who does not disclose to the suspect that he is working for the police), who by concealing his identity gains entry into the suspect's premises, the agent may make any observations permitted by the suspect. See *Lewis v. U.S.*, 385 U.S. 206 (1966), discussed extensively *infra*, p. 227.

2. **Misrepresentations of intentions:** Where the police do not conceal their identity from the suspect, but misrepresent their ***intentions***, the Supreme Court has not announced a rule. Lower courts have disagreed about whether and when such a misrepresentation prevents the defendant's consent to search from being valid.

F. **Physical scope of search:** A question related to the deception issues discussed above is raised where the police perform a ***broader*** search than that consented to by the suspect. The courts have usually been reluctant to find the broader-than-consented-to search valid.

1. **Plain view:** But if the police are proceeding to search only the area consented to, and they see in ***plain view*** an object outside of the consent area, they may seize it pursuant to the plain view doctrine, as long as no subterfuge is involved. *Bretti v. Wainwright*, 439 F.2d 1042 (5th Cir. 1971).

2. **Closed containers in autos:** Sometimes it will not be clear ***what*** the scope of the consent is. For instance, suppose a driver of an automobile consents to a police search of "your vehicle." Does this consent allow the police to examine ***closed containers*** inside the car? The Supreme Court has answered "yes" to this question — a consent to search a car will be deemed to cover any closed containers in the car, unless there is clear evidence that the consenter intended otherwise. *Florida v. Jimeno*, 500 U.S. 248 (1991). Thus in *Jimeno*, D's general consent to allow the police to search his car entitled the police to open a folded paper bag found on the floor, which turned out to contain cocaine. The prosecution was thus allowed to introduce the cocaine against D despite the officer's initial lack of probable cause.

   a. **Container owned by passenger:** However, the analysis in the prior paragraph applies only to containers ***owned by the person who consents***. Where a closed container is owned by a ***passenger***, the ***driver's*** consent to a search of the car and its contents will normally ***not*** cover the container. See *People v. James*, 645 N.E.2d 195 (Ill. 1994). (Third-party consent is discussed *infra*, p. 143.)

VIII. CONSENT BY THIRD PERSONS

A. **Importance of problem:** The previous section discussed the factors which are to be considered in determining whether a person's consent to search is sufficiently "voluntary" that the need for a search warrant is obviated. Where the search is made of the property of the consenter, and the incriminating evidence which is uncovered is used against the consenter, the "voluntariness" question is the only one which arises. But where the police seek ***the consent of one person for a search of the property of another***, or for the search of an area as to which another has an expectation of privacy, a new element is introduced. The material that follows discusses some of the more common difficulties relating to such ***"third-party" consent***.

B. Joint authority: Cases in which the defendant and a ***third person*** have ***joint authority*** over the premises pose special problems when the third person consents — is that consent binding on the defendant? We will consider two separate scenarios: (1) where D is ***absent*** at the time the third person consents; and (2) where D is ***present***, and ***refuses to consent***, while the third person consents.

By "joint authority," we mean a situation in which D and the third party have some sort of ***joint access to***, and some sort of ***joint expectation of privacy in***, the place to be searched. Common examples of joint authority are:

roommates, as to the common areas of the dwelling or any shared bedroom;

husband and wife, as to the marital dwelling;

a homeowner (or tenant) and his ***social guest***, where the homeowner gives the consent and the evidence is then used against the guest.

All of these scenarios are evaluated according to the same basic set of rules, as we discuss below.

1. D is absent when third person consents: First, let's consider this situation in which D is ***absent***, and the police ask for and receive consent of the third person to search the jointly-controlled (or what they believe to be the jointly-controlled) premises. Here, the basic rule is that the third party's consent is ***effective***, if that third party either (a) ***actually*** has or (b) is ***reasonably believed*** by the police to have, joint authority over the premises.

Example: Ms. Graff lives in a house together with D. The police show up at this house one day, arrest D in the front yard, and put him in a squad car nearby. They then knock on the front door, and Graff answers. They explain that they are looking for money and a gun from a recent bank robbery, and ask if they can search the house. Graff explains that she and D occupy a particular bedroom (the "east bedroom") as an unmarried couple, and gives consent to the police to search that bedroom. In the bedroom, the police find money and the gun from the robbery. At trial, D moves to suppress this evidence on the grounds that he had a reasonable expectation of privacy in the bedroom, and that Graff had no authority to consent to a search of that bedroom even though she too had legal access to it.

Held, for the prosecution. Joint authority exists when there is "mutual use of the property by persons generally having joint access or control for most purposes." By this standard, Graff had joint authority over the east bedroom. In such a scenario, "it is reasonable to recognize that *any of the co-inhabitants* has the right to permit the inspection in his own right and that the others have *assumed the risk* that one of their number might permit the common area to be searched." Therefore, Graff's consent was binding on D. *U.S. v. Matlock*, 415 U.S. 164 (1974).

a. Reasonable mistake: The third-party consent will be binding on the absent defendant even if the police were ***mistaken*** about whether the consenter in fact had joint authority over the premises, as long as the ***mistake was a reasonable one.*** For instance, if the consenting third person falsely tells the police that she lives in the premises to be searched, and the police reasonably believe her, the lie will not invalidate the consent.

Example: W tells the police that she has been beaten by D. She also tells the police that D is in "our" apartment on South California Street, and asks the police to go there with her to arrest D for the beating. The police do not get a warrant to arrest D or to search the apartment. Instead, they go with W to the apartment, get her consent to search it, have her let them in with her key, and find cocaine there. (D is asleep in the apartment at the time.) D challenges the validity of W's consent as against him.

Held, for the prosecution. It's true that W did not in fact have joint authority over the apartment; she was an "infrequent visitor" there rather than a "usual resident," so she did not have true authority to allow the police to make a warrantless entry or search. But this does not matter: so long as the police were ***reasonably mistaken*** in their belief that W had authority to consent, this is the same as if she had actually had such authority. That's because the Fourth Amendment bans only "unreasonable" searches and seizures, and where the police make a factual determination about a search, their reasonable mistake on the issue of authority to consent transforms the search into a "reasonable" one. *Illinois v. Rodriguez*, 497 U.S. 177 (1990).

2. **D is present and objecting when third person consents:** Now, let's consider the second scenario listed above: D is ***present*** when the third party consents to a search of the premises over which the two have joint authority, and D makes it clear that he, D, is ***not consenting.*** Here, as the result of a 2006 decision, the third party's consent will ***not be binding on D***, at least where it appears to the police that the third person and D have equal claim to the premises. So the fact that D is present and objecting at the time of the third-party consent (the situation being discussed here) — rather than absent and without the chance to object (the situation in *Matlock* and *Rodriguez* above) — makes all the difference.

Example: W, who is estranged from her husband D, returns to the former marital residence. There, she calls the police. When they arrive without a warrant, she tells them about a custody dispute she and D are having, and says that D is a cocaine user. Shortly thereafter, D arrives back at the house, and denies being a drug user. W tells the police that there are items showing D's drug use in the house. The police ask D for his consent to a search of the house, and he refuses. The police then ask W for consent and she readily gives it. In what W identifies as D's bedroom, the police find cocaine. D asserts that W's consent to the search was ineffective as to their shared bedroom, because it was given in the face of D's unequivocal refusal to consent.

Held (by a 5-3 vote), for D. Where as here the two parties are not living within some "recognized hierarchy" (like a household with parent and child, or military barracks housing people of different ranks), the co-tenant who wishes to open the door to a third person "has no recognized authority in law or social practice to prevail over a present and objecting co-tenant." Therefore, that co-tenant's "disputed invitation, without more, gives a police officer no better claim to reasonableness in entering than the officer would have been in the absence of any consent at all." Consequently, even though W may have had joint authority with D over the house, the police's warrantless entry in the face of D's express refusal to consent made this an unreasonable search. (Three members of the Court dissent, and a fourth Justice does not participate.) *Georgia v. Randolph*, 547 U.S. 103 (2006).

C. Other theories: Apart from the joint-authority scenario discussed above, there are at least three other theories under which consent by a third party will justify a search that would otherwise violate the rights of the defendant:

1. **Agency:** First, it may be the case, as a factual matter, that D has ***authorized*** the third person (let's call him X) to consent, even though X does not have direct ownership or control of the premises. If so, then by the doctrine of ***agency*** X's consent will bind D. For instance, suppose that D, a wealthy tycoon, gives X, his trusted valet, complete run of the premises, and also entrusts to X all decisions about who may be admitted to the premises. If in D's absence X gives the police consent to search, the court is quite likely to hold that by the law of agency X was authorized to consent on D's behalf, even if X had no title to or true "joint control" over the premises.

2. **Property of consenter:** Second, sometimes the police will want to search the ***property belonging solely to the consenter*** for evidence to be used against D. Here, if the property owner consents, this will generally validate the search even if the police know that D is not consenting.

   Example: Suppose that the police are investigating a murder, which they know to have been done by a Remington .33 caliber rifle. They learn from the records of a local gun store that such a rifle was purchased by and registered to X. They also independently suspect D, X's grandson, of the murder. If the police procure X's consent to their seizing and testing the rifle, D will not have a Fourth Amendment claim even though it is absolutely clear that he never consented to the seizure.

3. **Assumption of risk:** Finally, the relationship between the third party and D may be such that D will be found to have simply ***"assumed the risk"*** that the third person might see or scrutinize D's property. In this instance, a court is likely to find that this fact means that D simply had no justifiable expectation of privacy in the object. Here, too, D would probably have no Fourth Amendment claim if the police searched or seized the object.

   Example: D shares a duffle bag with his cousin Rawls. Rawls consents to a search of the bag. The prosecution claims that this consent is effective as against D. *Held*, for the prosecution: D "must be taken to have assumed the risk that Rawls would allow someone else to look inside." *Frazier v. Cupp*, 394 U.S. 731 (1969).

D. Husbands, wives, and lovers: Where one ***spouse*** (or spouse-equivalent, in the case of an umarried couple living together) consents to a search of their joint living area, that search will generally be upheld as against the non-consenting spouse. *Matlock*, *supra*, p. 144, is one example.

1. **Exceptions:** Several of the circumstances which might result in the consent's ***not*** being valid are as follows:

   a. **Personal effects:** If one spouse permits the search of the other's ***personal effects*** stored in a separate drawer, the third-party consent may be invalid.

   b. **No access to area:** Similarly, if one spouse consents to the search of a ***special area*** to which the consenting spouse would not normally have access (and which is used solely by the non-consenting spouse), the consent may be found to be without authority and thus invalid. For instance, if W consents to let the police break open and search

H's locked basement workshop, to which W has no key, this consent might be held invalid on the grounds that the basement was not "common" space as to which W had joint authority.

c. **Other spouse refuses to consent:** If the police know that the other spouse is objecting, the consent won't be effective. See *Georgia v. Randolph*, *supra*, p. 145.

E. **Parents and children:** Most courts have held that when a child is living at home with his parents, the parents may consent to a search of the ***child's room***.

1. **Consent by child:** The child, on the other hand, may ***not*** normally consent to a full-scale search of the parents' house.

F. **Landlords, tenants, and co-tenants:** A number of cases have discussed the right of a person to consent to the search of his tenant's, co-tenant's or landlord's room or premises.

1. **Consent by landlord:** A ***landlord*** may not consent to a search of his tenant's rooms, even though he has the right to enter them for cleaning. *Chapman v. U.S.*, 365 U.S. 610 (1961). But he probably may consent to a search of the areas of "common usage," such as hallways and common dining areas.

a. **Hotel guest:** *Stoner v. California*, 376 U.S. 483 (1964) indicates that a hotel guest is to be treated like any other tenant, and that the management may not consent to a search of the guest's room. But after the guest has ***checked out*** permanently, a hotel employee may consent to a search for items left behind.

2. **Consent by co-tenant:** If two or more people have equal right to or access to premises, one may generally consent to a search of the common premises when the other is absent. See *U.S. v. Matlock*, *supra*, p. 144.

a. **Exceptions:** But the particular circumstances may prevent the co-tenant's consent from being binding. Thus if one co-tenant is present, and ***objects***, the other's consent may not be sufficient to allow introduction of evidence seized against the objector. See *Georgia v. Randolph*, *supra*, p. 145.

i. **Defendant stands by without objection:** Conversely, if both co-tenants are present, and one of them (the defendant) ***stands by without objection*** while the other one consents, the defendant will generally be held to have implicitly consented as well.

b. **Non-paying guest:** Where a ***non-paying guest*** is present, the owner's consent will almost likely be binding on the guest, even if the guest refuses to consent. The guest may not usually consent to the search of the owner's property, except perhaps of the portion of the property over which the guest has a right of access. The same rules apply for a casual visitor.

Note: The situation in which a guest refuses consent, but the owner consents, illustrates that one person's consent may sometimes override another's refusal to consent, by virtue of the former's *superior property interest* in the premises. The evidence seized may then be used against the guest.

G. Employers and employees: Both an employer's consent to a search of his employee's work area, and employee's consent to a search of his employer's premises have been upheld in some circumstances.

1. **Employer's consent:** An ***employer*** has usually been allowed to consent to a search of his employee's work area if the search is for items ***related to the job***. But where the search is of areas where the employee is permitted to store non-work-related items, the employer's consent will probably not be binding.

2. **Employee's consent:** An ***employee*** may consent to a search of his employer's premises if he is in a position of substantial authority, (e.g., in an executive position). But where an employee is only temporarily in charge (e.g., a clerk or night watchman), he will not be able to consent for his employer.

H. Ignorance of consenter: It is irrelevant that the consenter has no idea of the purpose of the search (assuming no actual deception by the police), or mistakenly believes that the person for whom he is consenting is innocent and has nothing to hide.

> **Example:** The police, after arresting D, question his wife W about any guns that are in the house. Believing that her husband is innocent, and trying to clear him, W shows the police four guns. She remembers having seen D previously show some of his guns to the police, but did not notice that he only showed three of them; the fourth turns out to be the incriminating one. *Held*, the consent by W was not vitiated by her ignorance and mistake. Indeed, W's consent is of even greater validity than had W believed D to be guilty and shown the weapons only because she thought she had no choice legally. *Coolidge v. N.H.*, 403 U.S. 443 (1971).

IX. "STOP-AND-FRISK" AND OTHER BRIEF DETENTION

A. Nature of "stop-and-frisk": In nearly all of the kinds of arrest and search situations discussed in the present and previous chapters, the police are responding to past criminal conduct. Furthermore, most of the time they have probable cause either for an arrest or a search. (E.g., in the search-incident-to-arrest situation, the police must have probable cause for arrest, even though they do not necessarily have to have probable cause to believe that weapons or other evidence will be found in the search.) But suppose that the police are not investigating any particular crime, and are simply performing ***routine patrolling functions***, when they have a street encounter which although it makes them somewhat suspicious, does not give them probable cause to believe a crime has been committed. May they briefly detain the suspicious person without probable cause for arrest and without a warrant? If so, may they engage in a protective search for weapons? Such a detainment-and-weapons-search, popularly known as a ***"stop-and-frisk,"*** is permissible in certain circumstances as a result of the Supreme Court's decision in ***Terry v. Ohio***, 392 U.S. 1 (1968), and in a later case based on *Terry*, ***Adams v. Williams***, 407 U.S. 143 (1972).

B. *Terry:* In ***Terry***, the Court held that a stop-and-frisk could be constitutionally permissible ***despite the lack of probable cause for either full arrest or full search***, and despite the fact that a brief detainment not amounting to a full arrest was a ***"seizure"*** requiring some degree of Fourth Amendment protection.

1. **Facts:** In *Terry*, an experienced policeman, McFadden, observed the defendant and two others in what appeared to be the process of "casing" a store. He approached the suspects, identified himself as a policeman, and asked them to identify themselves. When they mumbled something that he could not hear, he grabbed the defendant, patted down the outside of his clothing, felt a pistol in the defendant's pocket, and removed it. The defendant was convicted on charges of carrying a concealed weapon.

2. **Court's holding:** The defendant in *Terry* contended that McFadden had lacked probable cause for arrest, that the "stop" had been an arrest, that the "frisk" was a Fourth Amendment search, and that the search was neither supported by probable cause nor incident to a valid arrest. The Supreme Court rejected this syllogism, and held the gun admissible.

   a. **Fourth Amendment involved:** The Court agreed that the detainment of the defendant on the street was a ***sufficient intrusion on his freedom that it was a "seizure" within the meaning of the Fourth Amendment***. The Court rejected "the notion that the Fourth Amendment does not come into play at all as a limitation upon police conduct if the officers stop short of something called a 'technical arrest' or a 'full-blown search'."

      i. **Frisk as search:** The Court also agreed that the ***"pat-down"*** of the defendant was a ***"search"*** within the meaning of the Fourth Amendment, even though it was not a full-scale body search.

   b. **Not unreasonable:** But the Court ***rejected the argument that because a Fourth Amendment seizure and search took place, "probable cause" was required***. This rejection of the probable cause requirement for such a "stop-and-frisk" constitutes the chief innovation of *Terry* and the cases based on it.

      i. **Distinguished from warrant situation:** The Court conceded that if the seizure and search had been conduct for which a warrant was required, probable cause would have been necessary, under the Fourth Amendment. But because the exigent circumstances (the need to act quickly) justified dispensing with the warrant requirement, the Court concluded that probable cause was not constitutionally required. Instead, the only constitutional test was whether the stop and/or frisk was ***"unreasonable."***

      ii. **Conduct reasonable:** The Court quickly concluded that the questioning of the defendant by McFadden was "reasonable": "It would have been poor police work indeed for an officer of 30 years' experience in the detection of thievery from stores in this same neighborhood to have failed to investigate this [suspicious] behavior further."

      iii. **Reasonableness of frisk:** The Court devoted much more discussion to the reasonableness of the ***frisk***, but concluded that it too had been reasonable, even though it was conducted before there was probable cause for either an arrest or a search. The Court stressed two facts about the particular frisk in *Terry*: (1) it was the product of McFadden's justifiable fears that the defendant might be armed and McFadden's safety threatened; and (2) it was no broader than necessary to find any weapons; no pockets not containing hard objects were examined, and nothing more than a pat-down was given to one of the other suspects who was not carrying anything that felt like a weapon.

c. **Summary:** The Court summarized its conclusions with the following language: "We merely hold today that where a police officer observes unusual conduct which leads him reasonably to conclude in light of his experience that criminal activity may be afoot and that the persons with whom he is dealing may be armed and presently dangerous, where in the course of investigating this behavior he identifies himself as a policeman and makes reasonable inquiries, and where nothing in the initial stages of the encounter serves to dispel his reasonable fear for his own or others' safety, he is entitled for the protection of himself and others in the area to conduct a carefully limited search of the outer clothing of such persons in an attempt to discover weapons which might be used to assault him. Such a search is a reasonable search under the Fourth Amendment, and any weapons seized may properly be introduced in evidence against the person from whom they were taken."

Note: The Court in Terry formulated a "balancing test" for determining the reasonableness of an intrusion into an interest protected by the Fourth Amendment. Because the invasion of privacy involved in a brief street-detention and pat-down is less than that which occurs in a full-custody arrest and body search, a lesser showing of social need to make the intrusion will suffice to make the intrusion "reasonable." The need to intrude (in Terry, the need to prevent and detect crime, and to protect the officer from physical harm) is thus to be "weighed" against the severity of the intrusion.

3. **Harlan's concurrence:** Justice Harlan, in a concurrence, emphasized that the effect of the *Terry* decision was to allow a ***forcible stop*** without probable cause, where some lesser but substantial degree of suspicion was present. Harlan noted that the issue with respect to the "stop" was not whether McFadden had had the right to ask questions of the defendant; any person, whether or not a policeman, may do that, since the person being questioned can simply walk away. Instead, the issue was whether McFadden had had the right to ***forcibly detain*** the defendant for purposes of questioning him; Harlan agreed with the Court that this detainment, although a Fourth Amendment seizure, was not unreasonable, since a quantum of suspicion was present that was substantial even though not probable cause for arrest.

4. **Douglas dissent:** Justice Douglas dissented (he was the sole dissenter) on the grounds that the effect of the majority's decision was to give the police more power when they act without a warrant than with one. As Israel and LaFave note (Nutshell, p. 161), this contention could have been answered by noting that probable cause, like reasonableness, can be determined by a balancing test based on the severity of the intrusion. (Thus a warrant for a routine inspection can be issued on a lesser showing of probable cause than a warrant to conduct a full-scale search of personal papers for incriminating evidence — see *Camara*, *infra*, p. 173.) Had a warrant been applied for in *Terry*, the Court could simply have held that there was probable cause for a brief detention and frisk, but not for a full-scale custodial arrest and full body search.

C. ***Adams: Adams v. Williams***, 407 U.S. 143 (1972), significantly broadened the *Terry* "stop-and-frisk" exception to the probable cause requirement by extending it to include suspicions not based on the officer's own observations, and by allowing the stop of a ***vehicle***. The opinion provoked a strong dissent by three members of the Court and much criticism by commentators.

1. **Facts of *Adams:*** In *Adams*, a policeman, Connolly, was in his patrol car when he was approached (or so he testified at trial) by an ***"informant"*** known to him, who stated that a person in a parked car nearby possessed a gun and narcotics. Connolly went over to the car, tapped on the window, and when the window was rolled down leaned in and removed a loaded pistol from the defendant's waistband. The pistol had not been visible to Connolly from outside, but when the window was rolled down it turned out to be in exactly the place that Connolly testified his informant said it would be. The defendant was arrested for illegal possession of a pistol, and in a subsequent search incident to arrest, narcotics were discovered on his person and in his car.

2. **Holding:** The Court (6-3) upheld, in an opinion by Justice Rehnquist, the validity of the seizure of the gun and the narcotics. The Court held that the informant's tip, although it did not establish probable cause for search or arrest under the *Aguilar-Spinelli* test (now abandoned; see *Illinois v. Gates*, *supra*, p. 57), had sufficient "indicia of reliability" to allow a forcible stop of the defendant's car. The chief "indicium" was the fact that the informant, under Connecticut law, could have been immediately arrested for making a false complaint.

   a. **Officer's personal observation not necessary:** The Court rejected the argument that the *Terry* rationale only applied to suspicious behavior witnessed by the police officer himself.

   b. **Search justified:** Given that the stop was reasonable, the seizure of the revolver was also justified for Connolly's safety, the Court held. The discovery of the weapon also constituted grounds for arrest for illegal possession, and the arrest in turn justified the search incident to arrest of the car.

3. **Dissent:** Justices Douglas (joined by Marshall) and Brennan dissented strongly. Brennan noted that it was not at all unlikely that the entire story of the "informant" was concocted after the fact, to justify the initial stop. There was absolutely nothing in Connolly's account of the tip to suggest that he had not made the whole thing up after the fact. Brennan also stated that he would not extend the *Terry* rationale to "mere possessory offenses," such as narcotics and weapons offenses.

   a. **Search:** Marshall and Douglas agreed with Brennan that the initial stop was unreasonable because not justified by sufficiently reliable information, and further contended that even after the discovery of the revolver, there was not probable cause for a weapons-possession arrest. They based this contention on the fact that under Connecticut law, possession even of a loaded weapon was illegal only if not permitted by a permit; Connolly testified that he had not asked whether the defendant had a permit before arresting him. Because the arrest was invalid, the dissenters argued, the subsequent search which uncovered narcotics did not fall within the search-incident-to-arrest exception and was invalid.

4. **Suspect required to leave car:** The "stop" of a driver that was approved in *Adams* was extended to allow the police to require that the stopped motorist ***leave his car***, in ***Pennsyl-***

vania v. Mimms, 434 U.S. 106 (1977). The Court held that requiring such an exit is a legitimate safety measure, in view of the large number of shootings of policemen committed by seated drivers. The Court relied on the fact that, given that the stop itself was allowable under *Adams*, requiring the driver to get out was an "additional intrusion [that] can only be described as *de minimis*."

a. **Pat-down allowable:** The Court in *Mimms* also held that once the driver got out of the car and was seen to have a bulge in his pocket which looked like a gun, the officer was justified in conducting a ***pat-down*** of the bulge.

b. **Passengers may be required to exit:** A post-*Mimms* case says that in any situation where a car is properly stopped and the driver required to step out, the ***passengers may also be required to step out.*** And that's true even if the passengers have done nothing whatsoever to give the police grounds to suspect wrongdoing by the passenger. See *Maryland v. Wilson*, 519 U.S. 408 (1997). The Court reasoned that the officer would be as much at risk from the passengers as from the driver, and that the additional intrusion on the passenger from being required to step out of the car was "minimal."

   i. **Pat-down of non-suspect passenger:** Similarly, if the car has been properly stopped and the occupants temporarily detained, the police are entitled to do a pat-down of any passenger — ***even if the police have no reason to suspect the passenger of wrongdoing*** — as long as the police have a reasonable suspicion that the passenger may be ***armed and dangerous***. *Arizona v. Johnson*, 129 S.Ct. 781 (2009).

   Example: Two officers pull over a car after a license plate check reveals that the car's registration has been suspended for an insurance violation. One of the three occupants is D, a passenger sitting in the rear seat. One officer, Treviso, notices that D is wearing clothing consistent with membership in the Crips gang. Treviso also learns early in the encounter that D has previously served time in prison for burglary. Treviso asks D to exit the car, suspects that D may have a weapon on him, and pats him down to ensure officer safety. While doing so, Treviso feels the butt of a gun near D's waist, which she seizes. D is charged with possession of a weapon by a convicted felon. D moves to suppress the gun.

   Held, for the prosecution: even though the officers had no grounds to suspect D of any wrongdoing when they made the (proper) stop of the car in which D was a passenger, and even though at the moment of the pat down Officer Treviso still had no reason to suspect D of wrongdoing, this did not make the pat down improper, or the gun inadmissible. As long as the police have made a proper traffic stop, they may perform a pat down of any passenger they reasonably suspect may be armed and dangerous, even if they have no grounds for suspecting the passenger of wrongdoing. (The Supreme Court assumes, without deciding, that Treviso reasonably believed D might be armed and dangerous.) *Arizona v. Johnson*, *supra*.

D. **Degree of probability required for stop:** *Terry* and *Adams* indicate that a stop may be constitutionally justified even if there is not classical "probable cause" to believe that the person to be stopped has committed a crime. But it is not clear ***what degree of probability*** of criminal conduct must exist before a stop is justified under *Terry* and *Adams*. Several Supreme Court cases shed some light on the question:

1. **Vague suspicion not sufficient:** In ***Brown v. Texas***, 443 U.S. 47 (1979), the Court held that a person may be stopped only if the officers have a "***reasonable suspicion***, based on ***objective facts***, that the individual is involved in criminal activity." In *Brown*, D was stopped on the grounds that : (1) he was walking in an area which had a "high incidence of drug traffic"; (2) he "looked suspicious"; and (3) he had not been seen in that area previously by the officers. The Court held that these considerations did ***not*** meet the "reasonable suspicion based on objective facts" test, and that the stop was therefore an unreasonable seizure in violation of the Fourth Amendment. This is so, the Court said, even though the officers' motive may have been only to ascertain D's identity.

2. **Modest degree of suspicion:** But a fairly ***modest amount of suspicion*** will be enough for a *Terry*-like stop. See, e.g., *U.S. v. Sokolow*, 490 U.S. 1 (1989). For instance, if a person engages in a number of acts which, viewed together, make it plausible to believe that he may be a ***drug courier***, this may be enough for a stop even though each act, taken alone, is entirely consistent with innocence. For example, in *Sokolow*, *supra*, agents of the Drug Enforcement Administration (DEA) stopped D as he left Honolulu International Airport after a flight from Miami. Seven members of the Court believed that the agents had enough reasons to suspect D of drug smuggling that he could be subjected to a *Terry* investigative stop.

   a. **Grounds for suspicion:** At the time they stopped D, the agents had the following reasons for suspecting D of smuggling:

      i. He had paid $2,100 for two airplane tickets from a roll of $20 bills that appeared to contain at least $4,000;

      ii. He had traveled under a name that did not match the name under which his telephone number was listed;

      iii. He had just completed a round trip between Honolulu and Miami, a "source city for illicit drugs";

      iv. He had stayed in Miami for only 48 hours, even though a round trip from Honolulu to Miami takes 20 hours of flying;

      v. He had appeared nervous during the trip (as reported to the agents by other narcotics agents who had surveilled his behavior during a stopover); and

      vi. He had not checked any of his luggage.

   b. **Sufficient for stop:** The seven Justices in the majority felt that these factors, taken together, gave the agents "reasonable suspicion that [D] was engaged in wrongdoing. . . . " The agents had to show "articulable facts" and "some minimal level of objective justification" for the stop, not just an "inchoate and unparticularized suspicion or 'hunch.'" But the majority believed that the facts known to the agents here satisfied this standard. And this was true even though each of these facts, taken by itself, was ***completely consistent with non-criminal behavior***. The point was that these facts when ***taken together*** created a possible scenario of drug smuggling.

c. **Drug courier profile:** The agents in *Sokolow* apparently did not make a carefully reasoned judgment, from scratch, that D's activities were suspicious. Instead, they relied on a ***"drug courier profile,"*** a set of factors established over many years by the DEA to predict which travelers might be smugglers. But the fact that D's actions matched a number of those specified in the profile was apparently ***not*** by itself constitutionally significant — the Court still conducted its own review as to whether a reasonable observer would suspect narcotics trafficking on these facts.

3. **Flight as a cause for suspicion:** The fact that an individual has ***attempted to flee*** when seen by the police will normally raise the police's suspicion, and may even without more justify the police in making a *Terry*-style stop. In any event, the combination of flight and presence in what the officer knows is a high-crime area will generally be enough for a stop. See *Illinois v. Wardlow*, 528 U.S. 119 (2000).

   a. **Facts:** In *Wardlow*, D fled as soon as he saw police officers patrolling the area where he was walking, an area known for heavy narcotics trafficking. The officers were part of a four-car caravan; as soon as D fled, two of the officers chased D down, conducted a protective pat-down weapons search, and thereby found an illegal gun.

   b. **Holding:** The Court concluded that the initial events gave the officers enough grounds for suspicion that they were entitled to make a *Terry* stop of D. The Court's opinion, by Chief Justice Rehnquist, said that the combination of D's presence in an area of heavy narcotics trafficking, plus his "unprovoked flight upon noticing the police," were enough to trigger a *Terry* stop. "Headlong flight — wherever it occurs — is the consummate act of evasion: it is not necessarily indicative of wrongdoing, but it is certainly suggestive of such."

      i. **Flight by itself probably not enough:** The majority did not seem to be saying that unprovoked flight, *by itself*, would necessarily be enough to justify a Terry stop. (A number of states as *amici* had urged the Court to say that it was.) Instead, it was the combination of unprovoked flight plus presence in a high crime area that seemed to have created enough suspicion to justify a stop in *Wardlow*.

4. **Tip from informant:** When the police want to make a stop based on an ***informant's tip***, they may similarly do so on "reasonable suspicion," and do not need to have probable cause. Whether the informant's tip is reliable enough to give rise to the required "reasonable suspicion" is to be determined by the ***"totality of the circumstances." Alabama v. White***, 496 U.S. 325 (1990). (This is the same test used to determine whether an informant's tip supplies "probable cause," see *supra*, p. 57, but the degree of reliability needed to create "reasonable suspicion" for a stop is obviously less than the reliability needed to furnish true probable cause.)

   a. **Prediction of future events:** When the court applies this "totality of the circumstances" test to evaluate information from an informant (especially an ***anonymous*** one) a key factor is whether the informant has ***predicted future events*** that someone without inside information would have been unlikely to know. Thus in *White*, the police received an anonymous tip that D would leave Apartment 235-C of a particular apartment building at a particular time carrying a brown attache case, that she would then enter a station wagon with a broken right tail light, and that she would then drive to a particular motel. The informant also stated that D would have an ounce of cocaine inside the attache case. The police saw a woman (D) leave the building containing unit 235-C, in a brown station wagon with a broken right tail light (although without an attache case), and saw her drive the most direct route to that motel. The police stopped D just short of the motel, and searched her; marijuana and cocaine were found during this automobile search.

b. **Holding:** The Court held that the tip in *White*, even though it was anonymous, created "reasonable suspicion" and thus justified the stop of D. Even though this anonymous tip was of low "reliability," the fact that the tip was extensively "corroborated" before the stop (i.e., D behaved as the informant predicted she would behave) was enough to create the reasonable suspicion needed for a stop. This was true even though not every detail of the tip panned out (e.g., D did not carry the attache case to the car before driving away).

c. **Tip without corroboration not enough:** The central principle of *White* seems to be that an anonymous tip will be sufficiently reliable to permit a stop if and only if, prior to the stop, the police have been able to ***verify that the informant's assertion that criminality is afoot*** is a ***reliable*** one. A post-*White* case shows that where by the moment of the stop the police have not been able to ***confirm*** that the anonymous informant has ***inside knowledge of criminality***, the tip does ***not justify*** the stop — the mere fact that the informant knows some innocent, publicly-knowable details about the suspect that turn out to be accurate (e.g., his physical appearance) will not suffice. *Florida v. J.L.*, 529 U.S. 266 (2000).

   i. **Facts:** In *J.L.*, the police got an anonymous phone call saying that a young black male standing at a particular bus stop and wearing a plaid shirt was carrying a gun. Two officers were dispatched to that bus stop, and saw three black males standing there, one of whom, D, was wearing a plaid shirt. The officers stopped and frisked D (as well as the other two), and found an illegal gun in D's pocket.

   ii. **Stop invalid:** In a rare unanimous vote, the Court concluded that the stop was ***not based upon reasonable suspicion***, as required by *Terry*. The anonymous call here "provided ***no predictive information***, and therefore left the police without means to test the informant's knowledge or credibility." It didn't matter that the tip about the gun turned out to be correct, because the reliability of the informant must be gauged *before* the stop. Here, all the police knew before the stop was that they should look for a black male in a plaid shirt at a bus stop. This may have indicated that the informant knew the suspect, but it did not furnish any reason to believe that the informant had knowledge of any "concealed criminal activity" by the suspect. "The reasonable suspicion here at issue requires that a tip be ***reliable in its assertion of illegality***, not just in its ***tendency to identify*** a determinate person."

   iii. **Suspicion of fabrication:** Here's another possible reason for the Court's unanimity in concluding that the stop in *J.L.* was not reasonable: the risk that the police ***completely fabricated the informant story*** was unusually high. The phone call supposedly came in to the police department of a major city (Miami), yet was not recorded; also, the informant was completely anonymous. The facts were thus completely consistent with the supposed tip's ***never having occurred at all*** — the police could have simply spotted three black men on a corner, stopped and frisked them all utterly without cause, and then made up an after-the-fact story about an anonymous informant. Notice how convenient it was for the police that the informant's tip implicated only the suspect who turned out to have an illegal weapon on him, not the other two black males who were stopped and frisked but not found with contraband. (The Court didn't mention any such suspicions in its opinion; I am just hypothesizing what may have been going on in some Justices' minds.)

This is not to say that the Court would not have come to the same conclusion — lack of cause for a stop — even had the Justices believed that the informant was real. But my scenario illustrates why, in the case of supposed anonymous informants, the risk of fabrication is unusually high. By contrast, where the police can show that they were in possession of some information before the stop that tended to corroborate the informant's assertion of criminality, the risk of police fabrication is smaller.

5. **Common-sense may be relied on (*Kansas v. Glover*):** As we've noted (p. 153), a fairly modest amount of suspicion will suffice for a *Terry* stop. Often, whatever level of suspicion an officer has, that suspicion will be based on the officer's law enforcement training. But an officer may have sufficient suspicion based instead on the sort of ***"common sense"*** that a non-lawyer might also have. That's what happened in *Kansas v. Glover*, 140 S.Ct. 1183 (2020), where the Court was called on to decide whether an indication that a driver was ***driving with a revoked license*** sufficed to create the level of suspicion that would make a *Terry* stop of the vehicle proper. The Court answered ***yes***.

   a. **Facts:** In *Glover*, a Kansas police officer (whom we'll call "O" for short) observed an individual (Glover) driving a pickup truck with Kansas license plate 295ATJ. (Apparently O did not recognize Glover.) O did not observe any violations of traffic laws. But without approaching the truck, O ran a license-plate search, which revealed that Glover was the registered owner of the truck, and that Glover's driver's license had been revoked. O then made the common-sense inference that any given vehicle has a more-than-trivial chance of being ***driven by its registered owner.*** That was enough, O believed, to give him a reasonable suspicion that Glover was the driver, and was driving with a revoked license. O therefore made a *Terry* stop of the truck. Once O verified that the driver of the truck was indeed Glover, O arrested him as a habitual violator of the law banning driving with a revoked driver's license.

   b. **Glover's defense:** The validity of this *Terry* stop depended on whether, prior to the stop, O had at least a ***"reasonable suspicion"*** that Glover was the registered owner and was driving with a revoked license.[11] Glover therefore claimed that O had merely had a ***"hunch"*** — something ***less than reasonable suspicion*** — that the driver was the registered owner. Consequently, he claimed, the stop violated his Fourth Amendment rights, and any fruit of the stop (here, the license-plate search that confirmed that Glover was indeed the registered owner of the vehicle) must be excluded.

---

11. For more about the "reasonable suspicion" standard for *Terry* stops, see *supra*, p. 153.

i. **Must be rooted in police expertise:** Glover based his argument on the theory that in determining whether reasonable suspicion existed, O's inference that the driver was the registered owner had to be based ***solely on O's law enforcement training or experience.***

c. **Court rejects D's argument:** But the Supreme Court squarely ***rejected*** Glover's argument. It said that when an officer is making inferences to determine whether there is reasonable suspicion adequate for a *Terry* stop, the officer is ***not limited to "knowledge gained only through law enforcement training and experience."*** To the contrary, the officer may make ***common-sense inferences.*** So here, "the inference that the driver of a car is its registered owner does not require any specialized training; rather, it is a ***reasonable inference made by ordinary people*** on a daily basis."

i. **Absent other information:** But the Court noted that the reasonableness of the inference that the driver of a car is its registered owner depends on the ***absence of other information pointing the other way.*** The Court gave this example: "[I]f an officer knows that the registered owner of the vehicle is in his mid-sixties but observes that the driver is in her mid-twenties, then the totality of the circumstances would ***not*** 'raise a suspicion that the particular individual being stopped is engaged in wrongdoing.' " But here, O possessed no information to rebut the reasonable inference that Glover was driving his own truck; therefore, O had the level of reasonable suspicion sufficient to support the stop.

E. **What constitutes a "stop":** It is not clear from either *Terry* or *Adams* ***what degree of interference*** with a person's mobility must exist before a Fourth Amendment "seizure" has occurred. Although the confrontations that occurred in *Terry* and *Adams* were specifically held to be Fourth Amendment seizures, it was not clear from those opinions whether there is a stop when, for example, the officer calls out "stop" to a person some distance away, or when he touches a person on the elbow and says "Hold it, sir, could I speak with you a second."

1. **"Reasonable person" test:** Since *Terry* and *Adams*, the Supreme Court has established the following test for determining whether an encounter constitutes a Fourth Amendment "seizure": "A person has been 'seized' within the meaning of the Fourth Amendment only if, in view of all of the circumstances surrounding the incident, a ***reasonable person*** would have believed that he was ***not free to leave.***" *U.S. v. Mendenhall*, 446 U.S. 544 (1980). The *Mendenhall* Court gave the following examples of circumstances that "might indicate a seizure, even where the person did not attempt to leave:" (1) the ***threatening presence*** of several officers; (2) the ***display of a weapon*** by an officer; (3) some ***physical touching*** of the person; or (4) the use of ***language*** or ***tone of voice*** indicating that compliance with the officer's request might be ***compelled.***

2. **Pursuit by police:** Suppose the police are ***chasing*** a suspect. Does this chase itself constitute a "seizure"? The answer seems to be that until the suspect ***submits*** to the chase (by stopping), there is ***no seizure***. More precisely, there will not be a seizure until two things happen: (1) the suspect ***stops*** in response to the chase or to police orders; and (2) a reasonable person in the suspect's position would believe that he was ***not free to leave*** once he stopped.[12]

a. ***Hodari* case:** This two-part rule was articulated for the first time in *California v. Hodari D.*, 499 U.S. 621 (1991).

i. **Facts:** In *Hodari D.*, police officers came upon four or five youths huddled around a parked car. When the youths saw the officers' car approaching, they panicked and took flight. One officer chased after D (one of the youths) on foot. Just before the officer came upon D, D tossed away what appeared to be small rock, which in fact turned out to be crack cocaine. D argued at trial that he had been seized as soon as the officer began the chase (since at that point, D realized that he was not free to leave); therefore, the drugs were the fruit of a seizure, and the evidence should be excluded because the officer lacked probable cause to make the seizure. The prosecution argued that the seizure had not occurred until the officer actually caught up with D and restrained him; on this view, D had abandoned the drugs, the drugs were lawfully recovered by the police, and they were admissible against D.

ii. **Holding:** By a 7-2 vote, the Court agreed with the prosecution — ***where a show of authority is made to a suspect, and the suspect does not yield, no seizure takes place***. "An arrest requires either physical force or, where that is absent, ***submission*** to the assertion of authority."

iii. **Dissent:** The two dissenters (Stevens, joined by Marshall) argued that submission by the suspect is not necessary for a seizure — once a reasonable person in the suspect's position would believe that he was not free to go, a seizure has occurred, even though the suspect himself has not yet submitted. The dissenters pointed out that by the majority's test it is the ***suspect's behavior***, not the behavior of the police, that determines whether a seizure has occurred. To the dissenters, this was illogical, since "the character of the citizen's response should not govern the constitutionality of the officer's conduct."

iv. **Significance:** The rationale of *Hodari D.* probably applies beyond the "chase" situation. It will presumable apply where:

[1] the officer says ***"freeze"*** or fires a warning shot;

[2] the officer, driving a police car, ***puts on his flashing lights or his sirens***; or

[3] in an airport setting, a narcotics agent approaches a group of passengers with his gun drawn, and announces a ***"baggage search."***

In all of these situations, if the suspect ***flees***, tries to ***dispose of evidence***, or does ***anything other than immediately submit,*** his actions will be ***admissible*** even though the initial encounter was made at a time when the police had no probable cause to make a stop or other seizure. That's because the police have not made a seizure for Fourth Amendment purposes.

b. **Exception for police shooting and other forcible "touchings":** As we just saw, in *Hodari D.* the police started their chase of D without having used any force against his

12. There is one major exception to this two-part rule: if the police ***shoot*** the suspect, then during the moment of shooting there is a "stop" even if the suspect then gets away; see *Torres v. Madrid, infra,* p. 159.

body; that fact led the Court to say that the start of the chase was not a Fourth Amendment "seizure." But what if the police <u>do</u> ***apply force to the body*** of the suspect, D, and D then ***escapes*** before he can be taken into custody? Does that brief application of force constitute a seizure? ***Torres v. Madrid***, 141 S.Ct. 989 (2021), establishes that the answer is ***"yes"***: a seizure occurs ***at the moment the officer applies force to the body of D, even if D then breaks away*** from that force.[13]

More specifically, *Torres* means that if the police ***shoot and wound a suspect***, that's a ***seizure*** even if the suspect ***flees*** rather than stopping.

i. **Facts of *Torres*:** Two New Mexico police officers approached Torres while she sat in her parked car. They were trying to serve an arrest warrant for a different person. When the officers attempted to speak to Torres, she did not realize the men were police officers; she thought they were carjackers trying to steal her car. She began to drive off, and the officers fired their pistols to stop her; two of their bullets hit and injured her. She nonetheless drove for 75 miles until she was hospitalized and arrested while in the hospital.

   (1) **§1983 suit:** Torres brought a suit against the officers under ***42 U.S.C. §1983,*** which allows for a civil suit for damages by a person whose ***constitutional rights have been violated*** by ***persons acting under color of state law.***[14] Her claim was that the officers used excessive force, making the shooting an unreasonable seizure under the Fourth Amendment. The officers claimed that because Torres was not successfully restrained by the shooting, she was not "seized" for Fourth Amendment purposes at all. (It was clear that a person can't recover under §1983 for excessive force by the police unless the force was used pursuant to a seizure.) Torres claimed that the shooting *did* constitute a seizure of her body, even though she then escaped rather than submitting to the officers' authority.

ii. **Holding:** The Supreme Court ***agreed with Torres*** by a vote of 5-3.[15] The majority opinion, by Chief Justice Roberts, posed the question as "whether a seizure occurs when an officer ***shoots someone who temporarily eludes capture*** after the shooting." And Roberts said that "The answer is ***yes:*** the application of physical force to the body of a person with intent to restrain is a seizure, even if the ***force does not succeed in subduing*** the person."

   (1) **Consistent with *Hodari*:** Roberts said that this conclusion was completely consistent with *Hodari D., supra*, even though in that case no physical contact between the police and the suspect occurred.

---

13. As the opinion in *Torres* makes clear, the rule that police application of force to the body of the suspect constitutes a seizure even if the suspect escapes applies only if the police's conduct ***"objectively manifests an intent to restrain[.]"*** So, for instance, if the officer taps D's shoulder in order to get her attention, no seizure occurs.

14. For more about §1983, see *infra*, p. 357. Civil suits using this provision are often brought by plaintiffs who say they have been the victims of ***police brutality*** (i.e., excessive use of force) during an arrest.

15. Justice Barrett did not vote, because the case was argued before she joined the Court.

(2) **Instantaneous, not continuing:** Roberts emphasized that unless the suspect "submitted" (i.e., let the officers take him into their custody), the seizure ***"lasts only as long as the application of force."*** In other words, he said, "the Fourth Amendment does not recognize any continuing arrest during the period of fugitivity." So once Torres ***continued driving*** after being shot, she was ***no longer "seized."***

(3) **Right to bring §1983 suit:** But the moment Torres was shot was nonetheless a seizure, no matter how brief. Therefore, since Torres was claiming that the shooting constituted excessive force by the police, she was ***eligible*** to raise her §1983 claim because she was seized "for the instant that the bullets struck her."[16]

iii. **Dissent:** The three most conservative members of the court ***dissented***. The dissent was by Justice Gorsuch, joined by Thomas and Alito. To the dissenters, the appropriate Fourth Amendment rule was that a seizure should be deemed to occur only when the suspect is in the ***"possession"*** of the police – a mere "touching" of the suspect, whether by a bullet or any other force, should not be deemed to be a seizure at all.

(1) **Pepper spray, etc.:** The majority's approach would be hard to administer, Gorsuch contended. For instance, he asked, what should count as a "touching" of the suspect (making the encounter a seizure if the police intended to restrain him)? Would a seizure occur when the officer deploys ***"pepper spray*** that enters a suspect's lungs as he sprints away?" And does a seizure occur when officers "detonate flash-bang ***grenades"*** that ***damage the suspect's eardrums*** even though he escapes? Lower courts will have to deal with these hard-to-resolve complications, he said.

3. **Search of buses:** Where the police board a ***bus***, and then question, or request to search, the passengers, when will a seizure of the passengers be deemed to have occurred? The Court has issued two opinions on this narrow subject. Taken together, these two opinions indicate that usually, ***no seizure will be found to have occurred.***

a. **"Feel free to decline" standard:** In the first opinion, the Court held that a seizure will be deemed ***not*** to have occurred if "a reasonable person would ***feel free to decline the officers' requests*** or otherwise terminate the encounter." *Florida v. Bostick*, 501 U.S. 429 (1991). The Court concluded that the test should not be whether a reasonable person would have felt "free to leave" (as it was in *Terry*), since a person on board a bus would not feel free to leave in any case.

b. **Police need not inform passengers of right not to cooperate:** In the second of the bus-questioning cases, the Court decided that when a court answers the question, "Did the passengers reasonably believe they were ***free not to cooperate***?" the fact that the

---

16. As Roberts pointed out while remanding the case to the lower court for further analysis, the fact that the shooting was a seizure of Torres would be only the first obstacle in Torres' §1983 suit. She would still have to show, on remand, that the seizure was unreasonable in the circumstances, and that the officers were not entitled to qualified immunity. For more about §1983 suits, see *infra*, p. 357.

officers ***failed to inform*** the passengers that they were free not to cooperate ***does not matter***. *U.S. v. Drayton*, 536 U.S. 194 (2002). As the result of *Drayton*, most interrogations of bus passengers will probably be found not to be seizures, and thus not to pose Fourth Amendment problems.

c. **Significance:** The two cases, *Bostick* and *Drayton*, seem to establish that the ordinary bus-based drug-interdiction scenario — in which multiple officers, whether in uniform or not, and whether visibly armed or not, explain that they are performing a drug interdiction effort and ask each passenger for permission to search his bags and person — will ***not constitute a Fourth Amendment seizure***. And if there is no seizure, ***any consent*** given will be ***valid*** even though the entire procedure was done without any individualized suspicion.

F. **"Stop" vs. arrest:** It is unclear ***how long*** the suspect can be detained and how intrusive the investigation can be, before the "stop" turns into a full-scale arrest requiring probable cause.

1. **Reasonableness of detention:** It is clear that the detention ***must not be longer than the circumstances which justified it require***. Thus where a person was stopped for jaywalking, and was detained for longer than was necessary to write out a ticket because the police wanted to radio headquarters on a completely unsubstantiated hunch that there was a warrant for his arrest, it was held that the detention was of unreasonable length. *U.S. v. Luckett*, 484 F.2d 89 (9th Cir. 1973).

2. **No more intrusive than necessary:** Not only must the stop be no longer than necessary to fulfill its purpose, it must also be ***no more intrusive than needed*** to verify or dispel the policeman's suspicions. This ***"least intrusive means"*** requirement is illustrated by an airport drug case, ***Florida v. Royer***, 460 U.S. 491 (1983).

a. **Facts:** In *Royer*, airport narcotics police stopped D because he fell within a "drug courier profile" used to indicate persons who are likely to be carrying drugs. They then stopped D, asked for and examined his ticket and his driver's license, and discovered that he was traveling under an assumed name. Without returning his ticket or license, they identified themselves as narcotics agents, told D that he was suspected of being a drug courier, and asked him to come with them to a separate police room about 40 feet away from the main concourse where the initial stop had taken place. While one officer sat with D in the room (described as a "large storage closet"), the other officer, using D's baggage check stubs, retrieved D's luggage from the airline and brought it back to the room. D was then asked if he would consent to a search of the suitcases; he took out a key and unlocked one of the bags, in which drugs were found.

b. **Unduly intrusive:** A majority of the Court concluded that, while the initial stop and questioning of D constituted a valid *Terry* stop, the subsequent conduct was ***more intrusive than necessary*** to carry out the limited investigation permitted by *Terry*. Since the police were mainly interested in gaining consent to search D's luggage, there was no need to remove him to the small room in order to gain that consent. (Had they moved him for reasons of "safety and security," the bounds of *Terry* would not have been crossed; but there was no indication that this was the reason for the move.) Similarly, the majority indicated, it would have been less intrusive to use trained dogs to conduct a "sniff test" of D's luggage (a procedure which the Court subsequently found not to violate the Fourth Amendment, in *U.S. v. Place*, *supra*, p. 51).

3. **Emphasis on "reasonableness":** A post-*Royer* case shows that the "least intrusive means" requirement will itself be qualified by a ***"reasonableness"*** approach. "The question is not simply whether some other [less intrusive] alternative was available, but whether the police acted unreasonably in failing to recognize or to pursue it." ***U.S. v. Sharpe***, 470 U.S. 675 (1985). The Court observed in *Sharpe* that where the police are acting in a "swiftly developing situation," the court "should not indulge in unrealistic second-guessing."

   a. **Application to facts:** Thus in *Sharpe*, the Court found it not unreasonable for the police to have detained D, a truck driver suspected of carrying marijuana, for ***20 minutes***. The reasonableness of this 20-minute stop was due in part to the fact that D's attempt to evade the stop had caused the two officers pursuing him to be separated, and the one who performed the stop waited 15 minutes for the other, more experienced one to arrive.

   b. **Law enforcement needs taken into account:** *Sharpe* also establishes that in determining whether the stop was of a length and intrusiveness that made it "unreasonable," the ***law enforcement needs*** of the officials who are performing the stop may be taken into account. Thus the fact that the stopping officer in *Sharpe* spent 15 minutes waiting for his more-experienced companion to arrive on the scene was a factor tending to make the duration of the stop reasonable. (Similarly, if a stop took longer than expected because the stopping officer had trouble radioing headquarters to find out whether the suspect was wanted for any crimes, this fact would help support the longer stop.)

4. **Demand for identification:** May the officer who is making an otherwise-proper *Terry* stop demand that the person being stopped ***identify himself***? The answer is ***yes***, as the result of *Hiibel v. Sixth Judicial Dist. Court*, 542 U.S. 177 (2004). There, Nevada enacted a statute that said that a person lawfully stopped under *Terry* "shall identify himself." By a 5-4 vote, the Court held that an officer demanding such identification was not violating the Fourth Amendment: a "request for identity has an immediate relation to the purpose, rationale, and practical demands of a *Terry* stop," and the particular request here was "reasonably related in scope to the circumstances which justified" the stop.

   a. **Limited effect:** But because of the highly limited scope of the Nevada statute, *Hiibel* does ***not*** establish that the police may demand that the person stopped supply an ***identification document*** (e.g., a ***driver's license***) — all it establishes is that the police may demand that the stoppee give an ***oral statement of his name.*** So we still don't know whether demanding a driver's license or other identification document goes beyond the reasonable scope of a *Terry* stop.

5. **On-scene fingerprinting:** Beyond the brief questioning of the suspect, other investigative measures may be permissible without turning the stop into an arrest (as to which probable cause would be required). For instance, the Court has indicated that the ***on-scene fingerprinting*** of a suspect might well be sufficiently unintrusive that it falls within *Terry*. This issue is discussed more extensively *infra*, p. 166. Clearly the examination of the sus-

pect's identification (at least where the suspect voluntarily hands it to the officer), and brief attempts to check out that I.D. (e.g., by radioing to the police station or the motor vehicle bureau) are, similarly, procedures which fall within the *Terry* framework. The suspect's property may also sometimes be taken from him and separately examined; see *infra*, p. 169.

6. **Alimentary canal smugglers:** The Court's increasing tendency to consider law enforcement needs when determining whether a stop was unreasonably long or intrusive, was illustrated by a case involving a traveler suspected of being an ***"alimentary canal smuggler."*** In that case, *U.S. v. Montoya de Hernandez*, 473 U.S. 531 (1985), the Court concluded that the detention of D, a traveler (who was suspected of having swallowed balloons containing drugs), for ***27 hours*** before agents found drugs in her rectum and arrested her, was nonetheless justified under a *Terry*-like rationale. (The delay was due to D's refusal to consent to an X-ray; she was then detained until a court order for a rectal exam could be obtained.)

G. **Frisk permissible under *Terry:*** *Terry* indicates that where the officer wishes to conduct a frisk in connection with a stop, he must follow a two-step process: (1) he must first merely pat down the outside of the suspect's clothing, to feel for hard objects which might be weapons; and (2) only if he feels such an object may he reach inside a pocket or article of clothing. Although no pat-down occurred before seizure of the gun in *Adams*, this can presumably be justified on the grounds that the "informant" had told the officer exactly where on the suspect the gun would be located.

1. **Limited purpose of frisk:** When the frisk does occur, it must be ***limited to the search for weapons.*** Thus items which could not be weapons may not be examined, and areas not within the control of the suspect may not be searched. For instance, if the officer feels something that he does not believe to be a weapon, but that he thinks might be ***contraband***, the officer may not expand the search (by removing the object) unless he already has probable cause to believe that the object is contraband.

Example: Officers spot D leaving a building that the officers know to be a "crack house." Based on D's evasive behavior, the officers suspect that D may be involved in the cocaine trade, though they do not have probable cause for this belief, merely reasonable suspicion. The officers stop D and frisk him. During the frisk, one officer feels a lump in D's nylon jacket. The officer realizes that the lump is probably not a weapon, but squeezes it and otherwise manipulates it to get a better sense of what it might be. Based on this squeezing, the officer decides that the lump may be crack. He therefore removes the lump from D's jacket, and sees that it is indeed crack. The crack is introduced against D at his drug-possession trial. D objects to this evidence, on the theory that the officer may have had the right to frisk him, but not the right to squeeze or manipulate the object once he realized that it was not a weapon.

Held, for D. The sole justification for a *Terry* frisk is to protect the officer or others nearby from danger posed by weapons. Therefore, once the officer realized that he was not feeling a weapon, he should have stopped the frisk, rather than expanding it by squeezing and manipulating the lump. The squeezing was an expansion of the search in violation of the Fourth Amendment, so the drug was the fruit of a poisonous tree (see *infra*, p. 324) and should not have been admitted against D. *Minnesota v. Dickerson*, 508 U.S. 366 (1993).

a. **"Plain touch" doctrine applies during frisk:** Recall that under the "plain view" doctrine (*supra*, p. 43), once the police legally view an object and recognize it to be contraband or evidence, they may ***seize*** it without a warrant. A ***"plain touch"*** variant of the "plain view" doctrine applies during a *Terry* frisk, so that if the officer, while staying within the narrow limits of a frisk for weapons, feels what he has probable cause to believe is a weapon, contraband or evidence, the officer may expand the search or seize the object. *Minnesota v. Dickerson, supra.*

Example: Suppose that in *Minnesota v. Dickerson*, the arresting officer, while staying within the confines of a *Terry* weapons frisk, had gained probable cause to believe that what he was feeling was cocaine. At that moment, the officer would have been justified in removing the object (thus "seizing" it) even without a search warrant and without having had probable cause to arrest D in the first place. On these hypothetical facts, the cocaine would have been "in plain touch" to the officer. (But in fact, at the moment the officer went beyond a pat-down and started manipulating and squeezing the lump, he did not have probable cause to believe cocaine was there, so the manipulation was itself an unlawful expansion of a search, just as the police may not move an object that they *see* in plain view in order to examine it further; see *Arizona v. Hicks*, *supra*, p. 128.)

2. **Reason to fear danger:** Even if a *Terry* stop is justified, the frisk may take place only if the officer has a ***reasonable belief*** that the suspect ***may be armed***. A reasonable belief that the suspect has ***contraband***, or that a frisk will turn up ***evidence of criminality***, is ***not sufficient.***

a. ***Ybarra*** **case:** Thus in ***Ybarra v. Illinois***, 444 U.S. 85 (1979) (also discussed *supra*, p. 70), the police had a valid warrant to search a bar and the bartender for heroin. While executing the warrant, the police performed a frisk of D, one of the bar's patrons; the officer felt a "cigarette pack with objects in it," which turned out to be tin foil packets holding heroin. The Supreme Court held that the initial frisk was not justified under *Terry*, because the police had ***no reasonable belief*** that D was ***armed or dangerous***. (For instance, D's hands were empty, he gave no indication of possessing a weapon, he made no gestures indicating an intent to commit an assault, and he "acted generally in a manner that was not threatening.") The Court expressly ***declined*** to allow frisks of persons who are on "compact" premises subject to a search warrant, where the police have a reasonable belief that the persons may be ***concealing contraband***.

H. **Search of automobile:** *Terry* involved merely a pat-down of the suspect's person. But the general doctrine of *Terry*, that Fourth Amendment searches and seizures of limited intrusion may sometimes be justified on less than probable cause, has been extended to allow a search for weapons in an ***automobile's passenger compartment***, even though the suspect is no longer inside the car. ***Michigan v. Long***, 463 U.S. 1032 (1983).

1. **Facts:** In *Long*, the police believed that D, who had driven his car into a ditch, was drunk. While D was out of the car, the police noticed a large hunting knife on the floor near the driver's seat. After performing a *Terry*-like pat-down of D, they searched the pas-

senger compartment (looking for weapons, they later claimed.) In so doing, they found a leather pouch on the front seat; they opened the pouch and found drugs.

2. **Search upheld:** Since D had not been arrested at the time of the search, the (later-overruled) doctrine of *New York v. Belton*, *supra*, p. 101, which at the time allowed the entire passenger compartment of a car to be searched incident to the driver's arrest, was not applicable. However, the Supreme Court upheld the search in *Long* on the rationale of *Terry*; just as the police may frisk the body of a suspect (even one who has not been arrested) if they reasonably believe that he may be armed, so they may ***search the passenger compartment of his car*** if two conditions are met: (1) they reasonably believe, based on "***specific and articulable facts***," that he is ***dangerous*** and ***may gain immediate control of weapons*** if these are in the car; and (2) they look ***only in those parts*** of the passenger compartment where weapons ***might be placed or hidden***.

   a. **Plain view:** If, while performing this extended *Terry*-type of weapons search, the police discover contraband or evidence of crime in a place where a weapon might have reasonably been placed, they may seize that evidence under the general "plain view" rule. In *Long*, the Supreme Court accepted the trial court's finding that the leather pouch might have contained a weapon. Therefore, the seizure of the drugs did not violate the Fourth Amendment.

   b. **Danger from suspect's return to car:** At the time the police searched D's vehicle, he was standing ***outside*** the car. Therefore, it is not immediately apparent why the police felt they had to protect themselves by looking for weapons ***inside*** the car. But the Supreme Court reasoned that D might have broken away from police control, re-entered the car and retrieved a weapon; or, after being permitted to return to the car (assuming that he was not arrested), he might have gotten the weapon and harmed the officers. In the Court's view, this latter danger existed precisely ***because*** the suspect was not being subjected to a full-scale custodial arrest.

3. **Dissent:** Justice Brennan (joined by Marshall) dissented in *Long*. He argued that the majority was continuing the process of "distorting *Terry* beyond recognition and [violating] the Fourth Amendment's fundamental requirement that searches and seizures be based on probable cause." He noted that no prior case had ever held that a *Terry*-type search (i.e., one based on less than probable cause) could extend past the body of the suspect; the search of a car's passenger compartment is much more intrusive and broad-sweeping than the limited pat-down permitted by *Terry*. Brennan was also critical of the Court's factual determination that the officers were reasonable in their belief that, even though D was obviously drunk, he might pose a danger to them while stopped by the roadside. And Brennan feared that the majority's limitation of such searches to places where weapons "may be placed or hidden" would not prove much of a limit, since a weapon may be located anywhere within the passenger compartment, including in any closed container (as was theoretically true of the leather pouch in which the drugs in *Long* were found.)

4. **Search may not be automatic:** *Long* does not mean that the police may search the passenger compartment of a car whenever they stop the driver. The theory of *Long* is that the police may protect themselves against the suspect's gaining access to hidden weapons. The police may search for such weapons only if they have a "reasonable belief based on

specific and articulable facts" which warrant them in believing that the suspect may be dangerous. It was the presence of the hunting knife in *Long*, for instance, which made the policemen's belief reasonable.

a. **Limited application:** Presumably *Long* will apply wherever the police find weapons on the suspect's ***person***, or wherever they discover a weapon in plain view in the car. But in the typical situation of a stop for a ***traffic violation***, the *Terry/Long* right-to-search-for-weapons will ***not*** apply. For instance, in *Knowles v. Iowa*, 525 U.S. 113 (1998) (also discussed *supra*, p. 139), the Court held that when an officer stops a motorist to issue a traffic ticket, and does not make a custodial arrest, the stop does not by itself entitle the officer to search the vehicle's interior.

I. **Brief detention at the station:** *Terry* and *Adams*, in holding that a Fourth Amendment seizure might sometimes be permissible on less than probable cause, spoke only of ***on-the-street*** encounters. If the suspect is required to come to the ***police station***, the *Terry/Adams* rationale will ***not apply***. The line dividing a *Terry*-like stop from an intrusion so severe that the full protection of the Fourth Amendment is triggered, is "crossed when the police, without probable cause or a warrant, forcibly ***remove a person from his home or other place in which he is entitled to be*** and transport him to the police station, where he is detained, although briefly, for investigative purposes." *Hayes v. Florida*, 470 U.S. 811 (1985). The *Hayes* Court noted that such station-house detention, even though brief and unaccompanied by interrogation, is "sufficiently like [an] arrest to invoke the traditional rule that arrests may constitutionally be made only on probable cause." (The case, which involved the fingerprinting of the defendant at the station-house, is discussed *infra*, p. 166.)

1. **Lack of actual arrest irrelevant:** Probable cause is necessary for a station-house detention accompanied by interrogation, ***even if no formal arrest is made***. Thus in ***Dunaway v. New York***, 442 U.S. 200 (1979), the defendant was asked to come to police headquarters, where he received his *Miranda* warnings, was questioned, and ultimately confessed. There was no probable cause to arrest him, but there was some reason for the police to suspect him in connection with the crime they were investigating.

a. **Holding:** The Court held that insofar as the defendant was ***taken into custody***, the intrusion on his privacy was much more severe than an on-the-street stop, and that the situation should therefore not be handled under the *Terry* "balancing test" approach. Instead, ***probable cause was required***, and since it was lacking, the confession was the tainted fruit of an invalid seizure. The mere fact that the defendant was not told he was under arrest, was not "booked," and would not have had an "arrest record" had the investigation proved fruitless, did not prevent the seizure from being serious enough to require probable cause.

2. **Fingerprinting:** Similarly, the rationale of *Terry* will not allow the police, acting without probable cause, to require a suspect to come to the station for ***fingerprinting***. *Hayes v. Florida*, 470 U.S. 811 (1985).

J. **Detention during search:** When the police are ***searching premises*** for contraband, pursuant to a ***search warrant***, they may ***detain the occupants*** while the search continues. ***Michigan v. Summers***, 452 U.S. 692 (1981).

1. **Less intrusion on individual:** In *Summers*, the Court reasoned that a "brief detention" was substantially less intrusive than a full-fledged arrest, and might therefore be made on less than the probable cause needed for a full arrest. In particular, the mere existence of a search warrant for the premises, the Court held, was ***by itself*** a sufficient "objective justification" for detaining the occupants during the search (assuming that the warrant itself was correctly issued on probable cause).

    a. **Regulatory interests:** In so holding, the Court relied on the "legitimate law enforcement interest in ***preventing flight*** in the event that incriminating evidence is found," plus the interest in making an ***orderly completion*** of the search; with respect to the latter, the Court noted that if the owner of the premises is present, he may be induced by self-interest to "open locked doors or locked containers to avoid the use of force . . . damaging to property. . . . "

2. **Dissent:** Justice Stewart, joined by Justices Brennan and Marshall, dissented. They contended that expansion of the situations in which detention may be made without probable cause should be strictly limited, and should be justified by either "an important purpose beyond the normal goals of criminal investigation" (e.g., the police officer's need to protect himself in *Adams v. Williams*, *supra*, p. 150) or by "an extraordinary obstacle" to the investigation. Neither of these considerations was present here, the dissent argued.

    a. **Other arguments:** Also, the dissent claimed that "If the police, acting without probable cause, can seize a person to make him available for arrest in case probable cause is later developed to arrest him, the requirement of probable cause for arrest has been turned upside down." Finally, the dissent observed that a search can sometimes take several hours, and that a detention during the conduct of such a search is hardly a "minor intrusion of brief duration."

3. **Right to use force to detain:** A post-*Summers* case shows that when the police exercise their right to detain the occupants while executing a search warrant, they may use ***reasonable force*** to carry out that detention. At least where what is being searched for is ***weapons***, reasonable force will automatically include the ***handcuffing of all occupants*** of the premises. See *Muehler v. Mena*, 544 U.S. 93 (2005).

4. **Applies only to immediate vicinity of arrest:** The holding of *Summers* — that while police are executing a search warrant, they may temporarily detain any persons present on the searched premises — applies only to persons who are detained either while they are ***on*** the premises or ***in the immediate vicinity of*** those premises. Once a person is permitted to ***leave*** the immediate vicinity of the premises being searched, the automatic "police may detain" rule of *Summers* no longer applies, ***no matter how "reasonable" it may be*** for the police to then detain that person under the circumstances. Instead, the usual Fourth Amendment procedures (including the rules on "stop and frisk") apply. That's the result of ***Bailey v. U.S.***, 133 S.Ct. 1031 (2013).

    a. **Facts:** In *Bailey*, police properly got a search warrant to search a basement apartment at 103 Lake Drive for a .380 caliber handgun. The police had been told by an informant who saw the gun in the apartment that a "heavy set black male with short hair" known as "Polo" was selling drugs from the apartment. (The warrant covered only a search for the gun, not for drugs.) While the officers were surveilling 103 Lake Drive but had not yet started their search, they observed a man (D) who conformed to the description of Polo leave the building with a companion and drive away.

i. **D is followed:** While some of the officers conducted the search of 103 Lake Drive, two detectives peeled away to follow D by car. About a mile from the 103 Lake Drive premises, the detectives stopped D's car and questioned him. D initially confirmed that he lived at 103 Lake Drive. But when he learned from the detectives that the police were currently searching those premises, he changed his story and denied residing there. The detectives, made more suspicious by this change of story, patted D down, and discovered in his pocket a key that turned out to open the door to 103 Lake Drive. Meanwhile, the officers searching 103 Lake Drive discovered drugs plus a gun.

ii. **D's suppression motion:** In D's prosecution for possession of the drugs and the gun, he moved to suppress the key (as well as his statements to the detectives made during the pat-down) as being the product of an illegal stop and search.

iii. **D loses below:** The lower courts found against D. They concluded that the stop and pat-down were justified by *Summers*, since D had been observed leaving the premises that were about to be searched and then detained relatively soon thereafter.

b. **D wins at Supreme Court** But by a 6-3 vote, the Supreme Court found that the lower courts were ***wrong***: the initial stop of D did ***not*** fall within the rule of *Summers*. The majority, in an opinion by Justice Kennedy, agreed that *Summers* permits the police to detain any occupant who is found ***on the premises*** during the execution of a search warrant, even absent any individualized suspicion of that person. This rule is justified by the law enforcement interest in "conducting a safe and efficient search," Kennedy said. But because the *Summers* exception gives the police substantial ***discretion*** to detain people "outside of the traditional rules of the Fourth Amendment," that exception must be ***"circumscribed."***

i. **"Immediate vicinity" rule:** Therefore, Kennedy said, *Summers* does not apply once the occupant is ***beyond the "immediate vicinity of the premises*** to be searched," and ordinary Fourth Amendment principles apply instead.

ii. **Application to facts:** Here, since the detectives did not stop D until he was about a ***mile*** from the premises being searched, he was no longer in the premises' "immediate vicinity." Therefore, the stop was not justifiable under *Summers*, and instead had to be justified, if at all, on traditional Fourth Amendment rules, including stop-and-frisk. (The Court sent the case back to the lower courts for a determination of (1) whether, when the detectives pulled over D's car, they had enough individualized suspicion of him to justify a *Terry*-style "stop" and (2) if so, whether their subsequent conversation with D gave them enough suspicion to search his person.)

c. **Dissent:** Three dissenters, in an opinion by Justice Breyer, said they would allow a detention under the *Summers* principle as long as it was carried out ***"as soon as reasonably practicable"*** under the circumstances, even if the detention occurred ***outside***

the "immediate vicinity" of the premises being searched. They thought this "reasonably practicable" rule was satisfied here.

K. Investigation of completed crime: All the stop-and-frisk situations discussed so far involved suspicion of crimes that were in the process of being carried out, or about to be carried out. But the Supreme Court has made it clear that the *Terry* exception to the requirement of probable cause also extends to an officer's attempts to investigate a serious crime that took place a significant time ***previously***. "If police have a reasonable suspicion, grounded in specific and articulable facts, that a person they encounter was involved in or is wanted in connection with a completed felony, then a *Terry* stop may be made to investigate that suspicion." *U.S. v. Hensley*, 469 U.S. 221 (1985).

1. **Application to facts:** The facts of *Hensley* illustrate the type of situation in which this extension of *Terry* to cover completed crimes may be significant. The police of Covington, Kentucky received a "wanted" flyer from another police department, stating that D was wanted for investigation concerning a robbery. (The flyer did not state that an arrest warrant had been issued for D.) Twelve days after the robbery, a police officer who knew D saw him in a car, stopped him, and during the stop noticed a gun in the car. The Supreme Court held that D could be convicted on gun charges, because the flyer furnished the requisite "reasonable suspicion, grounded in specific and articulable facts" that D was wanted in connection with the completed robbery.

L. Detention of property: Most cases relying on the *Terry* exception to the requirement of probable cause have involved seizures of the "person," i.e., stops. But the Supreme Court has also held the general *Terry* doctrine applicable to certain ***seizures of property***, so that these, too, can sometimes occur without probable cause.

1. **Incident to stop:** When the police perform a "stop" of a person pursuant to *Terry* (by definition a Fourth Amendment "seizure" of the person), they are also necessarily seizing whatever personal effects he has with him at the time (e.g., hand-carried luggage). It has always been assumed that this sort of incidental seizure poses no additional Fourth Amendment concerns. (But the stop of the person does not give the police the right to ***search*** the personal effects; only the unavoidable, *de facto*, seizure is treated as being merely incident to the stop.)

2. **Seizure as independent act:** But the Supreme Court has gone significantly further, by holding that *Terry* will sometimes justify the seizure of baggage and other personal effects, ***even where these are not incident to a* Terry*-justified stop of the items' owner***. This extension of *Terry* took place in *U.S. v. Place*, 462 U.S. 696 (1983) (also discussed *supra*, p. 51), an airport drug case.

   a. **Facts:** In *Place*, Miami Airport police became suspicious that Place might be transporting drugs in his luggage. However, they allowed him to check his bags and board the plane to New York's LaGuardia Airport. They then phoned federal Drug Enforcement Administration (DEA) authorities in New York about their suspicions, and the latter were waiting for Place at the arrival gate in New York. They identified themselves as federal narcotics agents, and asked Place to consent to a search of his luggage, which he refused. They then seized the bags, but not Place (whose name and address they had already obtained by inspecting his driver's license). The agents took the bags from LaGuardia to Kennedy Airport, where they used trained dogs to conduct a "sniff test" on the bags; the test was positive as to one of the bags. Ninety minutes elapsed between the initial seizure and the conducting of the sniff test. A search warrant was then obtained for the positively-tested bag, which was opened and found to contain cocaine.

b. **Initial seizure upheld:** The Supreme Court held that the initial seizure of Place's bags was ***justified*** under the rationale of *Terry*. There is a strong law enforcement interest in permitting brief investigative seizures of luggage suspected of containing drugs, because of the "inherently transient nature of drug courier activities at airports," and the need for police to stop the flow of narcotics into distribution channels.

c. **Brief and limited detention:** However, only a ***brief and limited*** detention and investigation may take place. The Court phrased its general rule as follows: "When an officer's observations lead him reasonably to believe that a traveller is carrying luggage that contains narcotics, the principles of *Terry* and its progeny would permit the officer to ***detain the luggage briefly*** to ***investigate*** the circumstances that aroused his suspicion, provided that the investigative detention is properly limited in scope."

i. **Unduly lengthy:** But the seizure in this case was ***too lengthy*** to qualify as the sort of "brief detention" authorized by *Terry*. The Court refused to set any outer time limit for the length of a *Terry* detention. But the ***90-minute*** delay here was clearly too long. Furthermore, the detention was made more burdensome by the agents' failure to tell Place where they were taking his luggage, how long they would have it, and how he could get it back if there were no narcotics in it. (But it was clear from the Court's opinion that the 90-minute delay by itself, without these other exacerbating factors, would have been sufficient to prevent the detention from qualifying under *Terry*.)

M. **Extensions of *Terry*:** Observe that the doctrine of *Terry*, which was originally limited to permitting the police to perform a brief stop and a very narrow search (the superficial pat-down of a suspect reasonably believed to be dangerous) has been gradually expanded by the Court, until it represents a major web of exceptions to the general principle that Fourth Amendment searches and seizures may only be performed upon probable cause. For instance, we've seen that the Court has held that:

The suspicion to support a stop need not be based on the officer's ***own observations.*** *Adams v. Williams.*

A suspicion of wrongdoing entitles the officer to stop a ***vehicle***, not just conduct an on-the-street stop of a pedestrian. *Adams.*

The officer may, pursuant to a vehicle stop, search the car's ***passenger compartment***. *Michigan v. Long.*

The stop may be accompanied by a temporary seizure of ***personal effects***, such as baggage. *U.S. v. Place*.

The detention may be made solely for purpose of ***investigating possible crime***, rather than for protection of officer. *Florida v. Royer.*

A stop is not unreasonable merely because it lasts for 27 hours. *U.S. v. Montoya de Her-*

nandez.

Cases permitting ***investigative*** and ***regulatory*** stops and searches to be made without probable cause, discussed in the next major section, are also part of this trend.

X. REGULATORY AND OTHER "SPECIAL NEEDS" SEARCHES

A. Focus of this section: Grouped in this section are various kinds of ***specific law enforcement activities*** which may invade areas protected by the Fourth Amendment, but whose special nature may justify dispensing with either ***probable cause***, a ***search warrant***, or both. These activities are commonly said to be ones presenting ***"special needs."*** Most of these activities have a ***"regulatory"*** rather than "investigation of crime" flavor.

The "special needs" activities that we'll examine here are:

1. ***health, fire*** and other ***safety-related inspections*** of ***physical premises*** by government inspectors who are ***not investigating suspected crimes***;
2. ***border*** and ***fixed checkpoint*** searches;
3. routine ***traffic stops***;
4. ***sobriety checkpoints***;
5. ***capturing the DNA*** of ***arrestees***;
6. searches of ***parolees and probationers***;
7. ***school searches***; and
8. office ***searches*** of ***government employees***.

B. Health and safety inspections of physical premises: The Supreme Court has laid down special rules governing how the Fourth Amendment restricts the circumstances under which government ***inspectors*** may perform inspections of physical premises to ensure that ***health, fire and other safety regulations*** are being complied with. We'll refer to this sort of premises inspection as a ***"building search."*** [17]

1. Summary of rules: Here is a summary of these special rules governing building searches:

[1] Most importantly, the inspector ***does not have to have any suspicion at all*** that there are health or safety violations at the particular premises to be inspected.

In other words, putting aside (for this rule [1]) whether the inspector has to obtain a *warrant*, the inspector is able to search, say, every building within a city, or every building having certain characteristics, without needing any ***reason to believe that any particular building or premises is in violation*** of any legal requirement. Thus

---

17. As you might expect, the inspector is always free to arrive at premises without any warrant or grounds for suspicion and to ask the owner or occupant to ***consent*** to a building search; if the latter agrees, then the search is lawful regardless of whether the inspector had any grounds for suspicion, and regardless of whether she had any kind of search warrant. Our discussion here focuses on the rules that apply if the owner/occupant *refuses consent*: what kind of suspicion must the inspector have, and must she have some sort of warrant, in order to perform the search over the owner/occupant's objection?

"area-wide building inspections" are possible.

[2] On the other hand, the inspector is ***not*** free to demand an inspection of premises ***without some sort of warrant.*** As we'll see in rule [3] below, the warrant can be of a special and easy-to-obtain sort, but the inspector cannot simply demand to inspect a particular building "empty handed," assuming there is no emergency.

[3] The required warrant is quite different from a standard "search warrant" as described in the warrant clause of the Fourth Amendment for use in criminal investigations. In the building-search context, here's how the warrant requirement (essentially a ***judge-made rule*** created by the Supreme Court in interpreting the Fourth Amendment's general "no unreasonable searches" clause, ***not*** the "warrant" clause) works:

[a] The official seeking the warrant does ***not*** have to show ***probable cause*** that the particular building to be inspected ***violates*** any health or safety regulation.

[b] Instead, the official merely has to show that government is proposing to conduct an ***"area inspection"*** that is ***reasonably tailored to making sure that the relevant health or safety codes are being observed.***

Example: The judicial officer being asked to issue the area-inspection warrant might find that the warrant was reasonable because it (i) covered all buildings in a city that had not been inspected for some predesignated length of time; *or* (ii) covered all multi-family dwellings, because of the greater risk of, say, faulty wiring in such dwellings; *or* (iii) covered all structures in an area of town in which building officials reasonably believe that there are special dangers (e.g., a large number of wood structures, close together, and built before modern fire codes took effect).

[c] The main function of the warrant requirement in this building-inspection context is to make sure that government inspectors are ***not given undue discretion*** that they can use to harass particular owners or occupiers for non-safety-related purposes.

Example: The need for an area-wide warrant would help prevent a corrupt building inspector from "shaking down" a particular restaurant owner — if the inspector wasn't required to have such a warrant, the inspector could threaten to conduct a bogus "for harassment only" health inspection of the restaurant premises twice a day for months if the owner didn't pay her a bribe.

[4] The inspector doesn't necessarily have to be in possession of the warrant at the time she ***first seeks to enter the premises.*** Instead, the inspector can take these steps in sequence:

[a] She asks the owner for ***consent*** to the search;

[b] If the owner refuses consent, the inspector can fill out an ***"administrative subpoena"*** stating the parameters of the proposed search (e.g., to inspect all recent occupancy records of a hotel) and hand it to the owner; and

[c] If the owner *still* refuses to permit an immediate inspection, the inspector can have the police temporarily safeguard the premises or records (to prevent the owner or confederates from destroying evidence of violations) while the owner exercises his constitutional right to try to persuade a judge to quash the subpoena before the owner has to allow the inspection.

See generally *Camara v. Municipal Court of San Francisco*, 387 U.S. 523 (1967) (setting forth the above rules, and rejecting a city's claim that no warrant at all should be required under the Fourth Amendment for housing inspections conducted to determine whether municipal housing codes are being complied with).

2. Houses and businesses, generally: The above rules, requiring an administrative "area-wide" warrant, apply both to ***housing inspections*** and to ***safety-related inspections of businesses generally***.

Example: A federal statute (the Occupational Safety and Health Act, or OSHA) purports to allow inspectors from the U.S. Dept. of Labor to search any workplace covered by OSHA during regular working hours, in order to inspect for violation of the OSHA's safety standards. The statute says that the inspector does not need a search warrant before demanding the inspection. D (the U.S. Dept. of Labor) asserts the right to conduct a warrantless search of P's electrical-contracting business premises to see whether OSHA violations are occurring there. P sues D for an injunction against the inspection, asserting that business owners have a Fourth Amendment right to be free of a warrantless non-emergency search of their business premises. D argues that safety inspections like the one proposed here are so important that they are "reasonable" (and therefore constitutional) even when done without a warrant.

Held (by the U.S. Supreme Court), for P. "The businessman, like the occupant of a residence, has a constitutional right to go about his business free from unreasonable official entries upon his private commercial property [and this right would be] placed in jeopardy if the decision to enter and inspect for violation of regulatory laws can be made and enforced by the inspector in the field without official authority evidenced by a warrant." Warrantless inspections of certain types of *closely-regulated* businesses may be permissible (a topic we discuss below), but the Fourth Amendment requires some sort of a warrant before a compulsory regulatory inspection of an ordinary business, such as the one here. *Marshall v. Barlow's, Inc.*, 436 U.S. 307 (1978).

3. Special rule for closely-regulated businesses: As the Court's opinion in *Marshall v. Barlow's*, *supra*, suggests, the Supreme Court has ***allowed*** governments to make warrantless regulatory inspections of certain types of ***closely-regulated businesses,*** though the Court's opinions in this area do not state a consistent rationale for why the fact of close regulation should nullify what would otherwise be a requirement of a search warrant. But a 2015 case says that the exception applies only to businesses that "pose[] a clear and significant ***risk to the public welfare."*** See *City of Los Angeles v. Patel, infra.*

a. What businesses are deemed "closely-regulated": The Supreme Court has, over many decades, identified only ***four types*** of businesses as falling within this "closely-regulated" category for which no prior inspection warrant is required:

[1] businesses that ***sell liquor*** on the premises (e.g., liquor stores and catering halls);

[2] ***firearms dealers***;

[3] ***mining*** businesses; and

[4] ***automobile junkyards***.

See *City of Los Angeles v. Patel*, 135 S.Ct. 2443 (2015) (discussed further *infra*, p. 174), where the Court listed the above four industries as the "only four industries that 'have such a history of government oversight that no reasonable expectation of privacy ... could exist for a proprietor over the stock of such an enterprise'."

Example of closely-regulated business: A New York statute requires that any "vehicle dismantler" (i.e., auto junkyard) must keep purchase and sale records of all vehicles and parts handled by the yard, and show those records on demand to any police officer even without a warrant.

Held, the statute does not violate the Fourth Amendment rights of junkyard operators. Auto junkyards are closely-regulated businesses in New York, and the Supreme Court has long recognized an exception to the requirement of a search warrant in the case of certain closely-regulated businesses. Furthermore, auto junkyards frequently buy stolen cars and stolen car parts, so a system of warrantless inspections is needed to combat car theft (since such inspections must be "unannounced" to be effective, and requiring a warrant would likely interfere with the ability of the police to make unannounced searches). *New York v. Burger*, 482 U.S. 691 (1987).

b. **Hotels are not closely regulated:** One category of business that the Court has held ***not*** to be "closely regulated" is ***hotels***. Therefore, inspectors who are not equipped with at least an administrative search warrant may not demand to make a regulatory inspection of a hotel's registry of guests. See *City of Los Angeles v. Patel,* 135 S.Ct. 2443 (2015), set forth in the following Example.

Example: D (the City of Los Angeles) enacts an ordinance requiring every hotel operator to keep a registry of information about each guest including name, address, license plate number, photographic ID if the guest pays in cash, and other guest data. The ordinance also requires every operator to make this registry available for inspection by any L.A. police officer on demand. The Ps, a group of motel operators, sue D, claiming that by requiring them to furnish such information to the police without a warrant and without any provision for pre-compliance judicial review, the ordinance violates their Fourth Amendment rights.

Held (by a 5-4 vote), for the Ps — the ordinance violates the Ps' Fourth Amendment rights. The ordinance here provides for an "administrative search," i.e., a search whose primary purpose is not crime control — rather, the main purpose is to let the police verify that the keep-a-guest-registry part of the ordinance is being complied with. But even administrative search schemes must normally give the person whose property is being searched the opportunity to have a neutral decision maker (not the officer seeking to do the search) review the reasonableness of the search before the property owner is required to comply.

It's true that owners of businesses in a few types of "closely-regulated" industries (e.g., liquor sellers, auto junkyard operators, etc.) may be subjected to warrantless searches without the owner's having a right to a pre-search review of the search demand by a magistrate. But the closely-regulated industries to which the Court has applied this special no-review regime are all ones which "pose[ ] a clear and significant risk to the public welfare." Nothing inherent in the operation of hotels poses such a risk. Therefore, the Ps have the right not to be searched unless and until a magistrate first reviews the propriety of the inspector's administrative subpoena. ***City of Los Angeles v. Patel***, 135 S.Ct. 2443 (2015).

C. **Immigration searches:** A number of different devices are typically used by ***immigration*** officials to control the influx of illegal aliens into the country, particularly from Mexico. The Supreme Court has held that some of these violate the Fourth Amendment.

1. **Search at border itself:** It is clear that immigration officials may search vehicles at the border itself. In *Almeida-Sanchez v. U.S.*, 413 U.S. 266 (1973), the Court quoted approvingly dictum from *Carroll v. U.S.*, 267 U.S. 132 (1925) to the effect that "Travellers may be stopped in crossing an international boundary because of national self protection reasonably requiring one entering the country to identify himself as entitled to come in, and his belongings as effects which may be lawfully brought in." Such searches may be conducted even if officials do not have any reason at all to suspect that a given vehicle contains illegal aliens or smuggled objects.

   a. **Limit on extent of search:** But the routine, non-probable-cause searches impliedly permitted by *Almeida-Sanchez* and *Carroll* extend only to baggage and vehicle searches, and to personal searches that are not deeply intrusive. Where a search requires the subject to undress, and particularly where anal and vaginal cavities are examined, officials must make a stronger showing of reason to believe that the particular suspect in question is concealing smuggled objects. (But even such "strip" searches may occur on something less than probable cause, especially where there is no less-intrusive way to conduct the search. See, e.g., *U.S. v. Montoya de Hernandez*, *supra*, p. 163, where a very intrusive non-probable-cause "stop" of a suspected "alimentary canal smuggler" was approved.)

2. **Interior patrols and check-points:** Where a search does not occur at the border or its "functional equivalent," however, a somewhat stronger showing of reasonable suspicion is required. A vehicle inside the border and ***not known to have recently crossed the border*** may be stopped and searched only if there is ***probable cause to believe aliens or smuggled objects are present***. *Almeida-Sanchez v. U.S.*, *supra*.

   a. **Roving patrol:** But where immigration officials, as part of a ***"roving patrol,"*** stop a car in the interior not to make a search, but merely to briefly question the occupants, ***probable cause is not required***. The officials must, however, be able to point to ***specific factors*** which give rise to some ***significant suspicion*** that an immigration violation has occurred. As the test is often phrased, there must be a ***"particularized*** and ***objective basis"*** for suspecting that the driver or passenger has committed an immigration violation. *U.S. v. Cortez*, 449 U.S. 441 (1981). The standard is thus similar to that applied in the usual *Terry* warrantless-stop situation. See, e.g., *Brown v. Texas*, *supra*, p. 153.

i. **Mexican appearance insufficient:** The ***Mexican appearance*** of the car's inhabitants is ***not by itself sufficient*** to allow even a brief stop for questioning. *U.S. v. Brignoni-Ponce*, 422 U.S. 873 (1975); *U.S. v. Ortiz*, 422 U.S. 891 (1975).

b. **Fixed checkpoint:** Where a ***"fixed checkpoint"*** is set up in the interior, the Supreme Court has held, ***all*** cars may be stopped. Officials may then refer particular motorists to a "secondary inspection area," where they can be questioned and, if necessary, their cars searched. *U.S. v. Martinez-Fuerte*, 428 U.S. 543 (1976) (dealing with the checkpoint at San Clemente, California).

i. **Criteria:** The criteria which may be used in making these "referrals" to the secondary area are even looser, the Court held in *Martinez-Fuerte*, than are necessary for a roving stop under *Brignoni-Ponce* and *Ortiz*. The Court permitted referrals made "largely on the basis of apparent Mexican ancestry," giving rise to the possibility that Mexican ancestry by itself might be enough to justify the referral.

ii. **No warrant needed:** The Court in *Martinez-Fuerte* also held that it was unnecessary for the authorities to obtain a warrant before setting up a checkpoint. The Court distinguished *Camara*, *supra*, p. 173, on the grounds that house searches are more intrusive than automobile stops, and that the need for preventing hindsight from "coloring the evaluation of the reasonableness of a search or seizure," a factor in the home-search situation, is not present in the car-stop case, where reasonableness is determined by such things as location and method of operation of the checkpoint, factors that are "not susceptible to the distortion of hindsight."

iii. **Dissent:** A dissent by Justice Brennan, joined by Justice Marshall, contended that only stops based upon "reasonable suspicion" were permissible under the Fourth Amendment, and that even if stops of all cars were permissible, referral to the secondary area should be permitted only upon "reasonable suspicion," and certainly not upon the mere fact of Mexican ancestry.

3. **Factory surveys:** Another device frequently used by immigration officials is the "factory survey," whereby agents pay surprise visits to factories and ask each employee questions designed to determine whether the employee may be an illegal alien. Assuming that the factory ***owner's*** Fourth Amendment rights are not violated by the survey (which will often be performed with the owner's consent), apparently no warrant at all will generally be necessary before the agents ask brief questions of the employees (e.g., "Where do you come from?" or "Where were you born?"). This type of brief questioning will normally not constitute a Fourth Amendment "seizure" of the worker at all, so that no "particularized and objective basis" for suspecting the worker of being an illegal alien need be shown. See *INS v. Delgado*, 466 U.S. 210 (1984), holding that no Fourth Amendment seizures occurred during two such factory surveys.

a. **Factual issue:** Of course, such questioning will always raise a factual issue about whether there has been a seizure, which will in turn depend on whether a reasonable person would have believed that he was free to walk away without responding. If such a seizure does take place, the Supreme Court has not yet decided whether the agents must have some particular articulable suspicion (as is required in the "roving patrol" situation) or whether on the contrary all workers at the particular factory may be briefly detained and questioned (as in the "fixed checkpoint" situation).

D. Protection of borders: Apart from immigration, the national interest in protecting the integrity of the nation's ***borders*** may justify other types of inspections where probable cause is lacking:

1. **Search of vessel in water:** Authorities may board for inspection of documents any ***vessel*** that is in waters which provide "ready access to the open sea." *U.S. v. Villamonte-Marquez*, 462 U.S. 579 (1983). They may do so even though they have ***no suspicion at all of wrongdoing***. In so concluding, the Court referred to cases permitting stopping of cars at fixed checkpoints (e.g., *U.S. v. Martinez-Fuerte*, *supra*, p. 176), and pointed out that such fixed checkpoints are not normally feasible in major waterways, since they can be easily evaded. Also, there is no mandatory international system of markings, distinguishing boats from cars, which bear standardized license plates. These distinctions justified treating random stops for document inspection as the analog to a fixed checkpoint for cars, and prevented such stops from being unreasonable searches or seizures under the Fourth Amendment.

2. **Opening of mail by customs agents:** ***Mail from abroad*** may be intercepted and opened by customs agents without a warrant, if there is "reasonable cause to suspect" that the envelope contains narcotics or other contraband. This is true even of first-class mail. This right, the Supreme Court has held, derives not from the fact that opening of the mail is an "exigent circumstance" (the source of the usual automobile exception to the warrant requirement) but from a long-standing, historically recognized exception to the warrant requirement for border searches. *U.S. v. Ramsey*, 431 U.S. 606 (1977).

   a. **Controlled delivery:** If customs agents discover contraband as part of such a warrantless search, they may reseal the package and carry out a "controlled delivery," by which the addressee can be identified when he receives the package, and prosecuted if appropriate. See *Illinois v. Andreas*, 463 U.S. 765 (1083).

E. Traffic stops for general criminal investigation: The problem of protecting the nation's borders, as we have just seen, justifies allowing random traffic stops. But where police want to use random warrantless traffic stops to pursue more ***general criminal investigative objectives***, the Court has generally said ***"no."*** For instance, in a 2000 case, the Court held that even if the police use a fixed highway checkpoint — thus reducing officers' discretion — they may not conduct warrantless traffic stops where the primary purpose is "to detect evidence of ***ordinary criminal wrongdoing***." ***Indianapolis v. Edmond***, 531 U.S. 32 (2000).

1. **Facts:** In *Edmond*, the police set up a series of six checkpoint locations, at each of which they stopped a predetermined number of vehicles. Although the officers checked each driver's license and registration, the primary purpose of the checkpoint was to check for illegal drugs. To this end, the officers conducted a plain view exam of each stopped vehicle from the outside, and a narcotics-detection dog walked around the outside of the vehicle.

2. **Seizure found unreasonable:** By a 6-3 vote, the Court ruled that the stops here, to the extent they were not accompanied by "individualized suspicion of wrongdoing," were unreasonable and thus violative of the Fourth Amendment. The majority opinion, written

by Justice O'Connor, conceded that the Court had authorized suspicionless checkpoint stops under certain circumstances (e.g., border crossings in *Martinez-Fuerte*, *supra*, and sobriety checkpoints in *Michigan v. Sitz*, *infra*, p. 180). But, O'Connor said, the Court had never approved a checkpoint program "whose primary purpose was to detect evidence of ***ordinary criminal wrongdoing***." The program here, since its primary purpose was to detect illegal narcotics, fell into this "ordinary criminal wrongdoing" class, and thus violated the Fourth Amendment.

a. **Rationale:** The majority feared that if the roadblocks here were found constitutional, "there would be little check on the ability of the authorities to construct roadblocks for almost any conceivable law-enforcement purpose. Without drawing the line at roadblocks designed primarily to serve the general interest in crime control, the Fourth Amendment would do little to prevent such intrusions from becoming a routine part of American life."

b. **Distinction:** But the majority made it clear that apart from the border-control and sobriety-checking contexts, other types of special-purpose checkpoints constructed so as to reduce police discretion would be found reasonable and thus constitutional. For instance, the Court indicated that a fixed checkpoint to check compliance with licensing, registration and vehicle-inspection requirements would be valid, so long as police discretion concerning which drivers to stop was minimized. (See *Delaware v. Prouse*, *infra*, p. 179, where the presence of unbridled police discretion was what caused a spot-check scheme to being validated.) Similarly, the majority indicated, the Fourth Amendment "would almost certainly permit an appropriately tailored roadblock set up to ***thwart an imminent terrorist attack*** or to ***catch a dangerous criminal who is likely to flee by way*** of a particular route."[18]

3. **Dissent:** Three members of the Court (Chief Justice Rehnquist, joined by Justices Thomas and Scalia), dissented. The dissenters acknowledged that the primary purpose of the roadblock was to interdict narcotics. But they pointed out that another of the purposes was to check driver's licenses and vehicle registrations. Since as even the majority acknowledged, this purpose would have made the stop valid had it been the sole purpose, the dissenters could see no reason why the presence of a second reason — the pursuit of narcotics — should change the analysis.

4. **Can seek third-party witnesses via roadblock:** In *Edmond*, the roadblock that was found unconstitutional was carried out for the main purpose of finding criminal activity (drug possession) committed by ***the very persons who were being stopped.*** But a post-*Edmond* case shows that *Edmond* will ***not*** cause a warrantless roadblock to be an automatic Fourth Amendment violation if the roadblock's immediate purpose is to seek ***witnesses*** — rather than ***suspects*** — to a ***recent crime***. In that case, *Illinois v. Lidster*, 540

18. The Court showed considerable foresight in making this remark. Less than a year later, in the immediate aftermath of the 9/11 attacks, the police set up various roadblocks, and stopped several passenger trains around the country. In each case, many people were apparently stopped without individualized suspicion, so that the police could check papers and identify anyone who might have participated in the attacks. Had the constitutionality of these stops been litigated, presumably the enormity and time-sensitivity of the law-enforcement need for them would have prevented these stops from being found to be unreasonable and thus Fourth Amendment violations.

U.S. 419 (2004), the Court approved by a 6-3 vote a warrantless roadblock whose purpose was to find witnesses to a recent fatal hit-and-run accident.

a. **Facts:** In *Lidster*, a highway motorist struck and killed a bicyclist just after midnight on a Saturday night; the motorist then drove off without identifying himself. About one week later, at the same time and place, the police set up a highway checkpoint to try to find witnesses to the accident — each driver was briefly stopped and handed a flier asking for help in identifying the driver. D, who had nothing to do with the hit-and-run accident, was arrested for drunk driving when an officer smelled alcohol on D's breath during the stop.

b. **Stop upheld:** A six-member majority, in an opinion by Justice Breyer, ***upheld*** the stop. Breyer's opinion began by holding that the case was distinguishable from *Edmond*. The checkpoint in *Edmond* had been for general "crime control" purposes, and was focused on whether the drivers were stopped were themselves committing a crime. Here, the information being elicited was to help police apprehend not the stopped vehicle's occupants, but ***third persons***. Therefore, *Edmond* did not control.

   i. **"Car not a castle":** Breyer noted that "the Fourth Amendment ***does not treat a motorist's car as his castle."*** Furthermore, *Edmond*'s requirement that cars not be stopped without "individualized suspicion" was irrelevant here, since the stops weren't designed to find suspects. Therefore, warrantless information-seeking stops like the one here were not per-se unreasonable seizures (as general-crime-fighting stops like the one in *Edmond* were), but must instead be evaluated on a ***case-by-case basis.***

   ii. **Reasonable in circumstances:** Breyer then concluded that judged on its ***individual circumstances***, the stop here was ***reasonable***. The "relevant public concern" was "grave." The checkpoint was appropriately tailored, since it took place at about the same day of the week, time and location as the death, making it most likely to turn up someone who had witnessed the accident.[19] Finally, the stop was very brief and nondiscriminatory (all cars were stopped). In sum, the stop was reasonable.

c. **Three partial dissents:** Even the three members of the Court who partially dissented in *Lidster* did not assert that the stop was necessarily unreasonable here. But these Justices would have remanded to the Illinois state courts for an initial determination of whether the stop here was reasonable.

F. **Discretionary stops to verify driver information:** Suppose the police, instead of pursuing general anti-crime objectives, conduct traffic stops in order to ensure that drivers are ***properly licensed*** and their ***cars correctly registered***. In a pre-*Edmond* case, ***Delaware v. Prouse,*** 440 U.S. 648 (1979), the Court indicated that fixed checkpoint stops for this purpose would be acceptable, but that random stops at the discretion of the police for the same purpose violate the fourth amendment.

---

19. Police believed that shift workers at local businesses would likely pass the accident spot at about the same time and day as in the prior week.

1. **Random stops invalidated:** In the scheme at issue in *Prouse*, the police conducted random traffic stops in order to check for proper driver's licenses and car registrations. The police conceded that they had not had probable cause, or even reasonable suspicion, to believe that any particular car stopped (including D's) was being driven in violation of any law. Accordingly, the Court held that the seizure from D's car of marijuana, seen in plain view by the officer as he walked to the stopped vehicle, was in violation of the Fourth Amendment.

2. **Checkpoint scheme to curb discretion:** The problem with the arrangement in *Prouse* was that virtually complete ***discretion*** was given to the police in deciding which cars to stop without suspicion. By contrast, the Court noted, it would probably be constitutionally permissible for the police to set up a check point at which ***every car*** would be stopped to verify compliance with licensing and registration laws. (In the later case of *Indianapolis v. Edmond*, *supra*, the Court quoted this language approvingly.)

G. **Sobriety checkpoints on highways:** Although highway police may not randomly stop cars in order to check for traffic violations, the police may set up a fixed ***checkpoint*** on the highway so as to test for ***drunkenness***. Even though a stop at such a ***"sobriety checkpoint"*** is a "seizure," such stops may be made of all drivers even though the police have no particularized suspicion about any one driver. ***Michigan Department of State Police v. Sitz***, 496 U.S. 444 (1990).

1. **No discretion:** *Sitz* apparently applies only where the police stop ***all*** cars passing the checkpoint. If the police stop less than all, presumably they must have some particularized suspicion before they may stop a specific person; otherwise, the case will be like *Delaware v. Prouse*, *supra*, where random auto stops without reasonable suspicion were disallowed by the Court.

H. **Summary on regulatory traffic stops and checkpoints:** So here's what can be said about the constitutionality of various types of traffic stops done according to a broad regulatory scheme:

Random stops: *Random stops* without individualized suspicion — even if made just for the purpose of verifying driver's license and related information — are ***not permissible***, because they give ***too much discretion*** to the officer. [*Delaware v. Prouse*]

Fixed checkpoint for driver verification: Stops of a ***predetermined number*** of vehicles at a ***fixed checkpoint***, if done for the primary purpose of ***verifying driver and vehicle information*** (license, registration, etc.) are probably ***allowable***, even without individualized suspicion. [Dictum in *Prouse* and *Edmond.*] The same is true of fixed-checkpoint stops for the primary purpose of ensuring ***driver sobriety***. [*Michigan v. Sitz.*] In both of these instances, the stop is being done for narrow regulatory purposes ***related to driving***, so the checkpoint is not unreasonable.

Fixed checkpoint for general crime-fighting: But stops of a predetermined number of vehicles at a fixed checkpoint, done for the primary purpose of ***general crime-fighting*** (e.g., ***finding narcotics***), are ***not allowable*** without individualized suspicion. Allowing such stops would swallow the rule requiring individualized suspicion for anti-crime stops. [*Edmond*]

I. **Capturing the DNA of arrested persons:** The police may, without a search warrant, ***take a DNA sample*** from ***anyone arrested for a serious crime***. That's the result of a 5-4 decision in ***Maryland v. King***, 133 S.Ct. 1958 (2013). *King* means that federal, state and local police may all ***build databases of the DNA of anyone they arrest*** for a "serious offense," and use that data to match suspects with prior or future unsolved crimes.

1. **"Most important":** Justice Alito, at oral argument in *King*, said that it was "perhaps the most important criminal procedure case" that the court had heard in decades. A,S,H,L&L, 2013 Supp., p. 96. Because of the case's obviously great significance, we'll look at it in considerable detail.

2. **Facts:** Alonzo King was arrested in Maryland in 2009 on assault charges — he menaced a group of people with a shotgun. Maryland's "DNA Collection Act" (the "Maryland Act") permitted police to collect DNA samples from any individual who was ***charged*** with an actual or attempted ***crime of violence or a burglary***, even if the person hadn't yet been convicted (or even arraigned). Since the assault charge against King involved a crime of violence, the police — as part of their ***routine booking procedures*** — collected King's DNA sample by ***swabbing the inside of his cheek*** (a ***"buccal sample"***).

   a. **Matches a previous rape:** King's DNA sample was matched against a national database, maintained by the FBI, of DNA samples collected from unsolved crimes. King's DNA turned out to match the DNA taken from a victim in an unsolved 2003 case of rape by a masked intruder. That match led authorities to charge King with the 2003 rape, for which he was eventually convicted.

   b. **D's argument:** King argued on appeal that Maryland law, by authorizing the taking of a DNA sample from him based on ***mere arrest*** — not yet followed by conviction — gave rise to an "unreasonable" search, and thus violated his Fourth Amendment rights. The highest court in Maryland agreed with him, saying that his expectation of privacy outweighed the state's interest in identifying a not-yet-convicted arrestee.

3. **Taking of sample upheld:** By a 5-4 vote, the Court upheld King's conviction, and ***upheld the Maryland Act***. The majority opinion was by Justice Kennedy, who was joined not only by three usually conservative justices — Roberts, Thomas and Alito — but also by the usually-liberal Justice Breyer. (As we'll see in a minute, though, the usually-conservative Justice Scalia dissented.)

   a. **Rationale:** Justice Kennedy agreed that the taking of a DNA swab from an arrestee without consent constitutes a Fourth Amendment search. But, he said, such searches are ***"reasonable"*** (and thus not violative of the Fourth Amendment) because they serve "[a] legitimate government interest[: ...] the need for law enforcement officers in a safe and accurate way to ***process and identify*** the persons and possessions they must take into custody." As Kennedy said at the conclusion of his opinion, the taking of a DNA swab is, ***"like fingerprinting and photographing***, a legitimate police ***booking procedure*** that is ***reasonable under Fourth Amendment***."

      i. **No genetic traits revealed:** Kennedy emphasized that the parts of a person's DNA that are currently stored as samples and used for identification consist solely of ***"noncoding regions"*** of the DNA. That is, the DNA "snippets" being used for matching have ***no known biological function***.[20] Therefore, he noted, the identifying patterns stored in the database, while perfect for identification, do not "show more far-reaching and complex characteristics like ***genetic traits***."

ii. Identification of arrestee, not unknown suspect: Kennedy then pointed to a number of distinct ***law enforcement interests*** that would be served by taking DNA samples from any arrested person. A major such interest is the interest in "***know[ing] who has been arrested*** and who is being tried." The arrestee "may be ***carrying a false ID*** or ***lie about his identity***," and "***criminal history records*** ... can be inaccurate or incomplete." Taking DNA samples will allow the police to check the suspect's criminal history; "[p]eople detained for minor offenses can turn out to be the most devious and dangerous criminals."

iii. Analogy to fingerprints: When police want to verify the identity and criminal history of a suspect whom they have in custody, Kennedy said, they have long used "accepted" means like "comparing the suspect's booking photograph to sketch artists' depictions of persons of interest, showing his ***mugshot*** to potential witnesses, and of course making a computerized comparison of the arrestee's ***fingerprints*** against electronic databases of known criminals and unsolved crimes." The comparison to the taking and matching of fingerprints was especially significant for Kennedy: "In this respect the ***only difference between DNA analysis and the accepted use of fingerprint databases is the unparalleled accuracy*** DNA provides."

iv. Prevention of flight and future crimes: An additional government interest supported by the taking of DNA samples of arrestees is the ***prevention of flight, and future crimes***, by the defendant. There have been "numerous cases in which felony arrestees ***would have been identified as violent*** through DNA identification matching them to previous crimes but who ***later committed additional crimes*** because such identification was not used to detain them."

v. Small burden: Against these weighty government interests, the intrusion posed by a "cheek swab to obtain a DNA sample" is "a ***minimal*** one," Kennedy said. Furthermore, the impact on an arrestee's ***justifiable expectation of privacy*** is relatively ***minor***. Unlike, say, a motorist whose privacy expectation means that he may not constitutionally be subjected to a suspicionless stop at an interior checkpoint,[21] persons arrested for serious crimes have a ***lesser expectation of privacy:*** "Once an individual has been arrested on probable cause for a dangerous offense that may require detention before trial ... his or her ***expectations of privacy and freedom from police scrutiny*** are ***reduced***. [Post-arrest] DNA identification thus does not require consideration of any unique needs that would be required to ***justify searching the average citizen***."

vi. Doesn't reveal genetic traits: Furthermore, Kennedy argued, the fact that the DNA samples being stored with today's technology are "noncoding" regions that

---

20. That's why these DNA portions are sometimes called ***"junk DNA."***

21. Kennedy pointed to *Indianapolis v. Edmond*, *supra*, p. 177, where the Court said that police could not conduct interior checkpoint stops of all drivers without ***individualized suspicion*** of wrongdoing.

"***do not reveal the genetic traits*** of the arrestee" means that the samples are not being used in the manner that poses significant ***privacy*** implications. "If in the future police analyze samples to determine, for instance, an arrestee's ***predisposition for a particular disease*** or other ***hereditary factors not relevant to identity***, that case would present ***additional privacy concerns*** not present here."

vii. Summary: Kennedy summarized the majority's holding this way: "DNA identification of arrestees is a ***reasonable search*** that can be considered part of a ***routine booking procedure.*** When officers make an arrest supported by ***probable cause*** to hold for a ***serious offense*** and they bring the suspect to the station to be ***detained in custody***, taking and analyzing a cheek swab of the arrestee's DNA is, like ***fingerprinting and photographing***, a ***legitimate police booking procedure*** that is reasonable under the Fourth Amendment."

4. Dissent: There were four ***dissenters*** in *King*. Perhaps the most strikingly unusual alignment was that the dissent was written by Justice Scalia, not commonly one to defend the rights of criminal suspects. Scalia's dissent was joined by three usually-liberal justices, Ginsburg, Sotomayor and Kagan.

a. Crime-investigation not a rationale for suspicionless search: Scalia argued that DNA sampling like the one here is ***not really done for the purpose of identifying the suspect***, as the majority claimed. Rather, the sampling is being done for the purpose of ***investigating crimes other than the crime of arrest*** — the previous or future crimes by ***not-yet-identified suspects*** that the police hope the sampling will help solve. Since the police, when they take a DNA sample from an arrestee, normally do not yet have reason to suspect the arrestee of these unspecified other crimes by unknown suspects, the taking of the sample is really a ***"suspicionless"*** search. And, he said, "[w]henever this Court has allowed a suspicionless search, it has insisted upon a ***justifying motive apart from the investigation of crime.***"

b. "Identification" rationale rejected: Scalia rejected the majority's claim that the DNA sampling was justified by the need to ***identify the suspect***. "The Court's assertion that DNA is being taken, not to solve crimes, but to identify those in the State's custody, ***taxes the credulity of the credulous***."

i. Logistics: Scalia described what he said were the "***actual workings*** of the DNA search at issue here." When D's DNA profile was sent to the FBI for matching, it was ***not*** matched against the FBI's database of the DNA of ***already-identified persons***. Rather, it was matched solely against a different FBI DNA database, the agency's "Unsolved Crimes Collection." This matching typically requires — and required here — ***several weeks***, which would inevitably culminate well after the suspect has been arraigned and ***released*** (or not) on bail. In sum, the search (the taking of D's DNA and matching it against samples) "***had nothing to do with identification***" of the arrested suspect. Rather, the purpose and value of the DNA sample-taking, here and in general, consist of "***matching old crime-scene evidence against the profiles of people whose identities are already known.***"

c. Consequence: This "matching old crime-scene evidence" use, Scalia contended, constitutes an ***"official investigation into a crime"*** (as Maryland's own DNA Collection Act characterizes the purpose of the state's DNA collection). But investigations into a crime are precisely the context in which the Fourth Amendment requires ***particularized suspicion*** if there is to be a search, he said.

i. **A "less noble" objective:** Scalia conceded that "[s]olving unsolved crimes is a noble objective[.]" But, he said, crime-solving "occupies a lower place in the American pantheon of noble objectives than the ***protection of our people from suspicionless law-enforcement searches.***"

d. **Prediction:** Scalia predicted that the majority's rationale would not stop at the sampling of persons arrested for what the majority called ***"serious crimes."*** If "identifying" a person arrested for a serious crime justified taking his DNA, why wouldn't the same be true of a person arrested for, say, a ***traffic offense***. He warned, "Make no mistake about it: As an entirely predictable consequence of today's decision, ***your DNA can be taken and entered into a national DNA database if you are ever arrested, rightly or wrongly, and for whatever reason.***"

i. **Protection of innocent:** He noted that no one was arguing against the right of the authorities to collect a DNA sample from anyone actually ***convicted*** of, say, assault (the crime on which D himself had been arrested) — the issue was whether samples could be taken of arrestees ***pre-conviction***. Ironically, he said, "The only arrestees to whom the outcome here will ever make a difference are those who ***have been acquitted of the crime of arrest (so that their DNA could not have been taken upon conviction)." So statutes like Maryland's — allowing for pre-conviction sampling*** — "manage[] to ***burden uniquely the sole group*** for whom the Fourth Amendment's protections ought to be most jealously guarded: ***people who are innocent*** of the State's accusations."

5. **Resolved issues:** Here are the main propositions that *Maryland v. King* seems to establish:

[1] When the police arrest a person for a ***"serious offense,"*** and they ***have probable cause to do so***, they may ***take a DNA swab*** from the arrestee's cheek. Doing so constitutes a "search" for Fourth Amendment purposes, but it is a ***"reasonable"*** search and thus does not violate the Amendment.

[2] At least in this scenario of an arrest for a serious offense based on probable cause, the taking of a DNA sample is ***justified as part of the police "booking procedure,"*** and is thus no different from taking an arrestee's fingerprints or mugshots.

[3] Once the police have validly taken a DNA swap under rule [1] above, they may then apparently (a) ***keep it forever***; and (b) attempt to ***match it with any other sample*** that ever comes into possession of any law enforcement agency. In particular, they may try to match it against DNA from ***unsolved crimes*** committed anywhere, and at any time, even if the unsolved crime has nothing to do with the crime for which the arrest occurred.

[4] Again, at least in this scenario of routine booking where the police have made an arrest for a serious crime with probable cause to do so, the police ***do not have to seek a search warrant*** to take the DNA sample. And it's pretty clear that that's true even if a warrant ***could be easily obtained***. This no-warrant-needed result follows from the *King* Court's finding that the taking of a DNA swab is a reasonable part of police

booking procedures, like the ***taking of fingerprints and mugshots*** (which don't require a search warrant, either). (However, in contrast to the taking of a fingerprint or mugshot, the taking of a DNA sample via cheek swab *is* a Fourth Amendment search.)

6. Open issues: *King* raises and leaves open a lot of issues. Here are some of them:

a. Non-serious crimes: Do the police have the right to take DNA samples from someone who is arrested for a ***"non-serious" crime***? The issue wasn't resolved by *King* itself, because the Maryland Act applied only to certain specified crimes that the majority described as "serious" (e.g., actual and attempted assault). And the majority's opinion seems to apply, explicitly, *only* to arrests for serious offenses. Thus the majority summarized its holding as applying where "officers make an arrest supported by probable cause to hold for a ***serious offense***[.]"

i. Misdemeanors: It's hard to predict whether the Court will eventually ***expand*** the police right to take DNA samples to situations in which the arrest is for, say, a ***misdemeanor***.

(1) Pros and cons: On the one hand, the more minor the crime of arrest, presumably the greater the suspect's ***reasonable expectation of privacy***. On the other hand, if the law-enforcement rationale being served is really to ***"identify"*** the suspect, as the majority claims (rather than to conduct an investigation into crimes other than the crime of arrest, such as "cold cases"), it's hard to see why the ***need*** for suspect identification is any less merely because the crime is minor.[22]

b. Eventual proof of lack of probable cause: Suppose that it later turns out that although the suspect (call him D) was arrested for a serious crime, the police ***lacked probable cause*** to make the arrest, and that the circumstances do not trigger the good-faith exception to the exclusionary rule (see *infra*, p. 348). Should this make a difference to the admissibility of the DNA against D for some other, previously-unsolved crime, that D is linked to by virtue of the computerized DNA matching process? For instance, in *King* itself, if the Court had determined that the police lacked probable cause in arresting D on the menacing/assault charge, would that have deprived the prosecution of the right to use the DNA match on the original unsolved 2003 rape?

i. Probably irrelevant: The answer will probably turn out to be ***"no."*** In general, the Court has been reluctant to extend the exclusionary rule to prohibit the ***"derivative"*** use of illegally-obtained evidence. For instance, where an illegal search leads the police to find a previously-unknown ***witness***, the Court will generally not bar use of the witness's testimony, at least if there's no indication that the original search was motivated by the desire to find such a witness. See *U.S. v. Ceccolini*, 435 U.S. 268 (1978) (*infra*, p. 337). So in the *King* context, as long as there is no evidence that the illegal arrest was ***motivated*** by a police desire to obtain the arrestee's DNA, the Court is likely to hold that the ensuing DNA match may be

22. Scalia's dissent makes this point: "If one believes that DNA will 'identify' someone arrested for assault, he must believe that it will 'identify' someone arrested for a traffic offense."

introduced as evidence of a different crime, even though the police might never have gotten the suspect's DNA without the illegal arrest.

c. National DNA database: If, as the majority asserts in *King*, the rationale for allowing DNA swabs is "identification," will such compulsory swabbing be allowed in ***non-criminal contexts***, too, as long as there is a demonstrated need for identification? Justice Scalia's parade of horribles — that warrantless compulsory DNA sampling for "identification" could constitutionally be required of air travelers, drivers and even public school students — does not seem (to me, anyway) so far-fetched. If that happens, then the long-standing national debate about whether we should have a ***national identification card*** may be made moot, because nearly all of us would likely end up with a Court-sanctioned "DNA identification profile" instantly accessible to any government agency.

i. Privacy interest: But this expansive possibility is not *required* by the majority's rationale. Remember, the majority claimed to be weighing the governmental benefits from "identification" against the impact on the subject's ***reasonable expectations of privacy***, and the fact that the suspect had been arrested on a serious charge was deemed to diminish his reasonable expectations. So perhaps the fact that a presumably-law-abiding citizen wants to fly on a plane, get a driver's license or attend public school will ***not*** be held to so diminish her reasonable expectations of privacy as to cause those expectations to be outweighed by the government's need for identification.

ii. Other ID devices: Notice that very similar issues are raised by ***other emerging identification technologies***. For instance, systems that recognize people based on their ***facial structure*** or the details of their ***retina*** are becoming commercially-available. If DNA swapping is an acceptable means of identification as part of a suspect-booking procedure, presumably facial-feature or retina identification, if reliable, quick and painless, will also be acceptable during booking. (And, indeed, if handheld devices to do this sort of identification become widespread, perhaps the police will be found to have the right to perform such an identification procedure on anyone they reasonably stop, even without an arrest.)

d. Retention for non-crime-ID purposes: *King* also does not say anything about whether the authorities may continue to ***store, and use,*** the DNA sample after the completion of the initial attempt to match samples from unsolved crimes. As far as the Court's present case law goes, the *only* government action with Fourth Amendment implications is the ***initial taking*** of the DNA sample — later government use of the sample seems not to be either a new search or a new seizure for Fourth Amendment purposes. But these later uses may constitute a much ***bigger "invasion of privacy,"*** in the ordinary sense of the term, than the original sample-taking.

i. Genetic traits: For instance, science is increasingly learning to decode information about ***genetic traits, and medical prognoses***, from DNA. Does a person whose DNA sample was taken for "identification" purposes after his arrest 10 years previously have a Fourth Amendment right (or any other constitutional right) to block government from, say, using this genetic/medical information to keep a close eye on people deemed to be ***genetically predisposed to criminal***

activity? The Court's case law does not, so far, indicate a constitutional right to block such use if the sample was originally constitutionally obtained.

ii. **Familial relationships:** A similar issue is posed by government's use of stored DNA samples to identify not the giver of the sample, but some ***relative*** of the giver. Again, there is no indication that government has to worry about the Fourth Amendment when it tries to do this, but the invasion-of-privacy issues are potentially large.

Example: Assume that *A* is properly arrested for a felony, and compelled to give a DNA sample, which is stored in a national database. Years later, an unknown rapist leaves a semen sample. Genetic analysis shows that the unknown rapist must be a first-degree *relative* (sibling, parent or child) of *A*. Therefore, the police closely scrutinize all of *A*'s first-degree relatives (e.g., by asking them to undergo "voluntary" interrogation), figuring that one of them must be the rapist.

Are the police free to do this without implicating the constitutional rights of either *A* or the relatives who are being scrutinized? The Supreme Court has never dealt with this issue or anything like this. But *King* seems to make it likely that the police investigation would be found to be "reasonable," since it's clear that the authorities are properly in possession of *A*'s sample as the result of the original proper arrest.

J. **Supervision of parolees and probationers:** ***Parolees*** and ***probationers*** may be subjected to warrantless searches by officials responsible for them, even if probable cause is lacking. *Griffin v. Wisconsin*, 483 U.S. 868 (1987).

1. **Rationale:** In so concluding, the Supreme Court, in *Griffin*, asserted that "special needs, beyond the normal need for law enforcement, make the warrant and probable cause requirements impracticable" in the parole and probation contexts. Just as there are special needs that justify dispensing with the warrant and probable cause requirements in the case of school searches (see *New Jersey v. T.L.O.*, *infra*, p. 188) and searches of government employees' offices (see *O'Connor v. Ortega*, *infra*, p. 190), so the need to ***supervise*** people who have committed crimes justifies dispensing with the warrant and probable cause requirements.

a. **Standard:** Instead of probable cause and a warrant, all that is required for the search of a probationer or parolee is that it be conducted pursuant to a ***valid regulation*** governing such persons. The regulation at issue in *Griffin* — which was interpreted by the state court system as allowing a search of D's house based upon a police officer's tip that D "had" or "may have had" an illegal weapon at his home — was, according to the Supreme Court, valid.

b. **Search on street:** In fact, the police may subject parolees to a warrantless stop and search at any time ***even if the officer has no grounds to suspect wrongdoing at all,*** so long as this condition is disclosed to the prisoner prior to his release on parole. ***Samson v. California***, 547 U.S. 843 (2006). (It's not clear whether this "no suspicion required" rule also applies to *probationers*, who seem to have greater constitutional rights than parolees.)

K. Pre-trial detainees may be searched: ***Pre-trial detainees*** have at most a ***"diminished"*** reasonable expectation of privacy. Therefore, the detainees may be subjected to cell searches, and may be prohibited from receiving packages or books received from other than publishers. Also, any inmate who receives a "contact" visit from a person outside the institution may be subjected to a strip search, plus a ***search of his body cavities***. *Bell v. Wolfish*, 441 U.S. 520 (1979).

1. **Dissent:** Three dissenters (Marshall, Stevens and Brennan) felt that each of these practices was unconstitutional, since the pre-trial detainee has not been convicted of any crime. The dissenters were especially critical of the body cavity searches, for which they found no pressing need, since all inmates are required to wear one-piece jump suits that would make insertion of contraband into a body cavity extremely difficult.

L. Searches in schools: There are at least some instances in which searches of ***students*** and their possessions ***may*** take place ***without a warrant and without probable cause.*** The Supreme Court has decided three cases on this topic, one involving a search of a student's pocketbook and the other two involving mandatory drug tests for various categories of students.

1. **School officials acting alone:** All three cases involved searches by ***school officials acting alone*** (i.e., not acting in concert with law enforcement authorities). Therefore, we still don't know what the rules are about when school authorities may act in conjunction with the police to perform searches on students without probable cause and without a warrant.

2. **Warrantless search for violation of school rules:** The first of the student-search cases was ***New Jersey v. T.L.O.***, 469 U.S. 325 (1985). In *T.L.O.* the Court held that school officials may search the person and property of a student ***without a warrant***. At the inception of such a search, all that is required is that there be "***reasonable grounds for suspecting*** that the search will turn up evidence that the student has violated or is violating either the ***law*** or the ***rules of the school***."

   a. **Search for smoking violations:** Thus the search at issue in *T.L.O.* (a principal's search of the pocketbook of a high school freshman suspected of violating the school's no-smoking rule) was justified even though there was no probable cause to suspect a criminal violation, because the facts were such that the principal reasonably suspected that he would find cigarettes in the purse.

   b. **Scope of search:** The Court in *T.L.O.* also set forth the standard for determining whether the ***scope*** of the search is reasonable (given that some sort of search is justified at the outset): the search will be permissible in scope "when the measures adopted are reasonably related to the objectives of the search and not excessively intrusive in light of the age and sex of the student and the nature of the infraction."

      i. **Application to facts:** The facts of *T.L.O.* show that a fairly intrusive search may be upheld despite the absence of probable cause. The principal found a pack of regular cigarettes in the student's purse, but at the same time noticed a package of rolling papers in the cigarettes. Because, in his experience, "possession of rolling papers by high school students was closely associated with the use of marijuana," the Court held that he was then entitled to search the purse more thoroughly for evidence of drug use. The Court found it reasonable for him not only to scrutinize the external appearance of other objects found in the purse, but also reasonable for him to open a zippered compartment in the purse, and to read two letters he found there (which implicated the student in marijuana dealing).

ii. **Uncertainty:** The Court in *T.L.O.* was probably *not* saying that a search as intensive as the one there (extending to the opening of the separate compartment in the purse and the reading of the letters) would be justified upon the mere suspicion that T.L.O. had violated school rules. It was apparently only because the official saw the rolling papers that he was allowed to search further for marijuana; similarly, it was only because he found the marijuana that he was entitled to open the zippered compartment and read the letters. Thus at some point, the official's suspicions probably ripened into probable cause to suspect a violation of the criminal law, and from then on the reasonableness of the search was probably dictated by ordinary rules governing criminal investigative searches. (The Court was vague on this issue, however.)

3. **Drug tests:** The other two student-search cases involved a school district's right to require that various categories of students ***submit to a drug test.*** As a result of these two cases, we now know that a school district may, at the least, require ***suspicionless drug tests*** of ***every student who wishes to participate in any competitive extracurricular activity,*** even if the district has ***not yet had a serious drug-use problem.***

a. **Drug tests for student-athletes:** The first of these cases was *Vernonia School Dist. v. Acton*, 515 U.S. 646 (1995), in which the Court held that a school district could require that all ***student athletes*** submit to drug tests, as a condition of participation in interscholastic sports, provided that the results were not shared with law enforcement authorities and the testing was conducted in a relatively unintrusive manner.

b. **Drug tests for all extra-curricular activities:** Then, the Court allowed random drug-testing of ***all middle- and high-school students who want to participate in any competitive extracurricular activity, regardless of whether the district has previously had a significant drug problem. Bd. of Educ. of Indep. School Dist. No. 92 v. Earls***, 536 U.S. 822 (2002).

i. **Facts:** In *Earls*, the small rural town of Tecumseh, Oklahoma imposed a drug-testing policy that required any middle-school or high-school student, before participating in any ***"competitive extracurricular activity,"*** to submit to random drug testing. The policy applied not only to athletics, but also to such interscholastic activities as the Academic Team, Future Farmers of America, Future Homemakers of America, band, choir, pom pon, and cheerleading.

ii. **Policy upheld:** By 5-4 vote, the Court upheld Tecumseh's testing policy. The majority opinion, by Justice Thomas, concluded that the intrusion was "reasonable," even though the drug tests here were imposed upon many more students than in the earlier *Vernonia* case, and even though the school district had far less of a drug problem than the district in *Vernonia.*

(1) **Interference with students not great:** The interference with students' privacy interests was not great, the majority concluded. Students in a public school generally have a ***"limited" privacy interest*** because of the state's

responsibility for maintaining discipline, health and safety. And just as the athletes in *Vernonia* had a lesser expectation of privacy because of the nature of those activities (e.g., the need to undress in locker rooms), so students who participate in "competitive extracurricular activities" "voluntarily subject themselves to many of the same intrusions on their privacy," such as the need for off-campus travel, communal undress, and regulation by faculty sponsors. And the drug tests interfered relatively little with that diminished expectation of privacy, since test results were not turned over to any law enforcement authority, the results were kept confidential, and the only sanction for failure was to limit the student's right to participate in the extracurricular activity.

(2) **Government's interest was great:** Conversely, the ***government's interest*** in being allowed to drug-test was ***substantial***. The majority conceded that the drug problem in tiny rural Tecumseh was not very serious. But, the Court said, "it would make little sense to require a school district to ***wait for a substantial portion of its students to begin using drugs*** before it was allowed to institute a drug testing program designed to deter drug use."

M. Office of government employee: Neither a warrant nor probable cause is required prior to the search of the office of a ***government employee*** by the employer, so long as the search is somehow ***work-related***. *O'Connor v. Ortega*, 480 U.S. 709 (1987). All that is required is that the search be "reasonable . . . under all the circumstances."

Quiz Yourself on
WARRANTLESS ARRESTS AND SEARCHES (ENTIRE CHAPTER)

26. The police had probable cause to believe that a particular recent burglary had been carried out by Wilson, who lived at a known address in the community. There was no reason to believe that Wilson would flee the jurisdiction. The police considered getting a warrant for Wilson's arrest. But before they got around to doing so, one officer saw Wilson walking down the street. The officer went up to Wilson and arrested him for the robbery. The officer then searched Wilson incident to the arrest, and found in Wilson's pocket proceeds from the robbery (namely, a ring). At Wilson's trial for the robbery, he seeks to suppress the ring, on the grounds that it was the unlawful fruit of an arrest that was made without a warrant where a warrant could have been obtained. Should Wilson's suppression motion be granted? ________________

27. Same basic fact pattern as the prior question. Now, however, assume that the police decided that, without getting a warrant, they would go to Wilson's house and arrest him. They rang his doorbell, but he did not answer the door. The police knocked down the door after Wilson didn't answer, and arrested him right inside the hallway. They informed him that he was under arrest, and he did not resist. During a search of Wilson's person they made incident to this arrest, they found the ring in his pocket, as in the above question. May the ring be suppressed on the grounds referred to in the prior question? ________________

28. Same facts as the prior question. Now, assume that the police learned that Wilson knew that they were on to him, and the police were reasonably worried that Wilson might flee. It was a small town, and after hours, so no magistrate was available. The police rang Wilson's bell, saw that there was no answer, knocked down his door and went into his bedroom, where they found him. They then searched the area around his immediate control, and found underneath his pillow a gun which turned out to have been used in the robbery. May the gun be suppressed as the fruit of an unlawful arrest? ________________

29. The police procured a validly-issued warrant for the arrest of Fred on an armed robbery charge. Two officers went to his house to execute the warrant. When Fred did not answer the doorbell, they broke down the door. (Assume that the police acted properly so far). They found Fred asleep in bed in one of the two bedrooms. The two officers handcuffed Fred to the wrought-iron bed. They then searched the rest of the premises, including the other bedroom. In the other bedroom, in a box the size of a package of cigarettes, they found five vials of crack. The robbery charge against Fred was ultimately dismissed, but he was tried for crack possession. At this trial, may he have the crack vials suppressed as being the fruits of an unlawful search? ________________

30. The police had probable cause to believe that a particularly vicious murder had been committed by Gerald. They therefore obtained a warrant to arrest Gerald. They knew that Gerald lived with his brother, Harold, who was also thought to be a pretty nasty character (but who was not directly implicated in the murder for which they were about to arrest Gerald). The three arresting officers rang Gerald's doorbell and received no answer. They broke into the house. In the basement, one of the officers found Gerald waiting with a knife in his hand; that officer disarmed Gerald and handcuffed him.

After this, another officer inspected the second floor of the house, calling out, "Harold, or anybody else who's there, come out with your hands over your head." He then looked in every room, and every closet large enough to hold a human being. In the closet of one of the bedrooms, he found a cache of weapons, which included what was eventually shown to be the murder weapon. It turned out that no one else was home, since Harold was away on vacation. At his murder trial, Gerald has sought to suppress the murder weapon found in the closet, on the grounds that it was the fruit of an unlawful search. Should Gerald's suppression motion be granted? ________________

31. Davies, a state trooper, had long suspected Johnson of illegally possessing and selling handguns without the proper license; Davies knew that Johnson didn't have either a handgun dealer's license or a license to possess a handgun, but Davies didn't have probable cause (just inchoate suspicion, based on local rumors) to believe that Johnson possessed and dealt in these items. While on routine patrol one day, Davies spotted Johnson driving his car with a blown headlight, a minor traffic violation. Davies did not have any reason to believe that Johnson had any handguns in his car at that particular moment. Nonetheless, hoping that he might be able to catch Johnson red-handed with some unlicensed guns in the car, Davies decided to stop him, using the blown headlight as a pretext. He pulled Johnson over and wrote out a ticket for the headlight. While writing the ticket, Davies looked through the car's window and saw a handgun partially hidden under the front passenger seat. Davies then searched the entire car and found a cache of handguns, for which Johnson didn't have the required licenses. Davies seized the handguns. At his trial for illegal possession and sale of handguns, Johnson has moved to suppress the handguns as the fruit of an unlawful search. Should this motion be granted? ________________

32. Two state troopers, Ginn and Cannon, who were sharing a single patrol car, spotted a car traveling 80 mph on a road where the speed limit was 55 mph. The officers pulled the car over, and ordered the driver, John, to get out. State law allowed officers to make a full custodial arrest of any driver driving more than 15 mph over the speed limit. Officer Ginn formally arrested John, put handcuffs on him, searched his body (found nothing incriminating) and placed him in the squad car, where Ginn remained with him. Officer Cannon then searched the entire passenger compartment of John's car. At the time of the search, Cannon did not have any cause to believe that any contraband or evidence of crime would be found. In the back seat of the car, Cannon found John's windbreaker. In the zippered pocket of the windbreaker, Cannon found a vial of crack. At his trial for crack possession, John has moved to suppress the vial of crack as the fruit of an unlawful search. Should his motion be granted? ________________

33. Two police officers, Genson and Hingham, received word that a warrant had just been issued for the arrest of Jim, a local resident, on charges of selling from his car vials of heroin, disguised in prescription-drug vials. The warrant mentioned that Jim customarily drove a late-model white Mercedes-Benz E350. Genson and Hingham happened to be passing Jim's house, and noticed a white Mercedes E350 pull into the driveway. While the driver was still inside, Genson and Hingham approached the vehicle, saw that the driver was Jim (whom they knew personally), told him he was under arrest pursuant to the warrant, asked him to exit the vehicle, handcuffed him, and placed him in the patrol car. Genson then asked Jim, "Do you have any drugs in the car — legal or illegal — or any prescription-drug bottles?" Jim responded, "I don't having any drugs, but in the trunk I've got a couple of empty vials that used to contain Valium." Genson asked for permission to search the trunk, and Jim said, "No way — go get a warrant if you want to do that." While Genson stayed with Jim in the patrol car, Hingham opened the trunk, and saw inside it two apparently-empty vials whose labels said that they contained Valium. (Assume that before Hingham opened the trunk, a reasonable officer in Hingham's position would have had a reasonable suspicion — not amounting to probable cause — that he might find prescription-drug vials there, and that the vials might contain trace evidence of heroin.) Hingham opened the vials, and saw tiny amounts of white powder inside. He submitted the vials for testing; they proved to contain trace amounts not of heroin, but of methamphetamine, a substance of whose sale or possession Jim had never previously been suspected. Jim was prosecuted both on the heroin charge covered by the warrant and an additional possession-of-methamphetamine charge. Jim moved to suppress the vials as evidence on the meth charge. Should the court grant the motion? ________________

34. Officer Glower, an undercover narcotics officer, observed Denton making a series of apparent drug sales on a street corner. Then, in response to Glower's offer to buy heroin from Denton, Denton took off his backpack, removed a plastic baggie containing a white substance, and handed the baggie to Glower in return for a $20 bill. Glower then announced that he was arresting Denton for drug trafficking, and handcuffed him. Glower seized the backpack, opened it, and saw that it contained a laptop computer. While still on the street corner where the transaction and arrest had taken place, Glower opened the laptop's cover, saw a listing for a file named "My Current Inventory," and used the laptop's word processing program to open the file. When opened, the file contained a numbered list of various types of illegal narcotics. While Glower's partner took Denton to the station house for post-arrest processing, Glower printed out a copy of the Current Inventory file and handed the printout to the prosecutor on duty. At Denton's drug trafficking trial, the prosecution has offered the printout as evidence. Denton, after citing the above facts and no other material ones, has moved to suppress the printout as having been obtained in violation of his Fourth Amendment rights. Should the trial judge grant the motion? ________________

35. The state of Calizonia has made it a crime, punishable by up to three years in prison, for a driver who has been properly arrested on drunk driving charges to refuse to submit to a breathalyzer test (which tests a person's Blood Alcohol Concentration or "BAC"). Della, while driving in Calizonia, was pulled over by Officer Graham after Graham saw her driving erratically. As Graham asked Della for her license and registration, Graham smelled liquor on Della's breath, and heard her slur her words. Graham told Della that he was arresting her for drunk driving.

(a) For this sub-question only, assume the following additional facts: Graham, after placing Della under arrest for drunk driving, told her that under state law she was required to submit to a roadside breathalyzer test using a portable machine that Graham had in his patrol car. Della refused to blow into the breathalyzer tube. Graham took Della into custody, and no other attempts were made to test her BAC levels. Della was then prosecuted for violating the compulsory-breathalyzer statute. (The prosecutor decided to drop the underlying drunk-driving charge because no BAC test was ever administered.) Della has now moved to have the breathalyzer charge dismissed, on the grounds that (1) it would have been a violation of her Fourth Amendment rights for the police, acting without a search warrant, to compel her to submit to the breathalyzer test; and (2) it would therefore be a violation of her Fourth Amendment rights to convict her for refusing to take the test. Should the judge grant Della's motion? _______________

(b) For this sub-question only, assume the following additional facts instead of the ones recited in sub-question (a): Graham normally carried a breathalyzer machine in his patrol car, but did not have it with him at that moment. He therefore handcuffed Della to the back of the patrol car, took her to a nearby hospital, and asked her to consent to have blood drawn so that her BAC could be measured. Della refused to consent. Graham and a colleague restrained Della while a nurse forcibly took a blood sample from her veins. (Graham made no attempt to get a warrant authorizing this test. There was in fact sufficient time available to seek and obtain a warrant, because BAC levels decline post-consumption at known rates, so the results of a sample taken even several hours after an arrest can be calibrated to show what the BAC was at the time of the arrest.) The compulsorily-drawn sample showed a BAC well in excess of permitted levels, and high enough to support a charge of drunk driving. When Della was prosecuted for drunk driving, she moved to suppress the blood test results on the grounds that the Fourth Amendment prohibited the police from performing the test without a warrant. Should the judge grant Della's motion? _______________

36. While Officer Griswold was cruising in his patrol car one day, he spotted a car that had apparently just crashed into a tree at the side of the road. He found the occupant, Denker, seriously injured but alive. There were several empty liquor bottles in the car, and Griswold thought he smelled liquor on Denker's breath. (Assume that this was enough to give Griswold probable cause to arrest Denker and test his blood for alcohol level.) Because of the serious injuries, Griswold immediately called an ambulance, and didn't immediately arrest Denker. Griswold thought that the ambulance would be taking Denker to Adams Hospital, so he (Griswold) drove to Adams to find and arrest Denker on drunk-driving charges. But it turned out that Denker had been taken to Bates Hospital instead. By the time Griswold could get to Bates, over two hours had elapsed since the accident.

At Bates Hospital, Griswold immediately placed Denker under arrest for drunk driving. Griswold also wanted to do a blood alcohol concentration (BAC) test on Denker, which requires the drawing of blood. Griswold realized that Denker's BAC had already receded a lot, and would continue to recede, so that as the taking of blood was further delayed it would become harder and harder to make a case for drunk driving. Therefore, without Denker's consent, and without procuring a search warrant (which in this rural area would have taken several hours at that time of night), Griswold instructed hospital officials to take a blood sample from Denker's finger. A BAC test on this blood sample showed that Denker was still past the point of intoxication. Denker was charged with drunk driving. He seeks to have the blood sample excluded from evidence as the fruit of an illegal warrantless search and seizure. Should his suppression motion be granted? _______________

37. Officer Henkle was an undercover "decoy" agent; it was her job to appear prosperous and relatively helpless, so as to induce muggers to attack her. Eugene, a mugger, tried to steal Henkle's purse and necklace. Henkle announced that she was a police officer, and Eugene immediately fled. Henkle followed him on foot until she saw him disappear into a private house. She went up to the front door of the house and, without knocking or ringing the bell, opened the door and went looking for Eugene. Before she found him, she noticed an open cardboard box filled with miscellaneous jewelry and purses, apparently the result of prior (more successful) muggings. She arrested Eugene in his bedroom, then seized the cardboard box. Eugene was charged with one of the prior muggings, and a purse found in the cardboard box was introduced as evidence. If Eugene tries to have the purse suppressed as the fruit of an unlawful search, should his motion be granted? ________________

38. Officer Johnson, while in his police cruiser, received a radio report that a robbery of a 7-Eleven store had just occurred, and that the robber was believed to now be escaping in a blue Ford two-door sedan. Near the scene of the crime, Johnson saw a car meeting that description traveling at a high rate of speed. He stopped the driver, Fred, on suspicion of being a robber, and arrested Fred for the robbery. (Assume that he had probable cause to do so.) Johnson did not search the car at that time for evidence of the crime. (Assume that he had probable cause to do so.) Johnson had the police department tow truck tow the car to the police station, where it was impounded. There, the next day, Johnson (without first having gotten a search warrant) searched the car's passenger compartment and trunk. In the trunk, he found a stocking mask and hold-up note, both of which turned out to have been used in the robbery. Fred has now moved to have these two items suppressed from his robbery trial. Should this motion be granted? ________________

39. For some time, the Ames police department had believed that the recent murder of George's wife, Karen, had been carried out by George. An informant notified the police that he believed Karen's dead body had been transported by George in the trunk of his 1996 maroon Pontiac. The police could have gotten a search warrant; they had probable cause to seize and search the car in connection with the murder investigation. However, they had not gotten around to procuring a warrant, when Officer Karloff spotted George driving the car one day. Karloff had probable cause to arrest George for the murder. Karloff stopped George, arrested him for the murder, and took him and the car to the police station. At the station, Karloff opened the trunk, and searched its contents for blood stains, which he found. These blood stains turned out to be the same type as Karen's blood, and they were introduced against George at his murder trial. May George have the blood stains suppressed as the fruit of an illegal search? ________________

40. Officer Jackson learned from a trusted informant that a white 1998 Buick driven by Harold, license number JRZ970, would be passing by a particular location at a particular time, and that it would contain heroin which Harold was planning to sell at retail. Jackson stationed himself at the appointed place and, sure enough, a 1998 white Buick with the correct license number drove by at the expected time. Jackson stopped the car (assume that he had probable cause to do so), but discovered that it was driven by Leonard, not Harold. Jackson did not arrest Leonard, because he had no probable cause for an arrest. He did, however, search the car, and found a zippered pouch in the trunk. He opened this pouch, and found heroin. The police eventually became convinced that Harold, not Leonard, was the owner of the drugs in the trunk, and Harold was charged with possession of illegal drugs. At his trial, he moved to suppress the zippered pouch as the fruits of a search that was unlawful because it was warrantless. Should Harold's suppression motion be granted? ________________

41. A car belonging to Marvin was towed by the police because Marvin had put insufficient coins in the parking meter, and time had expired. No search warrant was obtained, and the police did not have probable cause to perform a search. Once the car was in the police lot, the police unlocked and searched the car pursuant to a standard police procedure, by which all towed cars are searched, and a list made of all valuables in the car. The purpose of this procedure was to guard against theft by police employees, and also to prevent the owner of the car from making a false claim of theft by a police employee. When the police searched Marvin's car, they looked in the unlocked glove compartment, and found illegal drugs there. At his drug trial, may Marvin get the drugs suppressed as the fruits of an unlawful search? ________________

42. Officer Baines was the head of the Empire City Art Fraud Detection Bureau, a division of the Empire Police Department. Baines had heard rumors that a citizen of Empire, Norma, was forging and selling fake lithographs purporting to be by Salvador Dali. Baines knew that he did not have probable cause either to arrest Norma or to search her premises. Therefore, Baines decided to see if a more consensual approach would work. He rang Norma's doorbell, and when she answered, said to her, "Ma'am, we've heard that some fake Salvador Dali prints may be being made in your apartment. May I have a look around?" Baines did not tell Norma that forging art prints was a crime, and Norma believed that this was not a crime. Norma responded, "Sure, officer."

Baines at no time gave Norma *Miranda* warnings, or otherwise suggested to her that anything he might find could be used against her. Also, Baines did not tell Norma that she had a right to refuse consent, and that if she refused he would not conduct a search at that time because he had no warrant. After Norma approved, Baines took a look around the apartment, and immediately spotted a fake Dali print being manufactured; he left to get an arrest and search warrant, then came back and seized the fake print. At Norma's trial for art forgery, she moved to suppress all fruits of Baines' initial search, on the grounds that it violated the Fourth Amendment. Should her motion be granted? ________________

43. Same facts as the prior question. Now, however, assume that when Baines came to Norma's door, he was not wearing his police uniform. He said, "Ma'am, I'm a local art dealer, and I've heard that you've got a supply of fake Salvador Dalis that I could sell at a nice profit to tourists who don't know the difference between fake and real ones. Mind if I come in and take a look at your inventory?" Norma said, "Why, of course." At this time, she never dreamed that Baines was really a police officer working undercover. Baines spotted a fake print, then used this as the basis to get a search and arrest warrant. May the print be suppressed from Norma's ultimate trial? ________________

44. Same basic facts as the prior two questions. Now, however, assume that wearing his uniform, Baines went to Norma's door, rang the bell, and stated, "I have a search warrant. Will you consent to let me search your premises for fake Dali prints?" Norma responded, "O.K." In fact, Baines did not have, and had never applied for, a search warrant. Baines searched the apartment, found the fake print, and seized it. May Norma get it suppressed as the fruit of an unlawful search? ________________

45. Henry and Wanda were a married couple living together reasonably happily. Officer Lemon had a vague suspicion (but not probable cause to believe) that a rifle owned by Henry had been used to fire the fatal shot in an unsolved murder. Acting without a warrant, Lemon came to Henry and Wanda's house. Henry was not home, but Wanda was. Lemon asked whether Wanda or her husband had a rifle. Wanda replied that there was a rifle that she and her husband both owned and used from time to time. Lemon asked whether he could inspect the rifle and remove it for testing. Wanda, knowing that she herself was innocent of wrongdoing and believing that her husband was also, consented. Lemon looked at the rifle, took it away for testing, and discovered that it had indeed been used to fire the fatal shot. At his murder trial, may Henry get the rifle suppressed as the fruit of an unlawful search? ________________

46. Troy rented one room (a bedroom) in a house owned by Larry. Their arrangement permitted Larry to keep a key to Troy's room, and to enter that room in order to clean it once a week. The police suspected (without probable cause) that Troy possessed drugs. They came to the house, and found Larry (but not Troy) present. They asked Larry for permission to search Troy's room. Larry agreed, and let them use his key. In

Troy's room, the police found illegal drugs. At his drug possession trial, may Troy get the drugs found in his room suppressed? ________________

47. While Officer Noonan was patrolling his beat on foot one night, he saw a car with a broken window and the alarm blaring. When he looked inside the car's window, using his flashlight, he thought he could see that there was no radio in the spot where the radio would normally be. At about the same time, he noticed a young woman (who turned out to be Marla) walking away from the car at a rapid clip, carrying a shopping bag. Noonan did not have probable cause to believe that Marla had broken into the car, taken the radio, or committed any other offense. However, based on Noonan's 20 years on the police force, on the very fast rate that Marla was walking, on the fact that the alarm had only recently gone off, and on the bag Marla was carrying, Noonan had what could best be described as a "solid hunch" that Marla might have done the break-in and taken the radio.

Therefore, Noonan accosted Marla, asked her to stop for a moment, and asked her whether she had anything to do with the sounding of the car alarm. Noonan blocked Marla's way, in such a manner that it was clear to her that she would either have to answer his question or try to escape from him. Marla dropped the bag, apparently in a panic, and began to run. Noonan quickly looked in the bag, saw that it contained a car radio, and chased after Marla. He arrested her, and she was charged with burglary. At her trial, Marla has moved to suppress the radio, on the grounds that it is the fruit of a violation of her Fourth Amendment rights.

(a) What doctrine should the prosecutor cite in attempting to rebut Marla's suppression motion? ________________

(b) Should Marla's suppression motion be granted, in light of the rebuttal you listed as your answer to (a)? ________________

48. Officer Nelson, dressed in plain clothes, walked a foot beat around the neighborhood to try to spot criminal activity. His beat was a high crime area, in which there was an especially large amount of automobile theft. Nelson spotted a red Ferrari pull up and stop at a traffic light. Nelson could tell that the driver was a young black male. Nelson was quite prejudiced against blacks in general, and believed (in this case, quite irrationally) that few young blacks could afford Ferraris, and that this Ferrari was likely to have been stolen. (Not only did Nelson not have probable cause for this belief, but his belief would not even qualify as a "reasonable belief based upon objective criteria.")

Nelson went over to the car, asked the driver to roll down the window, and said, "Do you know where the nearest used-car dealer is?" Nelson was not in fact interested in getting an accurate answer to this question; he merely wanted to see whether the driver was nervous, whether there were lock-picking tools in the car, or whether there was any other sign of criminal wrongdoing. Nelson was prepared to let the car drive on if the driver didn't want to answer his question.

The driver had no idea that Nelson was a police officer. The driver (whose name was Vern) seemed extremely nervous; he tried to drive away, but the car stalled. Nelson saw through the rolled-up window that there did not seem to be a key in the ignition, but rather a series of loose wires hanging out. At that point, Nelson arrested Vern on charges of car theft. (Assume that by that time, Nelson had probable cause to believe that Vern had committed this crime.) At his trial, Vern has moved to suppress Nelson's testimony about what he saw, and any fruit of the subsequent search of the car, on the theory that all of this stemmed from an initial Fourth Amendment violation by Nelson in stopping Vern's car in the first place. Should Vern's motion be granted? ________________

49. Same basic facts as the prior question. Now, however, assume that: (1) Officer Nelson was in his police uniform, rather than in plain clothes; and (2) Nelson, instead of asking for directions, asked Vern for his driver's license and registration. If the rest of the episode transpired as described above, may Vern obtain suppression of evidence stemming from this encounter (including Nelson's testimony about the loose wires sticking out of the ignition)? ________________

50. Officer Mulroney was walking the night beat in a downtown area where there were a lot of office buildings and few nighttime pedestrians. At 1:00 a.m., she spotted a teenager, Evan, who was carrying a heavy desktop computer. Mulroney thought it was strange that someone, especially a teenager, would be carrying a heavy and expensive desktop computer through an office district late at night. Therefore, Mulroney stopped Evan and asked what he was doing. He said that he was borrowing the computer from a friend, and taking it to his apartment. Mulroney said, "Please come with me to the police station. I want to check the serial number of the computer, to make sure it's not stolen." (Assume that at this moment, Mulroney did not have probable cause to arrest Evan.)

Mulroney then escorted Evan to the police station; he made no attempt to resist. Evan was required to wait for 45 minutes while the police checked the serial number against a state-wide stolen property listing. It turned out that the computer was indeed stolen, and Mulroney so informed Evan. At that point, Evan confessed to being the thief. At his trial for burglary, Evan has moved to suppress his confession as the fruit of a Fourth Amendment violation. Should his motion be granted? ________________

51. Officer Pasternak was an experienced cop who had followed the same inner-city neighborhood beat for many years, and who knew almost everybody on that beat. In particular, he knew that Fiona sometimes used drugs (and even occasionally sold them), but he also knew that Fiona was as meek as a church mouse, and would never hurt anybody. One day, he spotted Fiona standing on a street corner, appearing to hand money to a stranger and to receive a package in return. Pasternak reasonably suspected (though he did not have probable cause to believe) that Fiona had just received drugs. He went up to Fiona, briefly detained her, patted the pocket of her coat, felt a soft parcel, and then reached inside. At no time did he suspect that Fiona was carrying a weapon; he did, however, suspect that the soft parcel he felt inside her coat pocket might well be drugs. The parcel did indeed turn out to contain cocaine, for which he arrested Fiona. At her drug-possession trial, Fiona has moved to suppress the parcel as being the fruit of a Fourth Amendment violation. Should her motion be granted? ________________

52. Same basic facts as the prior question. Now, however, assume that Pasternak did not know Fiona, and reasonably believed that Fiona might be carrying either a knife or a gun. After stopping her, he patted her coat pocket, and felt the soft parcel, which he deduced might be cocaine. He reached inside her coat and retrieved the parcel, confirming his suspicions. May Fiona get the parcel suppressed at her trial for drug possession? ________________

53. Every member of the Langdell Police Department had been told to be on the lookout for a blue car (make unspecified) with a license plate beginning with the letters "JQ." This was based on a description from a witness to a bank robbery, who had reported that a car having those characteristics was driven away by the sole robber. Since the robber had fired a shot (which did not hit anybody) during the bank robbery, the advisory said that the robber might be armed and presumed dangerous.

The day after the robbery, Officers Quarles and Ramon spotted a blue Ford whose license plate began with JQ. The officers waved the car over to the side of the street, and saw that it contained a driver (Gerard) and a front-seat passenger (Howard).

(a) Officer Quarles asked the driver, Gerard, to get out of the car. He then asked Gerard whether Gerard had had anything to do with the bank robbery the other day. Gerard denied this, but did so in a manner that did not allay Quarles' suspicion that this might indeed be the bank robber and the getaway car. Quarles then did a pat-down of Gerard, and did not find any weapons. He asked Gerard to put his hands on the front hood of the car, and looked inside the passenger compartment. Quarles' motive in doing so was to find any weapon that might be in the passenger compartment, to which Gerard might get access during their encounter. Underneath the rear seat, Quarles found a bag of marijuana. It later turned out that Gerard was not the bank robber, but he was charged with marijuana possession. At his trial, Gerard has moved to suppress the marijuana as the fruit of an unlawful search. Should his motion be granted?

____

(b) Simultaneously with Quarles' encounter with Gerard, Ramon asked the passenger, Howard, to exit the car on the passenger side. After Howard exited, Ramon noticed that he had a distinctive tatoo marking him as a member of the Tweets, a gang whose members were well-known for (1) usually carrying electronic devices from which they could use Twitter to arrange street crimes and (2) nearly always carrying switchblades. Although at the moment Howard exited the car Ramon had no probable cause to suspect Howard of wrongdoing, he patted down Howard's pockets to see if he was carrying a weapon. Ramon found something hard that he thought might be a switchblade; he removed it from Howard's pocket, and discovered it was a box cutter the possession of which by Howard was illegal due to Howard's status (unknown to Ramon at the time of the encounter) as a convicted felon. At Howard's trial for illegal possession of the box cutter, he has moved to suppressed the cutter. Should his motion be granted?

____

54. Police in the town of Langdell were concerned that a substantial number of drivers were driving without being properly licensed, and were driving unregistered vehicles. The Department embarked on a program of occasional, random "spot checks" to discover and deter this conduct. Each officer was told that approximately twice per day, he or she should pick a car at random, stop it, and ask to see the driver's license and registration. All officers were scrupulously careful to perform this task quite randomly, and thus did not discriminate against blacks, teenage males, or any other recognizable sub-group. Officer Turner randomly selected Donald for a stop; Turner had no objective basis for believing that Donald was especially likely to be driving without a license, driving an unregistered car, or otherwise committing any traffic violation. After Turner asked Donald for his license and registration, he observed that Donald's speech was somewhat slurred, and smelled liquor on Donald's breath. Donald indeed turned out to be driving while drunk, and was prosecuted for this offense. May Donald suppress all evidence resulting from the stop (and thus the entire case), on the grounds that it stemmed from a violation of his Fourth Amendment rights?

____

55. A statute of the state of Erewon provides that whenever a person is arrested for any of certain specified crimes — including rape, murder, aggravated assault and burglary — a sample of that person's DNA may be taken as part of police booking procedures. The statute specifies that the sample is to be taken by requiring the arrestee to open his mouth, and then swabbing the inside of his cheek to gather some cells. Acting with probable cause but without a search or arrest warrant, the police arrested Devon for having burglarized a private premises the night before. The arrest took place while Devon was walking through a park. At the police station, the police took a DNA swab in accordance with the statutory procedure. Devin was then released on bail. Meanwhile, the DNA sample was sent to an out-of-state laboratory. Three months later, the FBI reported that Devon's DNA matched a sample from the scene of a never-solved murder that had been committed in Erewon in 2008. At Devin's trial on the 2008 murder, the prosecution relied heavily on the DNA match, and conceded that without that match, the police would never have had occasion to suspect Devon of that murder. Devon now objects to the introduction of the DNA evidence, claiming that his Fourth Amendment rights were violated when the DNA sample was taken without a search warrant, under circumstances in which there were no exigencies preventing the police from getting such a warrant. Putting aside the issue of the proper remedy for any illegality, is Devon correct in asserting that the taking of the swab was a violation of his Fourth Amendment rights? _______________

Answers

26. No. Arrest warrants are as a general rule not constitutionally required. This is true even where the police have sufficient advance notice that procurement of a warrant would not jeopardize the arrest. See *U.S. v. Watson*.

27. Yes. The only situation in which an arrest warrant may be constitutionally required is where the police wish to ***enter private premises*** to arrest a suspect. If there are no exigent circumstances (e.g., a serious threat that the suspect will flee or will destroy evidence), the police may not enter a private home to make a warrantless arrest.

28. No, probably. The police may enter even private premises to make a warrantless arrest, if there are ***exigent circumstances*** that make it impractical for the police to delay the entry and arrest until they can obtain a warrant. Since the crime was a serious one here, and there was reason to believe that Wilson might flee at any moment, the requisite exigent circumstances seem present. If the police were entitled to enter Wilson's premises at all for this purpose, they were entitled to go throughout the house until they found him, so the fact that they intruded further than in the prior question is irrelevant. Once they arrested him, they were entitled to search the area around his control as a search incident to arrest (at least for purposes of protecting themselves), and were entitled to seize any weapon they found as a result of that limited search.

29. Yes, probably. The police will, of course, argue that the search took place incident to a valid arrest, and that the fact that there was no search warrant is therefore irrelevant. But the search-incident-to-arrest exception to the normal requirement of a search warrant (an exception that stems from *Chimel v. California*) covers only the area within the arrestee's ***possible control***. Since there were two officers, and since Fred was already handcuffed to the bed, it was very unlikely that Fred could get into the other bedroom to seize any weapon that might have been present there. Also, it was quite unlikely that any weapon would be in something as small as the container here. Therefore, it seems very unlikely that the search of that container aided the police's interest in protecting their safety or protecting against the destruction of evidence, the two reasons for the search-incident-to-arrest exception.

30. No, probably. The search of the closets here cannot be justified as a search incident to the arrest of Gerald, since the area of the search went far beyond any area to which Gerald could possibly have had ready access once he was handcuffed. But the Supreme Court has held that once an arrest takes place in the suspect's home, the officers may conduct a ***protective sweep*** of all or part of the premises, if they have a "reasonable belief" based on "specific and articulable facts" that ***another person*** who might be dangerous to the officer may be present in the areas to be swept. *Maryland v. Buie*.

While doing such a protective sweep, the police may not make a detailed search of the premises, merely a cursory look to make sure that there is no one else around who may be dangerous. This seems to be what the officer was doing, since Harold was known to live at that address and thought to be possibly dangerous; also, the degree of risk was magnified by the fact that Gerald was found in the basement holding a knife, indicating that he had somehow learned of the possibility of the arrest (so that he could have tipped off Harold as well). Since weapons were found in a closet large enough to hold a man, and thus large enough to be a proper subject of the protective sweep, the officer probably acted legally in opening that closet. Once he rightfully opened the closet, he had the right to seize anything that was in plain view, including the murder weapon.

31. No. A stop of a driver is not made "unreasonable" (and thus does not violate the Fourth Amendment) merely because the stop was based upon a minor traffic violation that served as a pretext for a stop made for some other purpose. *Whren v. U.S.* In other words, the real reason for the stop is ***irrelevant*** — once a police officer has probable cause to believe that even a minor traffic violation has occurred, he may stop the vehicle even though the stop is being used for the purpose of seeking evidence of some other crime for which the police officer has no probable cause or even reasonable suspicion. If the stop and its consequences then give the officer probable cause to believe that contraband or evidence of crime may be found in the car, the officer may go on to make a warrantless search.

In this "pretext stop" situation, you must look for ***two elements***: (a) a ***valid reason for the original stop*** (i.e., probable cause to believe some sort of offense has been committed, or at least an objective reason for suspecting criminality [see "stop and frisk," *supra*, p. 148]); and (b) something (perhaps something that only occurs as a result of the stop) that then gives the stopping officer ***probable cause*** to conduct a ***warrantless search***. For instance, suppose Davies had stopped Johnson, written the ticket, and then searched the entire car *without* first seeing the handgun under the front passenger seat. Under these facts, (b) would not be satisfied, and Davies would *not* have had probable cause to conduct a warrantless search of the car; therefore, the seizure of the handguns *would* be suppressed at trial. See *Knowles v. Iowa* (where officer makes stop for traffic ticket and does not make arrest, officer may not without more conduct search of car's interior).

32. Yes. The arrest of John was clearly proper — since the police directly observed the speeding, they had probable cause to arrest John for it. But the legal consequences of that arrest — in terms of what search of the car the police were entitled to perform — changed dramatically in 2009. Prior to 2009, the law (under *N.Y. v. Belton* (1981)) was that if the stop of a car and the arrest of the driver were valid, the police could automatically, incident to the arrest, make a search of the car's entire passenger compartment, and of the contents of any containers found in that compartment. But in *Arizona v. Gant* (2009), the Court effectively overruled *Belton*. *Gant* holds that even where the police make a custodial arrest of the driver, if they are able to secure the driver so that he cannot gain access to the passenger compartment, the police may not then use the search-incident-to-arrest rationale to search the compartment.

So here, where the arresting officers had handcuffed John to the patrol car, they did not have to worry that he could get access to the passenger compartment. Consequently, the officers could not search the passenger compartment incident to John's arrest, even though the arrest was proper. Nor was there any other exception justifying a warrantless and without-probable-cause search of the compartment; for instance, at the moment the police started that search they had no probable cause to suspect that drugs or contraband would be found. (On the other hand, if the police had found drugs on John's person when they properly searched his person pursuant to the arrest, then this discovery *would* have supplied probable cause to search the passenger compartment for drugs; there would still be an issue about whether a warrant was required, but the mobility of the car, and the easy destructibility of any evidence or contraband in it, meant that the circumstances qualified for the exigent-circumstances exception to the requirement of a warrant, in which event the follow-on search of the compartment would have been valid.)

33. No. The 2009 decision in *Arizona v. Gant* says that it is no longer the case that when the police make a valid custodial arrest of a driver and ensure he has no further access to the passenger compartment, they have the automatic right to search the entire compartment incident to that arrest. (By the way, even pre-*Gant*, the search-incident-to-arrest rule would have only extended to the passenger compartment, not to the trunk.) However, *Gant* also says that if the police who are making the arrest "reasonabl[y] believe that evidence *relevant to the crime of arrest* might be found in the vehicle," they may use the search-incident-to-arrest rationale as authority for searching any part of the vehicle (and any containers found in the vehicle) where such evidence might be found, even though vehicle is no longer within the immediate control of the arrested driver. This "reasonable belief that evidence might be found" standard is clearly less-demanding than "probable cause."

The police here qualify under this rule. The facts tell us that Officer Hingham had a "reasonable suspicion" that the trunk might contain prescription-drug vials, and that those vials, if they were found, might contain trace evidence of heroin. Since Jim was being arrested for selling heroin from prescription-drug vials, Hingham's suspicions related to the "crime of arrest." Therefore, even though Hingham did not have full probable cause to believe the vials would contain contraband or evidence of crime, he was entitled to make a search incident to arrest of the trunk (the place to which the "reasonable suspicion" pointed), and then to make a search of any containers in the trunk if such suspected evidence of the crime of arrest (heroin sales) might be found in those containers. Once he found the vials, any contraband they turned out to contain could be the basis for criminal charges as to a crime (meth distribution) different from the crime of arrest (heroin trafficking), to which the reasonable-suspicion pertained.

34. Yes. The Supreme Court has recognized an exception to the general search-incident-to-arrest doctrine for ***digital cell phone data***, and this exception would almost certainly be extended to cover digital data on laptops.

Under the general search-incident-to-arrest exception to the requirement of a search warrant, the Supreme Court has long allowed the arresting officer to seize and search any ***physical item*** found on the person of the arrestee, or within the arrestee's reasonable area of control. A backpack carried by the arrestee would almost certainly qualify, so Glower would have been justified in opening and examining, say, a letter or photo found in hard-copy form inside the backpack. But in a major 2014 decision, *Riley v. California*, the Court decided that the incident-to-arrest doctrine does ***not*** authorize the police to make a warrantless search of digital data on a cell phone, even incident to a perfectly legal arrest — the Court's rationale was that people carry such huge amounts of personal data on their cell phones that the interference with privacy that would result from warrantless searches of that data would be unreasonably large. Although *Riley* applies expressly only to data on cell phones, the Court's reasoning would almost certainly apply to the potentially even larger amounts of data on a laptop computer. Therefore, the Supreme Court would almost certainly hold that even though the arrest here was proper and made with probable cause, the police were required to obtain a search warrant before opening the laptop and examining its digital contents. If there were particular *exigent circumstances* present — e.g., if Glower had had reason to believe that the laptop was set up to erase itself within a short period of time — those circumstances might have justified Glower's immediate examination of the data without first seeking a warrant; but the fact pattern, by telling you that Denton did not allege any "other material facts" in his suppression motion, indicates that no such exigent circumstances existed.

35. (a) No. The Supreme Court has held that when the police have made a proper arrest for drunk driving (i.e., one supported by probable cause), they do not violate the arrestee's Fourth Amendment rights by requiring her to submit to a breathalyzer test as a form of search incident to arrest. *Birchfield v. North Dakota* (2016). That's because a breathalyzer test — which requires the suspect to blow into a tube for a few seconds — is relatively non-intrusive, and the governmental need to deter drunk driving is very great.

Since it would not be a violation of Della's Fourth Amendment rights for the police, after lawfully arresting her on drunk-driving charges, to make a warrantless demand that she undergo the breathalyzer test, it also was not a violation of her rights for the state to make her refusal to take such a test a crime. *Id.*

(b) Yes. In the same case referred to in part (a) above (*Birchfield v. No. Dakota*), the Supreme Court held that in contrast to a breathalyzer test, a *blood test* is so intrusive — and the information it supplies is so unlikely to be materially more useful than information from a breathalyzer test — that it *does* violate the Fourth Amendment rights of a drunk-driving arrestee to be forced to undergo such a test if the police have not procured a search warrant. In other words, in the case of drunk-driving arrests, the search-incident-to-arrest doctrine does *not* cover a search that takes the form of a blood test. Therefore, Graham either should have administered a warrantless breathalyzer test, or kept Della in custody until Graham was able to get a magistrate to issue a search warrant. (Had there been *exigent circumstances*, such as reasonable grounds to test for other substances of abuse that wouldn't be revealed by breathalyzer test, coupled with too little time to procure a search warrant before these other substances would likely have disappeared from Della's bloodstream, the exigent-circumstances exception to the warrant requirement might have applied; but there is no indication on our facts that any such exigent circumstances existed, and *Birchfield* makes it clear that the ordinary incident-to-arrest exception to the warrant requirement does not apply to blood tests.)

36. No, probably. The taking of the blood sample here clearly constituted a Fourth Amendment "seizure." Since it was done without a warrant, it violated Denker's Fourth Amendment rights unless some exception to the usual requirement of a search warrant applies. The search-incident-to-arrest exception does not apply, because there was no formal arrest (even though there was probable cause for one).

However, the Supreme Court has recognized that where probable cause to search exists, and where ***exigent circumstances*** make it impractical to take the time to procure a search warrant, an exception to the warrant requirement will be recognized. In the case of a Blood Alcohol Concentration (BAC) test to support a drunk-driving charge, the Court has held that the police do not have a "*per se*" or automatic right to carry out a warrantless taking of blood. *Missouri v. McNeely* (2013). Rather, each BAC-testing case is to be decided on its own facts — the trial ourt is to decide whether the facts of that particular situation indicated that a delay for getting a warrant would have substantially prejudiced the usefulness of the BAC test. *Id.*

Here, given Griswold's honest error about where Denker was being taken, the substantial loss of time before Griswold even got to the right hospital to make the arrest, and the unavailability of a quick warrant in this rural area, a court would probably hold that the likelihood of a further lowering of Denker's BAC constituted exigent circumstances, thus excusing the failure to take the time to get a warrant.

37. No. Normally, a police officer may not enter a private home to make a search, even with probable cause, unless a warrant has been procured. One of the common exceptions to this rule is for a search incident to arrest, but the police may ordinarily not enter a private dwelling to make an arrest without an arrest warrant. However, there is an exception to both the search warrant and arrest warrant requirements where the police enter a private dwelling in ***"hot pursuit"*** of a suspect. Since Henkle was in hot pursuit of Eugene at the time she entered the house, the exception applies. Since she was entitled to be in the house while looking for him, anything she saw there could be seized without a search warrant under the "plain view" doctrine. See *Warden v. Hayden*, allowing the seizure of evidence under similar "hot pursuit" circumstances.

38. No. This was a warrantless search, so Fred's motion must be granted unless some exception to the search warrant requirement applies. The search-incident-to-arrest rationale cannot apply, since the search took place a significant time after the arrest. Nor does the "routine inventory search" exception apply (see *Illi-*

nois v. Lafayette), since there is nothing in the facts to suggest that the car's contents were being subjected to a routine inventory itemization.

But in a series of cases, the Supreme Court has recognized a ***"vehicle impoundment"*** or "station house search" exception to the warrant requirement: where the police have probable cause to both search and seize the car, and they exercise the right to seize it by taking it to the police station, they need not get a warrant before later searching the car's contents. See, e.g., *Chambers v. Maroney*, allowing a warrantless station-house search of the impounded car under similar circumstances. This exception to the warrant requirement for an impounded vehicle seems to stem from the Supreme Court's perception that "one has a lesser expectation of privacy in a motor vehicle because its function is transportation and it seldom serves as one's residence or the repository of personal effects...." *U.S. v. Chadwick*.

39. No, probably. As set forth in the prior answer, the Supreme Court has generally recognized an exception (stemming from *Chambers v. Maroney*) to the search warrant requirement where an automobile is seized at the time of its owner's arrest, then taken to the police station and searched there. The question is whether the fact that the police had lots of time to get a warrant and didn't bother to do so makes a difference. *Florida v. White* strongly suggests that the answer is no, i.e., that the failure to get a warrant when there is time to do so does not make the eventual warrantless seizure unlawful. (In *Fla. v. White*, the police failed to get a warrant to seize a car that they knew was used for drug dealing; this failure did not make the police's later seizure of the car under state forfeiture laws a violation of the owner's Fourth Amendment rights.)

40. No, probably. For the police conduct here to be valid, two different rules must be combined. First, the doctrine of *Carroll v. U.S.* holds that where the police stop a car and need to perform a search in order to preserve evidence (because the car can quickly be driven out of the jurisdiction), they may search the car without a warrant even though no arrest has been made. (They must have probable cause to make the search, however.) Second, the Court held in *U.S. v. Ross* that where a warrantless search (with probable cause) of a lawfully-stopped vehicle is allowed (i.e., the *Carroll* doctrine applies), the police may also open any ***closed container*** which they find during the search, on the theory that the intrusion is not materially greater. Since Jackson had probable cause to stop the vehicle, and then probable cause to search it, he was also entitled to open containers that he found in it. This was true even though he had not arrested Leonard, so that the search-incident-to-arrest rationale does not apply.

41. No. If a car is impounded because it has been towed for some kind of traffic or parking violation, the car may be subjected to a warrantless ***"inventory search."*** This is true even though the police do not have probable cause at the time they make the search. *South Dakota v. Opperman*. (In fact, the police may even open closed containers found in the vehicle, if they do so as part of standardized procedures that apply to every towed or impounded car. *Colorado v. Bertine*.)

42. No. This is a classic situation demonstrating that where a person ***voluntarily consents*** to a search, any Fourth Amendment objections she might have are waived. Nothing in the facts suggests that Norma's consent was other than voluntary — there is no sign, for instance, of coercion or deception by Baines. The fact that Baines did not give Norma her *Miranda* warnings or otherwise advise her of the possible consequences of the search is irrelevant — there was no arrest, so *Miranda* warnings were not required, and the Supreme Court has never held that anything like the *Miranda* warnings must be given before permission to search is requested. Nor does it make any difference that Norma thought she had not committed a crime.

43. No. "When an individual gives consent to another to intrude into an area or activity otherwise protected by the Fourth Amendment, aware that he will thereby reveal to this other person either criminal conduct or evidence of such conduct, that consent is not vitiated merely because it would not have been given but for the non-disclosure or affirmative misrepresentation which made the consenting party unaware of the other person's identity as a police officer or police agent." L&I, p. 207. Here, Norma knew, at the time she let Baines into the house, that she would thereby expose her art fraud to him. The fact that she didn't know he was a police officer should make no difference. Her consent will be deemed "voluntary," and thus effective.

44. Yes. Where the consent to search was procured after the officer falsely stated that he had a search warrant, the consent will be deemed to be invalid. *Bumper v. North Carolina*. In this case, it is easy to see that the person's consent is not really "voluntary" — the person is or may be responding to the fact that a refusal to consent will be meaningless because the officer has a warrant.

45. No. If the third person and the defendant have joint authority over the premises or over an object, the third party's consent to a search (given while the defendant is absent) will normally be binding on the defendant. Where a husband and wife live together, they will almost always be presumed to have joint control over the premises, and the facts here tell us that Henry and Wanda both had ownership and control over the rifle. Therefore, Wanda had authority to consent to the search of the premises and the search and seizure of the rifle, so her consent will be binding on Henry. The fact that Wanda was mistaken about her husband's guilt or the danger from consenting to a search is irrelevant.

46. Yes. This is not a case in which the two parties, Troy and Larry, had "joint authority" over the premises. Instead, Troy had a vastly greater right of access to, and expectation of privacy in, his bedroom. Therefore, Larry did not have joint authority over the room, or even "apparent" authority (since it should have been clear to the police that Larry was merely a landlord, not a joint occupant, of the bedroom). Therefore, Larry's consent was not effective vis-a-vis Troy. See *Stoner v. California* (the management of a hotel may not consent to a search of a guest's room).

47. (a) The "stop and frisk" doctrine. By this doctrine, an officer may stop and briefly detain a person, even without probable cause for an arrest, if the officer has an ***articulable reason, based on objective facts,*** for suspecting that the person may have committed a crime. (The officer may also do a superficial frisk of the suspect if he has reason to believe the suspect dangerous, an aspect not at issue on these facts.)

(b) No. The "stop and frisk" doctrine applies here. The stop of Marla was certainly a Fourth Amendment "seizure," since it was reasonably apparent to Marla that she was not free to leave without answering Noonan's questions. However, this is a situation in which the "stop and frisk" doctrine makes the Fourth Amendment seizure a "reasonable" one even though there was not full probable cause for an arrest. Noonan certainly had a number of objective reasons for suspecting that Marla might have something to do with the break-in. The fact that the break-in had just occurred, that the alarm had just started, that Marla was walking more rapidly than a person usually would, and that she was walking away from the car holding a bag that might easily contain a radio — all of these factors were, when taken together, enough to raise the kind of "reasonable hunch" that would justify at least a brief stop. (For instance, *Ill. v. Wardlow* establishes that the fact that a person appears to be fleeing from the police is a factor that will usually significantly raise an officer's level of suspicion.)

And, by the way, the fact that each individual factor that Noonan relied on (e.g., fast walking away from a car) was "innocent" or "consistent with lawful behavior" doesn't change this — the reasonableness of the suspicion is evaluated under the ***"totality of the circumstances"*** standard (see *U.S. v. Arvizu*), and under the totality of circumstances here Noonan's suspicion was reasonable.

Then, once Marla refused to answer the questions, ran away, and left a bag holding a radio, Noonan of course now had probable cause to arrest her.

48. No. This question, at first glance, seems to involve the issue of whether Nelson had enough suspicion to make a "stop" of the *Terry* "stop and frisk" variety. However, in reality, no stop (or other Fourth Amendment seizure) occurred at all. In deciding whether a Fourth Amendment seizure has occurred, the Supreme Court uses a "reasonable person" test, by which a seizure has occurred only "if, in view of all of the circumstances surrounding the incident, a reasonable person would have believed that he was not free to leave." *U.S. v. Mendenhall.*

Vern did not know, initially, that Nelson was a police officer, or that he was anything other than what he purported to be, which was a civilian who wanted directions. Therefore, a reasonable person in Vern's position would have believed that he was free to disregard the request for information and to drive on. Since Vern's freedom of motion was not circumscribed, there was no Fourth Amendment "seizure" of his person or of his vehicle, up till the moment where Nelson saw the hot-wiring and made the arrest. Therefore, it didn't matter that Nelson had absolutely no rational grounds for suspicion at the time he walked up to the car and requested the information.

49. Yes, probably. Here, there was a true "seizure" within the meaning of the Fourth Amendment — Vern knew he was dealing with a police officer, and a reasonable person in his position would have understood that he was not free to disregard Nelson's request and drive away. Therefore, the "stop" violated the Fourth Amendment unless Nelson had a "reasonable suspicion, based on objective facts, that the [suspect] is involved in criminal activity." *Brown v. Texas*. The facts tell us that he did not — for instance, the fact that Vern "looked suspicious" and was seen driving in a high crime area will not suffice to justify a stop. Since Nelson would not have gotten his "plain view" through the window if he had not made the stop, and since the stop was an unreasonable seizure (even though it did not amount to a full arrest), presumably the fruits of that plain view will be suppressed.

50. Yes, probably. The initial stop probably did not violate the Fourth Amendment — the facts here suggest that Mulroney had "reasonable suspicion, based on objective facts" that the computer may have been stolen and that Evan either stole it or knew that it was stolen. She was therefore entitled to detain him briefly, and to question him briefly. But she was almost certainly not entitled to require him to come to the station house to answer additional questions — this was such a more intrusive procedure, and of such greater duration, that it probably raised the episode from a "stop" to a full-fledged arrest, for which probable cause was required. See *Hayes v. Florida*, holding that a station-house detention, even though brief and unaccompanied by interrogation, is "sufficiently like [an] arrest to invoke the traditional rule that arrests may constitutionally be made only on probable cause."

There is some chance that the prosecutor can succeed with the argument that the police worked as rapidly and unintrusively as possible, consistent with their need to discover whether a particular computer with a particular serial number was indeed stolen. But this argument will probably be rejected on the grounds that the time and distance were simply too great to constitute a stop. Since Evan confessed only after the police learned that the computer was stolen, he has a very good chance of having his confession ruled the fruit of the illegal pseudo-arrest.

51. Yes, probably. Pasternak was acting properly when he detained Fiona, since his suspicions were sufficiently reasonable and objective that they justified a "stop," even though not a full-fledged arrest. An officer, once he has made a lawful stop, is entitled to do a protective two-part frisk (first a pat-down, then a reaching under the surface if the pat-down discloses something), provided that the pat-down is for a ***weapon***. Even where an officer has made a legitimate stop, he may not perform a frisk whose sole purpose is to find contraband or evidence. *Ybarra v. Illinois*. Since Pasternak did not suspect that Fiona was armed or dangerous, and he was merely frisking her to find the contraband, this frisk was unlawful since he did not have probable cause to arrest her or probable cause to believe that he might find contraband. Because the frisk went beyond the bounds of the Fourth Amendment, the fruits from that frisk (the packet) must be suppressed.

52. Yes, probably. On these facts, as opposed to those of the prior question, Pasternak was at least justified in conducting the initial pat-down to discover whether Fiona carried a weapon. But since Pasternak was looking for a knife or a gun (and certainly knew that virtually any dangerous weapon would have to be hard), he could not have believed that the soft object he was feeling could be a weapon. The second stage of a frisk (the reaching in to take out the item that was located through the pat-down) may only be accomplished to take out something that might reasonably be a weapon. So Pasternak was not entitled to reach into Fiona's pocket to retrieve the soft parcel.

53. (a) No. First, the officers were justified in performing a "stop" of Gerard's car — relatively few cars are both blue and have a license plate starting with "JQ," so this combination of factors was enough to justify a stop, even though it did not amount to probable cause for a search or arrest. Quarles was also within his rights in asking Gerard to leave the car, since that was a reasonable safety measure; the description of the bank robber as "armed and presumed dangerous" was enough to justify Quarles in performing the pat-down of Gerard.

The Supreme Court has also held that in circumstances where the officer makes a *Terry*-like stop of a vehicle and believes that the driver may be dangerous, the officer can not only perform the pat-down but also check the inside of the passenger compartment (even if the driver has been asked to exit); see *Michigan v. Long*, to this effect. (And nothing in *Arizona v. Gant*, eliminating the police's automatic right to search the passenger compartment incident to a driver's arrest, changes this fact, since the search here was a *Terry/Long* officer-safety check, not a search incident to arrest.) Since Quarles had the right to look for weapons (although not to look for the purpose of finding contraband or evidence), he was entitled to seize any contraband that he found in plain view while performing this weapons scan. Therefore, the marijuana should be admissible.

(b) As discussed in part (a), the officers were justified in performing a "stop" of the car. Once a proper *Terry/Adams*-style stop of a vehicle occurs, the police are entitled to do a pat-down of any passenger — even one as to whom they have no suspicion of wrongdoing — as long as the police have a reasonable suspicion that the passenger may be armed and dangerous. *Arizona v. Johnson* (2009). Once Office Ramon saw Howard's tattoo and understood that it marked Howard as a member of the Tweets, Ramon's knowledge that Tweets members typically carry switchblades gave him a reasonable suspicion that Howard might be armed and dangerous. (In *Johnson* itself, for instance, the officer's discovery that the passenger was a member of the often-violent Crips gang and had been in prison was enough to create a reasonable suspicion that the passenger might be armed and dangerous.) Therefore, Ramon was permitted to pat Howard down for weapons. Since he thought the hard object he felt was a weapon, he was entitled to pull it (a Fourth Amendment seizure) from Howard's pocket. At that point, even though the item turned out to be a different sort of weapon than he had suspected, it was admissible since it had been obtained by proper stop-and-frisk procedures.

54. Yes. The Supreme Court has held that the police may not follow a practice of randomly stopping cars in order to check such things as licensing and registration. *Delaware v. Prouse*. Only if the officer has some objective suspicion that the particular driver has committed an offense, may he stop the car. (A checkpoint scheme where *every* car was stopped would pass muster; the problem comes where each officer is given discretion about which cars to stop randomly.)

55. No. The Supreme Court has held that when the police make an arrest on probable cause for a serious offense, they may collect a DNA sample from the inside of the arrestee's cheek as part of their routine booking procedure. *Maryland v. King* (2013). The taking of such a sample constitutes a Fourth Amendment search, but that search is deemed to be a ***"reasonable"*** one even though warrantless, because of the search's limited intrusiveness, its high value to law enforcement for identification of the person who has been arrested, and the reduced reasonable expectation of privacy on the part of one arrested for a serious crime. Once the police have properly collected the sample, *King* says that they may use it to match samples from unsolved crimes, apparently without there being any incremental Fourth Amendment implications. So nothing that happened here violated Devon's Fourth Amendment rights.

Exam Tips on ***WARRANTLESS ARRESTS AND SEARCHES***

Warrantless arrests and searches are a *very* big topic with examiners. Keep in mind the following:

Warrantless arrests are more common than those with a warrant. No arrest warrant is needed so long as the defendant is not taken into custody in his home. (With or without warrant, police can't arrest D unless they have probable cause to believe that D has committed a felony.)

Also, no arrest warrant is needed (even to go into a home) when the police are in ***"hot pursuit"*** or ***exigent circumstances*** exist (e.g., the defendant may flee the jurisdiction if not arrested immediately.)

Warrantless ***searches***, on the other hand, ***must fit within one of the exceptions to the warrant requirement to be valid.*** When you are faced with a warrantless search, consider each of these before deciding that the search was invalid. They are:

search ***incident to arrest***;

inventory search;

exigent circumstances;

plain view;

automobile searches;

consent searches;

stop and frisk; and

regulatory inspections (which sometimes actually require a warrant, but the standards to obtain a warrant aren't stringent).

Search incident to arrest: Police may ***search a suspect incident to a valid arrest*** — regardless of whether the officers actually fear for their safety or believe that evidence of a crime will be found.

Contrast this with a frisk in a ***"stop-and-frisk"*** situation. In stop-and-frisk, the police may pat down the suspect's outer garments to detect ***weapons only*** — they may ***not*** use a "frisk" as a basis to discover and seize anything other than a weapon, such as ***contraband.***

The police may also conduct a ***full body search*** prior to the defendant's incarceration, as long as they made a valid, full custodial arrest.

Police may also search the ***area within the suspect's immediate control*** pursuant to a valid arrest.

Example: Drug dogs sniff the baggage unloaded from an airplane, and alert police to Defendant's bag. Police wait for Defendant to claim her bag, then arrest her as she walks through the airport carrying her bag. They then open her bag and find marijuana. At her trial, the evidence is admissible. Police had probable cause to arrest Defendant based on the dogs' reaction to her bag. Pursuant to this valid arrest, police had the power to search the area within Defendant's immediate control, including the bag that she was carrying.

Remember that when a search is properly made incident to a lawful arrest, the police may examine ***items of personal property found on the person of the arrestee*** (e.g., a wallet or pocket diary).

But also remember that even if the police properly make a custodial arrest of a person who happens to be carrying a ***cell phone***, the incident-to-arrest doctrine does ***not*** permit the police to perform a ***warrantless search of the digital contents of the phone.*** Cite to the 2014 case of *Riley v. California* on this point. (This "no warrantless search" rule probably applies to laptops and other digital devices carried by the arrestee, not just cellphones.)

When the arrest is of a driver of a ***vehicle***, remember that the area deemed under the arrestee's control does ***not*** include the ***passenger compartment,*** so the police cannot use the search-incident-to-arrest exception to search the compartment. For more about this, see p. 212 *infra* (discussion of *Ariz. v. Gant*).

If the police have "specific and articulable facts" suggesting that ***another person may be present*** at the location of the arrest, the police may do a ***"protective sweep"*** of the entire premises, incident to the arrest.

Example: The police properly get a warrant to search for certain criminal evidence (a brown suitcase with leather straps, thought to contain cocaine) in the master bedroom of David's house. (They have information that David also possesses many weapons and is perhaps dangerous.) They knock on David's door, shout "Police," and get no answer. They force open the door and enter. Hearing noises in the basement, they go there, where they find David holding a brown suitcase with leather straps. They seize the suitcase, discover it contains cocaine, handcuff David, then search his person. They find a .22 caliber revolver, which they seize. David is charged with possession of an unlicensed revolver (the .22). David argues that the weapon is the fruit of an unlawful search, and must be suppressed.

David loses — the revolver was lawfully seized. The police entered the house validly (because of the search warrant). Once inside, they were entitled to conduct a protective sweep, since they had "specific and articulable facts" leading them to believe that David might be present and dangerous (knowledge that he possessed weapons). Therefore, they were entitled to go to the basement once they heard noises from there, since that indicated that this was where David or someone else might be. Once they saw David with the suitcase (the apparent object of the search warrant), they were entitled to seize the suitcase and to open it. Once they saw it contained contraband, they were entitled to arrest David, and to search him incident to that arrest. Since the gun was properly found by that search incident to arrest, it is admissible.

But remember that the protective sweep covers ***only places where a person might be hiding***, not areas ***too small*** for a person (e.g., a small box or suitcase).

Example: Same facts as prior example. After the police arrest David in the basement, they search the entire house. They find a small box on a shelf in the attic. They open it, and find an illegal Uzi submachine gun inside.

This evidence must be suppressed. Neither the search warrant nor the search incident to arrest nor the right to do a protective sweep entitled the police to open small boxes throughout the house. (The warrant didn't cover the box; the attic wasn't within the area possibly under David's control and was therefore not searchable incident to the arrest; the protective sweep didn't cover a shelf with a box, since no person could have been hiding in the box.)

Tests for drunk driving: Look out for scenarios where the police arrest a ***driver*** based on probable cause to suspect ***drunk driving,*** and the issue is whether the police can, without a warrant, require the driver to submit to either a ***breathalyzer test*** or a ***blood test***, in order to measure the driver's blood alcohol content (BAC). The answer is that (1) the police ***can*** require the ***breathalyzer*** test (and the states can ***make it a crime*** to refuse to take the test); but (2) they ***cannot*** require the ***blood*** test, because that test is so much more intrusive. Cite to *Birchfield v. No. Dakota* on this point.

Exigent circumstances: Evidence that tends to ***dissipate over time*** creates exigent circumstances that justify a warrantless search. (*Example:* Fire marshals can make an immediate warrantless search of the premises in which a suspicious fire has taken place, because if they wait for a warrant the smell of gasoline, and other clues, may dissipate.)

Destruction of evidence: Be on the lookout for situations in which the police reasonably suspect that if they don't enter the premises immediately, the people inside will ***destroy evidence*** (e.g., narcotics). This is a kind of exigency that justifies a warrantless search. (But if the police "manufacture" the emergency by violating or threatening to violate the Fourth Amendment, the destruction-of-evidence rationale doesn't apply.)

Plain view: If the police are in a ***place where they have the right to be,*** any item that they ***observe*** is "fair game" for seizure if it is evidence of criminal activity. This includes other contraband not named in the search warrant they see when properly executing a valid warrant.

Example: Police arrest D in front of his home for bank robbery. After he is handcuffed, he asks if he can go back into the house to telephone his wife. Officer accompanies him back into the kitchen, dials the number for him, and holds the receiver to his ear. While standing there, Officer notices the corners of three $20 bills protruding from a closed breadbox on the counter, and notices that the bills are all new with consecutive serial numbers. Officer, remembering that a number of $20 bills were taken in the robbery, opens the breadbox, discovers a total of 50 consecutively-numbered $20 bills, and seizes them. Later examination of the serial numbers proves that the bills were taken from the bank. The bills are admissible under the plain view doctrine. D impliedly consented to Officer's entry into his home by requesting to make a phone call (presumably he did not expect to be allowed to go by himself), so Officer was standing where he had a legal right to be when he saw the bills in plain view. His plain view of the bills (including their newness and their consecutive serial numbers) was then enough to give him probable cause to believe they were connected to the robbery, and thus probable cause to open the breadbox to explore further.

Automobile searches: In practical terms, all of the special constructions and exceptions carved out for searches of ***automobiles*** mean that police officers have considerable leeway to search them. When faced with a warrantless automobile search, consider each of the following:

General "automobile search" exception: Under the separate, free-standing "automobile exception," a police officer may ***search a motor vehicle without first getting a search warrant,*** as long as she has ***probable cause to believe that evidence or contraband is located in the vehicle.***

Example 1: Officer O has probable cause to believe that a car parked on the street in front of D's house is owned by D, and has heroin in it. Even if O would have plenty of time to get a search warrant, O may instead open the car's unlocked door to search the passenger compartment for the heroin. O may also open the trunk for the same purpose.

Closed containers: When the automobile exception applies to allow a warrantless search of a vehicle, the exception also allows the police to ***search any closed container inside the vehicle.*** (This assumes that the container might plausibly hold evidence or contraband relating to whatever it was that gave the police probable cause to stop and search the vehicle.)

Example 2: Same basic facts as Example 1 above. O may open a closed, opaque plastic bag in the trunk, to see if it contains heroin. And if it contains some other type of contraband, or evidence of crime, O can seize the bag without first getting a warrant.

Passenger's belongings: Also, if the automobile exception applies to allow a warrantless search of closed containers inside the vehicle, the police can search those containers ***even if they belong to a passenger*** (or to someone other than the vehicle's owner or driver), and even if there is no probable cause to believe that the container's owner has been involved in carrying the contraband or any other illegality.

Example 3: Same basic facts as Examples 1 and 2. Now, assume that (1) O knows that D (the vehicle's owner) is a man named "John Smith," and (2) O sees that a suitcase in the trunk has a luggage tag on it with the name "Mary Smith." O may open the suitcase to see if it, too contains heroin. And that's true even though O has reason to know that the suitcase does not belong to D, and even though O does not have probable cause to believe that Mary Smith has been involved in carrying heroin or any other illegality.

Search of vehicle parked on non-curtilage part of a home's driveway: If the vehicle is located not on a public street, but on a portion of a homeowner's ***residential property*** that is ***not*** part of the property's "***curtilage***," then the automobile exception will ***still apply***, assuming the police have probable cause to believe the vehicle contains contraband or evidence of crime.

Example 4: Same basic facts as Examples 1 through 3. Now, however, assume that the vehicle is parked on a part of D's driveway that's next to the front lawn, and not adjacent to the house. Since the place where the car is parked is not part of the house's curtilage, O may perform the searches in Examples 1 through 3 just as he could do if the car was parked on the street.

Search of vehicle parked on curtilage part of a home's driveway: But where the vehicle ***is*** located within the curtilage of a person's dwelling, the automobile exception will ***not apply*** to allow the warrantless search of the vehicle, even if the police have probable cause for a search. That's because the automobile exception ***does not "override"*** the special Fourth Amendment protections given to the "home" (and a home's curtilage is deemed part of the home, just as, say, any room inside the home would be).

Example 5: Same basic facts as Example 4, except that the vehicle is parked on a part of D's driveway that's adjacent to the house, and within the house's curtilage. Now, the automobile exception will ***not apply*** to allow the warrantless search of the vehicle, even if the police have probable cause for a search. That's because the automobile exception ***does not "override"*** the special Fourth Amendment protections given to the "home" (and a home's curtilage is deemed part of the home, just as, say, any room inside the home would be). [Cite to *Collins v. Va.*]

Search incident to arrest: Since 2009, the police can no longer automatically search the passenger compartment incident to the arrest of the driver. But they *can* search the compartment incident to the driver's arrest if *either*:

they have ***failed to secure*** the driver (e.g., with handcuffs), so that at the time of the search he might plausibly ***still gain access*** to the passenger compartment; or

they have ***"reason to believe"*** that the compartment (or any other part of the vehicle) ***"may"*** contain ***evidence of the crime*** for which the arrest occurred. (This is not likely in traffic-arrest cases, but might well work in drug-arrest cases, including arrests pursuant to an outstanding arrest warrant for drug trafficking.)

Cite to *Ariz. v. Gant* on these incident-to-arrest possibilities.

Inventory search (permissible anytime a vehicle is rightfully in police possession).

Example: D is validly arrested on a charge of drunken driving. Over his objection, police bring D's car to a police-owned lot and inventory the contents of the car. Under the front seat, the police find a plastic bag of heroin. In the back seat, police find a gun in a suitcase sealed by a zipper. The heroin and the gun are admissible. The search of the vehicle (including closed containers) was a valid inventory search, even though it was conducted long after D was arrested.

Plain view. Plain view will provide a basis for validating a search, ***so long as the stop of the vehicle was also valid.*** (If the stop was invalid, though, the officer's plain view into the car will also be insufficient, since it was acquired illegally.)

Example 1: Defendant murders a passenger in his car and disposes of the body. He is unable, however, to remove blood stains on the front seat. Several days later, he unknowingly drives with his hazard lights on. Officer notices Defendant's lights and stops him, not for a violation, but only to make him aware of the danger of the hazard lights. As Officer approaches the car, he sees the blood stains on the front seat. Since the stop was legal, and Officer got the plain view by being where he was legally entitled to be, he may now seize the car (since the evidence is affixed to it) under the plain view doctrine.

Example 2: Police institute a plan of randomly stopping vehicles in a high crime area between midnight and dawn. Pursuant to this plan, they stop Defendant. When Officer approaches the vehicle, he observes marijuana in the vehicle in "plain view." Because the initial stop was illegal (police cannot conduct roving random stops), the officer was not viewing the car's interior from a lawful vantage point, and the marijuana is inadmissible.

Consent searches: The three big issues for consent searches are the ***scope*** of the consent, whether ***deception*** nullifies the consent, and whether the person who consented had ***authority*** to do so.

Scope: "Consent" is broadly construed. Even when suspects are ***in custody***, you should find the consent to be voluntary and valid unless the police falsely assert or imply they have the right to make the search.

Example: Defendant is stopped for a traffic violation and taken into custody. He is patted down, and the police discover a vial of pills for which Defendant does not have a prescription. Officer then asks Defendant for permission to search the car, and Defendant replies, "Go ahead. Why not?" This consent is voluntary, thus valid.

Deception: Deception on the part of the police may or may not nullify the consent.

If the police say that they have a warrant when they don't, this will nullify the consent.

If the police ***misrepresent their identity,*** and thus procure consent, it's ***not clear*** whether the consent is valid. You should say that the case could come out either way.

Example: Police want to gain entry into D's house. During surveillance, they see D leave. They knock on the door of D's home, and his teenage daughter Terry answers. The police say they are friends of her father and want to talk to him. Terry lets them in and asks them to wait in the living room for her father to return. It's not clear whether Terry's consent to the police's entry into the home was valid, voluntary consent; certainly D has a decent chance of having the consent ruled involuntary because based on deception.

Authority: Be sure that police get consent from the right person, i.e., one who had ***authority*** to consent to a search of the particular premises. This is a common issue on exams.

A ***homeowner*** can consent to the search of the home even where the home is also being occupied by a ***social guest.*** (However, the homeowner probably cannot consent to the search of a ***suitcase*** or other small personal item as to which the guest has a high expectation of privacy.)

Example: Owner lets Stranger stay in Owner's house overnight, because Stranger says his car has broken down. Early the next morning, Owner gets suspicious of Stranger, and calls the police. Owner then lets the police into Owner's house, including the kitchen. While in the kitchen, the police see Stranger, and recognize him as a suspect in a pending robbery; they arrest him.

The arrest of Stranger is legal. Although the police would not have had the right to be in the position from which they recognized Stranger had it not been for Owner's consent, Owner had the right to give that consent to the police's entry into his kitchen. Therefore, at the moment when the police spotted Stranger in the kitchen, they were not engaged in an illegal search.

A ***hotel keeper*** or ***landlord cannot*** consent to the search of leased premises that are under the direct control of the guest/tenant.

A ***teenage or older child can*** consent as to the ***common areas*** of his parents' home (but generally not as to the private areas, such as the parents' bedroom).

An ***employer can*** consent to a search of the employee's work area.

Any of two or more ***joint occupants*** (e.g., husband and wife, or roommates) ***can*** consent to a search of the ***jointly occupied space*** if the other is ***not present.***

Example: Police suspect that Defendant is dealing marijuana from his home. They go to his home and his estranged wife W answers the door. (Defendant is not present.) The police ask for consent to search. W consents, saying "Search everywhere. That S.O.B. has ruined my life. I hate his guts." The police do so, including a detached garage, which has a lock that the police break to gain entry. They find marijuana in the garage. W's consent to the search of the house was valid, since she clearly had access and control over it. Whether her consent to the search of the garage was valid depends on whether the garage was used exclusively by Defendant. If it was, and he kept it locked even against W, W did not have authority to consent to the search. (And if Defendant had been *present* and objected to the house search, even W's consent to the house search would have been invalid as against Defendant.)

Stop and frisk: Remember that the police may make a brief "investigatory stop" — colloquially called "stop and frisk" — if they have ***reasonable suspicion***, based upon ***objective, articulable facts,*** that ***criminal activity may be afoot. This is a lesser standard than probable cause.***

If during questioning, the officer develops reason to believe that the suspect may be armed, he may ***frisk*** the suspect, but for weapons only (not for contraband or other objects).

Traffic stops are a great source of exam questions. Here are some general guidelines about traffic stops:

If the car has been stopped for a valid reason (e.g., a traffic infraction), the officer may request to see the driver's ***license***, and run a check on that license — this is a valid form of administrative search. (But an officer can't arbitrarily stop a car just to check whether the driver has a valid license.)

Stationary roadblocks are fine, so long as police use some ***objective, constant criteria*** to determine which cars they will stop. They can also stop every car to try to find ***witnesses*** to a recent crime. ***Random stops,*** on the other hand, are ***invalid***.

Police have the right to ***order all passengers out of the vehicle*** pursuant to a ***valid stop for an infraction*** (including a traffic infraction). If they have a reasonable belief based on specific and articulable facts that a passenger (or the driver) may be ***armed and dangerous***, they can also ***pat down*** the person's ***outer clothing*** to find weapons (but not non-weapon evidence of crime).

Be alert for situations in which, during the course of the traffic stop, the officer ***learns further information*** about some criminal activity. This further info must be taken into account in deciding whether the officer can take a further, more-intrusive, step.

Example: Officer stops D for not signalling. While writing D a ticket, Officer notices a plastic bag with white powder on the floor. At this point, Officer is entitled to search the bag, and the rest of the vehicle (even the trunk) — seeing the bag has given him probable cause to suspect drug offenses, so he can do a search that he wouldn't be authorized to do at the first moment of this non-custodial traffic stop.

Regulatory inspections: Here are the most important types of "regulatory searches," which don't require either probable cause to search, nor a warrant focusing on the particular person being searched:

Government inspectors may perform inspections of physical premises (***"building searches"***) to ensure that ***health, fire and other safety regulations*** are being complied with.

The inspector needs a warrant, but does ***not*** have to show ***probable cause*** that the particular building to be inspected ***violates*** any health or safety regulation. Instead, the inspector merely has to show that government is proposing to conduct an ***"area inspection"*** that is ***reasonably tailored to making sure that the relevant health or safety codes are being observed.*** The warrant then covers the whole area, or certain types of structures within the area — it doesn't have to mention individual addresses.

In the case of certain types of ***closely-regulated businesses, not even an area warrant is required*** for a premises search. This "closely-regulated business" exception applies only to businesses that "pose a clear and significant ***risk to the public welfare."*** (*Examples:* Liquor stores, firearms dealers and auto junkyards are "closely regulated" and thus subject to warrantless, suspicionless searches. But hotels are not.)

An important type of regulatory search is a ***"border search."*** Remember that police need not have probable cause or even reasonable suspicion to conduct a search of a person or his belongings at a fixed border checkpoint.

One topic that crops up with border searches for drugs is ***alimentary canal smuggling.*** Police can perform an ***intrusive body cavity search*** if they have a particularized and objective basis for suspecting a traveler of alimentary canal smuggling.

Example: Inspector sees D speaking to Anon as the two walk across the international border into the United States. Inspector recognizes Anon as someone who has previously been convicted of smuggling narcotics. Inspector searches the pair's luggage and finds a large quantity of drugs in Anon's bag and drug paraphernalia in D's. Inspector orders a male physician to conduct a body cavity search of D. This search is permissible — the total of facts known to Inspector created a particularized and objective basis for believing that D might be smuggling drugs in his alimentary canal.

If the police properly arrest someone for a ***serious offense*** (e.g., a violent felony), remember that they may take a ***DNA sample*** from the arrestee's cheek, as part of the routine booking process. [*Maryland v. King.*]

Other examples of regulatory searches:

metal detection in ***airports.***

school searches (e.g., searches of student lockers). The test is generally that school officials must have a reasonable basis for suspecting criminal conduct or a violation of school rules. (*Example:* School officials can't randomly search lockers, but can search lockers of those students as to whom the officials have a particularized basis for suspecting possession of contraband.)

But ***drug tests*** in schools may be required as a condition of participation in most ***extracurricular activities,*** as long as the results are not shared with the police. That's true even if school officials don't have any basis for suspecting that any particular student is using drugs.

Searches of ***parolees*** and people on ***probation*** — parolees (and probably probationers) can be stopped at any time or place even without suspicion of wrongdoing, and searched without a warrant.

CHAPTER 4

ELECTRONIC SURVEILLANCE AND SECRET AGENTS

ChapterScope

This chapter examines the rules that police must follow when trying to gather evidence against a suspect through covert means, that is, surveillance and secret agents. The Fourth Amendment applies to some of these situations, just as it applies to conventional searches and seizures.

Electronic surveillance: There are two main forms of electronic surveillance — ***wiretapping*** (listening to phone conversations) and ***bugging*** (listening to non-telephonic voice conversations). Both forms normally ***constitute Fourth Amendment searches.***

Probable cause and warrant rules: Consequently, if the conversation is one in which both participants had a reasonable expectation of privacy, the ***probable cause*** and ***search warrant*** requirements must be met before government can wiretap or bug it.

"Secret agents": The use of a ***"secret agent"*** — i.e., an undercover operative or informant who the suspect does not realize is working for the government — normally does ***not*** pose Fourth Amendment problems. So long as the suspect is aware that a person is present, the presence of that other person ***does not constitute a "search,"*** even though the suspect does not realize that the other person is a police agent.

No need for probable cause or warrant: Therefore, conversations with the undercover agent may be introduced in court ***without*** there ever having been probable cause or a search warrant.

Entrapment: A suspect may claim that a secret agent "entrapped" him. This can be a valid defense, but only if the agent induced the suspect to commit a crime which the suspect was not otherwise predisposed to commit.

I. HISTORICAL BACKGROUND

A. ***Olmstead:*** The first telephone wiretap case to reach the Supreme Court was ***Olmstead v. U.S.***, 277 U.S. 438 (1928), in which a 5-4 majority held that messages passing over telephone wires were not within the Fourth Amendment's protection against unreasonable search and seizure.

1. **Physical trespass doctrine:** The *Olmstead* Court held that the wiretap, which was placed on the telephone wires outside of the defendant's house, failed in two respects to invade an area protected by the Fourth Amendment:

   a. **Conversations not seizable:** First, the Fourth Amendment applied only to "places" and "things." Since the tap intercepted only intangible conversations, the Amendment was not violated.

b. **Trespass:** Furthermore, the Amendment could only be violated by ***physical trespass*** onto the subject's property. Since the tap in *Olmstead* had been placed on wires outside the defendant's premises, no Fourth Amendment violation could have occurred, even if conversations could sometimes be protected by the Fourth Amendment.

Note: Both of these rationales were later rejected in *Katz v. U.S.*, discussed *infra*, which held that a wiretap could violate the Fourth Amendment even though it involved only intangible conversations and no trespass onto defendant's property occurred.

2. **Dissent:** Justice Brandeis, in a dissent to *Olmstead*, warned against the great threat to privacy posed by telephone wiretapping and argued against "an unduly literal construction" of the Fourth Amendment. Brandeis said that "the right to be let alone" is "the most comprehensive of rights and the right most valued by civilized man."

a. **"Dirty Business":** Justice Holmes added his belief that wiretapping, here in violation of a state law, was a "dirty business," and contended that "it is a less evil that some criminals should escape than that the government should play an ignoble part."

B. **Eavesdropping:** The *Olmstead* physical trespass rationale was extended to the use of ***electronic eavesdropping equipment*** unconnected with the telephone system. In ***Goldman v. U.S.***, 316 U.S. 129 (1942), the Court held that a microphone placed against the wall of a private office was not a physical trespass, and that therefore no Fourth Amendment violation could have occurred.

1. **Some protection:** But in 1961, the Court held that electronic surveillance accomplished through physical trespass violated the Fourth Amendment, despite the fact that intangible conversations, not "places" or "things," were affected. In ***Silverman v. U.S.***, 365 U.S. 505 (1961), a unanimous Court held that listening to a conversation via a "spike mike" inserted ***into*** a house constituted an illegal search and seizure.

a. **Douglas concurrence:** Justice Douglas concurred in *Silverman*, maintaining that "the depth of the penetration of the electronic device . . . is not [the] measure of the injury. Our concern should not be with the trivialities of the local law of trespass."

i. **Note:** Justice Douglas' views in *Silverman* were later to be adopted by the Court in its *Katz* decision.

II. FOURTH AMENDMENT PROTECTION OF *KATZ*

A. ***Katz:*** In ***Katz v. U.S.***, 389 U.S. 347 (1967), *supra*, p. 16, the Supreme Court by a 7-1 decision expressly rejected *Olmstead* and *Goldman*, and held that ***unauthorized electronic eavesdropping is an illegal search and seizure***, even though it involves only intangible conversations, and even though no physical trespass onto the speaker's property occurs.

1. **Facts:** The defendant was convicted of illegally transmitting wagering information via telephone from Los Angeles to Miami and Boston. Admitted into evidence at his trial were recordings of his conversations made by a device attached to the outside of a telephone booth by FBI agents. There was no actual physical intrusion into the booth.

2. **Rationale:** The majority, *per* Stewart, said that the question was not whether the telephone booth was a "constitutionally protected area," since ***"the Fourth Amendment protects people, not places."*** Constitutional protection must be accorded to a person who justifiably relies upon the privacy of a particular place, be that a home, office, car, or telephone booth.

3. **Judicial approval required:** The *Katz* Court indicated that a proper judicial authority could have approved the procedure used upon an adequate showing of need and for the narrow purpose of ascertaining whether Katz was indeed transmitting wagering information as had been alleged.

   a. **National security cases:** A footnote to the majority opinion noted that "a situation involving the national security is a question not presented by this case."

B. **The reliance test:** Under *Katz*, an unauthorized wiretap violates the Fourth Amendment if the subject places ***justifiable reliance*** on the privacy of the particular place. The Court made clear that such reliance may be placed "even in an area accessible to the public." See Harlan's "justifiable expectation of privacy" concurrence, discussed *supra*, p. 16.

C. **Participant monitoring:** *Katz* is silent on the question of the constitutionality of ***participant monitoring of conversations***, i.e., wiretapping or eavesdropping with the consent of one of the parties. Most lower courts have taken this silence, along with a footnote by Justice White expressly approving of participant monitoring, to ***allow*** such procedures.

III. THE FEDERAL WIRETAPPING AND STORED-COMMUNICATIONS STATUTES

A. **Two statutes covered:** In this section III, we consider ***two federal statutes*** that impose non-constitutional limits on the ways in which state and federal governments can perform wiretaps, and can access certain electronically-stored messages and files. In Pars. (A) through (G), we cover the federal ***wiretapping*** statute, known as "Title III." In Par. (H), we cover a different federal statute, the ***"Stored Communications Act,"*** that deals with electronic messages that are stored on computers not owned by the creator or recipient of the message.

B. **Title III of the Crime Control Act:** *Katz* indicated that wiretapping could be constitutionally permissible if authorized by a judicially-issued warrant. Partly in response to *Katz*, Congress enacted ***Title III*** of the Omnibus Crime Control and Safe Streets Act of 1968, authorizing the issuance of ***warrants for electronic surveillance*** in certain situations. Title III is codified at ***28 U.S.C. §§2510-22***, and is sometimes referred to as the ***"Wiretap Act."*** (We'll call it "Title III" here.)

C. **Operation of Title III:** Here is an overview of how Title III operates:

1. **Application to federal crimes:** §2516 of the Act authorizes the Attorney General or a specially designated Assistant Attorney General to apply to any federal judge for an order permitting the FBI or other appropriate federal agency to intercept ***"wire or oral communications"*** to gather evidence of certain enumerated federal crimes. The reference to "wire or oral communications" makes it clear that the Act applies both to ***wiretapping*** and to ***electronic eavesdropping*** (i.e., "bugging").

   a. **Crimes covered:** Included in the list is any crime for which the federal government has jurisdiction, such as violations relating to labor unions, public officials, espionage or treason, counterfeiting, bankruptcy fraud, narcotics, or gambling.

2. **State crimes:** Title III also permits electronic surveillance in certain ***state*** law enforcement contexts. The Title permits a state prosecutor to seek judicial authorization for surveillance where evidence of certain enumerated felonies is to be gathered. The Title permits such authorization only in states which have passed enabling legislation.

3. **Other interceptions unlawful:** Any willful interception not complying with the Act is made a federal crime punishable by five years imprisonment or a $10,000 fine or both. Also, evidence from such interceptions is ***not admissible in any state or federal proceeding.***

4. **Presidential authority:** §2511(3) expressly exempts from restriction the President's constitutional power to protect against certain ***foreign threats***. (See *infra*, p. 222.) But the Supreme Court has held that this power does not allow the President to authorize interceptions in ***domestic*** security cases. *U.S. v. U.S. District Court*, 407 U.S. 297 (1972).

5. **Procedure:** Under §2518, a judge may authorize an intercept only if he finds that:

   a. there is ***probable cause*** to believe that a ***specific individual*** has committed one of the enumerated crimes;

   b. there is probable cause to believe that the interception will ***furnish evidence about the crime***;

   c. normal investigative procedures have been tried and have failed or reasonably appear likely to fail or to be dangerous; and

   d. there is probable cause to believe that the facilities from which, or the place where, the interception is to be made are or will be ***used in connection with the offense*** or are ***linked to the individual under suspicion*** (e.g., leased to him, frequently used by him, etc.).

   e. **Emergency allowance:** Interception without prior judicial authorization is permitted when an ***emergency situation*** exists with respect to conspiratorial activities of ***organized crime*** and there are grounds upon which an order could be obtained otherwise. But this decision may only be made by a specially-designated law enforcement officer, and a judicial order must be applied for within 48 hours of the start of the interception unless the communication sought is obtained before the end of the 48-hour period.

6. **Participant monitoring allowed:** Wiretapping or eavesdropping conducted with the ***consent of a party to the communication*** is specifically ***exempted*** from the Act. Of course, such consensual surveillance must still meet Fourth Amendment requirements, discussed below.

7. **Minimizing interception of innocent material:** §2518(5) of Title III requires that every judicial wiretap order state that the surveillance must be "conducted in such a way as to ***minimize*** the interception of communications not otherwise subject to interception." That is, law enforcement officials must make efforts to minimize the interception of ***innocent***, non-criminal, communications.

8. **Covers "real-time" access only:** Title III covers ***only "real-time" access*** to communications, ***not*** access to ***"stored communications."*** If the authorities want to obtain and search "stored communications" — electronic communications that occurred previously, and that are now stored on a third party's computers — they must proceed according to a different statute, the ***Stored Communications Act,*** which is discussed *infra*, p. 222.

D. Covert entry allowed: Officials who obtain a Title III order authorizing bugging of private premises may constitutionally make a ***covert entry*** into those premises to ***install the bug***. In *Dalia v. U.S.*, 441 U.S. 238 (1979), FBI agents entered the defendant's place of business secretly at midnight to install the bug, and entered again to remove it several weeks later. The Supreme Court held that:

1. Covert entry into private premises to install a bug is not *per se* unreasonable, or violative of the Fourth Amendment.

2. Congress intended, in Title III, to give courts authority to approve covert entry, even though Title III nowhere explicitly so states. Authorization of such entry is implicit in the Act's limited approval of buggings and other electronic surveillance, since such surveillance frequently cannot be accomplished without it.

3. Nor is it required that the authorizing court explicitly approve covert entry in its order permitting the bug.

E. Consenting party exception: Title III does not apply where an interception takes place with the ***consent*** of one of the parties to a communication; in such a situation, no warrant is needed.

1. **Police officer impersonates owner of tapped phone:** The Supreme Court has indirectly indicated that this "consenting party" exception applies where a police officer answers calls coming into a tapped phone, and ***"impersonates"*** the owner of the tapped phone.

    Note: It is important, when analyzing wiretapping and other electronic surveillance (e.g., the planting of "bugs"), to distinguish between the question whether the intercept falls within Title III and meets its requirements, and the question whether the intercept is a Fourth Amendment search or seizure (and if so, whether it is a "reasonable" one).

    Title III's requirements must be met where applicable, regardless of whether the interception constitutes a Fourth Amendment search and seizure, even a reasonable one. Conversely, an interception is not legitimate merely because it is authorized by a judge acting under Title III, if the interception constitutes an unreasonable search or seizure under the Fourth Amendment, or if the warrant does not meet the "probable cause" and "particularity of description" requirements of the Fourth Amendment. And electronic surveillance not covered by Title III (as where one party "consents" to the surveillance) must nonetheless satisfy applicable Fourth Amendment tests (although the material which follows indicates that the Amendment has not been construed to protect against "bugged informants").

F. Title III in practice: The state-level surveillance-enabling provisions of Title III have been surprisingly little used. Twenty-eight states have not even passed legislation authorizing surveillance, as they must do if their law enforcement officials are to use Title III; these states include California, Illinois, Pennsylvania, Michigan and Ohio. Over 80% of the surveillance practiced by state police occurs in New York and New Jersey, apparently aimed mostly at organized crime.

1. **Federal use limited:** Nor has the federal government made particularly widespread use of Title III. Most federal uses are in gambling and drug cases.

2. **Conviction rate low:** Reported figures show that less than one-third of the intercepts produce convictions, perhaps indicating that surveillance is not an effective anti-crime technique and thus accounting for its low current use.

G. **Foreign threats:** §2511(3) of Title III provides that Title III does ***not limit*** the ***"constitutional power of the President*** to take such measures as he deems necessary to protect the Nation against actual or potential ***attack*** or other ***hostile acts*** by ***foreign powers***, to obtain foreign intelligence information deemed essential to the ***security*** of the United States, or to protect national security information against foreign intelligence activities."

1. **Separate statute:** This section of Title III doesn't make it clear whether and when the President may conduct wiretaps without court order in order to protect national security. But Congress has, in a separate statute, given the Executive Branch some power to do this. The Foreign Intelligence Surveillance Act of 1978, 50 U.S.C. §1801 *et seq.*, allows the Attorney General to authorize wiretapping ***without a court order*** if the surveillance is directed solely at ***communications between or among foreign powers***, and "there is no substantial likelihood that the surveillance will acquire the contents of any communication to which a United States person is a party." If a U.S. citizen or a resident alien is involved, warrantless surveillance may not occur, but a warrant may be obtained from a special court.

H. **The Stored Communications Act (SCA):** As we noted on p. 221 *supra*, Title III is limited to ***"real-time surveillance"*** — it sets the rules for when law enforcement may wiretap telephone calls and other electronic communications ***as those communications are occurring.*** A completely different statute, the ***Stored Communications Act*** (the ***"SCA"***) was adopted by Congress in 1986, at the dawn of the Internet era, to set the procedural rules for when and how government may access non-real-time records, i.e., ***historical records,*** of electronic communications. The SCA is codified at 18 U.S.C. §§ 2701-11.

1. **Brief treatment:** The SCA is quite complex, so we will touch only on a few key aspects of it here.

2. **Out of date:** The SCA is widely regarded as being ***out of date***. When it was enacted in 1986, Internet usage was just beginning, and people used the Internet in much more limited ways than they do now. Therefore, some of the key procedural distinctions embedded in the SCA don't really make much intuitive sense in light of today's usage patterns, and whether or how the SCA applies to a particular modern-day scenario is often unclear.

3. **Some applications are unconstitutional:** Some practices that the SCA authorizes have been found by the Supreme Court to be ***violations of the Fourth Amendment.*** As the result of the landmark case of ***Carpenter v. U.S.***, 138 S.Ct. 2206 (2018) (discussed in detail beginning *supra*, p. 34), when law enforcement wants to request or demand that a third party wireless carrier's ***cell-site location information (CSLI)*** covering seven days or more of an individual's cell-phone movements, a search warrant is required, even though

the SCA says that the lesser requirements for a "§ 2703(d)" court order" (p. 223 below) will suffice.

a. **Possible application to other contexts:** The rationale of *Carpenter* may well apply to other sorts of third-party-maintained stored communications beyond CSLI (e.g., digital records of credit card charges, or digital lists of email addresses on either end of a person's email communications); thus it remains to be worked out by post-*Carpenter* courts whether the SCA's application to these sorts of communications, too, violates users' Fourth Amendment rights.

4. **"ISPs":** The SCA applies to different types of third parties that hold stored communications created by someone else. ***Email service providers*** like Gmail and Yahoo, ***cloud-storage providers*** like Dropbox and Google Drive, and ***wireless cellphone carriers*** that keep non-content records about calls, are among the categories that are at least implicitly covered by SCA.[1] For ease of reference, we'll refer to all service providers that hold on their computers stored communications belonging to others as being "Internet Service Providers" or ***"ISPs,"*** even though that's not really the correct Internet-era designation for some types of services that are or may be covered by the SCA.

5. **Main provisions:** What follows is a short discussion of what law enforcement needs to do under the SCA in order to access "stored communications," i.e., electronic communications created by a person or business and then stored on the systems of a ***third-party ISP.*** The SCA does not set the rules for government to access messages stored on the computer of the ***creator or recipient*** of the message — it applies *only* to messages stored on those ***third-party*** service-providers that we're loosely calling ISPs.

a. **Types of orders:** To begin with, the SCA recognizes three different types of documents that, depending on the circumstances, law enforcement may need to generate, or else procure from a court, to compel a third party to turn over a stored communication. In descending order from "hardest-to-get" to "easiest-to-get," these documents are:

[1] A conventional ***search warrant,*** issued by a neutral magistrate, of the sort that would suffice for a search implicating Fourth Amendment rights. As we've seen (*supra*, p. 63), the Fourth Amendment's "warrant" clause requires that a warrant be issued by a neutral-and-detached magistrate, that the government should ***"probable cause"*** for the warrant, and that the warrant ***"particularly describ[e]"*** the information to be seized.

[2] A so-called ***"§ 2703(d) order."*** This is a court order of a special sort, as described in § 2703(d) of the SCA. A § 2703(d) order is in effect a cross between a subpoena (see [3] below) and a search warrant ([1] above). To obtain the order, the government has to show ***"specific and articulable facts"*** demonstrating that there are ***"reasonable grounds to believe"*** that the contents of the stored communication are ***"relevant and material*** to an ongoing criminal investigation." So this "reasonable suspicion" standard is less demanding than the "probable cause"

1. Note, however, that broad-based publicly-accessible cloud storage providers like Dropbox did not even exist when the SCA was adopted in 1986, and even public email services were much less-developed than they are today.

required for a search warrant, but it requires government to furnish a statement of reasonable grounds for believing the record is relevant to a criminal investigation, an action that government does not have to take when it issues a subpoena. If the judge is convinced that this reasonable-suspicion standard is met, the judge signs the order, and the government serves it on the third party who holds the stored communication.

Note on *Carpenter*: But remember, by virtue of the Supreme Court's 2018 holding in *Carpenter v. U.S.*, *supra*, p. 34, some court orders issued under § 2703(d) will be ***violations of the Fourth Amendment rights*** of the persons to whom the stored communications pertain.

[3] A ***subpoena***, drafted and signed by the law enforcement agency that is seeking the stored record. A subpoena does not need to ***state any reason*** why the issuer thinks that the subpoenaed materials are relevant to a criminal investigation, and does not need to be signed or approved by a ***judge*** (or anyone outside the agency that's issuing the subpoena).

b. **Emails:** A big function of the SCA is to give people who write or receive ***emails*** some meaningful statutory protection against law enforcement's right to compel the ISP to turn over copies of past emails held on the ISP's systems. Here's a brief summary, ordered by type-and-age of the material, of the ***least***-difficult-to-obtain document that law enforcement must create or procure in order to compel the ISP to turn over the email item:[2]

   i. **Older than 180 days and never opened:** If the recipient of the email ***never opened,*** retrieved or downloaded it, and has left it in unopened form on the ISP's systems ***for more than 180 days,*** a ***subpoena*** is all that's required to compel disclosure of the email's ***full contents.***[3]

      (1) **Rationale:** The SCA reflects the view that if the email has remain unopened by the recipient for 180 days, it has effectively been ***abandoned*** by both the sender and the receiver, so that it should be subject to the lowest of the three levels of protection.

   ii. **Newer than 180 days and never opened:** If the recipient of the email never opened, retrieved or downloaded it (i.e., same condition as Par. (i) above), but the email has been left on the ISP's systems for ***180 days or less,*** the email receives the ***highest level of protection*** recognized by the SCA: law enforcement must obtain a ***conventional search warrant*** to force the ISP to turn over these "recent" emails.

---

2. The SCA's definitions are often confusing (and obsolete) as they apply to modern email systems. Therefore, the "rules" given in the text are merely best guesses by commentators about how the SCA would be interpreted as applied to various categories of emails. See generally Kerr, "A User's Guide to the Stored Communications Act, and a Legislator's Guide to Amending It," 72 Geo. Wash. L. Rev. 1208 (2004).

3. However, in most cases the government must also give simultaneous ***notice*** to the ISP's customer or subscriber that the subpoena is being issued.

(1) **Rationale:** So relatively ***"recent"*** emails (6 months old or less) get the same high protection as, say, a ***first-class letter*** that had not yet been delivered by the Postal Service would receive, whereas older emails (more than 6 months old) are treated as semi-abandoned materials for which a subpoena to the ISP will suffice.

(2) **Criticism:** These age-of-email-based categories may have made sense when the SCA was adopted in 1987, because in those days a person usually "dialed in" to "retrieve" her emails, and one who didn't retrieve an email for 180 days might plausibly be viewed as having abandoned it. Today, where emails are often automatically downloaded to the recipient's device (but still kept for backup on the ISP's server), this distinction between "old" and "new" emails — where only "new" ones get much protection, and only until the message has been "opened" by the recipient (see Par. (iii) below) — doesn't match up very well with most people's intuitive privacy expectations.

iii. **Opened emails:** If the email has been ***"opened"*** or downloaded by the recipient from the ISP, but kept in that opened form on the ISP's computers, probably the ***lowest*** level of protection applies, by which a ***subpoena*** is sufficient. See Kerr, *infra*, footnote 4, at 1222-23.

iv. **Noncontent "metadata" data about emails:** The creation of any email also produces certain ***"noncontent"*** information about that email. Noncontent information (sometimes called ***"envelope"*** information or ***"metadata"***) is information that the ISP uses to ***route and keep track*** of the email. Noncontent information about emails includes such data as the ***email addresses of the sender and recipient***, information about ***when*** the email was ***sent and/or retrieved***, and the ***size*** of the message.[4]

(1) **Mid-level treatment:** In any event, noncontent information receives ***mid-level protection***: the government must get a ***§ 2703(d) order*** based on reasonable suspicion. And that seems to be true whether the email to which it pertains is older or younger than 180 days, and whether the email was or wasn't ever opened. See Kerr, *supra*, footnote 4, at 1223.

c. **Other types of files:** Today, when many people make use of ***"cloud storage,"*** the SCA's treatment of non-email files that a user has ***permanently*** stored[5] stored becomes important. Unfortunately, the SCA was drafted when cloud storage did not exist in its present form; therefore, it's not completely clear from the SCA's text what government has to do to compel an ISP to turn over permanently-stored files stored on its servers.

i. **Probably lowest protection:** Most likely, non-email files that a user has permanently stored "in the cloud" receive, under the SCA, the ***lowest level*** of protection: a mere ***subpoena*** issued by law enforcement probably suffices to force the ISP to

---

4. The "Subject" line is generally considered content, not noncontent.

5. I mean "permanently stored" as opposed to "temporarily stored during transit to a recipient," which is the status of emails or other files that might be stored on a third-party server while en route to a recipient.

turn over the files. And that's likely true whether the file is "recent" (stored by the ISP for less than 180 days) or older than 180 days. Cf. Kerr, *supra*, footnote 4, at 1222-23.

IV. THE USE OF SECRET AGENTS

A. **Problem generally:** *Olmstead, Goldman, Silverman,* and *Katz* (*supra*, pp. 217-219) all involved the use of electronic surveillance equipment to monitor conversations between persons who were both unaware of the surveillance. But suppose the police place a "bug" on an informer, with his consent, to enable him to transmit to them the conversations he has with the individual under investigation. Or suppose a police agent is "wired," and induces the suspect to take him into his confidence. Does the Fourth Amendment apply? The Supreme Court has generally answered this question in the negative. It has similarly held that the use of "unbugged" agents and informers, who merely report (and perhaps testify) as to conversations they have with suspects, does not involve the Fourth Amendment.

B. **Pre-*Katz* view of "bugged agents":** The Supreme Court held, in two different pre-*Katz* cases, that the use of secret agents equipped with electronic surveillance equipment was not eavesdropping and thus could not possibly violate the Fourth Amendment.

1. ***On Lee:*** In ***On Lee v. U.S.***, 343 U.S. 747 (1952), an informant was "wired for sound," and a conversation between him and the defendant, occurring within the defendant's house, was transmitted by radio to a narcotics agent. The agent testified at trial to the substance of the conversation. The Supreme Court, 5-4, held this testimony admissible.

   a. **No trespass:** The majority rejected the claim that either the informant or the agent had "trespassed" on the defendant's property, and held that in the absence of physical trespass there was no "search and seizure."

   b. **Dissent:** The four dissenters said that the words spoken were ***within the defendant's house*** and thus entitled to protection.

2. ***Lopez:*** The use of a tape-recorder by a secret agent was approved in ***Lopez v. U.S.***, 373 U.S. 427 (1963). The Court emphasized that the recorder "was used only to obtain the most reliable evidence possible of a conversation in which the government's own agent was a participant and [thus] fully entitled to disclose."

   a. **Distinguished from *On Lee:*** Chief Justice Warren concurred, but distinguished *Lopez* from what he said was the wrongly decided *On Lee. On Lee*, he contended, denied the defendant his right to cross-examination, since only the agent and not the wired informant testified.

   b. **Dissent:** The three dissenters to *Lopez* stated that "there is a grave danger of chilling all private, free, and unconstrained communications if secret recordings . . . are competent evidence of any self-incriminating statements the speaker may have made." They saw no difference between *On Lee* and *Lopez*.

C. **Pre-*Katz* use of "unbugged agents":** In two additional pre-*Katz* cases, the Court approved the use of "unbugged" secret agents and informants; the Court held that the use of such agents (who testify at trial from recollection as to the incriminating statements made to them), involves no intrusion by the government but only ***"misplaced trust"*** by the suspect in the agent or informant.

1. ***Lewis:*** In ***Lewis v. U.S.***, 385 U.S. 206 (1966), a federal narcotics agent told the defendant he wanted to buy narcotics; the sale occurred in the defendant's house. The Supreme Court found no Fourth Amendment violation because the defendant "invited the undercover agent to his home for the specific purpose of executing a felonious sale of narcotics"; furthermore, the agent did not "see, hear, or take anything that was not contemplated and in fact intended by petitioner as a necessary part of his illegal business."

   a. **Waiver:** The Court held that the defendant had ***waived*** his Fourth Amendment rights in his home since he had converted it to a "commercial center."

   b. ***Gouled*** **distinguished:** The Court distinguished *Gouled v. U.S.*, 255 U.S. 298 (1921), on the grounds that there the agent exceeded the scope of the invitation to him. The agent in *Gouled*, a business acquaintance of the defendant, came into the latter's home as a guest but conducted a surreptitious search and seizure of certain papers in the house. In *Lewis*, the agent did not commit any acts that were beyond the scope of the business for which he had been invited into the house.

2. ***Hoffa:*** The Supreme Court's affirmance of Jimmy Hoffa's bribery conviction was based on reasoning similar to that of *Lewis.* ***Hoffa v. U.S.***, 385 U.S. 293 (1966). In *Hoffa*, a Teamster-turned-informant became a regular visitor to Hoffa's hotel room and overheard conversations concerning Hoffa's plans to bribe jurors. As in *Lewis*, the Court found Hoffa's statements "totally voluntary." No Fourth Amendment search or seizure occurred; Hoffa's "misplaced trust" was his own fault, and did not vitiate his consent to the informant's entry into the hotel suite (admittedly an area as to which Hoffa was entitled to Fourth Amendment protection).

D. **Reaffirmation after *Katz:*** Doubts about the continued vitality of *On Lee, Lopez, Lewis*, and *Hoffa* arose after the *Katz* decision and its expectation-of-privacy test. But these doubts were put to rest in ***U.S. v. White***, 401 U.S. 745 (1971).

1. **Facts:** In *White*, an informer was wired to transmit to narcotics agents conversations with the defendant occurring in a restaurant, in the defendant's home, and in the informer's car. As in *On Lee,* the informer did not testify at the trial, but the agent who received the transmissions testified as to their content.

2. **Holding:** A four-man plurality held that no Fourth Amendment right had been involved. The Court based its conclusion on the following syllogism:

   a. **No expectation of privacy:** When a person misplaces his trust, and makes incriminating statements to an "unbugged" informer, he does not have any "justifiable expectation of privacy" which has been violated; there is no Fourth Amendment protection for "a wrongdoer's misplaced belief that a person to whom he voluntarily confides his wrongdoing will not reveal it."

   b. **Wiring irrelevant:** Given this premise, it makes no difference whether the informer is "bugged" or not; the addition of recording or transmitting equipment merely enhances the reliability of the evidence.

3. **Concurrence:** Justice Black concurred on the basis of his dissent in *Katz*, believing the Fourth Amendment inapplicable to conversations. Justice Brennan concurred only because he did not believe that *Katz* should be retroactively applied.

4. **Dissent:** All three dissenters believed that "*On Lee* and *Lopez* are of a vintage opposed to *Berger* and *Katz*" and thus should be overruled. Justice Douglas asked whether "now that the discredited decisions in *On Lee* and *Lopez* are resuscitated and revived, must everyone live in fear that every word he speaks may be transmitted or recorded and later repeated to the entire world?" He expressed fear about the "chilling effect" *White* would have on free speech and social intercourse.

5. ***Katz* eroded:** There can be little doubt that the *White* decision eroded the "justifiable reliance" concept of *Katz*, since *White* necessarily assumes that a person cannot "justifiably" trust and talk to anyone, regardless of how close.

   a. **New test:** *White* really changes the operative test from *Katz*'s "reasonable expectation of privacy" to one based on a "possible risk of disclosure."

6. **Dissent's distinction:** Even the dissenters in *White* seemed satisfied that the *Lewis-Hoffa* rule, holding unbugged conversations not to be entitled to Fourth Amendment protection, remained valid after *Katz*. The dissenters distinguished *White* from *Lewis* and *Hoffa* on the grounds that the threat of hidden recording and transmitting equipment is more chilling of the right to privacy than the threat that an informant will later try to reformulate from memory the language of an obscure conversation.

   a. **Distinction unjustified:** But whether a person is "bugged" or not has nothing to do with his "expectation of privacy." As one commentator has observed: "Both [bugged and unbugged] surveillance tend to repress in the same way: by making people distrustful and unwilling to talk to one another. The only difference is that under electronic surveillance you are afraid to talk to anybody in your office or even on the phone, while under a spy system you are afraid to talk to anybody at all." Amsterdam, *Perspectives on the Fourth Amendment*, 58 Minn. L. Rev. 349 (1974).

E. **Title III:** The use of undercover agents, both "bugged" and "unbugged," is not covered by Title III, since that Act expressly exempts the interception of conversations with the consent of a party. See *supra*, p. 221.

F. **Right to counsel:** The use of a bugged or unbugged informer against a suspect who has already been indicted may violate the latter's ***Sixth Amendment right to counsel***. See *infra*, p. 399.

V. ENTRAPMENT

A. **Meaning of entrapment:** Undercover agents do not generally wait passively for the suspect who has taken them into his confidence to make incriminating statements. Generally, the undercover agent plays to at least a small degree the role of "*agent provocateur*," inducing the suspect to make statements or commit offenses which, were it not for the agent's presence, would not occur. While the solicitation of mere statements will almost never be objectionable, the agent's inducement to the suspect to perform a criminal act may sometimes be sufficiently coercive that the suspect will be able to assert the defense that he was ***"entrapped"*** into committing the crime.

1. **Definition:** The Supreme Court has defined the entrapment defense this way: the government "may not ***originate a criminal design***, implant in an ***innocent person's mind*** the ***disposition*** to commit a criminal act, and then ***induce*** the commission of the crime so that the government may prosecute. Where the government has induced an individual to break the law and the defense of entrapment is at issue . . . the prosecution must prove beyond a reasonable doubt that the defendant was ***disposed*** to commit the criminal act ***prior*** to first being approached by government agents." *Jacobson v. U.S.*, 503 U.S. 540 (1992).

    Example: D orders some sexually explicit material from a California bookstore, which contains pictures of nude pre-teen and teenage boys. At the time D places the order, receipt of such materials is not illegal. Shortly thereafter, federal law is changed to make receipt through the mails of sexually explicit pictures of children (such as those received by D) illegal. For the next two years, two separate government agencies, acting through five fictitious organizations and a bogus pen pal, engage in an elaborate "sting" operation in which they send many phony direct-mail solicitations to D. By means of these mailings, the government attempts to induce D to order sexually explicit photos of children in violation of the new law. D finally places an order, and is arrested after the materials are delivered to his home. D asserts that he was entrapped.

    Held (by the Supreme Court), for D. The government "overstepped the line between setting a trap for the 'unwary innocent' and the 'unwary criminal'. " The government did not prove that D's decision to order the materials was independent of the attention that the government had directed at D. "The Government [may not play] on the weaknesses of an innocent party and beguile him into committing crimes which he otherwise would not have attempted." *Jacobson v. U.S., supra.*

B. **Constitutional basis for entrapment defense:** Although the Supreme Court has reversed federal convictions on the ground that they were based on entrapment (as in *Jacobson, supra*), the Court has never recognized any ***constitutional right*** to the entrapment defense; the federal reversals have been justified by reference to the Court's supervisory powers over the administration of justice by the federal courts. In *U.S. v. Russell*, 411 U.S. 423 (1973), the Court flatly stated that the entrapment defense ***"is not of a constitutional dimension."*** Therefore, the Court is likely to continue to respect state law on the entrapment defense, and not to reverse state convictions on the ground of any constitutional right to the defense.

Quiz Yourself on
ELECTRONIC SURVEILLANCE AND SECRET AGENTS *(ENTIRE CHAPTER)*

56. The FBI had been trying to put organized-crime kingpin Lewis "Fat Louie" Lenkowitz away for a number of years, without success. Finally, the federal agents decided that the right kind of electronic "bug" might be just the thing. The agents knew that Louie often transacted business at a neighborhood social club. With the help of local police officials, a phony fire scare was arranged at the club, and all patrons were temporarily evicted. Federal agents disguised as firefighters went into the club, and clipped a bug on the wall of the room where Louie was known to transact business. This bug transmitted sounds in the room out to the local FBI office one block away. No permission of any judge or magistrate was sought or received for this operation.

Shortly thereafter, Louie mentioned in passing, while at the club, "You remember when we put the cement shoes on old Jimmy Boffa?" Federal agents immediately charged Louie with the murder of Boffa, which had occurred some years earlier. They then sought to introduce Louie's statement against him at his trial. Louie has moved to have the statement suppressed on the grounds that it was obtained in violation of his Fourth Amendment rights. Should his motion be granted? _______________

57. Langdell police were convinced that Melvin had murdered his wife Wanda, who had disappeared one night after the two had been overheard arguing. However, the police had no direct evidence that Melvin did it. Harriet, an attractive young member of the Langdell force, volunteered for an undercover assignment to try to get evidence against Melvin. She arranged to "run into" Melvin at a local singles bar, and to become romantically involved with him. Soon, he invited her to move in with him. She did, but only after placing a "bug" under his bed, which transmitted to the police station everything spoken in the bedroom. Several nights later, after a particularly passionate interlude, Melvin mentioned to Harriet that he had murdered Wanda. The police's tape of this statement, recorded at the police station via the bug, was introduced against Melvin at his subsequent murder trial. Can Melvin have this tape suppressed on the grounds that it was obtained in violation of his rights? _______________

Answers

56. Yes. Bugging and wiretapping are "searches," as the term is used in the Fourth Amendment. Therefore, absent exigent circumstances, bugging and wiretapping may not occur except on probable cause, and with a warrant. In fact, a federal statute, so-called "Title III," (18 U.S.C. §§ 2510-20) prohibits all eavesdropping and wiretapping without a court order. So the bugging here clearly violates both Title III and the Fourth Amendment, and Louie can keep his bugged statement out of evidence.

57. No. The Supreme Court has held that ***"secret agents"*** — that is, people who engage in conversations with a suspect, without the suspect's knowing that the other party is a police officer or informant — are not conducting "searches," and thus cannot violate the Fourth Amendment. This is true whether the agent is "bugged" or "unbugged." See, e.g., *U.S. v. White*. Furthermore, the prohibitions against bugging and wiretapping contained in Title III expressly exclude (and thus permit) interceptions made by or with the ***consent of a party to the conversation.*** So even though Harriet was a police officer, and Melvin did not know this, the recording of Melvin's statement does not violate either the Fourth Amendment or Title III. (However, if the bug had been used to record a conversation between Melvin and someone else, at which Harriet was not present, then Title III would apply and the statement could not be used — what makes the difference here is that Harriet was a party to the communication being intercepted.)

Exam Tips on
ELECTRONIC SURVEILLANCE AND SECRET AGENTS

Here are some of the ways issues discussed in this chapter can appear on exams:

Electronic surveillance questions are rare because the rules are based on statutes.

The most important thing to remember is that electronic surveillance (e.g., bugging or wiretapping) ***without a warrant*** is ***improper unless one of the parties to the conversations consents.***

Example: Suspecting that students are using illegal drugs, a college president arranges for local police to put concealed microphones in several dormitory suites. The police do not get a search warrant. With these microphones, officers record an offer by D (one of the students) to sell drugs to another student. The tapes are inadmissible against D at his trial for dealing in narcotics, because electronic surveillance requires a warrant.

You are much more likely to get an exam question about ***secret agents***, an area in which there have been a number of cases on point.

Remember that ***before there has been an indictment,*** a defendant ***assumes the risk of his own misplaced trust,*** that is, the risk that the person in whom he confides will relay the information to police.

Example: Police recruit Brother (D's brother) in an attempt to catch D gambling. Brother wears a recording device and meets D to place a bet. D takes the bet and the conversation is recorded. The tape is used against D at his gambling trial. D's constitutional rights have not been violated; he assumed the risk that Brother would not keep his confidences.

After indictment, the state is very ***limited*** in how it can use secret agents to gather evidence to use in the criminal prosecution. States can only use passive "listening post"–type secret agents; any ***active conduct*** to elicit information — even if it's not a direct question — will violate a defendant's ***Sixth Amendment right to assistance of counsel.***

Example: D and X are involved in a bomb plot. After D is arrested and charged, the government turns X against D, and sends X to visit D in jail. During the meeting, X says to D, "Gee, I was surprised to hear they nabbed you." D's response is inadmissible, because it was obtained in violation of D's Sixth Amendment right to counsel: the purpose of X's comment was to elicit a response, impermissibly transforming X's conduct from passive to active. Since D had already been indicted, he was entitled not to have the government try to elicit information from him in the absence of his lawyer.

Entrapment is sometimes a hidden issue. To make a claim for entrapment, the defendant must show that the police ***planted the suggestion*** of the crime in D's mind. If D had a ***"predisposition"*** to commit this type of offense, his entrapment defense will ***fail***.

Example: Burglar, who has prior convictions for burglary, meets Undercover Agent, who is posing as a "fence." Undercover Agent suggests a plan of a staged burglary to Burglar, with the two of them splitting the profits. Burglar agrees, then is charged with conspiracy to burgle. Because of Burglar's prior prior convictions, he will probably not be able to argue that he was an innocent person not predisposed to commit this criminal act. Thus his entrapment defense will probably fail.

CHAPTER 5

CONFESSIONS AND POLICE INTERROGATION

ChapterScope

This chapter examines the rules about confessions and police interrogations. The most important rule in this context is the *Miranda* rule; we will spend most of the chapter exploring its parameters.

Voluntariness: In order for a confession to be admissible against the defendant at trial, it must be ***voluntary.***

Miranda* rule:** When a suspect is questioned in custody by the police, his confession will be admissible against him ***only if he has received the four "Miranda" warnings.

Custody: *Miranda* warnings must be given only if the suspect is in ***custody.*** "Custody" exists only if a reasonable person in the suspect's position would believe that he is ***not free to leave*** at that moment.

Interrogation: *Miranda* warnings must be given only if the police are ***interrogating*** the suspect. Interrogation includes both direct questioning and its "functional equivalent." ***Volunteered statements*** do ***not*** qualify.

"Public safety" exception: *Miranda* warnings are unnecessary where the questioning is "reasonably prompted by a concern for the ***public safety***" (e.g., questioning that occurs while the police are trying to find a bomb that they think is set to go off).

Waiver: A suspect may impliedly or expressly ***waive*** any or all of his *Miranda* rights.

Impeachment of defendant: The *Miranda* rule applies principally to the government's ***"case in chief."*** It does ***not*** apply to evidence used to ***impeach*** the defendant's credibility on cross-examination.

I. INTRODUCTION

A. **Major area of controversy:** Police interrogation of suspects, and the use in evidence of confessions obtained by interrogation, have been the subject of extensive judicial and popular discussion during the last 30 years.

1. **Dilemma:** Underlying all of the cases decided in this area is the policy dilemma between the need to protect the individual against coercive or brutal police tactics and the need to have an effective police system not hamstrung in its role of fighting crime.

2. **Role of confessions:** Also at issue is the role that confessions play in our criminal system. There is dispute about whether confessions are necessary for effective law enforcement; the statistics are equivocal. (Nutshell, p. 197).

   a. **Confessions as bad for society:** Many believe, as Justice Goldberg wrote for the Court in *Escobedo v. Illinois*, 378 U.S. 478 (1964), "that a system of criminal law enforcement which comes to depend on the 'confession' will, in the long run, be less reliable and more subject to abuses than a system which depends on extrinsic evidence independently secured through skillful investigation."

b. **Need for police flexibility:** But others believe that if the use of confessions is cut back, the police system will, as Justice White put it in his dissent to *Escobedo*, "be crippled and its task made a great deal more difficult . . . for unsound, unstated reasons which can find no home in the provisions of the Constitution."

B. **Historical development:** The use of ***coerced confessions*** in federal prosecutions has been barred since before the turn of the century, but only since 1936 has the Supreme Court restricted the use of confessions in state trials. During the post-1936 period, the Court has relied *seriatim* on several different theories for deciding whether a particular confession should be allowed in a state trial.

1. ***Miranda* rule:** Today, the admissibility of most confessions in either federal or state trials is governed by the Supreme Court's ruling in *Miranda v. Arizona*, 384 U.S. 436 (1966), which will be extensively discussed below.

2. **Not all cases covered by *Miranda:*** The *Miranda* decision, however, does not render earlier Supreme Court cases on confessions irrelevant. A few of the situations in which these earlier cases, rather than *Miranda*, are relevant, follow:

a. **Consent searches:** The ***voluntariness*** of ***consent to allow a search*** (see *supra*, p. 139) is often determined by reference to factors similar to those governing the voluntariness of confessions. *Miranda* has no effect on this consent-to-search problem, so that pre-*Miranda* confession cases, which emphasized the importance of the voluntariness of the confession, must be consulted.

b. **Involuntary confessions never admissible:** The *Miranda* decision described certain fairly technical requirements (e.g., the reciting to the suspect of his right to remain silent) that must be met if a confession is to be valid. Even if these requirements are met, a confession may still be inadmissible if it does not meet the test of earlier case-law. In other words, compliance with *Miranda* requirements is a necessary but not sufficient condition for the admissibility of a confession. A confession which is ***involuntary***, for instance, is not admissible despite compliance with *Miranda.*

i. **Must be police coercion:** However, in recent years, the test for determining the "voluntariness" of a confession has been dramatically watered down. For instance, it is now apparently the case that the only thing that can prevent a confession from being found to be "voluntary" is ***police coercion***. Neither ***coercion by non-government personnel***, nor serious ***mental illness*** on the defendant's part, is at all relevant in determining whether his confession is "voluntary." See, e.g., *Colorado v. Connelly*, discussed *infra*, p. 264 (fact that suspect's confession was in large part due to his psychotic, schizophrenic state, and that he confessed because the "voice of God" told him he should do so, is irrelevant; confession was admissible because there was no police or other governmental wrongdoing).

c. **Collateral use:** Although a confession obtained in violation of *Miranda* may not be introduced in the prosecution's case in chief, it may be used to impeach the defendant's testimony. But if such a confession was obtained by coercion, it may not be admitted even for impeachment purposes. See *Mincey v. Arizona*, 437 U.S. 385 (1978), discussed *infra*, p. 278. Pre-*Miranda* case law is relevant to the question of what constitutes coercion.

II. PRE-*MIRANDA* CONFESSION CASES

A. ***Brown v. Mississippi:*** The first time the Supreme Court prevented the use of a coerced confession in a state trial was in *Brown v. Mississippi*, 297 U.S. 278 (1936). In *Brown*, a confession obtained by brutally beating the suspect was set aside on the theory that interrogation is part of the state conviction process and is thus subject to the Fourteenth Amendment's due process requirements. The *Brown* Court held that the due process requirement meant that "state action, whether through one agency or another, shall be consistent with the fundamental principles of liberty and justice which lie at the base of all our civil and political institutions." The confession in *Brown*, because it was the product of utter coercion and brutality, was held to have been obtained in violation of due process.

1. **Fifth Amendment not discussed in *Brown:*** The *Brown* decision did not hold that the Fifth Amendment's freedom against compulsory self-incrimination applied to state trials and had been violated. Rather, it held that some kinds of police brutality are so shocking that they violate the Fourteenth Amendment right of due process, whether or not these police methods violate the Fifth Amendment. The *Brown* Court thus applied the "fundamental rights" approach to coerced confessions (see *supra*, p. 2) — the right to be free of coercion in police interrogation was so important that it was a "fundamental right" as to which the Fourteenth Amendment applied.

B. **The "voluntariness" test:** The Fifth Amendment was not specifically held applicable to the states until 1964, in *Malloy v. Hogan*, 378 U.S. 1 (1964). From *Brown* until *Malloy*, the Supreme Court used the fundamental rights approach to review the admissibility of confessions in state trials. In determining whether the admission of a particular confession would violate the suspect's fundamental rights, the Court attached great importance to whether the confession was voluntary. For this reason, the test applied between *Brown* and *Malloy* has often been referred to as the ***"voluntariness" test.***

1. **Factors in voluntariness test:** In applying the so-called "voluntariness" test, the Court did in fact attach great importance to whether the confession was a product of the defendant's "free and rational choice." See, e.g., *Lisenba v. Cal.*, 314 U.S. 219 (1941). However, the "voluntariness" of a confession is a hard notion to define, let alone measure, and the Court during the *Brown*-to-*Malloy* years allowed several different factors to enter into its decisions on the admissibility of particular confessions:

a. **Reliability:** Some confessions were disallowed because the means by which they were obtained made their ***reliability*** doubtful.

Example: In cases of police brutality, such as *Brown*, there was good reason to suspect that the defendant had confessed not because of his guilt, but in order to escape further beating. The unreliability of a particular confession was often further indicated by the lack of any corroborating evidence.

b. **Offensive police practices:** Other confessions were disallowed despite their apparent reliability, because the police practices by which they were obtained offended the Court's sense of ***fundamental decency***.

Example: In *Rogers v. Richmond*, 365 U.S. 534 (1961), the police induced the defendant to confess by pretending to arrest his sick wife. The state court allowed the confession to be introduced, on the grounds that the police's trickery was not likely to have produced an unreliable confession. The Supreme Court reversed, holding that the reliability of the confession was not the only issue. The Court stated that confessions obtained by subterfuge and force must be disallowed "not because such confessions are unlikely to be true but because the methods used to extract them offend an underlying principle in the enforcement of our criminal law: that ours is an accusatorial and not an inquisitorial system."

c. **Confessions not the product of free will:** Finally, some confessions were disallowed because they were not the product of the defendant's ***free choice***, even though these confessions were apparently reliable, and even though the practices by which they were obtained did not strike the Court as being inherently objectionable or indecent.

Example: In *Townsend v. Sain*, 372 U.S. 293 (1963), the suspect, who was sick, was given a drug by the police that happened to have the effects of a truth serum. The police were unaware of the drug's effects, and obtained a confession from the suspect after questioning him. The Supreme Court held that the confession was not admissible, despite the fact that it appeared to have been reliable and was not the result of conscious wrongdoing by the police: "Any questioning by police officers which *in fact* produces a confession which is not the product of free intellect renders that confession inadmissible."

2. **"Totality of the circumstances" examined:** In applying the "voluntariness" test during the *Brown*-to-*Malloy* years, the Supreme Court, and the state courts attempting to follow it, made their decisions on the admissibility of confessions on a case-by-case basis. In each case, the courts considered the ***"totality of the circumstances"*** in order to determine whether any of the three factors listed in (1.) above vitiated the confession. In their examination of the overall facts of each case, the courts attached greatest importance to the following factors:

   a. the number of interrogators;

   b. the length of questioning;

   c. the place of questioning;

   d. whether the right to counsel was denied; and

   e. the characteristics of the subject (e.g., age, physical and mental condition, education, and experience.)

C. **Criticism of the voluntariness test:** For the nearly 30 years during which the "voluntariness" test was applied, it was frequently criticized for giving defendants insufficient protection. Because the test was applied by examining the "totality of the circumstances," a great deal of discretion was left to the trial judge, and decisions varied greatly. It was in part to give more precise guidelines to the police that the Supreme Court issued its *Miranda* decision, discussed below.

D. Pre-*Miranda* rules for federal prosecutions: Because the admissibility of confessions in state trials during the *Brown* to *Malloy* period was determined by reference not to the Fifth Amendment but to the Fourteenth Amendment fundamental right of due process, the state and federal tests were not, strictly speaking, the same.

1. **Use of voluntariness test:** The Supreme Court, during the *Brown* to *Malloy* period, generally used the voluntariness test in the few cases in which it reviewed the use of confessions in federal trials.

2. ***McNabb-Mallory* rule:** In addition to excluding involuntary confessions, the Court also excluded from federal trials confessions obtained by federal officers where the confession was obtained during a period of "unnecessary delay" in taking the suspect before a U.S. magistrate for arraignment. This rule preventing the federal use of confessions obtained during lengthy custody was known as the ***McNabb-Mallory rule***, after the cases in which it was enunciated, *McNabb v. U.S.*, 318 U.S. 332 (1943) and *Mallory v. U.S.*, 354 U.S. 449 (1957).

    a. **Repeal of rule:** The *McNabb-Mallory* rule was formulated not as a constitutional doctrine but as an exercise by the Supreme Court of its discretionary right to supervise the federal courts. It was never extended to the states, and was repealed from federal practice by the Omnibus Crime Control Act of 1968, Title II, 28 U.S.C. 3501(a).

III. *ESCOBEDO* AND THE RIGHT TO COUNSEL

A. Pre-*Escobedo* cases: The cases described above, which applied the "totality of the circumstances" test in determining the admissibility of confessions, did not address great importance to whether the suspect was permitted to have a lawyer with him during the interrogation. However, in several cases during the late 1950s and early 1960s, the Supreme Court began to pay increasing attention to the issue of ***right to counsel*** during the interrogation process.

1. ***Crooker:*** In *Crooker v. California*, 357 U.S. 433 (1958), a confession was held to have been voluntary and therefore admissible, despite the fact that the accused had unsuccessfully requested the right to call his lawyer. But four members of the Court dissented, stating that "the accused who wants a counsel should have one at any time after the moment of arrest."

2. ***Spano:*** In *Spano v. N.Y.*, 360 U.S. 315 (1959), a majority of the Court found a confession obtained after an overnight, eight-hour questioning session, to have been involuntary. The majority opinion applied traditional "involuntariness" criteria.

    a. **Concurrence:** But four Justices, in a concurrence, stated that the confession should have been excluded on right-to-counsel grounds. The concurrence, written by Justice Stewart, noted that the defendant in *Spano* had already been indicted by the time of the questioning; the concurrence argued that because an indicted suspect has the right to counsel at the arraignment which should immediately follow the indictment, he has the right to counsel at a police interrogation conducted during the period when the arraignment should have taken place.

3. ***Massiah:*** In *Massiah v. U.S.*, 377 U.S. 201 (1964), an indicted defendant, while out on bail and in his co-defendant's car, made incriminating remarks which were overheard by the police via a concealed radio transmitter planted with the co-defendant's co-operation. The incriminating statements were held inadmissible.

   a. **Need for counsel:** The 6-3 majority held that the overheard conversation was in effect a surreptitious investigation; the opinion noted that the right-to-counsel rationale of the concurrence in *Spano* applied as forcefully to an undercover use of police tactics as it did to a jailhouse interrogation. Therefore, the right to counsel applied, and the confession must be barred, the Court held.

B. ***Escobedo:*** In the *Crooker, Spano*, and *Massiah* cases discussed above, it became clear that at least four, and in *Massiah* five, members of the Court attached great importance to a defendant's right to counsel in certain pre-trial confrontations with the police. But it was not until ***Escobedo v. Illinois***, 378 U.S. 478 (1964), that a ***confession obtained in a police stationhouse*** was held ***inadmissible because of deprivation of the right to counsel***.

1. **Facts:** The *Escobedo* confession was obtained after defendant made repeated requests to see his lawyer, and after the lawyer had actually come to the police station and been turned away.

2. **Holding:** The Court's holding was a very limited one: "We hold . . . that where, as here, the investigation is no longer a general inquiry into an unsolved crime but has begun to focus on a particular suspect, the suspect has been taken into police custody, the police carry out a process of interrogations that lends itself to eliciting incriminating statements, the suspect has requested and been denied an opportunity to consult with his lawyer, and the police have not effectively warned him of his absolute constitutional right to remain silent, the accused has been denied 'the Assistance of Counsel' in violation of the Sixth Amendment to the Constitution as made obligatory upon the States by the Fourteenth Amendment, . . . and that no statement elicited by the police during the investigation may be used against him at a criminal trial."

3. **No use of "totality of circumstances" test:** The *Escobedo* opinion departed from the previous practice of examining the "totality of the circumstances" in judging the admissibility of confessions. Under *Escobedo*, if the right to counsel was not respected, the confession could not be admitted even though all circumstances taken together indicated the voluntariness of the confession and an absence of offensive police conduct.

4. **Effect of *Malloy* on *Escobedo:*** The abandonment of the "totality of the circumstances" test in *Escobedo* was due in large part to the decision, only a few months earlier, in *Malloy v. Hogan*, 378 U.S. 1 (1964). In *Malloy*, which did not involve a confession, the Court held that the Fifth Amendment privilege against self-incrimination applied to state trials as well as to federal ones.

   a. **Fifth Amendment in *Escobedo:*** As a result of *Malloy*, it was unnecessary for the Court to use the vague "totality of the circumstances — voluntariness" test in determining the admissibility in state court of the *Escobedo* confession. Although *Esc-*

obedo dealt mainly with the Sixth Amendment right to counsel, the court's concern with the Fifth Amendment right against self-incrimination was indicated by its reference to "the right of the accused to be advised by his lawyer of his privilege against self- incrimination." (Indeed, subsequent cases have viewed *Escobedo* as being based on the right against self-incrimination *instead of* the Sixth Amendment right to counsel.)

IV. *MIRANDA* GENERALLY

A. Impact of *Miranda:* The *Escobedo* holding was narrowly confined to its facts; that case applied only to situations in which the accused was in custody, asked for and was refused a lawyer, and was not warned of his right to remain silent. But in ***Miranda v. Arizona***, 384 U.S. 436 (1966), the Supreme Court broadened the right against self-incrimination to cover ***virtually all custodial police interrogations***. Furthermore, the Court established extremely specific ***procedural safeguards*** which must be followed during custodial police interrogations in order to avoid violation of the self-incrimination privilege.

1. **Continued validity of *Miranda:*** *Miranda*, which is probably the most important case decided in the 1960s, continues to be of utmost importance today. And in 2000, the Court expressly declined to overrule the case; see *Dickerson v. U.S.*, *infra*, p. 241. There are, however, indications that the present Court is unhappy with the breadth of *Miranda*, and will cut it back wherever occasion presents; this trend is discussed *infra*, p. 278.

B. General setting of *Miranda:* The *Miranda* decision is not narrowly confined to its facts, and in fact involves four distinct companion cases. The language of the decision is of a breadth not usually seen even in Supreme Court opinions — as one of the dissenters to *Miranda* put it, the majority opinion set forth "a constitutional code of rules for confessions."

C. Holding of *Miranda:* The Court in *Miranda* summarized its decision in the following words: "We hold that when an individual is ***taken into custody*** or otherwise ***deprived of his freedom by the authorities in any significant way*** and is subjected to ***questioning***, the ***privilege against self-incrimination is jeopardized***. Procedural safeguards must be employed to protect the privilege, and unless other fully effective means are adopted to notify the person of his right of silence and to assure that the exercise of the right will be scrupulously honored, the following measures are required. [The suspect] must be warned prior to any questioning

1. that he has the right to remain silent,
2. that anything he says can be used against him in a court of law,
3. that he has the right to the presence of an attorney,
4. and that if he cannot afford an attorney one will be appointed for him prior to any questioning if he so desires."

D. Custodial questioning only: The *Miranda* warnings are necessary only where an individual "is taken into custody or otherwise deprived of his freedom by the authorities in any significant way and is subjected to questioning." The circumstances in which the requisite deprivation of freedom has occurred will be discussed more fully *infra*, p. 243.

1. **No distinction between confessions and exculpatory statements:** The *Miranda* rules apply to ***any statement*** made by the suspect while in custody. "No distinction can be drawn between statements which are direct confessions and statements which amount to 'admissions' of part or all of an offense. The privilege against self-incrimination protects the individual from being compelled to incriminate himself in any manner; it does not distinguish degrees of incrimination. Similarly, for precisely the same reason, no distinction may be drawn between inculpatory statements and statements alleged to be merely 'exculpatory'. "

E. **May be exercised at any time:** The right to remain silent and to have a lawyer present may be exercised at any time during the questioning. Thus even if the suspect at first indicates that he waives his right to silence and to a lawyer, if he changes his mind the interrogation must cease.

F. **Waiver:** The suspect may waive his right to remain silent and to have a lawyer, but this waiver is effective only if it is knowingly and intelligently made. The suspect's silence may not be taken as a waiver. (The problems of waiver will be discussed more fully, *infra*, p. 259.)

1. **Where suspect already aware of rights:** The police must give the *Miranda* warnings even if they have reason to believe that the suspect is aware of his rights. "No amount of circumstantial evidence that the person may have been aware of [these] rights will suffice. . . . "

G. **Right to counsel:** If the suspect indicates that he wants a lawyer, and can't afford one, the police must obtain one for him, before they conduct the interrogation.

1. **Right applies only where questioning occurs:** The police do not have an absolute duty to provide counsel for all suspects who wish one; the police can avoid the need for procuring counsel by simply not conducting the interrogation. But if they wish to interrogate, they must supply a lawyer to whomever wants one.

2. **Indigence presumed:** The police do not have to warn the suspect that he has a right to counsel appointed for him, if they know for a fact that he can afford a lawyer of his own, or that he has already retained one. But "the expedient of giving a warning is too simple and the rights involved too important to engage in *ex post facto* inquiries into financial ability when there is any doubt at all on that score."

3. **Right to lawyer's presence:** The right to counsel imposed by *Miranda* is not merely the right to consult a lawyer prior to the questioning, but the right to ***have the lawyer present*** while the questioning goes on.

   a. **Rationale:** The Court emphasized that if a lawyer is merely consulted before the questioning starts, the suspect's will can quickly be overborne by the questioners once the lawyer is no longer present. The Court noted that the presence of counsel during interrogation will also act to prevent police coercion, and will "help to guarantee that the accused gives a fully accurate statement to the police and that the statement is rightly reported by the prosecution at trial."

H. **Inadmissibility:** Any statement obtained in violation of the *Miranda* rules will be ***inadmissible*** as prosecution evidence, regardless of whether other factors indicate that the statement would meet traditional "voluntariness" criteria.

1. **Impeachment use:** A confession obtained in violation of the *Miranda* rules cannot be introduced as part of the prosecution's case in chief. But it may generally be introduced for purposes of ***impeaching*** testimony which the defendant has given. See *infra*, p. 277.

I. Fifth Amendment basis for *Miranda:* The *Miranda* decision relies more heavily on the Fifth Amendment right against self-incrimination than on the Sixth Amendment right to counsel. The essence of the Court's holding is that custodial interrogation is ***inherently coercive***, and that because of such inherent coercion, "no statement obtained from [a] defendant [in custody] can truly be the product of his free choice." The right to have a lawyer present, although related to the Sixth Amendment, is important in the custodial interrogation context ***because uncounseled questioning is likely to induce confessions in violation of the Fifth Amendment***, not because there is a general right to have a lawyer when one is in jail. (If the police do not interrogate, they do not have to supply a lawyer.)

1. **Rejection of voluntariness test:** *Miranda* represents a complete rejection of the "voluntariness" test for judging confessions. The failure to give required *Miranda* warnings constitutes an ***irrebuttable presumption*** that the confession was involuntary; no evidence showing that the suspect was aware of his rights, or that he truly desired to make his confession, can overcome the failure to give the required warnings.

2. **Dissent's criticism:** The majority's complete rejection of the voluntariness test provoked a strong dissent by Justice White, with whom Justices Harlan and Stewart joined (Justice Clark wrote a partial dissent). The dissent argued that the Fifth Amendment only protects persons against being ***compelled*** to testify; the dissent stated that while some custodial interrogations are indeed coercive, not all are, and sometimes a suspect may confess in a purely voluntary manner. The dissent advocated that the traditional "totality of the circumstances" test for determining voluntariness be maintained.

   a. **Other methods suggested:** The dissent also suggested that other methods than a complete ban on questioning could help the courts determine which confessions were voluntary: "Transcripts or observers could be required, specific time limits, tailored to fit the case, could be imposed, or other devices could be utilized to reduce the chances that otherwise indiscernible coercion will produce an inadmissible confession."

3. **Constitutional basis:** Two key decisions bearing on the constitutional status of *Miranda* are *Dickerson v. U.S.*, immediately *infra*, and *Vega v. Tekoh, infra,* p. 358. Taken together, these two cases seem to conclude that *Miranda* is only ***indirectly*** a constitutional holding: some, but not all, all scenarios in which *Miranda* warnings are required but not given are a violation of the suspect's Fifth Amendment rights.

J. Congress did not successfully substitute for the *Miranda* warnings (*Dickerson*): The *Miranda* majority stated that the warnings listed in *Miranda* must be given "unless other fully effective means are devised to inform accused persons of their right to silence and to assure a continuous opportunity to exercise it[.]" The Court thus implied that a legislature, either state or federal, could enact other procedural safeguards against involuntary self-incrimination, which would replace the *Miranda* warnings. But as a 2000 case, ***Dickerson v. U.S.***, showed, an attempt by Congress to substitute for the *Miranda* warnings in federal prosecutions failed.

1. **Congressional response:** Not long after *Miranda*, Congress tried to take the Court up on its invitation to devise such "other fully effective means . . . to inform accused persons of

their right to silence. . . ." Congress did this by enacting Title II of the Omnibus Crime Control and Safe Streets Act of 1968. Title II governed the admissibility of confessions in federal courts, and purported to repeal the strict warning requirements of *Miranda* for federal prosecutions.

a. **Voluntariness test reinstated:** Title II stated a simple and exclusive test for admissibility: a confession was admissible in evidence in federal prosecutions ***"if it is voluntarily given."*** So even where the *Miranda* warnings were not given, the federal judge was free to (indeed required to) admit the confession if he found it to be voluntary, according to Title II.

2. **Court strikes down statute:** From the beginning, there were grave doubts about whether Title II was constitutional. Mostly for that reason, federal prosecutors almost never relied on it, and for over 30 years the Supreme Court was never called upon to say whether it was constitutional. But in *Dickerson v. U.S.*, 530 U.S. 428 (2000), that issue finally arose. The Court responded by striking down the statute as ***unconstitutional***. In so doing, the Court: (1) made it clear that *Miranda* was at least indirectly ***based upon the Constitution***; and (2) ***declined to overrule*** *Miranda*.

a. **Holding:** By a 7-2 vote, the Court found that Title II was an improper effort by Congress to supersede *Miranda*. The Court's opinion, by Justice Rehnquist, said that the majority in *Miranda* "thought it was announcing a constitutional rule." Since that case was a holding about what the Constitution requires, it could not be superseded by Congress — that's because it is up to the Court, not Congress, to determine the scope of constitutional guarantees.

i. **Stare decisis:** In declining to overrule *Miranda*, the Court relied heavily on the principle of ***stare decisis.*** The majority hinted that it might well not agree with *Miranda*'s reasoning and rule "were we addressing the issue in the first instance." But it said that *Miranda* "has become ***embedded in routine police practice*** to the point where the warnings have become ***part of our national culture***." Therefore, *stare decisis* "weigh[s] heavily against overruling it now."

b. **Dissent:** Two justices, Scalia joined by Thomas, dissented. Scalia believed that *Miranda* did not hold that the *Miranda* warnings were constitutionally-required. Therefore, he believed that Congress should be free to overturn the requirement of *Miranda* warnings in federal cases, as Congress had attempted to do in Title II. Scalia also believed that the Court was itself violating the constitution by imposing the not-constitutionally-required *Miranda* warnings on the states.

c. **What the case means:** There are three plausible interpretations of what *Dickerson* means about the constitutional underpinnings of *Miranda*:

[1] **Interpretation 1:** that *Miranda* is a ***direct constitutional holding.*** That is, the Court was holding in *Dickerson* that in any situation in which the *Miranda* warnings were not given, admission of a confession is ***necessarily a violation*** of the Fifth Amendment privilege against self-information and/or the Sixth Amendment right to counsel.

[2] **Interpretation 2:** that *Miranda* is only ***indirectly*** a constitutional holding. That is,

the *Dickerson* Court concluded that where *Miranda* warnings are not given, the admission of many (but by no means all) of the resulting confessions would violate the Constitution. Therefore, *Miranda* rested on the Court's power to the Court exercise the ***prophylactic*** power to avoid constitutional violations, by setting out a ***"bright-line" rule*** requiring warnings in all cases to prevent constitutional violations in some.

[3] **Interpretation 3:** that *Miranda* is ***not a constitutional holding at all*** — it merely reflects the Court's supervisory powers over the nation's judicial system.

d. **Interpretation [2] selected (*Vega v. Tekoh*):** A post-*Dickerson* decision, *Vega v. Tekoh*, 142 S.Ct. 2095 (2022)[1] seems to confirm that a majority of the Roberts Court has ***chosen Interpretation [2]*** as the correct interpretation of what Dickerson says about the constitutional status of *Miranda*.

   i. **Consequence:** In *Vega*, the Court conceded that *Dickerson* says that the *Miranda* rules are "constitutionally based," and have "constitutional underpinnings." But, the Court indicated, *Dickerson* and other precedents mean that where required *Miranda* warnings are not given, the admission of the resulting confession ***will not necessarily violate*** the Fifth or Sixth Amendment rights of the suspect.

V. WHAT IS A "CUSTODIAL" INTERROGATION

A. **Language of *Miranda:*** The *Miranda* opinion applies only to "custodial" questioning. The Court stated that "By custodial interrogation, we mean questioning initiated by law enforcement officers after a person has been taken into custody or otherwise deprived of his freedom of action in any significant way." Post-*Miranda* cases have raised numerous difficulties with deciding when questioning is "custodial."

B. **"Focus of investigation" test abandoned:** In a footnote to the language quoted in (A.) above, the *Miranda* Court stated that "[Custodial interrogation] is what we meant in *Escobedo* when we spoke of an investigation which had ***focused*** on an accused." However, several subsequent Supreme Court cases indicate that this footnote is not to be taken literally, and that ***the mere fact that an investigation has "focused" on a particular suspect does not make it custodial*** for *Miranda* purposes.

Example: D is suspected of tax fraud. IRS agents visit D at his house at 8 a.m., and interview him for 3 hours. D is not (and knows he is not) in "custody," and that he is free at any time to discontinue the interview. He makes certain statements that are later used against him at trial. At trial, D argues that because the tax fraud investigation had already "focused" on him before the interview, he should have been entitled to *Miranda* warnings. He reasons that the same psychological pressures present in a jailhouse interrogation were present when the agents interviewed him.

Held, for the prosecution. The fact that the investigation had "focused" on D was irrelevant to whether he was entitled to Miranda warnings. The only thing that mat-

1. For a full discussion of *Vega*, see *infra*, p. 358.

tered was whether D was in custody. Since he wasn't, and knew he wasn't, the agents didn't need to give him the warnings. *Beckwith v. U.S.*, 425 U.S. 341 (1976).

1. **Undercover agents:** The irrelevance of whether the investigation has "focused" on D is especially significant in analyzing whether D's conversations with ***undercover agents*** or ***government informants*** must be preceded by warnings. If the defendant talks to an undercover agent or informant ***without knowing*** he is talking to a law enforcement agent, no "custodial interrogation" has taken place. This is true even if the defendant is ***in jail*** at the time.

   Example: D is in jail pending trial on a charge of aggravated battery. The police suspect him in an unrelated murder (of Stephenson). The police therefore place in D's cell an undercover agent. The agent befriends D, and purports to plot with D for them both to escape. The agent asks D if D has ever killed anybody (apparently to get D to prove to the agent that D is sufficiently ruthless to kill in the course of the escape, if necessary). D responds by admitting to and describing the Stephenson murder. At his trial for the Stephenson murder, D tries to have his statements excluded on the grounds that he made them to a law enforcement officer (the agent), and did so without the benefit of *Miranda* warnings.

   Held, this was not a custodial interrogation in the *Miranda* sense, so *Miranda* warnings were not necessary. The rationale for requiring *Miranda* warnings is that a suspect will feel compelled to speak when he is in a "police-dominated atmosphere." When a suspect, even an incarcerated one, speaks freely to one who he believes to be a fellow inmate rather than an officer, this coercive atmosphere is lacking. *Illinois v. Perkins*, 496 U.S. 292 (1990).

   a. **Sixth Amendment:** However, the use of undercover agents, although it will never cause a *Miranda* violation, may lead to a violation of the suspect's ***Sixth Amendment*** right to ***counsel***. Once a suspect has been ***indicted*** or otherwise charged, it will be a violation of his right to counsel for a secret agent to deliberately obtain incriminating statements from him in the absence of counsel, and to pass these on to the prosecution. See, e.g., *Massiah v. U.S., supra*, p. 238. But there was no right-to-counsel problem in *Perkins, supra*, because D had not been indicted or arrested on the charge to which his statements related (the murder) at the time he made the statements; the fact that he was under indictment for an unrelated charge was irrelevant.

C. **Objective "reasonable suspect" test:** Whether a suspect is or is not in "custody" as of a particular moment is to be determined by an ***objective "reasonable suspect"*** test. In other words, the issue is ***whether a reasonable person in the suspect's position would believe that he was (or was not) in custody at that moment.***

   1. **Ignore parties' own beliefs:** Thus the ***unexpressed intent*** of the police officer to hold (or not hold) the suspect against his will is ***irrelevant***. Similarly, the suspect's own subjective belief that he is or is not free to go, to the extent that that belief is not one that would be shared by a reasonable person, is irrelevant. See, e.g., *Berkemer v. McCarty*, 468 U.S. 420 (1984), discussed further *infra*, p. 248.

   2. **Cuts both ways:** This "objective" rule cuts both ways.

a. **Officer intends not to hold suspect:** Thus suppose the officer has subjectively decided ***not*** to hold the suspect in custody, but has not indicated (directly or indirectly) this fact to the suspect. Here, the suspect ***is*** in custody for *Miranda* purposes if a reasonable person in the suspect's position would think that he was not free to leave. The same is true if the interrogator hasn't decided whether the person being interrogated is a "serious" suspect, and thus hasn't decided whether to hold him — what counts is what one in the suspect's position would think, not what the interrogator thinks.

Example: Police are trying to solve the rape-murder of V, a 10-year-old girl. They have reason to believe that V talked to two ice cream truck drivers (X and D) shortly before her death. The police initially focus on X, but ask D to come to the station to see if he can shed any light on the crime. There, officers ask D a number of questions, to which he gives answers. At one point, D mentions that on the day of V's death he left his trailer home about midnight in his housemate's turquoise American-made car. This fact causes the questioners to suspect D much more intensely, because another witness has tied a turquoise American-made sedan to the crime. Shortly thereafter, the questioners advise D of his *Miranda* rights, and he stops talking. His pre-*Miranda* statements are admitted against him at trial. The prosecution argues that the fact that the questioners had not yet focused on D as a suspect at the time he gave the answers should be entitled to significant weight in determining whether D was in custody at the time he gave those answers.

Held, for D. "An officer's subjective and undisclosed view concerning whether the person being interrogated is a suspect is irrelevant to the assessment whether the person is in custody. . . . [A]n officer's view's concerning the nature of an interrogation, or beliefs concerning the potential culpability of the individual being questioned, may be one among many factors that bear upon the assessment whether that individual was custody, but only if the officer's views or beliefs were somehow manifested to the individual under interrogation and would have affected how a reasonable person in that position would perceive his or her freedom to leave." (Case remanded for a determination of whether a reasonable person in D's position would have thought that he was free to leave the station.) *Stansbury v. California*, 511 U.S. 318 (1994).

b. **Officer intends to hold suspect:** Conversely, suppose the interrogating officer has subjectively decided that D *is* a serious suspect who should be formally arrested and not allowed to leave. Here, too, this undisclosed belief will be irrelevant — if a reasonable person in the suspect's position would think he was free to leave, D is not in custody.

Example: Suppose that O, an officer, knows that a 6'5" man with a dragon tattoo on his left wrist is being sought in connection with a recent robbery. O sees D walking on the street, and notices that D is very tall and bears such a tattoo. Assume further that D does not know that the police are looking for a tattooed or tall person as the suspect in the case. O stops D and asks him an innocuous question (e.g., "Excuse me, sir, may I ask you where you're going?"). Assume that even prior to this question, O has already decided not to let D go unless D shows affirmatively that he was not the robber. So long as O has not communicated to D his intent to detain D, a reasonable person in D's position would think he was free to go. Therefore, D is not in "custody," and is thus not entitled to *Miranda* warnings.

3. **Suspect is minor:** Suppose that the suspect is a ***child***. When the objective "reasonable suspect" test is being applied, should the child's ***age be taken into account*** in determining whether a reasonable person in the suspect's position would believe he was in custody? The Supreme Court's answer is ***yes***, the child's age should be taken into account — so the younger the child, the quicker the court will be to conclude that a reasonable person of that child's age would have believed that he was in custody and not free to leave. ***J.D.B. v. North Carolina***, 131 S.Ct. 2394 (2011), a 5-4 decision.

   a. **Facts:** In *J.D.B.*, the suspect J.D.B. was a 13-year-old boy who was removed from his classroom and questioned by the police in a school conference room. The questioning concerned two recent home break-ins, and merchandise stolen from them that had later been spotted in J.D.B.'s possession at the school. The interrogation lasted 30-45 minutes, during which J.D.B. was not given *Miranda* warnings, was not permitted to speak to his legal guardian (his grandmother) and was not told that he could leave the room. He eventually confessed, at which point he was given *Miranda* warnings. The question was whether J.D.B.'s young age should be taken into account in deciding whether a reasonable person in his position would have believed, at the moment of confession, that he was free to leave the conference room (in which case he was not in "custody" and thus not entitled to *Miranda* warnings).

   b. **5-4 vote:** By a 5-4 vote, the Court held that the age of a minor who is a suspect ***should be taken into account*** in performing the objective analysis of whether the suspect was in custody. The majority opinion pointed out that "reasonable person" analysis in various areas of the law has always taken into account the age of the subject; in negligence cases, for instance, the age of the defendant is considered. The same should be true in the custody analysis, the majority said, since "a reasonable child subjected to police questioning will ***sometimes feel pressured to submit when a reasonable adult will feel free to go."*** Therefore, the child's age should be taken into account, at least where that age is "***known*** to the officer at the time of the interview, or would have been ***objectively apparent*** to any reasonable officer[.]"

   c. **Dissent:** The four dissenters (Alito, joined by Roberts, Scalia and Thomas) argued that a bright-line "***one-size-fits-all*** *Miranda* custody rule" would be ***easier to administer*** than a system where the child's age — but not other individual characteristics like intelligence — has to be taken into account. Any danger of coercion due to the suspect's youth could be handled by paying special attention to whether the incriminating statements were truly ***voluntary*** rather than coerced.

D. **Place of interrogation:** The ***place*** in which the interrogation takes place will often have an important bearing on whether "custody" exists. The test is always whether a reasonable person in D's position would believe he was free to leave, and this will depend in part on the locale.

   1. **Station-house:** Thus interrogations that take place in a ***station-house*** are more likely to be found "custodial" than those in, say, the defendant's home.

      a. **Arrest:** If D has been told that he is "under arrest" and is escorted to the police station, that's virtually dispositive — D is clearly in custody, because a person under arrest is not free to leave (at least until further steps, such as arraignment, have taken place).

b. **Placed in patrol car:** Similarly, if D has been placed in a ***patrol car*** under circumstances suggesting that D has been arrested, he is clearly in "custody."

c. **Voluntary station-house questioning:** A suspect who ***"voluntarily"*** comes to the police station in response to a police request is normally ***not*** in custody, and is therefore not entitled to *Miranda* warnings. *Oregon v. Mathiason*, 429 U.S. 492 (1977).

   i. **Facts:** In *Mathiason*, a burglary case, the police became suspicious of a parolee, who then came to the station in response to an officer's message that the latter would "like to discuss something with you." The suspect was told that he was not under arrest, that the police believed he was involved in the burglary, and (falsely) that the police had found his fingerprints at the scene. The suspect admitted the theft, and was then given his *Miranda* warnings, after which he made a taped confession.

   ii. **Holding:** The Court, in a *per curiam* opinion, held that the suspect had not been in custody at the time he made his initial confession, and had thus not then been entitled to *Miranda* warnings.

d. **Lack of formal arrest not dispositive:** However, the mere fact that there has been ***no formal arrest*** will ***not*** by itself suffice to prevent a station-house questioning from being custodial. If the surrounding circumstances would indicate to a reasonable person in D's situation that he was not free to leave the station house, then the questioning is "custodial" however voluntary D's initial decision to come to the station may have been. For instance, if during the course of the "voluntary" questioning the police let D know that they ***now consider him the key suspect*** in the crime, this is likely to be enough to convince a reasonable person in D's position that the police are about to arrest him; if so, D is already in custody.

2. **Street encounters:** The issue of whether D is in custody often arises where the encounter takes place on the ***street***. Here, there is no general rule. If it should be clear to one in D's position that the police seriously suspect him of a felony, D is probably in custody. But if it appears that the police's suspicions are minor, or if the crime for which D is being questioned is so minor that arrest is unlikely, then probably D is not in custody.

   a. **Scene-of-the-crime questioning:** It is clear that the police may engage in a general questioning of persons ***near the scene of a crime*** without giving *Miranda* warnings. The *Miranda* decision itself stated that the decision "is not intended to hamper the traditional function of police officers in investigating crime. . . . General on-the-scene questioning as to facts surrounding a crime or other general questioning of citizens in the fact-finding process is not affected by our holding."

      i. **Focus on suspect:** But if the police seize one particular suspect fleeing the scene of the crime, the "general on-the-scene questioning" to which *Miranda* referred is not present, and the warnings presumably have to be given.

   b. **D acts suspiciously:** The police may sometimes detain a person not as part of a general "scene of the crime" investigation for a specific known crime, but because the person is ***acting suspiciously***. The ***"stop and frisk,"*** discussed in the context of arrest and search, *supra*, p. 148, is typical of such detention. Such encounters are probably not custodial, even where the suspect is frisked for the policeman's safety; see *Berkemer v. McCarty*, below (in which the Supreme Court referred to "the absence of any suggestion in our opinions that *Terry* stops are subject to the dictates of *Miranda*").

i. **Possible exceptions:** However, if the circumstances of a particular street encounter create a coercive atmosphere, the *Miranda* warnings might nonetheless be necessary. Thus if the police outnumber the suspects, or if the on-the-street questioning is sustained and intense, the questioning might be deemed custodial. The Supreme Court alluded to this possibility in *Berkemer v. McCarty*, where it noted that a suspect will be deemed to be in "custody" as soon as his "freedom of action is curtailed to a 'degree associated with formal arrest'. "

3. **Traffic stops:** Stops of ***motorists*** for ***minor traffic violations*** will normally ***not*** be "custodial." Here, as in other contexts, the test is whether one in the motorist's position would believe that he was or was not free to leave. Usually a driver in this position would reasonably believe that he was free to leave after a ticket had been issued to him.

Example: D, a motorist, is stopped and required to get out of his car. At the moment D has finished stepping out of the car, the arresting officer has decided to arrest D for driving while intoxicated, but has not yet communicated this fact to D. The issue is whether D is, at that moment, in custody.

Held, D was not yet in custody for *Miranda* purposes at the moment he stepped out of the car. "A [police officer's] unarticulated plan has no bearing on the question whether a suspect was 'in custody' at a particular time; the only relevant inquiry is how a reasonable person in the suspect's position would have understood his situation." *Berkemer v. McCarty*, 468 U.S. 420 (1984).

a. **Rationale:** So how does a reasonable person in the position of a motorist stopped for a traffic offense understand her situation? In *Berkemer*, *supra*, the Court answered by saying that typically, the reasonable person thinks he is not in custody: a traffic stop is ***"presumptively temporary and brief,"*** and the motorist knows that "in the end he most likely will be allowed to continue on his way" (in contrast to the typical station-house interrogation).

i. **Public:** Another factor making traffic stops less likely to be found "custodial" is that they usually occur in ***public***, and involve at most one or two police officers. This in turn means that the atmosphere is "substantially less police dominated" than the typical station-house interrogation. *Berkemer*, *supra*.

b. **Arrest:** Of course, if the police notify the motorist that he is ***under arrest***, he is immediately deemed to be in custody. Thus the defendant in *Berkemer, supra,* was held to have been in custody "at least as of the moment he was formally placed under arrest and instructed to get into the police car."

4. **Interview at home:** If the encounter takes place at D's ***home***, while he has not been placed under arrest, D is probably ***not*** in custody. See, e.g., *Beckwith v. U.S., supra*, p. 244,

in which D was not in custody while being questioned for three hours in his home on tax-fraud charges.

a. **Rationale:** In cases involving interrogation at D's home or workplace, courts have emphasized the familiar atmosphere in which the questioning is taking place, the lack of isolation from the outside world, and the absence of the "police-dominated" ambiance with which *Miranda* was so concerned.

5. **Airport smuggling investigations:** The stop of a ***suspected smuggler*** at an ***airport*** may in a particular situation be held to be custodial. Such a stop has aspects of a "scene of the crime" questioning, which, as noted, is usually not custodial. But if it is clear to the suspect that he is not free to leave, or if a large number of police are present so that a coercive atmosphere is created, custody may be found. See, e.g., *Florida v. Royer*, 460 U.S. 491 (1983), discussed *supra*, p. 161.

a. **Search:** If the smuggling suspect is ***searched***, the court is even more likely to hold that there has been custody. See, e.g., *U.S. v. McCain*, 556 F.2d 253 (5th Cir. 1977)

E. **Purpose of interrogation:** *Miranda* applies even when the ***purpose*** of the custody is ***unrelated*** to the purpose of the interrogation.

Example: D is in jail on a state offense. An IRS agent interrogates him about a tax crime completely unrelated to the one D is in jail for. *Held*, the interrogation was "custodial," so D was entitled to the Miranda warnings. *Mathis v. U.S.*, 391 U.S. 1 (1968).

VI. MINOR CRIMES

A. **No "minor crimes" exemption:** There is ***no "minor crimes"*** exception to the *Miranda* requirement — if an interrogation meets all of the standard requirements for *Miranda* warnings (especially the requirement that the suspect be "in custody"; see *supra*, p. 243), these warnings must be given ***no matter how minor the crime***, and ***regardless of the fact that no jail sentence may be imposed for it***. *Berkemer v. McCarty*, 468 U.S. 420 (1984).

1. **Traffic stops:** Probably the most important application of this rule is that suspects charged with ***minor traffic violations*** must be given *Miranda* warnings prior to custodial interrogation. *Berkemer* itself, for instance, involved an arrest for driving while intoxicated; even though the offense was only a misdemeanor under local law, *Miranda* warnings were required.

2. **Rationale:** In refusing to grant an exemption from *Miranda* for minor crimes, the *Berkemer* court relied principally on the rationale that such an exemption would significantly undermine the ***"clarity"*** of the *Miranda* rule. The Court pointed out that the police are often unaware at the time of an arrest whether the suspect has committed a misdemeanor or felony, and "it would be unreasonable to expect the police to make guesses as to the nature of the criminal conduct at issue before deciding how they may interrogate the suspect." Furthermore, "investigations into seemingly minor offenses sometimes escalate gradually into investigations into more serious matters," and an exception for minor crimes would force the police and courts to make difficult determinations about the point in such an escalation at which the *Miranda* warnings were required. Conversely, the dan-

ger that the *Miranda* rule was designed to deal with (that the police will coerce suspects into incriminating themselves) may certainly be present even in investigations into "minor" crimes.

VII. WHAT CONSTITUTES INTERROGATION

A. **Volunteered statements:** The *Miranda* Court emphasized that ***"volunteered statements*** of any kind are not barred by the Fifth Amendment and their admissibility is not affected by our holding today."

1. **Non-custodial statements:** Clearly no *Miranda* warning is required when a person simply walks up to a police officer on the street or into a police station and makes an incriminating statement. (See Nutshell, p. 224.)

2. **Voluntary custodial statements:** The *Miranda* decision, although it bars custodial ***interrogation*** where the warnings are not given, does not necessarily bar all unwarned statements by persons in custody. A suspect in custody might, for instance, volunteer a statement without any questions having been asked of him at all. But because of the coercive possibilities of a station-house atmosphere, the courts will be skeptical of any prosecution claim that no warnings to a suspect in custody were necessary because no questions were asked.

3. **Indirect questioning:** Usually, interrogation will take the form of a direct question addressed to the suspect. However, there are other techniques of eliciting information by ***indirect means***. In ***Rhode Island v. Innis***, 446 U.S. 291 (1980), the Supreme Court held that interrogation, for purposes of *Miranda*, occurs "whenever a person in custody is subjected to either express questioning or its ***functional equivalent***. That is to say, the term 'interrogation' . . . refers not only to express questioning, but also to any words or actions on the part of the police (other than those normally attendant to arrest and custody) that the police ***should know are reasonably likely to elicit*** an ***incriminating response*** from the suspect."

   a. **Application in *Innis* case:** The Court then concluded that in the particular facts of *Innis*, there had been ***no interrogation***. In *Innis*, D was arrested for a murder which had been committed by means of a sawed-off shotgun. D was transported in a police car by three officers. During the trip, one officer said to the others that there was a school for handicapped children near the scene of the murder, and that "God forbid one of [the handicapped children] might find a weapon with shells and they might hurt themselves." D then interrupted the conversation, stating that the officers should turn the car around so that he could show them where the gun was located.

      i. **Holding:** D claimed that he had been "interrogated," in violation of his *Miranda* right to have all interrogation cease until a lawyer was present. (See *supra*, p. 240.) But the Supreme Court held that there was no interrogation, because the officers should not necessarily have known that their conversation was "reasonably likely to elicit an incriminating response." The Court relied on the fact that there was nothing to suggest that the officers were aware that D was "peculiarly susceptible to an appeal to his conscience concerning the safety of handicapped children," or to suggest that they knew that D was "unusually disoriented or upset." Thus they had no reason to expect their remarks to produce an incriminating response.

ii. **Reference to *Brewer*:** The facts of *Innis* are reminiscent of those in *Brewer v. Williams* (discussed *infra*, p. 408), in which a policeman told a murder suspect that the victim was entitled to a "Christian burial," thus inducing the suspect to lead police to the body. In *Brewer*, the Court held that the suspect's right to counsel was violated by this exchange. But the Court in *Innis* held that *Brewer* was ***irrelevant*** to the *Innis* situation, insofar as *Brewer* involved the Sixth Amendment right to counsel, not the Fifth Amendment right against self-incrimination implicated by *Miranda*; the Court noted that the definitions of "interrogation" under the Fifth and Sixth Amendments are "not necessarily interchangeable, since the policies underlying the two constitutional protections are quite distinct."

b. **Intent of police:** The ***intent*** of the police is not dispositive under *Innis*. If the police intend to provoke an incriminating response, but the ploy is not reasonably likely to be successful, under the *Innis* test there would not be interrogation. Conversely, if the eliciting of an incriminating response is not intended, but the officers negligently fail to realize that this is likely to be the result, there will be deemed to be an interrogation. (As to the first point, Justice Stevens dissented in *Innis*, arguing that "*Miranda* protects a suspect in Innis' position not simply from interrogation that is likely to be successful, but from any interrogation at all.")

c. **Dissents:** Justice Marshall (joined by Justice Brennan) dissented in *Innis*, on the grounds that although the Court's test was a proper one, it should have led to a finding that the officers' remarks ***were*** reasonably likely to elicit an incriminating response. Justice Stevens dissented both on this ground, and also on the ground that any statement or action that is likely to elicit ***any*** response (not just an incriminating one) should be treated as interrogation.

4. **Police set up meeting with spouse:** Suppose the police conduct consists not of statements or questions to D, but rather the ***arranging of a situation*** in which the police believe it likely that D may "volunteer" an incriminating remark. Is this "interrogation"? For instance, suppose the police set up a meeting between D and his spouse under circumstances such that they reasonably believe that D may make an incriminating remark to her. In a 1987 case on these facts, the Court, by a 5-4 vote, held that there was ***no*** interrogation, because "officers ***do not interrogate a suspect simply by hoping that he will incriminate himself***." *Arizona v. Mauro*, 481 U.S. 520 (1987).

a. **Facts:** In *Mauro*, D had previously told the police that he would not speak to them without a lawyer present. D's wife came to the station, and the police decided to let her speak to her husband, but only in the presence of an officer and with a tape recorder running. Without telling D that his wife was present and wanted to speak to him, one of the officers showed the wife into the room, seated himself at the desk, and put a tape recorder in plain sight on the desk. During their short conversation, D made incriminating remarks to his wife.

b. **No "interrogation" found:** A majority of the Supreme Court found that no "interrogation" had taken place. True, *Innis* had treated, as falling within *Miranda*, police conduct that was the "functional equivalent" of interrogation, including "any words or actions on the part of the police . . . that the police should know are reasonably likely to elicit an incriminating response from the suspect." However, this was not what happened here. First, there was no evidence that D's wife was sent in to see her husband ***"for the purpose"*** of eliciting the statements — the conversation took place at the wife's request, and the officers had initially tried to discourage her from talking to her husband. Also, the police conduct here was less like interrogation than the police conduct in *Innis* (which the Court had held not to be interrogation).

c. **Dissent:** The four dissenters disagreed with the majority on essentially factual grounds. They believed that the police *had* intended to try to elicit an incriminating response by D. The dissenters pointed out that the police failed to give D any advance warning that his wife was coming to talk to him, that an officer would accompany her, or that the conversation would be recorded. The police thus arranged the situation so that there would be maximum surprise to D. This was a "powerful psychological ploy," by which the police intentionally "set . . . up a confrontation between [D and his wife] at a time when he manifestly desired to remain silent." Since the police knew or should have known that the encounter was "reasonably likely to produce an incriminating response," it amounted to interrogation even though D's response did not stem from anything the police said to him.

d. **Significance:** *Mauro* probably does not establish new law. The *Innis* test — by which the police conduct an "interrogation" whenever their conduct is "reasonably likely to elicit an incriminating response" — remains the law after *Mauro*. However, the case illustrates that a majority of the Court will lean over backwards to find that the *Innis* test has not been satisfied.

   i. **Significance of intent:** Also, *Mauro* may mean that the police's ***intent*** is more important than formerly. *Mauro* seems to mean that if the police do not ***intend*** to try to elicit incriminating remarks, their conduct does not constitute "interrogation," even if a reasonable person would have found the conduct likely to produce an incriminating result. This seems to be a change from *Innis*, in which the Court held that its test "focuses primarily upon the perceptions of the suspect, rather than the intent of the police."

5. **Clarifying questions:** A statement may be volunteered, and not the product of "interrogation," even though the police ask ***clarifying questions***. But the follow-up questions must be truly intended for clarification, and must not be designed to induce the defendant to state facts which he originally intended not to divulge.

B. **Identification questions:** Since the privilege against self-incrimination is not applicable to physical identification procedures, such as line-ups or fingerprinting (see *infra*, p. 200), routine questions of a suspect for ***identification only*** should not require warnings.

1. **Unsolicited responses:** When routine or identification questions are asked, an incriminating response not solicited by the question should be considered volunteered as long as no impression is created that the suspect must incriminate himself. Thus routine questions asked during the ***booking*** of a suspect have not usually been held to require *Miranda* warnings. See, e.g., *Pennsylvania v. Muniz*, 496 U.S. 582 (1990) (plurality holds that ques-

tions to D regarding name, address, height, weight, etc. did not require *Miranda* warnings, even though a videotape of the questions and D's answers was introduced at trial to show that D was drunk).

C. Emergency questions: Questions asked by police in ***emergency circumstances***, such as when tending or rescuing a victim, or for the police's own immediate protection, have generally been held to be non-interrogative. However, the "public safety" exception established by the Supreme Court in *New York v. Quarles*, *infra*, p. 254, means that *Miranda* will not apply in emergency situations, whether or not these could fairly be said to be "interrogation."

D. Questions by non-police: In *Miranda*, the Court limited its holding to "questioning initiated by law enforcement officers." Most courts have used this language to admit incriminating statements made in response to interrogation by ***non-police***, including private investigators and victims. (Nutshell, p. 228.)

1. **Probation officers:** The courts are split on whether this exception includes parole and probation officers, since they are usually viewed as "law enforcement officers" by parolees and probationers.

2. **IRS agents:** The Supreme Court has implied that ***IRS agents***, when conducting tax investigations, are to be treated as law enforcement officials. See *Beckwith v. U.S.*, 425 U.S. 341 (1976), *supra*, p. 244. However, most of the time interviews by IRS agents will take place in a non-custodial situation (i.e., a voluntary interview in an office or home, as in *Beckwith*) and *Miranda* warnings will in that case not be needed.

3. **Psychiatric examination:** Similarly, a court-ordered ***psychiatric examination*** to determine the defendant's competency to stand trial may trigger the right to *Miranda* warnings, depending on how the prosecution later attempts to use the results of the examination.

   a. **Results used to determine penalty:** If the results of the psychiatric exam are to be used in determining the ***penalty*** in a capital case, *Miranda* warnings must be given. Thus in ***Estelle v. Smith***, 451 U.S. 454 (1981), the defendant was tried for first-degree murder, for which the death penalty could be imposed. The court ordered that the defendant undergo a psychiatric examination to determine his competence to stand trial; the defendant made no request for the examination, and, although counsel had been appointed for him, counsel was not advised that the examination would take place. The defendant was not given any sort of *Miranda* warnings prior to the interview.

      i. **Psychiatrist's testimony:** The psychiatrist testified that he found the defendant competent to stand trial. But the more significant testimony arising from the examination was that after the defendant was convicted of the charge, in a separate ***penalty phase*** on the issue of whether capital punishment should be applied, the psychiatrist testified that the defendant was a continuingly dangerous person, who had no remorse for what he had done. Since continuing dangerousness was one of the elements which by statute had to be found before the death penalty could be imposed, the psychiatric testimony played a material role in the jury's ultimate conclusion that the death penalty should be imposed on the defendant.

b. **Holding:** The Supreme Court held that the prosecution was ***not entitled*** to use the psychiatrist's testimony in the penalty phase, because the defendant had not been told that he had a right to remain silent during the examination and that anything he said could be used against him. The Court saw no reason to distinguish between the guilt and penalty phases of the trial.

c. **Results used to assess competency or sanity:** But the Court conceded that no *Miranda* warnings (at least with respect to Fifth, rather than Sixth, Amendment rights) would have been required had the results of the examination been used only on the competency issue. Nor would such warnings have been required had the defendant placed his sanity in issue pursuant to an insanity defense. Furthermore, the Court left open the possibility that if the defendant had used testimony from a different psychiatrist to show that he was not continuingly dangerous, the prosecution might have been entitled to introduce the state psychiatrist's testimony.

Note: The Court in *Estelle* also held that the defendant's Sixth Amendment right to the effective assistance of counsel had been violated (an aspect of the decision discussed further *infra*, p. 385).

VIII. THE "PUBLIC SAFETY" EXCEPTION

A. **Background:** Suppose that while a suspect is under interrogation, the police believe that there is a loaded weapon nearby, that a victim is being held, that a bomb may go off, or that some other ***imminent threat to public safety*** exists. The police wish to question the suspect about the gun, victim, bomb, etc. Until 1984, the police in this situation had to make a choice:

1. **One option:** They could try to maximize the likelihood that the defendant would answer, by not giving him his *Miranda* warnings before the questioning; but if they did so, the response could not be admitted into evidence against him.

2. **Other option:** Alternatively, they could give him his *Miranda* warnings, thereby reducing the likelihood that he would answer, but preserving their ability to admit his statements if he did (as well as evidence derived from those statements).

B. **The "public safety" exception:** But in 1984, the Supreme Court dissipated this dilemma, by holding that *Miranda* warnings are simply ***unnecessary*** prior to questioning that is "reasonably prompted by a concern for the ***public safety***." Furthermore, the existence of such a reasonable concern for the public safety is to be determined ***objectively***, not by examining the subjective motivation of the officer. ***New York v. Quarles***, 467 U.S. 649 (1984).

1. **Consequences:** These two propositions, taken together, mean that, in a fairly large portion of interrogations that take place soon after the suspect is placed in custody (including many interrogations occurring at the scene of a crime), *Miranda* warnings will not be required.

2. **Facts:** The breadth and practical impact of this holding are illustrated by the facts of *Quarles* itself. Four armed officers accosted D, a suspected rapist, in a grocery store. When he saw the officers, he ran towards the back of the store, where he was caught and handcuffed; a frisk showed that he was wearing an empty shoulder holster. One officer,

without giving D *Miranda* warnings, asked him where the gun was; D answered "The gun is over there," nodding towards some nearby empty cartons. The loaded gun was found in the cartons, and D's statement, as well as the gun, were sought to be admitted by the prosecution.

3. **Holding:** The Court in *Quarles* created a new exception to the *Miranda* requirement for situations in which there are ***"overriding considerations of public safety,"*** and held that this exception was applicable on these facts.

   a. **Rationale:** The Court began by observing that the *Miranda* requirements are merely ***"prophylactic"*** measures, which are "not themselves rights protected by the Constitution but [are] instead measures to ensure that the right against compulsory self-incrimination [is] protected." Since the *Miranda* warnings (in the majority's view) were not directly required by the Fifth Amendment, the Court was free to engage in a ***cost-benefit analysis***. The Court observed that whereas in the typical custodial interrogation context, the only cost of giving *Miranda* warnings is the possibility of fewer convictions, in an emergency situation there is the additional cost of protecting the public. Therefore, the majority concluded, "The need for answers to questions in a situation posing a threat to the public safety outweighs the need for the prophylactic rule protecting the Fifth Amendment's privilege against self-incrimination."

   b. **Objective standard:** The Court also determined that the existence of a threat to the public safety should be determined by an ***objective***, rather than subjective, standard. That is, the questioning officer's subjective belief that there is or is not a significant threat to the public safety should be ***irrelevant***; the test is whether a ***reasonable officer*** in that position would conclude that there was such a threat. Here, an officer would reasonably have believed that D had just removed a gun from his holster and had concealed it somewhere in the supermarket, where "an accomplice might make use of it [or] a customer or employee might later come upon it." (The Court's rejection of a subjective standard enabled it to overcome strong evidence that the interrogation was ***not in fact prompted*** by the officers' concern for their own or the public's safety.)

   c. **"Bright line" becomes blurry:** The majority acknowledged that its decision "to some degree . . . lessen[s] the desirable clarity of [the *Miranda*] rule." Formerly, the *Miranda* rulings were simply mandatory in any custodial interrogation. Now, in many if not most situations, there will be a plausible claim that "public safety" required some of the questions. The former "bright line" represented by the traditional *Miranda* rule has thus now become a blurred one; just how blurry is illustrated by the fact that New York's highest court and the U.S. Supreme Court disagreed about whether the public's safety was at stake on the facts of *Quarles* itself.

   d. **May still show compulsion:** The majority was careful to observe that its holding does not prevent the suspect from showing that his answers were ***actually coerced***; if he can make such a showing, he will still be entitled to have those answers excluded. Whether such "actual compulsion" exists will be determined under "traditional due process standards." (See *supra*, p. 235, for a brief summary of these traditional standards.) For instance, on the facts of *Quarles*, the suspect might well be able to show that when handcuffed and surrounded by four armed police officers, his answer to the question "Where is the gun?" was not a voluntary one.

4. **Dissent:** Four members of the Court dissented from at least the creation of a "public safety" exception to *Miranda*. The principal dissent was by Justice Marshall, joined by Brennan and Stevens. The dissenters objected not only to the new "public safety" exception, but also to the way in which the majority applied that exception to the facts of *Quarles* itself.

   a. **Objection to rationale:** The dissenters saw the majority's new rule as being in sharp conflict with *Miranda's* "constitutional presumption that statements made during custodial interrogations are compelled in violation of the Fifth Amendment and are thus inadmissible in criminal prosecutions." The fact that public safety may be threatened in a particular case does not make it any less likely that the suspect's response has been coerced. *Miranda* was a way of making sure that coerced confessions are not admitted, not a way of "balancing" the suspect's interest in his Fifth Amendment rights against society's need for his information. The majority's use of such a cost-benefit analysis was thus, according to the dissenters, unfaithful to the "logic of *Miranda*."

   b. **Coercion:** The dissenters also observed that the cost-benefit argument behind the creation of the public safety exception amounted to arguing that "by deliberately withholding *Miranda* warnings, the police can get information out of suspects who would refuse to respond to police questioning were they advised of their constitutional rights." Therefore, the dissenters noted, "The 'public-safety' exception is efficacious precisely because it permits police officers to coerce criminal defendants into making involuntary statements." Thus in those situations where the public-safety exception makes a difference, it does so by what the dissenters viewed as a direct violation of the Fifth Amendment.

   c. **Difficulty of administration:** Lastly, the dissenters predicted that the new public-safety exception would "destroy . . . forever the clarity of *Miranda* for both law enforcement officers and members of the judiciary." Given that New York's highest court and the U.S. Supreme Court disagreed about whether public safety was at stake on the facts of *Quarles* itself, how could the police officer on the street be expected to determine when the exception should apply?

5. **O'Connor's view:** Justice O'Connor agreed with Marshall, Brennan and Stevens that the majority's departure from *Miranda* principles was unwarranted. However, she believed that even though the defendant's statement about the gun should not be admitted, the gun itself could be, on the theory that the gun was "non-testimonial," and that the "fruits of the poisonous tree" doctrine (*infra*, p. 324), should not be strictly applied where the constitutional violation is merely a failure to meet the technical requirements of *Miranda*, rather than an actual compulsion of testimony.

IX. WARNINGS REQUIRED UNDER *MIRANDA*

A. **Adequacy of warnings:** The *Miranda* warnings must be given in a clear and unambiguous manner so that the individual understands his rights and feels free to exercise them. The police do not have to quote the exact words of the *Miranda* decision, but their rendition of the warnings must convey the substance of the decision. (See, however, the discussion of *Duckworth v. Eagan*, *infra*, p. 257, indicating that some degree of ambiguity in the warning will be allowed.)

1. **Right to attorney:** The warning must make it clear to the suspect that he has a right to have a lawyer present ***during the questioning.***

   a. **"If and when you go to court":** The essence of the warning about an attorney is ***not*** that a suspect has an ***automatic right*** to have the police provide him with a lawyer while they hold him in custody — all the police must do is to ***choose*** between providing a lawyer or questioning, so they are always free to defer their questioning until some later date if they can't (or don't want to) provide a lawyer. Consequently, the warning merely has to get this fact across. Thus so long as the police indicate that they won't question the defendant without a lawyer unless he waives this right, the warning does not become inadequate merely because the police say the sentence, "We will provide a lawyer for you if and when you go to court." See *Duckworth v. Eagan*, *infra*, p. 257.

2. **Right to remain silent:** The warning must convey to the suspect both that he has the ***right to remain silent***, and that ***anything he says may be used against him***.

   a. **Consequences of silence:** The *Miranda* Court noted that many suspects will when questioned feel that "silence in the face of accusation is itself damning and will bode ill when presented to a jury." If this is so, it would be desirable to tell the suspect not only that he has the right to remain silent, but also that his ***silence will not be used against him***.[2] But the Supreme Court has never imposed such a requirement, even though the suspect may be left with the impression that the prosecution *may* somehow introduce his silence in the police station into evidence.

3. **Ambiguity in warning:** Perhaps because a majority of the Court since the Rehnquist era has had doubts about the wisdom of the *Miranda* rule, the Court appears to be willing to find that the police have complied with *Miranda* in a particular situation even if the warnings given are somewhat ***ambiguous***. For instance, in *Duckworth v. Eagan*, 492 U.S. 195 (1989), the police gave D warnings that included these sentences: "You have a right to talk to a lawyer for advice before we ask you any questions, and to have him with you during questioning. You have the right to the advice and presence of a lawyer even if you cannot afford to hire one. ***We have no way of giving you a lawyer, but one will be appointed for you, if you wish, if and when you go to court."*** Five members of the Court found this warning ***adequate*** even though it was somewhat ambiguous.

   a. **Defendant's claim:** The defendant in *Duckworth* argued that the warnings given to him were inadequate because they left him in doubt about whether he was entitled to a court-appointed lawyer ***before interrogation*** — D claimed that the sentence, "We have no way of giving you a lawyer, but one will be appointed for you, if you wish, if

---

2. For instance, it might be helpful to the suspect to be told that in the event of an eventual trial, the prosecution would not be able to suggest that the jury should draw an adverse inference from the suspect's invocation of his right to remain silent. The prosecution is in fact not permitted to make such a suggestion; see *Doyle v. Ohio*, infra, p. 280.

and when you go to court," reasonably suggested to him that if he couldn't afford his own lawyer, he would have to undergo interrogation without a lawyer present. Further, he claimed, this language suggested that he would not receive a court-appointed lawyer until he actually went to trial, and that if he wasn't taken to trial he would never receive a lawyer at all. All of this, D argued, contributed to his decision to confess rather than ask for a lawyer.

b. **Majority view:** But five Justices believed that the warning was adequate despite this "if and when you go to court" language. In the majority's view, a suspect who has just received *Miranda* warnings will often ask *when* he will obtain counsel; the "if and when you go to court" advice "simply anticipates that question." Therefore, someone in D's position should have understood the whole set of warnings to mean that: (1) D would not be given a court-appointed lawyer until he had to appear in court (though he could have his own lawyer present at any time); but (2) the police would not ask him questions if he said that he did not want to answer questions without a lawyer present. Since the total set of warnings, although they did not match the exact form prescribed in *Miranda*, constituted a "fully effective equivalent," D's confession (and the physical evidence derived from it) were admissible.

c. **Dissent:** The four dissenters in *Duckworth* thought that the warnings here were clearly inadequate under *Miranda*. They believed that the "if and when you go to court" language had led D to believe that a lawyer would not be provided for him until some indeterminate time in the future ***after questioning***. In fact, a defendant hearing the phrase "go to court" would typically believe that no lawyer would be provided until trial, an event that might never occur. Also, the dissenters criticized the majority's lawyer-like one-sentence-at-a-time parsing of the warnings — the dissenters pointed out that people in D's position will generally be "frightened suspects unlettered in law, not lawyers or judges or others schooled in interpreting legal or semantic nuance."

B. **Where police think suspect aware of rights:** The warnings must be given even if the police have reason to believe that the suspect is already ***aware*** of his right to remain silent and to have a lawyer. As the *Miranda* Court put it, "The Fifth Amendment privilege is so fundamental to our system of constitutional rule and the expedient of giving an adequate warning as to the availability of the privilege so simple, we will not pause to inquire in individual cases whether the defendant was aware of his rights without a warning being given."

1. **Right to appointed counsel:** An exception to the above rule is that where the police are absolutely sure that the suspect has his own lawyer, or has the money for one, they do not have to tell him that one can be appointed for him. But this exception does not apply "when there is any doubt at all" (in the words of *Miranda*) as to the suspect's financial ability.

2. **Where lawyer present:** If the suspect's lawyer happens to be present during the interrogation, the *Miranda* warnings apparently do not have to be given. This may be deduced from *Miranda* itself, in which the Court stated that "the presence of counsel . . . would be the adequate protective device necessary to make the process of police interrogation conform to the dictates of the privilege. His presence would ensure that statements made in the government-established atmosphere are not the product of compulsion."

3. **Warnings cut off by suspect:** Suppose the police are in the process of reading the *Miranda* warnings, and the suspect interrupts with words like "You don't have to read that to me — I know my rights." Most courts have held that the officer must nonetheless finish the warnings.

4. **Warnings about nature or seriousness of crime:** There is nothing in *Miranda* itself that indicates that the police must tell the suspect the nature or seriousness of the crime with which he is charged. But if the suspect is unaware of the seriousness of his crime (e.g., where the victim of an assault dies while the suspect is in custody), he may be more willing to make a confession than if he knew how serious the charge was. Nonetheless, the courts have not imposed a requirement that the police inform the suspect of the nature or seriousness of his crime. Indeed, the Supreme Court has held that the failure of the police to tell a suspect who was arrested on minor charges that he would also be questioned on much more serious (murder) charges did not nullify the suspect's decision to waive his *Miranda* rights. See *Colorado v. Spring*, discussed *infra*, p. 262.

   a. **Trickery barred:** But the police probably may not ***intentionally trick*** the suspect into thinking his crime is less serious than it is, in order to induce him to confess. *Miranda* states "any evidence that the accused was threatened, tricked, or cajoled into a waiver [of his right to silence or to a lawyer] will, of course, show that the defendant did not voluntarily waive his privilege." The Supreme Court has expressly declined to decide whether an affirmative misstatement by the police, as to the seriousness of the crime (or the scope of the interrogation that is about to begin), would nullify the suspect's decision to waive his *Miranda* rights. *Colorado v. Spring*, *infra*, p. 262.

X. WAIVERS AND INVOCATIONS OF *MIRANDA* RIGHTS

A. **Waivers and invocations:** After being read the *Miranda* warnings, a suspect may ***waive*** his right to a lawyer and his right to remain silent. Conversely, the suspect may of course ***invoke*** his *Miranda* rights.

B. **Special waiver and invocation issues:** The waiver and invocation of *Miranda* rights is perhaps the most complicated area in all of constitutional criminal procedure. Therefore, we'll spend a considerable time looking at the intricacies of waivers and invocations. These problems may be divided into several main areas:

   [1] when will the suspect be deemed to have ***waived*** a *Miranda* right?;

   [2] when will the suspect be deemed to have ***invoked*** (i.e., asserted, the opposite of waived) a *Miranda* right?; and

   [3] once a *Miranda* right has been invoked, what rules govern the police-suspect interaction ***thereafter***?

   We cover these areas in Paragraphs (2), (3) and (4), respectively, below.

1. **Two different rights:** To begin with, keep in mind that there are ***two distinct Miranda rights*** that may be the subject of a waiver or invocation: the right to have ***questioning cease*** until the suspect can ***consult a lawyer***, and the right to ***remain silent***. The rules on waiver and invocation are similar, but not identical, as between the two contexts. The most

important difference relates to police conduct after the right has been invoked: when what is invoked is the right to *counsel*, the police may not initiate any attempt to get a waiver for some significant period of time, whereas if what is invoked is the right to *remain silent*, the police may continue to question, or to attempt to get a waiver (with the proviso that anything the suspect says prior to making a valid waiver may not be used against him at trial).

2. **Determining whether a waiver occurred:** Let's turn now to the rules for determining ***whether a suspect has waived*** one or both of his *Miranda* rights.

   a. **"Knowing and voluntary":** For the suspect to be deemed to have waived either *Miranda* right (silence or counsel), the prosecution will have to show that the waiver was ***"knowing and voluntary."***

      i. **Meaning of "knowing and voluntary":** Here is how the Supreme Court has explained the meaning of the phrase "knowing and voluntary": "First, the relinquishment of the right must have been ***voluntary*** in the sense that it was the product of a ***free and deliberate choice*** rather than intimidation, coercion, or deception. Second, the waiver must have been made with a full ***awareness*** both of the nature of the right being abandoned and the ***consequences*** of the decision to abandon it." ***Moran v. Burbine***, 475 U.S. 412 (1986).

         (1) **Fact of confession not enough:** The mere fact that the suspect ***answered questions*** after being given his *Miranda* warnings will not, without more, constitute the required proof of knowing and voluntary waiver. There must in addition be affirmative evidence of both the voluntary element (i.e., lack of coercion) and the knowing element (understanding of at least some of the consequences of waiving). Cf. S&C (9th), pp. 743-74.

         Example: At a hearing on whether D in fact waived his *Miranda* rights before speaking to the police, the arresting officer O testifies that he read D his *Miranda* warnings from a printed card, and that D then confessed when asked whether he was involved in the crime in question. O testifies that he cannot remember whether he asked D if he understood the rights, or whether O made an effort to determine if D was capable of understanding these warnings.

         Held, this testimony is not enough to demonstrate waiver, because it does not satisfy the "knowing" element. The mere fact that warnings were read to the suspect, and that the suspect thereafter immediately confessed, does not establish that he understood the nature of the rights he was waiving. *Tague v. Louisiana*, 444 U.S. 469 (1980).

         (2) **Sufficient extra information:** On the other hand, waivers can be ***implied*** (for more about this, see *infra*, p. 261). Not much is required to create an implied waiver that satisfies the "knowing and voluntary" requirement beyond the fact that the suspect was read the warnings and confessed — the only other needed ingredient is that the defendant be shown to have *understood* the warnings. For instance, suppose the interrogating officer testifies that, "After I read D the warnings, I asked him whether he understood them, and he said he did. I then asked him whether he was willing to speak to us, and he said 'ask your

questions, and I'll decide whether to answer as we go.' " That testimony, unless its truthfulness is successfully attacked by the defense, will almost certainly be sufficient to create an implied waiver that meets the knowing-and-voluntary requirement; the fact that D did not sign a waiver form, or indicate that he would necessarily answer any given question, will not be enough to nullify his knowing and voluntary status.

b. Waivers can be express: Waivers can, of course, be "*express*." For instance, if a suspect signs a standard waiver form, that's an express waiver. Express waivers can be oral, too; if the suspect says to the police, "I understand these rights but I'm willing to talk to you," that's an express waiver. Express waivers will be ***valid*** as long as there is no indication of ***coercion*** or of basic ***lack of understanding*** by the suspect.

c. Implied waivers: But ***"implied"*** waivers are also possible, and, indeed, common.

i. Validity of implied waivers: The Supreme Court has explained the validity of implied waivers this way: "An express written or oral statement of waiver of the right to remain silent or of the right to counsel is usually strong proof of the validity of that waiver, but is ***not*** inevitably either ***necessary or sufficient*** to establish waiver. ... The courts must presume that a defendant did not waive his rights; ... but in at least some cases waiver can be clearly ***inferred*** from the ***actions and words*** of the person interrogated." *North Carolina v. Butler*, 441 U.S. 369 (1979),

Example: D is interrogated by the FBI. The officers learn that D has an 11th grade education and is literate. He is given an FBI document containing the *Miranda* warnings, which he reads. He is asked if he understands his rights, and he says that he does. The officers then tell D that he doesn't have to speak or sign the form but that they would like him to talk to them. D responds "I will talk to you but I am not signing any form." D never requests counsel, and never attempts to terminate the questioning; he then makes incriminating statements in response to the questions.

Held, the fact that D refused to sign the form did not prevent him from being deemed to have impliedly waived his rights. An intent to waive can be inferred from the actions and words of the person being interrogated. Case remanded to the state courts to determine whether D's actions here in fact constituted an implied waiver. *North Carolina v. Butler*, *supra*.

ii. Answering of questions: The most common form of implied waiver comes when the suspect is read his warnings, indicates that he understands them, never expressly says that he is waving his rights, and then ***answers one or more questions***. As a lower court said about this situation, "a defendant's subsequent willingness to answer questions after acknowledging his *Miranda* rights is ***sufficient to constitute an implied waiver.*** ... Even though [D] never 'formally' waived his *Miranda* rights, such cooperation, when coupled with his acknowledgment of his *Miranda* rights, constituted a valid waiver." *U.S. v. Frankson*, 83 F.3d 79 (4th Cir. 1996), quoted in S&C, p. 744.

iii. Additional factors: Here are two additional factors that will make it more likely that an implied waiver will be found to have occurred:

D was ***familiar with the criminal justice system*** by virtue of his having been arrested and interrogated on multiple recent occasions. This familiarity makes it more likely that D understood his rights and understood the consequences of waiving them. Cf. S&C, p. 744.

D answers ***some*** questions but refuses to answer others. This selective response makes it more likely that D understood his rights and intended to waive them. *Id.*

d. Information about scope of questioning: For a waiver to be valid, how much, if anything, does the suspect need to be told about the ***scope*** of the proposed questioning? The answer seems to be, ***"not much,"*** as long as the police do not intentionally mislead the subject on this point. So for instance, suppose the suspect believes that the upcoming interrogation will focus only upon the ***minor crime*** for which he has been arrested, and waives his rights to permit the interrogation. If the police suddenly change the questioning to cover a different, much more major crime, does this vitiate the waiver? The Supreme Court answered ***"no,"*** in ***Colorado v. Spring***, 479 U.S. 564 (1987).

i. Facts: Thus in *Spring*, D was arrested on federal firearms charges in Missouri. Federal Alcohol, Tobacco and Firearms (ATF) agents got D to waive his *Miranda* rights; D seems to have believed that the questioning would focus solely on the firearms transactions, since that's what he knew he was being arrested for. The agents indeed questioned him first on the firearms transactions. But after D incriminated himself on these, the agents switched to asking him about a murder in Colorado. This questioning led to a later questioning session in which D confessed to the Colorado murder.

ii. Waiver upheld: By a 7-2 vote, the Supreme Court held that D's initial waiver was ***not nullified*** by the fact that he mistakenly believed that the interrogation would focus only on the federal firearms charges, not the Colorado murder charges. The majority noted that the police did ***not*** make any ***affirmative misstatements*** about their intent; they merely neglected to tell D that the Colorado murder charges would be part of the interrogation. "Mere silence" by officials as to the subject of an interrogation is ***not "trickery"*** sufficient to invalidate a suspect's waiver of *Miranda* rights, the Court said. All that is needed for a valid waiver of *Miranda* rights is that the suspect ***understand the nature*** of his constitutional right — here, his right to remain silent — and there is no need to disclose information that would be ***"useful"*** to him in deciding whether relying on the right would be ***wise***.

iii. Dissent: The two dissenters in *Spring* contended that a suspect's awareness of the ***subject*** of the interrogation should be included among the factors that are considered in determining whether the waiver was ***voluntary***. Here, there was evidence that the police had designed an elaborate psychological ploy by which D would first be interrogated about the minor charges, then confronted with the murder charges after he incriminated himself on the former. The unexpected shift in questioning injected a major coercive aspect into the situation, the dissenters argued.

e. **Knowledge that D's lawyer is trying to contact him:** Suppose the suspect is ***represented by an attorney who is trying to see him,*** and this fact is known to the police but not to the suspect. Does the existence of such retained counsel change the requirements for the suspect to be deemed to have waived his *Miranda* rights? The question is particularly likely to arise where the lawyer has been retained ***on the suspect's behalf*** not by the suspect himself but by a ***friend or family member***, and the suspect does ***not even know*** that the retention has occurred. As the result of a dramatic and controversial Supreme Court case, the answer seems to be ***"no."*** More specifically, the suspect's waiver of his *Miranda* rights will be ***effective*** even though the police: (1) ***decline to tell*** the suspect that a lawyer has been retained for him or is trying to see him; and (2) ***prevent***, or by use of trickery discourage, the lawyer from seeing his client. ***Moran v. Burbine***, 475 U.S. 412 (1986).

   i. **Facts:** In *Moran*, D was arrested by the Cranston (Rhode Island) police in connection with a local burglary. While D was in custody, the police learned facts which made them suspect him in a prior Providence murder case; Providence police officers arrived in Cranston to question D about the murder. Meanwhile, D's sister, who knew only of the burglary charge, retained a Public Defender to represent him. The lawyer called the Cranston police station, and said she would represent D in person if the police intended to question him. The officer on the phone falsely told her that the police would not be questioning D or putting him in a line-up that night; he did not tell her that D was a suspect in a murder case or that Providence police officers were present. ***Nor did the officers ever tell D that his sister had retained a lawyer for him.*** Shortly after this conversation with the lawyer, the police read D his *Miranda* rights, and procured a signed waiver of those rights. He then confessed to the murder.

   ii. **Waiver upheld:** By a 6-3 vote, the Supreme Court ***upheld*** the validity of the waiver. It did so in a very broad manner, by holding that ***"events occurring outside of the presence of the suspect*** and entirely ***unknown*** to him surely ***can have no bearing*** on the capacity to comprehend and knowingly relinquish a constitutional right." Knowledge that a lawyer had been retained for him "would have been useful to [D]; perhaps even it might have affected his decision to confess. But we have never read the Constitution to require that the police supply a suspect with a flow of information to help him calibrate his self interest in deciding whether to speak or stand by his rights."

      (1) **Police state of mind irrelevant:** The ***motives*** of the police were totally ***irrelevant***, the Court held: "[E]ven ***deliberate deception*** of an attorney could not possibly affect a suspect's decision to waive his *Miranda* rights unless he were at least aware of the incident." Police trickery could only affect the constitutional validity of a waiver "if it deprives a defendant of knowledge essential to his ability to understand the nature of his rights and the consequences of abandoning them." Because D had been told, and understood, everything that *Miranda* requires the police to convey, the deception of the attorney, and the failure to tell D that there was an attorney, were simply irrelevant.

(2) **Sixth Amendment claim rejected:** The majority also rejected D's claim that his ***Sixth Amendment*** right to counsel was violated by police efforts to interfere with his dealings with his attorney. D contended that a suspect's right to have the police not interfere with his dealings with his lawyer should attach as soon as the suspect is placed in custodial interrogation. But the Court held that cases establishing that the right to appointment of counsel does not attach until the initiation of ***"adversary judicial proceedings"*** also meant that ***no aspect*** of the Sixth Amendment right to counsel is triggered prior to initiation of formal charges (and the arrest and questioning here did not constitute the initiation of formal proceedings — only an arraignment or the equivalent could do that).

iii. **Dissent:** Justice Stevens, joined by Brennan and Marshall, dissented in *Moran*. The dissenters took the broad view that "the right to counsel at custodial interrogation is infringed by police treatment of an attorney that prevents or impedes the attorney's representation of the suspect at that interrogation."

(1) **Rationale:** The dissenters saw *Miranda* as an attempt to reduce the inherently coercive nature of incommunicado interrogation. Consequently, any police interference with consultation between lawyer and suspect was directly contrary to the purpose behind *Miranda*. Furthermore, "*Miranda* clearly condemns ***threats or trickery*** that cause a suspect to make an ***unwise waiver*** of his rights even though he fully understands those rights" — the trickery here (both the lying to the lawyer and the failure to inform the suspect about the lawyer) was no different from any other trickery that would vitiate the waiver.

f. **Mentally ill defendant:** Suppose that a suspect who waives his *Miranda* rights is ***mentally ill***, and his illness in some sense causes him to waive his *Miranda* rights and confess. Assuming that there is no police coercion, does the fact that the suspect's decision to waive his rights is not fully rational make the waiver invalid? The Supreme Court has answered this question in the negative — ***no matter how irrational the suspect's decision to waive his Miranda rights, the waiver will stand so long as there was no police coercion***. This conclusion was reached in ***Colorado v. Connelly***, 479 U.S. 157 (1986).

i. **Facts:** Uncontradicted evidence in *Connelly* showed that D was a chronic schizophrenic, and was in a psychotic state on at least the day before he walked up to a police officer, waived his *Miranda* rights, and confessed. Other evidence showed that D, in confessing, thought he was following the "voice of God." However, there was no evidence that the officer who gave the warnings and took the confession knew of D's mental state, or used any coercion.

ii. **Rationale:** Seven members of the Court (all but Brennan and Marshall) believed that D's waiver of his *Miranda* rights was valid. "*Miranda* protects defendants against ***government coercion*** leading them to surrender rights protected by the Fifth Amendment; it goes ***no further*** than that. [D's] perception of coercion flowing from the 'voice of God,' however important or significant such a perception may be in other disciplines, is a matter to which the United States Constitution does not speak."

(1) **Standard of proof:** The majority also established, for the first time, the standard of proof for analyzing the voluntariness of a waiver of *Miranda* rights: The state need merely establish the voluntariness of the waiver by a ***preponderance of the evidence***.

(2) **Admissibility of confession:** Similarly, the majority found the confession itself to be "voluntary," again, because it was not the product of police coercion. ***"[C]oercive police activity is a necessary predicate*** to the finding that a confession is not 'voluntary' within the meaning of the Due Process Clause of the Fourteenth Amendment."

iii. **Significance:** *Connelly*, taken together with *Spring* (*supra*, p. 262) and *Moran* (*supra*, p. 263), illustrates the present Court's refusal to ***consider anything but police coercion*** in determining whether a waiver of *Miranda* rights is "voluntary."

(1) **Wrongdoing by third parties:** Indeed, taken to its logical extreme, the Court's approach would mean that if a non-government actor (e.g., the suspect's spouse, or a store detective) persuades the suspect to waive his rights and confess, the fact that this third party may have used ***torture***, duress, brainwashing, or any other factor that overbears what is ordinarily thought of as the free will, would make absolutely no difference — as long as the *police* were innocent of wrongdoing, the waiver would be deemed voluntary, and the confession could be admitted without violating due process.

3. **Invocation must be "clear and unequivocal":** Just as a *waiver* of either *Miranda* right must be ***"clear and unequivocal,"*** so an ***invocation*** of either right must be clear and unequivocal. Consequently, until a clear and unequivocal invocation of either right has occurred, the police may ***continue to question the suspect*** and/or to ***repeatedly request a waiver.*** The Court imposed this "clear and unambiguous" requirement for invocation of the rights in multiple decisions, first as to the right to counsel and then as to the right to silence.

a. **Right to counsel:** The ***right-to-counsel*** case was ***Davis v. U.S.***, 512 U.S. 452 (1994). There, the Court held that if the suspect makes an ***ambiguous*** request — which a reasonable observer would think might or might not be a request for counsel — the questioning does ***not*** have to stop.

Example: D, while in custody, is interrogated about a murder in which he is a suspect. About an hour and a half into the interview, D says, "Maybe I should talk to a lawyer." The agents doing the questioning indicate that if D wants a lawyer, they will stop questioning until he gets one, and ask him to clarify whether he wants a lawyer or not. He then says, "No, I'm not asking for a lawyer." The interrogation continues, and D makes incriminating statements. Finally, he asks unequivocally for counsel, and questioning ceases. D argues that once he made his ambiguous statement ("Maybe I should talk to a lawyer"), questioning should have automatically ceased, and that his later incriminating statement is therefore inadmissible.

Held, for the prosecution. The obligation to stop questioning once the suspect asks for a lawyer (see *Edwards v. Ariz.*, discussed *infra*, p. 267), applies only where the suspect "articulate[s] his desire to have counsel present ***sufficiently clearly*** that a reasonable police officer in the circumstances would understand the statement to be a request for an attorney." If the statement does not meet this level of clarity, the officers ***need not stop questioning the suspect.*** Here, D's initial statement was at best an ambiguous one, and the interrogators were therefore not required to stop asking him questions. *Davis v. U.S., supra.*

i. **Clarifying questions:** In fact, when the suspect makes an ambiguous request regarding his desire for counsel, not only do the police not have to stop the questioning, they do not even have to make attempts to ***clarify*** whether the suspect is requesting a lawyer. Thus on the facts of *Davis, supra,* although the police there did try to clarify whether D was really asking for a lawyer, they were *not required* to do so: they would have been entitled to just keep on questioning D until he made an unambiguous request for a lawyer.

b. **Right to silence:** In a post-*Davis* case, the Court then held that the same requirement that the invocation of the right be clear and unequivocal applies where the right is to ***remain silent*** rather than to have counsel. In ***Berghuis v. Thompkins***, 130 S.Ct. 2250 (2010), a 5-4 decision, the majority said that "there is no principled reason to adopt ***different standards*** for determining when an accused has invoked the *Miranda* right to remain silent and the *Miranda* right to counsel at issue in *Davis*. [There] is good reason to require an accused who wants to invoke his or her right to remain silent to do so unambiguously."

i. **Rationale:** The majority reasoned in *Thompkins* that if the police were required to cease questioning based on an ambiguous statement or act, they would be required to "make difficult decisions about an accused's unclear intent and face the consequences of suppression 'if they guess wrong'." That would impose too heavy a burden on law enforcement efforts, while not materially furthering *Miranda*'s main goal of dispelling the compulsion inherent in custodial interrogation.

Example: D is interrogated by Detective Helgert and another detective in connection with a fatal shooting one year earlier. They give D a document containing the four standard *Miranda* warnings and a related fifth warning. They then ask him to read aloud the fifth warning, to ensure that he understands English. He does so. The detectives then read the first four items aloud to D, and ask him to sign the document. D makes an ambiguous indication about whether he understands the rights listed on the document, and refuses to sign the form. The police interrogate him for two and three-quarter hours, during which he mostly remains silent but occasionally gives a one-word non-incriminating answer. Then, Helgert asks D, "Do you believe in God?" D says yes, and his eyes fill up with tears. Helgert asks, "Do you pray to God?", to which D answers yes. Then, Helgert asks, "Do you pray to God to forgive you for shooting that boy down?" D answers yes, and looks away. D later tries to have this last remark suppressed from his trial, arguing that when he gave an ambiguous statement about whether he understood his right to remain silent and was invoking it, the police were required to clarify his intent before they resumed questioning.

Held, the incriminating remark is admissible. Just as an invocation of the *Miranda* right to counsel must be unambiguous, so an invocation of the right to *remain silent* must be unambiguous. If D had said that he wanted to remain silent, or that he did not want to talk to the police, this would have been unambiguous enough to invoke his right to cut off questioning. But here, D made neither statement. His conduct was ambiguous as to whether he was asserting his right of silence, so he will be deemed not to have asserted that right. Since there is no evidence that he was coerced, the police were entitled to continue questioning him up until the incriminating remark. *Berghuis v. Thompkins*, *supra*.

(1) **Mere answering of questions:** Notice that under *Berghuis v. Thompkins*, the prosecution must demonstrate only three things in order to establish an implied waiver of the right to silence:

[1] that the police gave the suspect *Miranda* warnings;

[2] that the suspect ***answered*** one or more questions following the warnings; and

[3] that the suspect ***understood*** the warnings.

If they can show these three things, then the fact that the police ***continued to interrogate*** the suspect at length after he made an ambiguous indication about whether he was invoking his right to silence will not matter. That's how it came about in *Thompkins* that D, despite his refusal to sign the waiver form and despite his near-total silence for 2 3/4 hours of questioning, was deemed to have waived his right of silence by virtue of giving a couple of one-word responses, only one of which was incriminating.

4. **Waiver after successful invocation of the right:** Suppose now that the suspect *does* invoke with sufficient clarity either his right to remain silent or his right to counsel. Can his later words or conduct be deemed to be an ***undoing*** of that invocation, and if so, under what circumstances? The rules for undoing an invocation of the right to counsel are somewhat stricter than those for undoing an invocation of the right to remain silent; we consider each of these rights in turn.

a. **Desire to prevent badgering:** Before we do that, though, notice that once a suspect has invoked either right, if the courts make it too easy for the suspect to undo the invocation, the police will have a strong incentive to continue trying to get the suspect to ***change his mind***. In other words, the police will have a large incentive to ***badger*** the suspect. The rules on what police conduct is permissible following an invocation of either right have been developed so as to reduce this incentive-to-badger.

b. **Right to counsel:** Where the defendant asserts in the first session that he ***wants a lawyer***, the Supreme Court has made it ***very hard*** for the prosecution to establish that this demand has subsequently been waived. In ***Edwards v. Arizona***, 451 U.S. 477 (1981), the Court set forth a "bright line" rule that "An accused . . . having expressed his desire to deal with the police only through counsel, is ***not subject to further interrogation*** by the authorities ***until counsel has been made available to him***, unless the ***accused himself initiates*** further communication, exchanges or conversations with the police."

i. **Response to questioning:** Waiver will not be established, the *Edwards* Court held, by the mere fact that the suspect ***responded*** to later ***police-initiated*** interrogation (even if that interrogation was preceded by a new reading of the *Miranda* warnings).

ii. **"Initiating the conversation" test:** *Edwards* is an important case, because it means that once a suspect indicates a desire to have a lawyer, any subsequent ***waiver*** of that right will not be measured by the usual tests for waiver (the "knowing and voluntary" standard; see *supra*, p. 260). Instead, the only way the suspect may waive a previously-asserted desire to have a lawyer present at interrogation is by ***initiating the conversation*** with the police.

iii. **Application in *Edwards:*** Thus in *Edwards* itself, Edwards asserted, on the night of his arrest, a desire to consult with a lawyer before making a "deal" with the prosecution. The questioning ceased, and the police came back the next morning. They gave Edwards his *Miranda* warnings a second time. Because Edwards knew that he had already been implicated by another suspect in the crime, he gave an incriminating statement.

(1) **Invalid waiver:** Since this second encounter with the police was not initiated by Edwards, the Supreme Court found it invalid because it was not made in the presence of the previously-requested lawyer. This was true even though Edwards might have known of his right to a lawyer and of the dangers of not insisting on one, and made a perfectly rational decision to waive his previously-exercised right to one. (In *Edwards* itself, Edwards began the second day of questioning by stating that he did not want to talk to anyone, but he was told that he "had to." However, the holding of *Edwards* goes beyond these facts, to include any questioning that is initiated against a suspect who on a previous occasion has requested counsel.)

iv. **Concurrence:** Although there were no dissenters in *Edwards*, three Justices (Burger, Powell and Rehnquist) concurred only in the result. All of the concurring Justices agreed that Edwards had not voluntarily and knowingly waived his right to counsel on this particular set of facts. But all three also rejected the notion that the only way a waiver of a previously-asserted right to counsel could take place was by initiation of conversation by the defendant. Justices Powell and Rehnquist, for instance, argued that a "routine" conversation begun by the police concerning "unrelated matters" should not preclude a waiver by the defendant; similarly, they contended, "police legitimately may inquire whether a suspect has changed his mind about speaking to them without an attorney."

v. **"Bright line" guidance:** The majority's position in *Edwards* has the advantage of setting a very bright-line rule: ***once the suspect has asserted a desire to have counsel, the police may never question him again prior to supplying him with that counsel.***[3] All they may do is wait, and hope that the suspect will come to

---

3. The later case of *Maryland v. Shatzer*, *infra*, p. 271, however, holds that a ***14-day release*** from custody will suffice to nullify the application of *Edwards*, and allow the police to re-initiate questioning.

them to confess or otherwise talk about the crime. This approach means that police officers will not have to evaluate difficult concepts of "knowing and intelligent waiver" before deciding whether to take a suspect's statement without supplying previously-requested counsel.

Note: Keep in mind that the *Edwards* opinion does not apply to the *initial* decision on the part of a suspect to waive his right to counsel. That sort of waiver continues to be judged on general "knowing and voluntary" waiver principles. Similarly, the *Edwards* decision has no effect on the situation where the suspect initially waives the right to a lawyer, but asserts his right to remain silent rather than being questioned; *Michigan v. Mosley* (discussed *infra*, p. 272) means that so long as the police wait a substantial period, they may initiate another questioning session (at least if they give a second set of *Miranda* warnings).

vi. Request must be unambiguous: *Edwards* only applies where the suspect ***clearly*** asserts his right to have counsel present during a custodial interrogation. If the suspect makes an ***ambiguous*** request — which a reasonable observer would think might or might not be a request for counsel — the questioning does ***not*** have to stop. See the discussion of *Davis v. U.S.*, *supra*, p. 265.

vii. Meaning of "initiates": Under *Edwards*, the police may not interrogate a suspect who had demanded a lawyer unless the suspect "***initiates*** further communication, exchanges, or conversations with the police." There will therefore sometimes be an important factual issue about whether such "initiation" has occurred. In ***Oregon v. Bradshaw***, 462 U.S. 1039 (1983), the Supreme Court stretched to find that the suspect had initiated a dialogue entitling authorities to resume questioning him.

(1) Facts: In *Bradshaw*, D was suspected of manslaughter in a drunken-driving fatality; he denied his involvement and requested an attorney. While the police were transferring him from the police station to the jail, D asked one of the policemen "Well, what is going to happen to me now?" The officer then said "You do not have to talk to me," and told D that since he had demanded a lawyer, any further discussion had to be at D's own free will. D said that he understood, and began discussing with the officer where he was being taken and what crime he would be charged with. The officer suggested that D might ***help himself by taking a lie-detector test***; D did so, failed the test, and then confessed.

(2) Holding: By a 5-4 vote, the Supreme Court held that the conversation in which the officer suggested a lie detector test was ***not in violation*** of D's *Miranda* rights. Four of the five, in a plurality opinion, applied the *Edwards* test and concluded that D had ***initiated the conversation*** which led to the polygraph suggestion.[4]

---

4. The fifth vote for the state came from Justice Powell, who did not take a position on whether *Edwards* had been violated, but agreed that D had validly waived his *Miranda* rights.

(3) **Routine requests:** The plurality noted that some statements or requests by a suspect are so ***"routine"*** that they will not be enough to trigger *Edwards*, and to permit interrogation to begin anew. For instance, a request for a drink of water or for use of a telephone are "routine incidents of the custodial relationship," and will therefore be meaningless under *Edwards*. What is required is a statement by the accused that "represent[s] a desire on the [suspect's] part . . . to open up a ***more generalized discussion relating directly or indirectly to the investigation***." According to the plurality, D's question "Well, what is going to happen to me now?" represented an overture for such a generalized discussion about the investigation.

(4) **Two-step process:** Thus, the plurality said, when the suspect initially requests a lawyer, any further incriminating statement by him will be judged according to a ***two-step*** test: (1) Did the suspect initiate discussion with the police, indicating that he wanted to talk about the investigation?; and (2) if so, was there a knowing and intelligent waiver of the right to counsel, judged by the totality of the circumstances? The plurality answered "yes" to both questions on the facts here.

(5) **Dissent:** The four dissenters in *Bradshaw* agreed with the plurality that the suspect must reopen dialogue with police in a way indicating a desire to talk about the investigation. But unlike the plurality, the dissent believed that this had ***not*** happened in *Bradshaw*. In the dissenters' view, D only wanted to find out where the police were going to take him, a normal reaction to being taken from the police station and put in a police car without being told where he was going.

viii. **Questioning about different crime:** As noted, under *Edwards* a suspect who asks for a lawyer may not be interrogated thereafter, unless it is the suspect who initiates the further discussion. The Supreme Court has held that this bright-line rule applies even where the police subsequently wish to question the suspect about a ***different crime*** than the one they were questioning him about when he first requested the lawyer. *Arizona v. Roberson*, 486 U.S. 675 (1988).

Example: D is arrested at the scene of a just-completed burglary, is given his *Miranda* warnings, and states that he wants a lawyer before answering any questions. While still in custody, a different police officer (who is not aware that D had previously asked for counsel) asks D about a different burglary, gives him his *Miranda* warnings, and obtains an incriminating statement about that different burglary.

Held, *Edwards* prevented the second officer from initiating discussions about the second burglary, just as it would have prevented the officer from initiating discussions about the original burglary. *Roberson*, *supra*.

ix. **Questioning after a suspect has consulted lawyer:** Suppose that the suspect asks for a lawyer, ***consults*** with this lawyer, and is subsequently interrogated by the police outside the lawyer's presence. In this situation, the rule of *Edwards* (that a suspect who asks for a lawyer may not be interrogated thereafter, unless it is the suspect who initiates the further discussion) will be deemed to be ***violated***. In other words, the lawyer must be present ***during the subsequent questioning***, and a mere consultation before the questioning will be no substitute for this. *Minnick v. Mississippi*, 498 U.S. 146 (1990).

Example: D is arrested on charges of murder after escaping from the county jail. D requests counsel, and consults with a court-appointed attorney two or three times. Later, police interrogate D, in sessions initiated by the police. D's lawyer is not present during these questioning sessions. During the questioning, D makes incriminating statements. *Held*, the statements made by D under interrogation must be suppressed. *Edwards* requires the attorney's presence at all subsequent questioning, once counsel has been requested — D's prior consultation with the lawyer is not a substitute. *Minnick v. Mississippi, supra.*

x. **Break in custody:** The *Edwards* "no police-initiated questioning after invocation of the right to counsel" rule ***ceases to apply*** once there has been a substantial ***break in custody.*** In this narrow situation, the Supreme Court has laid down a very bright-line rule: once the suspect has been ***out of custody for at least 14 days***, *Edwards* ***no longer applies***, and the police may initiate questioning even though they never furnished counsel in response to the suspect's initial request for it. ***Maryland v. Shatzer***, 130 S.Ct. 1213 (2010).

(1) **Facts:** The facts of *Shatzer* illustrate how the break-in-custody issue can arise. In August 2003, while D was already in prison on an unrelated crime, a detective tried to question him about allegations that he had sexually assaulted his son. D invoked his right to counsel; questioning ceased, and D was returned to the general prison population. (Apparently D was never given access to counsel; his *Miranda* rights were respected by the cessation of questioning; see *supra*, p. 240.) Then, in March, 2006, a different detective learned new information about the assault incident, and decided to question D again. D, who was still in prison, was brought to a small conference room in the prison, with no other prisoners present. He signed a written waiver of his *Miranda* rights, and then underwent several questioning sessions during which he incriminated himself.

(2) **The issue:** The issue was whether *Edwards* still applied at the moment of the March, 2006 re-interrogation. It was clear that D, by asking for counsel back in August 2003, initially became entitled under *Edwards* not to be subjected to further police-initiated questioning. But did the 2 1/2 year break between the 2003 and 2006 questioning sessions — during which time D was part of the general prison population — cause the *Edwards* rule to stop applying?

(3) ***Edwards* ceased to apply:** The Supreme Court answered "yes" — the break in custody was sufficiently long that the ***coercive effect*** of the initial interrogation, which had led D to invoke his right to counsel, should be deemed to have ***dissipated***. In fact, the Court said, any break in custody longer than ***14 days*** would have sufficed to make *Edwards* inapplicable, so the 2 1/2 year gap here fell easily on the sufficiently-long side of the line.

(4) **Rationale:** The Court reasoned that "[When] a suspect has been released from his pretrial custody and has ***returned to his normal life*** for some time before the later attempted interrogation, there is little reason to think that his change of heart regarding interrogation without counsel has been coerced. He has no longer been isolated. He has likely been able to seek advice from an attorney, family members, and friends. ... [I]t is far-fetched to think that a police officer's asking the suspect whether he would like to waive *Miranda* rights will any more 'wear down the accused' than did the first such request at the original attempted interrogation — which of course is not deemed coercive."

(5) **Length:** *Shatzer* establishes that a "break in custody" has to be of "sufficient duration to dissipate [the] coercive effects" of the original interrogation session. Since *Edwards* itself was a Court-made prophylactic rule (not, the Court had previously held, a constitutionally-required rule), the Court was free to shape the confines of the rule as it wished. And it was now deciding, somewhat arbitrarily, that a break in custody would be sufficiently long to nullify *Edwards* if the break was 14 days or more. That period "provides plenty of time for the suspect to get reacclimated to his normal life, to consult with friends and counsel, and to shake off any residual coercive effects of his prior custody."

(6) **Return to prison population:** In *Shatzer* itself, D was not ***out of prison*** during the 2 1/2 year gap between interrogations; rather, he was part of the general prison population. But the Court decided that this was the ***equivalent*** of not being in custody at all: "Without minimizing the harsh realities of incarceration, we think lawful imprisonment imposed upon conviction of a crime does not create the coercive pressures identified in *Miranda*." When a prisoner is released back into the general prison population, he returns to his accustomed surroundings and daily routine, and is not "isolated with [his] accusers" as in the standard *Miranda* scenario. So D's time in prison between the two interrogations was to be treated as if he were not in custody at all.

c. **Right to silence:** Let's now leave the topic of the police's right to initiate a new interrogation after the suspect has invoked his right to counsel, and turn to the related topic of when the police may initiate a new interrogation after the suspect has invoked his ***right to silence***. As we'll see, in the right-to-silence scenario there is no equivalent of the bright-line "police may not initiate questioning" rule of *Edwards*.

i. **"Scrupulously honored" standard:** Instead, the Court applies a much-weaker standard: ***"scrupulously honored."*** In a 1975 case that interpreted *Miranda*'s language about the consequences of an assertion of the right to silence, the Court said that "the admissibility of statements obtained after the person in custody has decided to remain silent depends [on] whether his 'right to cut off questioning' was 'scrupulously honored.'" ***Michigan v. Mosley***, 423 U.S. 96 (1975).

(1) **Outcome:** In *Mosley*, the Court concluded that even though the second interrogation was initiated by the police, the circumstances made it clear that the

suspect's right to silence had indeed been scrupulously honored, so the second interrogation was valid.

(2) **Facts of *Mosley*:** *Mosley* involved a defendant, Williams, who was interrogated about two robberies after receiving his *Miranda* warnings, and who said he did not want to answer police questions. Questioning was then immediately terminated. Several hours later, Williams was taken to a different floor of the building where he was being held, and, after again being given his *Miranda* warnings, was questioned by a different officer about a fatal shooting which had occurred in a third robbery. Williams implicated himself. At trial, he moved to strike his statements on the ground that they were procured in violation of his right not to be questioned after he initially exercised his *Miranda* rights.

(3) **Holding:** The Court, in a 7-2 decision, held that Williams' right not to be questioned had ***not been violated*** by the resumption of questioning. The Court applied its "scrupulously honored" standard, and concluded that the second interrogation satisfied the standard. The Court observed that "This is not a case ... where the police failed to honor a [suspect's] decision ... to cut off questioning, either by refusing to discontinue the interrogation upon request or by persisting in repeated efforts to wear down the suspect's resistance and make him change his mind." Rather, the police here "***immediately ceased*** the interrogation, resumed questioning only after the passage of a ***significant period of time*** and the provision of a ***fresh set of warnings***, and restricted the second interrogation to a crime that had not been the subject of the earlier interrogation."

(4) **Significance:** *Mosley*, although it is a 1970s decision, represents the Court's only holding on the procedures to be followed after a suspect successfully invokes his right to remain silent. It's hard to know which of the factors cited by the Court were dispositive. But subsequent lower-court cases interpreting *Mosley* have indicated that the police must satisfy ***three requirements*** in order to be deemed to have "scrupulously honored" the suspect's invocation of his right to remain silent:

The police must ***immediately cease the interrogation*** once the suspect invokes his right;

The ***gap*** between the cessation of questioning and the initiation of the new session must represent a ***significant passage of time*** (a ***"cooling off"*** period); and

Prior to the second interrogation, the police must give a ***second set*** of *Miranda* warnings.

KLIK&K (12th) p. 630.

(5) **Limits:** Conversely there are apparently two things that the police *can* do without violating the suspect's right of silence:

First, although the second interrogation in *Mosley* was about a ***different***

crime, this does not seem to be a constitutional requirement. So the police can, assuming they wait for a significant period and re-issue *Miranda* warnings, question the suspect about the ***same crime*** as was the subject of the first interrogation.

Second, unlike the situation in which the suspect invokes the right to counsel, the police are permitted to ***re-initiate*** questioning in the right-to-silence scenario. In other words, the bright-line rule of *Edwards* — that when a suspect has invoked the right to counsel, any new questioning session must be initiated by the suspect, not the police — does ***not apply*** where the right being invoked is the right to silence.

Example: On the facts of *Mosley*, suppose that the defendant Williams had said that he wanted a lawyer before undergoing further questioning. In that event, the steps followed by the police — cessation of questioning, passage of several hours, and a new set of *Miranda* warnings — would *not* have sufficed, because the second session was initiated by the police, something that *Edwards* forbids. But because what was at issue was the right to remain silent rather than the right to counsel, the second questioning was legal even though police-initiated.

ii. Must occur during custody: Even the relatively weak "scrupulously honored" standard applies only where the first interrogation was a ***custodial*** one. If the first encounter was a ***voluntary non-custodial*** discussion between the police and the suspect, in which *Miranda* warnings were not required or given, the suspect has ***no right to silence*** to invoke, and therefore does not get the benefit of the "scrupulously honored" standard for a second interrogation. This means, most significantly, that there does ***not have to be a cooling off period*** between the two sessions.

Example: The day after a robbery at 123 Main St., Officer stands in front of the building, asking passersby whether they know who committed the robbery. One of those passersby is D, who Officer has no particular reason to suspect was involved. D tells Officer, "I don't have anything to say to you — I never talk to the police." Three minutes later, while D is still standing nearby, another pedestrian comes up to Officer, points to D, and says, "He told me that he and his friend committed the robbery at 123 Main." Officer concludes that he now has probable cause to arrest D, so he does so. (Assume that Officer's conclusion is correct, and that the arrest is lawful.) Officer puts D in the patrol car and reads him his *Miranda* warnings immediately. Officer then asks questions, and elicits an incriminating response. At trial, D moves to suppress that response, on the grounds that in the initial street encounter, he invoked his right of silence, and there was no significant period of cooling off before the arrest and second questioning.

It is very unlikely that D will win with this argument. During the first encounter, he was not (nor could he reasonably have believed that he was) in custody, i.e., he was free to leave at any time. Therefore, he had no *Miranda* rights at that point to invoke or waive. Consequently, the post-arrest questioning in the police car was the *first* custodial interrogation, not the second, and it was to be treated the way any other initial custodial interrogation would be treated. So the fact that there was no significant cooling off period between the initial questions and the true custodial interrogation does not matter, and D's entitlement to have his right to remain silent be "scrupulously honored" was not violated by the custodial interrogation.

iii. **Ambiguous invocation of right:** If the police give the *Miranda* warnings and the suspect gives an ***ambiguous*** response as to whether he means to assert his right to silence, two things happen:

The ambiguous response does ***not*** constitute an invocation of the right (because only unambiguous invocations count; see *Berghuis v. Thompkins, supra*, p. 266); and

The police may ***continue asking questions*** to the suspect, rather than either stopping the interrogation or even trying to clarify the suspect's intent.

Taken together, these two facts mean that until the police receive an unambiguous indication that the suspect wants to remain silent and not be further questioned, the police have an ***incentive to continue asking questions***. Perhaps the suspect will make some response that incriminates himself or that at least unambiguously signals that he has waived his right to remain silent. In that case, the response will itself be a valid implied waiver of the right to remain silent (assuming he understood the original *Miranda* warnings). In the worst case, the suspect remains silent, but even here there is effectively no downside to the police for having continued the questioning.

Example: Consider the facts of *Berghuis v. Thompkins, supra*, p. 266: The police present D with a multi-paragraph form containing the *Miranda* warnings; D indicates his understanding by reading one of the paragraphs and listening to the police reading of the other paragraphs; but D then refuses to sign the form. However, the police ask D lots of questions anyway, over a long period, in response to which D remains virtually silent. Finally, after 2 3/4 hours of this, D gives three one word answers to questions, the last of which is incriminating.

Held, the police have behaved properly, and the incriminating answer is admissible. D's refusal to sign the form was not an unambiguous invocation of his right to silence, so it had no effect. Therefore, the police were entitled to keep on questioning D. Once he answered, the fact of answering, taken together with proof that he understood the warnings, was enough to constitute an implied waiver of the right to remain silent.

5. **Summary of waiver differences as between counsel and silence:** In summary, the operation of *Miranda* waivers and invocations is similar, but not identical, as between the right to counsel and the right to silence.

   a. **Waiver must be unambiguous:** As to both rights, any waiver claimed by the prosecution must be shown to have been ***unambiguous***.

   b. **Implied:** Also as to both rights, any waiver may be ***implied*** rather than express. That is, the suspect's waiver of the right may be shown by his conduct and the circumstances. This doesn't happen very often in the right to counsel, since it's hard for a suspect to engage in conduct that implicitly but clearly suggests that he desires counsel; but it is theoretically possible. In the case of the right to silence, the fact that the suspect, after being given the warnings, ***answers*** one or more questions, is likely to be held to constitute an implied waiver of the right to remain silent (as in *Berghuis v. Thompkins*, *supra*, p. 266).

c. **Invocation must be unambiguous:** As to both rights, any ***invocation*** of the right, like a waiver of it, must be ***unambiguous***.

   i. **Consequences:** Once the suspect makes an ***ambiguous*** invocation of either right, the rules governing the police are the same in the two situations: the police may continue to question the suspect, and need not to try to clarify his intent.

d. **Consequences of invocation:** The most important ***difference*** between the right-to-counsel and the right-to-silence scenarios comes after the suspect makes the requisite unambiguous invocation of the right. In the case of the right to ***counsel***, the questioning must immediately cease, and may ***not be reinitiated*** by the police unless the suspect is ***released from custody*** for at least 14 days. In the case of the right to silence, the police must cease questioning, but may then re-initiate it as long as they wait a ***"significant period"*** (a cooling-off period) between questioning sessions, during which period the suspect may continue to be held in custody — then, if the suspect answers questions at any point in the resumed questioning, he will be deemed to have waived the right to silence.

   i. **Easier for police in right-of-silence scenario:** So it's considerably easier for the police to re-institute questioning after the suspect clearly invokes the right to remain ***silent***, than after he invokes the right to ***counsel***.

XI. THE *MIRANDA* RIGHTS OF GRAND JURY WITNESSES

A. **Grand jury questioning generally:** All of the discussion above has concerned interrogation by police officers. But in some cases, the ***prosecution*** will attempt to question suspects, by subpoenaing them before a ***grand jury***. There is dispute about the applicability of *Miranda* to such grand jury questioning; most courts have held *Miranda* not to be applicable.

   1. **General right against self-incrimination:** It is well settled that a witness summoned before a grand jury may refuse to answer on the grounds that his answer might be self-incriminatory.

   2. **Witness must appear:** The witness must, however, appear before the grand jury and be sworn, even if he refuses to testify on Fifth Amendment grounds. Because the witness must come before the grand jury, it may be argued that the setting is "custodial" in the *Miranda* sense.

B. **Warnings not generally required:** Most post-*Miranda* cases have concluded that the grand jury witness does not have to be warned of his right to remain silent or to have a lawyer present.

   1. ***Dionisio*** **analogy:** Of the courts holding *Miranda* not applicable to grand jury witnesses, some have based their conclusions on the Supreme Court's holding in *U.S. v.*

Dionisio, 410 U.S. 1 (1973), which held that a grand jury subpoena is not an "unreasonable seizure" within the meaning of the Fourth Amendment; these courts have argued that if the subpoena is not an "unreasonable seizure," it is not "custodial" in the *Miranda* sense either.

2. **"General fact-finding" rationale:** Other courts have based their refusal to require *Miranda* warnings on the fact that the grand jury inquiry is a "general questioning of citizens in the fact-finding process," a kind of questioning specifically excluded in *Miranda.*

3. **Perjury not excused:** Even in a jurisdiction holding that *Miranda*-type warnings must be given to some or all grand jury witnesses, the prosecution's failure to give such warnings will not be a defense to a subsequent prosecution for ***perjury*** committed before the grand jury. As the Supreme Court noted in *U.S. v. Mandujano*, 425 U.S. 564 (1976), perjury is not an acceptable response even to a violation of one's constitutional rights (assuming that no gross violation of due process has occurred).

   a. **Full *Miranda* warnings not required:** In *Mandujano*, the Court declined to decide whether a grand jury witness must be told he has a right to remain silent. But the Court did hold that two aspects of the *Miranda* warnings (the right to appointed counsel if one is indigent, and the right to have questioning cease completely) do ***not apply*** to grand jury witnesses.

   Note: In many instances, the problem of *Miranda* warnings for grand jury witnesses is obviated by the granting of *immunity* to the witness. When such immunity is granted, the witness may not plead the Fifth Amendment. The immunity granted can be either *"transactional"* (i.e., preventing prosecution for any offense to which the testimony relates) or *"use"* (i.e., preventing the introduction of the compelled testimony and other evidence derived from it, but not preventing all prosecution of offenses to which the testimony relates based on independently-derived evidence.) The Supreme Court held in *Kastigar v. U.S.*, 406 U.S. 441 (1972), that a witness granted use immunity *may constitutionally be prevented from asserting the Fifth Amendment*; the Court stated that the scope of use immunity was "co-extensive" with the Fifth Amendment privilege at trial. If the witness can be compelled to testify by granting him immunity, the *Miranda* warnings are obviously unnecessary.

XII. OTHER ADMISSIBILITY ISSUES RELATING TO *MIRANDA*

A. ***Wong Sun* and *Miranda:*** Suppose a suspect is illegally arrested and given his *Miranda* warnings, and he then confesses. Have the *Miranda* warnings ***"purged the taint"*** of the illegal arrest, so that the "fruit of the poisonous tree" doctrine of *Wong Sun* does not apply? The Supreme Court has held that a state rule providing that the giving of the warnings automatically purges the taint in all circumstances, is invalid. *Brown v. Illinois*, 422 U.S. 590 (1975). *Brown* is treated more fully *infra*, p. 331.

B. **Admissibility for impeachment:** *Miranda* clearly prevents a confession obtained in violation of the *Miranda* rules from being introduced as part of the prosecution's case in chief. But in ***Harris v. New York***, 401 U.S. 222 (1971), the Supreme Court, by a 5-4 vote, significantly undermined *Miranda* by permitting prosecution use of such statements for ***impeachment purposes*** at trial.

1. **Facts:** The defendant was indicted for selling heroin on two occasions. Testifying in his own behalf, he emphatically denied making one of these sales. The prosecution then read a statement, obtained in violation of *Miranda*, in which the defendant admitted making both sales. The Supreme Court held that the use for impeachment purposes of the statement was permissible, despite the lack of *Miranda* warnings. "The shield provided by *Miranda* cannot be perverted into a license to use perjury by way of a defense, free from the risk of confrontation with prior inconsistent utterances."

2. **Criticism:** This case has been widely criticized as ignoring the explicit guidelines of *Miranda*, especially since the evidence admitted ostensibly for impeachment purposes seemed to prove the defendant's guilt if believed by the jury; juries are notoriously incapable of separating the "impeachment" value of testimony from its substantive value, even where the judge instructs them to consider only the former.

   a. **Distortion charged:** The Nixon-appointed majority of *Harris* has also been criticized for distorting the facts of the case, since there was strong evidence that Harris did not give his statement voluntarily. The statement was made while Harris was in the hospital suffering from drug-withdrawal and from the effects of an accident. The defendant's condition was ignored in the majority opinion.

3. **Cutting-back of *Miranda:*** *Harris*, like *Quarles* (p. 254), *Moran* (p. 260) and *Duckworth* (p. 257) has seemed to many observers to indicate that the conservative bloc on the Court is unhappy with the *Miranda* rule, and will seek to restrict its applicability wherever possible.

4. **Involuntary confession:** Although a statement obtained in violation of *Miranda* may be admissible for impeachment purposes under *Harris*, it may ***not*** be used even for this purpose if it was the product of ***coercion***, or was ***involuntary*** for some other reason. Such an involuntary confession was found to exist in *Mincey v. Arizona*, 437 U.S. 385 (1978).

   a. **Facts:** The defendant was interrogated by police while he was in the intensive care unit of a hospital, with bullet wounds, partial paralysis, tubes in his throat and nose, a catheter in his bladder, and various drugs in his system. He asked repeatedly that the questioning stop until he could get a lawyer, but nonetheless answered the questions by writing on pieces of paper, all the while claiming that his pain was "unbearable." The answers themselves bore significant signs of confusion.

   b. **Holding:** The Court held that the confession was not the product of "a rational intellect and a free will," that it was taken from a "seriously and painfully injured man on the edge of consciousness," and that the defendant's will was "simply overborne." Therefore, the confession was involuntary and could not be admitted even for purposes of impeachment.

   c. **Dissent:** Only Justice Rehnquist dissented from this conclusion, arguing that there was other evidence that the confession was voluntary, despite being the product of intense pain.

C. Use of defendant's silence: So far in this chapter, we've talked mainly about whether the prosecution can make use of the defendant's ***statements***, including ones made under custodial interrogation and thus requiring *Miranda* warnings. But a serious issue of admissibility can also arise with respect to the defendant's ***silence*** — when may the prosecution call to the jury's attention at trial the fact that the defendant has ***remained silent at some prior point,*** thus raising a reasonable ***inference of guilt?*** The answer depends heavily on the situation in which the silence occurred.

We will consider four different situations, not all of which involve custodial police questioning:

[1] Failure to take stand: Whether the prosecution may comment at trial on the fact that D has ***chosen not to take the stand at the trial***, and has thus elected not to refute the prosecution's allegations. (See Par. 1 below.)

[2] Silence under custodial interrogation: Regardless of whether D takes the stand, whether the prosecution may attempt to disprove D's defense (e.g., his alibi defense) by showing that ***under custodial interrogation*** (and thus after receiving *Miranda* warnings), D chose to remain silent, in circumstances in which (the prosecution asserts) an innocent man would have explained his innocence to the police. (See Par. 2 below.)

[3] Silence under non-custodial interrogation: Regardless of whether D takes the stand, whether the prosecution may cast doubt on D's innocence by pointing out that ***while D was being subjected to non-custodial*** (and thus ***voluntary***) police questioning, he remained silent, in a way that (the prosecution asserts) is inconsistent with his defense at trial. (See Par. 3 below.)

[4] Failure to come forward: Regardless of whether D takes the stand, whether the prosecution may call to the jury's attention the fact that ***before D was ever subjected to police questioning***, he ***failed to come forward to tell his story to the police***, in a way that is inconsistent with his defense at trial. (See Par. 4 below.)

1. Comment on D's failure to take the stand: Where D exercises his Fifth Amendment right ***not to take the stand at his trial***, the Supreme Court has imposed a very simple bright-line rule: the Fifth Amendment itself ***prevents the prosecution from pointing out to the jury*** that D ***could have taken the stand*** to "tell his story" and elected not to do so. ***Griffin v. California***, 380 U.S. 609 (1965). Similarly, the trial judge ***may not instruct the jury*** that D's silence (his failure to take the stand) constitutes evidence of guilt. *Id.*

a. Rationale: As the Supreme Court reasoned in *Griffin*, allowing comment on the defendant's refusal to testify at trial would be "a ***penalty imposed by courts for exercising a constitutional privilege***. It cuts down on the privilege by ***making its assertion costly***. ... [T]he Fifth Amendment ... forbids either ***comment by the prosecution*** on the accused's silence or ***instructions by the court*** that such silence is evidence of guilt."

2. Impeachment by showing D's silence during custodial interrogation: Now, suppose D raises a particular defense at trial (e.g., an alibi defense), and the prosecution would like to disprove that defense and/or impeach D's credibility as a witness, by showing that while D was ***being subjected to custodial interrogation***, he ***remained silent***, in a way that is inconsistent with his "story" at trial. We'll assume that D was properly given his *Miranda* warnings, and either terminated the questioning immediately, or started answering questions and then at some point stopped answering or terminated the questioning.

a. **D does not take the stand:** Where D does ***not even take the stand***, it's always been clear, since *Miranda* itself, that the prosecution ***may not comment*** on the fact that D invoked his right to remain silent during questioning. And that's true even if D is asserting at trial (through third-party witnesses) an alibi that an innocent suspect would be likely to have explained to police during the interrogation.

b. **Impeachment of D's credibility:** Now, let's suppose that D *does* elect to take the stand, and recites his present version of the facts (e.g., an ***alibi***). On cross-examination, may the prosecution attempt to impeach D's credibility by saying, in effect, "If your story is true, ***why didn't you tell that story to the police*** when they had you in custody and gave you your *Miranda* warnings"? Here, too, the Supreme Court has laid down a bright-line rule: the prosecution ***may not refer, directly or indirectly, to D's silence under custodial questioning,*** even if that silence is inconsistent with D's present trial testimony. ***Doyle v. Ohio***, 426 US. 610 (1976).

   i. **Rationale in *Doyle*:** In reaching this conclusion, the court in *Doyle* said, "While it is true that the *Miranda* warnings contain no express assurance that silence will carry no penalty, such assurance is ***implicit to any person who receives the warnings.*** In such circumstances, it would be ***fundamentally unfair*** and a deprivation of due process to allow the arrested person's silence to be used to impeach an explanation subsequently offered at trial."

3. **Silence under non-custodial questioning:** Now, let's suppose that at a time when the police have ***begun to suspect D*** of a particular crime, but ***before*** they have ***arrested*** him, they ask him to ***undergo voluntary questioning*** and he agrees. If D then refuses to answer a particular question or to discuss a particular topic, may the prosecution comment on that refusal at trial? The answer depends on whether D is found to have ***formally invoked*** his ***Fifth Amendment*** rights during the questioning: (1) if he *has* formally invoked those rights, it's not yet clear as of this writing whether the prosecution may comment on his silence (though the odds are that the Court will ultimately bar comment), but (2) if he has ***not*** explained why is remaining silent (so that he is ***not found to have invoked*** his Fifth Amendment rights), it's clear that the prosecution ***may*** comment on that silence.

a. **Illustration in *Salinas* case:** Proposition (2) above — that if a suspect voluntarily undergoes non-custodial (and un-*Mirandized*) questioning but then remains silent ***without expressly invoking*** his Fifth Amendment rights, the prosecution ***may comment on this silence*** at trial — is demonstrated by a 2013 case, ***Salinas v. Texas***, 133 S.Ct. 2174 (2013).

   i. **Facts:** In *Salinas*, two victims were murdered in their home. D had been a guest at a party hosted by the victims the night before they were killed. Police recovered shotgun shell casings at the crime scene. Their investigation led the police to suspect D; they therefore visited D at his home. During that home visit, D agreed to hand over his shotgun for ballistic testing. The police then asked D if he would voluntarily accompany them to police headquarters, where they would ask him some questions.

(1) D answers questions: D agreed to go to the police station for questioning. There, the officers did not arrest or charge him, and did not read him his *Miranda* warnings. For the most part, D answered the officers' questions. But when the police asked him whether his shotgun "would match the shells recovered at the scene of the murder," D declined to answer. Instead, as the officers later testified, D looked down at the floor, shuffled his feet, clenched his hands, and began to tighten up. Eventually, the police arrested D for the murder.

(2) Use at trial: At trial, D did not take the stand. The prosecution introduced testimony by the officers about D's silence (and physical reactions) during the questioning about shell-matching. The issue before the Supreme Court was whether this testimony violated D's Fifth Amendment privilege against self-incrimination.

ii. Held against D: By a 5-4 vote, the Supreme Court held ***against*** D. The Court had been expected to decide whether, on the assumption that D had invoked his Fifth Amendment rights in this non-custodial-questioning scenario, the prosecution was permitted to comment on D's silence. But in a surprise move, a plurality of the Court decided that ***D had not even invoked his Fifth Amendment privilege at all***, so that the Court could (and did) uphold the prosecutor's evidence without *reaching* the issue of whether the evidence would have violated D's Fifth Amendment rights had he invoked them.[5]

(1) Rationale: In an opinion for a three-Justice plurality,[6] Justice Alito said that a witness normally cannot invoke his Fifth Amendment privilege against self-incrimination "by simply standing mute." Silence in the face of *custodial* interrogation presents a special case — there, because of the risk of ***coercion*** stemming from arrest, *Miranda* and cases decided under it prevent the prosecution from commenting on the defendant's silence even if he did not expressly say that he was invoking his Fifth Amendment right. But where, as here, a suspect is engaged in a ***"voluntary"*** rather than custodial interrogation, the suspect must "put the police ***on notice*** that he is relying on his Fifth Amendment privilege," and merely remaining silent under questioning does not do that, Alito said. For instance, a defendant might decline to answer a question during voluntary questioning "because he is trying to ***think of a good lie***, because he is embarrassed, or because he is ***protecting someone else***." It's

---

5. Only a three-Justice plurality found that D had failed to invoke his Fifth Amendment rights. But another two justices, concurring in the result, held that it didn't *matter* whether D had invoked his Fifth Amendment rights, because they would allow prosecutorial comment on a defendant's pre-custody silence even if he *had* made such an invocation. Thus five members of the Court agreed that whatever Fifth Amendment right against self-incrimination D might have had in this situation, that right was not violated by the prosecutor's comment on his silence.

6. See the prior footnote.

up to the suspect make it clear that his silence is due to his invocation of his privilege against self-incrimination, not to some other motive.

iii. Dissent: The four dissenters (Breyer, joined by Ginsburg, Sotomayor and Kagan), said that this was one of those cases in which courts should ***infer from the circumstances*** that the defendant was invoking his privilege against self-incrimination.

(1) Distinguished from other situations: The dissenters conceded that there are some situations in which ***express*** invocation of the Fifth Amendment is required in order to gain the Amendment's protections; for instance, the questioner might have a special need to know whether the defendant was relying on the Fifth Amendment (e.g., in a grand jury investigation, where the government needs to know whether the witness is remaining silent in order to protect some other person — a situation *not* entitling the witness to rely on the Fifth Amendment — or to avoid incriminating *himself*, a situation in which the Amendment *would* apply).

(2) Invocation should be inferred: But here, the police had already ***informed D that he was a suspect in the murder***, the interrogation was taking place in a police station, and other factors, too, would have made it clear to D that the police were trying to get him to incriminate himself. Therefore, the circumstances "[gave] rise to a reasonable ***inference*** that [D's] silence derived from an exercise of his Fifth Amendment rights." Thus, the dissenters said, D should be ***deemed to have invoked*** those rights — and thus been free from prosecutorial comment on his silence — even though he did not expressly mention the Fifth Amendment as his reason for remaining silent.

b. Significance of *Salinas*: It seems likely that five members of the *Salinas* Court (the three members of the *Salinas* plurality plus the two who concurred in the judgment) believe that in this ***non-custodial "voluntary" interrogation*** scenario, unless the suspect ***expressly mentions*** that he is remaining silent "because of the Fifth Amendment" or for the purpose of "self-incrimination," the prosecution is ***free to comment*** on his silence at trial. If so, a defendant who simply refuses to allow the police to start questioning him on a voluntary basis, or who ends the "interview" in mid-stream, will not be able to prevent the prosecutor from commenting on his silence at trial.

i. Incentive: Notice that this gives the police a huge ***incentive*** to ***do as much "voluntary" questioning of a suspect as possible***, and to ***delay arrest*** (and the giving of *Miranda* warnings) ***as long as possible***. Under *Salinas*, any *pre*-arrest silence not accompanied by the suspect's express invocation of the Fifth Amendment *can* be used against D at trial. But *post*-arrest (and post-*Miranda*), the suspect's silence — whether accompanied by an express invocation of the Fifth Amendment or not — *cannot* be so used. So even if the police fully intend to arrest D for a particular crime as to which they already have probable cause, they should (and in real-world practice apparently often *do*) start by telling D that he is ***not*** under arrest, and asking him whether he would "voluntarily" answer some questions. In fact, the police often, as part of their request for "cooperation," tell D that his cooperation will help them ***"eliminate you as a suspect."***

(1) Consequence: It will be the ***rare*** suspect who has enough presence of mind not only to decline to answer the "voluntary" police questions, but to explicitly say (as *Salinas* requires) that he is doing so ***"to avoid self-incrimination."*** Thus *Salinas* makes it likely that in years to come, there will be a lot of prosecution comments at trial on the defendant's pre-arrest silence in the face of non-custodial police questioning.

ii. D expressly invokes rights: In any event, it's quite possible that even where the suspect *does* formally invoke his Fifth Amendment rights prior to "voluntary" (non-custodial) interrogation, a majority of the Court will nonetheless hold that the prosecution is allowed to comment on his silence. Neither *Salinas* nor any other Supreme Court opinion answers that question. But at least two members of the Salinas Court (the two who concurred in the result) would allow prosecutorial comment in this "rights formally invoked" situation.

4. D's silence without interrogation: Finally, let's consider the fourth situation: D has never been subjected to questioning (voluntary or custodial), but has simply ***failed to come forward*** to tell the police his "story," under circumstances in which an innocent and truthful person would likely have done so. In this situation, like the "voluntary questioning" situation addressed in *Salinas*, *supra*, the prosecution ***will be permitted to comment*** on the defendant's initial silence. *Jenkins v. Anderson*, 447 U.S. 231 (1980).

a. Silence prior to arrest: In *Jenkins*, D raised a ***self-defense claim*** at his murder trial. The prosecution impeached this claim by pointing out that for two weeks after the murder, ***D failed to go to the authorities*** to surrender himself or explain the self-defense incident. The Supreme Court held that *Doyle* (*supra*, p. 280) was inapplicable to these facts, and that D's pre-arrest silence *could* be used to impeach the defendant's testimony. The Court distinguished *Doyle* by noting that here, ***"no governmental action induced [D] to remain silent*** before arrest." Nor was D in custody during the period of silence. The Court conceded that its holding might dissuade a defendant from taking the stand because of the risk of cross-examination, but said that "this is a choice of litigation tactics."

Quiz Yourself on ***CONFESSIONS AND POLICE INTERROGATION*** *(ENTIRE CHAPTER)*

58. One night in Central Park, police officers in a roving patrol car suddenly heard muted cries that sounded like they were coming from an animal. They discovered a young woman lying beaten by the side of the path, her head terribly bloody. The officers immediately scouted around the area. They found a young man who was carrying a baseball bat, which appeared to have some dark, sticky substance on it. The officers arrested the young man, whose name was Claude, and took him to the police station. The officers did not say anything to Claude, either at the time of the arrest or during the trip, except, "Come on, guy, we're gonna have to take you into the police station."

At the station, Claude was booked on charges of committing the beating, and put in a temporary holding cell until he could be arraigned. Shortly after Claude was put in the cell, a police detective walked in, and without any preamble said, "We know you beat that girl in the park. Did you rape her too?" Claude responded, "No, I only hit her on the head once with the bat, to try to stun her." Claude was tried on aggravated assault charges, and the prosecution sought to introduce his confession as the main part of their case against him. May the confession be admitted, and why or why not? ________________

59. The police had long believed that Dennis had murdered his wife, but they had no proof. One day, an officer happened to catch Dennis driving through a red light. Local law permitted a prison term for that offense. Dennis was arrested, taken to the station house, arraigned, and held in a cell pending trial, because he couldn't make the $200 bail. The police wanted to take advantage of this happy situation, so they put an undercover police officer, Alan, into Dennis' cell — Alan was dressed in regular prison garb, and was coached to tell Dennis that he, Alan, was in for car theft.

Alan hoped that Dennis would incriminate himself in his wife's murder without any prompting, but this did not happen. Therefore, during their second day as cellmates, Alan said to Dennis, "You know, once I get out again — and I'm sure I'm gonna beat this rap — I'd love to have a partner to do bank robbery jobs with, which are what I'm really good at. But I can't have a wimp as a partner; I could only use somebody who would kill if the need arose. Did you ever kill anybody?" Dennis had always dreamed of getting a chance to commit a lucrative crime or two with an expert as mentor. So he replied, "Well, as a matter of fact, about two years ago, I murdered my wife, and they never pinned anything on me."

Dennis was then charged with murdering his wife, and Alan was called to testify about what Dennis had told him in the cell. Dennis asserts that admission of this testimony would violate his rights, since he never got any *Miranda* warnings before he made his incriminating statement to Alan. Should Alan's testimony be suppressed on this ground? ________________

60. The police suspected (reasonably and accurately, as it turned out) that Elvira had committed a recent burglary of a valuable diamond-and-pearl necklace. The police decided to take a direct approach. Bess, one of the better detectives on the local force, was sent to Elvira's house. When Elvira answered the door, Bess inquired whether she could ask Elvira some questions about "a burglary that took place the other night, involving a necklace." Elvira invited Bess in. Bess questioned Elvira for nearly an hour and a half, about the burglary and about Elvira's movements on the night of the burglary. At no time did Bess give Elvira any *Miranda* warnings.

About 45 minutes into the interview, Elvira said, "I've really got to get to the grocery store before it closes in another 10 minutes." Bess replied, "No, I think we really have to get to the bottom of this." Elvira reluctantly agreed to stay, in part because she wasn't sure she had any choice. Near the end of the interview, Elvira said, "Anyway, I'd never bother to steal a necklace where the largest diamond was only one-quarter carat and the total weight was only two carats." Since the police had never released these details about the necklace, and Elvira had claimed that she did not know the owner and had never seen the necklace, this remark was incriminating. At Elvira's trial for burglary, the prosecution tried to introduce the statement against her. Elvira has objected, on the grounds that the statement was obtained from her in violation of her *Miranda* rights. Should the statement be allowed into evidence? ________________

61. While the *USS Nebraska* was docked in San Diego, her officers discovered one of the sailors dead in his bunk, cause unknown. The police were immediately called, and sealed off the gangway, so that no one could leave or enter the ship. At the time, there were 15 men aboard. The police then said, "We're not sure whether this death was murder, accident, or natural causes, but nobody leaves the ship until you've answered our questions." Each seaman was then taken privately to a cabin where one of the police officers questioned him about what, if anything, he knew concerning the death. No seaman was given *Miranda* warnings.

One of the seamen, Frank, when asked, "Did you have anything to do with the sailor's death?" answered, "Well, he was being mean to me all the time, so I put a pillow over his face while he was asleep, till he stopped breathing." At Frank's trial for murder, this confession is sought to be introduced into evidence against him. The prosecution argues that since at the time of Frank's questioning it was not known whether there even had been a crime, and the investigation certainly had not focused on Frank, *Miranda* warnings should not be applicable. Should Frank's confession be excluded from evidence against him?

____

62. Officer Nelson was on traffic patrol. He spotted a car driving with one tail light missing. (It was part of Nelson's job to stop and warn motorists of even minor infractions — he usually just warned them, and let them go on their way.) Nelson flashed his lights and pulled the car over. The car was being driven by Jermaine. He asked Jermaine for her driver's license and for the car's registration. Jermaine produced both. Nelson noticed that the owner of the car, according to the registration, was John Jones, not Jermaine. He asked Jermaine, "How do you come to be driving a car registered to John Jones?" Jermaine, suddenly very nervous, replied, "Well, I borrowed it from him. I was going to bring it back pretty soon." Nelson asked, "Does he know you have the car?" Jermaine said, "No, but I'm sure he wouldn't mind." This was enough to make Nelson quite suspicious. He radioed headquarters, where he found that the car had been reported stolen by Jones 12 hours before. Jermaine was charged with car theft, and her earlier statement to Nelson was admitted against her to show that she knew that she did not have authority to take the car. Jermaine has moved to have her statement excluded from evidence as rendered in violation of *Miranda*. Should the statement be excluded? ________________

63. Ike was getting into a parked car, when Officer Quentin, of the Arbortown police, noticed that the registration on the car's front windshield had expired. As Ike drove away, Quentin stopped him, and arrested him for driving with an expired registration sticker. (Driving with an expired registration sticker is, under local law, punishable by at most a $200 fine, and a jail term may not be imposed for it. Normally, a driver would not be arrested for this offense, but merely given a citation; however, local law did permit an arrest in this situation.) Quentin was known as an especially tough "law and order" type. Therefore, he took Ike back to the police station, where he was booked and then held for several hours pending arraignment. During this time, the police ran a routine ID check on Ike, and discovered that he was wanted by the police of another town (Elmont), for a burglary at 123 North Avenue in Elmont.

Officer Quentin went up to Ike and said, "Did you commit a burglary at 123 North Avenue in Elmont two weeks ago?" Ike responded, "Hey, officer, I didn't go in the house, I just drove the getaway car on that one." At no time during this exchange (or prior to it) did anyone give Ike any *Miranda* warnings. Ike was charged by the Elmont police with being an accomplice to the North Avenue burglary. His statement to Quentin was introduced against him. Ike protested that the statement was made in violation of the *Miranda* rules. The prosecutor argued in rebuttal that *Miranda* warnings need not be given where a person is in custody for a misdemeanor or other non-felony crime. Must Ike's confession be excluded from evidence against him? ________________

64. Police were investigating a murder in which the victim, Molly, was found dead of stab wounds in her apartment. It turned out that Molly had been having an affair with a married man, Herb. Herb's wife, Jill, was known to the police to be a jealous sort who had become enraged in the past when Herb had carried on affairs with other women, though the police did not know whether Jill had been aware of the Herb-Molly affair. Finally, the police got a break — they found a couple of red hairs embedded in the carpet near Molly's body; since Molly was a brunette and Jill was a redhead, they were able to persuade a judge that this constituted probable cause for issuing a warrant for Jill's arrest. (Assume that the arrest warrant was properly issued.) They then arrested Jill for Molly's murder, and brought her to the police station.

The detective in charge of the case, Detective Reynolds, came into Jill's holding cell. Reynolds did not give Jill any *Miranda* warnings. Reynolds said, without preamble (and without Jill's saying anything to him first), "Look, we know you did it. We know all about the affair between Herb and Molly, and we've got evidence that you knew about that affair too. Furthermore, we've got several red hairs found at the crime scene, embedded in the carpet right near where the body was found. It would make life a lot easier for everybody if you would just confess." Jill responded, "Well, I went to Molly's apartment that night, and had a drink with her while I tried to talk her into stopping the affair. But I didn't kill her."

At Jill's murder trial, the prosecution, as part of its case in chief, introduced this statement to show that Jill was present at the murder scene. By then, Jill had changed her story, and claimed that she was never at the apartment. Therefore, Jill's lawyer objected to the introduction of the statement, on the grounds that it was obtained in violation of Jill's *Miranda* rights.

(a) What argument should the prosecutor make for holding that *Miranda* is inapplicable to Jill's station-house statement? ________________

(b) Will this argument be successful? ________________

65. Nell, a wealthy businesswoman, disappeared suddenly one day. Shortly thereafter, her family received a ransom demand for $1 million, together with instructions about where and when the money should be delivered. Nell's husband, Lee, decided to pay the money, but to bring the police in on the ransom payment. Lee showed up at the ransom "drop" at the appointed time with the money. Police staked out the area.

Soon thereafter, Ken picked up the ransom, and began to drive away. The police, led by Officer Stone, stopped him, handcuffed him and put him in the back of the police cruiser. There, Stone, said to him, "If anything happens to Nell, you'll get the chair under the Lindberg law. Tell us where she is, and save your life. Where is she?" Ken replied, "I've got her tied up in an apartment I've rented," and took the police there. At Ken's later kidnapping trial, the prosecution anticipated that Ken might claim that his only involvement was to pick up the ransom, not to participate in capturing or holding Nell. Therefore, the prosecution sought to introduce Ken's statement to Stone, to show that Ken was the main or sole criminal. Ken has objected on the grounds that his statement to Officer Stone was taken in violation of his *Miranda* rights.

(a) What doctrine should the prosecution assert, in opposition to Ken's objection? ________________

(b) Will this doctrine apply to render *Miranda* inapplicable and the confession thus admissible? ________________

66. Nestor was arrested on armed robbery charges, and taken to the station house. He was read a complete set of *Miranda* warnings. Nestor made no statement or even gesture indicating that he understood the warnings and was waiving his rights. The police immediately began questioning him. Nestor answered their questions, thus incriminating himself. May his statements be introduced against him at trial as part of the prosecution's case in chief? ________________

67. Same basic facts as prior question. Now, however, assume that after Nestor was read his Miranda warnings, the police officer said, "Do you understand these rights?" and Nestor replied, "Yes," but did not elaborate further. The police asked him questions without any response for half an hour, and then asked the question to which he gave an incriminating response. May his response be introduced against him at trial as part of the prosecution's case in chief? ________________

68. Omar was a 21-year-old man who lived at home with his parents. A well-documented facet of his personality was that he was very much influenced by any older man in whose company he happened to be at the time. Omar was arrested by the police on charges of participating in a burglary, in that he drove the getaway car for the principal burglar, Bob, an older man. The police arrested Omar at his house, in front of his mother. Omar was taken to the station, and given his *Miranda* warnings. Simultaneously, Omar's mother (unbeknownst to Omar) arranged to have the family lawyer, Ralph, go to the station house.

Ralph arrived at the station house while Omar was being read his *Miranda* warnings. The officers at the front desk did not let Ralph see his client. Nor did they inform Omar that Ralph had been retained for him by his family, or that Ralph was there waiting to see him. Omar was read the *Miranda* warnings and said, "I don't want to hide anything"; he proceeded to answer questions concerning his role in the burglary. At Omar's burglary trial, his lawyer seeks to suppress statements made at the station house. The defense demonstrates that because of Omar's impressionable nature, there is a very high probability that had Ralph been permitted to see Omar, Omar would have taken Ralph's advice to remain silent. Must Omar's statement be excluded from the case against him? ________________

69. Same basic fact pattern as the prior question. Now, however, assume that: (1) no lawyer had been retained for Omar and thus none was waiting at the station; and (2) the officer interrogating Omar said to Omar (after giving him his *Miranda* warnings), "The guy you pulled the burglary with, Bob, has already confessed that you were in it with him. So you have nothing to lose by confessing, and it may even shorten your sentence for having cooperated with us." The officer knew that this was a complete lie (Bob had not even talked to the police about anything), and the sole purpose of the officer's statement was to induce Omar to waive his *Miranda* rights. Omar agreed to answer questions, and confessed. Must Omar's confession be excluded from evidence as a violation of his *Miranda* rights? ________________

70. The police arrested Quentin on a murder charge, booked him, and put him in jail because he could not make bail. Shortly after he was first jailed, Detective Angstrom read Quentin his full *Miranda* rights, and asked if he would answer some questions regarding the murder with which he was charged. Quentin responded, "I want a lawyer, and I might talk to you after I talk to the lawyer." Over the weekend, while Quentin was still in jail, a court-appointed lawyer visited him, and discussed the charges. (The lawyer did not anticipate that Quentin would be questioned again, so he did not tell Quentin that he should remain silent if questioning resumed.) On Monday morning, Detective Butts came into Quentin's cell, ascertained that Quentin had met with the lawyer, gave Quentin his *Miranda* warnings again, and asked him if he would now discuss the case. Quentin agreed to do so. In response to questions by Butts, Quentin implicated himself. May these incriminating statements be introduced against Quentin at trial? ________________

71. On October 1, the police arrested Quincy on a robbery charge, and brought him to police headquarters. There, they read him his *Miranda* warnings; Quincy responded that he wanted to deal with them only through an attorney that he asked the police to arrange to have appointed for him. The police decided that it was too much of a bother to get an attorney appointed right away, so they released him. On November 1, after the police got more evidence implicating Quincy on the robbery charge, they brought him back into custody, and once again read him his *Miranda* rights. Quincy orally agreed to waive those rights, made no reference to his prior request for a lawyer, and gave an incriminating response. May this response be introduced against Quincy at trial? ________________

72. Raymond was arrested on suspicion of having committed a burglary in New York City on March 10. At the station house, the detective stupidly forgot to give Raymond his *Miranda* warnings, then interrogated him. In response to the detective's questions, Raymond confessed that he had indeed done the burglary. (This questioning did not take place in a particularly coercive manner, and under all the circumstance, a court would conclude that Raymond gave the confession "voluntarily.")

At Raymond's trial on the burglary charges, he took the stand in his own defense. Under questioning by his lawyer, Raymond asserted an alibi defense — he claimed that he had been in Chicago on the day and time when the burglary took place. On cross-examination, the prosecutor showed Raymond a transcript of his confession, and asked him, "If your alibi defense is true, how come you confessed to the crime, instead of either remaining silent, or telling the police about your alibi defense?" Over an objection by Raymond's lawyer, the judge let the question stand, and Raymond replied, "The confession is phony — I just gave it to get the police off my back. In fact, I was in Chicago that day, as I've just said."

The trial judge instructed the jury that they should consider this material only for purposes of evaluating Raymond's credibility as a witness, and not as bearing directly on the substantive issue of whether Raymond committed the crime. The jury found Raymond guilty. On appeal, should the appeals court order a new trial on the grounds that the material was admitted in violation of Raymond's *Miranda* rights?

____

73. On August 25, Stan was arrested on suspicion of being the masked rapist who had assaulted a woman in Boston on the evening of August 10. He was driven to the police station, booked, and then taken into a room used for interrogations. There, he was given his *Miranda* warnings. After reading him the warnings, Dave, the lead detective, said to him, "If you have any evidence that will help us exclude you as a suspect, you might want to help us out by answering a few simple questions, like where you were on the night of the 10th." Dave said, "No, I don't want to talk to you." The case went to trial. At the trial, Stan took the stand and testified that he could not have committed the rape because he was in New York the entire evening on which the rape occurred. On cross-examination, the prosecutor asked him, "If your story about being in New York was true, why didn't you tell that story to the police when they had you in custody, instead of refusing to answer any of their questions?" Stan's lawyer has objected to the question as an infringement of Stan's rights under *Miranda*. Should the court sustain the objection?

____

74. Same basic facts as the prior question. Now, however, assume that after the police came to suspect Stan of being the masked rapist, Dave visited Stan at his house and asked him if he would voluntarily come to the police station to answer some questions, "so that we can clear you as a suspect." Stan agreed, and accompanied Dave to the police station. At an interrogation room at the station, Dave did not read Stan any *Miranda* warnings. Instead, he said to Stan (in front of what Stan knew was a video recorder), "Stan, you've agreed to this voluntary interview, which you may terminate at any time. Is that correct?" Stan answered, "yes." Stan then answered various questions asked by Dave. At one point, Dave asked him, "Were you in Boston throughout the evening of August 10, when we know the rape occurred?" Stan replied, "I'm tired of answering your questions, and I'm terminating this interview." Stan gave no other indication of why he was cutting off the questioning. Dave let Stan leave the police station, then immediately arrested him for the rape. At trial, Stan took the stand to offer the same "I was in New York" alibi as in the prior question. The prosecution attempted to rebut this testimony by offering testimony by Dave that Stan had suddenly terminated the voluntary interview when Dave asked about Stan's whereabouts on the evening in question. Stan's lawyer has objected on the grounds that this impeachment use of Stan's silence would violate Stan's privilege against self-incrimination. Should the court sustain this objection?

Answers

58. No, because Claude was not given his *Miranda* warnings. This is a classic illustration of when *Miranda* warnings must be given: The suspect was in custody, and he was questioned by the police; therefore, the police were required to tell him: (1) that he had the right to remain silent, (2) that anything he said could be used against him in a court of law, (3) that he had the right to have an attorney present before any questioning, and (4) that if he could not afford an attorney, one would be appointed for him before questioning, if he wished. Since Claude was not given these warnings, nothing he said may be used against him. It doesn't matter that Claude's confession was in a sense "voluntary," rather than "coerced" — *Miranda* is a "bright line," i.e., automatic, rule.

59. No. It is true that Dennis was in "custody" at the time he made his statement, and that his statement was in response to a question asked by someone who was in fact a police officer. Thus the formal requirements for *Miranda* (custody and police interrogation) seem to be met. However, the Supreme Court has held that where the defendant talks to an undercover agent or a government informant, and the defendant does not ***know*** that he is talking to a law enforcement officer, no "custodial interrogation" will be deemed to have taken place, even if the exchange occurs while the defendant is in jail. Therefore, *Miranda* warnings do not have to be given in this situation. See *Illinois v. Perkins*, involving facts similar to those in this question.

60. No, probably. The issue, of course, is whether Elvira was "in custody" at the time she made the statement. The Supreme Court follows an "objective" standard for determining whether somebody is in custody for *Miranda* purposes: the suspect will be deemed to have been in custody if a ***reasonable person*** in the suspect's position would have ***understood that he or she was not free to go.*** See *Berkemer v. McCarty*, establishing this test.

Here, the situation probably amounted to custody by this standard — a reasonable person in Elvira's positions, after being told that she could not (or at least should not) go to the grocery store, would probably have felt that she was not free to leave or to evict Bess whenever she wanted. Since Elvira was in custody, and since Bess was a police officer interrogating her (and Elvira knew that Bess was a police officer), the requirements for *Miranda* warnings were satisfied. Since those warnings were not given, her statement may not be introduced against her as part of the prosecution's case in chief.

61. Yes. The requirement of *Miranda* warnings is triggered wherever the police conduct a custodial interrogation of someone who they think *may* have something to do with or know something about a possible crime. The fact that the police are not certain that a crime has been committed, or the fact that the investigation has not "focused" on the person being interrogated, does not make a difference. See *Stansbury v. California*. Since Frank was clearly in custody here (in the sense that a reasonable person in his position would have known that he was not free to leave without answering the questions), and since he was clearly being interrogated by a police officer, *Miranda* warnings needed to be given.

62. No, probably. Again, the issue is whether this interrogation was "custodial." The Supreme Court has held that ordinary stops of a driver for minor traffic violations normally will not constitute a taking into custody, for *Miranda* purposes. See *Berkemer v. McCarty*, holding that since such stops are generally temporary and brief, and the motorist knows that he will probably be allowed to go on his way, *Miranda* warnings do not have to be given. Here, Jermaine had no reason to believe (at least, no reason apart from her own knowledge that she had committed a crime) that this was anything other than a routine traffic stop that would allow her to go on her way when she promised to get the tail light fixed. She had no reason to believe that she had been arrested or would be arrested. Therefore, the coercive element usually associated with custodial interrogation was not present here, and it is unlikely that the court would find that *Miranda* warnings had to be given.

63. Yes. There is no ***"minor crimes"*** exception to the *Miranda* requirement — if an interrogation meets all of the standard requirements for *Miranda* warnings (especially the requirement that the suspect be "in custody"), these warnings must be given no matter how minor the crime, and regardless of the fact that no jail sentence may be imposed for it. *Berkemer v. McCarty*.

64. (a) That Jill's statement was not in response to any "interrogation." It is not enough that the suspect makes an incriminating statement while in custody — *Miranda* only applies where there is "interrogation" during the custody. The prosecutor should argue that Detective Reynolds may have made statements, but he did not ask questions, so that there was no interrogation.

(b) No, probably. The Supreme Court has held that there can be "interrogation" even though there is no direct questioning. The Court has held that "the term 'interrogation'... refers not only to express questioning, but also to any words or actions on the part of the police (other than those normally attendant to arrest and custody) that the police ***should know are reasonably likely to elicit*** an ***incriminating response*** from a suspect." *Rhode Island v. Innis*. Here, Reynolds, by going into such detail about the evidence the police had against Jill, and by mentioning how desirable it would be if Jill were to confess, should probably have known that some incriminating response was likely to be made by Jill in response. The fact that Reynolds volunteered the information on his own, without stating it in response to a question by Jill, further reinforces the argument that Jill must have understood Reynolds' statements as an attempt to get her to talk.

65. (a) The "public safety" exception to *Miranda*. The Supreme Court has recognized a "public safety" exception to the *Miranda* rule — *Miranda* warnings are simply unnecessary prior to questioning that is "reasonably prompted by a concern for the public safety." *New York v. Quarles*.

(b) Yes. Ken was certainly in custody at the time he made the statement, and he certainly made the statement in response to interrogation. But since it was quite possible that other accomplices were holding Nell, and that time might be of the essence in saving her from further harm, the court would almost certainly find that the "public safety" exception applied here.

66. No. The defendant's silence and his subsequent answering of questions, without anything more, will never be held to be a valid waiver of the right to remain silent or of the right to have a lawyer present.

67. Yes. Waivers of *Miranda* rights may be implied, not just express. In particular, there are situations in which the suspect's actions and words justify the inference that he waived his right to silence. As the prior question shows, a suspect's mere silence, followed by the answering of a question, is not enough to demonstrate a waiver. But the conduct of answering, when coupled with proof that the suspect *understood* his *Miranda* right to remain silent, *does* qualify as an implied waiver, as long as nothing indicates that there was police coercion. Furthermore, an *invocation* of a *Miranda* right must be unambiguous; Nestor's initial silence after being read his warnings was not sufficiently clear to be an invocation of his right to silence. Therefore, in contrast to the prior question, the fact that Nestor said that he understood his rights after they were read to him, when added to the fact that he eventually answered a question, gave rise to an implied waiver of the right to remain silent.

68. No. In a case involving similar facts, the Supreme Court held that the defendant's waiver was "knowing and voluntary," and thus effective. *Moran v. Burbine*. Even though the defendant might have reached a different decision about whether to waive his rights if he had known that a lawyer had been retained and was trying to reach him, the *Moran* Court felt that this was irrelevant — the defendant knew his rights and made a conscious decision to waive them; this was all that mattered. So Omar will be held to have knowingly waived his rights, and the confession will be admitted against him.

69. No. The Supreme Court has never dealt with whether police trickery regarding the strength of their case voids a *Miranda* waiver. However, almost certainly the decision in *Moran v. Burbine* (see prior answer) would be binding in this situation as well, since the fact that the police have a strong or weak case has no bearing on whether the defendant understands his rights and has consciously chosen to waive them. Lower courts that have considered this "trickery regarding the strength of the police case" issue have generally held that the waiver is nonetheless effective.

70. No. On almost precisely these facts, the Supreme Court has held that the resumption of questioning without the suspect's lawyer present violates *Miranda* and the post-*Miranda* case of *Edwards v. Arizona*. See *Minnick v. Mississippi*: "When counsel is requested, interrogation must cease, and officials may not reinitiate interrogation without counsel present, regardless of whether the accused has consulted with his attorney." So observe that Quentin does better by asking for a lawyer than he does by merely asserting that he wants to remain silent — he scores a clear "win" (whereas if he had remained silent, and was later re-questioned, the admissibility of his statements would turn on the length of time between the two sessions, whether the second interrogation concerned the same crime, and other factors. See *Michigan v. Mosley*.)

71. Yes. The normal rule laid down by *Edwards v. Arizona* is that once a suspect asserts his right to counsel, all questioning must cease until the requested lawyer is made available, and the police may not reinitiate questioning before then. However, in the post-*Edwards* case of *Maryland v. Shatzer*, the Court set out a bright-line exception to *Edwards*: once the suspect has been out of custody for at least 14 days following his invocation of the right to counsel, *Edwards* no longer applies, and the police *may* re-initiate questioning even though they never furnished counsel in response to the initial request. The facts here qualify for this *Shatzer* exception. Therefore, since the police reinitiated their questioning of Quincy more than 14 days after he had been released from custody, they were entitled to re-arrest him, give him a new set of *Miranda* warnings, procure a waiver, and start the entire process of interrogation anew even though they had never furnished a lawyer following Quincy's original request for one.

72. No. The Supreme Court has held that where the defendant takes the stand and makes a statement, the prosecution may use a confession obtained in violation of *Miranda* to ***impeach the defendant's credibility*** as a witness. *Harris v. New York*. (But if the statement was not only obtained in violation of *Miranda*, but also was coerced or was involuntary, then it cannot be used even for impeachment purposes. See *Mincey v. Arizona*. However, there is no evidence of coercion or involuntariness on the facts here.)

73. Yes. Once a suspect has been taken into custody and given his *Miranda* warnings, if the suspect declines to answer questions the prosecution may not comment on that silence at trial. *Doyle v. Ohio*. That's true even if the defendant takes the stand and affirmatively gives testimony whose truthfulness would be impeached by a showing that the defendant elected not to answer police questions while in custody. In *Doyle*, the Supreme Court said that even though the *Miranda* warnings contain no express assurance that silence will carry no penalty, such an assurance is "***implicit*** to any person who receives the warnings" and that allowing the silence to be used later to impeach the defendant's testimony would be "fundamentally unfair."

74. No. The fact pattern here is very similar to that in *Salinas v. Texas* (2013). In *Salinas*, a 5-justice majority held that the defendant's invocation of his right to silence during a voluntary (non-custodial) interrogation *may* be commented upon by the prosecution, at least if the defendant never ***expressly invoked*** his Fifth Amendment privileges. (A three-justice plurality in *Salinas* said that in this voluntary-interrogation scenario, a defendant who does not expressly invoke his Fifth Amendment rights, but remains silent, won't be inferred to have relied on those rights; therefore, the prosecution may comment on the silence. Another two members said that whether the defendant does or doesn't expressly invoke the Fifth Amendment, as long as the questioning is voluntary the prosecution may comment about the silence. So a majority of the *Salinas* Court believed that a defendant who simply cuts off voluntary questioning can't prevent the prosecution from commenting on that fact.) Thus here, given that Stan agreed to the voluntary questioning but then suddenly ended the interview, and given that he did this without expressly invoking his privilege against self-incrimination, under *Salinas* the prosecution may (1) present evidence at trial showing that Stan refused to answer a particular question, and (2) encourage the jury to infer that a person with a true alibi in that situation would not have refused to answer.

***Exam Tips** on*
CONFESSIONS AND POLICE INTERROGATION

Here's what to look for in questions about confessions and police interrogation:

Although *Miranda* requires four different warnings, even when some of these are ***omitted*** the warnings as will not be deemed inadequate, if the message as a whole was ***clear and unambiguous.***

Example: D is arrested and told that anything he says can be used against him in court; that he has the right to consult an attorney before questioning; and that counsel will be appointed for him if cannot afford to retain one. D initially makes no statements, then later changes his mind and confesses. At trial, D tries to have his statements suppressed, on the grounds that he was never told he had the right to remain silent. D will probably lose, since he was warned that what he said could be used against him, he did not in fact make any statements at that time, and the omission of the "right to remain silent" language probably didn't affect his conduct.

Remember the one clear, bright-line rule of law that applies to *Miranda* rights: ***once a defendant has invoked his right to counsel, police cannot question him further until they provide one.*** (Of course, the prosecution can always argue that the defendant did not clearly invoke the right, or that the defendant initiated subsequent questioning.)

Example: Officer arrests D for possession of stolen property. She knows D has other property concealed. She advises D of his *Miranda* rights, and he responds that he will not say anything until he speaks with an attorney. Officer then tells D that he will not be subject to further charges if he speaks up immediately and tells her the location of the remainder of the property. D speaks. D's *Miranda* rights have been violated by the attempt to elicit information from him after he invoked his right to counsel.

However, police can still take a statement from D after D requests counsel if (1) D ***initiates*** the conversation and (2) D makes a ***knowing and intelligent waiver*** of her right to counsel.

Remember that *Miranda* only applies to ***custodial interrogation.*** Therefore, it's important for you to determine, as a preliminary matter, whether the defendant was in custody. The general test is ***whether a reasonable person in the suspect's position would believe he is in custody at that moment.*** Some examples of how this test has been applied on exams include:

Being held by the police at ***gunpoint*** (in any situation) — probably custody.

Roadside questioning of the operator of a motor vehicle who has been stopped for a ***traffic violation*** — probably not custody.

Participation in a lineup before being charged with a crime — probably not custody.

Example: D voluntarily agrees to participate in a lineup. After being identified by the victim, he states, "This isn't my day. I might as well confess." This statement is admissible, in spite of the lack of *Miranda* warnings, because D was not in custody at the time.

Conversations with ***undercover or secret agents*** — not custody.

Voluntarily coming to police headquarters — not custody.

Remember that if the suspect is a ***minor***, his age is considered as part of the "reasonable person's belief" test — so a reasonable young child taken from a classroom to be questioned might well think he is not free to leave (and thus be in custody) where a reasonable adult would have believed he was free to leave.

The other part of the foundation for a *Miranda* challenge is that there must have been ***interrogation***. Interrogation need not be direct questioning — any comment by police that is ***reasonably likely to produce an incriminating response*** qualifies.

Example 1: D is arrested for theft and placed in a "holding cell." Meanwhile, the police search his car. Later, Officer comes to D's cell and holds up an envelope of stolen merchandise that was found in the car and says, "You're in big trouble now." D blurts out, "Donna was the one who did it." Officer's comment probably (though not certainly) constituted interrogation and thus triggered D's *Miranda* rights, because a defendant in this situation would be reasonable likely to make an incriminating response.

Example 2: D is arrested and brought in for booking. The booking officer is D's neighbor. On seeing D, Booking Officer says, "Hey, what are you doing here?" D makes an incriminating response. Booking Officer's question probably does not qualify as interrogation, because Booking Officer did not know any facts to suggest that his innocuous comment was reasonably likely to elicit an incriminating statement.

The two most important situations that are ***not interrogation*** (and therefore do not require *Miranda* warnings for the defendant's statement to be admissible) are:

General factual inquiries at a ***crime scene***;

Example: Officer, standing outside a bar, hears gunshots inside. She rushes in, gun drawn, and asks "What the devil happened here?" Defendant responds, "I shot them in self-defense." Although Defendant may argue that this was custodial interrogation because Officer had her gun drawn, her question was more in the nature of a general inquiry to those present, not directed at any particular person for any particular purpose. Therefore, it won't be considered "interrogation" that triggered the right to *Miranda* warnings.

Volunteered statements. Questions on this issue often use the term "blurt out." If your question describes a defendant as "blurting out" something, you should discuss whether the statement was volunteered (and you should probably find that it was.)

Example: Police arrest D and give her *Miranda* warnings. D states that she wants to call her lawyer and is told that she can do so as soon as she is fingerprinted. While being fingerprinted, D blurts out "Paying a lawyer is a waste of money because I know you guys have me." Her statement was volunteered, not the product of interrogation. Therefore, even though it was obtained at a time when D had not yet consulted with the lawyer she asked for, the statement was not obtained in violation of *Miranda*.

Remember that there are various scenarios under which *Miranda* either doesn't apply, or doesn't block use of the non-*Mirandized* statement:

Even if a statement is inadmissible because of a *Miranda* violation, it can still be used to ***impeach*** the defendant — it just can't be used in the prosecution's case in chief.

Example: Officer takes D into custody, and without giving her *Miranda* warnings asks her where she was at the time of the theft. D responds that she was present at the scene of the crime, but saw nothing. At trial, the prosecution cannot use this non-*Mirandized* statement for its case-in-chief. D then testifies at trial that she was not at the scene at the time of the crime. The prosecution may now offer D's non-*Mirandized* statement for impeachment purposes only.

A ***second***, *Mirandized* confession following a first non-*Mirandized* confession will be admissible. The first confession does not taint the second (even though D may have made the second only because he felt that "the cat was already out of the bag").

Miranda does not require police to tell the defendant ***what crime*** he is being charged with. It also does not prohibit questioning about a ***different crime*** than the one the defendant thought he was being charged with at the time he received the warnings.

And don't forget the (limited) ***public safety exception*** to *Miranda* — if the statements are voluntary and the questions are prompted by a concern for public safety, they will be admissible even though no *Miranda* warnings are given.

Example: Police chase Suspect, who they think has committed armed robbery. After they arrest him and don't find the gun that they believe he used, they ask him, "Where's the gun?" D gives the location of the discarded gun. Assuming that this question was or might have been motivated by concern for public safety, D's response is admissible under the public-safety exception.

Be careful to spot the issue of whether D ***waived*** his Miranda rights.

A waiver of *Miranda* rights (especially the right to ***remain silent***) can be ***implied*** from D's actions. For instance, suppose D is given (and understands) his right to remain silent, but not does expressly agree to answer questions. The police ask him lots of questions, and after remaining silent for all of them, he finally ***answers*** one, with an incriminating response. This will be an implied waiver of D's right to remain silent.

A waiver of *Miranda* rights is ***valid*** even if D suffers from a mental illness that interferes with his ability to understand his rights and make rational choices. The critical factor in these cases is the behavior of the police. As long as the statement was not made as a result of police coercion, the fact that D may have been subjected to third-party force (e.g., mental illness, or pressure from a relative) that overbore his free will won't be enough to vitiate the waiver.

Evidence of an accused's ***silence*** after he has received *Miranda* warnings is generally ***not admissible.***

Example: D is arrested and charged with murder. She is read her *Miranda* rights, and refuses to give a statement. At trial, she takes the stand and gives a lengthy alibi defense. On cross-examination, the prosecutor asks her why, if her story was true, she did not tell it to police at the time of her arrest. The prosecutor's question was impermissible: D's election to exercise her *Miranda* rights and remain silent cannot be used against her at trial. [Cite to *Doyle v. Ohio*.]

On the other hand, if a suspect agrees to undergo ***voluntary (i.e., non-custodial) interrogation***, and therefore does not receive the *Miranda* warnings, his general silence or refusal to answer a particular question ***may*** be put into evidence by the prosecution. Only in the unusual situation where D ***formally mentions his privilege against self-incrimination*** as the reason he's refusing to continue the voluntary interrogation will the prosecution be prevented from using the silence.

Example: D is suspected of a murder that took place on the evening of April 5. The police ask him to come to the police station voluntarily to answer some questions. D agrees, and starts to answer questions. But when the police ask him, "Where were you on the evening of April 5?" D refuses to answer and cuts off the questioning without further comment. At trial, D offers an alibi defense for the evening of April 5. The prosecution *may* prove that D refused to answer when he was asked his whereabouts. Since D was not in custody at the time of the questioning, and did not formally invoke his privilege against self-incrimination when he cut off the questioning, he's not entitled to block this evidence that he remained silent. [Cite to *Texas v. Salinas.*]

CHAPTER 6

LINEUPS AND OTHER PRE-TRIAL IDENTIFICATION PROCEDURES

ChapterScope

A number of challenges can be made to lineups and pre-trial identification. This chapter examines the major arguments that defendants have made.

Fifth Amendment: A defendant may argue that an identification procedure violates his right against ***self-incrimination.*** However, physical identification procedures (e.g. a lineup or a voice sample) will generally ***not*** trigger the Fifth Amendment privilege against self-incrimination.

Sixth Amendment: A defendant may argue that an identification procedure violates his Sixth Amendment right to ***counsel.*** A defendant has the right to have counsel at a ***pre-trial lineup*** that occurs ***after the institution of formal proceedings against him.***

Due Process: A defendant may be able to argue that an identification procedure, such as a lineup, was so unfair as to violate his right to ***due process of law.*** To do this, the defendant must show that, viewed by the "totality of the circumstances," the identification procedure was so ***"unnecessarily suggestive"*** and so conducive to mistaken identification as to be deeply unfair to him.

I. IDENTIFICATION PROCEDURES GENERALLY

A. **Various identification procedures:** There are a number of methods by which the police may procure a physical identification of a suspect to link him with a particular crime. These include ***lineups, fingerprints, blood samples, voice-prints, the use of photographs***, etc. Defendants who have been identified by these methods have frequently raised one or more constitutional objections to them. Among the more frequently raised objections are the following:

1. **Self-incrimination:** that such identification procedures violate the suspect's ***privilege against self-incrimination***;

2. **Search and seizure:** that such procedures constitute an ***unreasonable search or seizure in violation of the Fourth Amendment***;

3. **Right to counsel:** that when such procedures are used without the defendant having a lawyer present, the ***Sixth Amendment right to counsel*** is violated; and

4. **Due process:** that such procedures in many cases violate the general Fifth or Fourteenth Amendment (depending on whether state or federal law enforcement officials are involved) ***right to due process***.

B. **Recent treatment of these claims:** Of the four kinds of claims listed above, the most successful has been the assertion of the right to counsel, to which the major part of this chapter is addressed. The Fourth Amendment arguments, which have generally been unsuccessful, are discussed *supra*, in various places. See, e.g., *supra*, p. 166, for a discussion of whether suspects may be fingerprinted in the absence of either probable cause or a search warrant.

II. LIMITATION OF THE PRIVILEGE AGAINST SELF-INCRIMINATION

A. ***Schmerber:*** In ***Schmerber v. California***, 384 U.S. 757 (1966), the Supreme Court held (5-4) that an ***involuntary blood test*** did not violate the Fifth Amendment right against self-incrimination, because that Amendment protects only against compulsion to give ***"testimonial or communicative"*** evidence.

1. **Facts:** The defendant was arrested for drunken driving, and a blood sample was taken from him over his objection, by a physician acting under police direction.

2. **Majority opinion:** The five-man majority opinion, which held that the forced blood test was not a violation of the Fifth Amendment right against self-incrimination, stated that that Amendment protects only against the compulsion of "communications" or "testimony," and not against "compulsion which makes a suspect or accused the source of 'real or physical evidence'."

   a. **Difficult cases:** The Court acknowledged that the line between "testimonial" and "physical" evidence might not always be an easy one to draw. The Court noted that "Some tests seemingly directed to obtain 'physical evidence,' for example, lie detector tests measuring changes in body functions during interrogation, may actually be directed to eliciting responses which are essentially testimonial."

   b. **Testimonial by-products:** The Court also acknowledged, in a footnote, that in some circumstances compelling a suspect to furnish physical identification might produce testimonial by-products. Thus if a suspect was opposed to blood tests on religious grounds, or was terrified by the pain of the intrusion, he might choose to confess rather than to submit to the procedure. The Court stated that compulsion might not be permissible in such a case, or that at least the government might have to forego the testimonial by-products of the identification procedure. The Court stressed that the *Schmerber* situation did not itself involve such a problem.

3. **Minority:** Four dissenters objected that blood involuntarily extracted is indeed "communicative" and obviously self-incriminatory. The dissenters claimed that articles such as private papers and diaries, covered under the Fifth Amendment, are no more revealing than a person's own blood, and that therefore the right against self-incrimination should apply here with equal force.

   a. **Due process argument:** One dissenter, Justice Fortas, also asserted that the due process clause prohibits the state from committing "any kind of violence upon the person . . . and the extraction of blood, over protest, is an act of violence."

B. **Extension:** *Schmerber* has subsequently been the basis for holding various physical identification procedures to be outside the privilege against self-incrimination.

1. ***Wade:*** In *U.S. v. Wade*, 388 U.S. 218 (1967), discussed more fully *infra*, p. 299, the Court said that the privilege did not apply to a defendant forced to appear in a ***lineup*** and to ***speak for identification***.

2. **Other procedures:** *Schmerber* has since been applied to find the privilege against self-incrimination not applicable to ***fingerprinting, DNA sampling, photography, measurements, physical movements, handwriting analysis***, and even ***examination by ultraviolet light***.

   a. **Voice:** In fact, the defendant may even be required to ***speak***, without this necessarily violating his privilege against self-incrimination. For instance, the defendant may clearly be required to give a ***voice sample*** for voiceprint analysis, with no self-incrimination problems. See *U.S. v. Dionisio*, 410 U.S. 1 (1973). Similarly, a drunk-driving suspect may be required to answer questions to test his mental acuity (e.g., "In what year did you have your sixth birthday?") without violating his self-incrimination rights. See *Pennsylvania v. Muniz*, 496 U.S. 582 (1990), validating this "sixth birthday" question.

C. **Refusal to cooperate:** A suspect does ***not*** have a right to ***refuse to participate*** in an ***identification procedure*** since under *Schmerber* such procedures are not within the privilege against self-incrimination.

1. **Consequences of non-cooperation:** A suspect may be held in contempt of court, and indefinitely jailed, for his refusal to cooperate.

2. **Prosecution's comment on defendant's refusal to cooperate:** Since identification procedures do not involve the right against self-incrimination, the rule that the prosecution may not comment on the accused's refusal to testify (*Griffin v. California*, 380 U.S. 609 (1965)) does not apply. Thus the prosecution may comment on the defendant's refusal to cooperate in the identification procedure. For instance, in *South Dakota v. Neville*, 459 U.S. 553 (1983), the Supreme Court upheld a state statute permitting the prosecutor to comment on a drunk-driving defendant's refusal to submit to a *Schmerber*-type blood test. Since the state had the right to force the defendant to take such a test, it had the right to offer him a choice between taking the test and some other alternative (in this case, having his refusal to take it be brought to the attention of the trier of fact).

III. THE RIGHT TO COUNSEL

A. **The *Wade-Gilbert* rule:** In the co-cases of ***U.S. v. Wade***, 388 U.S. 218 (1967), and ***Gilbert v. California***, 388 U.S. 263 (1967), the Supreme Court announced the rule that a suspect, at least ***after indictment***, has an ***absolute right to have counsel present at any pretrial confrontation procedure***. Such confrontations include both ***lineups*** (in which a witness picks the suspect out of a group of persons, usually resembling each other) and ***one-man show-ups***, in which the witness is shown only the suspect and asked whether the suspect is the perpetrator.

1. **Rationale:** The Court identified such pretrial confrontations as a ***critical stage*** in the prosecution, and said that the "presence of counsel at such critical confrontations, as at the trial itself, operates to assure that the accused's interests will be protected consistently with our adversary theory of criminal prosecution."

a. **Danger of eyewitness identification:** In both *Wade* and *Gilbert*, the Court emphasized the notorious unreliability of eyewitness identification. The Court cited the many cases of mistaken identification on record, and pointed to the strong possibility that the police will influence (either consciously or unconsciously) the witness's identification.

b. **Facts of *Wade*:** In *Wade*, two eyewitnesses picked the defendant out of a lineup only after they saw (according to their own subsequent testimony) the defendant standing in the station-house hallway surrounded by FBI agents.

c. **Facts of *Gilbert*:** The lineup in *Gilbert* was conducted in an auditorium in which some 100 witnesses to the several alleged offenses of the defendant made wholesale identification of the suspect in the presence of each other, a procedure "fraught with dangers of suggestion."

d. **Right of confrontation:** The presence of counsel at these identification procedures is necessary, the *Wade-Gilbert* Court held, to protect the defendant's constitutional right to confrontation. The Court cited several respects in which the presence of a lawyer at the lineup is necessary if the right of confrontation is not to be forever lost.

   i. **Other participants unrecorded:** The names of the other participants in a lineup are usually unrecorded, and are often either police officers or suspects of other crimes, neither a class of persons likely to protest any prejudice in the proceeding.

   ii. **Witnesses unreliable:** Also, witnesses to lineups are not likely to be schooled in the detection of suggestive influences. Moreover, a victim is likely to be a particularly unreliable source of objective information because excited by vengeful or spiteful motives.

   iii. **Suspect incapacitated:** The suspect will, because of his tension, not be in a good position to identify prejudicial practices, and probably would not be believed at trial even if he did testify to the prejudicial nature of the confrontation.

2. **Improper identification inadmissible:** The Supreme Court therefore laid down a *per se* rule that ***any identification which occurs without the presence of counsel*** (except where there has been an effective waiver, discussed *infra*, p. 386) ***must be excluded as evidence at trial***.

   a. **In-court identification:** If the lineup is improper, not only may the prosecution not introduce into evidence at trial the fact that the defendant was picked out of a lineup, but the prosecution will even have to make a special showing before the witness who made the lineup identification will be allowed to testify in court that the person sitting in the dock is the person observed by the witness at the scene of the crime.

      i. **Reason for burden:** The Court observed that "A rule limited solely to the exclusion of testimony concerning identification at the lineup itself, without regard to admissibility of the court-room identification, would render the right to counsel an empty one. The lineup is most often used . . . to crystallize the witnesses' identification of the defendant for future reference. . . . The State may then rest upon the witnesses' unequivocal courtroom identification, and not mention the pretrial identification as part of the State's case at trial." In order to strengthen the rule excluding improperly-conducted lineup identifications, the Court imposed a special burden on the prosecution to show that the courtroom identification by a witness who participated in such a lineup is not "tainted" by the lineup identification.

ii. Nature of burden: In order for the witness to be permitted to make such an in-court identification if the lineup itself was improperly conducted, the prosecution must show by ***"clear and convincing evidence"*** that the in-court identification is not the "fruit of the poisonous tree" (i.e., the product of the improper lineup identification). In determining whether the in-court identification is "purged of the taint" of the improper lineup, the court should consider a number of factors: "the prior opportunity [of the witness] to observe the alleged criminal act, the existence of any discrepancy between any pre-lineup description and the defendant's actual description, any identification prior to lineup of another person, the identification by picture of the defendant prior to lineup, failure to identify the defendant on a prior occasion, and the lapse of time between the alleged act and the lineup identification."

iii. Black's dissent: Black's partial dissent in *Wade* protested against the majority's requirement that the prosecution demonstrate that an in-court identification is not tainted by an earlier improper lineup, and asserted that such a " 'tainted fruit' determination . . . is practically impossible. How is a witness capable of probing the recesses of his mind to draw a sharp line between a courtroom identification due exclusively to an earlier lineup [and] one due to memory not based on the lineup?"

iv. Lower courts' response: Most lower courts dealing with the in-court identification problem have held that the particular in-court identification in question meets the requirements of *Wade*, despite the improperly-conducted lineup. Most courts have based their finding on the fact that the witness had ample opportunity to see the crime and its perpetrator. See K,L,I&K, p. 766.

B. *Wade-Gilbert* rule reaffirmed in *Moore*: The Supreme Court reaffirmed the validity of the *Wade-Gilbert* rule in several respects, in ***Moore v. Illinois***, 434 U.S. 220 (1977).

1. **Facts of *Moore:*** The defendant, suspected of rape, was brought before the judge at a ***preliminary hearing***, the purpose of which was to determine whether there was probable cause to seek an indictment and to fix bail. He was not represented by counsel. While he was standing before the bench, the victim was asked to say whether she saw her assailant in the courtroom, and she predictably enough said that it was the defendant. At trial, the court allowed the victim to testify that the defendant was her assailant, and that she had identified him at the preliminary hearing.

2. **Holding:** The Supreme Court held that the victim should ***not have been allowed to testify as to her earlier identification***. (The Court did not reach the question whether she should have been allowed to testify that the man in the courtroom was the man who raped her.) The Court rebutted several contentions by the prosecution:

   a. **Preliminary hearing:** In response to the prosecution's argument that there had been no indictment, and that therefore the right to counsel had not attached at the time of the preliminary hearing, the Court noted that *Kirby v. Illinois* (*infra*, p. 303) provided for a right to counsel in identification procedures commencing with the "initiation of adversary judicial criminal proceedings," and the hearing was clearly such a proceeding — at that point, "the government had committed itself to prosecute," and the defendant was "faced with the prosecutorial forces of organized society. . . . " (quoting *Kirby).*

b. One-man show-up: The Court also rejected the prosecution's argument that there was no right to counsel at a ***one-man show-up*** (as opposed to a multi-person lineup) — "Indeed, a one-on-one confrontation generally is thought to present greater risks of mistaken identification than a lineup."

c. Judicial proceeding: Nor was the right to counsel barred by the fact that the identification took place during the course of a ***judicial proceeding*** (the preliminary hearing). The Court noted the extreme suggestiveness involved in telling the victim that she would view the suspect, letting her see him when he was standing before the bench, and letting her hear the judge summarize the alleged evidence against him.

d. Independent source: Finally, the Court affirmed the ***"per se"*** rule of *Gilbert* that the existence of the identification could not be alluded to at trial, even if it could be shown that that identification had an ***"independent source."*** Thus the fact that, according to the prosecution, the victim had prior to the hearing picked out a picture of the defendant (as well as several other pictures) was irrelevant.

C. Meaning of the right to counsel: Although the Supreme Court in *Wade-Gilbert* did not detail what role counsel should play at the lineup, most commentators believe the attorney should at the very least observe the proceedings (taking notes or making a recording) and record his objections to it as part of the identification record. (K,L,I&K, p. 764.)

1. Adversary model: Others have suggested that the lineup procedure is to be an adversary proceeding in which counsel for the suspect may question the witnesses, make objections, and have reasonable recommendations respected by the police.

D. Waiver: The Court in *Wade* indicated that there could be an ***"intelligent waiver"*** of the right to the presence and consultation of an attorney.

1. Requirements: Although the *Wade* opinion does not discuss the requirements of a valid waiver, it would seem that the *Miranda* model must be followed. Thus a suspect must apparently be fully advised of his right to have a lawyer present, and a "heavy burden" rests on the government to show an express waiver. See the discussion of waiver under *Miranda*, *supra*, at p. 259.

E. Substitute counsel: In both *Wade* and *Gilbert*, the indicted suspect had had counsel appointed for him before the holding of a lineup was contemplated, and the Court implied that in the normal situation it is this previously retained or appointed attorney who must be notified about the lineup so that he may be present at the lineup. However, *Wade* indicated that in an emergency situation where immediate identification is required, a ***substitute attorney*** may be adequate for purposes of the confrontation.

F. Crime Control Act: The Omnibus Crime Control and Safe Streets Act of 1968 (of which Title III on electronic surveillance, discussed *supra*, p. 219, is a part) provides in §3502 that: "The testimony of a witness that he saw the accused commit or participate in the commission of the crime for which the accused is being tried shall be admissible in evidence" in any federal trial.

1. **Doubtful constitutionality:** In purporting to "repeal" the in-court identification portion of the *Wade-Gilbert* rule, which rests on the Sixth Amendment, this section of the Crime Control Act is probably unconstitutional.

2. **Practical effect:** Most lower courts appear to consider themselves bound by the Supreme Court's reading of the Constitution rather than by that of Congress, and have ignored the statute. (See K,L,I&K, p. 769.)

IV. EXCEPTIONS TO THE RIGHT TO COUNSEL

A. **Pre-indictment identifications:** The defendants in both *Wade* and *Gilbert* had been indicted before they were subjected to uncounselled lineup identification. The Supreme Court has refused to extend the *Wade-Gilbert* rule to lineups conducted ***before the institution of formal proceedings against the suspect***. In ***Kirby v. Illinois***, 406 U.S. 682 (1972), the Court, 5-4, limited the right to counsel in lineups and showings to a time "at or after the initiation of adversary judicial criminal proceedings — whether by way of formal charge, preliminary hearing, indictment, information or arraignment."

1. **Rationale:** The Court's opinion (a four-vote plurality, since one Justice concurred only in the result) stated that only at "the initiation of judicial criminal proceedings" does the defendant find himself "faced with the prosecutional forces of organized society, and immersed in the intricacies of substantive and procedural criminal law."

   a. **Dissent:** The dissenters pointed out that the *Wade-Gilbert* rule was not limited to "an abstract consideration of the words 'criminal prosecutions' in the Sixth Amendment," but was rather meant to protect the "most basic right [of] a criminal defendant — his right to a fair trial at which the witnesses against him might be meaningfully cross-examined."

   b. **Criticism:** The Court in *Miranda* recognized that the accusatory forces of the police begin immediately upon custody. It therefore seems inconsistent and unrealistic to suggest, as the *Kirby* plurality opinion does, that only after indictment have "the adverse positions of government and the defendant . . . solidified."

2. **"Initiation" of proceedings:** The *Kirby* decision supplies only partial clarification as to what constitutes "the initiation of judicial criminal proceedings." The Court listed "formal charge, preliminary hearing, indictment, information or arraignment" as being means of commencing formal judicial proceedings. Most lower courts have held that the ***issuance of an arrest warrant*** triggers *Wade-Gilbert*. Where the only police action against the subject has been a ***warrantless arrest***, however, most courts have held the *Wade-Gilbert* right-to-counsel-at-lineup rule not to be triggered. (See Nutshell, p. 254.)

B. **Photographic identifications:** In ***U.S. v. Ash***, 413 U.S. 300 (1973), the Supreme Court ruled that the right to counsel ***does not apply where witnesses view still or moving pictures of the suspect for identification purposes***.

1. **Rationale:** The Court noted that unlike the lineup situation, the suspect is not present when the witness views photographs. Since, according to the Court, the major purpose of the right-to-counsel in the *Wade* lineup situation is to prevent the suspect from being

penalized for his ignorance and inability to ascertain and object to prejudicial conditions, there is no need for counsel when the suspect is not himself present.

a. **Witness interviews:** Furthermore, the Court noted, it would be impossible to impose a right-to-counsel wherever the prosecution conducts interviews with prospective witnesses. Since the identification-through-photographs is merely one kind of interview, there is no reason to distinguish that form of identification from other procedures used by the prosecution in interviewing witnesses.

2. **Dissent:** The three dissenters objected that the "impermissible suggestiveness" present in the lineup context was an equal danger in the case of photographic identifications, and that the lack of presence of the accused simply meant that any unfairness was unlikely to come to light.

C. **Scientific methods:** In *Schmerber*, *supra*, p. 298, the Court held that no Sixth Amendment right to counsel attaches where a blood sample is extracted from a suspect. In *Wade*, the Court distinguished between ***"scientific methods,"*** such as the use of blood samples in *Schmerber*, and the inherently unscientific use of eye-witness identifications. The *Wade* Court held that the right to counsel did not apply to the scientific examination of the accused's fingerprints, blood sample, clothing, hair, and the like. "Knowledge of the techniques of science and technology is sufficiently available, and the variables in techniques few enough, that the accused has the opportunity for a meaningful confrontation of the Government's case at trial through the ordinary processes of cross-examination of the Government's expert witnesses and the presentation of the evidence of his own experts."

1. ***Gilbert*** **handwriting sample:** In *Gilbert*, the Court used this analysis as the basis for holding that the taking of a ***handwriting exemplar*** was not a "critical stage" of the proceedings entitling the defendant to the assistance of counsel.

V. DUE PROCESS LIMITATIONS

A. ***Stovall:*** In ***Stovall v. Denno***, 388 U.S. 293 (1967), the third case in the *Wade-Gilbert* "trilogy," the Supreme Court established that "a recognized ground of attack independent of any right to counsel claim" is whether a confrontation "was so ***unnecessarily suggestive and conducive to irreparable mistaken identification***" as to deny a suspect ***due process of law.***

1. **Facts:** In *Stovall*, the defendant was found when keys discovered at the murder scene were traced to him. He was arrested, handcuffed to a police officer, and presented alone in a ***show-up*** before a hospitalized victim, who identified him after he spoke a few words. The suspect was the only black in the room. The victim's life was at the time in severe jeopardy, but she recovered to make an in-court identification.

2. ***Wade-Gilbert*** **not retroactive:** In *Wade-Gilbert*, the Court declined to apply the right to counsel ***retroactively***, i.e., to lineups occurring before the date of the decision. Therefore, the *Wade-Gilbert* rationale could not be used to hold the show-up in *Stovall* invalid. However, the *Stovall* Court recognized that an identification procedure could be so prejudicial that it violated the defendant's right to due process, independently of whether the right to have counsel at the proceeding attached.

3. **Test in *Stovall:*** The *Stovall* Court established the following test for determining whether an identification procedure violated due process: "a claimed violation of due process of law in the conduct of a confrontation depends on the ***totality of the circumstances surrounding it. . . .***"

   a. **Special facts in *Stovall:*** The *Stovall* Court noted that "the practice of showing suspects singly to persons for the purpose of identification, and not as part of a lineup, has been widely condemned," due to the extreme suggestion inherent in showing only the suspect. However, in the factual situation presented by *Stovall* itself, the Court concluded that the possible unfairness of a show-up was mitigated by the urgent need for the confrontation proceeding, since the hospitalized witness (who was the only living eyewitness) was in danger of dying at any moment.

4. **Holding followed:** The lower courts have generally allowed uncounseled show-ups in similar cases of serious injury to the victim or witness.

B. **Suggestive identification admissible if reliable:** In ***Neil v. Biggers***, 409 U.S. 188 (1972), the Court showed a greater willingness to allow show-ups than had seemed to be the case in *Stovall*. In *Biggers*, the Court found a show-up not violative of due process ***even though it was not justified by exigent circumstances***.

1. **Facts of *Biggers:*** The victim in *Biggers* was a nurse who was first assaulted in her dimly lit kitchen, then forced from the house and raped under a bright, full moon. The entire incident took 15 to 30 minutes, and the victim gave a general description of the height, weight, build, age, voice, hair and complexion of the assailant immediately after the event. She then went through many photographs, believing that one looked similar to her assailant. Several lineups and show-ups were conducted with the victim making no identification. Finally, the police brought a suspect (ultimately the defendant) alone before the victim seven months after the crime. She said she had "no doubt" in her identification of him, and that she could never forget the assailant's face.

2. **Identification admitted:** Despite the extreme suggestiveness inherent in the final show-up procedure, the Court held that the identification was lawful. The Court applied the "totality of the circumstances" test, and concluded that any prejudice inherent in the show-up was countered by (1) the length of time of the victim's exposure to the assailant, (2) the adequate light during the crime, (3) the personal nature of the crime, (4) the unlikelihood that others witnessed the crime, (5) the "more than ordinarily thorough" description first offered by the victim, and (6) the certainty expressed by the victim.

3. **Criticism:** The show-up procedure used in *Biggers* was rejected by both the District Court and Court of Appeals because it was ***unnecessary***; the victim's life was not in danger, and even the five-man majority of the Supreme Court admitted that the "police did not exhaust all possibilities" in seeking a lineup.

C. **Use of photos:** In ***Simmons v. U.S.***, 390 U.S. 377 (1968), the Court held that where a witness ***identifies the suspect through the use of photographs***, the "totality of the circumstances" test applies for determining whether due process is violated. (The Court later held in *Ash*, *supra*, p. 303, that no right of counsel exists during the use of such photographic identification procedures.)

1. **Facts of *Simmons:*** A bank robbery suspect was identified by each of five witnesses (each acting outside of the presence of the others) from six photos, all of which pictured the suspect in the presence of others. (The photos had been obtained from a relative the day after the crime.) This procedure was followed by an in-court identification.

2. **Balancing need:** Balancing the need against risks, the Court concluded that the use of the photos was ***not "unnecessarily suggestive."*** The Court found the need and the risks to be as follows:

   a. **Need:** A serious felony had occurred, the perpetrators were still at large, and it was essential that the FBI be put on the right track quickly so as to apprehend the suspect;

   b. **Risks:** Conversely, the risk of mistaken identification was not large. The FBI agents did not disclose which of the persons in the photos was under suspicion. Also, the witnesses had had an excellent opportunity for viewing the suspect because of the good light and the substantial period of time (five minutes) during which the witnesses and the perpetrator were both at the scene of the crime.

3. **In-court identification:** Just as *Wade* prohibited certain tainted in-court identifications, so *Simmons* implies that if due process is violated by a pre-trial confrontation or photographic identification, the prosecution may be barred from allowing the identifying witness to make an in-court identification of the defendant (even if no reference is made in court to the objectionable pre-trial identification). In fact, in *Simmons* the prosecution never introduced the fact that a photographic identification had been made, and the procedural aspects of the case revolved around whether the pre-trial identification had destroyed the witnesses' ability to make a correct in-court identification. The Court noted that "[I]mproper employment of photographs by police may sometimes cause witnesses to err in identifying criminals. . . . Regardless of how the initial mis-identification comes about, the witness thereafter is apt to retain in his memory the image of the photograph rather than of the person actually seen, reducing the trustworthiness of subsequent lineup or courtroom identification."

   a. **Test for reversal:** However, the Court held, an in-court identification would constitute reversible error "only if the photographic identification procedure was so impermissibly suggestive as to give rise to a ***very substantial likelihood of irreparable misidentification."*** For the reasons cited above, the Court held that this was not the case here.

D. **Further leniency in *Brathwaite:*** The Court gave an even more lenient interpretation of due process requirements for photographic identifications in ***Manson v. Brathwaite***, 432 U.S. 98 (1977).

1. **Facts:** In *Brathwaite*, an undercover narcotics agent had a tip that drugs were being sold in a particular apartment unit, and went with his informant to what eventually turned out to be a different unit in the same building, where he made a purchase. He then returned to the station house, and gave a general description of the seller ("colored man, approximately five feet eleven inches tall, dark complexion, black hair, short Afro style, and having high cheekbones, and of heavy build") to one of his co-officers. The latter said that he thought he had seen a man conforming to that description in the area of the sale on several occa-

sions, and pulled a photograph of this person from the files. The undercover agent identified this photograph as being of the seller.

2. **Use at trial:** At trial, the agent was permitted not only to make an in-court identification, but also to testify that he had identified a photograph as being the defendant, and that he was sure that this photograph was indeed of the defendant. When the issue reached the Supreme Court on *habeas corpus*, the defendant argued that both the in-court identification and the testimony as to the photographic identification were improper.

3. **Defendant loses:** The Court rejected both of these contentions, although it acknowledged that the procedure was ***"suggestive"*** because only one photograph was used, and ***"unnecessary"*** because there was no emergency preventing the use of multiple photographs. The Court cited *Simmons*' requirement that there be "a very substantial likelihood of irreparable misidentification," and held that this was not the case here, in view of the agent's training, the time he spent looking at the seller during the transactions (five to seven minutes, by the majority's interpretation of the evidence), the good light, the accuracy and detailed nature of the description, the agent's "level of certainty," and the relatively short time (two days) between the crime and the identification.

4. **Dissent:** Justice Marshall (joined by Justice Brennan) dissented on two grounds.

   a. **First ground of disagreement:** Marshall argued first that the Court had in the past correctly distinguished between the test for allowing testimony about a pre-trial identification, and the test for allowing an in-court identification. Even if a "totality of the circumstances" test were appropriate for determining whether an in-court identification should be allowed, he contended, a *per se* rule requiring automatic exclusion of all unnecessarily suggestive pre-trial identifications should be, and had been, imposed.

   b. **Second ground of disagreement:** Secondly, the dissent argued, even if a "totality of the circumstances" test were to be applied to testimony about pre-trial identification as well as to in-court identification, the pre-trial identification in this case could not pass the test. Marshall disagreed with the majority's interpretation of the facts in several respects, including the length of time that the agent had to view the seller, and the specificity of his description, which, Marshall noted, omitted any indication that the seller spoke with a marked Caribbean accent (the defendant had come to the U.S. from Barbados as an adult). Also, Marshall disputed the majority's contention that the agent's degree of certainty, and his training as an agent, made his identification more reliable. He concluded that there was indeed "a very substantial likelihood of misidentification."

E. **Present uncertainty of due process doctrine:** The varied application of due process by the Supreme Court, and the general reluctance of the lower courts to exclude eyewitness identifications, suggest that the present impact of the *Stovall* due process requirement for identification procedures is both uncertain and limited.

   1. ***Foster:*** However, in extreme cases, the courts have nonetheless been willing to exclude eyewitness identifications on due process grounds. Thus in ***Foster v. California***, 394 U.S. 440 (1969), the Supreme Court found a confrontation violative of due process.

a. **Facts of *Foster*:** In *Foster* an identification was procured in the following manner: **(a)** the suspect was lined up with men several inches shorter than he; **(b)** only the suspect wore a jacket similar to that of the robber; **(c)** when the lineup produced no positive identification, the police used a one-man show-up of the suspect; and **(d)** because even the show-up identification was tentative, the police several days later used a second lineup, in which only the suspect was a repeater from the last lineup.

b. **Held unconstitutional:** The Court held that all of the identifications of the *Foster* suspect were violative of due process, since the procedures were such that an identification of the suspect was "all but inevitable."

2. **Lower courts:** The lower courts, in applying *Stovall, Biggers, Simmons,* and *Brathwaite*, have rarely found due process violations in identification procedures, even when extreme practices were followed.

Examples: Lower courts have upheld **(1)** a lineup in which the suspect wore jail coveralls while the others wore street clothes; **(2)** a photo identification in which only one photograph was shown; **(3)** photo identifications in which the suspect's photograph was made to stand out (e.g., in color or full length); and **(4)** multiple identifications (where the witness views the suspect in more than one identification procedure).

Quiz Yourself on
LINEUPS & OTHER PRE-TRIAL ID PROCEDURES *(ENTIRE CHAPTER)*

75. One day, the Ames Police Department received a call from an unidentified male caller, who stated, "You'd better evacuate the courthouse building. It will be blown up at 2:00 p.m." This call was automatically recorded, as are all incoming calls to the Department. The police evacuated the courthouse as urged, and tried (but failed) to find a concealed bomb. There was one, and it went off at 2:00 p.m., destroying the court house. Based on an informant's tip, the police focused their investigation on Stan. They arrested Stan for the bombing, and asked Stan to give them a "voice print" — they wanted him to speak into a telephone the same words that the unidentified caller had spoken, so they could have an expert produce a print-out of the sound waves from the two recordings and determine whether they were made by the same person. Stan refused, and the police got the court to order that he give the voice print or else be held in contempt. Stan reluctantly complied. At Stan's trial, the prosecution seeks to introduce the voice prints from the two recordings, together with the expert's testimony that the same voice appears on both recordings. Stan objects on the grounds that use of this information would violate his Fifth Amendment privilege against self-incrimination. Should the court exclude the evidence on the basis urged by Stan? ________________

76. Based on the testimony of an accomplice, Tom was indicted for carrying out a particular burglary. He was then arrested, and brought to the police station. Because the owner of the burglarized house, Sheila, had gotten a brief look at Tom as he ran out of the house, the police decided to perform a lineup. They put Tom together with five other people (non-uniformed police officers) who approximately resembled Tom in terms of age, race, height, etc. Sheila was asked to look at the six men through a one-way mirror, and to state whether she could identify the burglar. She quickly picked Tom out of the lineup. At no time prior to or during this transaction did any police officer or other government officer say anything to Tom. At Tom's burglary trial, the prosecution offered into evidence the fact that Sheila had picked Tom out of the lineup. What, if any, constitutional right of Tom's would be violated by the admission of this evidence? ________________

77. Same basic fact pattern as the prior question. Now, assume that the results of the lineup were ruled by the court to be inadmissible. Assume further that at the trial, Sheila took the stand, and was asked, "Can you identify the burglar as being somebody in this courtroom?" Over the defense's objection, the court permitted Sheila to answer, and she said, "Yes, it's the defendant." Sheila did not refer to the fact that she had made an earlier identification of Tom in the lineup. Neither side presented any evidence showing the reliability (or unreliability) of Sheila's in-court identification of Tom as being the burglar. Has the trial judge erred in permitting Sheila in court to identify Tom as the burglar? ________________

78. The First National Bank of Ames was robbed at gunpoint by a dark-haired woman wearing sunglasses. One of the tellers stepped on the "panic button," sending an alarm to police headquarters, so the police got an early jump on the case. One officer who rushed to the scene saw a car traveling away from the bank at a suspiciously high speed, so he stopped the car. The car was driven by Ursula, who had sunglasses and was dark-haired. The officer made a warrantless arrest of Ursula. (Assume that the officer did not violate Ursula's Fourth Amendment rights in doing so.) The officer then took Ursula to the police station. It was now too late in the day to have Ursula brought before a magistrate, so she would have to stay in jail for the night. The police decided, however, that they should conduct a lineup while witnesses' memories were fresh.

Therefore, the police put Ursula in a lineup with five other women of approximately similar appearance, and asked two of the bank tellers to see if they could pick the robber out. Ursula protested prior to and during this lineup that she wanted to have her lawyer present during the lineup, but the police refused, telling Ursula that her lawyer would only delay the proceedings and make trouble. One of the tellers, Arlene, picked Ursula out of the lineup. At Ursula's bank robbery trial, she seeks to have this lineup identification excluded from evidence against her, on the grounds that the police's refusal to allow her attorney to be present violated her right to counsel. Should the lineup identification be excluded on this ground? ________________

79. Same basic fact pattern as the prior question. Now, however, assume that Ursula was formally charged with the bank robbery, given a preliminary hearing, and then arraigned (at which time she pled not guilty). Shortly thereafter, detectives working on the case interviewed Bruce, another teller who had been present during the robbery. The detectives showed Bruce six photographs, each of a different woman, and asked him whether he recognized any of them as being the robber. Bruce picked out Ursula's photograph immediately. (Neither Ursula nor her lawyer knew that this photographic identification session was going to take place, and the lawyer was not present during it.) At Ursula's trial, the prosecution has offered into evidence the fact that Bruce picked Ursula's picture out of the bunch. Ursula objects, on the grounds that the photo ID session was carried out in the absence of her lawyer and thus violated her right to counsel. Should the fact that Bruce identified Ursula from the photos be excluded on this ground? ________________

80. Tina was brutally raped one night in a poorly lit parking lot. She told police, shortly after the crime, that the rapist was not someone she recognized, that he was an Asian about six feet tall, and that he wore a "New York Mets" jacket. Because Vincent was found wandering near the scene of the crime several hours later, and had a previous conviction for rape under similar circumstances, he was arrested, charged and arraigned.

Two days after the crime, the police asked Tina to come to a lineup. There were six men in the lineup; Vincent was the only Asian, and he was taller than any of the others by at least five inches. The police made Vincent wear a New York Mets jacket, and none of the other men in the lineup had any kind of sports jacket. Vincent was given a court-appointed lawyer who was present at the lineup. Tina stated that she could not be sure whether her assailant was one of those in the lineup.

Three days later, the police asked Tina to come to another lineup. This time, there were six men, including two Asians; Vincent was the only person who was in both lineups. Vincent's lawyer was again present, and protested several ways in which the lineup was unduly suggestive (e.g., that Vincent was the only one who was in both lineups, that there were only two Asians, that Vincent was taller than everyone else, etc.). The police disregarded his complaints. This time, Tina picked Vincent out as her assailant. At Vincent's rape trial, the prosecution sought to introduce into evidence the fact that Tina picked Vincent out of the second lineup.

(a) What argument should Vincent's lawyer make about why this lineup identification should be excluded from evidence? ________________

(b) Will the argument you recommend in part (a) succeed? ________________

81. While jogging one night, Upton was struck and seriously injured by a car, whose driver drove away rather than render assistance. Upton told the police that in the split second before the impact, he had gotten a very brief glimpse at the driver, who was a young blond-haired woman. Based on an informant's tip, the police came to believe that Wendy was the hit-and-run driver. They procured Wendy's photo from her license application at the Department of Motor Vehicles. They then went to Upton's hospital room, and showed him the picture of Wendy. They did not show him any pictures of other possible suspects (i.e., they did not conduct any photo array). As the detective handed Upton Wendy's picture, he said to Upton, "We think this is the woman. Can you identify her from this photo?" Upton replied, "Yes." At Wendy's trial for leaving the scene of an accident and vehicular negligence, the prosecution has sought to introduce into evidence the fact that Upton recognized Wendy from her photo in his hospital room. Wendy seeks to exclude this evidence. Should the court find that the evidence would violate Wendy's constitutional rights, and therefore exclude it? ________________

Answers

75. No. The privilege of self-incrimination applies only to responses by the suspect that are essentially ***"testimonial."*** A wide variety of physical identification procedures have been held not to be testimonial, and thus not subject to the privilege against self-incrimination. For example, the suspect may be ordered, against his will, to furnish a blood sample. *Schmerber v. California*. Similarly, a person arrested for a serious crime may be required to furnish a DNA sample. *Maryland v. King*.

76. The Sixth Amendment right to counsel. The Supreme Court has held that a suspect has an absolute right to have ***counsel present*** at any pre-trial confrontation procedure (e.g., lineup or show-up), if "adversary judicial criminal proceedings" have commenced against him (e.g., an indictment). *U.S. v. Wade*; *Kirby v. Illinois*. Since Tom had already been indicted, and thus "adversarial judicial criminal proceedings" had commenced against him, he had an absolute right to have a lawyer (a court-appointed lawyer if necessary) present to advise him and to make sure that the proceedings were not unduly suggestive. Because the police did not honor this right, the fruits of the lineup will be excluded, even though nothing in these facts suggests that the lineup was in fact unduly suggestive or otherwise unfair to Tom.

77. Yes. Where a lineup is held without the presence of counsel, and thus violates the rule of *U.S. v. Wade*, not only may the prosecution not introduce at trial the fact that the defendant was picked out of a lineup, but the prosecution will even have to make a special showing before the witness who made the lineup identification will be allowed to testify in court that the person sitting in the dock is the person observed by the witness at the crime scene. The prosecution must show by "clear and convincing evidence" that the in-court identification is not the "fruit of the poisonous tree," i.e., not the product of the improper lineup identification. Here, the prosecution has made no showing that Sheila's in-court identification does not stem from her lineup identification. (That is, the prosecution has not shown that Sheila had a long time to identify Tom during the burglary, that she correctly described Tom before the lineup, or anything else to dispel the possibility that Sheila may be remembering Tom's face from the lineup, not from the earlier burglary). The prosecution therefore loses.

78. No. As noted above, the right to have counsel present in lineup proceedings only attaches when "adversary judicial criminal proceedings" have commenced against the defendant. An indictment, a formal charge, a preliminary hearing, an arraignment — any of these would constitute the initiation of adversary judicial criminal proceedings. But the mere making of a warrantless arrest, even when coupled with taking the defendant to the police station and holding her in custody, does ***not*** amount to adversary judicial criminal proceedings, according to nearly all lower courts that have considered the issue (although the Supreme Court has never decided this point). So even though Ursula actually requested her lawyer, and even though the risk to her of unfairness from the lineup was arguably just as great as if she had already been, say, arraigned, she is deemed to have no right to counsel. Therefore, the lineup results may be admitted against her (at least if the way the lineup was carried out was not grossly unfair judged by the "totality of the circumstances").

79. No. Even after adversary judicial criminal proceedings have begun against the defendant, the defendant has no right to have counsel present where witnesses view still or moving pictures of the suspect for ID purposes. In other words, picking Ursula's photo out of a "photo array" is deemed to be something quite different from picking Ursula herself out of a lineup — in the former situation, there is no right to have counsel present, whereas in the latter there is. See *U.S. v. Ash.*

80. (a) That the identification violated Vincent's right to due process. If a lineup identification (or other confrontation) is so ***"unnecessarily suggestive*** and conducive to irreparable mistaken identification" that it denies the suspect ***due process of law***, that identification will not be admitted into evidence. Whether the identification procedure was so unfair as to amount to such a due process violation is determined by looking at the "totality of the circumstances" surrounding it. *Stovall v. Denno.*

(b) Yes, probably. It is very hard for the defendant to show that the lineup procedure was so suggestive and unfair that it amounted to a violation of his due process rights. But one of the very rare cases in which the Supreme Court so held involved facts quite similar to these (and in fact, the lineup here was probably even more suggestive, since Vincent was the only Asian the first time). See *Foster v. California*. In *Foster*, the Court concluded that the procedures were so suggestive that an identification of the defendant as the perpetrator was "all but inevitable" — this seems to be an accurate description of the procedures here as well. (Also, courts take into account the likely ***reliability*** of the identification, not just the degree of suggestiveness. Here, since the place where the crime took place was very poorly lit, Tina's ability to clearly perceive the rapist and thus later correctly identify him was somewhat impaired, making it more likely that the court would find a due process violation.)

81. Yes, probably. Just as a lineup or show-up may be excluded on the grounds that it is so suggestive that it violates the defendant's due process rights, so a photographic identification may be that suggestive. Here, the photo ID was equivalent to a one-person show-up — the police did not see whether Upton could pick out Wendy's picture from among a group of photos, but rather, handed him just one photo and also said, "We think this is the woman." In that situation, it was almost certain that Upton would identify Wendy.

Also, given the short period of time that Upton had to glimpse the driver, there is additional reason to doubt the reliability of his identification.

But such due process issues are determined by the "totality of the circumstances," and there are no hard-and-fast rules. So a court might conclude that the photo ID, although suggestive, was not so unfair as to be a due process violation. See, e.g., *Simmons v. U.S.*, finding that a photo ID did not violate the defendant's due process rights, even though he appeared, together with others, in all six of the photographs shown to the victim.

Exam Tips on *LINEUPS & OTHER PRE-TRIAL ID PROCEDURES*

Lineups and pretrial-identification questions allow an examiner to test your knowledge of several constitutional rights of criminal defendants. In your answer, be sure to demonstrate that you know that many rights are implicated. In particular, look for the following:

Every time you have a lineup or pretrial identification procedure in your facts, consider all ***four*** constitutional protections that a defendant can assert:

self-incrimination (Fifth Amendment)

search and seizure (Fourth Amendment)

right to counsel (Sixth Amendment)

due process (Fifth or Fourteenth Amendment)

Remember that defendants have no Fifth Amendment protection against being required to provide exemplars of ***physical attributes.*** Thus they can be made to ***speak certain words*** at a lineup, or to provide ***handwriting samples.*** (The Fifth Amendment protects only ***testimonial*** communications.) There is also ***no right to have counsel present*** when these procedures are done (assuming that D hasn't been arrested or indicted yet), since the procedures are not deemed to be a "critical phase" of the prosecution.

Example: Witness, who sees a murder, tells police that the murderer uttered, "Good Lord, what will the stock exchange think of me!" At the lineup, D (who hasn't been charged yet) and the others in the lineup can be required to repeat that phrase so that Witness can identify the perpetrator by voice. Also, D has no right to have counsel present during this procedure.

Exam questions often require you to figure out whether D has the ***right to counsel*** at a lineup or other pre-trial identification procedure. This generally turns on ***whether "adversarial judicial proceedings" have already been initiated.*** Look for whether the defendant has been indicted, arrested, or otherwise formally charged. If so, the defendant had the right to counsel. If not, he did not.

Example: On the facts of the above example, if D had been arrested for the murder prior to the lineup, he'd have a right to have counsel present during the lineup, and the lineup results would not be admissible if this right were not honored.

Two primary ***exceptions*** to the right to counsel are also frequently tested. These are:

scientific tests to establish identity

Example: Defendant is arrested for possession and use of heroin, and over his objection, is subjected to a blood test to determine if he is currently using heroin. Defendant has no right to have counsel present when blood is drawn.

photographic identification procedures, in which a witness is asked to pick the perpetrator from among a group of photos. (There's no right to counsel here even after the suspect has been indicted.)

A pretrial identification violates ***due process*** only if two requirements are met: 1) the procedure is ***unduly suggestive***; and 2) there is substantial likelihood of ***irreparable mistaken identification***.

There is no *per se* test for when a lineup is unduly suggestive. Here are some of the factors that are likely to constitute undue suggestiveness plus risk of irreparable mistake in identification:

there is a great disparity in ***height*** between the defendant and all others in the lineup;

the police ***address a specific question*** to the witness about one of the lineup participants (e.g., "Look closely at suspect 3 — is he the one?");

there is a disparity of ***race, gender or age*** between D and all others in the lineup;

the police require only the suspect to ***dress to match*** a witness' description of the perpetrator.

Identifications made by victims on their ***deathbed*** are a good source of issues on an exam. In these cases, defendants often have pretty good arguments that their Sixth Amendment right to counsel was violated and that the procedure violated due process because it was unduly suggestive.

Of course, you should say that the prosecution can counter this with evidence that there was no time to arrange a more objective procedure (because the victim was about to die) and/or that the victim saw the attacker well enough that misidentification would be unlikely.

CHAPTER 7

THE EXCLUSIONARY RULE

ChapterScope

This chapter examines the parameters of and exceptions to the "exclusionary rule," the principal means by which courts enforce the constitutional rights of defendants. The exclusionary rule provides that evidence obtained by violating the defendant's constitutional rights may generally not be introduced by the prosecution at the defendant's criminal trial.

Standing: A defendant may assert the exclusionary rule only to bar evidence obtained through violation of his ***own*** constitutional rights, not to bar evidence obtained through violation of the rights of some third party.

"Fruit of the poisonous tree" doctrine: Even evidence that is only ***indirectly*** obtained by a violation of a defendant's rights is subject to exclusion. Once the original evidence is shown to have been unlawfully obtained, all evidence ***stemming from*** it is equally unusable. This is the ***"fruit of the poisonous tree"*** doctrine. The doctrine has several important ***exceptions***:

Independent source: When the police have an ***independent source*** for the evidence, which does not involve illegality, the evidence is not barred by the exclusionary rule.

Inevitable discovery: Evidence which would ***inevitably have been discovered anyway*** through other police techniques may be admitted at trial.

"Purged taint": Where ***intervening factors*** are significant enough to ***purge the taint*** of the original illegal police conduct, the exclusionary rule will not apply.

Collateral use exception: The exclusionary rule only applies to exclude the evidence from the prosecution's case-in-chief. Therefore, illegally-obtained evidence may normally be used to ***impeach*** the defendant, if he takes the stand.

"Good faith" exception: The exclusionary rule does not bar evidence that was obtained by officers acting in ***reasonable reliance*** on a ***search warrant*** issued by a proper magistrate but ultimately found to be unsupported by probable cause.

I. PURPOSE AND FUNCTION OF EXCLUSIONARY RULE

A. **Function:** Suppose the police seize evidence in violation of one of the constitutional guarantees discussed previously. That is, suppose they obtain a confession without giving the required *Miranda* warnings, or seize evidence from premises without procuring the required search warrant, or conduct an invalid lineup which produces an identification of the defendant. It would do the defendant little good to be able to show that his constitutional guarantees had been violated, if the illegally obtained evidence could still be used against him in court. A judge-made doctrine, however, called the ***exclusionary rule***, provides that evidence obtained by violating the defendant's constitutional rights ***may not be introduced by the prosecution***, at least for purposes of providing direct proof of the defendant's guilt.

1. **Violation of regulation but not Constitution:** The exclusionary rule applies only where evidence is obtained in violation of the ***Constitution***; the rule is not triggered, for instance, by the gathering of evidence in violation of an ***administrative regulation***. Thus in *U.S. v. Caceres*, 440 U.S. 741 (1979), an IRS agent recorded a conversation between a taxpayer and the agent, in which the taxpayer attempted to bribe the agent. IRS electronic surveillance regulations required advance approval of such recording to be obtained from high IRS officials. (Yet because the agent himself was a party to the conversation, no constitutional violation occurred; see *supra*, p. 226.)

   a. **Holding:** The Supreme Court held that the fact that the evidence was obtained in violation of the regulations did not require it to be excluded from the taxpayer's criminal trial. The Court noted that application of the exclusionary rule to such a regulatory violation could inhibit the formulation of standards for prosecutorial or police procedures; "the result might well be fewer and less protective regulations." The rationale of *Caceres* would presumably also apply to evidence obtained in violation of a ***statute***, assuming that the statute itself did not provide for exclusion of the evidence.

B. **Other remedies:** There are other remedies available in some circumstances for violation of the rights previously described. These include tort and criminal actions against the officials involved, as well as the possibility of injunctive relief. But exclusion of the illegally seized evidence is by far the most commonly used remedy of persons whose Bill of Rights guarantees have been violated.

1. **Indictment may not be dismissed:** One of the possible "other remedies" apart from the exclusionary rule, ***dismissal of the indictment***, was explicitly rejected by the Supreme Court as an inappropriate response to even grievously unconstitutional police procedure.

   a. **Demonstrable prejudice:** In *U.S. v. Morrison*, 449 U.S. 361 (1981), the Court held that an indictment may not be dismissed as a remedy for police misconduct, unless there is "demonstrable prejudice [to the defendant], or substantial threat thereof." This is true, the Court held, even though the violation of the defendant's rights may have been ***deliberate***.

      i. **Application in *Morrison*:** Thus in *Morrison*, federal agents, aware that the defendant had retained counsel, disparaged her choice of counsel, suggested she would get better representation from the public defender, and repeatedly attempted to interrogate her outside of counsel's presence. Although the Supreme Court noted that it was not condoning the "egregious behavior" of the government agents, the absence of any prejudice to the defendant (since she did not incriminate herself during these interrogations) precluded dismissal of the indictment.

C. **Theory behind exclusionary rule:** Courts have given two principal rationales for refusing to admit evidence obtained in violation of the defendant's constitutional rights:

1. **Deterrence:** First, such exclusion will act as a ***deterrent*** to violations of the Constitution, since in many cases the police will have no motive to conduct an unlawful search, interrogation, etc., if they know that they will not be able to use its fruits in evidence.

   Note: Observe that the deterrent function of the exclusionary rule will operate only where the police are interested in bringing an individual to trial. Where the police violate a person's constitutional rights as part of a pattern of harassment, or in order to discourage future criminality, the exclusionary rule will have little deterrent value, since the police do not contemplate the formal use of evidence in court.

2. **Fairness:** Secondly, the ***integrity of the judicial system*** requires that the courts not be made "party to lawless invasions of constitutional rights of citizens by permitting unhindered governmental use of the fruits of such invasions." *Terry v. Ohio*, 392 U.S. 1 (1968). (But in a 1984 major opinion, a majority of the Court made no mention of "judicial integrity" as a rationale supporting the exclusionary rule. See *U.S. v. Leon*, *infra*, p. 348.)

D. **Basis for rule:** Until 1984, it was not clear whether the exclusionary rule was required by the Constitution, or was merely a judge-made method of assisting the protection of constitutionally-guaranteed rights. The Supreme Court resolved this issue in *U.S. v. Leon* (*infra*, p. 348), by holding that the rule ***is not required by the Constitution***. Rather, it is merely a judicially-created method of deterring violations of the Fourth and other Amendments.

E. **Future of rule:** The number of situations in which the exclusionary rule is applied has steadily dwindled over the last ten years. The latest, and most substantial, inroad upon the rule came in *U.S. v. Leon*, (*infra*, p. 348), when the Court held that the prosecution may introduce illegally-obtained evidence as part of its case-in-chief against the person whose rights were violated, if the police obtained the evidence by relying upon a search warrant which they reasonably (but erroneously) believed to have been valid. Much of this chapter is devoted to a discussion of the areas in which the exclusionary rule does not apply.

F. **Topics to be covered:** In this chapter, four distinct issues will be treated: **(1)** May the exclusionary rule be asserted by defendants who were not themselves the direct victims of the constitutional violation?; **(2)** Does the exclusionary rule apply to evidence which was indirectly derived from a constitutional violation?; **(3)** Does the rule apply only to direct proof of guilt at trial, or does it also apply to impeachment testimony at trial and to grand jury and quasi-criminal proceedings?; and **(4)** Does the fact that the police reasonably (but erroneously) believe their conduct to be constitutional ever cause the rule not to apply?

II. STANDING TO ASSERT THE EXCLUSIONARY RULE

A. **General standing issue:** It is well accepted that the exclusionary rule does not give a particular defendant freedom from the introduction of evidence derived through violation of all other people's constitutional rights, without regard to whose rights those are. As a general rule, the defendant may assert the exclusionary rule only to bar evidence obtained through violation of ***his own constitutional rights***. The requirement that the rights violated be those of the defendant has historically been referred to as a rule of ***standing*** to raise a constitutional claim. (But the Supreme Court's decision in *Rakas v. Illinois*, discussed *infra*, p. 321, transforms this requirement from a separate inquiry about "standing" into a generalized Fourth Amendment question: did the defendant have a legitimate privacy interest in the things seized or premises searched?)

1. **Interpretation in *Alderman:*** The Supreme Court's major discussion of the general standing requirement for the exclusionary rule was in ***Alderman v. U.S.***, 394 U.S. 165 (1969).

a. **Facts:** *Alderman* involved the admissibility against one co-defendant of evidence obtained from an illegal wiretap of another co-defendant's conversation. The former conceded that the wiretap had not been a violation of his own constitutional rights. He contended, however, that even if the Constitution did not require the exclusion of evidence derived from the violation of ***any*** person's rights, it at least required the exclusion of evidence derived from violation of a co-conspirator's or co-defendant's rights.

b. **Holding:** The Court rejected this argument. It stated that "The established principle is that suppression of the product of a Fourth Amendment violation can be successfully urged only by those whose rights were violated by the search itself, not by those who are aggrieved solely by the introduction of damaging evidence. Coconspirators and codefendants have been accorded no special standing."

   i. **Deterrence:** The Court conceded that to prevent introduction of evidence against one defendant obtained through violation of the rights of another might have some deterrent effect. "But we are not convinced that the additional benefits of extending the exclusionary rule to other defendants would justify further encroachment upon the public interest in prosecuting those accused of crime and having them acquitted or convicted on the basis of all the evidence which exposes the truth."

   ii. **Dissent:** Two dissenters, Fortas and Douglas, contended that no evidence obtained in violation of the Fourth Amendment should be admissible in the trial of one "against whom the search was directed." Thus the dissenters would not bar the use in all trials of all illegally seized evidence, but would prevent the government from deliberately violating the Fourth Amendment rights of one person for the purpose of obtaining evidence against another.

2. **Not constitutionally imposed one way or other:** The Supreme Court stated in *Alderman* that the rule against "vicarious" assertion of constitutional rights is neither imposed nor prohibited by the Constitution. Thus the state courts, and both state and federal legislatures, are free to allow defendants to block the admission of evidence derived through violations of the constitutional rights of others.

   a. **California approach:** For instance, California appears to apply the exclusionary rule in at least some situations in which it is not constitutionally required. In *People v. Martin*, 290 P.2d 855 (Cal. 1955), the California Supreme Court held that evidence obtained from an illegal search and seizure could not be introduced in ***any*** trial, regardless of whether it was the defendant's, or some other person's, Fourth Amendment right that was violated.

   b. **ALI Model Code:** Similarly, the *ALI Model Code*, in Section 290.1(5), allows a defendant to object to the unconstitutional search and seizure of evidence from a member of his family, a co-conspirator, a business partner, or a co-resident.

   c. **Use of supervisory powers to exclude evidence:** But the ***federal courts***, although they have general supervisory powers over the conduct of litigation, do ***not*** have authority to allow a defendant to block the admission of evidence derived through violations of the constitutional rights of others. This was the express holding of ***U.S. v. Payner***, 447 U.S. 727 (1980). In *Payner*, the IRS believed that a particular bank in the Bahamas was being used for tax evasion by numerous Americans. An IRS agent made a completely illegal seizure of a briefcase belonging to an officer of the bank, and copied 400 documents in it; one of these ultimately led to an investigation of D, a customer of the bank, and to his prosecution for tax evasion. Since D had no privacy interest in the briefcase or the documents in it, he was not entitled as a constitutional matter to have the evidence suppressed. But the lower courts held that because of the government's knowing, willful and bad-faith violation of the suitcase owner's constitutional rights, the federal courts' supervisory powers could be used to exclude the evidence.

i. **Holding:** The Supreme Court held, however, that "the supervisory power does not authorize a federal court to suppress otherwise admissible evidence on the ground that it was seized unlawfully from a third party not before the court." The Court noted that its previous decisions on standing, including *Rakas v. Illinois*, *infra*, p. 321, "have established beyond any doubt that the interest in deterring illegal searches does not justify the exclusion of tainted evidence at the instance of a party who was not a victim of the challenged practices. . . . The values assigned to the competing interests do not change because a court has elected to analyze the question under the supervisory power instead of the Fourth Amendment. In either case, the need to deter the underlying conduct and the detrimental impact of excluding the evidence remain precisely the same."

ii. **Dissent:** A dissent (by Justices Marshall, Brennan, and Blackmun) argued that there was ample precedent for allowing the supervisory power of the federal court to be used to suppress evidence obtained by the government through misconduct (e.g., the *McNabb/Mallory* involuntary confession rule, *supra*, p. 237). Also, the dissent noted, this was not a case of an inadvertent "blunder" by law enforcement officials, but rather, an intentional violation of the law for the explicit purpose of obtaining the evidence in question. "If the federal court permits such evidence, the intended product of deliberately illegal government action, to be used to obtain a conviction, it places its own imprimatur upon such lawlessness and thereby taints its own integrity."

B. **Confession cases:** The general rule that a defendant may, for purposes of the exclusionary rule, assert only his own constitutional rights, is fairly easy to apply in the case of an illegally-obtained ***confession: it is only the person who makes the illegally-obtained confession who may have it barred by the exclusionary rule***.

1. **Implication of other parties:** Thus if one suspect, A, confesses without being given the required *Miranda* warnings, and in his confession implicates B, only A may assert his Fifth Amendment rights and have the confession barred. It may still be introduced in evidence against B.

C. **Search and seizure cases:** Where the case involves a possible Fourth Amendment ***search*** or ***seizure***, however, the rule that only the person whose rights have been violated may assert the exclusionary rule is more difficult to apply than in the case of confessions. Several people's rights may be violated by one illegal search or arrest; for instance, an illegal entry and seizure of evidence on particular premises may violate the Fourth Amendment rights of both the owner of the premises and the owner of the particular items seized.

1. ***Rakas v. Illinois:*** Prior to 1978, several fairly broad classes of persons were entitled to raise the claim that a search or seizure violated the Fourth Amendment. "Standing" to assert such a claim was possessed by anyone who: (1) had a possessory interest in the ***premises searched***; (2) had a possessory interest in the ***items seized***; or (3) was ***"legitimately present"*** at the scene of the search. (However, having "standing" was no guarantee that the claim itself would be successful; it would not be if there was no legitimate expectation of privacy involved on the defendant's part.) But in ***Rakas v. Illinois***, 439 U.S. 128 (1978), the Supreme Court abandoned this traditional two-step process of first determining whether the defendant has standing, and secondly determining whether he had a legitimate expectation of privacy that was unreasonably affected by the search. Instead, the Court articulated a simple ***one-step*** rule: ***a defendant may seek to exclude evidence derived from a search or seizure only if his "legitimate expectation of privacy"*** (the *Katz* test) ***was violated.***

   a. **Result:** Thus a mere possessory interest in the premises searched, or mere presence at the scene of the search, will not confer "standing," if the defendant had no legitimate expectation of privacy that was violated by the search. For instance, the Court held that the defendants in *Rakas*, several automobile passengers, had no legitimate expectation of privacy with respect to the car's interior. (This aspect of the case is discussed *infra*, p. 321, in the treatment of "presence at the search.")

2. **Possessory interest in premises:** Prior to *Rakas*, a ***possessory interest in the premises*** which are searched was automatically sufficient to confer standing to object to that search. After *Rakas*, the question became, did the holder of the possessory interest have a legitimate expectation of privacy with respect to the premises?

   a. **Privacy interest normally exists:** Normally, the answer will be "yes." But cases where the answer will be "no" can be imagined; for instance, suppose the defendant owned a house, but furnished free or paid lodging to a large number of transients, each of whom had complete run of the premises. A court might well hold that in these circumstances, the owner no longer had a reasonable expectation of privacy with respect to the premises as a whole, and that he could therefore not object to a search of the premises.

3. **Possessory interest in items seized:** Similarly, originally a ***possessory interest in the items seized*** was by itself automatically enough to permit a challenge to the constitutionality of the seizure. But in ***Rawlings v. Kentucky***, 448 U.S. 98 (1980), the Supreme Court held that possession of the seized items must be evaluated like any other basis for a Fourth Amendment claim, i.e., it will be relevant ***only*** if it confers a legitimate expectation of privacy with respect to the item and the search.

   a. **Facts of *Rawlings:*** In *Rawlings*, D was a visitor to a house belonging to one Marcuess. The police arrived with a warrant to arrest Marcuess on drug charges; while there, they conducted a search of D and of several other visitors, including Cox, a friend of D's. In Cox's handbag, they found 1,800 tablets of LSD and other drugs, ownership of which was immediately claimed by D.

   b. **Court's holding:** The Supreme Court, without discussing the legality of the search, held that D could not challenge that search because no Fourth Amendment rights of his were violated by it (regardless of whether Cox's rights may have been violated). The Court conceded that D owned the drugs that were seized, but stated that this was ***irrelevant***; the question was whether D had a legitimate expectation of privacy with respect to Cox's purse and its contents. Because D: (1) had apparently stuffed the drugs in Cox's purse only moments before the police arrived; (2) had no right to exclude others (e.g., Cox's other friends) from looking through Cox's purse; and (3) admitted that he had had no subjective expectation that the purse would remain free from governmental intrusion, D had no legitimate expectation of privacy with respect to the purse's contents.

i. **Effect of *Rakas:*** The Court acknowledged that this was a change from pre-*Rakas* law, but denied that this made a change in the final result: "Prior to *Rakas*, [D] might have been given 'standing' in such a case to challenge a 'search' that netted those drugs but probably would have lost his claim on the merits. After *Rakas*, the two inquiries merge into one: whether governmental officials violated any legitimate expectation of privacy held by [D]."

4. **Presence at scene of search:** Before 1978, standing to object to a search was ***automatically*** conferred upon a person who was ***legitimately on the premises*** where the search took place.

a. ***Rakas v. Illinois:*** But in ***Rakas v. Illinois***, 439 U.S. 128 (1978), the automatic standing given to anyone who was "legitimately present at the scene" was explicitly ***overturned.***

i. **Facts of *Rakas:*** In *Rakas*, police stopped a car in which the Ds were riding as passengers, suspecting that the vehicle might have been the getaway car in a recent robbery. The police searched the interior of the car and found a sawed-off rifle under the front passenger seat and a box of rifle shells in the locked glove compartment. The Ds never asserted a property interest in the items seized. Instead they asserted that: (1) any defendant at whom a search is "directed" has standing to contest the legality of that search (a so-called "target" theory); and (2) since the Ds were "legitimately on the premises" at the time of the search, they had standing to object to it.

ii. **Target theory rejected:** First, the Supreme Court quickly rejected the "target" theory, both because it would involve practical difficulties (e.g., the problem of determining the person at whom a search was directed, which might be difficult indeed in the case of, say, a bug on a telephone used by a large number of people) and because it would represent a further extension of the exclusionary rule and a corresponding suppression of probative evidence.

iii. **New approach to standing:** Then, the Court articulated its new one-step analysis of Fourth Amendment cases, by which the standing issue no longer exists as a distinct question, but is instead handled as part of a single inquiry into whether the defendant had a legitimate expectation of privacy which was unreasonably violated by the search. (See *supra*, p. 321.)

iv. **Presence at search not automatically sufficient:** Finally, the Court expressly overturned its prior view that legitimate presence on the premises searched would by itself be automatically enough to allow a constitutional challenge to that search.

v. **Application to facts of *Rakas:*** On the particular facts of *Rakas*, the Court found, the Ds did ***not*** have such a legitimate expectation of privacy with respect to the areas where the items were found; neither the glove compartment nor the area under the car seat are areas in which a passenger as such would normally have a legitimate expectation of privacy. (The Ds did not make any special showing that they had a legitimate privacy expectation in these particular areas.)

5. **Social guest:** But a ***social guest*** normally *does* have standing to object to a search of the premises where he is visiting, even though *Rakas* establishes that mere "presence at the scene" of a search does not confer standing.

   a. **Overnight guest:** Thus the Court has held that an ***overnight*** guest has standing to object to the police's warrantless entry of the premises where the guest is staying. See *Minnesota v. Olson*, 495 U.S. 91 (1990), *supra*, p. 29.

   b. **Business visitor:** On the other hand, the Court has held that a ***business visitor*** to premises will normally ***not*** have standing to object to a search of the premises, at least where the visit is a ***brief one*** unaccompanied by any real personal relationship between guest and host. See *Minnesota v. Carter*, 525 U.S. 83 (1998), *supra*, p. 29. This is true even where the visit takes place at a home rather than office or other traditional place of business.

   c. **Non-overnight social guests:** But *Carter*, *supra*, also established that five members of the Court there believed that a ***social guest***, even one who is only ***briefly*** on the premises (and who has not become a "temporary resident" of the premises, as an overnight guest becomes) normally has an expectation of privacy in her host's home. Therefore, such a short-term social guest normally has standing to object to a search of the common areas of the host's home. See *Carter*, *supra*, p. 29.

6. **Vehicle searches:** When the police stop a ***vehicle***, both the ***driver*** and ***all passengers have standing*** to challenge the constitutionality of the vehicle stop.

   a. **Passengers:** As to passengers, the Court so held in *Brendlin v. California*, 551 U.S. 249 (2007): "When a police officer makes a traffic stop, the driver of the car is seized within the meaning of the Fourth Amendment. [Any] passenger is ***seized as well*** and so may challenge the constitutionality of the stop."

   b. **Where D is not the owner of the vehicle:** Now, consider what happens where the owner is absent, the driver is ***driving with the owner's consent*** when the car is stopped, and the driver claims that the search violated her Fourth Amendment rights. Here, too, the Court has held that in most instances, such a non-owner nonetheless ***has a reasonable expectation of privacy*** with respect to the vehicle, and consequently has standing to assert a Fourth Amendment claim. We discuss the topic in an earlier chapter; see *supra*, pp. 30-32.

7. **No automatic standing for co-conspirators:** Where one member of a ***conspiracy*** is stopped and/or searched, the ***other members of the conspiracy*** do ***not*** automatically get

standing to object to the stop or search by virtue of their membership. That is, membership in a conspiracy adds nothing to the standing equation, and each member must independently show that he had an expectation of privacy or a property interest that was interfered with by the stop or search. *U.S. v. Padilla*, 508 U.S. 77 (1993).

Example: D1 is stopped and searched while driving a Cadillac; the search discloses 560 pounds of cocaine in the trunk. D1 is arrested. D1's cooperation leads agents to D2, D3, and D4, who are arrested as being involved in the drug scheme. These three defendants argue that because they were involved in the conspiracy that D1 was pursuing at the time of his stop, and because they were responsible for making the arrangements for D1 to drive the Cadillac, they automatically have standing to protest the stop and search of the Cadillac.

Held, for the prosecution. The fact that D2, D3, and D4 may have been part of the conspiracy, or had joint control or responsibility for the transportation aspect of the conspiracy, adds nothing to the issue of standing. Unless each of these defendants can show that he had a property interest or expectation of privacy in the Cadillac or the drugs, he or she will not have standing to object to the stop or the search. *U.S. v. Padilla*, *supra*.

D. Wiretaps: Where a Fourth Amendment violation concerns the illegal use of ***wiretaps*** or other eavesdropping equipment, rather than the search and seizure of tangible property, the standing issues are somewhat different.

1. **Parties to conversation:** The persons whose conversation is overheard clearly have the right to object, "since their conversation was the subject of the search" (Nutshell, p. 300), and since their privacy is the most immediately affected by the interception.

2. **Owner of premises:** It is not clear when the ***owner of premises*** may object to the illegal interception of conversations taking place on those premises (assuming that the owner is not one of the parties to the conversation).

   a. ***Alderman* case:** A pre-*Rakas* case, ***Alderman v. U.S.***, 394 U.S. 165 (1969) concluded that the owner of premises has automatic standing to contest the legality of an interception made of a conversation on those premises. But the rationale of *Alderman* was that conversations should receive the same protection as tangible objects; when *Alderman* was decided, the law was that the owner of premises had automatic standing to contest any search made of those premises (even if the owner was not present, and the objects seized were not his). Since ownership of the premises no longer gives rise to automatic standing under *Rakas* when tangible objects are seized, there is no reason to believe that such ownership will be automatically sufficient when a conversation is at issue. Thus the question will probably be: Did the owner of the premises have a legitimate expectation that the conversations occurring on his premises (but in which he did not participate) would remain private? It would certainly seem that where the owner is ***present*** during the conversations (even though he does not participate), his privacy claim will be stronger than where he is not.

   b. **Wiretaps distinguished from "bugs":** It is also not clear whether there will be a distinction between "bugs" (which pick up a conversation in which both parties are on the premises) and wiretaps (which pick up a telephone conversation). One would think that a homeowner would normally be entitled to presume that neither telephonic nor non-telephonic conversations will be subject to surveillance.

III. DERIVATIVE EVIDENCE GENERALLY, AND THE "INDEPENDENT SOURCE" AND "INEVITABLE DISCOVERY" EXCEPTIONS

A. **Derivative evidence generally:** The exclusionary rule clearly applies to evidence which is the direct result of a violation of the defendant's rights. Thus if the seizure of evidence from defendant's premises is a violation of his Fourth Amendment rights, its admission against him is barred. But suppose that the connection between the constitutional violation and the evidence in question is a more tenuous one. Suppose, for instance, that an illegal search is conducted and the defendant's diary seized, the diary contains the names of persons who are aware of the defendant's criminal activities, and the police interview these persons, obtaining from them statements incriminating the defendant. Is the testimony of these witnesses, obtained indirectly through the illegal search, barred just as the objects seized in the search are barred? The general question of the admissibility of evidence obtained indirectly through constitutional violations — the problem of ***"derivative evidence"*** — has produced an extensive body of case law.

B. ***Silverthorne:*** The first Supreme Court case to discuss the admissibility of derivative evidence issue in any detail was ***Silverthorne Lumber Co. v. U.S.***, 251 U.S. 385 (1920).

   1. **Facts:** In *Silverthorne*, federal agents unlawfully seized certain documents belonging to the Silverthornes and gave them to a grand jury that had already indicted both Silverthornes and their company. A federal court ordered the documents returned, but photographs of them were kept, and the prosecution induced the grand jury to then issue a subpoena to regain them.

   2. **Holding:** The Supreme Court, *per* Holmes, held that the subpoena was invalid, because it was issued based on knowledge illegally obtained (i.e., the knowledge of the documents' contents derived from their unlawful seizure). The Court stated broadly, "The essence of a provision forbidding the acquisition of evidence in a certain way is that not merely evidence so acquired shall not be used before the Court but that it ***shall not be used at all***" (emphasis added).

C. **"Fruits of the poisonous tree" doctrine:** The doctrine that when an item of evidence is obtained by violating a person's rights, further evidence derived from that first item may not be admitted against the person, is popularly called the ***"fruits of the poisonous tree"*** doctrine. That is, once the original evidence is shown to have been unlawfully obtained (making that evidence an inadmissible ***"poisonous tree"***), all evidence whose discovery ***stems from that evidence, the "poisoned fruit," should be equally inadmissible.***

   1. **Modern Court is generally hostile:** But as we'll see, since at least the Rehnquist Court, a majority of the Supreme Court has been relatively hostile to the poisonous-tree doctrine, and has steadily narrowed the doctrine's reach.

D. **Approach used in our discussion:** Below, we begin with a discussion of the two major exceptions to the application of the poisonous-tree doctrine: (1) the "independent source" exception (in Par. (E) below); and (2) the "inevitable discovery" exception (in Par. (F) below, beginning on p. 327). The two exceptions are closely related; each is premised on the idea that unless the police wrong-doing was the but-for cause that allowed the police to gain access to particular "derivative" evidence, there is no reason to punish the government by making the derivative evidence inadmissible.

1. **"Purging the taint":** After we discuss these two major exceptions, we discuss (in section IV, beginning on p. 330) the possibility by which events occurring between the police illegality and the eventual discovery of derivative evidence may be deemed to be sufficient to ***"purge the taint"*** of the illegality, so that the "fruit" (the derivative evidence) is rehabilitated, and not treated as inadmissible.

E. **Independent source exception:** The Court in *Silverthorne, supra,* recognized that the "fruits of the poisonous tree" doctrine should not apply where the secondary facts in question ***came from two sources, only one of which was related to the original illegality.*** The Court's opinion noted that facts obtained indirectly through constitutional violations "[do not] become sacred and inaccessible. If knowledge of them is gained from an ***independent source*** they may be proved like any others, but the knowledge gained by the Government's own wrong cannot be used by it in the way proposed." This language permitting the use of information discovered in two ways, only one of which was the product of illegality, has given rise to what is known as the ***"independent source"*** exception to the "fruits of the poisonous tree" doctrine.

> **Example:** Suppose that in *Silverthorne*, the government had initially become aware of the contents of the documents through the illegal seizure (as it did), but that during the subsequent course of its investigation of the Silverthornes, the government had been told by witnesses of the documents' contents. If the government had been able to show that these interviews with witnesses had had nothing to do with the original illegal seizure, and that the witnesses' testimony about the documents thus constituted an "independent source" for the government's desire to subpoena them, the "fruits of the poisonous tree" doctrine would not have applied.

1. **Expanded view:** The "independent source" exception has become increasingly important, as the result of the Court's use (and arguably, misuse) of the exception in ***Segura v. U.S.***, 468 U.S. 796 (1984).

   a. **Facts:** In *Segura*, the police had probable cause to arrest D for narcotics violations, and probable cause to search his apartment for evidence of those violations. They arrested him outside of the apartment, but did not obtain a search warrant (even though there were no "exigent circumstances" justifying a warrantless entry). The officers then entered the apartment with D, where they saw narcotics paraphernalia (and also saw several other people who were later arrested). A search warrant was not obtained until 18 or 20 hours later, due to "administrative delays"; during this time, two agents remained in the apartment to make sure that no evidence was removed or destroyed. When the warrant was finally obtained, the agents found and seized narcotics and other evidence, which they had not previously observed.

   b. **Holding:** D argued that since the initial entry into the apartment was unlawful (a fact not contested by the government), and since the agents' 18-hour stay in the apartment was unlawful, the evidence that was finally seized was "tainted fruit," which should be excluded. But the Supreme Court rejected this argument. It reasoned that prior to the illegal entry, the police already knew enough to obtain a search warrant; therefore, they could have staked out the apartment from the outside (which would have been legal), gotten the warrant, and seized the very same evidence. The police thus had an "independent source" for that evidence, the Court ruled.

c. **Dissent:** Four Justices dissented from the conclusion that the "independent source" exception was applicable here. In an opinion by Justice Stevens, they pointed out that D's claim was not that the information leading to the issuance of the search warrant was tainted, but that the agents' ***access*** to the evidence was tainted — had the agents not been in the apartment during the 18-hour period, it was highly likely that the other persons there (who were not arrested, and of whose existence the agents only became aware when they made the illegal entry) would have surmised that D had been arrested and would have destroyed the evidence. In the dissent's view, any time the police's illegal conduct gives them access to evidence, the "independent source" exception should not apply if the evidence would have been removed or destroyed by the time lawful procedures had justified the search or seizure.

   i. **Majority's response:** But the majority answered the dissent by saying that the dissent's view would "extend the exclusionary rule, which already exacts an ***enormous price*** from society and our system of justice, to further 'protect' criminal activity. . . . The essence of the dissent is that there is some 'constitutional right' to destroy evidence."

2. **"Rediscovery" of evidence:** In *Segura*, the evidence in question was not discovered until the police were conducting their final search-with-warrant. But *Segura* has since been extended to cover the situation where the police are illegally on premises, they discover particular evidence, they apply for a warrant, and they ***"rediscover"*** the evidence. In this scenario, as long as the trial court is convinced that the illegal entry did not contribute either to the officer's decision to attempt to get a warrant or to the magistrate's decision to grant the warrant, the evidence will be ***admissible*** even though its initial discovery was illegal. *Murray v. U.S.*, 487 U.S. 533 (1988).

   a. **Facts:** Thus in *Murray*, police arrested drug traffickers outside a locked warehouse. Instead of immediately getting a warrant, they forced open the warehouse and saw bales of marijuana inside. They then submitted a warrant application to a magistrate, in which they did not mention that they had already been inside the warehouse and seen marijuana. The magistrate granted the warrant; the officers re-entered the warehouse, "rediscovered" the marijuana, and seized it.

   b. **Holding:** By a 4-3 vote, the Court ruled that so long as the prosecution could show on remand that the officers would have applied for and properly received a warrant even had they not first entered the warehouse, the marijuana could be admitted under the independent source exception. It did not make any difference that, unlike *Segura*, the present case involved evidence that was ***actually discovered during the initial warrantless entry.*** To exclude the evidence "would put the police (and society) not in the ***same*** position they would have occupied if no violation occurred, but in a ***worse*** one."

c. **Dissent:** But three dissenters argued that the majority's view gives the police a ***strong incentive to make warrantless entries***. Anytime the police have probable cause to obtain a search warrant but are uncertain about whether useful evidence will in fact be found, they can make a warrantless entry, see whether there is anything worthwhile there, and only go to the time and bother of getting a search warrant if there is. In *Murray* itself, for instance, it is unlikely that the police would have gone to the trouble of getting a warrant had they discovered that the warehouse was empty.

3. **Scope:** So *Segura* and *Murray*, taken together, appear to allow admission of evidence under the "independent source" exception when three requirements are satisfied:

a. **Illegally on premises:** First, the police must have been on the premises ***illegally*** at the moment they discovered the evidence or contraband in question. Perhaps they arrested D in his home without a required arrest warrant, and then "searched incident to arrest" (making the search invalid; see *supra*, p. 108). Or, as happened in *Murray*, perhaps they forced open the premises without a search warrant and saw the evidence or contraband there. Whatever the sequence, the point is that the police ended up in premises for which they did not have a search warrant, and as to which no exception to the search warrant exists.

b. **Probable cause for search warrant:** Second, although the police did not have a search warrant, at the moment of entry they must have had knowledge that would have ***entitled*** them to ***procure*** a search warrant. That is, they had probable cause to believe that contraband, or evidence of crime, would be found on the premises. This theoretical availability of a warrant is the "independent source" that justifies the admission of the evidence even though the police were acting illegally at the moment they seized the evidence.

c. **Police would have applied for warrant:** Finally, the police must show that they would probably have ***eventually applied for a search warrant*** even had they not engaged in the illegality. (Thus suppose the police had probable cause for a search warrant, but let a long time lapse without getting a warrant. If they then discovered contraband while illegally on the premises, and the court determines that without the illegal entry and discovery the police would never have bothered to get a warrant, *Murray* indicates that the "independent source" exception won't apply.)

F. **The "inevitable discovery" exception:** The Supreme Court has recognized a second exception to the poisonous-tree doctrine, related to the "independent source" exception: the ***"inevitable discovery"*** exception. Under this exception, evidence may be admitted if it would ***"inevitably"*** have been discovered by ***other police techniques*** had it not first been obtained through the illegal discovery. The main case discussing the inevitable discovery exception is ***Nix v. Williams***, 467 U.S. 431 (1984).

1. **Prosecution bears proving of qualifying for exception:** It is the ***prosecution*** that bears the burden of showing, by a preponderance of the evidence, that the information would inevitably have been discovered by lawful means. Nix, supra.

2. **Applies where derivative evidence is a weapon or a body:** The "inevitable discovery" rule is most often applied where the possibly-poisoned fruit is a ***weapon*** or a ***body***, whose location the police learn about from an illegal search or improperly-obtained confession.

a. **Facts of *Nix v. Williams*:** Evidence of a body was what was at issue, for instance, in *Nix v. Williams, supra. Nix* involved a later stage of a prosecution begun in the child-murder case of *Brewer v. Williams* (discussed at length *infra*, p. 408). In *Brewer*, the Supreme Court held that the police, by urging D to "help that little girl receive a Christian burial" had intentionally and unconstitutionally elicited from D the location of the girl's body. After the Supreme Court in *Brewer* remanded the case to the trial court for a new trial, D sought to exclude the *corpus delecti* itself from the trial, i.e., to exclude evidence of the finding of the victim's body, the fact of her death, and other evidence discovered on or near the body.

b. **Trial court lets the body's discovery be introduced:** The trial court concluded that the ***body would inevitably have been found*** (and soon after it in fact was) even had D *not* told the police where to find it. The trial court noted that search parties were already looking for the body, and that at the time D made his confession, had come quite near to it. Therefore, the trial court allowed the prosecution to introduce various items of evidence about the finding of the body, its condition, and the like.

c. **Supreme Court affirms:** The Supreme Court ***agreed*** that the trial court had properly allowed this evidence about the body into evidence: even had the police not unconstitutionally elicited from D the location of the body, the police inevitably would have soon discovered the body anyway.

   i. **Rationale:** The Court's rationale in *Nix* for the inevitable discovery exception was that such a doctrine ***does not violate the core rationale for the exclusionary rule.*** That rationale is that in order to deter illegal police conduct, the prosecution ***should not be placed in a better position*** than it would have been in had there been no illegality. Where the evidence would inevitably have been discovered (just as where the evidence is in fact discovered through an "independent source"), admitting the evidence by hypothesis does ***not*** place the prosecution in a better position than it would have been in had there been no illegality. Indeed, keeping the evidence *out* actually places the prosecution in a ***worse*** position, a result for which there is no sound rationale.

   ii. **Absence of bad faith not required:** The Court in *Nix v. Williams* refused to make it a condition of the "inevitable discovery" exceptions application that the prosecution prove an ***absence of bad faith*** on the part of the police. Refusing to allow evidence that would inevitably have been discovered anyway merely on the grounds that the police used bad faith in obtaining that evidence would place the prosecution in a worse position than had there not been illegality; furthermore, such a "good faith" requirement would ***"fail . . . to take into account the enormous societal cost of excluding truth[.]"***

d. **Dissent:** Even the two Justices who dissented in *Nix v. Williams* (Brennan and Marshall) agreed that there should be an "inevitable discovery" exception to the exclusionary rule. However, the dissenters believed that the government should be put to a ***sterner burden of proof*** than that advocated by the majority, before such evidence should be allowed. The dissenters would have required ***"clear and convincing evidence"*** (rather than a mere "preponderance of evidence") that the information would inevitably have been discovered.

3. **Scope of exception:** The inevitable discovery exception, as it applied in *Nix*, meant that evidence obtained in violation of the defendant's ***Sixth Amendment right to counsel*** could be admitted. It seems quite clear, however, that the exception also applies to evidence which is obtained in violation of ***other*** constitutional guarantees. Thus evidence obtained in violation of the Fourth Amendment's ban on unreasonable searches and seizures, or in violation of the Fifth Amendment right of a suspect in custody to ***remain silent***, could similarly be introduced if it were shown that this evidence would inevitably have been discovered had the illegality not occurred.

4. **Factual issue:** But observe that a delicate factual question will always be presented when an "inevitable discovery" claim is made by the prosecution. The showing that must be made by the prosecution is that the particular ***evidence*** in question would have been discovered. Thus where the prosecution seeks to enter evidence about the ***condition of a body***, it will not be enough for the prosecution to prove that the body would eventually have been found; the prosecution must also prove that the particular ***forensic finding*** sought to be introduced would have been available.

   Example: For instance, suppose *Nix* had occurred in the summertime, when a body could be expected to decompose relatively rapidly (rather than in December, as actually happened). In that event, presumably the prosecution would have borne the burden of demonstrating the latest time by which the body would have been found, and the further burden of showing that all evidence sought to be introduced concerning the hour and manner of death would still have been intact at that time.

   a. **Meaning of "inevitable":** It's not clear what standard the Court will use to determine the "inevitability" of the evidence's discovery. In particular, it's not clear whether the steps that the trial judge believes that the police would (inevitably) have taken had the police not committed the ***unconstitutional action*** may be considered. That is, can the police argue that had they not behaved unconstitutionally, they would "inevitably" have taken some other (constitutional) action — like applying for a search warrant — that would have produced the same evidence anyway, making the exception applicable?

      (1) **Failure to get warrant:** The issue is most likely to arise when the police identify particular premises as likely containing evidence of criminality, and they mistakenly believe that the case fell into one of the many ***"no warrant required"*** situations. Therefore, they conduct a warrantless (and illegal) search rather than applying for a warrant for which they had probable cause, i.e., a warrant to which they would have been entitled. Can the prosecution successfully argue that a proper search inevitably would have occurred, because the police inevitably would have asked for, and received, a warrant had they not performed the illegal warrantless search?

      i. **Never answered:** The Court has never decided a case involving this sort of fact pattern and issue. But in view of the present Court's hostility to the fruit-of-the-poisonous-tree doctrine, and the majority's view that the "social costs" of excluding obviously-relevant but illegally-obtained evidence are very high, it seems likely that the court would be quick to find that the police ***would indeed have***

sought and received a search warrant, entitling them to treat the fruits of their illegal warrantless search as falling within the inevitable-discovery exception."

IV. "PURGING THE TAINT" OF POLICE ILLEGALITY — THE SIGNIFICANCE OF SUBSEQUENT INDEPENDENT EVENTS

A. The "purged taint" exception in general: Suppose that the police obtain a piece of evidence indirectly through a constitutional violation, and that neither the independent source nor the inevitable discovery exceptions seems to apply. In such a situation, it may nonetheless be the case that the exclusionary rule does not apply, due to a long-recognized judicial exception known as the ***"purged taint"*** doctrine.

1. **Doctrine defined:** The principle of the purged taint doctrine is that if enough ***additional factors intervene*** between the original illegality and the final discovery of evidence, neither the "deterrence" nor "judicial fairness" rationales behind the exclusionary rule applies. Therefore, the evidence may be admissible despite the fact that it would not have been discovered "but for" the illegality.

2. ***Wong Sun* formulation:** The Supreme Court's initial major discussion of the "purged taint" doctrine was in ***Wong Sun v. U.S.***, 371 U.S. 471 (1963). In *Wong Sun*, the Court stated that the applicability of the "fruit of the poisonous tree" doctrine is determined by "whether, granting establishment of the primary illegality, the evidence to which instant objection is made has been come at by ***exploitation of that illegality*** or instead by means ***sufficiently distinguishable to be purged of the primary taint."***

B. *Wong Sun:* *Wong Sun*, *supra*, arose out of a complicated fact situation, and demonstrates both the application of the "fruits of the poisonous tree" doctrine to exclude evidence obtained indirectly through constitutional violations, and the use of the "purged taint" exception to allow other evidence, even though "but for" the illegality that evidence would not have been found.

1. **Facts of *Wong Sun:*** Acting on a tip, federal narcotics agents broke into Toy's apartment, and handcuffed him. The entry was (as the Supreme Court held) without probable cause and therefore illegal. Immediately after the entry Toy made a statement accusing one Yee of selling narcotics. The agents went immediately to Yee, who surrendered heroin to them, and made a statement that he had been sold the drugs by Toy and one Wong Sun. Wong Sun was arrested (again without probable cause, as the Court later held), and both he and Toy were arraigned and released on their own recognizance. Several days later, Wong Sun was interrogated at the offices of the Bureau of Narcotics, where he was warned of his right to remain silent, and told that he could have a lawyer. Wong Sun responded by making a confession, but refusing to sign it.

2. **Issues of admissibility:** The Supreme Court, in reviewing the conviction of Toy and Wong Sun, considered, among other issues, the following:

   a. whether the statement made by Toy immediately after the illegal entry of his house could be used against him;

b. whether the drugs seized from Yee could be used against Toy, or were instead "fruits of the poisonous tree" (the illegal entry of Toy's house);

c. whether these same drugs could be used against Wong Sun; and

d. whether Wong Sun's confession was an excludable fruit of his illegal arrest.

3. **Use of Toy's statement against him:** The Court held that Toy's statement, made right after the invasion of his house, could ***not*** be used against him because it was a "fruit" of the illegal invasion. The Court ***rejected*** the government's argument that the statement, although closely following the invasion, was nonetheless admissible because it resulted from "an intervening independent act of a free will" (i.e., Toy's decision to speak). The Court cited the fact that six or seven officers had participated in the break-in, at a time when Toy's wife and children were asleep, and that Toy had been immediately handcuffed. "In such circumstances it is unreasonable to infer that Toy's response was sufficiently an act of free will to purge the primary taint of the unlawful invasion."[1]

4. **Use of drugs against Toy:** The Court also disallowed the use against Toy of the drugs seized from Yee. The seizure was the direct result of Toy's statement, which itself was, the Court had held, an inadmissible fruit of the illegal invasion; the seizure was therefore "come at by the exploitation of [the] illegality." The relationship between the original illegal entry, Toy's statement implicating Yee, and the seizure of drugs from Yee was so close that nothing had occurred to "purge the taint" of the illegal entry. Therefore, the drugs could not be used against Toy.

   a. Use of drugs against Wong Sun: The drugs were, however, ***admissible*** against *Wong Sun*, even though their seizure had been the direct product of the illegal entry into Toy's house. The admissibility of the drugs against Wong Sun was due to his ***lack of standing*** to object to their seizure.[2]

5. **Use of confession:** The Court then turned to whether ***Wong Sun's own confession*** could be used against him. The Court conceded that his arrest had been without probable cause, and therefore illegal. But because Wong Sun had been ***released*** for several days after the arrest, and because he had returned voluntarily to make the statement, "the connection between the arrest and the statement had 'become ***so attenuated as to dissipate the taint***.' "

C. Standards for determining if intervening events "have purged the taint": Today, the Court considers ***three factors*** in deciding whether an event (or even the passage of time) occurring between the illegal conduct and the police's acquisition of the possibly-tainted fruit

1. Today, the admissibility of Toy's statement would be governed by the three-factor test of the post-*Wong Sun* decision in *Brown v. Illinois*, *infra*, p. 331. Under that test, the result would almost certainly be the same: the taint would not be found to be purged, given the short time between the illegal entry into Toy's house and his statement, and the lack of any intervening event.

2. The admissibility of the drugs against Wong Sun and not against Toy points to the critical importance of observing ***whose rights have been violated***. It does not matter to how great an extent particular evidence is the "fruit" of an illegal arrest or search; if the illegality did not violate the constitutional rights *of the defendant himself*, he will never be able to argue the "fruits of the poisonous tree" doctrine. See the treatment of standing *supra*, p. 324.

is sufficient to ***"purge the taint"*** of the illegality. The three factors were set forth in ***Brown v. Illinois***, 422 U. S. 590 (1975). In *Brown*, the illegality was an arrest that violated the Fourth Amendment, and the possibly-tainted "fruit" was a *confession* by the arrestee; but the Court has since indicated that these factors are to be applied in other types of derivative-evidence scenarios as well.

According to *Brown*, here are the three factors the Court will take into account in deciding whether the taint from the illegality has been "purged":

[1] The ***"temporal proximity"*** of the illegality to the fruit (in *Brown*, the proximity of the illegal arrest to the confession by the arrestee);

[2] The "presence of ***intervening circumstances***" between the illegality and the fruit; and

[3] Of "particular" importance, "the ***purpose and flagrancy*** of the ***official misconduct."***

1. **Application in *Brown*:** *Brown* itself demonstrates a common scenario in which an intervening event will ***not*** be enough to purge the taint — an illegal ***arrest*** followed quickly by a custodial station-house interrogation and ***confession***.

   a. **Facts:** In *Brown*, D was arrested without probable cause, so that he could be questioned concerning a murder. After the arrest, he was taken to the police station, given the *Miranda* warnings, and interrogated. Within two hours of his arrest, he made an incriminating statement. Several hours after that, in a second interrogation session (prefaced by a new set of *Miranda* warnings), he made a *second* incriminating statement.

   b. **Both confessions tainted:** The Supreme Court concluded that ***neither confession*** could be admitted, because there had been no purging of the taint of the illegal arrest as to either. The Court focused mainly on the first confession (which is what we'll concentrate on here). All three factors listed by the Court favored a finding that the taint ***had not been purged*** by the time of the first confession, the opinion said:

      i. **Temporal proximity:** As to ***temporal proximity,*** the fact that the first confession was separated from the illegal arrest ***"by less than two hours"*** cut strongly against purging of the taint. (The Court compared this brief time with the situation in *Wong Sun*, *supra*, where the taint of Wong Sun's own confession was purged in part because it came "several days" after the illegality.)

      ii. **Intervening events:** As to ***"intervening events,"*** the Court's view was that there had been "no intervening event of significance whatsoever" between the arrest and the first confession. So neither the police's act of taking D to the police station, nor their then reading him his *Miranda* warnings, constituted intervening events of any significance.

      iii. **Purpose and flagrancy:** Lastly, the ***"purpose and flagrancy"*** of the illegal police conduct similarly cut strongly against a finding that the taint was purged. The illegality "had a ***quality of purposefulness"*** — the police conceded that their purpose in arresting D without probable cause was ***solely investigatory***, making this an "expedition for evidence in the hope that something might turn up." And such a purpose constituted flagrant wrongdoing, the Court concluded.

2. **Illegal stop is followed by discovery of outstanding arrest warrant:** The main case in which the Court has applied the *Brown* three-factor test is a 2016 case posing the issue of whether the taint of an illegal stop will be purged by the officer's discovery that there is an ***outstanding arrest warrant*** for the suspect. Based on that case, the Court seems inclined to find that discovery of the warrant is normally a sufficiently important intervening event that the discovery will ***suffice to purge the taint*** of the stop, thereby permitting the police to ***make an arrest*** on account of the warrant and then a ***search incident to that arrest.*** That case is ***Utah v. Strieff,*** 579 U.S. 232 (2016), a 5-3 decision.

   a. **Facts:** In *Strieff,* police got an anonymous tip that narcotics were being sold in a particular residence. Detective Fackrell conducted surveillance of the house, and noticed that various visitors arrived at the house and left a few minutes later; this pattern caused him to suspect that narcotics activity was indeed going on there. At one point, he observed D (Strieff) leave the house and walk towards the parking lot of a nearby convenience store.[3]

      i. **Stop in parking lot:** In the store's parking lot, Fackrell stopped D, demanded that D tell him what he had been doing at the residence,[4] and then demanded D's ID. When D gave him a state ID card, Fackrell called in the information on it to a police dispatcher, who reported that D had an outstanding arrest warrant for a traffic violation. Fackrell then arrested D on the warrant, searched him incident to the arrest, and discovered narcotics on D's person, for which D was then prosecuted.

      ii. **D's unsuccessful contention at trial:** D sought to suppress the fruits of the search, based on the argument that the initial stop had not been based upon reasonable suspicion. The prosecution answered that even if this was true, Fackrell's discovery of a valid outstanding arrest warrant was enough to "attenuate" the connection between the unlawful stop and the resulting search (i.e., enough to "purge the taint" of the stop). The trial court ***agreed with the prosecution*** and allowed in the fruits of the search, after which D pleaded guilty but reserved the right to appeal the purging-of-the-taint ruling.

   b. **Taint found to be purged:** By a 5-3 vote,[5] the Supreme Court ***sided with the prosecution*** — discovery of the outstanding warrant was indeed ***enough to purge the taint*** of the illegal stop, based on the three-factor test of *Brown, supra.* In an opinion by Justice Thomas, the Court applied the three *Brown* factors this way:

      [1] **Temporal proximity: *"Temporal proximity"*** between the stop and the search cut in favor of suppression, Thomas said. The proximity factor will favor suppression unless "substantial time" elapses, and here, the search took place ***"only minutes"***

---

3. Fackrell later conceded that he didn't see D enter the house, so he didn't know whether the visit was in fact short enough to justify a suspicion that D may have been conducting a drug transaction. That lack of knowledge was what led all parties, and eventually the Supreme Court, to assume that Fackrell's subsequent stop of D was illegal.

4. It's not clear from the Supreme Court opinion how D answered the question, if at all. The issue didn't matter, in view of the Supreme Court's assumption that the stop itself had been made without adequate suspicion and thus was illegal.

5. The Court consisted of only eight justices, following Justice Scalia's death earlier that year.

after the illegal stop, which was *not* a substantial time.

[2] **Intervening circumstances:** On the other hand, the second factor — "the presence of ***intervening circumstances"*** — ***"strongly favors the State,"*** Thomas said. The outstanding warrant predated Fackrell's investigation and was "entirely ***unconnected with the stop."*** Plus, once Fackrell discovered the warrant, he had an ***"obligation"*** to arrest D, making the arrest a "ministerial act" (i.e., not within Fackrell's discretion).

[3] **"Purpose and flagrancy of misconduct":** The final factor — the "purpose and flagrancy of the official misconduct" — also ***"strongly favors the State,"*** Thomas wrote. Fackrell was ***"at most negligent,"*** and his main error — making the stop without knowing whether D's visit to the house had been a short one — was a ***"good-faith mistake."*** Furthermore, Thomas continued, there was "no indication that this unlawful stop was ***part of any systemic or recurrent police misconduct."*** To the contrary, he said, "all the evidence suggests that the stop was an ***isolated instance of negligence*** that occurred in connection with a bona fide investigation of a suspected drug house."

Since two of the three *Brown* factors cut strongly in favor of a finding that the taint from the unlawful stop was "sufficiently attenuated" by the preexisting arrest warrant, Thomas said, the fruits of the search incident to the arrest on the warrant were ***not required to be excluded.***

c. **Dissent:** Justices Sotomayor and Kagan wrote separate dissents, and Justice Ginsburg joined most of the Sotomayor dissent. Both dissents argued that ***discovery of an outstanding warrant should not be considered a significant intervening event.*** Both reasoned that because ***large segments of the population*** are covered by such warrants, treating the discovery of a warrant as purging any taint from an illegal stop will give the police a ***large incentive*** to make suspicionless stops — the police collectively will know that many such stops will turn up an outstanding warrant, thereby retroactively justifying an arrest and an incident search.

i. **Sotomayor's dissent:** The principal dissent was by Justice Sotomayor. She wrote that the majority's approach "allows the police to stop you on the street, demand your identification, and check it for outstanding traffic warrants — even if you are doing nothing wrong." She continued, "If the officer discovers a warrant for a fine you forgot to pay, courts will now ***excuse his illegal stop*** and will ***admit into evidence anything he happens to find by searching you*** after arresting you on the warrant."

(1) **Widespread warrants:** Sotomayor especially disagreed with the majority's conclusion that the illegal stop here was ***"isolated,"*** and that there was "no indication that [the stop] was part of any ***systemic or recurrent police misconduct."*** She pointed out that outstanding warrants are "surprisingly common," and that the vast majority are for minor offenses (e.g., missing a fine payment on a traffic ticket). And, she said, police departments frequently capitalize on the large number of outstanding warrants; many stops-plus-warrant-checks are "the product of ***institutionalized training procedures."*** Furthermore, ***"people***

of color are disproportionate victims" of these suspicionless searches. She disagreed, therefore, with the majority's conclusion that suspicionless stops are "isolated."

d. **Significance of *Strieff*:** The dissenters in *Strieff* seem correct in warning that the majority opinion will likely give police departments a ***major incentive to make large numbers of stops*** of questionable validity.

   i. **Incentives for police:** Under *Strieff*, every stop becomes an opportunity to determine whether the person stopped has an outstanding arrest warrant, no matter how old or minor the offense might turn out to be. And once the existence of the outstanding warrant is confirmed, the officer is free (indeed, probably *required* by law) to arrest the suspect. At that point, the officer can do a search incident to the arrest, and any contraband or evidence of criminality she finds — whether or not it has anything to do with the reason for the stop — can serve as admissible evidence in a new prosecution predicated on that evidence.

   ii. **Facts in *Strieff* itself:** In *Strieff* itself, the Court's main legal conclusion (that the taint of the illegal stop was not purged) seemed to be premised on three ***factual findings*** by the majority about the conduct of the particular police officer, Fackrell, and his department. And each of those findings tended to exculpate the officer and the police department generally. As the majority put it:

      [1] Officer Fackrell, was "at most ***negligent***";

      [2] The illegality of the stop was a ***"good-faith mistake"***; and

      [3] There was "no indication that [the] unlawful stop was part of any ***systemic or recurrent police misconduct."***

      So in theory, a person illegally stopped (call her D) in a post-*Strieff* case might convince the court that the taint in her own case should *not* be deemed to have been purged, if she can show that one or more of these three factual findings made in *Strieff* cannot be made about the police conduct in her own case.

      (1) **Hard showing to make:** But in the typical illegal-stop scenario, it will be very ***difficult*** for D to make any of these showings. Even where there *was* the sort of misconduct that the *Strieff* majority found not to have existed there, how would D — from her position outside the police department — *know about it* and be able to *prove* it?

      (2) **Sotomayor's dissent:** Sotomayor's dissent hints at the problems a post-*Strieff* defendant would face; she writes that the majority "does [not] offer guidance for ***how a defendant can prove that his arrest was the result of 'widespread' misconduct."*** It seems clear that such a proof of widespread police misconduct would take statistical and discovery resources far beyond those of a typical criminal defendant.

D. **Particular scenarios:** In Pars. (E)-(J) below, we focus on particular scenarios that pose the issue of whether the taint of an original police illegality has been purged by the time the police eventually uncover evidence that they would likely not have found but for the illegality. These scenarios are:

[1] The police illegality leads the police to ***become aware of a new suspect.*** (Par. E, p. 336).

[2] The police are investigating one crime, and an illegal action they commit leads them to evidence of a ***completely different crime***. (Par. F, p. 336).

[3] The police's illegal conduct versus D leads to their discovery of the ***existence of witnesses*** who can give testimony against D. (Par. G, p. 337).

[4] An illegal police action against D (e.g., an improper arrest or search) leads the police to obtain a ***confession*** from D that he probably would not have made absent the illegality. (Par. H, p. 337).

[5] There are ***two successive confessions*** (by the same suspect), and the issue is whether the second confession is tainted by the fact that the first one was illegally obtained. (*Example:* D is legally arrested, is given insufficient *Miranda* warnings, confesses, is then given adequate *Miranda* warnings, and confesses again. The first confession is inadmissible against D, but what about the second one: does the taint from the first one taint the second one?) (Par. I, p. 338).

[6] A confession obtained in violation of *Miranda* furnishes the police with ***leads to additional evidence***, such as ***physical evidence*** (e.g., stolen property, or a murder weapon) or to ***witnesses***, and the issue is whether the additional evidence is tainted. (Par. J, p. 342).

E. Illegality leading the police to focus on a particular suspect: In some cases, the illegal search, arrest, lineup, etc., will lead the police to ***become aware of a suspect*** whom they had not suspected previously. Although this first lead to the suspect may not itself be strong evidence against him, the police may end up getting good evidence against him solely because of their luck in being pointed toward him in the first place.

1. **Taint easily purged:** The Supreme Court has never decided a case involving this scenario. But in this situation in which an illegality leads the police to focus on a suspect, the lower courts have been quite ready to find that the ***full-scale investigation*** of the suspect ***purged the taint*** of the original illegality and of the tip stemming from it. As one court expressed it, an unconstitutional action that only induces the police to "focus" on one particular person should not in effect grant him "immunity from prosecution." *Gissendanner v. Wainwright*, 482 F.2d 1293 (5th Cir. 1973).

F. Leads to different crime: Suppose the police are investigating one crime, and an illegal action they commit leads them to evidence of a ***completely different crime***. As in the situation of the "discovered suspect" discussed above, the Supreme Court has never decided a case posing the issue, but the lower courts have been quite willing to find the taint of the original illegality ***purged***.

> **Example:** The police return to the scene of an illegal arrest, and during their search for co-conspirators on the premises, notice a newspaper clipping referring to a completely separate crime. They conduct an investigation into the crime described in the clipping, and obtain evidence against a suspect, who is then tried.
>
> *Held*, the connection between this evidence and the original arrest is "so attenuated as to dissipate the taint." *Gregory v. U.S.*, 231 F.2d 258 (D.C. Cir. 1956).

G. Leads to witnesses: One of the fruits of police illegality may be the discovery of the ***existence of witnesses*** who can give testimony against the defendant. In determining whether such "witness leads" are tainted, The main Supreme Court case on the subject suggests that the taint of the illegality will often be found to be ***purged*** by the time the police and prosecution are ready to use the witness testimony, so that the testimony can be used at trial.

1. ***Ceccolini* case:** That Supreme Court case allowing use of an illegally-obtained witness lead is ***U.S. v. Ceccolini***, 435 U.S. 268 (1978).

   a. **Facts of *Ceccolini:*** In *Ceccolini*, a policeman happened to be in the defendant's flower shop, talking to a friend, when he noticed an envelope with money sticking out of it lying on the cash register. He picked it up, looked inside it, and discovered not only money but also policy slips. He then asked his friend, Hennessey, whom the envelope belonged to. She said that it was the defendant's and that he had asked her to give it to someone. The policeman eventually passed this information along to the FBI. An FBI agent went to Hennessey's house, where she agreed to describe these events. She later testified as to the events, leading to the defendant's perjury conviction.

   b. **Holding:** The Supreme Court held that, although the policeman's search of the envelope was clearly illegal, and although the path from this search to Hennessey's testimony was "straight and uninterrupted," the taint was nonetheless ***attenuated***, and Hennessey's testimony therefore admissible. The Court noted the general fact that witnesses often ***voluntarily come forward*** to testify, and that therefore, there is generally less of an incentive for police to make an illegal search for such witnesses, as opposed to a search for physical evidence. The Court also relied on the fact that ***four months elapsed*** between the search and the interview by the FBI agent, the fact that there was no coercion of the witness, and the absence of any evidence that the policeman, in making his original illegal search, was motivated by the desire to find a witness to or even evidence of crime.

      i. **Summary:** The Court summed up its holding by stating that "the exclusionary rule should be invoked with ***much greater reluctance*** where the claim is based on a causal relationship between a constitutional violation and the discovery of a ***live witness*** than when a similar claim is advanced to support suppression of an inanimate object."

H. Confessions as tainted fruit: In many cases, the most devastating direct or indirect product of police illegality is a ***confession***. Most frequently, such a confession will be the result of an illegal arrest; but it may also result from an illegal search of a suspect's premises, or from confronting the suspect with the results of an illegal wiretap or lineup identification.

1. **Confessions in *Wong Sun:*** *Wong Sun*, *supra*, p. 330, furnishes an example both of (1) a confession (by Toy) so closely related to police illegality that it is itself tainted, as well as (2) a confession (by Wong Sun) sufficiently separated from illegality by intervening factors as to be "purged" of its taint. The two confessions in *Wong Sun* reflect almost opposite ends of the spectrum of "taintedness." [6]

   a. **Toy's confession:** Toy's confession, which followed immediately after the police's illegal entry into his house and their handcuffing of him, was so closely tied to the illegal acts that it was "fruit of the poisonous tree." The presence of "oppressive circumstances" made it easier for the Court to find the confession tainted, but in footnote 12 the Court implied that the taint might have been fatal even had the police behaved in a less threatening manner; the closeness in time and place between the illegal entry and the confession might have been enough to render the confession an inadmissible fruit of the illegal entry.

b. Wong Sun's confession: Wong Sun's confession, however, although it followed his illegal arrest, was given (1) after he had been ***free on his own recognizance for several days,*** (2) after he had ***returned voluntarily*** to the Narcotics Bureau offices for interrogation, and (3) after he had been ***warned of his right to a lawyer*** and to remain silent. These three facts, taken together, were more than adequate to "purge the taint" of Wong Sun's illegal arrest, the Court held.

2. *Brown v. Illinois:* The two confessions in *Wong Sun*, because each was so obviously at one end or the other of the spectrum of "taintedness," furnished relatively little guidance to courts faced with the necessity of deciding whether a particular confession was the inadmissible fruit of a poisonous tree. But the facts of a post-*Wong Sun* case, *Brown v. Illinois* (*supra*, p. 331), pose a "confession as potentially poisonous fruit" situation that's closer to the dividing line between "taint purged" and "taint not purged" than either of the confessions in Wong Sun. In *Brown*, the Supreme Court set forth a three-factor test for determining the taintedness of a confession. There, if you'll recall, the Court found that the taint had ***not*** been purged as to either confession, so both were excluded.

3. Confession where arrest made with probable cause, but no arrest warrant: In the cases of "confessions as tainted fruit" that we've discussed so far, the confession was the fruit of an arrest made ***without probable cause***, and the confession was found to be tainted fruit from that arrest; in this situation, as we've seen, the court applies the poisonous-tree analysis and sometimes excludes the confession as poisoned fruit. Suppose, however, that the police arrest D ***with*** probable cause, but that the arrest is unconstitutional because it is made ***without an arrest warrant*** in a situation where a warrant is required (e.g., D is arrested in his house, and there are no exigent circumstances).

a. No "poisonous fruit" analysis at all: In this "probable cause but no arrest warrant" situation, the Supreme Court has ***refused*** to apply the "fruit of the poisonous tree" analysis to any resulting confession, and has held that a voluntary confession given by D in the station-house after the warrantless arrest ***automatically escapes exclusion.*** *New York v. Harris*, 495 U.S. 14 (1990).

I. Second confession as fruit of the first: Sometimes a case involves ***two successive confessions*** (by the same suspect); suppose that the only issue regarding the second confession is whether it is tainted by an ***earlier confession*** that is not the fruit of any still-earlier illegality, but that is itself an illegally-obtained "poisonous tree." This question may arise, for instance, where the defendant is ***legally arrested***, is given insufficient *Miranda* warnings, confesses, is then given adequate *Miranda* warnings, and confesses again. The second confession is, if con-

---

6. *Wong Sun* was decided well before the Court in *Brown v. Illinois*, *supra*, p. 331, adopted its current three-factor test for deciding when a taint of illegality has been purged. But it's likely that each confession would be decided the same way today, under the three-factor test, as it was decided in *Wong Sun*.

sidered by itself, valid; but is it nonetheless the tainted fruit of the earlier, unlawful, confession?

As the result of a pair of cases separated by 19 years, the answer is ***"not usually."*** More specifically:

> The second confession will not be deemed tainted as long as it was ***"voluntarily made,"*** and the Court will ***presume*** that the second confession is indeed voluntary if made after warnings, even though that confession followed an earlier unwarned confession. (*Oregon v. Elstad, infra*)
>
> The second confession is more likely to be deemed to be voluntarily made if the underlying circumstances do not make that second confession a ***mere continuation*** of the first. (So, for instance, the second is more likely to be found voluntary if the two were meaningfully ***separated*** by ***time, place, or interrogator***, or if it was made clear to the suspect that the first, unwarned, confession would not be admissible.) (*Elstad*)
>
> The second confession is less likely to be deemed tainted if the failure to warn prior to the first confession was the result of an ***inadvertent mistake*** by the police (*Elstad*)
>
> But where the police follow an ***intentional "two-step" practice*** of eliciting an unwarned confession, then immediately giving a warning under circumstances that lead the suspect to believe that ***even the already-made confession can be used against him*** (so that the suspect sees no reason not to repeat the confession after the warning), the second confession *will* probably be deemed involuntary and thus ***tainted*** (*Missouri v. Seibert, infra*).

1. ***Elstad*** **rejects the general "cat out of the bag" theory:** The first, and more general, of the two cases on sequential confessions was ***Oregon v. Elstad***, 470 U.S. 298 (1985). There, the Court announced that instead of presuming that the second confession is tainted fruit of the first, *Miranda*-less, confession, the Court would analyze solely whether the second confession was ***"knowingly and voluntarily made."*** If the confession (or other statement) satisfied this "knowingly and voluntarily made" standard, ***it would not be invalidated merely because there was a prior, illegally-obtained confession having the same substance.***

   a. **Facts:** In *Elstad*, D was a young suspect who was arrested at his house on a burglary charge. In a brief encounter in D's living room, an officer told D that he thought D had been involved in a burglary, and D acknowledged that he had been at the scene. This exchange occurred without *Miranda* warnings, apparently because the officer did not think that D was in custody at that moment. D was then taken to the police station, given *Miranda* warnings, and subjected to a much more thorough interrogation, after which he confessed. The issue was whether this second confession was tainted fruit from the earlier questioning that should have been Mirandized but wasn't.

   b. **Second confession held admissible:** By a 6-3 vote, the Court held that D's second confession was ***admissible***, because ***no causal connection*** between the first and second confessions had been demonstrated.

   c. **"Cat out of the bag" theory rejected:** In upholding the admissibility of the second confession, the *Elstad* Court ***rejected*** what might be called the ***"cat out of the bag"*** theory. Under this theory, once the suspect has confessed without having received the *Miranda* warnings to which he was entitled, this unwarned confession is likely to have a psychologically corrosive effect on his decision whether to remain silent at the second interrogation — he may feel that since he has already "let the cat out of the bag," there is little to be gained by remaining silent the second time. To the *Elstad* majority, "the causal connection between any psychological disadvantage created by [a suspect's] admission and his ultimate decision to cooperate is ***speculative and attenuated*** at best. It is difficult to tell with certainty what motivates a suspect to speak. ..."

i. **No duty to warn of prior statement's inadmissibility:** In fact, the *Elstad* majority even declined to impose a requirement (imposed by some lower courts and advocated by the dissenters) that the suspect be ***told*** that his earlier unwarned confession may turn out not to be admissible.

d. **No need for passage of time or intervening events:** Almost no one proposed that once an unwarned confession is made, no subsequent warned confession should be admitted. Rather, lower courts had often held (and the dissent urged) that the two confessions must be separated by either the ***passage of a significant amount of time***, or some kind of break in the chain of events, before the second, warned, confession could be deemed free of taint. But the *Elstad* majority ***rejected*** any such requirement. All that matters, under *Elstad*, is whether the second statement was ***"voluntarily made."*** Furthermore, not only will there not be a presumption that the second statement was involuntary, there will apparently be a presumption of ***exactly the opposite:*** "The fact that a suspect chooses to speak after being informed of his rights is, of course, ***highly probative.***"

e. **Brennan's dissent:** Three Justices (Brennan, Marshall, and Stevens) dissented in *Elstad*. The principal dissent, authored by Justice Brennan, contended that the decision was a "potentially crippling blow to *Miranda* and the ability of courts to safeguard the rights of persons accused of crime." Brennan argued that "the hopeless feeling of an accused that he has nothing to lose by repeating his confession" can vitiate the voluntariness of the subsequent confession.

i. **Incentives:** Brennan believed that the majority's holding would furnish the police with a substantial ***incentive to avoid giving Miranda*** warnings.

2. **Intentional "two-step" approach struck down (*Seibert*):** Justice Brennan's warning in *Elstad* that the majority's approach would give the police a large incentive to intentionally solicit unwarned confessions followed by warned ones turned out to be ***prescient***. Many police departments in the years after *Elstad* adopted a ***conscious "two step" approach*** to interrogation, in which the police would ***intentionally procure an unwarned*** (and inadmissible) confession, give *Miranda* warnings, and then hope to get the suspect to give an (admissible) ***confirmation of what he had already confessed to.*** But in a 2004 decision, the Court by a 5-4 vote — and without five votes for any single rationale — held that this two-step approach will at least sometimes lead to a ***tainted, and inadmissible, second confession***. ***Missouri v. Seibert***, 542 U.S. 600 (2004).

a. **Facts:** In *Seibert*, D was afraid of being prosecuted for neglect when her son Jonathan, who had cerebral palsy, died in his sleep. In D's presence, two of her other sons, teenagers, devised a plan to conceal Jonathan's death by burning his body while burning the family's mobile home. They planned to leave Donald, a mentally ill teenager living with the family, in the mobile home during the burning, so that it would not appear that Jonathan had been unattended at his death. One of D's sons set the fire together with a friend, and Donald died in it.

i. **First questioning of D:** Five days after the fire, the police awakened D at 3:00 a.m. at a hospital. The arresting officer intentionally refrained from giving D Miranda warnings. D was then transported to the police station, where a different officer, Hanrahan, questioned her for 30 or 40 minutes without giving her *Miranda* warnings. He pressed D to admit that the plan had always been for Donald to die in the fire. D made that admission. Hanrahan then gave D a 20-minute break, turned on a tape recorder, gave D *Miranda* warnings, and tried to get her to repeat her earlier (unwarned) statement that Donald was to die in his sleep in the fire. For a while, D resisted repeating this statement. But finally, in answer to Hanrahan's statement "Didn't you tell me that [Donald] was supposed to die in his sleep?" D answered "yes." D's answer was admitted against her in a prosecution for Donald's murder, and she was convicted.

ii. **Conscious decision to delay warnings:** At a suppression hearing before D's trial, Hanrahan testified he had made a ***"conscious decision"*** to withhold *Miranda* warnings until he got favorable information. He did this pursuant to an interrogation technique he had been taught, under which he would "question first, then give the warnings, and then repeat the question 'until I get the answer that she's already provided once'."

b. **Plurality strikes on objective grounds:** By a 5-4 vote, the Court decided that D's second confession here ***should not have been admitted.*** However, the five justices in the majority could not agree on a rationale. A four-justice plurality, in an opinion by Justice Souter, applied an ***"objective"*** analysis, from ***D's point of view:*** under the circumstances here, a reasonable person in D's position "would ***not have understood*** [the *Miranda* warnings] to convey a message that [D] ***retained a choice*** about continuing to talk."

i. **Conclusion:** Souter concluded that D's post-warning statements here were inadmissible "because the question-first tactic effectively threatens to ***thwart Miranda's purpose*** of ***reducing the risk that a coerced confession would be admitted***, and because the facts here do not reasonably support a conclusion that the warnings given could have ***served their purpose***[.]"

c. **Fifth vote from Kennedy:** The decisive fifth vote to exclude D's post-warning statements came from Justice Kennedy. Kennedy concurred in the result, but not in the plurality's reasoning.

i. **Inadvertent failure:** Kennedy voted for a ***subjective*** approach, in which the intent of the interrogating officer will make the difference: If the failure to warn initially is inadvertent (as in *Elstad*), then there will be a presumption that there is no causal relationship between the first (unwarned) confession and the second (warned) one. But if the initial failure to warn is part of a ***"calculated [technique]*** to undermine the *Miranda* warning," then the post-warning statements relating to the same subject matter as the pre-warning interrogation must be excluded, he said, "unless corrective measures are taken" before the post-warning statement is made. (For instance, Kennedy said, either a ***"substantial break in time and circumstances"*** between the two interrogations, or "an additional ***warning*** that ***explains the likely inadmissibility*** of the ***pre-warning*** custodial statement," might suffice as a "curative measure.")

d. **Dissent:** Four Justices (O'Connor, joined by Chief Justice Rehnquist and Justices Scalia and Thomas) ***dissented*** in *Seibert*. O'Connor agreed with the plurality that an objective standard — one not dependent upon the interrogating officer's state of mind — should be applied. (Thus she rejected Kennedy's subjective "intent to undermine *Miranda*" approach.)

   i. **"Voluntariness under all the circumstances":** But she believed that the plurality gave too little deference to *Elstad*. For O'Connor, assuming that the first confession was unwarned and thus inadmissible, *Elstad* supplied the correct test — essentially ***"voluntariness under all the circumstances"*** — for determining whether the "taint" of that first confession was dissipated by the time of the second (warned) confession.

   ii. **Would leave issue to lower court on remand:** O'Connor would have left it to the Missouri courts to apply the *Elstad* test on remand. But she indicated that the fact that Officer Hanrahan referred to D's unwarned statement during the second part of the interrogation — "Didn't you tell me that [Donald] was supposed to die in his sleep?" — cut against a finding of voluntariness.

3. **Where we are now:** So as the result of the pairing of *Oregon v. Elstad* and *Missouri v. Seibert*, we are left with two main rules for cases involving both an initial unwarned and a subsequent warned confession:

   We have a general rule that where a pre-warning statement is followed by a post-warning statement, there will be a ***presumption*** that the giving of the warning has ***dissipated any taint*** from the earlier statement, making the post-warning statement admissible (*Elstad*); but

   We also have a possible exception: where the post-warning statement is a virtual ***continuation*** of the pre-warning one, and a reasonable person in the suspect's position might ***not have understood that the pre-warning statement was inadmissible***, the Court may conclude that the ***warnings were not effective***, in which case the post-warning statement will be excluded (*Seibert*).

J. **Confession as a "poisonous tree":** In many cases, a confession obtained in violation of *Miranda* furnishes the police with ***leads to additional evidence***, such as ***physical evidence*** (e.g., stolen property, or a murder weapon) or ***witnesses***. Until 2004, there had been substantial disagreement about the extent to which such additional evidence is tainted by being the product of an illegally-obtained confession.

But as the result of ***U.S. v. Patane***, 542 U.S. 630 (2004), it is now clear that such additional evidence will virtually ***never be treated as tainted fruit*** merely because that evidence derived from a non-Mirandized confession. By a 5-4 vote, the Court held in *Patane* that *Miranda* exists only to guard against violations of the suspect's Fifth Amendment right not to be coerced into ***testifying*** against himself, and that the admission of ***additional fruits*** of a non-Mirandized (but voluntary) confession — in that case, ***physical evidence*** — therefore ***cannot violate Miranda.***

1. **Facts:** In *Patane*, police acted on a tip that D, a convicted felon, illegally possessed a Glock pistol. They arrested D at his house for a different offense (violating a restraining order). One of the arresting officers, Detective Benner, tried to advise D of his *Miranda* rights, but before he could finish doing so, D interrupted and said that he knew those rights. Benner then asked D about the Glock, and D eventually told him that it was in D's bedroom, and gave Benner permission to retrieve it. (D seems not to have known that it was a felony for him to possess the gun.) D was charged with the federal crime of possessing a firearm by a convicted felon, and tried to have the gun suppressed as the tainted fruit of a confession obtained in violation of *Miranda*. The prosecution conceded that the confession itself could not have been admitted against D because the *Miranda* warnings were not completed; the only issue was whether D was correct in arguing that physical evidence such as the gun, when seized as a direct result of a confession given in violation of *Miranda*, should be excluded as fruit of the poisonous tree.

2. **5-4 vote allows admission:** Five members of the Court agreed that the gun should ***not be excluded***, although they did not agree on a single rationale.

   a. **Plurality opinion by Thomas:** A three-justice plurality, in an opinion by Justice Thomas, took a broad view of the problem, a view that would ***completely prevent the fruit-of-the-poisonous-tree doctrine of* Wong Sun *from <u>ever</u> being used to exclude a piece of evidence derived from a non-Mirandized confession.***

      i. **Concurrence by Kennedy:** The final two votes needed to admit the evidence came from a concurrence by Justice Kennedy, in which O'Connor joined. These two justices agreed with the central proposition of the three-justice plurality opinion: as long as what is being introduced is ***physical evidence*** deriving from a non-Mirandized confession, rather than the ***confession itself, exclusion of the evidence is not required***.

   b. **Dissent:** Four justices dissented in *Patane*, mainly in an opinion by Justice Souter (joined by Stevens and Ginsburg). Souter argued that the result in the case "adds an important ***inducement*** for interrogators to ***ignore***" *Miranda*. Souter conceded that there was a "price for excluding evidence[.]" But, he said, "the Fifth Amendment is worth a price, and in the absence of a very good reason, the logic of *Miranda* should be followed: a *Miranda* violation raises a presumption of coercion ... and the Fifth Amendment privilege against compelled self-incrimination ***extends to the exclusion of derivative evidence[.]"*** He concluded that "there is no way to read this case except as an ***unjustifiable invitation to law enforcement officers to flout Miranda*** when there may be physical evidence to be gained."

3. **Probable extension to third-party witness' testimony:** *Patane* clearly means that for a majority of the Court that decided that case, ***physical evidence*** deriving directly from a non-Mirandized confession will never be excludable as fruit of the poisonous tree, so long

as the confession is not coerced. But the logic of *Patane* should dictate a broader result, that fruit-of-the-poisonous-tree treatment should be denied for *any* evidence deriving from a *Miranda* violation, other than a confession by the non-Mirandized suspect himself. For example, the logic of the case seems to mean that ***third-party witness testimony*** that the police obtain only by virtue of a *Miranda* violation ***should not be excluded*** as fruit of the poisonous tree.

V. COLLATERAL USE EXCEPTIONS

A. Collateral use exceptions generally: All of the material above has concerned the prosecution's use of illegally-obtained evidence at the defendant's trial, as part of the prosecution's case-in-chief. There are, however, other contexts in which the admissibility of illegally-obtained evidence has arisen. A number of these will be considered below.

B. Impeachment at trial: In ***Harris v. N.Y.***, 401 U.S. 222 (1971) (also discussed *supra*, p. 277), the Supreme Court held that a defendant's confession, obtained in violation of *Miranda*, could be introduced to ***impeach the defendant's trial testimony***, even though it could not be used in the prosecution's direct case. Thus the exclusionary rule does not generally apply to the use for impeachment purposes of illegally-obtained confessions.

1. Statements made in direct testimony: *Harris* allowed the use of an illegally-obtained confession to impeach statements made by the defendant ***during his direct testimony*** only. The case thus did not present the question of whether such evidence could be used to impeach statements made by the defendant during ***cross-examination.***

a. Statements during cross-examination: Because *Harris* did not involve impeachment of statements made during cross-examination, many lower courts felt that admission of illegal evidence for this purpose was prohibited by the Supreme Court's earlier decision in *Agnello v. U.S.*, 269 U.S. 20 (1925). But in ***U.S. v. Havens***, 446 U.S. 620 (1980), the Supreme Court held that the rationale of *Harris* ***permits use of illegally-obtained evidence*** to impeach even those statements that are made by the defendant only on ***cross-examination*** (and which are therefore elicited by the prosecution).

i. Facts: In *Havens*, D and one McLeroth (both lawyers!) were stopped by customs officials as they arrived in Miami after a flight from Lima, Peru. Both were searched; cocaine was found in several makeshift pockets sewn onto a tee-shirt McLeroth was wearing. In D's baggage, the officials found no drugs, but seized a tee-shirt from which pieces had been cut that matched the pieces that had been sewn into McLeroth's tee-shirt. At D's trial, in his direct testimony he simply denied being involved in smuggling on the trip in question; he did not testify at all as to the tee-shirt incident. On cross-examination, he was asked whether he had had anything to do with the sewing of the cotton swatches to make pockets on McLeroth's tee-shirt (which he denied) and whether he had a certain tee-shirt with missing swatches in his luggage when he came through customs (which he also denied). The prosecution then sought to introduce the tee-shirt with the missing pieces to impeach D's testimony; the trial court admitted this for the limited purpose of impeaching D's credibility.

ii. **Supreme Court approves:** The Supreme Court upheld the admission of the tee-shirt for impeachment purposes. The Court noted that the questions on the tee-shirt "would have been suggested to a reasonably competent cross-examiner by [D's] direct testimony; they were not 'smuggled in'." The rationale of *Harris* and *Oregon v. Hass*, *infra*, p. 345, that "truth is a fundamental goal of our legal system . . . [and] that when defendants testify, they must testify truthfully or suffer the consequences," is just as applicable to statements made on cross-examination as it is to those made on direct testimony.

iii. **Dissent:** Four Justices (Brennan, Marshall, Stewart, and Stevens) dissented. The dissent stressed that there was a major difference between allowing impeachment of direct testimony and that of testimony made on cross-examination. If impeachment were allowed only of statements made on direct testimony, defense counsel could avoid admission of particular illegally seized evidence or confessions by foregoing certain areas of questioning. But when impeachment of statements made on cross-examination is allowed, this "passes control of the [*Harris* impeachment] exception to the government, since the prosecutor can lay the predicate for admitting otherwise suppressible evidence with his own questioning." Since counsel is usually given substantial latitude in cross-examining opposing witnesses, the majority's holding "allows even the moderately talented prosecutor to 'work in' . . . evidence on cross-examination . . . as it would in its case in chief . . . " To avoid this consequence, the defendant will be compelled to forego testifying at all on his own behalf.

2. ***Harris* extended:** The use of illegally-obtained confessions for impeachment purposes was reaffirmed, and even extended, in *Oregon v. Hass*, 420 U.S. 714 (1975). Whereas in *Harris* the defendant had not been given his *Miranda* warnings at all, in *Hass* he received his warnings, ***asked for a lawyer***, and was ***questioned before the lawyer was provided***. The majority held that his confession could be used to impeach his testimony, as in *Harris*. The dissent (Brennan and Marshall) contended that this use was even worse than in *Harris* — once the warnings are given and a lawyer is requested, the dissent said, the police have almost nothing to lose by continuing their questioning, since they know that as soon as the lawyer arrives, he will almost certainly advise his client to remain silent, and obviously a confession usable for impeachment purposes is better than no confession at all.

3. **Non-confession evidence:** The *Harris/Havens* rule allows impeachment use not only of illegally-obtained confessions, but also of evidence obtained through any kind of constitutional violation. Thus in *Havens*, the evidence was an item (the tee-shirt) seized in an illegal search.

4. **Use of silence for impeachment:** Suppose that the prosecution wishes to introduce for impeachment purposes not a prior statement of the defendant, but rather the fact that the defendant ***remained silent*** when illegally arrested or questioned. Does *Harris* apply to permit the prosecution to introduce the fact of the defendant's silence?

a. ***Doyle:*** The Supreme Court held in ***Doyle v. Ohio***, 426 U.S. 610 (1976), that the prosecution may ***not***, even in cross-examination, constitutionally elicit the fact that the defendant remained silent during custodial questioning. In *Doyle*, the required *Miranda* warnings had been given and the arrest was legal; presumably *a fortiori* the accused's silence could not be used to impeach him where the arrest or questioning was illegal. (But if the prosecution asks, "Did you keep silent when you were arrested and questioned?" and the defense ***successfully objects*** to the question, there is no violation of *Doyle* because there has been no "use" of the fact of the accused's silence. See *Greer v. Miller*, 483 U.S. 756 (1987)

Note: For more about the prosecution's right to comment on the fact that the defendant remained silent at some earlier time, see *supra*, pp. 279-283.

5. **Impeachment of defense witnesses:** *Harris* allows the prosecution to use illegally-obtained evidence to impeach the defendant. But illegally-obtained evidence may ***not*** be used to impeach the testimony of ***defense witnesses*** other than the defendant himself. The Supreme Court so held in ***James v. Illinois***, 493 U.S. 307 (1990), a 5-4 decision.

   a. **Facts:** In *James*, D, a murder suspect, told police (without *Miranda* warnings) that on the day of the murder his hair had been reddish-brown and slicked-back, and that the next day he had had it dyed black and curled. At trial, D did not testify, but called as a witness W, a family friend. W testified that D's hair had been black on the day of the shooting. (Witnesses for the prosecution testified that the murderer had "reddish" slicked-back hair.) The prosecution impeached W's testimony by introducing D's police statement.

   b. **Holding:** A majority of the Court held that this impeachment should ***not*** have been allowed. The main reason cited by the majority was that allowing impeachment of defense witnesses would have a chilling effect on a defendant's ability to present his defense: a defendant would have to worry both that hostile witnesses called by him might willingly invite impeachment, and that friendly witnesses might through simple carelessness subject themselves to impeachment. Also, whereas the defendant himself rarely fears a perjury prosecution (the substantive charge against him is usually much more frightening) a witness other than the defendant will normally fear a prosecution for perjury, so the need to deter perjured testimony is less than where the witness is the defendant himself.

   c. **Dissent:** Four dissenters in *James* (led by Justice Kennedy) argued that tainted evidence should be usable to impeach defense witnesses. The majority rule, the dissenters argued, "grants the defense side in a criminal case broad immunity to introduce whatever false testimony it can produce from the mouth of a friendly witness."

6. **Use of statements compelled under immunity:** Where testimony before a ***grand jury*** is compelled by a grant of immunity, that testimony may not be used even to impeach statements made by the defendant at a subsequent trial. In *New Jersey v. Portash*, 440 U.S. 450 (1979), the Court held that *Harris* and *Hass* did not apply to this situation; in those cases, the statements involved were not coerced or involuntary. Here, by contrast, since the testimony was given in response to a grant of immunity, it was coerced; otherwise, the defendant could have been sent to jail for contempt of court. The fact that the testimony given before the grand jury may have been as reliable as a voluntary confession made to police is irrelevant.

C. **Grand jury testimony:** In ***U.S. v. Calandra***, 414 U.S. 338 (1974), the Court held that a ***grand jury witness cannot refuse*** to answer questions on the ground that they were based on evidence which had been illegally seized. The majority stressed that the deterrence function of the exclusionary rule would not be furthered by barring evidence which could not be used at trial; the dissent (Brennan, Douglas and Marshall) argued that to allow the indirect use of the evidence to compel testimony "thwarts [the witness's] Fourth Amendment protection and 'entangles the courts in the illegal acts of Government agents' — consequences that *Silverthorne* (*supra*, p. 324) condemned as intolerable."

1. **Extent of holding:** The *Calandra* Court noted that "our conclusion necessarily controls both the fruits of an unlawful search and seizure and any question or evidence derived therefrom." Thus the prosecution may present to the grand jury any evidence regardless of the legality of the means by which it was seized, and the grand jury may question the witness based on the illegally-obtained material.

2. **Fifth Amendment:** Recall, however, that the ***Fifth Amendment protection against self-incrimination*** applies to grand jury witnesses (*supra*, p. 276.) The defendant in *Calandra* did not have the Fifth Amendment claim available to him, since he had been granted transactional immunity (*supra*, p. 277.)

    Note: Observe that *Calandra* significantly cuts back the holding in *Silverthorne*, *supra*, p. 324, which was one of the first cases to bar the indirect fruits of illegally-obtained evidence. The *Calandra* Court distinguished *Silverthorne*, chiefly on the grounds that there the grand jury had already indicted the defendants, permitting them to "invoke the exclusionary rule on the basis of their status as criminal defendants."

D. **Other contexts:** The applicability of the exclusionary rule has arisen in several other contexts. These include sentencing, parole hearings, juvenile proceedings, and deportation proceedings.

1. **General principle:** In all of these collateral contexts, the determination of whether the rule should apply must be made by "weigh[ing] the likely ***social benefits*** of [exclusion] against the likely ***costs***." *U.S. v. Janis*, 428 U.S. 433 (1976). On the "benefits" side, the principal, and perhaps even sole, function of the rule (in the present Court's view) is to "deter future unlawful police conduct." On the "costs" side, there are generally two related harms: (1) the loss of evidence which is often probative; and (2) less accurate, or at the very least more cumbersome, adjudications. *Id.*

2. **Sentencing:** Most courts have held that the exclusionary rule does not apply to bar consideration of illegally-obtained evidence for purposes of ***sentencing*** a convicted defendant. (See Nutshell, p. 286). But if the evidence is obtained from a special investigation made solely for the purpose of enhancing the possibility of a heavy sentence, the exclusionary rule may apply. See, e.g., *U.S. v. Schipani*, 315 F. Supp. 253 (E.D.N.Y. 1970). Also, the courts may be unwilling to allow the use of ***coerced confessions*** for sentencing purposes, since such confessions are inherently unreliable and their introduction at the sentencing stage may in itself violate the privilege against self-incrimination.

3. **Parole revocation hearings:** The exclusionary rule will ***not*** be applied to evidence used in ***parole revocation proceedings.*** In *Pennsylvania Board of Probation v. Scott*, 524 U.S. 357 (1998), the Court (by a 6-3 vote) reasoned that application of the exclusionary rule would "both hinder the functioning of state parole systems and alter the traditionally flexible administrative nature of parole revocation proceedings."

4. **Juvenile proceedings:** Most lower courts have applied the exclusionary rule in ***juvenile proceedings which may lead to institutional commitment***. These courts have based their exclusion of unlawfully-obtained evidence on *In re Gault*, 387 U.S. 1 (1967), which held several constitutional rights (e.g., the right against self-incrimination and the right to counsel) applicable in such juvenile proceedings.

5. **Deportation proceedings:** The exclusionary rule does ***not*** apply where the illegally-obtained evidence is sought to be used in ***deportation*** proceedings. The Supreme Court so concluded in *INS v. Lopez-Mendoza*, 468 U.S. 1032 (1984).

VI. OTHER EXCEPTIONS – THE "GOOD FAITH WARRANT" AND "KNOCK-AND-ANNOUNCE VIOLATION" EXCEPTIONS

A. **Exceptions generally:** We now examine two additional exceptions to the exclusionary rule: (1) an exception for the fruits of a search issued pursuant to an otherwise-proper search or arrest warrant applied for in ***"good faith"*** that turns out not to be supported by probable cause; and (2) an exception for the fruits resulting from an entry into a dwelling where the police were required to ***"knock and announce"*** themselves and failed to do so.

B. **The "good faith warrant" exception:** Prior to 1984, the exclusionary rule was found inapplicable in a significant number of contexts, many of them summarized above. These included the grand jury context, impeachment of the defendant's statements at the criminal trial, situations where the "taint" was deemed "purged," and a number of others. But it remained the case that if evidence was obtained in violation of the defendant's rights, that evidence could not be introduced at the defendant's criminal trial as part of the prosecution's ***case-in-chief***. Then, in 1984, in the most dramatic development in criminal procedure in many years, even this previously inviolate principle was abandoned by the Burger Court, in favor of what can loosely be described as a limited ***"good faith" exception*** to the exclusionary rule.

1. ***Leon*** **case:** The exception was originally formulated in ***U.S. v. Leon***, 468 U.S. 897 (1984), a 6-3 decision. As articulated in *Leon*, the exception was fairly limited: the exclusionary rule was modified "so as not to bar the use in the prosecution's ***case-in-chief*** of evidence obtained by officers acting in ***reasonable reliance*** on a ***search warrant*** issued by a detached and neutral magistrate but ultimately found to be ***unsupported by probable cause***." (But the exception has been extended to cover the situation where the police rely on what they think is an outstanding *arrest* warrant that is not in fact outstanding; see *Arizona v. Evans*, *infra*, p. 356.)

   a. **Facts:** In *Leon*, the police, in preparing an affidavit to obtain a search warrant, relied on both information from a confidential informant as well as their own investigations. A facially-valid warrant was issued, and several premises were searched pursuant to it, yielding evidence of various narcotics violations. The two lower courts reviewing the case concluded that the police affidavit had not established probable cause (both because it relied on stale information and because it did not establish the informant's credibility under the then-applicable two-pronged test, *supra*, p. 57). The Supreme Court could have reviewed the lower courts' finding that there was no probable cause, and might well have concluded that the new rule of *Illinois v. Gates*, *supra*, p. 57

(which relaxed the standards for determining probable cause in cases involving informants) meant that the warrant was valid. Instead, it assumed that there was no probable cause, and went on to formulate its new "good faith" exception to the exclusionary rule.

b. Not constitutionally-based: The majority's opinion began by asserting that, in search and seizure cases, the exclusionary rule is ***not required by the Fourth Amendment*** (or by any other constitutional provision). The rule is a "judicially created remedy, [not] a personal constitutional right of the person aggrieved." Once an illegal search or seizure takes place, the Fourth Amendment violation is "fully accomplished," and use of the fruits of that search or seizure at trial "work[s] no new Fourth Amendment wrong."

c. Deterrent effect: The majority then asserted that the sole function of the rule is to safeguard Fourth Amendment rights ***through its deterrent effect on the police***. In the Court's view, the rule is "designed to deter police misconduct rather than to punish the errors of judges and magistrates."

d. Cost/benefit analysis: Therefore, the majority believed, the decision whether to allow use in the prosecution's case-in-chief of "inherently trustworthy tangible evidence obtained in reliance on a search warrant issued by a detached and neutral magistrate that ultimately is found to be defective" should be based on a ***cost/benefits analysis.***

i. Costs: On the "costs" side of the ledger, there are "substantial social costs" exacted by the rule, namely, that "some guilty defendants may go free or receive reduced sentences. . . . "

ii. Benefits: By contrast, the "benefits" of the exclusionary rule are minor, at least where the police act in "objectively reasonable reliance" on a neutral magistrate's issuance of a warrant. The only possible benefits that the majority could see were a deterrent effect on the issuing judge or magistrate, and a deterrent effect on the police officer seeking the warrant. In the Court's view, neither effect could be major:

(1) Issuing magistrate: Issuing magistrates could not be deterred by the rule because they "are not adjuncts to the law enforcement team; as neutral judicial officers, they have no stake in the outcome of particular criminal prosecutions."

(2) Police officers: Nor could the police officer seeking the warrant be deterred by exclusion of the evidence, since by hypothesis the officer is acting in the "objectively reasonable belief that [his] conduct did not violate the Fourth Amendment." In the case of a warrant later found to be defective, the error will always be that of the magistrate, not the police officer, since it is up to the magistrate to determine whether the officer has articulated probable cause. Therefore, "[p]enalizing the officer for the magistrate's error, rather than his own, cannot logically contribute to the deterrence of Fourth Amendment violations."

e. **Development of Fourth Amendment law:** One of the arguments to which the majority felt compelled to respond was that the new "good faith" exception would ***freeze Fourth Amendment jurisprudence*** in its present state, because defendants would have no incentive to litigate Fourth Amendment claims as long as there was "objectively reasonable reliance" by the police on a warrant, and because courts would tend to decide the objectively-reasonable-reliance issue without ever reaching the issue of whether there had been a Fourth Amendment violation. The majority answered this argument by asserting that where the underlying constitutional issue is a significant one, the courts could and should decide the basic Fourth Amendment issue *before* turning to the good-faith issue.

f. **Exceptions:** The majority in *Leon* took pains to point out that its new good-faith exception did not mean that the exclusionary rule would be inapplicable wherever an officer obtains a warrant and abides by its terms. The Court foresaw several types of situations in which the officer ***will not have reasonable grounds to believe that the warrant was properly issued***, and in which the exclusionary rule will therefore still apply:

   i. **Misleading affidavit:** The exception will not apply if the officer who prepared the affidavit on which the warrant is based ***knows*** that the information in it is ***false***, or ***recklessly disregards*** its truth or falsity;

   ii. **"Rubber-stamping" magistrate:** Nor will the exception apply if the magistrate "wholly abandon[s] his judicial role." For instance, if the magistrate fails to take a "neutral and detached" stance, and instead becomes part of the investigation, the exception will not apply; the Court cited *Lo-Ji Sales* (*supra*, p. 62), in which the magistrate helped the police execute the search warrant, as an illustration of such non-neutral conduct.

   iii. **Inadequate affidavit:** The underlying affidavit may be "so lacking in indicia of probable cause as to render official belief in its existence entirely unreasonable." For instance, if the affidavit merely states, in a conclusory fashion, that the police have probable cause to believe that there is evidence of a particular crime at a particular place, and does not supply any of the facts on which that belief is based, it will not be reasonable for the officer to rely on the resulting warrant.

   iv. **Facially deficient warrant:** The warrant may be ***so facially deficient*** that the officers who execute it cannot reasonably presume it to be valid. For instance, the warrant might so completely fail to specify the items to be seized (a violation of the "particularity" clause of the Fourth Amendment) that reliance will be unreasonable. (But this exception will apparently not be read narrowly, since in a companion case to *Leon, Massachusetts v. Sheppard*, *infra*, the Court held that a warrant describing drugs rather than evidence of a murder could still be reasonably relied on, because the underlying affidavit correctly described the items to be searched for.)

g. ***Massachusetts v. Sheppard:*** The companion case to *Leon*, *Massachusetts v. Sheppard*, 468 U.S. 981 (1984), illustrates another facet of the "good-faith" exception. In that case, the police prepared an adequate affidavit showing probable cause to believe that evidence connecting the suspect with a murder would be found at the premises. Because the application was made on a Sunday, and the proper type of warrant form could not be found, the magistrate used a form appropriate for narcotics searches. The warrant therefore did not "list with particularity" the things to be seized. (However, the officers who did the searching were the ones who had prepared the affidavit, and therefore knew what the warrant was intended to cover; they in fact only seized evidence covered by the affidavit). The consequence of the new "good-faith" exception was that since the police had received assurances from the magistrate that he would amend the warrant form to reflect the fact that murder evidence rather than narcotics was involved, their reliance on the resulting warrant (which they did not inspect) was objectively reasonable. Therefore, the evidence was not to be excluded from trial.

h. **Dissents in *Leon*:** Three Justices bitterly dissented from the majority's decision in *Leon* to recognize the new "good-faith" exception. Justice Brennan's dissent was joined by Justice Marshall; Justice Stevens wrote a separate dissent (though he believed, for different reasons than the majority, that the evidence in the companion case of *Massachusetts v. Sheppard* should not be excluded).

i. **Brennan dissent:** Brennan's dissent disagreed with almost every proposition made by the majority. Among his arguments were the following:

   i. **Constitutional violation:** He disagreed that the exclusionary rule is merely a "judicially created remedy" rather than a constitutional imperative. In his view, the Fourth Amendment, like the rest of the Bill of Rights, "restrains the power of the government as a whole; it does not specify only a particular agency and exempt all others. The judiciary is responsible, no less than the executive, for ensuring that constitutional rights are respected." Brennan pointed out that the principal motive for most searches and seizures is precisely to ***obtain evidence to use in court***; therefore, "police and the courts cannot be regarded as constitutional strangers to each other. . . . " He also argued that only if the exclusionary rule were held to be directly required by the Fourth Amendment could the holding in *Mapp v. Ohio*, *supra*, p. 4 (that the Fourteenth Amendment requires that state courts exclude illegally-obtained evidence) be correct.

   ii. **Deterrence rationale rejected:** Therefore, Brennan rejected both the majority's assertion that deterrence is the principal function of the exclusionary rule, and its assertion that a cost-benefit analysis is appropriate. Furthermore, he contended, the fact that some criminals will go free is not a cost of the exclusionary rule, but rather, a cost ***of the Fourth Amendment itself***: "[S]ome criminals will go free not . . . 'because the constable has blundered' . . . but rather because official compliance with Fourth Amendment requirements makes it more difficult to catch criminals."

   iii. **Benefits outweigh costs:** Even accepting the majority's determination that the desirability of the "good-faith" exception should be determined by a cost-benefit analysis in which the benefit is "deterrence," Brennan disagreed that the costs of the status quo outweighed its benefits. On the costs side, he asserted, prosecutors rarely drop cases because of search and seizure problems. On the benefits side, he conceded that the police officers involved in any particular warrant request would not be deterred by application of the exclusionary rule to that very case, if the officers began with an objectively-reasonable belief in the constitutionality of their conduct. But he saw the deterrence rationale as having a much broader function than deterring the individual officers whose conduct is at issue in a particular prosecution; the chief deterrent function of the exclusionary rule "is its tendency to promote ***institutional compliance*** with Fourth Amendment requirements on the part of law enforcement agencies generally."

(1) **Explanation:** That is, Brennan argued, police departments ***nationally*** will better educate their officers in the requirements of the Fourth Amendment, and will adopt procedures that are more constitutional, if they know that the overall system is one in which unconstitutionally-obtained evidence may not be admitted. The new exception, Brennan feared, "will tend to put a premium on police ignorance of the law. . . . Police departments will be encouraged to train officers that if a warrant has simply been signed, it is reasonable, without more, to rely on it."

j. **Stevens' dissent:** Justice Stevens, too, dissented from the establishment of the new "good-faith" exception (though he agreed with the majority that in the companion case of *Massachusetts v. Sheppard*, *supra*, p. 350, the evidence was correctly admitted). Like Justice Brennan, Stevens believed that the majority's rule would weaken police observance of constitutional requirements, because it would "encourage . . . the police to seek a warrant even if they know the existence of probable cause is doubtful. . . ." Also, he observed, in any case in which the "good-faith" exception applied, the police would also be ***immune from civil damages*** (because "qualified" immunity applies where there is good faith); therefore, the result would be that in these situations there would be ***no remedy at all*** for what was by definition a violation of the defendant's constitutional rights. The Bill of Rights had been transformed into "an unenforced honor code that the police may follow in their discretion;" in fact, "Bill of ***Rights***" had now become a misnomer.

2. **Broadened to cover reliance on arrest warrant:** There is at least one ***additional context*** — beyond reliance on a search warrant — in which evidence seized in violation of the Fourth Amendment will be admissible due to the police's good-faith and reasonable belief that they are complying with that Amendment. If the police reasonably (but mistakenly) believe that there is an ***arrest warrant outstanding*** for a particular suspect and arrest him, evidence found during a ***search incident to this wrongful arrest*** will be ***admissible***, at least where any police misconduct consists of ***"nonrecurring and attenuated negligence."*** *Herring v. U.S.*, 129 S.Ct. 695 (2009). Two Supreme Court cases, one involving an error by a judicial system and the other by a police department, illustrate this good-faith-belief-in-an-arrest-warrant extension to the good-faith-reliance-on-a-search-warrant exception.

a. **Error by court system:** The first case involved an error by a ***court system***. In *Arizona v. Evans*, 514 U.S. 1 (1995), an officer spotted D committing a traffic infraction and stopped him. The officer entered D's name into a computer terminal in his patrol car, and received a message that there was an outstanding misdemeanor warrant for D's arrest. The officer therefore arrested D, saw D drop marijuana during the arrest, searched the car, and found marijuana in the car. It turned out that the arrest warrant had been quashed by a judge, but the court system had apparently negligently failed to inform the police computer operators of this fact.

i. **Good-faith exception:** The Supreme Court held in *Evans* that the "good faith" exception of *Leon* should be ***extended*** to this situation. The Court reasoned that the exclusionary rule was not constitutionally-required, and should apply only where it would help ***deter future Fourth Amendment violations***. Here, where the error was probably made by court personnel (who failed to report the quashing to the police) rather than by the police, it was very unlikely that applying the exclusionary rule would deter similar future violations: "[B]ecause court clerks are not adjuncts to the law enforcement team ... they have no stake in the outcome of particular criminal prosecutions," and so were unlikely to be deterred from similar failures by the threat that evidence would be excluded.

b. **Non-systemic negligence by police:** Then, in 2009, the Court ***extended*** the exception for good-faith reliance on an apparently-outstanding arrest warrant to a situation in which, unlike in *Evans*, the error was ***committed by the police department***. The majority reasoned that since the error was unintentional, and arose from "nonrecurring and attenuated negligence" by the police, suppressing the evidence would not have a deterrent effect on police misconduct, and therefore should not be required. The case was ***Herring v. U.S.***, 129 S.Ct. 695 (2009).

i. **Facts:** In *Herring*, D drove to the Coffee County Sheriff's Department to retrieve something from his impounded truck. Officer Anderson, knowing that D had had law enforcement issues before, checked with his own county and a nearby one to see whether there were any outstanding warrants for D's arrest. A clerk in neighboring Dale County reported to Anderson that her database showed that there was an active arrest warrant out for D. Anderson therefore stopped D as he drove out of the impound lot, arrested him on the Dale County warrant, searched his body, and found contraband on him. But it turned out that there *was* no outstanding Dale County warrant — the warrant had been recalled five months earlier, but this fact had not been entered by the Dale County Sherriff's Department into its database. Therefore, D moved to suppress the evidence as the fruit of a search incident to an illegal arrest.

ii. **Court refuses to suppress:** By 5-4 vote, the Supreme Court held that the "good faith exception" of *Leon* and *Evans* should be extended to this scenario, even though this time ***the error was made by the police*** rather than (as in *Evans*) the judicial system. In an opinion by Chief Justice Roberts, the Court again noted that the exclusionary rule existed only to deter official wrongdoing; "the abuses that gave rise to the exclusionary rule featured intentional conduct that was patently unconstitutional." An error arising from ***"nonrecurring and attenuated negligence,"*** Roberts said, should not trigger the exclusionary rule; the rule should be triggered only by "police conduct [that is] ***sufficiently deliberate that exclusion can meaningfully deter it,*** and ***sufficiently culpable*** that such deterrence is ***worth the price paid by the justice system***." The exclusionary rule serves to deter ***"delib-***

erate, reckless, or grossly negligent conduct, or in some instances ***recurring or systemic negligence***." The error here did not rise to that level, he said.

(1) Objective test: Roberts also stressed that when the courts assess deterrence and culpability, the analysis should be an *objective* one: " 'whether a reasonably well-trained [arresting] officer ***would have known that the search was illegal*** in light of all the circumstances.' " Thus, he said, "If the police have been shown to be ***reckless*** in maintaining a warrant system, or to have ***knowingly made false entries*** to lay the groundwork for future false arrests, exclusion would certainly be justified ... should such misconduct cause a Fourth Amendment violation. ... In a case where ***systemic errors*** were demonstrated, it might be ***reckless for officers to rely*** on an unreliable warrant system." But here, there was no evidence that errors in Dale County's warrant system were routine or widespread, so Anderson's reliance on the system was not unreasonable.

(2) Conclusion: Roberts summarized the Court's reasoning this way: "[W]hen police mistakes are the result of ***negligence*** such as that described here, ***rather than systemic error or reckless disregard of constitutional requirements,*** any marginal deterrence ***does not 'pay its way.'"***

iii. Dissent: The main dissent in *Herring* was by Justice Ginsburg (joined by Stevens, Souter and Breyer). Ginsburg rejected the majority's premise that the exclusionary rule will result in only marginal deterrence where the error is merely careless, rather than intentional or reckless. Ginsburg believed that just as the prospect of tort liability imposed by the doctrine of *respondeat superior* causes employers to ***supervise*** their employees' conduct more carefully, so the risk of exclusion of evidence would lead police departments, and the overseers of police computer systems, to supervise operations in a way that minimizes negligent data entry errors. And, she argued, by restricting the exclusionary rule to bookkeeping errors that are "deliberate or reckless," the majority was leaving Herring and others like him with ***no effective remedy*** for violations of their constitutional rights.

c. Summary: So *Evans* and *Herring*, taken together, establish a couple of principles:

If a police officer believes that there is a ***valid outstanding arrest warrant*** for a suspect, and the officer's belief is ***reasonable*** under all the circumstances as known to him, a search done pursuant to that arrest will not be invalidated even though there was really no warrant, and even though the incorrect information given to the officer was the result of ***negligence*** by the court system or by the police themselves.

The focus is on the facts ***as the arresting officer reasonably believed them to be.*** Thus if a reasonable person in the arresting officer's situation would have known that the warrant records were ***riddled with systemic errors***, the officer's reliance on the information that a warrant was outstanding might be "***reckless***" and thus not in good faith.

It will be very difficult for a suspect to ever get an arrest based on a warrant — and the consequent search incident to that arrest — thrown out on grounds that the warrant did not exist or was improperly issued. It won't be enough for the suspect to show that the incorrect information that the warrant existed was due to negligent data-entry or systems-maintenance by the police department itself. The suspect will apparently have to show two additional hard-to-prove things:

(a) that information in the police arrest-warrant system was either ***filled with deliberate falsehoods*** or so ***systemically riddled with negligent errors*** as to make the system's operation ***reckless***; and

(b) that the falsity or systemic error-proneness was so ***widely known*** within the department that the arresting officer could ***not reasonably have had confidence*** in the information he was given.

3. **Reliance on later-overruled legal principle:** *Leon* (*supra*, p. 348) and cases decided under it have usually involved what you can think of as "factual" mistakes. But there is another type of error that can also entitle the prosecution to make use of the *Leon* good-faith-error exception to the exclusionary rule: a reasonable error about ***what the appropriate legal rule is.*** Thus in ***Davis v. U.S.***, 131 S.Ct. 2419 (2011), the Court held by a 7-2 vote that when the police conduct a search that is legal under a binding legal precedent that is later ***overruled***, the police and prosecution get the benefit of *Leon*, so that the exclusionary rule will not be applied to keep out the results of the search.

   a. **Broader significance:** More broadly, *Davis* means that *Leon* will be applied (preventing application of the exclusionary rule) whenever the police obtain evidence "as a result of ***non-culpable, innocent police conduct.***" And police reliance on a binding judicial precedent that makes the search in question legal will be enough to meet this "non-culpable, innocent police conduct" standard, even though a later decision overrules that precedent before the case is concluded.

   b. **Facts of *Davis*:** The facts of *Davis* show how the overruling-of-precedent scenario can arise. In April, 2007, the police made a routine traffic stop of a car in which D was a passenger and X was the driver. Both were handcuffed and placed in the back of separate patrol cars. The police then searched the passenger compartment of the vehicle, and found a revolver inside the pocket of a jacket belonging to D. The incident happened in Alabama, which is part of the Eleventh Circuit.

      i. **Original law:** At the time of the search, most federal courts (including the Eleventh Circuit) interpreted *New York v. Belton* (*supra*, p. 101) to hold that in all situations in which the occupants of the vehicle are arrested, the police may then, incident to the arrest, search the passenger compartment, regardless of whether the arrestee was within reaching distance of the vehicle. So under Supreme Court precedent as it was interpreted in the states of the Eleventh Circuit in April, 2007, the search that found D's revolver was perfectly legal because it was incident to D's and X's arrest.

      ii. **Change in law:** But then, after D was convicted but while his appeal was still pending in front of the Eleventh Circuit, the Supreme Court decided *Arizona v. Gant* (*supra*, p. 101). The *Gant* decision clarified — and essentially overruled — *Belton*, by validating searches incident to the arrest of a vehicle's occupants *only* if the arrestee was within reaching distance of the vehicle during the arrest. So under

Gant's clarification of *Belton*, the search here was no longer a valid search incident to arrest, because at the time of the search D and X, being handcuffed in a police car, could not have gotten access to the passenger compartment.

iii. **Holding:** Thus the question posed by *Davis* was, if the police rely on a binding legal precedent that makes a search legal (here, that precedent was *Belton* and the Eleventh Circuit caselaw interpreting it to always allow a passenger-compartment search following a valid arrest of a vehicle's occupants), does the *Leon* good-faith exception apply if that precedent is later overruled, so that the search would be illegal? The Supreme Court found for the prosecution. The Court decided that the police and prosecution should ***get the benefit of the precedent on which they relied***, even though while the case was still pending the precedent turned out to be bad law.[7]

(1) **Rationale:** The *Davis* majority reasoned that the *Leon* good-faith exception should ***apply,*** "because suppression would do ***nothing to deter*** police misconduct in these circumstances, and because it would come at a ***high cost*** to both ***truth*** and the ***public safety.***" So police reliance on what turns out to be an erroneous — but is at the time, binding — appellate decision falls within the general rule that the good-faith exception applies to all ***"nonculpable, innocent police conduct."***

C. **Exception for "knock-and-announce" violations:** Under most circumstances, when the police wish to enter a private dwelling — for instance, to execute a search warrant — they are required by the Fourth Amendment to ***"knock and announce."*** That is, they are required to knock first, announce that they are the police, and give the occupant a chance to answer the door — only if the occupant does not answer within a reasonable time may the police enter forcefully. (See *supra*, p. 67, for more about the knock-and-announce requirement.) But as the result of a 2006 decision, even if the police violate the knock-and-announce rule, ***the exclusionary rule will not apply. Hudson v. Michigan***, 547 U.S. 586 (2006). Therefore, even if the defendant can show that certain evidence would not have been acquired by the police but for their failure to wait for the door to be answered, the evidence will still be admissible against him.

1. **Facts:** In *Hudson*, the police arrived at D's house with a warrant to search the house for drugs and firearms. They knocked and announced their presence, but then waited only a very short time — apparently just three to five seconds, not enough time for anyone to answer — before they entered forcibly. Once inside, they discovered cocaine and a firearm. D claimed that these fruits should be excluded on account of the police's failure to honor the knock-and-announce rule (which prior Supreme Court cases had concluded was imposed by the Fourth Amendment).

2. **D loses:** In one of the Roberts' Court's first decisions, a 5-4 majority decided that the exclusionary rule should ***not apply*** to knock-and-announce violations.

---

7. It doesn't seem as though the Court in *Davis* was saying that there must be actual police reliance — nothing in the record suggested that the arresting officer *knew* of the Eleventh Circuit precedent on the relevant point. It seems to be enough that the police took Action X, where under applicable precedent Action X was lawful, whether the police knew of the precedent or not. Cf. KLIK&K, 2011 Supp., pp. 56-57.

a. **Majority's rationale:** The majority, in an opinion by Justice Scalia, reasoned that the exclusionary rule should apply only "where its deterrence benefits outweigh its 'substantial social costs.' " In the case of the knock-and-announce rule, Scalia said, the social costs of applying the exclusionary rule would be large. For one thing, there would be a "constant flood" of litigated claims, because "the costs of entering this lottery would be small, but the jackpot enormous: suppression of all evidence, amounting in many cases to a get-out-of-jail-free card."

   i. **Small benefits:** On the other side of the scale, the deterrence benefits from applying the exclusionary rule here would be small, Scalia said. The resident whose rights had been violated could still bring a civil damage suit against the police under 42 U.S.C. § 1983 for violating his rights "under color of law," and the possibility of such a suit would provide (Scalia assumed) an effective deterrent, making the further deterrent of exclusion unnecessary. Also, Scalia said, the "increasing professionalism of police forces," and the increasing accountability of the police, lessened the need for the exclusionary rule as a deterrent in this scenario.

b. **Dissent:** The dissenters, in an opinion by Justice Breyer, argued that the deterrent effect of exclusion was in fact quite necessary for knock-and-announce violations, since the possibility of civil liability was not a good alternative deterrent. (Breyer pointed to the absence of evidence that any plaintiff had ever recovered more than nominal damages under § 1983 for a knock-and-announce violation.)

3. **Significance:** *Hudson* suggests that the Roberts Court will be even more hostile to the exclusionary rule — and more eager to find occasions to cut it back — than were the Burger or Rehnquist Courts.

VII. THE RIGHT TO SUE FOR CIVIL DAMAGES (§1983)

A. **Right to sue officers:** As we've just seen, many exclusionary-rule cases have involved the defendant's Fourth Amendment right to be free of unreasonable searches and seizures; the exclusionary rule will often give the defendant the remedy of having any evidence deriving from the unreasonable (and thus illegal) search or seizure ***excluded*** from the criminal case against him.

   But another important consequence of a Fourth Amendment violation is that the violation may entitle the suspect to bring a ***civil suit for money damages against the officer(s) who committed the illegal action.*** Therefore, we'll take a brief look at when the victim of such illegality may recover civil damages.

B. **§1983:** An important federal statute, ***42 U.S.C. §1983***, allows a person to bring a civil tort action against any person who, ***"under color of" state law,*** deprives the plaintiff of "any ***rights***, privileges, or immunities" ***secured by the federal Constitution or a federal statute.*** So the basic effect of §1983 is to permit a ***tort suit*** by anyone who is injured when a ***state or local official violates the plaintiff's federal rights,*** typically her constitutionally-guaranteed civil rights.

1. **Fourth Amendment violations:** Many §1983 actions allege that state or local officials have violated the Fourth Amendment's prohibition of ***unreasonable searches and seizures.***

   Example: Suppose that Officer, an officer in the City police force, arrests P without probable cause, and then brutally beats P in an unsuccessful attempt to extract a confession. P is likely to be able to recover tort damages from both Officer and City under §1983. Officer has acted "under color of" state law — that is, he has used his official position as justification for his acts. And Officer's conduct amounts to an "unreasonable seizure" under the Fourth Amendment. So Officer will have ***direct civil liability*** for violating §1983 (assuming the affirmative defense of qualified immunity, discussed below, p. 000, doesn't apply). Then, City is likely to be ***vicariously liable*** for Officer's §1983 violation, under the tort doctrine of *respondeat superior*.

2. **No remedy for *Miranda* violations (*Vega v. Tekoh*):** Now, suppose that the claim raised by a plaintiff in a §1983 suit is based not on a state official's violation of the plaintiff's Fourth Amendment's protection against unreasonable searches and seizures, but instead on the official's violation of ***plaintiff's Miranda rights.***[8] That is, suppose P's un*Mirandized* confession is improperly used against him at his criminal trial, but P is nonetheless ***acquitted***; may P then recover damages under §1983 for this violation of his *Miranda* rights? The Supreme Court answered ***"no"*** in ***Vega v. Tekoh***, 142 S.Ct. 2095 (2022).

   a. **Holding:** The vote in *Vega* was 6-3, with Justice Alito writing the majority opinion. He said that under the Court's prior decisions, the requirement of *Miranda* warnings is ***merely "prophylactic,"*** not required by the Fifth Amendment.

      i. **Cost/benefit:** Therefore, Alito said, since a violation of *Miranda* is not necessarily a violation of the Fifth Amendment, people whose *Miranda* rights have been violated ought to be allowed to recover under §1983 only if the ***"benefits*** [of allowing such a recovery] ***outweigh the costs."*** And, he concluded, the benefits of allowing a §1983 recovery for *Miranda* violations "would be ***slight***," whereas "the costs would be ***substantial***."[9]

   b. **Dissent:** The three liberal members of the Court ***dissented***, saying that *Miranda* is a ***"constitutional rule."*** Therefore, she continued, an officer who causes a suspect's un*Mirandized* confession to be improperly used against him at trial has deprived the suspect of a constitutional right under color of law, entitling the suspect to recover under §1983.

   c. **Constitutional significance of *Vega*:** So *Vega* means that a majority of the Roberts Court now believes that the right to *Miranda* warnings is ***not constitutionally required.*** That is, not all scenarios in which the police fail to give give a suspect required *Miranda* warnings will be a violation of the suspect's Fifth (or Sixth) Amendment rights.[10]

---

8. For our discussion of *Miranda* rights, see *supra*, p. 239.

9. Alito listed several costs of allowing such a recovery. For instance, "judicial economy" would be damaged because it would require a federal judge or jury to "adjudicate a factual question" (whether the civil plaintiff was in custody when questioned), even though that question "had already been decided by a state court."

3. **Implied right of action against federal officials:** Section 1983 by its terms allows only actions against ***state and local*** government officials, ***not federal ones.*** However, when a federal official violates a citizen's constitutional rights, the citizen is often permitted to bring a ***federal tort-like suit*** against the official. This occurs because the court finds that the citizen has an ***"implied private right of action"*** for violation of those constitutional rights.

   a. **Fourth Amendment violation:** For example, suppose that a federal law-enforcement official violates P's Fourth Amendment right to be free from unreasonable searches and seizures. The Supreme Court has held that P may then bring a federal civil damages suit against the official for this violation. See *Bivens v. Six Unknown Named Agents of FBI*, 403 U.S. 388 (1971) (civil suit for money damages allowed against FBI agents for search and arrest made without probable cause).

4. **Qualified immunity:** Even if a police officer violates a suspect's Fourth or Fifth Amendment rights, any §1983 suit by the suspect must overcome a significant obstacle: the defendant officer's ***"qualified immunity."***

   a. **Nature of immunity:** The Supreme Court has described qualified immunity this way: "The doctrine of qualified immunity shields officers from civil liability so long as their conduct does not violate ***clearly established*** statutory or constitutional rights of which a ***reasonable person would have known."*** *City of Tahlequah v. Bond*, 142 S.Ct. 9 (2021).

      i. **Consequence:** Qualified immunity protects "all but the ***plainly incompetent*** or those who ***knowingly violate the law***." *Id.* This gives the officer lots of protection.

      Example: Suppose state law enforcement officer O arrests D on the belief that there is probable cause to believe that D has just committed a crime. O then conducts a search of D incident to that arrest, and finds incriminating evidence. At D's criminal trial, the judge finds that the arrest was unlawful because O did not in fact have probable cause; the judge therefore excludes the evidence found in the search, and D goes free. Now, D sues O under §1983.

      The mere fact that O was wrong about whether the arrest was justified is not sufficient to overcome O's qualified immunity. If the judge hearing the §1983 claim believes that the lawfulness of the arrest was a moderately close question (even if that judge believes that the criminal-court judge was correct in finding it unlawful), O will be protected by qualified immunity. That's because D conduct did not violate "clearly established statutory or constitutional rights"; nor can it be said that O was "plainly incompetent" or "knowingly violate[d]" the law. Cf. *City of Tahlequah v. Bond, supra*.

---

10. For more about the constitutional underpinnings of *Miranda*, see *supra*, p. 242.

Quiz Yourself on
***THE EXCLUSIONARY RULE** (ENTIRE CHAPTER)*

82. The First National Bank of Pound was robbed by two masked gunmen, and for two months the police had no useful clues. Then, in an episode unrelated to the bank investigation, Officer Jackson of the Police Department learned from an informant that Albert possessed some illegal weapons in his apartment. The informant had proved unreliable in the past, so this tip did not give Jackson probable cause to obtain a warrant to search Albert's apartment, or to arrest Albert. Jackson decided to set forth without a warrant, since he knew he couldn't get one. At a time when he knew Albert was not home, he broke into Albert's apartment, and began ransacking the place. In a closed box underneath Albert's bed, Jackson found a batch of letters, which he started reading more from voyeuristic curiosity than for any other reason. The first letter, written by Bertha to Albert, contained one sentence which read, "When Carter and I robbed the First National Bank of Pound last month, we got away with $89,000 in loot, so I'd like to spend some of this money on one of the weapons you're selling."

Jackson immediately realized that this was probably the key to the bank job, so he took the letter and left Albert's apartment. Solely because of the letter, Bertha was charged with doing the bank job. At her trial, the prosecution sought to introduce the letter into evidence. Bertha objected, on the grounds that the letter was seized in violation of the Fourth Amendment. Must the judge exclude the letter from evidence? ________________

83. Bart was a master drug smuggler, who specialized in importing cocaine from Colombia. Bart was smart enough never to smuggle the cocaine in himself. Instead, he used various "mules." On one occasion, Bart recruited Karen to serve as a mule — Bart attached a kilogram of cocaine owned by Bart to the inside of Karen's thigh. Bart and Karen traveled on the same plane from Colombia to Miami. (They took the same flight so that Bart could immediately retrieve the cocaine after the flight and market it at retail.) At Miami Airport, Drug Enforcement Administration (DEA) agents focused their attentions on Karen not because of any objective grounds for suspicion, but merely because one of them thought that Karen "looked shifty and nervous." In violation of the Fourth Amendment, the DEA agent stopped Karen, took her into a private room, and performed a strip search on her. There, the agent found the cocaine. Bart was implicated because he showed up on the airline's computer reservation system as having been Karen's traveling companion.

At Bart's trial for cocaine smuggling, the prosecution plans to offer the cocaine into evidence against him. At a suppression hearing, Bart has moved to exclude the evidence on the grounds that it is the fruit of the detention and searching of Karen, in violation of the Fourth Amendment; Bart also points out that the cocaine belongs to him. Should Bart's suppression motion be granted? ________________

84. Officer Katz had many prejudices, especially ones concerning blacks and women. One day, he spotted an expensive late-model Porsche being driven by Danielle, a black woman. Katz believed that no black woman could possibly have come to drive such a car except by stealing it, earning it through prostitution, or otherwise behaving unlawfully. Because of this belief and not because of any other objective clues, Katz pulled Danielle over and asked to see her license and registration. Both seemed in order, but Katz nonetheless believed that Danielle must be lying when she said she owned the car and had paid for it with honestly-earned money. Therefore, Katz arrested her on charges of prostitution (thinking that she had paid for the car through this means), even though there was not a shred of evidence to support this.

At the station house, Katz questioned Danielle, after first reading her her *Miranda* warnings. Under questioning, Danielle suddenly admitted that a large part of the money to buy the car had come from cocaine smuggling done by her and her boyfriend. Danielle was then charged with drug smuggling. At her trial, the prosecution sought to introduce her confession against her. Danielle has moved to suppress the confession on the ground that it is the fruit of a violation of her Fourth Amendment rights. Should Danielle's suppression motion be granted? ________________

85. Federal prosecutors were trying to make an insider trading case against Gordon and Ivan, both wealthy and famous arbitrageurs. They began by breaking into Ivan's office at night, and seizing all of the records in his office, which they then carted to a warehouse. They did this without probable cause and without a warrant. Buried among these documents (and not seen by authorities until much later) was a copy of a July 1 letter from Ivan to Gordon concerning trading in the stock of ABC Corp.; the letter made it clear that Ivan and Gordon were both guilty of insider trading in that transaction. The federal authorities were so busy building their case that they did not go through the documents seized from Ivan's office, and merely kept them boxed in a government warehouse.

Shortly thereafter, federal agents arrested Gordon without a warrant and without probable cause, and then questioned him without first giving him his *Miranda* warnings. Under the questioning, Gordon broke down, confessed to the ABC transaction, and gave police a copy of the July 1 Ivan-to-Gordon letter. The agents realized that they had gotten the letter from Gordon by violating his Fourth and Fifth Amendment rights, and that they might have a hard time introducing the letter into evidence against him. However, since they now knew about the letter, and saw that it was from Ivan to Gordon, they went back into the warehouse, and discovered Ivan's copy of it in one of the boxes.

At Gordon's trial for insider trading, prosecutors offered into evidence against Gordon the copy Gordon had given them of the Ivan-to-Gordon July 1 letter. Gordon has moved to suppress this document on the grounds that it was obtained as the fruit of an unlawful search and interrogation of him.

(a) What doctrine should the prosecution cite in opposing Gordon's suppression motion?

____

(b) If the prosecution uses the doctrine you recommend in (a), should Gordon's motion be granted?

____

86. The police received a tip from a reliable informant that cocaine was being processed at a warehouse at 481 Main Street. The informant explained that he knew this because he had been a member of the operation, until he quarrelled with the other principals. The police went to the 481 Main address, and discovered a locked warehouse that could plausibly have been a cocaine processing factory. At this point, they knew they had probable cause to get a search warrant, and would normally have done so. Normally, they would have staked out the building while they got the warrant (so that no one could remove or destroy evidence). But to save time and to eliminate the need for a stakeout, they decided to see if they could break in first. They successfully broke into the building, and saw that it was indeed a cocaine-processing factory.

At that point, without touching anything, they re-locked the premises, applied for a warrant (using only the information that they had had prior to the break-in), received the warrant, went back to the building, broke in again, and seized the cocaine and other evidence. This evidence was introduced against Jerry, one of the principals, in his trial for drug-related offenses. Jerry has moved to suppress the evidence, on the grounds that it was obtained in violation of his Fourth Amendment rights (since he was the owner of the building, as well as one of the owners of the processing operation). Should Jerry's motion be granted?

____

87. Harry, a wealthy industrialist, was on his way to work in his chauffeured limousine one day, when two masked gunmen suddenly attacked the vehicle, spewing bullets into its tires. The gunmen then opened the door and forcibly abducted Harry. Shortly thereafter, Harry's family received a ransom demand, which the family complied with. Harry was released unharmed; however, since his captors had blindfolded him while they transported him to their hideaway, and kept masks on at all times, Harry was not able to help the police determine who had committed the crime. Starting shortly after the kidnapping, the police ballistics lab analyzed the bullets found in the car, and discovered that these had come from a Smith & Wesson .38 revolver, of a type manufactured between 1980 and 1988.

The police immediately began examining the records of every gun dealer and pawn shop in the metropolitan area, figuring that there was a good chance that the owner (or at least original purchaser) of the gun used in the abduction would be listed in these records. The police then began to interview each Smith & Wesson .38 gun owner shown in the records, and to test each of his or her guns. After the police had checked about 10% of the listed guns, they happened to get a call from an anonymous informant, who said, "You'll find evidence of a serious crime at 1025 South Avenue."

The police realized that this did not furnish them with probable cause to obtain a search warrant for that address. Therefore, they decided to wing it. They went to 1025 South Avenue, rang the bell, and broke in when there was no answer. They ransacked the house, and in so doing, found a Smith & Wesson .38 revolver. Just on a hunch that this might have been the gun used in the Harry kidnapping case, they seized the gun and took it back to the police station. (They did not find any other evidence of criminality.) The department ran a ballistics test on the revolver and, lo and behold, it turned out to be the gun that had fired the bullets into Harry's car. The police went back to 1025 South Avenue, staked it out, and eventually arrested the owner, Kent, when he entered one day. Meanwhile, it turned out that Kent was the registered owner of the gun, and that his name appeared on the records of a local pawn shop as being the owner of that gun. The 1025 South Avenue address was listed as Kent's address in the pawn shop records.

At Kent's trial for kidnapping, the prosecution seeks to enter the gun into evidence, and to tie it to the kidnapping by showing that it fired the bullets found in the car. Kent moves to suppress, on the theory that the police's possession of the gun stems directly from their illegal break-in of 1025 South Avenue at a time when they did not have probable cause or a warrant.

(a) What doctrine should the prosecution cite in support of its opposition to Kent's suppression motion?

____

(b) If the prosecution cites the doctrine you referred to in part (a), should the court grant Kent's suppression motion? ________________

88. Leslie reported to the Ames police that her apartment had been burglarized. Officer Kaplan was sent to investigate the complaint. Leslie showed Kaplan into her home office, and had him sit in front of her desk. At one point during the interview, Leslie excused herself to go to the bathroom. Kaplan, with no evil purpose in mind, just curiosity, picked up a stack of letters from Leslie's desk. In the middle of the stack was a letter to Leslie stating, "Sis, I know you poisoned our mother to get her insurance money, but I so far can't bring myself to turn you in. I want you to know that I know, though. [signed] Morton." Kaplan deduced that this might be a clue to a murder case.

After leaving Leslie's apartment, Kaplan ascertained that Leslie indeed had a brother named Morton, and that their mother had died the month before; no one outside the family suspected foul play. Kaplan contacted Morton, who said, "Well, now that you're here, yes, I'd be happy to talk about why I think Leslie murdered our mother." Morton then described facts that made the police believe that Leslie had indeed killed her mother. Leslie was tried for this murder. At the trial, the prosecution relied heavily on Morton's testimony as to incriminating actions by Leslie. Leslie has moved to suppress Morton's testimony, on the grounds that the prosecution learned of Morton's existence only through Kaplan's illegal ransacking of Leslie's mail. Should Leslie's motion be granted? ________________

89. Nelson's wife, Marie, disappeared without ever being heard from again. The police were convinced that Marie had been murdered, and that Nelson had done it. However, they did not have a shred of hard evidence to prove this. They therefore decided that they would have to play "hardball" to get anywhere with the case. Without probable cause and without a warrant, they arrested Nelson at his home, and took him down to the police station. They dutifully read him his *Miranda* warnings. He agreed to listen to their questions, though not necessarily to talk. After two hours of grilling, Nelson finally confessed that he had done it, and described the method used. A videotape was made of this interrogation session, and it is clear that Nelson's confession was "voluntary." Nelson was tried for murder, and the prosecution sought to introduce the videotape of Nelson's confession. Nelson has moved to suppress this confession, on the grounds that it was the fruit of the police's prior illegal arrest of him. Assuming that the arrest was indeed a violation of Nelson's Fourth Amendment rights, should Nelson's suppression motion be granted? ________________

90. Officer Quell, while walking a downtown beat in City, saw Diego, a young male in his early twenties look repeatedly into the window of a jewelry store. Based solely on Quell's hunch that young males walking alone who look into the windows of jewelry stores are often up to no good, Quell approached Diego and demanded to see some ID. Diego (who was in fact considering buying an engagement ring displayed in the window and was thus completely innocent) complied by handing his driver's license to Quell. Quell radioed back to headquarters Diego's name and date of birth as shown on the license; after a brief pause, the dispatcher informed Quell (accurately) that a warrant had been issued six years previously for Diego's arrest, on the grounds that he had not paid a $100 fine for a minor traffic violation. Quell, acting pursuant to a City police department directive that any person discovered to have an outstanding arrest warrant should be immediately arrested regardless of the age or seriousness of the offense, told Diego that Diego was under arrest on the warrant. Quell then searched Diego's person incident to that arrest. As part of the search, Quell reached into Diego's pocket, pulled out a plastic bag, and saw that the bag contained a white powdered substance that reasonably appeared to Quell as though it might be heroin. The contents of the bag indeed turned out to be heroin, and Diego was prosecuted on a charge of heroin possession with intent to distribute. Diego moved to suppress the heroin from evidence on the grounds that the substance was discovered only as the direct result of an illegal stop of Diego by Quell. The prosecution con cedes that the stop was illegal based on the facts known to Quell at the time of the stop.

(a) If you are the prosecutor, what argument would you make about why the heroin should be admissible notwithstanding the illegal stop? ________________

(b) Assuming you make the argument you mention in your answer to (a), should the court nonetheless grant Diego's suppression motion? ________________

91. Officer O'Brien was irrationally prejudiced against young males with long hair, and against anyone who looked like a "hippie." O'Brien spotted Peter and Rachel walking down the street hand in hand, and developed a hunch, based solely on their long hair and style of clothing, that the two were probably in possession of drugs. He arrested them both on drug charges, and escorted them to the station house. There, each was subjected to a "clothing search," which was done to every arrestee in order to inventory their possessions and to protect against concealed weapons. The two were searched simultaneously. In Rachel's purse, five marijuana cigarettes were found. Rachel looked imploringly at Peter when this occurred. Peter then said, "I can't let Rachel take the rap for this — those cigarettes are mine." Peter was charged with marijuana possession, and the prosecution sought to use his station-house confession against him. Peter objected on the grounds that this statement was a direct fruit of his unlawful arrest. Should the court grant Peter's suppression motion? ________________

92. The police had probable cause to believe that Veronica was the masked gunman who had recently robbed the local branch of the First National Bank. They properly procured a warrant for her arrest, and arrested her at her house. They handcuffed her, and brought her to the police department. There, Detective Usher questioned her about the robbery, without first giving her *Miranda* warnings. (He had learned from his personal experience that suspects often clam up when read their *Miranda* warnings, and are somewhat more likely to speak if not given the warnings. Therefore, he developed a standard practice of conducting his interrogations in two steps: question without warnings, obtain an admission, warn, then get the suspect to repeat the earlier admission.) In response to Usher's questions — but not in response to any overt coercion or trickery — Veronica confessed that she was the robber. Usher left the room briefly to get a police stenographer, then returned. At this point, he read Veronica her *Miranda* warnings, and did not mention to her that her earlier confession would be inadmissible because unwarned. He then reviewed her earlier answers to his questions, and asked her to confirm those answers.

Veronica, reasoning that she had already "let the cat out of the bag" by confessing, decided that there was no point in refusing to answer the same questions again, this time before the stenographer. Therefore, she confirmed her earlier answers, again confessing to being the robber. The stenographer recorded these answers, and Veronica then signed the confession. At Veronica's bank robbery trial, the prosecution seeks to enter the signed transcript of the second confession into evidence against Veronica. (The prosecution concedes that the first confession is inadmissible.) Veronica has moved to suppress that second confession as the fruit of the earlier, non-*Mirandized* confession. Should Veronica's suppression motion be granted?

____

93. Over the course of a year, three co-eds at Ames State University were found, each in her own off-campus apartment, each stabbed to death. The police believed that a single killer was at work. Detective Johnson of the Ames police force received an anonymous tip that Bernard, who the caller said lived at 141 West Street in Ames, was the killer. This information did not amount to probable cause to arrest Bernard or search his house. Nonetheless, Johnson felt that he had to act. After telephoning Bernard and ascertaining that he was out, Johnson broke into Bernard's house, and carefully searched it from corner to corner. He happened upon three separate snapshots, which he recognized instantly as being of the three dead girls. He immediately seized these photos, and left the house. Based in part on other evidence not illegally obtained, the police were eventually able to charge Bernard with the murder of one of the girls, Kelly.

At Bernard's murder trial, the prosecution did not use the snapshot of Kelly (or anything else derived from Johnson's illegal search of Bernard's house) as part of its direct case. The defense then put on its case. Its only witness was Bernard. On direct, Bernard denied committing the murder of Kelly and said nothing more. On cross-examination, the prosecutor asked, "Did you ever meet Kelly?" Bernard responded, "No." The prosecution asked, "Did you ever obtain a photograph of Kelly?" Again, Bernard answered, "No." Then, the prosecutor showed Bernard the snapshot and asked, "Isn't it true that this photo of Kelly was found in your house?" Bernard's lawyer objected to the prosecution's use of this photo, on the grounds that the photo was the direct fruit of an illegal search, and must thus be barred by the exclusionary rule. Should the trial judge sustain this objection? ________________

94. The police suspected that Egon was the person who had killed Gerald, a business associate of Egon's. However, they did not have probable cause to arrest Egon or to search his premises. Instead, they simply broke into Egon's house one day while he and his wife were away, and seized the most interesting item they found, a Remington .33 revolver. This gun was of interest to the police because they had already determined, from ballistics tests, that Gerald had been shot with a Remington .33. Ballistics tests later showed that the seized pistol was indeed the murder weapon. The police knew that their seizure of the gun was illegal, and they had no other way to prove that Egon had owned the murder weapon. However, they had enough other circumstantial evidence of Egon's guilt that Egon was prosecuted for the murder anyway.

In the prosecution's direct case, only this circumstantial evidence, not the fact that Egon owned the murder weapon, was introduced. During the defense case, Egon did not take the stand. However, Fran, Egon's wife, did take the stand. She stated on direct examination, "So far as I know, Egon never kept a gun at our house." The prosecution, on cross-examination, then showed Fran the Remington seized from the house, and asked, "Don't you recognize this gun as one that was in your house up until several months ago?" Egon's lawyer immediately objected to this evidence on the grounds that it was the fruit of the unlawful entry into Egon's house. Must the court sustain Egon's objection? ________________

95. Detective Lawrence of the Langdell police force received an anonymous call, in which the caller stated, "The occupant of apartment 3B in my building is selling drugs from that apartment. I live at 1865 Center Street." The caller did not say how he came by this information. Lawrence believed that this information was enough to establish probable cause to search apartment 3B at the 1865 Center Street address. He went before a neutral and detached magistrate, and presented the above facts to her in an affidavit. Lawrence did not conceal any relevant facts. The magistrate agreed with Lawrence that the facts here established probable cause, and the magistrate therefore issued a warrant to search apartment 3B of 1865 Center Street "for drugs or any paraphernalia associated with drugs." Lawrence executed the warrant by its terms (breaking into the apartment when there was no answer), and strictly confined his search to the scope of the warrant. He found cocaine that seemed to be held for resale, and seized it.

The occupant of the apartment turned out to be Herb. Herb was tried for a variety of drug charges. The prosecution offered the seized drugs as part of its case-in-chief. Herb moved to suppress the seized drugs, on the grounds that they were the fruits of an illegal search, since there was in fact no probable cause to support issuance of the search warrant. The trial judge has agreed with Herb that the warrant was issued without probable cause, because there was no indication that the informant was either generally reliable or reliable in this case, so that by the "totality of the circumstance" test (*Illinois v. Gates*), probable cause for the warrant did not exist. However, the trial judge has also concluded that Lawrence reasonably believed, on the facts known to him, that probable cause existed; the judge also believes that the magistrate similarly made a reasonable mistake as to the existence of probable cause. Must the trial judge order the drugs suppressed from Herb's trial? ________________

96. As of 2010, Supreme Court precedents left it unclear whether police use of a GPS device to track all the movements of a suspect's vehicle over an extended period constituted a search requiring a warrant. At that time, the binding precedent on this issue in states of the federal First Circuit was a 2009 First Circuit decision, *Adams v. U.S.* (not a real case), holding that even extended use of a GPS tracking device attached to a suspect's car was not a "search" and therefore did not require a warrant. In mid-2010, federal DEA agents in Massachusetts (part of the First Circuit) attached a GPS to the vehicle of Devin, who was suspected of being part of a drug-smuggling ring. They did not request a warrant, but they had probable cause to believe that tracking Devin's vehicle would lead to proof that Devin was involved in the ring. The agents were not aware of the *Adams* ruling, but believed no warrant was needed because no search would occur. After 15 days of surveillance, data gathered via the GPS revealed multiple trips by Devin to the home of another known member of the ring. At Devin's federal criminal trial in late 2010, this GPS data was allowed into evidence by the judge, who relied on the *Adams* decision. Devin was convicted. In 2012, while Devin was about to appeal his conviction, the Supreme Court decided in *U.S. v. Jones* (a real case) that use of a GPS tracking device attached to a suspect's property (such as a vehicle) automatically constitutes a search, and thus requires a warrant. Devin then argued, during a timely appeal to the First Circuit, that he should get the benefit of the *Jones* ruling, in which case the DEA use of the GPS search was illegal without a warrant, justifying a new trial. Should the First Circuit grant Devin's new-trial motion? ________________

Answers

82. No. It is true that the exclusionary rule allows evidence seized in violation of the Fourth Amendment to be suppressed ("excluded") from criminal trials. However, the defendant may only obtain suppression of materials that were seized in violation of ***her own*** expectation of privacy. This is the rule of ***"standing."*** See *Alderman v. U.S.* The break-in by Officer Jackson, made without probable cause and without a warrant, was clearly illegal and a violation of Albert's Fourth Amendment rights. But that break-in did not violate *Bertha's* rights, since she had no possessory interest in Albert's apartment, was not present there, and did not "own" the letter once she had sent it. Since no reasonable expectation of privacy on Bertha's part was violated by the search, the illegality cannot serve as the basis for suppression of the letter in her trial.

83. No. As in the prior question, Bart's problem is that he lacks standing to object to the unlawful seizure and search of Karen. The fact that Bart had a possessory interest in the cocaine seized is not by itself enough to allow him to challenge the constitutionality of the seizure. Only if Bart's possession of the cocaine gave him a legitimate expectation of privacy with respect to that item will Bart be allowed to protest. *Rawlings v. Kentucky*. Here, once Bart put the cocaine on Karen's person, where any customs agent might look at it, and where Karen might have shown it to third persons (e.g., her friends), Bart almost certainly lost any expectation of privacy he had regarding that cocaine. The facts here are similar to those in *Rawlings* (D put his drugs in X's handbag, which was then illegally searched; D was held to have no right to object to the search and seizure of the drugs).

84. Yes. Where evidence is indirectly derived from a violation of the defendant's constitutional rights, that evidence will often be suppressed — this is the ***"fruit of the poisonous tree"*** doctrine, by which an initial constitutional violation (the "tree") will be deemed to "taint" the evidence that is indirectly found because of it (the "fruit"). Here, Danielle's confession would almost certainly be found to be tainted fruit from the "tree" of the stop made without probable cause, and the arrest made without probable cause. If Katz had never made his illegal stop of Danielle's car, and his illegal arrest, she never would have been in a position to confess at the station house.

In cases where the confession derives from an illegal arrest or stop, the prosecution can sometimes show that the taint was ***"purged"*** by intervening events. But the mere giving of *Miranda* warnings, and the suspect's "voluntary" decision to confess, are generally held not to be the kind of intervening events that will purge the taint. So here, the relation between the confession and the prior illegal stop/arrest is so strong, and the police wrongdoing so great, that the "fruits of the poisonous tree" doctrine will almost certainly be applied. See, e.g., *Wong Sun v. U.S.* (illegal arrest of D was followed by his confession; the confession must be suppressed because it was the fruit of the illegal arrest).

85. (a) The "independent source" doctrine. If a particular piece of evidence comes from two sources, only one of which derives from the illegality that the defendant complains of, the exclusionary rule does not apply.

(b) No. Since the government has an "independent source" for the contested evidence, the illegality is not the "but for" cause of the evidence's availability, and the illegality is thus ignored. Here, the prosecution already had the July 1 letter in its possession, so this constituted an "independent source" for that letter. The fact that the government did not focus on the document, and learned of the document's significance only due to the illegal questioning of Gordon, will probably not prevent the independent source doctrine from applying here. Also, although the government acted illegally in getting Ivan's copy of the letter, Gordon does not have standing to object to the violation of Ivan's rights. So even though every step taken by the federal agents was grossly illegal, they end up with evidence they can use to convict Gordon.

86. No. Here, as in the prior question, the "independent source" exception saves the prosecution. On very similar facts, the Supreme Court held that since the police ultimately seized the evidence based on a properly issued warrant, the fact that they first viewed the evidence by an illegal break-in was irrelevant — the subsequent with-warrant seizure was an "independent source." See *Murray v. U.S.*

If the court believed that the police would not have bothered to get a warrant had they not first broken in and seen the evidence, the result might be otherwise. But here, the facts tell us that if the police had been unable to break in, they would have taken the extra trouble to get a warrant anyway. That being the case, the second entry is viewed as an independent source. The fact that the first break-in made life easier for the police (in the sense that had they not discovered anything wrong once they broke in, they would not have bothered to get the warrant) is viewed as irrelevant.

87. (a) The "inevitable discovery" doctrine. Under this exception, evidence may be admitted if it would "inevitably" have been discovered by other police techniques had it not first been obtained through the illegal discovery. The prosecution bears the burden of showing, by a preponderance of the evidence, that the information would inevitably have been discovered by lawful means. *Nix v. Williams.*

(b) No. This is a situation in which the "inevitable discovery" rule should apply. The police were in the process of examining the records of every local pawn shop and gun shop, to check on anyone who had bought a Smith & Wesson .38. Although they had not yet found Kent's name, the police would inevitably have gotten to that particular pawn shop, and would then have found Kent's name and address. Therefore, they would have looked for Kent until they found him, and would have then either discovered the gun or become increasingly suspicious of Kent if he couldn't produce it. So a court would probably be satisfied that the police really would have inevitably discovered the gun even had no illegality taken place.

88. No, probably. It is true that the police's lead to Morton as a witness (and, indeed, the entire police knowledge that a crime was committed) stemmed directly from Kaplan's illegal look at Leslie's mail. (Kaplan may have had the right to sit at Leslie's desk, since he was there to investigate a burglary reported by her. But this consent clearly did not extend to Kaplan's ransacking through a stack of letters on Leslie's desk, so what he did went beyond the scope of the consent and constituted an illegal search.) However, the courts are extremely reluctant to find that a ***"witness lead"*** is the tainted fruit of a poisonous tree. As the Supreme Court has put it, "The exclusionary rule should be invoked with much greater reluctance where the claim is based on a causal relationship between a constitutional violation and the discovery of a live witness than where a similar claim is advanced to support suppression of an inanimate object." *U.S. v. Ceccolini.*

Since Kaplan was not actively looking for evidence against Leslie when he stumbled upon it, and since

Morton was in fact anxious to testify (and thus was a most "voluntary" witness) it is unlikely that the court will view Morton's testimony as the tainted fruit of the admitted poisonous tree (the illegal search). (The facts here are somewhat similar to those of *Ceccolini*, where the witness' testimony was admitted.)

89. Yes. This is a classic illustration of the "fruit of the poisonous tree" doctrine. The confession derived directly from the arrest — without the arrest, Nelson would not have been subject to station house questioning by the police, and would therefore not have confessed. Furthermore, there was a quality of "purposefulness" in the police's conduct — they knew they were violating Nelson's right to be free of unreasonable seizures, yet they violated that right precisely in order to have the chance to question him and thus the chance to get a confession. In this situation, a court is very unlikely to hold that the taint of the illegal arrest was "purged" by any subsequent event. The giving of the *Miranda* warnings, and the fact that the confession was "voluntary" rather than "coerced," will almost never by themselves be enough to purge the taint of an illegal arrest. See *Brown v. Illinois*, excluding a confession derived from a similar illegal arrest.

90. (a) That Quell's discovery of the outstanding warrant, and his arrest of Diego on that warrant, were sufficient to "purge the taint" of the illegal stop.

(b) No. Even if a search that discloses a piece of evidence comes about as the result of a stop conducted in violation of a person's Fourth Amendment rights, events occurring after the illegal stop may be sufficient to ***"purge the taint"*** of the illegality. The Supreme Court considers three factors in deciding whether the taint of illegality has been purged by the time the search occurs: (1) the "temporal proximity" between the illegal stop and the search (so that the longer the passage of time, the more likely the taint is to be found purged); (2) the "presence of intervening circumstances" (so that if events truly independent of the illegal stop bring about the search, that factor cuts in favor of a finding that the taint was purged); and (3) the "purpose and flagrancy of the official misconduct" (so that if the illegality was the result of a good faith mistake and not the product of "systemic police misconduct," that factor cuts in favor of a finding that the taint was purged). *Brown v. Illinois*.

In an arrest-on-an-old-warrant case with facts fairly similar to the ones here, the Supreme Court applied the three-factor test and concluded that the taint of the illegal stop was purged by the discovery of the arrest warrant, making the evidence found incident to the warrant arrest there admissible. See *Utah v. Strieff* (2016). Applying the three factors to our present facts, here's how a court would likely analyze the situation in light of *Strieff*: (1) the "temporal proximity" cuts in favor of Diego, since the Supreme Court's case law suggests that a gap of less than two hours between illegality and search will normally be too brief for purging the taint, and the gap here (as in *Strieff*) was just a couple of minutes. (2) The "intervening events" factor cuts strongly in favor of the government, because the outstanding warrant long pre-dated the illegal stop, and was thus logically completely independent of that stop (as was the warrant in *Strieff*). (3) The "purpose and flagrancy of the official misconduct" also cuts in favor of the government; Quell's mistaken belief that he had enough objective indicia of suspicion to justify an investigative stop seems to have been at most negligent (i.e., nothing in the facts suggest that Quell *knew* the stop was unlawful), and there's no indication of systemic official misconduct by the City police department (as there would be if, for instance, the heads of the department instructed officers to make many stops that they knew were invalid in the hopes of finding outstanding warrants that could serve as pretexts for searches). (Again, the type of police misconduct here is comparable to that in *Strieff*.) Therefore, two of the three *Brown v. Illinois* factors favor the government, and a lower court here would probably thus conclude (as the Supreme Court did in *Strieff*) that any taint from the illegal stop had been purged by the time the search incident to the arrest on the warrant occurred.

91. No. Clearly there was some connection between the illegal arrest, and Peter's self-incriminating statement. But this does not automatically mean that the statement is the tainted fruit of the illegal arrest. The issue is always whether there have been intervening events sufficient to "purge" the taint. Here, the fact that Peter's statement was somewhat voluntary, and was not in response to any questioning, is a factor strongly tending to purge the taint. On very similar facts, in *Rawlings v. Kentucky*, the Supreme Court concluded that the spontaneous outburst was not the tainted fruit of the admittedly illegal arrest.

92. Yes, probably. In this "two confession" scenario, the second confession will not *normally* be deemed to be the tainted fruit of the earlier poisoned confession. *Oregon v. Elstad* says that if the second confession was "knowingly and voluntarily made," it will not be invalidated merely because there was a prior, illegally-obtained confession having the same substance. And that's true even if the suspect reasons that the "cat's out of the bag" — the fact that the suspect may be at a psychological disadvantage from having already confessed is ordinarily irrelevant, so long as the second confession was "knowingly and voluntarily made." But the post-*Elstad* case of *Missouri v. Seibert* says that where the police make a conscious decision to ***follow a two-step process whose purpose is to undermine Miranda*** — doing unwarned questioning until they get a confession, then giving the *Miranda* warnings, then asking the suspect to repeat the confession — there will be a presumption that the warnings were not effective as to the second confession. That's what happened here, so *Seibert* means that the warnings will probably be found to be ineffective, in which case the second confession will be found inadmissible.

93. No. The Supreme Court has held that evidence obtained in violation of the Fourth Amendment may always be used to ***impeach*** statements made by the defendant. This is true even if the illegal evidence is used to impeach statements elicited by the prosecution from the defendant on cross-examination. See *U.S. v. Havens*. This is what happened here. So even though it was only in response to the prosecution's questions on cross-examination that Bernard denied having the photo, the prosecution is able to impeach Bernard's testimony by presenting that illegally-seized photo. (Of course, Bernard is entitled to a jury instruction stating that the snapshot should only be considered as evidence of Bernard's trustworthiness as a witness, not as direct evidence of whether he committed the crime. But it is questionable whether the jury will truly disregard the snapshot when deciding Bernard's guilt.)

94. Yes. The prosecution may use evidence obtained in violation of the Fourth Amendment to impeach the defendant on cross-examination. But illegally-obtained evidence may ***not*** be used to impeach the testimony of ***defense witnesses*** other than the defendant himself. *James v. Illinois*. Since the testimony being impeached here was that of Fran, not the defendant, *James* means that Egon may successfully object to use of the gun to impeach the testimony. (If the prosecution can convince the judge that the "inevitable discovery" exception, or some other exception to the exclusionary rule, is applicable, then the result would be different. But there is nothing on these facts to suggest that the prosecution can make such a showing.)

95. No. The Supreme Court has held that the exclusionary rule does not bar the use, even in the prosecution's case-in-chief, of evidence obtained by officers who acted in ***reasonable reliance*** on a search warrant that was issued by a detached and neutral magistrate but that was ultimately found to be unsupported by probable cause. *U.S. v. Leon*. Since the facts tell us that Lawrence reasonably believed that he had probable cause, furnished an affidavit stating everything he knew, and got the affidavit approved and the warrant issued by a neutral and detached magistrate, the requirements for the special "good faith" exception of *Leon* are satisfied. The net result is that the prosecution gets to use evidence in its case-in-chief that was seized in direct violation of the Fourth Amendment's prohibitions on warrants issued without probable cause.

96. No. *U.S. v. Leon* says that in some circumstances, if the police have a good faith belief that the search they are doing is lawful, the fact that it turns out not to be lawful does not trigger the exclusionary rule. This principle has been extended to the situation in which the police rely on a particular binding (and applicable) precedent that makes the search legal, but where that precedent gets overruled before the present case has been finally decided. *Davis v. U.S.* (2011). This principle applies here: for a search done in 2010 in Massachusetts, the applicable constitutional rule on the issue of whether GPS tracking for an extended period requires a warrant was the rule set forth in *Adams*, that no warrant was required. The fact that this rule was overturned by the Supreme Court while D's case was still pending does not prevent the evidence from being admisible despite the exclusionary rule. So Devin ends up not getting the benefit of the law as it exists at the time of his appeal.

Exam Tips on ***THE EXCLUSIONARY RULE***

The concepts from this chapter go hand-in-hand with those in Chapters 2 and 3. Make sure you understand how all of these relate to one another. Here are some tips to help you with exclusionary rule questions:

The exclusionary rule is very basic: ***if the evidence in question was seized in violation of the defendant's constitutional rights, it is inadmissible at the defendant's criminal trial.***

Example: The police are looking for a bank robber. Officer sees D sitting on his front porch, and on a mere hunch that D "looks like the type who might rob banks," arrests D. Officer then frisks D, feels a soft container in D's pocket, pulls out the container, and discovers cocaine. The cocaine will not be admissible against D, because it was seized in violation of D's Fourth Amendment rights: the arrest of D was made without probable cause, so the search of him incident to arrest was also invalid. (The drugs are "fruit of the poisonous tree," i.e., the illegal arrest.)

A key point to remember on exams is that you must check for ***standing***: a defendant does ***not*** have standing to object to the violation of a ***third party's*** constitutional rights. Thus a defendant may only exclude evidence that was obtained in violation of *that defendant's* own constitutional right.

Questions on this issue frequently involve a party attempting to contest the search of ***another person's car, person, or clothing.*** The objecting party does not have standing to object to any of these searches.

Example: D sells Customer some bagged heroin. Customer is later stopped for a traffic violation and the heroin is found in the vehicle, in a bag whose markings indicate that it was supplied by D. Even if the traffic stop violated Customer's Fourth Amendment rights, this does not help D: D may not challenge the search of Customer's car, because he had no reasonable expectation of privacy in someone else's car and thus lacked standing to object to the stop and search.

But if D *does* have a ***reasonable expectation of privacy*** in the place or property searched, he can get the evidence excluded if it was obtained pursuant to an unreasonable search or seizure,

Example: Store is having problems with shoplifting. It stations Officer at a vantage point from which she can see into the ladies' dressing rooms. D takes a dress into the dressing room and stuffs it into her purse. Officer apprehends D at the front of the store. The dress will be inadmissible at trial, because D was stopped only because Officer knew D had taken the dress, and Officer's knowledge came from a violation of D's reasonable expectation of privacy in the dressing room she was occupying.

An often-tested area involves ***items held out to the public.*** Much personal information that we would not necessarily want people to know about us will still be determined to be "held out to the public" and thus ***not*** subject to a reasonable expectation of privacy. For instance, ***garbage put out for collection***, ***tax returns***, ***bank statements*** held in the bank's records, and registers of the ***telephone numbers*** called from a home telephone are all items as to which there is generally no expectation of privacy. Another is the ***view into our homes*** from a public area, obtained either with the naked eye or with binoculars.

A gray area concerns matters that the public ***could conceivably view,*** but only with great difficulty. If this issue arises on an exam, you should weigh the factors and determine whether it would be reasonable for a defendant to expect privacy in the area.

Example: D's home has a window nine feet above the ground. Passers-by cannot see into the house through the window, but a neighbor could, if he climbed onto his roof. The police climb on to the neighbor's roof to have this view. Although people could theoretically see in the window, D probably has a reasonable expectation of privacy in this area of his home, because it would be very unlikely that his neighbor would attempt to look inside his home this way.

Keep in mind the possibility that the ***"inevitable discovery"*** theory may apply: Even if the evidence was illegally seized and there is no independent lawful basis for its discovery, if it would have inevitably been discovered it is admissible.

Example: D shows Undercover Agent stolen guns that he has in the trunk of his car. Undercover Agent reports this to her superiors. Instead of getting a warrant, the superiors immediately order a search of the trunk of D's car, which is parked in D's driveway. The search reveals the stolen guns. D challenges the admissibility of the guns, on the theory that they were the fruit of the warrantless search. A court might well hold that the guns are admissible because a search warrant would "inevitably" have been issued for the car based on Undercover Agent's information, and the guns would then inevitably have been discovered.

If a search warrant turns out to be invalid, keep in mind that this may not make the seized evidence inadmissible. Remember that the evidence will still be admissible if (1) there was a ***substantial basis*** for issuing the warrant, and (2) the officers executing it objectively and in good faith ***believed*** that the warrant was valid.

"Purging the taint of the illegality": Even where you conclude that a stop, arrest or questioning violated the suspect's constitutional rights, don't presume that evidence derived from it necessarily will be excluded. Keep in mind the ***"purged taint"*** doctrine: if significant ***additional events intervene*** between the original illegality and the final discovery of evidence, that may be enough to ***"purge the taint"*** of the ***original illegal police conduct.***

Here are the ***three factors*** the Court takes into account in deciding whether the taint from the illegality has been "purged" by the time the evidence in question is discovered:

[1] The ***"temporal proximity"*** of the illegality to the fruit (so the ***longer the time*** between the illegality and the discovery of the ultimate evidence, the more likely it is that the taint has been purged);

[2] The nature of any "***intervening circumstances***" that occurred between the illegality and the fruit (so that events that are truly *independent* of the illegality are more likely to produce a purging of the taint);

[3] The ***"purpose and flagrancy*** of the ***official misconduct"*** (so that an illegal stop or arrest arising from a good-faith police mistake as to probable cause is more likely to lead to a purging of the taint than an arrest/stop that the officer *knows* is illegal).

Example of purging the taint: Officer genuinely (but unreasonably and inaccurately) believes that he has sufficient objective grounds to stop D to investigate whether D has just shoplifted. from a store. D is in fact completely innocent of shoplifting. As part of the stop, Officer demands photo ID from D, which D supplies. Officer radios to headquarters with D's name, and is told that there is a 6-year-old warrant outstanding for D's arrest for an unpaid traffic ticket. Officer arrests D on the warrant (pursuant to police department policy requiring arrest of anyone found to be the subject of an outstanding arrest warrant), and searches D's person incident to the arrest. That search discovers heroin in D's pocket.

In D's prosecution for heroin possession, the heroin (the fruit of the search incident to the arrest) will be admissible, even though Officer's discovery of it stemmed directly from the illegal stop. That is, the ***taint*** of the illegal stop will be found to have been ***"purged"*** by the discovery of the arrest warrant. Of the three factors mentioned above governing when the taint is deemed purged, two favor a purging. (The "intervening circumstance" was the discovery of the arrest warrant, and the warrant's existence was causally independent of the illegal stop, cutting in favor of a finding of purging. And the "official misconduct" inherent in the stop was at most a negligent but good-faith mistake by Officer, not an intentional act of wrongdoing by Officer or a product of systemic police wrongdoing, so that, too, cuts in favor of a finding of purging.) Cite to *Utah v. Strieff*, whose facts are similar.

Evidence that's the ***fruit of a confession*** given in custody without required *Miranda* warnings generally ***won't be inadmissible*** as fruit of the poisonous tree. That is, any taint from the lack of warnings will likely be deemed purged. So ***physical evidence*** — or ***leads to third-party witness testimony*** — won't be inadmissible even if they stem directly from a *Miranda* violation (as long as the confession is "voluntary"). *U.S. v. Patane*.

Example: D is arrested for domestic violence. He's questioned without *Miranda* warnings, and reveals that he's in possession of an unregistered pistol, whose location he shows the police. The gun will be admissible against D — the fact that the police would never have found the gun had D not confessed to its location during unwarned custodial questioning is irrelevant, because an unwarned confession won't ever be a "poisonous tree" with respect to physical fruits (or third-party witness testimony) derived from that confession.

Evidence that derives from an ***illegal arrest*** is not *per se* inadmissible. Even if the arrest was illegal, if there were ***significant intervening factors*** that broke the chain of causation between the illegal arrest and the evidence, this will be enough to trigger the doctrine of "purging the taint" of the illegality, in which case the evidence will be admissible. Look for ***remoteness in time or place*** from the illegality.

Example: D is illegally arrested on Tuesday, and released on bail. On Wednesday, the police question D at his home after giving him *Miranda* warnings, and he confesses. The confession will be admissible: even though the confession derived from the initial illegal arrest, the passage of time, and D's freedom from custody, will be enough to purge the taint of the illegal arrest.

Illegally-seized evidence can always be used to ***impeach*** the defendant, even though it is inadmissible in the prosecution's case-in-chief.

Example: D is arrested and charged with distributing controlled substances. As part of its case, the prosecution wants to introduce a 20 kilos of cocaine that were seized at D's summer home. The drugs, however, are ruled inadmissible because they were discovered pursuant to a warrantless search. At trial, D takes the stand and testifies that, while his brother is heavily involved in the drug trade, he himself has never even been in possession of a small amount of cocaine. The prosecution asks on cross, "How come 20 kilos of cocaine were discovered by police at your summer home?" This question is proper, as impeachment, even though the drugs were illegally seized. If D denies that any drugs were found, the prosecution will be allowed to introduce the drugs themselves, again as impeachment rather than as substantive evidence.

CHAPTER 8

THE RIGHT TO COUNSEL

ChapterScope

The Sixth Amendment says that "In all criminal prosecutions, the accused shall enjoy the right . . . to have the Assistance of Counsel for his defense." Here are the key concepts regarding the right to counsel:

Right to counsel: The right to counsel means the right to ***retain*** (hire) counsel. Also, if the defendant is ***indigent***, it means the right to have counsel ***appointed*** (and paid for by the government), in any case in which the defendant can be sent to jail.

Critical stage: The right to counsel applies to ***all critical stages*** of the proceedings. A stage is critical if the defendant is compelled to make a decision which may later be formally used against him.

Waiver: A defendant may ***waive*** his right to counsel, but he must do so "knowingly and intelligently."

Effectiveness of counsel: The Sixth Amendment entitles a defendant to the ***effective assistance*** of counsel. Counsel is ineffective if: (1) her performance is ***deficient***, that is, she was not a "reasonably competent" attorney; *and* (2) the deficiencies were ***prejudicial***, that is, there is a "reasonable probability" that but for counsel's errors, the result of the proceeding would have been different.

I. INTRODUCTION

A. **Sixth Amendment:** The Sixth Amendment provides in part that "in all criminal prosecutions, the accused shall enjoy the right . . . to have the Assistance of Counsel for his defense." This right was made applicable to the states, via the Fourteenth Amendment, in *Gideon v. Wainwright*, 372 U.S. 335 (1963).

B. **Right to appointed counsel:** The focus of this chapter is upon the right of an ***indigent*** defendant to have counsel ***appointed for him by the state***, and upon the scope and limitations of this right. The vast majority of decisions under the Sixth Amendment have dealt with appointed, rather than retained, counsel. (However, as we'll see in greater detail below, p. 376, a criminal defendant also has a Sixth Amendment right to be represented by the *retained*, i.e., non-court-appointed, counsel of his choosing.)

C. **Right to counsel in other contexts:** The right to the presence of an attorney, appointed or retained, also has been established in certain ***pre-trial*** settings, such as in post-charge lineups (see *supra*, p. 299) or during police in-custody interrogations (see *supra*, p. 240). Other pre-trial situations in which the right attaches will be discussed *infra*.

   1. **Appointed vs. retained counsel:** In those situations where an indigent defendant would have the right to appointed counsel, a non-indigent defendant has *a fortiori* a right to have his own retained counsel present. But the converse is not necessarily true — the fact that

no right to appointed counsel exists does not mean that no right to have retained counsel present exists. For instance, although the Supreme Court held in *Ross v. Moffitt* (discussed *infra*, p. 379) that a state may refuse to provide counsel to aid in the preparation of applications for second-level discretionary appeals, it does not follow that the state may prevent a convicted defendant from paying his own lawyer to aid with such applications.

II. RIGHT TO RETAINED COUNSEL OF ONE'S CHOICE

A. **Right generally:** The Sixth Amendment guarantees the right of a criminal defendant who does not need appointed counsel to ***hire private counsel of her own choosing*** to represent her. See, e.g., *Caplin & Dysdale v. U.S.*, 491 U.S. 617 (1989): "The Sixth Amendment guarantees a defendant the right to be represented by an otherwise qualified attorney whom that defendant can ***afford to hire***, or who is willing to represent the defendant even though he is without funds."

1. ***Per se* right:** If the private counsel chosen by defendant is qualified, the court's denial of permission for the lawyer to conduct the defense is ***automatically reversible error*** — the defendant does not even need to demonstrate on appeal that the denial of counsel of choice is likely to have ***affected the outcome***. *U.S. v. Gonzalez-Lopez*, 126 S.Ct. 2557 (2006).

   Example: D, who is charged with narcotics distribution, attempts to hire an out-of-state lawyer, Low, to represent him. The trial judge, mistakenly believing that Low has violated a local court rule in a different case, refuses to consent to the representation. D is represented by a different lawyer, is convicted, and appeals. The government argues that even though D's Sixth Amendment right to be represented by a paid attorney of his choice was violated, the violation should be deemed harmless error unless D can show that the substitute lawyer's representation of D so adversely affected the outcome as to constitute "ineffective assistance of counsel" (see infra, p. 386).

   Held, for D: the conviction is reversed without any showing of whether Low's presence as lawyer would have made any difference. "Where the right to be assisted by counsel of one's choice is wrongly denied … it is unnecessary to conduct an ineffectiveness or prejudice inquiry to establish a Sixth Amendment violation. Deprivation of the right is 'complete' when the defendant is erroneously prevented from being represented by the lawyer he wants, regardless of the quality of the representation he received." *U.S. v. Gonzalez-Lopez*, *supra*.

2. **Federal or state:** This right to a counsel of one's own choosing, imposed by the Sixth Amendment, applies to ***both state and federal*** trials.

3. **Limitations:** But the theoretically "unqualified" right to be represented by one's own retained attorney is ***not really so absolute***.

   a. **Ability to pay may be blocked:** For instance, the government may place limits on the mechanism by which the defendant ***pays*** his retained lawyer. For example, federal "civil ***forfeiture***" statutes allow the government to seize and keep any property used in, or money earned from, violations of drug or other laws. The Supreme Court has held that such forfeiture statutes may be enforced even where the forfeited property is the only property with which the defendant could pay his retained lawyer, and even if the effect of enforcement is that the lawyer refuses to represent the defendant because of the difficulty in obtaining payment. See *Caplin & Drysdale, Chartered v. U.S.*, 491 U.S. 617 (1989).

b. **Conflict:** Similarly, a defendant's right to a lawyer of his own choosing does not give him the right to choose a lawyer where this would result in a ***conflict*** between the lawyer's representation of the defendant and his representation of some other co-defendant. This is true even where all defendants are willing to "waive" the conflict. See *infra*, p. 398.

III. THE INDIGENT'S RIGHT TO APPOINTED COUNSEL

A. ***Powell* and capital crimes:** An indigent has a constitutional right to ***appointed*** counsel in felony cases (and in certain misdemeanor cases too). The first case finding such a right as to a *state* felony trial was ***Powell v. Alabama***, 287 U.S. 45 (1932).

1. **Limited holding:** *Powell* involved a ***capital crime***, and the Supreme Court, in finding that the indigent defendants there had a constitutional right to an appointed lawyer, emphasized that its holding was limited to capital crimes, and to those capital crimes where the defendant was "incapable adequately of making his own defense because of ignorance, feeble-mindedness, illiteracy or the like."

2. **Due process rationale:** The holding in *Powell* was based ***not*** on the Sixth Amendment right to counsel, but on the Fourteenth Amendment right to ***due process***. The absence of counsel in the case at hand was found to have been so prejudicial to the defendants as to have rendered the trial fundamentally unfair.

B. ***Betts v. Brady:*** From *Powell* (1932) until *Gideon v. Wainwright*, 372 U.S. 335 (1963), the Supreme Court determined the existence of the right to appointed counsel in particular state trials by the due process test. The Sixth Amendment right to counsel, although held in *Johnson v. Zerbst*, 304 U.S. 458 (1938) to require the appointment of counsel for all indigent defendants in federal felony trials, was held in ***Betts v. Brady***, 316 U.S. 455 (1942) ***not to apply to state trials***.

1. ***Betts* rationale:** In declining to apply the Sixth Amendment right to appointed counsel automatically to all state trials, the *Betts* Court stated that "while want of counsel in a particular case may result in a conviction lacking in . . . fundamental fairness [as in *Powell*], we cannot say that the amendment embodies an inexorable command that no trial for any offense, or in any court, can be fairly conducted and justice accorded a defendant who is not represented by counsel."

   a. **Fair trial obtained:** The *Betts* Court decided that in the case before it the lack of appointed counsel did not result in a denial of due process to the defendant, since the trial for robbery rested on the "simple issue" of judging the truth of testimony establishing an alibi. The defendant was a man of "ordinary intelligence and ability" who had once before been in court and thus was "not unfamiliar with criminal procedure."

2. **Dissent:** The three dissenters called for application of the Sixth Amendment to the states. They also alluded to an equal protection argument by asserting that "a practice cannot be

reconciled with 'common and fundamental ideas of fairness and right' which subjects innocent men to increased danger of conviction merely because of their poverty."

3. **Erosion of *Betts:*** In the 20 years following *Betts*, the Court decided over 30 cases involving application of the *Betts* due process standard. In all but a few, compelling circumstances were found to entitle the defendant to an attorney to ensure the "fundamental fairness" of the trial. See Nutshell, p. 324.

C. ***Gideon:*** Finally, *Betts* was overruled and the ***Sixth Amendment held applicable to the states***, in ***Gideon v. Wainwright***, 372 U.S. 335 (1963). The Court relied principally on the broad language of *Powell* and said that "*Betts* departed from the sound wisdom upon which the Court's holding in *Powell* rested."

1. **Facts:** The defendant was charged with the robbery of a poolroom. At trial he was denied his request for appointed counsel, despite his indigence. He conducted his own defense, and was convicted and sentenced to five years imprisonment.

    a. ***Per se* rule announced:** The Supreme Court held that Gideon had been denied a fair trial because "in our adversary system of criminal justice, any person haled into Court, who is too poor to hire a lawyer, cannot be assured a fair trial unless counsel is provided for him." Therefore, the Sixth Amendment (as incorporated in the Fourteenth Amendment) automatically entitles an indigent defendant to appointed counsel, at least in felony cases.

    b. **Subsequent acquittal:** The retrial of Gideon itself provides a nice example of the importance of counsel. In the second trial, with appointed counsel representing him, Gideon was acquitted by a jury. The attorney was able to discredit the prosecution's sole witness and to emphasize the need for proof "beyond a reasonable doubt." See Lewis, *Gideon's Trumpet*, pp. 223-238 (1968).

D. **Equal protection:** While *Gideon* was based on the Sixth Amendment, appointment of counsel has also been held to be compelled in certain situations by the ***equal protection clause*** of the Fourteenth Amendment.

1. ***Griffin:*** The equal protection rationale is founded on ***Griffin v. Illinois***, 351 U.S. 12 (1956), in which the Supreme Court held that a state must provide a ***free transcript of the trial proceedings*** when submission of a transcript is a prerequisite to appeal.

    a. **Black's concurrence:** There was no majority opinion in *Griffin*, but a frequently-cited concurrence by Justice Black noted that "It is true that a State is not required by the federal constitution to provide appellate courts or a right to appellate review at all. . . . But that is not to say that a State that does grant review can do so in a way that discriminates against some convicted defendants on account of their poverty. . . . There can be no equal justice where the kind of trial a man gets depends on the amount of money he has."

2. ***Douglas:*** The "*Griffin* principle" of equal protection was held in ***Douglas v. California***, 372 U.S. 353 (1963) to require that ***counsel be appointed*** to assist indigent defendants in preparing the ***first appeal*** from a conviction, at least where this first appeal is available as a matter of right to every convicted defendant.

a. **Rationale:** *Douglas* based its requirement of counsel on the reasoning that "where the merits of the one and only appeal an indigent has as of right are decided without the benefit of counsel, we think an unconstitutional line has been drawn between rich and poor."

b. **Limited holding:** *Douglas* explicitly declined to decide whether the right to counsel attaches to ***discretionary higher appeals*** (i.e., appeals which the court has discretion to accept or refuse, as is the case with certiorari by the U.S. Supreme Court). The holding in *Douglas* was limited to "the first appeal, granted as a matter of right to rich and poor alike, from a criminal conviction."

3. ***Ross:*** In ***Ross v. Moffitt***, 417 U.S. 600 (1974), the Supreme Court adopted a narrow view of the *Griffin-Douglas* equal protection principle, in holding that an indigent does ***not*** have a right to appointed counsel on his applications for ***discretionary review*** by the state supreme court or on his petition for certiorari to the United States Supreme Court.

a. **Rationale:** The 6-3 majority, *per* Rehnquist, stressed that the defendant did not need an attorney to have "meaningful access" to the higher appellate courts. Discretionary appeals, the Court noted, are accepted or rejected usually on the basis not of the likelihood that the original determination of guilt was wrong, but on the importance of the legal issues involved, a question which can be evaluated from the record of the intermediate appellate proceedings (during which by *Douglas* the defendant had the assistance of counsel).

i. **No need for absolute equality:** The opinion observed that the concept of equal protection does not require absolute equality, so that "the fact that a particular service might be of benefit to an indigent does not mean that the service is constitutionally required." The question whether the lack of appointed counsel denied equal protection to poor defendants as against rich ones was "not one of absolutes, but one of degrees." Since the defendant in *Ross* was not "denied meaningful access" to the North Carolina Supreme Court, he was not denied equal protection. Nor was he denied meaningful access to the U.S. Supreme Court by a lack of counsel to assist in his petition for certiorari.

b. **Dissent:** The three dissenters to *Ross* (Douglas, joined by Brennan and Marshall) relied heavily on the unanimous opinion by the Fourth Circuit, in which Judge Haynesworth had been able to find "no logical basis for differentiation between appeals of right [as in *Douglas*] and permissive review procedures in the context of the Constitution and the right to counsel;" the Haynesworth opinion had in fact found an even greater need for counsel on higher appeal because of the "highly specialized aspect of appellate work."

i. **Criticism:** *Ross* seems entirely inconsistent with the holding in *Douglas*, which the *Ross* majority distinguished merely by saying that the nature of higher appeal makes "this relative handicap [lack of counsel] far less than the handicap borne by the indigent defendant denied counsel on his initial appeal."

4. **Right to "effective" assistance:** In those proceedings where the right to counsel on appeal does apply (i.e., appeals as of right), this right includes the right to ***effective*** assistance. *Evitts v. Lucey*, 469 U.S. 387 (1985). Thus in *Evitts*, D's appointed counsel's failure

to file a required "statement of appeal," leading to dismissal of the appeal, so clearly deprived him of effective assistance that he was entitled to a new appeal. (The *Evitts* Court did not discuss the standard for measuring effectiveness of appellate counsel; see the discussion of effectiveness of trial counsel *infra*, p. 386.)

E. The concept of indigence: The only description of "indigent persons" furnished by the Supreme Court is those "lacking funds to hire a lawyer." The lower courts have generally determined the existence of indigence on a case-by-case basis, without developing formal standards.

1. **Number qualified:** In state felony cases, as of the early 1990s about 80% of defendants received appointed counsel, indicating that states are not imposing a stringent means test for proving indigency. K,L,I&K, p. 79, n. g.

2. **ABA standard:** The ABA has recommended the following test for determining whether counsel should be appointed for a particular defendant: "Counsel should be provided to any person who is financially unable to obtain adequate representation without substantial hardship to himself or his family. Counsel should not be denied to any person merely because his friends or relatives have resources adequate to retain counsel or because he has posted or is capable of posting bond." (ABA Standards, *Providing Defense Services*, §6.1.)

3. **Reimbursement:** Many states have recoupment laws requiring indigent defendants to ***reimburse the state*** for the cost of the legal services provided if they are later able to do so.

   a. **May not discriminate:** In *Rinaldi v. Yeager*, 384 U.S. 305 (1966), the Supreme Court struck down one such statute which required only those sentenced to prison to repay; the law was held to work an "invidious discrimination" between defendants sentenced to prison and others given only a suspended sentence or a fine.

   b. **Limits on recovery:** The Court has also held that a recoupment statute (which applied whether the defendant was convicted or not) violated equal protection because it did not allow the defendant to make use of the limits on wage garnishment, and other exemptions and protections, given to civil judgment debtors. *James v. Strange*, 407 U.S. 128 (1972).

   c. **Condition of probation:** But in *Fuller v. Oregon*, 417 U.S. 40 (1974), the Court ***upheld*** an Oregon statute which required repayment to the state of the costs of a free defense as a ***condition of probation***. The Court relied on the fact that the statute required payment only from those defendants who subsequently gain the ability to repay the expenses.

IV. PROCEEDINGS IN WHICH THE RIGHT TO COUNSEL APPLIES

A. Misdemeanors: In ***Argersinger v. Hamlin***, 407 U.S. 25 (1972), the Supreme Court extended the right to counsel to ***all indigent misdemeanor defendants faced with a potential jail sentence***.

1. **Rationale:** The Court held that the Sixth Amendment, in granting a right to counsel, did not distinguish between felonies and misdemeanors (as it did in providing a right to jury trial). "There is nothing in the language of the [Sixth] Amendment, its history, or in the decisions of this Court, to indicate that it was intended to embody a retraction of the right [to counsel] in petty offenses. . . . "

    a. **Equal need:** The opinion also rejected any contention that the need for counsel is any less because of shorter penalties, since some misdemeanor trials can "bristle with thorny constitutional questions." Moreover, difficult questions of legal tactics, such as the advisability of a guilty plea, will usually be present in such cases.

    b. **Jail not petty:** The Court also noted that *any* jail sentence can hardly be viewed as "petty."

2. **Jail sentence possible but not imposed:** As long as an indigent defendant is not ***sentenced*** to imprisonment, the state is not required to appoint counsel for him, even if the offense is one which is ***punishable*** by imprisonment. *Scott v. Illinois*, 440 U.S. 367 (1979). This holding means that even if the offense charged is a felony under state law, the state does not have to supply an indigent with counsel as long as the judge is willing merely to impose a fine.

    a. **Dissent:** Four Justices dissented in *Scott*. Three of them (Brennan, Marshall and Stevens) argued that society's view of the moral stigma associated with a particular offense is more clearly indicated by the authorized sentence than by the actual one imposed; in the present case, for instance, the defendant was charged with "petty larceny," an offense carrying substantial stigma. Therefore, counsel should be required wherever a jail sentence is authorized by law. Justice Blackmun, also dissenting, argued for a "bright line" rule that would require appointed counsel whenever the offense was punishable by more than six months' imprisonment ***or*** resulted in any actual imprisonment.

3. **Use to increase sentence for later crime:** An uncounseled misdemeanor conviction ***may*** be used to ***increase*** a permissible sentence for a ***subsequent*** conviction. *Nichols v. U.S.*, 511 U.S. 738 (1994).

    a. **Facts of *Nichols:*** Thus in *Nichols*, D was convicted in 1983 of state misdemeanor charges of driving under the influence; he was not offered a lawyer, pleaded guilty, and was fined $250 but not jailed. Then, in 1990, D pleaded guilty to federal drug conspiracy charges. Under federal Sentencing Guidelines, D's DUI misdemeanor conviction was counted, raising his Criminal History Category from one category to another. Consequently, the sentencing judge was allowed to (and did) add an extra 25 months to D's sentence.

    b. **Holding:** By a 5-4 vote, the Supreme Court held that the early uncounseled misdemeanor conviction could be used to increase D's jail term for the subsequent felony. D was not being punished for his earlier conviction, but rather, for the second one, the majority asserted. Since sentencing judges have always been allowed to take into consideration a broad range of factors in setting a defendant's sentence (e.g., past criminal behavior that did not result in a conviction), there was no Sixth Amendment violation in allowing the prior conviction to be used to increase D's sentence.

c. **Dissent:** The four dissenters in *Nichols* argued that "a conviction that is invalid for imposing a sentence for the offense itself remains invalid for increasing the term of imprisonment imposed for a subsequent conviction." To the dissenters, the issue was reliability: "an uncounseled misdemeanor . . . is not reliable enough to form the basis for the severe sanction of incarceration."

4. **Suspended sentence:** Suppose D is charged with a misdemeanor, not provided with counsel, convicted, but given a ***suspended sentence and probation***, so that a probation violation will trigger his imprisonment under the no-longer-suspended sentence. Can the state meet its Sixth Amendment obligation by not furnishing D with counsel until the probation-revocation hearing? The brief answer is "no" — unless the state furnishes counsel prior to the ***initial trial***, it gives up the right to imprison D when and if he violates his probation. See *Alabama v. Shelton*, 535 U.S. 654 (2002) (discussed more fully *infra*, p. 385).

B. **Quasi-criminal proceedings:** The Supreme Court has extended the right to appointed counsel to a ***juvenile delinquency proceeding*** in which institutional commitment was a possibility. ***In re Gault***, 387 U.S. 1 (1967). The *Gault* holding seems equally applicable to other proceedings which are "comparable in seriousness to a felony prosecution."

1. **Civil commitment:** *Gault* has been extended by several courts to ***civil commitment*** proceedings in which a significant deprivation of freedom is involved.

V. STAGES AT WHICH RIGHT TO COUNSEL ATTACHES

A. **Problem generally:** Distinct from the question of whether a right to counsel attaches in certain kinds of cases (e.g., misdemeanors, quasi-criminal proceedings, etc.) is the question of the ***stage*** of the proceedings at which the right to counsel begins and ends. May a defendant have counsel appointed for him at the preliminary hearing? At the sentencing hearing? Several of the more important non-trial stages of criminal proceedings are discussed below.

B. **Police investigation:** The preceding chapters have discussed several situations in which a suspect has a right to counsel during the period in which the police are ***conducting an investigation***. Thus the suspect has a right to appointed counsel if he is to be questioned by the police in custody, according to *Miranda* (see *supra*, p. 240). Similarly, a suspect against whom formal proceedings have been initiated has the right to a lawyer at a lineup or show-up (see *supra*, p. 299). And in *Massiah* (*infra*, p. 399), an indicted suspect was held to have the right not to have incriminating statements elicited from him by undercover agents in the absence of his lawyer. But with the exception of these several situations, a suspect does not usually have the right to appointed counsel during the investigative stage of a prosecution.

1. **Not Sixth Amendment right:** In any event, the right to counsel in the situations just described apparently does *not* derive from the Sixth Amendment at all, but rather from the ***Fifth*** Amendment right against self-incrimination. In *Moran v. Burbine*, 475 U.S. 412 (1986) (discussed more extensively *supra*, p. 263), the Court made this clear. In fact, the Court held that even if a suspect has already, prior to police questioning, ***established an attorney-client relationship*** (by the use of retained rather than appointed counsel), he has ***no*** Sixth Amendment right to have the police ***not interfere*** with that relationship. Thus in *Moran*, D's Sixth Amendment rights were not violated when, shortly after D was arrested

and before any formal proceedings had begun, the police declined to tell D that his family had retained a lawyer who was trying to contact him, or when the police falsely told the lawyer that D would not be interrogated until the following day.

C. **Initial appearance:** A defendant's first contact with the judiciary in a criminal case is usually his ***initial appearance*** before a magistrate, which generally occurs soon after his arrest. At the initial appearance, the defendant is informed of the charges against him, and told of his right to remain silent, to have the assistance of counsel, and, if the case is a felony case, to have a preliminary examination. The magistrate also usually sets bail. (Nutshell, p. 340.)

1. ***White* case:** In ***White v. Maryland***, 373 U.S. 59 (1963), the Supreme Court held that the initial appearance is a "***critical stage***" of the proceedings, and ***requires the appointment of counsel***, if the defendant is compelled to make a decision which may later be formally ***used against him.***

   a. **Facts of *White*:** In *White*, the defendant had been compelled to make an initial, non-binding, plea. He pleaded guilty without the assistance of counsel, but then at his arraignment (*infra*, p. 384) was assisted by appointed counsel and changed his plea to not guilty. Although the change of plea was allowed, the original guilty plea was introduced against him at trial.

   b. **Holding:** The Supreme Court found that the use of the guilty plea as evidence against the defendant made the initial appearance a critical stage, requiring that appointed counsel be made available; such counsel was needed to help the defendant to "plead intelligently."

2. **Where no binding decision made:** Even if the defendant is not compelled at the initial appearance to make decisions which may be formally used against him at trial, there is still a possibility that he may in particular circumstances have a right to appointed counsel. *Coleman v. Alabama* (discussed *infra*) indicates that the setting of bail is one of the factors that makes a preliminary examination a critical stage requiring access to appointed counsel; since bail is often set at the initial hearing, the *Coleman* rationale might be applied to require the appointment of counsel to assist the defendant in arguing that low or no bail should be set. (See Nutshell, p. 341.)

D. **Preliminary hearing:** Some time (at least a few days) after the initial appearance, a "***preliminary hearing***" or "preliminary examination" is conducted, also by a magistrate. The chief function of this hearing is to determine whether there is probable cause to "bind over" or "hold" the accused for prosecution (although it is the prosecutor who makes the final decision whether to prosecute).

1. ***Coleman:*** The preliminary hearing ***is a critical stage*** of the prosecution. Therefore, the denial of appointed counsel at the preliminary hearing is a violation of the accused's Sixth Amendment rights. ***Coleman v. Alabama***, 399 U.S. 1 (1970). The Court reasoned in *Coleman* that counsel can perform several important functions at the preliminary-hearing stage, including the cross-examination of witnesses and the reduction of bail.

   a. **"Harmless error" possibility:** However, the denial of counsel at the preliminary hearing does not necessarily require reversal of the subsequent conviction, because that denial will constitute ***"harmless error"*** unless the defendant can show that the presence of counsel would have changed some specific occurrence or omission at the hearing having a direct impact at trial. *Coleman, supra.*

i. **Illustration of non-harmless error:** The Court in *Coleman* gave as an example of such a prejudicial (non-harmless) occurrence the situation in which "important testimony of a ***witness unavailable at trial*** could have been ***preserved*** had counsel been present."

ii. **Illustrations of harmless error:** On the other hand, the *Coleman* Court said, it would ***not*** be enough for the defendant to show that counsel might have persuaded the magistrate to ***dismiss the case***, or for him to show that counsel would have been ***more familiar with the case at trial*** had he been present at the hearing. These advantages were, the Court said, too speculative to require reversal of an otherwise valid conviction. The Court therefore remanded for a consideration of whether the denial of counsel there had been harmless error.

E. **Indictment:** In some states, the formal criminal process is commenced by a grand jury's return of an ***indictment*** charging the defendant with a particular crime (generally a felony). It has long been established that the return of an indictment triggers the accused's right to appointed counsel.

F. **Arraignment:** After an information or indictment is issued, an ***arraignment*** takes place. At the arraignment, the charges are read, and the defendant enters a plea.

1. **Where no prejudice can occur:** The arraignment is a critical stage requiring counsel, but the denial of counsel is harmless error as long as the defendant is not required to bind himself in any way. Thus if he is asked to enter a plea, but is permitted to change his plea later without any prejudice (e.g., without having the change of plea introduced against him as in *White*, *supra*, p. 383) the absence of appointed counsel is harmless error, and the conviction will not be reversed.

2. **Where not harmless error:** But if certain defenses or pleas are lost to the defendant as the result of entering a particular plea, or if the plea is otherwise prejudicial to him, the denial of counsel at the arraignment is not harmless error, and the conviction will be reversed. Thus in *Hamilton v. Alabama*, 368 U.S. 52 (1961), the defendant lost, by state law, the right to assert an insanity defense by not raising it at arraignment; the Supreme Court held that the denial of appointed counsel at the arraignment therefore required reversal.

G. **Plea-bargaining:** ***Plea-bargaining*** is a critical stage of criminal proceedings. Therefore, a defendant who is considering whether to accept or decline an offer of a plea bargain from the prosecution is entitled to have an attorney assist him.

1. **Effective assistance:** Recall that if D has a right to an attorney, he has right to have that attorney render "effective assistance" (see *supra*, p. 379 and *infra*, p. 386). In the plea-bargaining context, this means that D has the right to effective assistance whether he ends up ***accepting*** or ***rejecting*** the plea bargain. See, e.g., *Missouri v. Frye* and *Lafler v. Cooper* (both *infra*, p. 391), twin cases in which the Court held that there is a right to effective assistance of counsel during the plea-bargaining process even if D ends up rejecting (or never learning about) a plea offer.

H. Sentencing a "critical stage": ***Sentencing*** is a "critical stage" of criminal proceedings, requiring the right to an attorney. ***Mempa v. Rhay***, 389 U.S. 128 (1967).

1. **Rationale:** The Court held in *Mempa* that "appointment of counsel for an indigent is required at every stage of a criminal proceeding where ***substantial rights*** of a criminal accused may be ***affected***." Counsel was therefore required for the sentencing, clearly a crucial part of the criminal proceeding as far as the defendant was concerned.

2. **Suspended sentence:** Suppose D is convicted of a crime, and is given a ***suspended sentence***, under which he is ***placed on probation*** and will be imprisoned if and only if he later violates the terms of the probation. Does he have the right to appointed counsel during the process that leads to the suspended sentence? The Supreme Court has answered ***"yes"*** to this question. ***Alabama v. Shelton***, 535 U.S. 654 (2002).

   a. **Misdemeanor cases:** *Shelton* means that states are limited in how they handle minor crimes, especially non-serious ***misdemeanors***. If the state wants to be able to ask the judge to impose a suspended sentence and probation, to be followed by imprisonment if D violates the probation, then the state will have to ***choose*** between (1) providing counsel in all such minor cases; or (2) ***giving up the right to impose a jail sentence*** if D ***violates*** the probation (making the threat of imprisonment for probation violations relatively toothless). In other words, *Shelton* forbids the state from saying, "We'll deny appointed counsel in the initial trial that ends in the suspended sentence, but we'll then supply counsel if and when we propose to imprison D for violating the probation."

3. **Probation revocation not part of process:** There is no automatic right to appointed counsel in a ***probation revocation*** proceeding. *Gagnon v. Scarpelli*, 411 U.S. 778 (1973).

   a. **Special circumstances:** So assuming D does not make a serious argument that he didn't commit the probation violation, nor a serious argument that there are mitigating circumstances, D is not entitled to appointed counsel at the probation-revocation proceeding, even though an order of revocation will result in imprisonment. But in such a revocation hearing, D *is* "presumptively" entitled to counsel if he makes a "timely and colorable claim" that (1) he ***did not commit*** the violation, or (2) there are ***mitigating circumstances*** making revocation inappropriate. *Gagnon.*

I. Psychiatric examination a "critical stage": A ***psychiatric examination***, if used by the prosecution to establish that a murder defendant remains dangerous and should receive the death penalty, is a "critical stage" to which the Sixth Amendment right to the effective assistance of counsel attaches.

1. ***Estelle v. Smith:*** In *Estelle v. Smith*, 451 U.S. 454 (1981) (discussed more fully *supra*, p. 253), the Court unanimously held that, since counsel for the defendant had already been appointed, the Sixth Amendment required that counsel be notified (1) that a psychiatric examination had been ordered by the court; and (2) that the results of this examination might be used during the penalty phase of the trial on the issue of the defendant's future dangerousness.

   a. **Rationale:** The Court expressly refrained from deciding whether the defendant had a right to have his lawyer ***with him*** at the examination (though the Court implied that such a right probably did not exist); rather, the opinion was based on the theory that the defendant "was denied the assistance of his attorneys in making the significant decision of whether to submit to the examination and to what end the psychiatrist's findings could be employed."

J. Appeals: A convicted defendant has the right to appointed counsel for his first ***appeal as of right*** (i.e., appeal made available to all convicted defendants). See *Douglas v. California*, 372 U.S. 353 (1963) (discussed *supra*, p. 378). But there is no right to have counsel appointed for attempts to obtain ***discretionary review*** of the conviction (e.g., review by the state supreme court, or petitions for certiorari to the U.S. Supreme Court). See *Ross v. Moffitt*, 417 U.S. 600 (1974) (discussed *supra*, p. 379).

K. Collateral proceedings: A ***prisoner*** has a limited right to legal assistance for the purpose of pursuing ***collateral proceedings*** (e.g., federal *habeas corpus*). In ***Bounds v. Smith***, 430 U.S. 817 (1977), the Supreme Court held that "the fundamental constitutional right of access to the courts requires prison authorities to ***assist inmates*** in the preparation and filing of meaningful legal papers by providing prisoners with ***adequate law libraries*** or adequate ***assistance*** from persons trained in the law."

1. **Fulfillment of obligation:** This obligation may be fulfilled, the Court held, by any of the following: (1) adequate law libraries; (2) the training of inmates as paralegal assistants to work under lawyers' supervision; (3) the use of paralegals and law students; and (4) the use of lawyers, either on a volunteer, part-time consulting, or full-time staff basis.

2. ***Ross v. Moffitt* distinguished:** The Court in *Bounds* distinguished the collateral attack situation from the situation at issue in *Ross v. Moffitt* (*supra*, p. 379) (discretionary review by the state supreme court or petition for certiorari to the U.S. Supreme Court). In the latter case, prisoners have already had counsel for their initial appeals as of right, and are thus likely to have appellate briefs written on their behalf, trial transcripts and other sources to use in preparing petitions for review. In the collateral attack situation, however, the claim (a constitutional one) is often being advanced for the first time, and the need for legal assistance is therefore greater.

3. **Dissents:** Three Justices (Rehnquist, Stewart and Burger) dissented, each in a separate opinion. The dissenters took general issue with the majority's statement that there is a "fundamental constitutional right of access" to the federal courts for the purpose of collaterally attacking state convictions.

VI. RIGHT TO EFFECTIVE ASSISTANCE OF COUNSEL

A. Effectiveness of counsel generally: The Sixth Amendment does not merely entitle the defendant to have a lawyer. It entitles him to the "***effective assistance*** of counsel." Therefore, even a defendant who has been actually represented by counsel may show that his Sixth Amendment right was violated. Such a claim is known as an ***"ineffective assistance"*** claim.

B. Standard for judging effectiveness: The standard for evaluating a defendant's claim that the representation he received was not "effective" is given in ***Strickland v. Washington***, 466 U.S. 668 (1984). Under *Strickland* (which remains very much in force), a defendant whose lawyer has actually participated in the trial must make ***two showings*** in order to sustain his Sixth Amendment claim:

[1] **First prong:** that counsel's performance was ***"deficient,"*** in the sense that counsel was ***not*** a ***"reasonably competent*** attorney"; and

[2] **Second prong:** that the deficiencies in counsel's performance were ***prejudicial*** to the defense, in the sense that there is a "***reasonable probability*** that, but for counsel's unprofessional errors, the ***result*** of the proceeding ***would have been different***."

1. **Objective standard:** For the ***first*** of these prongs (***competence***), the defendant must show that the advice given by counsel was not "within the ***range of competence*** demanded of attorneys in criminal cases." It will not be enough for D to show that some or even most defense lawyers would have handled the matter differently, since there are "countless ways to provide effective assistance in any given case." Furthermore, the court should apply a ***"strong presumption" that the lawyer's conduct fell within this wide range.***

2. **Prejudice:** Even if the defendant has shown that counsel's work at the trial was hopelessly incompetent, under the ***second prong*** of *Strickland* he must still show that this incompetence led to ***prejudice***. This means that if the facts showing the defendant's guilt are so overwhelming that even the most competent lawyering would be unlikely to have obtained an acquittal, the Sixth Amendment claim ***fails***. In particular, the requirement of a showing of prejudice means that the defendant must show that there was "a ***reasonable probability*** that, but for counsel's unprofessional errors, the ***result of the proceeding would have been different.***" This requirement that prejudice be shown is often referred to as the "second prong" of *Strickland.*

   a. **Meaning of "reasonable probability":** A "reasonable probability" is a probability that is "***sufficient to undermine confidence*** in the outcome." *Strickland.* In the usual case where the issue is the defendant's guilt or innocence (as distinguished from an appropriate sentence), the issue is therefore "whether there is a reasonable probability that, absent the errors, the factfinder would have had a ***reasonable doubt*** respecting guilt." *Id.*

C. **Advice as to plea-bargaining:** The right to effective assistance of counsel applies during the ***plea-bargaining*** process. There are two distinct scenarios, in either of which counsel might be found to have failed to furnish effective assistance:

[1] Due to poor advice from counsel, the defendant ***agrees to accept a plea bargain***, when going to trial would likely have led to a better outcome (e.g., acquittal, conviction on a lesser charge than the one pleaded to, a shorter sentence upon conviction, etc.).

[2] Due to poor (or no) advice from counsel, the defendant ***fails to accept a plea bargain*** offered by the prosecution, ***goes to trial***, gets convicted, and receives a ***longer sentence*** than the one offered under the plea bargain.

We'll consider each of these scenarios separately.

1. **D accepts a "bad" plea-bargain offer:** One branch of the Court's decisions on whether there can be a right to effective assistance of counsel during the plea-bargaining process has involved the defendant's ***acceptance*** of a "bad" plea bargain. These decisions establish

that in at least some circumstances, the ***result*** of the plea bargain taken under bad advice — compared with the result that would likely have occurred at trial — can be ***so dramatically worse*** that the defendant will be deemed to have been deprived of effective assistance and perhaps entitled to ***withdraw the plea*** and get a new trial.

Example: D is a non-citizen who has resided lawfully in the U.S. for 40 years, and has served in Vietnam. He is charged by a state court with marijuana smuggling. His lawyer does not tell him that if he pleads guilty to the charge, he will be automatically ***deported*** under federal immigration law; indeed, the lawyer says that D does not have to worry about the immigration consequences of a guilty plea because he has been in the country so long. D pleads guilty, and then discovers that he is automatically and immediately deportable. He argues that had he known of this consequence, he would have insisted on going to trial, and that his lawyer's failure to tell him about the deportation risk constituted ineffective assistance of counsel.

Held (at least in part) for D. The automatic deportation consequences of a guilty plea here were so great that the lawyer's inaccurate advice deprived D of his Sixth Amendment right to effective assistance of counsel. However, to be entitled to withdraw his plea and go to trial, D will have to show on remand that he has suffered "prejudice" (the second prong under *Strickland, supra,* p. 387). ***Padilla v. Kentucky***, 130 S.Ct. 1473 (2010).

a. **How D can show prejudice from taking the "bad" plea deal:** In *Padilla, supra,* the Supreme Court held that D's counsel's failure to warn D that if he took the proposed plea bargain he was certain to be deported, constituted ineffective assistance. But, the Court noted, D would still have to make, on remand, a second showing, that the advice ***caused him "prejudice."*** Therefore, we need to understand what constitutes "prejudice" in this situation where D accepts a bad plea bargain based on ineffective assistance.

   i. **Second prong of *Strickland*, generally:** You'll recall that the need for D to show that he has "suffered prejudice" as the result of the ineffective assistance is often referred to as the ***"second prong"*** of *Strickland* (*supra*, p. 387). There, the Court gave this general formulation of what the second prong requires the defendant to show: "a reasonable probability that, but for counsel's unprofessional errors, ***the result of the proceeding would have been different."***

   ii. **Application of this prong in various contexts:** In the case of tactical errors made by counsel *at trial* that lead to D's conviction, for D to make the required showing that the "result of the proceeding" would probably have been different, D would need to show a reasonable probability that, absent the errors, "the factfinder would have had a ***reasonable doubt respecting guilt***" (i.e., a reasonable probability of ***acquittal***). But this standard doesn't really make sense in the context of whether D was prejudiced by taking a possibly-unwise *plea bargain* — even if it's unlikely that D would have been acquitted had the case been tried, the plea bargain might nonetheless entail such negative consequences that D can plausibly argue that had he known of these consequences, he would have rejected the plea offer, and has therefore suffered "prejudice."

iii. **What is the standard for plea bargain cases:** So, then, if D claims prejudice from not being accurately advised about the potential negative consequences of a plea bargain, what *does* D need to do to make the required showing of "a reasonable probability that, but for counsel's unprofessional errors, ***the result of the proceeding would have been different"*** (the *Strickland* formulation)?

iv. **The "I would have insisted on going to trial" standard:** The Supreme Court has given a very crisp (and relatively ***pro-defendant***) answer to this question. The defendant does *not* have to show that had he not taken the "bad" plea-bargain, he would probably have been acquitted at trial. Instead, he ***merely*** has to make a much easier showing: a ***"reasonable probability that,*** but for counsel's errors, he ***would not have pleaded guilty and would have insisted on going to trial."*** *Hill v. Lockhart*, 474 U.S. 52 (1985).

v. **Decision to go to trial in the case of probable deportation:** The issue of what constitutes prejudice when D takes a bad plea bargain arises most often in cases where D is not a U.S. citizen, and pleads guilty to an offense that (unbeknownst to D) makes it likely or certain that he will be ***deported***. *Padilla*, supra, was an example of such a "guilty plea leads to deportation" scenario. A 2017 case, ***Lee v. U.S.,*** 137 S.Ct. 1958 (2017), is another example, one that illustrates how the "I would have insisted on going to trial" is to be ***applied***.

(1) **Facts of *Lee*:** In *Lee*, D was a permanent resident (but non-citizen) of the U.S. who pleaded guilty to a narcotics crime in order to get a somewhat shorter sentence (16 or 17 years) than he would have gotten if convicted at trial (18 years). Before D took the plea, his lawyer erroneously assured him that he would not be deported if he pleaded guilty. (In reality, deportation was not just possible but ***mandatory***, whether he pleaded guilty or was found guilty at trial.) After taking the plea, D discovered the error and unsuccessfully tried to withdraw his plea.

(2) **Government's proposed prejudice standard:** When the case got to the Supreme Court, the government argued that no one in D's position – i.e., one who takes a plea in return for less prison time than he would receive after a conviction at trial – could make the required showing of prejudice unless he could show that he ***had "a viable defense"*** to the original charges. Without a "viable defense," the government argued, D couldn't show he would have been better off going to trial: in either case, D was certain to be deported after a jail sentence, and the only result of going to trial would be a longer imprisonment prior to the inevitable deportation. Therefore, the government argued, the Court should adopt "a *per se* rule that a defendant with no viable defense cannot show prejudice from the denial of his right to trial."

(3) **Court rejects this approach:** But the Supreme Court ***rejected*** this *per se* rule urged by the government. The decision whether to plead guilty does not turn solely on the "likelihood of success at trial," the Court said. Rather, the decision also involves "assessing the respective consequences of a conviction after trial and by plea." If those consequences are, from the defendant's per-

spective, "***similarly dire***," then ***"even the smallest chance of success at trial may look attractive."***

(4) D's claim was backed by the evidence: This *didn't* mean, the Court said, that the court was required to ***take at face value*** D's claim that he would have rejected the plea had he known it would trigger mandatory deportation. But here, there was ***"substantial and uncontroverted evidence"*** in the record that D would indeed have rejected the plea had he known it would lead to mandatory deportation. The record showed that:

(1) Lee had ***strong connections*** to this country and no connections to any other (including his native South Korea);

(2) D's behavior during the plea negotiations showed that deportation was the ***"determinative issue"*** for him; and

(3) The length of D's prison sentence was ***only "a year or two more"*** if he were to lose at trial instead of taking the plea.

In sum, D's decision whether to plead involved the difference between "certain" deportation (if he took the plea) and "almost certain" deportation (if he tried the case).

(5) D's decision was not "irrational": The Court then had to decide whether the above factors were sufficiently compelling that the Court should accept as true D's claim that he would have rejected the plea had he known it would trigger mandatory deportation. The Court conceded that not everyone faced with D's choice would conclude that the difference between "certain" and "almost certain" deportation justified risking an extra year or two of prison time. But that was not the issue.

Rather, the issue was whether it would have been ***irrational*** for D to choose to go to trial in the circumstances. And the Court decided that it "***cannot say*** it would be irrational" for D to do so. Since D might rationally (even if not wisely) chosen to throw the "Hail Mary pass" of going to trial had he known the deportation consequences of his choice, that was enough to establish that the ***ineffective assistance had caused him "prejudice."*** Consequently, D was entitled to a new trial.

2. **D rejects a good plea-bargain offer:** Now let's consider the opposite situation: the prosecution offers the defendant a particular plea bargain, and due to counsel's bad advice (or total lack of advice), the defendant ***doesn't take the offer***, goes to trial, gets convicted, and gets a longer prison term than the one originally offered under the plea-bargain. Until 2012, the Supreme Court had never decided whether there could be ever be a violation of the right to effective assistance in this "plea-bargain-not-accepted" scenario. But two important decisions that year — decided on the same day — establish that there can indeed be a violation of the Sixth Amendment right to effective assistance when the defendant is offered a plea bargain and declines it.

We'll consider these two cases as a single unit, not only because the Court decided them on the same day by identical 5-4 votes, but also because the majority applied essentially the same approach to both.

a. **The cases:** The cases are ***Missouri v. Frye***, 132 S.Ct. 1399 (2012) and ***Lafler v. Cooper***, 132 S.Ct. 1376 (2012). In *Frye*, defense counsel did not even ***inform*** the defendant of the prosecution's offer until after it expired; in *Lafler*, defense counsel told the defendant about the offer, but ***gave bad advice*** that resulted in the defendant's declining the offer, going to trial, and getting a longer sentence than had been available under the offer. In both cases, the Court concluded that the defendant had been denied the effective assistance of counsel, though the Court left to the lower courts on remand what the precise effect of this denial would be.

b. **Facts:** Here is a brief summary of the facts of the two cases:

   i. ***Frye*:** In *Frye*, Frye was charged with driving on a revoked license. Because he had three prior convictions for that same offense, he was vulnerable to a felony conviction with a four-year maximum prison sentence. The prosecution sent a letter to Frye's lawyer offering to take a misdemeanor plea and to recommend a 90-day sentence. The lawyer never told Frye about the offer, and it expired. Soon after the expiration, Frye was arrested again for driving on a revoked license. Probably because of this new arrest, the prosecution refused to re-offer the original plea bargain. Frye stood trial, was convicted, and was sentenced to three years in prison. He argued on appeal that had he been told about the misdemeanor offer, he would have accepted it, and that counsel's failure to tell him about it violated his right to effective assistance. The Missouri appellate court agreed.

   ii. ***Lafler*:** In *Lafler*, Cooper, who had shot the victim four times, was charged with assault with intent to murder as well as three other offenses. The prosecution offered to dismiss two of the charges, and to recommend a sentence of 51 to 85 months in prison on the remaining two, in return for a guilty plea. Cooper rejected the plea, based on his lawyer's obviously-bad advice that the prosecution would not be able to show that he had had an intent to kill because all four of his shots ***hit the victim below the waist***. Cooper was then convicted of all four offenses, and received a mandatory minimum sentence of 185 to 360 months in prison. He argued (on federal habeas corpus) that he had been denied effective assistance of counsel. The lower federal courts agreed, and ordered an unusual remedy: ***"specific performance"*** of the original plea offer (i.e., a carrying out of the original 51-to-85 month sentence).

   Note: So notice that in both *Frye* and *Lafler*, the defendant ***succeeded*** in the court(s) below with his claim of denial of effective assistance. Thus in both cases, it was the *prosecution* that persuaded the Supreme Court to grant cert.

c. **Right to effective assistance:** In both cases, Justice Kennedy, joined by the four liberal justices (Ginsburg, Breyer, Sotomayor and Kagan) held that a defendant ***has a Sixth Amendment right to the effective assistance of counsel during the plea-bargaining process***, even in the situation in which the defendant ends up ***not taking the plea bargain*** and then either gets convicted at trial or later pleads guilty under a worse (or no) plea deal.

i. **Large proportion of plea bargains:** Kennedy noted in *Frye* that the ***overwhelming majority*** of criminal cases in both the federal and state systems are ***resolved by plea-bargaining***: 97% of federal convictions and 94% of state convictions are the result of guilty pleas.

(1) **Centrality of plea-bargaining:** Therefore, Kennedy said, "plea bargains have become ***so central*** to the administration of the criminal justice system that ***defense counsel have responsibilities*** in the plea bargain process, responsibilities that must be met to render the adequate assistance of counsel that the Sixth Amendment requires[.]" (*Frye*.)

ii. **Longer sentences:** Kennedy also cited, approvingly, a commentator's assessment that "[Defendants] who do take their case to trial and lose ***receive longer sentences*** than even Congress or the prosecutor might think ***appropriate***, because the longer sentences ***exist on the books largely for bargaining purposes***." For Kennedy, these ultra-long available sentences made it even more important that defendants receive effective assistance of counsel during the plea-bargaining process.

d. **Specifics of rulings:** The two cases stand for two main propositions about what defense counsel must do when the prosecution makes an offer for a plea bargain.

i. **Rule requiring communication of offer:** In *Frye*, Kennedy announced the rule that would deal with the situation where (as in *Frye*) counsel ***does not even inform the defendant*** about the prosecution's plea offer: "as a general rule, defense counsel has the ***duty to communicate formal offers*** from the prosecution to accept a plea on terms and conditions that may be favorable to the accused." Since Frye's lawyer did not do that, Frye was denied his right to effective assistance (though as we'll see below, that denial was not enough to guarantee him an effective remedy).

ii. **Rule governing bad advice:** And in *Lafler*, Kennedy announced a comparable rule governing the situation which the defendant is told about the plea offer, but ***not given competent advice about whether to take it***: "If a plea bargain has been offered, a defendant has the right to effective assistance of counsel in ***considering whether to accept it***."

e. **Showing of prejudice:** But a defendant who can show that he was denied effective assistance during the plea-bargaining process under the *Frye* and *Lafler* decisions will not necessarily be entitled to any practical ***relief***. In both cases, the majority continued to impose the two-prong rule of *Strickland* (*supra*, pp. 386-387), under which a defendant claiming ineffective assistance must show not only that counsel's performance was incompetent, but also that this incompetence ***resulted in "prejudice"*** to the defense. "Prejudice" means, in general, that but for the incompetence, there is a reasonable probability that the ***result of the proceeding would have been different.***

i. **How to show prejudice:** A defendant who claims that he failed to accept an offered plea bargain due to defense incompetence must show several things in order to satisfy this "prejudice" prong of *Strickland*. As the *Frye* majority expressed the requirements, a defendant must show ***all*** of the following:

[1] "a ***reasonable probability*** [the defendant] ***would have accepted*** the earlier plea offer had [he] been afforded effective assistance of counsel";

[2] "a reasonable probability the plea would have been ***entered without the prosecution canceling it***" (assuming the prosecution had the power under state law to make such a cancellation); and

[3] "a reasonable probability the plea would have been entered ***without ... the trial court refusing to accept it***" (again assuming the prosecution had the power under state law to refuse to accept the plea).

(1) Summary: As Kennedy's opinion in *Frye* summarized the effect of these three rules, in cases where the defendant doesn't take the offered plea bargain, he will have to demonstrate "a ***reasonable probability*** that the ***end result*** of the criminal process would have been ***more favorable*** by reason of [either] a ***plea to a lesser charge*** or a ***sentence of less prison time***."

f. Nature of relief: If the defendant *does* manage to jump through both hoops of *Strickland* — i.e., he shows (1) deficient performance of counsel and (2) a reasonable probability that without the deficiency the result would have been different — the court that is ultimately deciding the Sixth Amendment issue will be forced to decide the not-necessarily-obvious issue of the ***appropriate remedy***.

The majority opinion in *Lafler* discusses the remedy issue, and shows that the choice of remedies will depend on whether the charges in the never-consummated plea offer are or are not the ***same*** as in the ultimate guilty plea or conviction at trial. In other words, the choice-of-remedy problem depends on whether the case involves only so-called ***"sentence bargaining"*** by the prosecutor or instead also (or alternatively) involves ***"charge bargaining."*** Therefore, we'll consider these two situations separately.

i. "Sentence bargaining" First, let's consider the simpler situation, the situation involving only ***"sentence bargaining."*** As Kennedy described it in *Lafler*, this is the situation in which "the ***sole advantage*** a defendant would have received under the plea is a ***lesser sentence*** ... [because] the ***charges*** that would have been admitted as part of the plea bargain are the ***same*** as the charges the defendant was convicted of after trial."[1]

(1) Formula for sentence-bargaining cases: For such sentence-bargaining cases, Kennedy's *Lafler* opinion says that if the defendant jumps through the two prongs of *Strickland*, the appropriate relief is that "the court may ***exercise discretion*** in determining whether the defendant should receive the ***term of imprisonment the government offered*** in the plea, the ***sentence he received at trial***, or ***something in between***." (Kennedy assumed that under state law, the

1. "Sentence bargaining" was essentially what was at issue in *Frye*. Frye was faced with a single felony charge, for driving with a revoked license. Although the more attractive of the offers in *Frye* would have substituted a misdemeanor for a felony, no charges would really have been "dropped" (there was only the one charge of driving with a revoked license), and the benefit to Frye from the offer would have been a reduction from a maximum four-year prison term to a maximum one-year term.

trial judge would have had discretion to reject the plea bargain, as is apparently the case in most states.)

(2) **Small comfort:** Notice that this formula ***gives virtually no guaranteed relief*** to the defendant who succeeds with an effective-assistance claim in a sentencing-bargaining case. Typically, the ***same judge*** who conducted the trial will be reassigned the case for resentencing. And as a matter of Sixth Amendment law, *Lafler* says that that judge has ***"discretion"*** to decide that the defendant should be given the ***same sentence*** as the one imposed at the trial, ***not*** the previously-offered plea bargain sentence or anything in between. You may wonder how often that judge will give the defendant who succeeds in climbing the *Strickland*-imposed mountain (i.e., shows both counsel incompetence and prejudice) any relief other than ***re-imposing the original sentence.***

ii. **"Charge bargaining" (plea agreement drops some charges):** Now, let's look at the ***"charge bargaining"*** scenario. This is, at least approximately, the situation that Kennedy's *Lafler* opinion described as one in which "[the] offer was for a guilty plea to a count or counts ***less serious*** than the ones for which a defendant was convicted after trial, or [where] a ***mandatory sentence*** confines a judge's sentencing discretion after trial[.]" Here, Kennedy said, "it may be that ***resentencing alone*** will ***not be full redress*** for the constitutional injury."

(1) **Specific performance:** In this situation, what contract law would call an order of ***specific performance*** may be constitutionally required. As Kennedy put it, where resentencing would not give full redress, the proper remedy "***may be to require the prosecution to reoffer the plea proposal.***" Then, he said, once the re-offer has occurred, the judge can ***exercise discretion*** in deciding whether to vacate the conviction from trial and ***accept the plea*** or leave the conviction undisturbed."

(2) **Little practical relief:** So here, too (as in the sentence-bargaining-only situation) the defendant may receive little or no practical relief.

Example: In *Lafler* itself, the Supreme Court held that the lower federal courts had decreed the wrong remedy; the state prosecutor should have been required to re-offer the original plea agreement (which Cooper would undoubtedly accept). But then, because the state trial judge had the discretion to reject this plea agreement when it was originally offered, that judge would have the same discretion this time around, too. So the judge can either "vacate the conviction from trial and ***accept the plea*** or leave the conviction undisturbed." *Lafler*, *supra*.

Note: So Cooper's reward for all the (successful) work of showing counsel's incompetence and prejudice might well end up being nothing more than having the trial judge reimpose the original 185-month-minimum sentence.

3. **Significance:** So, in brief, *Hill* (p. 389), *Lee* (p. 389), *Frye* (pp. 391-393), and *Lafler* (pp. 391-394) establish these propositions about the denial of effective assistance in connection with whether to accept a plea bargain offer made by the prosecution:

[1] A defendant has the ***right to the effective assistance of counsel*** during the plea-bargaining process;

[2] This right can be violated if the defendant ***accepts a plea*** and ends up worse off due to the lack of effective counsel;

[3] The right can also be violated if the defendant ***rejects*** the plea (or ***never learns*** of it), and ends up worse off due to the lack of effective counsel;

[4] For the defendant to establish an effective-assistance violation under rule [2] above, he will have to show that he ***suffered "prejudice"*** (i.e., ended up being "worse off") from not accepting the plea. Making such a showing will typically require him to overcome multiple obstacles (e.g., showing that the prosecutor and/or judge would not have canceled the plea agreement if D had accepted it); and

[4] For the defendant to establish an effective-assistance violation under rule [3] above, he will have to show that he ***suffered "prejudice"*** from accepting the plea. Making such a showing will require the defendant to show a ***"reasonable probability that,*** but for counsel's errors, he ***would not have pleaded guilty and would have insisted on going to trial."*** D doesn't have to show that had he gone to trial, he likely would have *won* – all he needs to show is that ***it would not have been irrational*** for him to try the case. For instance, mandatory deportation in the event of a conviction either by plea or trial might well be enough to make it not-irrational for D to try the case as a type of "Hail Mary pass" hoping for a long-shot acquittal. (*Lee*.)

D. Insufficient time to prepare: The requisite ineffective assistance, and prejudice, may be due to the fact that the court has refused to grant a ***postponement*** to allow a newly-appointed lawyer ***adequate time to prepare*** for trial.

1. Shortness of time without more: In rare cases, the shortness of the preparation time may by itself be enough to give rise to a presumption of ineffectiveness and prejudice; this was the case, for instance, in *Powell v. Alabama*, 287 U.S. 45 (1932) (*supra*, p. 377), where counsel for poor illiterate black defendants on trial for rape of a white woman was appointed only moments before trial began — counsel's actual performance at trial was not even examined, because the surrounding circumstances made it so unlikely that any lawyer could provide effective assistance that ineffectiveness was properly presumed. (See the Supreme Court's more recent analysis of *Powell* in *U.S. v. Cronic*, 466 U.S. 648 (1984).)

a. Ordinary delay: Generally, however, the fact of delay will not eliminate the need for showing ***actual ineffectiveness and prejudice***. See, e.g., *Chambers v. Maroney*, 399 U.S. 42 (1970) (no per se rule that late appointment of counsel, even a few minutes before trial, automatically amounts to ineffective representation.) See also *U.S. v. Cronic*, *supra* (25 days for counsel to prepare defense, compared with 4 1/2 years for government to develop prosecution, did not justify abandonment of the requirement of a showing of ineffectiveness and prejudice.)

E. Right of consultation: The defendant's lawyer must be given a ***reasonable right of access*** to his client. Thus in *Geders v. U.S.*, 425 U.S. 80 (1976), the Supreme Court held that a trial court order preventing D from consulting with his counsel about anything during a seventeen-hour overnight recess between his direct and cross-examination violated D's right to counsel. The Court conceded that there was a danger that the lawyer would "coach" the defendant's answers for cross-examination, but held that this danger must be dealt with in other ways (e.g., allowing the prosecutor to cross-examine D to develop whether coaching occurred).

F. No right to "meaningful relationship": The Sixth Amendment does not include any right to a ***"meaningful attorney-client relationship." Morris v. Slappy***, 461 U.S. 1 (1983). This is true whether the attorney is appointed or retained (though the question is much more likely to arise in the case of an appointed lawyer, as in *Morris*).

1. **Substitution of counsel:** In *Morris*, D's originally-appointed lawyer, who had prepared to try the case, became hospitalized; different counsel was appointed to try the case, over D's objection. The Supreme Court seems to have held that the trial court was not required to consider D's interest in having the original lawyer rather than the replacement try the case. (However, if the replacement lawyer was appointed so late that he had no opportunity to prepare the case, it would probably be a violation of the Sixth Amendment to deny a continuance; this was not the situation in *Morris.)*

G. No right to have lawyer present perjured testimony: The Sixth Amendment entitles the defendant to a lawyer who will represent him loyally and vigorously. But that amendment of course does ***not*** entitle the defendant to a lawyer who will knowingly present ***perjured testimony***.

> **Example:** D, who is charged in state court with murder, plans to assert self-defense. In preparing for the case, D at first repeatedly tells his court-appointed lawyer, L, that he did not see a gun in the victim's hand. Just before trial, D tells L that he plans to testify that he saw "something metallic" in the victim's hand. L tells D that this would be perjury, that he, L, cannot and will not knowingly put perjured testimony on the stand, and that if D insists on giving this testimony, L will disclose the perjury and withdraw from the case. D reluctantly omits the "something metallic" testimony, and is convicted. He then argues that L's refusal to allow him to testify as he wanted violated his right to counsel.
>
> *Held*, for the prosecution. The rules of professional ethics in force in the state prohibited L from putting on D's proposed testimony, so L acted in accordance with the rules. It cannot be a violation of D's Sixth Amendment rights for his counsel to act in accordance with professional rules. *Nix v. Whiteside*, 475 U.S. 157 (1986).

H. Death penalty cases: The Supreme Court seems somewhat more likely to uphold an ineffective-counsel claim when the case is a ***capital case*** and the defendant is in fact ***sentenced to death***. Nothing in Supreme Court doctrine states that the tough standards for a successful ineffective-assistance claim should be relaxed in such cases, but defendants seem nonetheless to prevail more often here than in non-capital cases. Success is particularly likely based on ineffective assistance during the ***penalty phase*** of the trial. For instance, the Court will be quick to find ineffective assistance when counsel fails to ***conduct an adequate "social history" investigation of the defendant's life***, and thus ***fails to show mitigating evidence*** — such as parental ***abuse*** — that would have been discovered by a proper investigation.

Example: D is charged with murdering a 77-year-old woman by drowning her in her bathtub. After D is convicted, his two public defenders tell the jury that during the sentencing phase they will hear mitigating evidence about D's difficult life. However, the lawyers never introduce such evidence. Nor do the lawyers ever hire a forensic social worker to conduct a "social history" of D's life, even though public funds are available for this. (Counsel merely consult some Maryland Dept. of Social Services records documenting D's long history in the state's foster care system.) Had a social history been compiled, it would have shown that D's mother was a chronic alcoholic who frequently left him alone for days (so that he and his siblings had to beg for food and eat garbage), that the mother placed him in foster care at age six, that D's first and second sets of foster parents abused him physically and sexually, and that D had lived on the streets since age 16. D claims that his lawyers' failure to investigate, and present evidence of, D's dysfunctional background constituted ineffective assistance of counsel.

Held, for D. Counsel's decision not to investigate beyond the DSS records "fell short of the professional standards that prevailed in Maryland" at the time. (For instance, ABA guidelines at the time said that in the death penalty phase counsel should consider presenting evidence of "family and social history.") Counsel had no reason to believe that conducting a social history — for which public funds were available — would have been unproductive or counterproductive. Furthermore, counsel's failure to investigate seems to have been caused by "inattention, not reasoned strategic judgment." Lastly, since the mitigating evidence that an investigation would have discovered was "powerful," there is a "reasonable probability" that, but for counsel's unprofessional failure to investigate, the result of the proceeding would have been different (i.e., a sentence of life imprisonment rather than death). Therefore, D's death sentence is reversed. *Wiggins v. Smith*, 539 U.S. 510 (2003).

I. **Conflict in multiple representation:** Particularly where appointed counsel is involved, the right to counsel may be violated if the lawyer represents ***multiple defendants***, and the interests of these defendants ***conflict.***

1. **Objection by lawyer:** If the ***lawyer objects*** to the fact that he is being required to represent multiple defendants whose interests conflict, or one of the defendants objects, the trial judge ***must investigate*** whether there is an actual conflict. If he does not make such an investigation, and one of the defendants is convicted, that defendant must on appeal merely make a ***minimal showing*** that he "may" have been prejudiced by the multiple representation, and he will be entitled to a reversal of the conviction. *Holloway v. Arkansas*, 435 U.S. 475 (1978).

2. **No objection:** But if neither the defendant nor the lawyer objects to the multiple representation, the trial judge (at least in state trials) is ***not required*** to make any inquiry into possible conflict, unless he "knows or reasonably should know that a particular conflict exists." *Cuyler v. Sullivan*, 446 U.S. 335 (1980).

   a. **Showing on appeal:** Furthermore, where no objection is made at the trial level, the defendant will have to make a much stronger showing on appeal in order to obtain a reversal, than he would if a trial-level objection had been made and refused. He must demonstrate that an "actual conflict of interest adversely affected his lawyer's performance." *Cuyler v. Sullivan, supra*. However, once the defendant makes such a showing of actual conflict adversely affecting performance, he is ***relieved*** of the need to make the two showings required by *Strickland, supra*, p. 386, for ordinary "ineffective assistance of counsel" claims. That is, he does not have to show that the lawyer's work fell outside the "wide range of professional competence"; perhaps even more importantly, he is relieved of showing that there was ***actual prejudice*** (i.e., a "reasonable probability" that the result would have been different). But the basic requirement that the conflict have "adversely affected" the lawyer's performance does mean that the lawyer must be shown to have ***performed differently***, and less well, because of the conflict.

i. **Illustration:** The facts of *Cuyler* illustrate one way in which such a showing of adverse effect on the lawyer's performance might be made. In *Cuyler*, two lawyers jointly represented three defendants; since D had no money, his fee was entirely paid by the other two defendants. D was tried first, and his defense rested without putting on any witnesses. One of the two lawyers later testified that he had declined to put on a case for D because he did not want to expose the defense's witnesses for the other two trials that were coming up. The Supreme Court implied (though it did not decide) that if this consideration was in fact a reason why no defense was presented, the requisite showing of an adverse effect on counsel's performance would be satisfied.

3. **No right to waive the conflict:** Cases like *Cuyler* illustrate that it can be a violation of the right to counsel for one lawyer to represent multiple defendants who have conflicting interests. Now, consider the converse problem: If co-defendants all want to be represented by the ***same*** lawyer, and ***waive*** their rights to object to the conflict, does the court violate each defendant's Sixth Amendment rights by ***refusing*** to allow the multiple representation? The answer is ***"no"*** — so long as there is a reasonable possibility of a conflict, the court may prohibit the same lawyer from representing two or more defendants, without violating the Sixth Amendment rights of the defendant who loses access to his first choice. *Wheat v. U.S.*, 486 U.S. 153 (1988).

Note: One of the reasons the Supreme Court has given trial courts the ability to disallow multiple representation even where all defendants waive the conflict is that without such an ability, the trial court may be ***"whipsawed"*** on appeal. That is, if the trial court allows the multiple representation, one of the defendants may claim on appeal that his waiver was not a "knowing" one (e.g., it was forced upon him by, say, the "king pin" co-defendant who was paying all parties' legal bills); appeals courts sometimes grant a retrial in these circumstances. If the trial court did not allow the multiple representation, the defendant who did not get his choice of counsel would appeal on that ground. Therefore, the Supreme Court has determined that the only way to avoid this whipsawing is by establishing a blanket rule that wherever there is a reasonable possibility of a conflict, the trial court may insist on separate representation. (The Court's opinion in *Wheat, supra*, discusses the whipsawing problem extensively.)

J. **Expert assistance:** Most lower courts have held that a defendant is entitled to the appointment of ***experts*** when necessary to present an effective defense. (See K,L&I (9th), pp. 96-99.) The Supreme Court has dealt with this issue only in the context of the right to an expert ***psychiatrist.***

1. **Right to psychiatrist:** In the psychiatric context, the Court has continued to hold that there are at least two instances in which the defendant has the right to a psychiatrist's assistance at state expense: (1) when he makes a preliminary showing that his ***sanity*** is likely to be a ***significant factor*** in his defense; and (2) when, in a capital sentencing proceeding, the state tries to justify the ***death penalty*** by showing that the defendant is likely to ***remain dangerous*** in the future. *Ake v. Oklahoma*, 470 U.S. 68 (1985).

   a. **Scope of right:** In these two situations, the defendant does not have a constitutional right "to choose a psychiatrist of his personal liking or to receive funds to hire his own." What he does have is the right to have the state appoint a psychiatrist to examine him, and to have that psychiatrist's evidence available at trial to rebut the state's evidence on sanity or dangerousness.

K. **Fees and transcripts:** The Supreme Court has extended broadly the *Griffin* equal protection principle to invalidate any ***fees*** that are required to obtain access to state appellate or collateral proceeding courts. The Court has also required that all ***transcripts and records*** necessary to present an effective appeal or petition be given to an indigent without charge.

1. ***Mayer:*** The Court in *Mayer v. Chicago*, 404 U.S. 189 (1971), extended the *Griffin* principle further in the case of transcripts than has yet been required with respect to appointment of counsel. The Court held in *Mayer* that the right to a "record of sufficient completeness" attaches regardless of whether the penalty faced by the defendant is merely a fine.

2. **Preliminary hearing:** In *Roberts v. La Vallee*, 389 U.S. 40 (1967), the Court held that an indigent defendant must receive a free transcript of a ***preliminary hearing*** even though he had his attorney present at the hearing. Denial of such a transcript would, the Court held, fail to meet the established test "that differences in access to the instruments needed to vindicate legal rights, when based upon the financial situation of the defendant, are repugnant to the Constitution."

L. **Secret agents:** Once a suspect has been indicted and has counsel, it is a violation of his ***right to counsel*** for a ***secret agent*** to deliberately obtain incriminating statements from him in the absence of counsel, and to pass these on to the prosecution. ***Massiah v. U.S.***, 377 U.S. 201 (1964), discussed more fully *supra*, p. 238.

1. **Must be "deliberately elicited":** The Supreme Court has continued to impose the requirement stated in *Massiah* that the secret agent ***"deliberately elicit"*** the incriminating testimony. In *U.S. v. Henry*, 447 U.S. 264 (1980), Nichols, a paid informant to the FBI, was incarcerated in the same jail cell as D. He told his FBI contact of this fact, and the FBI man told him to be alert to any statement made by D, but not to begin any conversation with or questioning of D about the crime for which D was currently under indictment (a bank robbery). At D's trial, Nichols recited several incriminating statements made to him by D while they were in jail together.

   a. **Holding:** The Supreme Court held that these facts were sufficient to establish that the government and Nichols had ***violated*** D's right to counsel. The Court stressed that, under *Massiah*, a Sixth Amendment violation would exist only if Nichols "deliberately elicited" the incriminating information. Since Nichols was paid on a contingent fee, was ostensibly no more than a fellow inmate of D, and was in custody with him, the Court found it probable that Nichols deliberately used his position to secure the incriminating information. The fact that the FBI officer may have told Nichols not to initiate any questioning is irrelevant, since the officer "must have known" that Nichols was likely to do so anyway.

b. **Passive listening:** The Court in *Henry* left open the possibility that in the future it might extend *Massiah* to cover cases where the information is gleaned by an "inanimate electronic device" which has no capability of leading the conversation onto any particular subject, or where it is obtained by an informant who "is placed in close proximity but makes no effort to stimulate conversations about the crime charged." But in *Kuhlmann v. Wilson*, discussed *infra*, p. 401, the Court made it clear that *Massiah* will not be extended in this way, and that only the "deliberate eliciting" of information is barred by the Sixth amendment.

c. **No "interrogation" required:** *Henry* apparently means that a violation of the *Massiah* right to counsel may occur even if there is no ***"interrogation"*** at all (provided that a non-inquisitive but deliberate means of eliciting information is used). This should be contrasted to the rule in *Miranda* cases, where an interrogation is absolutely necessary. See, e.g., *Rhode Island v. Innis*, *supra*, p. 250.

2. **Limited holding:** The protection against uncounseled statements to informants, recognized by *Massiah* and *Henry*, has not been extended to ***pre-indictment*** situations. Thus in *Hoffa*, *supra*, p. 227, the Court rejected Hoffa's contention that the informant's eavesdropping on Hoffa's incriminating statements violated the *Massiah* rationale. The Court conceded that at the time the eavesdropping occurred, the government had sufficient evidence against Hoffa to indict him; but this did not mean that he had the same Sixth Amendment right as the actually-indicted defendant in *Massiah*. "There is no constitutional right to be arrested. The police are not required to guess at their peril the precise moment at which they have probable cause to arrest a suspect, risking a violation of the Fourth Amendment if they act too soon, and a violation of the Sixth Amendment if they wait too long."

   a. **Alternative motives by police:** Suppose that while D is under indictment for one crime, the police employ a secret agent against him as part of an investigation into a ***separate*** crime on which there has been no indictment. May the prosecution use information obtained by the secret agent in its case on the first indictment? The Supreme Court answered ***"no"*** to this question in *Maine v. Moulton*, 474 U.S. 159 (1985).

      i. **Rationale:** In reaching this conclusion, the Court in *Moulton* reasoned that a contrary rule "invites abuse by law enforcement personnel in the form of fabricated investigations and risks the evisceration of the Sixth Amendment right. . . . " Three dissenters would have allowed the evidence to be admitted so long as the use of the secret agent took place merely "in spite of," rather than "because of," the pending charge.

      ii. **Result:** Where there is a pending indictment on the one hand and an ongoing investigation into additional charges on the other, the police are thus free to use a secret agent who elicits information from the suspect. However, that information may be used ***only*** in prosecutions for offenses that have not yet reached the indictment stage.

3. **Active/passive distinction:** The Supreme Court continues to distinguish between the ***active*** eliciting of information by the agent and the mere ***passive receipt*** of information — the right to counsel can only be violated by the former. Two cases, decided in the same term, illustrate this distinction.

   a. **Passive listening:** In one of the cases, *Kuhlmann v. Wilson*, 477 U.S. 436 (1986), a jailhouse informant was placed in the same cell as D, and told not to ask D any questions but simply to "keep his ears open" for information. The informant listened to D's account of the crime, and did not ask any questions, though he did tell D that his initial alibi "didn't sound too good." D ultimately told the informant information that the police found useful, though this happened only after (and probably directly because of) a jailhouse visit by D's brother. The Court found that D's right to counsel had not been violated, and allowed the information to be used against him.

      i. **Rationale:** The Court held that *Massiah* and *Henry* only apply where there occurs "secret interrogation by investigatory techniques that are the equivalent of direct police interrogation." A defendant must show that the police and their informant "took some action, ***beyond merely listening***, that was designed deliberately to elicit incriminating remarks."

      ii. **Dissent:** Three dissenters in *Kuhlmann* contended that this was not a case in which the informant really served as an impassive "listening post": the dissenters pointed out that the police deliberately placed D in a cell overlooking the scene of the crime, in the hopes that this would trigger an inculpatory comment to the informant; also, the informant's comment that D's alibi did not "sound too good", and his attempts to establish a relationship of camaraderie with D, went far beyond the bounds of passive listening.

   b. **Deliberate eliciting of information:** In the other case, the informant, a co-defendant of D, prompted D to repeat the facts of the crime to a hidden transmitter. The Court held that there was a violation of the right to counsel, because the informant had "deliberately elicited" the information. This was so even though the meeting at which D made the statements was one requested by D rather than by the police or the informant. "[K]nowing exploitation by the State of an opportunity to confront the accused without counsel being present is as much a breach of the State's obligation not to circumvent the right to the assistance of counsel as is the intentional creation of such an opportunity." *Maine v. Moulton*, 474 U.S. 159 (1985).

4. **Presence at attorney-client conference:** The presence of an undercover agent at a ***conference*** between a suspect and his ***lawyer*** will also be a violation of the suspect's right to counsel, if material from this conference is ***used by the prosecution***.

   a. **Informant doesn't tell prosecution:** But the Supreme Court has ***refused*** to hold that an undercover agent's participation in such a pre-trial attorney-client conference constitutes a ***per se*** violation of the right to counsel, even where the agent never passes on any information to the prosecution. In *Weatherford v. Bursey*, 429 U.S. 545 (1977), Bursey (the defendant) and Weatherford (an undercover agent) were charged with vandalizing a selective service office; the purpose of charging Weatherford was to preserve his cover vis-à-vis Bursey. Bursey's lawyer asked Weatherford to participate in two pretrial meetings with Bursey and the lawyer, but Weatherford did not pass on to the prosecution anything learned at these meetings. Weatherford testified as a witness against Bursey, but only as to events prior to the attorney-client meetings; nor did he refer to anything said at these meetings.

i. **Holding in *Weatherford:*** The Supreme Court declined to hold that the mere presence of Weatherford at the attorney-client meetings constituted a violation of Bursey's right to counsel, and noted that there was no evidence that Weatherford's presence contributed in any way to the conviction of Bursey. Also, the Court argued, had Weatherford declined to participate in the meetings, he would probably have unmasked himself as an informer. (The Court also indicated, however, that if Weatherford had gone to the meeting for the ***purpose*** of spying, there would probably have been a Sixth Amendment violation even if no information was passed to the prosecution; but here, it was at Bursey's lawyer's request that Weatherford came to the meetings, and there was no evidence that he was motivated by a desire to spy.)

ii. **Dissent:** Two Justices (Marshall and Brennan) dissented, arguing that a *per se*, prophylactic, rule against any "spying upon attorney-client communications" should be adopted. Even where the agent does not pass on what he learns to the prosecution, he will be able to prepare his own testimony better, and anticipate questions. Also, fear of informants may deter defendants from using their right to communicate candidly with their lawyers. Finally, proof that the agent was present for the purpose of spying, or that he passed information to the prosecution, is likely to be almost impossible to obtain.

5. **May be used for impeachment of D's testimony:** Even where the police or prosecution violate D's Sixth Amendment rights by deliberately having an undercover informant elicit incriminating statements from D outside the presence of D's counsel, the prosecution may ***use*** these statements to ***impeach D's trial testimony.*** That's the holding of ***Kansas v. Ventris***, 129 S.Ct. 1841 (2009). In other words, just as statements elicited from the defendant in violation of *Miranda* may be used to impeach that defendant's trial testimony (see *Harris v. N.Y., supra,* p. 344), so statements elicited by informants in violation of *Massiah* (*supra*, p. 399) may be used for this same purpose.

a. **Facts of *Ventris*:** The facts of *Ventris* show how powerful this prosecution right to make impeachment use of the fruits of a Sixth Amendment violation can be in those situations where the defendant decides to testify. D and Theel confronted V in V's home. One or both ended up shooting V to death with a .38 revolver, and stealing V's truck and $300. Theel got the murder charges against herself dropped in exchange for her agreement to testify at D's upcoming murder trial that D was the shooter. After D's indictment and pre-trial imprisonment, officers planted an informant in D's cell. The informant elicited from D the statement that D was the shooter, and was the one who had stolen the truck and cash.

i. **Use at trial:** At D's trial, D took the stand and blamed both the shooting and robbery entirely on Theel. The prosecution called the informant to contradict D's testimony; the informant proposed to tell the jury that D had confessed that D himself had done the shooting and robbery. The judge allowed the testimony even though the prosecution acknowledged that the use of the informant to elicit D's statements had probably violated D's Sixth Amendment rights. The jury actually acquitted D of the murder charges, but convicted him on the robbery. D argued on appeal that because his statements had been obtained in violation of his Sixth Amendment rights, the prosecution shouldn't be entitled to use them against him even for impeachment.

b. **Use allowed:** But the Supreme Court, by a 7-2 vote, rejected D's argument. In an opinion by Justice Scalia that relied on the rationale of cases allowing impeachment use of illegally-obtained evidence in other contexts (e.g., *Harris*, *supra*, p. 344, regarding evidence derived from *Miranda* violations), the Court said, "Our precedents make clear that the game of ***excluding tainted evidence for impeachment purposes*** is ***not worth the candle***. ... Once the defendant testifies in a way that contradicts prior statements, denying the prosecution use of 'the traditional truth-testing devices of the adversary process' ... is a high price to pay for vindication of the right to counsel at the prior stage."

   i. **Little deterrence:** Preventing impeachment use of statements taken in violation of *Massiah* would have very little deterrent value, Scalia said. That's because, in order for such a rule against impeachment use to act as a deterrent, "[a]n investigator would have to anticipate both that the defendant would choose to testify at trial (an unusual occurrence to begin with) and that he would testify inconsistently despite the admissibility of his prior statement for impeachment. Not likely to happen[.]"

VII. THE CLIENT'S RIGHT TO CONTROL THE DEFENSE

A. **The right generally:** In the prior section (VI), we answered the question, "What kind of lawyering conduct does or doesn't constitute the 'effective assistance of counsel' that the Sixth Amendment guarantees to criminal defendants?" In the present section, we discuss a related but distinct issue: "Which decisions about the defense are the province of the lawyer, and which ones are ***reserved to the defendant?"***

1. **Two categories:** As we'll see, many types of decisions are deemed to be matters of "trial strategy," as to which counsel, not the defendant, gets to call the shots. But other types of decisions – especially ones relating to ***determining the objectives*** the defense should be trying to achieve – are ***reserved to the client.*** As to this latter category, if counsel ignores the client's wishes, the client will be found to have been ***denied his right*** to the effective assistance of counsel.

2. **How we'll proceed:** We'll consider the two categories of decisions separately, beginning with the category of decisions that are deemed to be matters of trial strategy, and that are therefore the province of the lawyer.

   Note on self-representation: A defendant's right to ***represent himself*** does not really fall into either of the two categories. We consider this right separately *infra*, p. 411.

B. **Rights reserved to lawyer:** Assuming the defendant chooses to have a lawyer manage and present her case, then many of the decisions about how the case should be defended – typically decisions that can be described as matters of ***"trial strategy"*** – are ***reserved to the lawyer,*** not the client.

1. **Consequence:** If a decision falls within this "trial strategy" category, two important Sixth Amendment consequences follow:

   [1] the ***lawyer*** is entitled to ***make the decision on her own***, and need not follow the wishes of the client; and

   [2] the fact that the lawyer has made her own decision rather than following the client's wishes ***will not constitute ineffective assistance of counsel.***[2]

2. **Decisions falling into the "lawyer's prerogative" category:** Decisions will be found to fall within this "province of the lawyer" category if the decision is primarily about the ***strategies or tactics to be used by the defense,*** rather than about what the ***objectives*** of the defense should be. As the Court said in a 2018 case, "***Trial management*** is the ***lawyer's province:*** Counsel provides his or her assistance by making decisions such as 'what ***arguments*** to pursue, what ***evidentiary objections*** to raise, and what ***agreements to conclude*** regarding the admission of evidence." *McCoy v. Louisiana*, 138 S.Ct. 1500 (2018).

   a. **Examples:** Therefore, counsel – not the client – is empowered to make decisions about the following issues, all of which are deemed to be matters of "trial management":

      [1] whether to move to ***suppress prosecution evidence*** obtained by a constitutional violation (e.g., evidence from searches that violated D's Fourth Amendment rights);

      [2] whether to have D ***wear civilian clothing*** rather than prison garb during the trial;

      [3] whether to ***object*** to an improper ***jury instruction***;

      [4] whether to ***forgo cross-examination*** of a witness;

      [5] whether to ***call a witness*** (other than D himself) at trial.

      See KLIKK&P, p. 196.

C. **Decisions that belong solely to the client:** In contrast to the above category of "trial management" decisions, as to which the lawyer has control, there is a category of decisions that are so ***"fundamental"*** that the Supreme Court confers the decision-making power on the ***client***, not the lawyer. The Court has never articulated exactly where or how the dividing line should be drawn between these two categories. But the Court's decision in a 2018 case, *McCoy v. Louisiana*, suggests approximately where the line should be drawn.

1. **What *McCoy* says:** According to *McCoy*:

   [1] if the decision consists of "***strategic choices*** about ***how best to achieve a client's objective***," the decision belongs to the ***lawyer***; *but …*

   [2] if the decision concerns "***what the client's objectives in fact <u>are</u>***" (emphasis in origi-

2. Of course, the lawyer's decision may be ***so ill-advised*** that it constitutes ineffective assistance. But when a reviewing court is later trying to decide whether the decision amounted to ineffective assistance, that court will essentially ignore the fact that the client objected to the decision.

nal), then it's the ***client***, not the lawyer, who holds the right to make the decision.

2. **Examples where client has the decision-making power:** In the Court's most recent discussion in this area, *McCoy*, the Court gave a list of choices that fall within the "what are the client's ***objectives***?" category and thus ***belong to the client***. The list included the following types of choices:

   [1] whether to ***"self-represent"***;

   [2] whether to ***plead guilty***;

   [3] whether to ***waive a jury***;

   [4] whether to ***testify in one's own behalf***;

   [5] whether to ***take an appeal***; and ...

   [6] whether to ***concede guilt*** in the context of a capital-murder proceeding (the issue posed by *McCoy* itself).

D. Conceding the client's guilt as a Sixth Amendment violation (*McCoy*): The Court's most recent discussion of the defendant's authority to make "what are my objectives?" choices is ***McCoy v. Louisiana***, 138 S.Ct. 1500 (2018). *McCoy* was a capital murder case, in which the trial was divided into a guilt phase and a penalty phase. The Court concluded that the defendant held the absolute right to ***maintain his factual innocence*** during the guilt phase, despite his lawyer's belief that this strategy would be disastrous.

1. **Facts of *McCoy*:** The defendant in *McCoy*, Robert McCoy, was charged with the capital murder of three members of his estranged wife's family. McCoy's family retained Larry English as McCoy's trial counsel. English concluded that the evidence against McCoy was overwhelming, and that his only chance to avoid being sentenced to death at the penalty phase would be to ***concede guilt during the guilt phase***. McCoy vociferously opposed this strategy; he wanted English to present an alibi defense (that McCoy was out-of-state at the time the murders occurred in-state), and to contend that the victims were killed by corrupt police officers as result of a drug deal that went wrong.

2. **English refuses:** English allowed McCoy to testify in his own defense; McCoy did so, by maintaining his innocence and pressing his theory that the victims were killed by corrupt police. But English told the jury in his opening statement that the evidence was "unambiguous," and that ***"my client committed three murders."*** After the jury returned a unanimous verdict of first-degree murder on all three counts and the penalty phase began, English again conceded that McCoy was the killer. But English urged the jury to spare McCoy the death penalty in view of his "serious mental and emotional issues." The jury, however, returned a death verdict as to all three killings.

3. **Contention on appeal:** In post-trial proceedings and on appeal, new lawyers for McCoy argued that he should get a new trial because English had violated McCoy's Sixth Amendment rights by conceding, over McCoy's objection, that McCoy had committed the murders.

4. **Court agrees:** By a 6-3 vote, the Supreme Court ***agreed with McCoy*** – it was unconstitutional for the court to allow defense counsel to concede guilt in the face of the defen-

dant's "intransigent and unambiguous objection." The majority opinion was by Justice Ginsburg.

a. **What choices belong to the client:** Ginsburg began her opinion by explaining the distinction between decisions that are the province of the lawyer and those that are reserved to the client.

   i. **Decisions belonging to the lawyer:** She described the category of decisions reserved to the lawyer this way: "***Trial management*** is the lawyer's province: Counsel provides his or her assistance by making decisions such as 'what arguments to pursue, what evidentiary objections to raise, and what agreements to conclude regarding the admission of evidence.'"

   ii. **Decisions belonging to the client:** But there are other decisions, Ginsburg said, that are ***"reserved for the client."*** This category includes, she said, "whether to plead guilty, waive the right to a jury trial, testify in one's own behalf, and forgo an appeal." What these decisions have in common is that they are ***not*** "strategic choices about how best to *achieve* a client's objectives; they are choices about ***what the client's objectives in fact are***."

b. **Which category conceding guilt fits into:** The heart of Ginsburg's opinion was her conclusion that the decision whether to concede guilt in a capital case falls into the "reserved to the client" category, because it is a decision about what the client's objectives in the case should be, not a choice about how best to achieve those objectives.

   i. **Explanation:** Ginsburg explained why this was so. McCoy's lawyer, English, had assumed that the objective of the defense here should be to avoid the death penalty. Given that assumption, it followed that conceding guilt at the outset would be the best way to achieve that objective. But, Ginsburg said, a client in McCoy's situation "may not share that objective."

      (1) **Alternative objectives:** Ginsburg listed a couple of ***alternative objectives*** that a defendant in McCoy;s situation – a death penalty case with overwhelming evidence against the defendant – might rationally view as the main objective the defense should pursue. The defendant "may wish to avoid, above all else, the ***opprobrium*** that comes with ***admitting he killed family members.***" Or, the defendant "may hold ***life in prison not worth living*** and prefer to risk death for any hope, however small, of exoneration."

      (2) **Consequence:** In any event, Ginsburg said, in the case at hand McCoy had made an ***"intransigent and unambiguous objection"*** to counsel's plan to concede guilt. Therefore, the case involved McCoy's "***autonomy*** to decide that the objective of the defense is to assert innocence," and his choice to pursue that objective placed the case into the "reserved for the client" category.

   ii. **No need to show prejudice:** Ginsburg then turned to the issue of what else McCoy was required to show – beyond a violation of his right to determine what the objective of the defense should be – in order to be entitled to relief on his Sixth Amendment claim. Ordinarily, Ginsburg said, to obtain redress for "attorney error," a defendant must ***"show prejudice."*** (She cited *Strickland v. Washington*, *supra*, p. 387, on this point.)

(1) **"Structural error":** But the error here – "violation of a defendant's Sixth Amendment-secured ***autonomy***" – fell into a separate category of errors, ones that previous Supreme Court decisions had called ***"structural."*** A structural error "affect[s] the ***framework within which the trial proceeds***," as distinguished from "a lapse or flaw that is 'simply an ***error in the trial process*** itself.'"

(2) **Reasons for labeling an error as structural:** One type of error that will be ranked as "structural," Ginsburg said, was "if the right at issue is not designed to protect the defendant from ***erroneous conviction*** but instead protects ***some other interest***," such as "the fundamental legal principle that a defendant must ***be allowed to make his own choices about the proper way to protect*** his own liberty." Here, English's admission of McCoy's guilt, over McCoy's vigorous objection, "block[ed] the defendant's ***right to make the fundamental choices about his own defense."*** Therefore, the admission was a "structural error."

(3) **"Harmless error" doesn't apply:** The last part of Ginsburg's opinion dealt with what the ***consequences*** would be of the fact that the error here was a structural one. The court's previous decisions had held that a structural error "is ***not subject to harmless-error review***." McCoy therefore did not have to ***show how the error caused him prejudice:*** the error here was a structural error, and when an error is structural, "a ***new trial*** is the ***required corrective."***

E. No obligation to argue all issues (*Jones v. Barnes*): Another question is whether the client, once he has been convicted, is entitled to insist on his own view of ***which arguments should be raised*** on ***appeal.*** The Supreme Court answered ***"no,"*** in *Jones v. Barnes*, 463 U.S. 745 (1983).

1. **The issue in *Barnes*:** In *Barnes*, the defendant D wanted his counsel to raise on appeal a collection of seven arguments that D had identified. The lawyer, however, selected for the appeal only the three arguments that the lawyer felt had the greatest merit.

2. **Holding in *Barnes*:** The Court held that Barnes' Sixth Amendment rights were ***not violated*** by the lawyer's disregarding Barnes' wishes on which issues to raise on appeal. An appellate lawyer is ***not required*** by the Sixth Amendment to ***raise all issues which his client would like him to argue,*** the Court said. Rather, the lawyer is permitted to ***use his own professional judgment*** about what issues have the best probability of success, and there will be no Sixth Amendment violation even if other issues urged by the client are later found to be non-frivolous.

VIII. WAIVER OF THE RIGHT TO COUNSEL

A. Standards: Any ***waiver*** of the Sixth Amendment right to counsel must be made ***"knowingly and intelligently."*** (See the discussion of waiver of *Miranda rights*, *supra*, p. 259, in which the "knowingly and intelligently" requirement is also imposed.)

1. **Preponderance standard:** The government must merely prove by a ***preponderance of the evidence*** (not, say, beyond a reasonable doubt) that the defendant knowingly and intelligently waived his right to counsel. *Colorado v. Connelly*, 479 U.S. 157 (1986) (also discussed *supra*, p. 264).

2. **Factual test:** In determining whether there has been an effective waiver, the courts look to the facts and circumstances of each case, including the defendant's age, physical and mental condition, and education and experience, in addition to the setting in which the alleged waiver occurred.

3. **Police coercion required:** Even if the facts and circumstances cast doubt on whether the defendant's decision to waive the right to counsel was the product of a free and rational mind, the waiver probably will be upheld if there is no ***police coercion***. In *Colorado v. Connelly*, *supra*, p. 264, the Court held that coercive police activity is a "necessary predicate to the finding that a confession is not 'voluntary' within the meaning of the Due Process Clause"; the Court will almost certainly reach the same conclusion with respect to the voluntariness of a waiver of the right to counsel.

4. ***Miranda* warnings suffice:** If the defendant is given his ***Miranda*** warnings, and does not ask for counsel, this will normally be treated as a valid waiver of the right to counsel, even though the *Miranda* warnings do not refer especially to the Sixth Amendment post-indictment right to counsel. In other words, even though the *Miranda* warnings are designed only to protect the defendant's ***Fifth*** Amendment right against self-incrimination, those warnings inform the defendant that he has the right to have counsel present during interrogation; if he declines such assistance, the police may treat this as a waiver, and interrogate him, even though the formal Sixth Amendment right to counsel has attached. *Patterson v. Illinois*, 487 U.S. 285 (1988).

5. **Actual relinquishment:** For a waiver of the Sixth Amendment right to counsel to exist, it must be shown not only that the defendant understood that he had such a right, but also that he ***intended to relinquish it***. This latter requirement is demonstrated by a controversial Supreme Court case, ***Brewer v. Williams***, 430 U.S. 387 (1977).

   a. **Facts of *Brewer*:** *Brewer* involved the abduction and murder of a 10-year-old girl in Des Moines, Iowa. After the girl's disappearance, police suspicion focused on the eventual defendant, Williams, an escapee from a mental hospital. The day after a warrant for Williams' arrest was issued, a Des Moines lawyer for Williams told the police there that he had received a long-distance phone call from Williams from Davenport, Iowa, 160 miles away, and that he had advised Williams to turn himself in to the Davenport police. Williams did in fact turn himself in in Davenport, and was given his *Miranda* warnings by the Davenport police. Williams then talked by phone from Davenport to his lawyer, who was still at the Des Moines police station. He was told by his lawyer not to say anything to any police until he was returned to Des Moines. Williams also consulted with a local Davenport lawyer, who similarly advised him not to say anything until he was returned to Des Moines and was with his lawyer.

      i. **The police make a promise:** Two Des Moines policemen, including a detective named Leaming, then drove to Davenport to pick Williams up; before leaving Des Moines, they agreed with Williams' lawyer that they would not question him until he was back in Des Moines with his lawyer. Once the police got to Davenport, the local lawyer there again got the police to promise not to interrogate Williams on the return trip, and also tried unsuccessfully to gain permission to ride back to Des Moines with the police and Williams.

ii. The "Christian Burial speech": During the return trip, Williams stated several times that he would tell the police "the whole story" when he got back to Des Moines and was with his lawyer. Detective Leaming, who knew that Williams was deeply religious, made a statement to Williams which came to be known in the subsequent proceedings as the "Christian burial speech." Addressing Williams as "Reverend," Leaming said "I want to give you something to think about while we're traveling down the road . . . Number one, I want you to observe the weather conditions. . . . They are predicting several inches of snow for tonight, and I feel that you yourself are the only person that knows where this little girl's body is, that you yourself have only been there once, and if you get a snow on top of it you yourself may be unable to find it. And, since we will be going right past the area on the way into Des Moines, I feel that we could stop and locate the body, that the parents of this little girl should be entitled to a Christian burial for the little girl who was snatched away from them on Christmas Eve and murdered. . . . I do not want you to answer me. I don't want to discuss it further. Just think about it as we're riding down the road."

iii. He shows them the body: As the car approached Des Moines, Williams had the police stop in a town called Mitchellville, where he led them to the body.

b. Evidence introduced at trial: At Williams' trial, the court allowed Williams' statements during the trip, and the fact that the body was found where Williams said it would be, to be introduced into evidence. It did so over the objections of Williams' lawyer, who claimed that the evidence was gathered through a violation of an express agreement between the lawyer and police that Williams would not be so interrogated, and that the interrogation violated Williams' Sixth Amendment right to counsel. The court ruled that Williams had indeed had a right to counsel, but that he had ***waived*** this right to have an attorney present by volunteering information as he did.

c. Supreme Court reverses: The U.S. Supreme Court, in a *habeas corpus* proceeding (see *supra*, p. 5), held that the trial court's waiver theory was erroneous, and ordered a new trial. The vote was 5-4 (Burger, White, Blackmun and Rehnquist dissenting).

i. *Miranda* not reviewed: The majority began by refusing the request of the State of Iowa (and 21 other states who submitted *amicus curiae* briefs) that the *Miranda* doctrine be overruled. The Court did not uphold the *Miranda* doctrine, but said that consideration of that doctrine was unnecessary in this case, because a new trial was necessary on Sixth Amendment right-to-counsel grounds (rather than on Fifth Amendment *Miranda* privilege-against-self-incrimination grounds).

ii. No waiver: The Court then held that the State had ***failed to show*** that Williams had effectively waived his right to counsel. The Court quoted the definition of waiver it had given in an earlier case: waiver is an "intentional relinquishment or abandonment of a known right or privilege." *Johnson v. Zerbst*, 304 U.S. 458 at

464 (1938). Concededly, Williams had been informed of and seemed to understand his right to counsel (making it a "known right" in the language of *Johnson v. Zerbst*). But the prosecution had completely failed to show that he ***intended to relinquish that right***.

iii. **Reasons:** This lack of relinquishment was demonstrated, the Court said, by Williams' having made the effort to contact two lawyers prior to the trip, and by these lawyers' having instructed the police not to interrogate him. But the clearest indication of a lack of waiver, the Court stated, was the fact that Williams told Leaming that he would tell him the "whole story" ***after*** consulting with his lawyer in Des Moines.

d. **Significance:** *Brewer* stands for the proposition that where a suspect has appropriately asserted the Sixth Amendment right to counsel (e.g., by retaining a lawyer, or having one appointed for him by the court), he will be deemed to have later waived that right only if the prosecution shows that he not only understood that he had the right, but that he ***intended*** to relinquish that right.

B. **Waiver after pre-trial appointment of counsel:** One scenario in which the rules governing waiver of the right of counsel become important is where a suspect has been formally charged, and is represented by counsel (retained or appointed); trial has not yet begun, and the police want to ***question the suspect outside of the presence of his counsel.*** In this scenario, may the police ask the suspect whether he is willing to answer their questions, and treat his willingness to answer as constituting a waiver of his right to have his counsel present at any questioning? According to ***Montejo v. Louisiana***, 129 S.Ct. 2079 (2009), the answer is "***yes***."

1. **Prior decision in *Jackson* overruled by *Montejo*:** In *Montejo*, a 5-4 decision, the Court flatly ***overruled*** a prior case, *Michigan v. Jackson,* 475 U.S. 625 (1986).

a. **What *Jackson* said:**. *Jackson* had held that once formal proceedings start against a suspect by an arraignment, indictment or comparable step, if the suspect requests a lawyer the police ***may not subsequently initiate conversations with him outside of that counsel's presence.*** (If the police violated this rule, the answers couldn't be used against the suspect, at least in a trial on the crime(s) to which the formal proceedings related.)

b. ***Jackson* found to be a "prophylactic" rule:** But in *Montejo*, the majority opinion by Justice Scalia characterized *Jackson* as applying merely a ***"prophylactic rule"*** — the Sixth Amendment did not *require* the presumption (applied by the *Jackson* Court) that any suspect who invokes his right to counsel at an arraignment did not thereafter voluntarily waive the right unless he initiated conversation with the police; the "must voluntarily initiate" rule was merely a ***non-constitutionally-required*** method of reducing the risks of a Sixth Amendment violation (i.e., the risk that a post-appointment-of-counsel police interrogation would occur where the suspect did not intelligently and knowingly waive his right to counsel). To Scalia, the danger that the *Jackson* prophylactic rule was designed to combat was the danger of ***police badgering*** — the police might continually ask the suspect to talk to them outside the presence of counsel until his will to resist was worn down.

c. **Cost/benefit analysis:** Since the rule of *Jackson* was merely a prophylactic one, Scalia said, the Court was free to revisit the rule and re-weigh the rule's benefits against its costs. He did such a re-weighing, and concluded that "the ***marginal benefits*** of *Jackson* (the number of confessions obtained coercively that were suppressed by its bright-line rule and would otherwise have been admitted) were ***dwarfed by its substantial costs*** (hindering 'society's compelling interest in finding, convicting, and punishing those who violate the law[.]')"

2. **Significance:** The significance of *Montejo* is somewhat ***limited,*** because the case does not overrule *Edwards v. Arizona* (*supra*, p. 267). In other words, in the common scenario in which the suspect (i) has not only had counsel appointed for him at an arraignment or other formal proceeding (the *Jackson/Montejo* scenario) but has also, while in custody, been given *Miranda* warnings during which he asserted that he wanted to have counsel; and (ii) is still in custody, then *Edwards* still applies, and requires that there be no custodial interrogation unless either counsel has been appointed or the suspect initiates the encounter.

   a. **Suspect not in custody:** On the other hand, *Montejo* is quite ***important*** in those cases where the suspect has been ***released from custody.*** That's because, in this situation, *Edwards* ***doesn't apply*** — it applies only to waivers of *Miranda* rights, which are rights that apply only during *custodial* interrogation. So *Montejo* means that the police can knowingly approach an indicted defendant outside of his lawyer's presence and freely interrogate him if he consents, as long as they don't do so in custody.

C. **Entry of plea:** If a purported waiver of the right to counsel is followed by entry of a ***guilty plea,*** courts are especially skeptical of whether the wavier was "knowingly and intelligently" made, as it is required to be.

1. **Knowledge required:** Thus in *Von Moltke v. Gillies*, 332 U.S. 708 (1948), a plurality of the Court said that "[t]o be valid such waiver must be made with an apprehension of the nature of the charges, the statutory offenses included within them, the range of allowable punishments thereunder, possible defenses to the charges and circumstances in mitigation thereof, and all other facts essential to a broad understanding of the whole matter."

   a. **Minimum requirements:** Although most lower courts have not examined every factor within the *Von Moltke* list quoted above, virtually all courts have held at least that the defendant must be ***aware of the charges against him*** and must ***understand the full significance of his decision*** to waive counsel.

D. **Right to conduct one's own defense:** The Sixth Amendment guarantees the right of a defendant to proceed ***pro se*** (i.e., to ***represent himself without counsel).*** See ***Faretta v. California***, 422 U.S. 806 (1975),

1. **Rationale:** The Court reasoned in *Faretta* that the rights guaranteed by the Sixth Amendment are personal to the accused, ***not*** to the accused's counsel. Unless a defendant willingly accepts the decisions of counsel, the defense presented is not in any "real sense" that of the accused.

   a. **Free choice paramount:** The majority rejected the view of the dissent that the state's interest in providing a fair trial permits it to insist upon representation by counsel; the majority asserted that the right of free choice was paramount in the eyes of the draftsmen of the Sixth Amendment.

2. **Waiver required:** *Faretta* emphasized that the defendant who proceeds *pro se* must ***"knowingly and intelligently"*** waive his right to appointed counsel.

   a. **Must respect rules:** The Court also said that the choice of self-representation was "not a license" for disrespect either of the courtroom or of the rules of procedural and substantive law.

   b. **No right of appeal:** When a defendant knowingly elects to represent himself, the Court said, he cannot thereafter complain that his own defense amounted to ineffective assistance of counsel — that defense is waived on any appeal.

3. **Mentally incompetent defendant:** If the defendant has a ***severe mental illness*** that prevents her from being competent to conduct her own defense, the state may ***insist on appointing counsel***, notwithstanding *Faretta*. See *Indiana v. Edwards*, 128 S.Ct. 2379 (2008): "[T]he Constitution permits States to insist upon representation by counsel for those competent enough to stand trial ... but who still suffer from severe mental illness to the point where they are not competent to conduct trial proceedings by themselves."

Quiz Yourself on
THE RIGHT TO COUNSEL *(ENTIRE CHAPTER)*

97. Kathy was charged with shoplifting. Under state law, shoplifting, where the amount involved is less than $100, is classified as a misdemeanor. A jail sentence of up to six months is authorized. Kathy was indigent, and requested a lawyer for her trial. However, due to a shortage of funds, the county declined to provide one. Kathy was convicted, and sentenced to one night in jail. She has appealed her conviction (and has not done the one night in jail, pending the outcome of the appeal). She argues on appeal that the county's refusal to provide her with a lawyer for the trial, in these circumstances, violated her Sixth Amendment rights. Is Kathy's contention correct? ________________

98. Same basic fact pattern as the prior question. Now, however, assume that because of the relatively large ($250) amount involved, Kathy was charged with petit larceny, a felony. The maximum sentence authorized for petit larceny is two years in prison. Because she was indigent, Kathy requested a court-appointed lawyer. The county declined to provide one due to budget constraints. Kathy was tried and convicted. The judge decided not to sentence her to jail, but sentenced her to pay a $100 fine. Have Kathy's Sixth Amendment rights been violated? ________________

99. Lester was arrested for burglary, a felony, late one Friday afternoon. He was taken to the station house, booked, and then held in a cell at the county jail because no magistrate was available. Lester's confinement lasted from Friday afternoon until Monday morning. The police did not give Lester his *Miranda* warnings, or make any attempt to question him. On Friday evening, Lester stated that he was indigent (which was true), and demanded that the authorities furnish counsel for him. They refused to do so. (Lester wanted a lawyer over the weekend because he believed that a lawyer might be able to get him released. In fact, there were some special emergency procedures available, under which a knowledgeable lawyer might indeed have gotten Lester released over the weekend.) On Monday morning, Lester was taken to an initial appearance before a magistrate, at which time the charges were read to him, he entered a non-binding plea of not guilty, and counsel was appointed for him. Did Lester's confinement without counsel over the weekend violate his Sixth Amendment rights? ________________

100. Norman was charged with murdering his second wife. While he was under arrest and kept at the police station, he was given his *Miranda* warnings, and made an extensive confession that was videotaped. In the confession, Norman disclosed facts that only the killer could have known. Since Norman was indigent, he requested and was given a court-appointed lawyer, Larry. The prosecution's case at trial rested mainly on the videotaped confession, which was shown to the jury. Larry presented a defense for Norman that fell far below the usual standards of competence. For instance, he put Norman on the stand without warning Norman that Norman's past criminal record could be used to impeach his testimony; as a result, Norman's prior conviction for murdering his first wife was brought out on cross-examination to impeach Norman. Nor did Larry object to the use by the prosecution of the videotaped confession; a more competent lawyer would probably have objected (though it is unlikely that the court would have excluded the confession from evidence even had the best available arguments been presented for exclusion). Needless to say, Norman was convicted on the murder charge. On appeal, he has argued that his lawyer's performance was so bad as to deny him the effective assistance of counsel, as guaranteed by the Sixth Amendment. Should the appellate court agree with Norman, and grant a new trial? ________________

101. Otto was arrested on state-law charges of robbing two different Getty gas stations, one on July 4 and the other on July 5. In plea negotiations with Otto's court-appointed lawyer, Loretta, the state prosecutor, Pamela, disclosed that the principal piece of evidence that the prosecution intended to introduce at trial was a statement that Otto had made to a friend, Fred, who unbeknownst to Otto was a police undercover agent. As Pamela told Loretta, if the case went to trial Fred would testify that on July 10, Otto told Fred, "I'm the one who did both the Getty robberies last week." Pamela offered the following plea bargain: she would drop one of the two robbery charges, and would recommend a sentence of 25-to-30 months on the other. (Under state law, the trial judge would have discretion about whether to accept or reject this or any other plea bargain.) If Otto did not take the plea bargain, Pamela said, the prosecution would go to trial on both charges; if Otto was convicted of both, the prosecution would attempt to obtain two sentences of 35-to-40 months each, to be served consecutively. Loretta passed the offer on to Otto, but advised him not to take the offer because "It's very likely that we can keep Fred's testimony out of evidence because your Fifth Amendment privilege against self-incrimination protected you against having a government agent secretly elicit a confession from you." This was in fact blatantly legally-incorrect advice, because the Fifth Amendment privilege does not apply where the suspect does not know he is speaking to a government agent, and any competent criminal defense lawyer would have known this.

Otto unwisely took Loretta's advice, rejected the plea agreement, and soon thereafter went to trial. The Trial judge correctly admitted Fred's testimony, and the jury convicted Otto on both counts. The judge sentenced him to two 40-month sentences (in the middle of the appropriate range for robbery under the state's advisory sentencing guidelines), to be served consecutively. In federal *habeas corpus* proceedings, Otto now argues that he was deprived of the effective assistance of counsel by Loretta's bad legal advice, and that the appropriate remedy is an order by the federal court that the state court reinstate the original single-count plea-bargain and under it, sentence Otto to no more than 30 months' imprisonment.

(a) Did Otto have a Sixth Amendment right to the effective assistance of counsel while he was deciding whether to accept the proffered plea bargain? ________________

(b) Assuming for this sub-part (b) only that Otto had a right to the effective assistance of counsel, what fact(s) must he prove to show that he is entitled to relief? And what are the chances that he can prove whatever he is required to prove? ________________

(c) Assuming for this sub-part (c) only that Otto has made whatever showing you mentioned in your answer to part (b), is Otto entitled to the remedy he has asked for (an order that the state-court judge reinstate the original plea-bargain)? If not, what remedy is Otto entitled to? (Assume that whatever relief the federal judge orders, the case will be remanded for enforcement to the same state court judge who set the original sentence.) ________________

102. Oliver was charged in state court with the first-degree murder of his ex-wife, Vivian, by stabbing her to death in her apartment. Oliver and his court-appointed lawyer Les agreed that the best way to defend the case would be to raise the alibi defense that Oliver was out of state when the killing took place. As it happened, 12 years prior to the trial, in 2008, Oliver was convicted of stabbing his girlfriend Jane to death. Under the relevant state evidence rules in force at the present trial: (1) if Oliver took the stand to testify in his own defense, the prosecution would be permitted to ask him, "Isn't it true that you were convicted in 2008 of stabbing your girlfriend Jane?"; but (2) if Oliver did not take the stand, the prosecution would not be permitted to ask him about this conviction or to introduce any evidence of it. Oliver wanted to take the stand, because he thought that doing so would improve the odds that the jury would buy his alibi defense. Les, however, told Oliver that if he took the stand, the prosecution would be sure to bring up the Jane stabbing, and in Les's view the results would be disastrous. Over Oliver's vociferous objection, Les tried the case without calling Oliver to the stand, and Oliver was convicted. On appeal, Oliver now seeks a new trial, claiming that Les's refusal to call him to testify violated his Sixth Amendment right to the effective assistance of counsel.

(a) Did Les's refusal to put Oliver on the stand violate Oliver's Sixth Amendment right to effective assistance of counsel? ________________

(b) For this sub-part (b), assume (whether the assumption is accurate or not) that the answer to sub-part (a) is yes. What else, if anything, will Oliver need to establish on appeal, beyond the above facts, in order to be entitled to a new trial? ________________

103. Osmond and Paula were co-indicted for bank robbery by a state grand jury, and arrested by local police. Since Osmond claimed to be indigent, counsel was appointed for him by the court. Osmond and Paula were then released from jail on their own recognizance. While both were out of jail, Osmond asked Paula if the two of them could meet to discuss their defense, without any lawyers present. Unbeknownst to Osmond, Paula had in fact already turned state's evidence. At the request of prosecutors, Paula wore a concealed transmitter to the meeting with Osmond. At that meeting, Paula said, "Don't you think we might be better off pleading guilty — you and I both know that we pulled this heist, and a jury's gonna believe we did too." Osmond replied, "You and I may know we did it, but a jury doesn't have to know. I want to plead not guilty and defend this thing all the way." Shortly thereafter, Paula pled guilty. At Osmond's trial, the tape of his statement to Paula was played before the jury. Osmond argues that the use of this tape violated his Sixth Amendment rights, since his lawyer was not present at the meeting where Paula elicited the statement from Osmond. Should the court exclude the tape on this ground? ________________

104. Same facts as the prior question. Now, however, assume that Osmond had not been arrested or charged on the bank robbery charges, but he knew that the police regarded him as the principal suspect. The police knew that Osmond had consulted his long-time attorney about the charges that seemed likely to be filed against him. The police sent Paula to Osmond's house, so that they could discuss what to do if charges were in fact filed. Unbeknownst to Osmond, Paula had already turned state's evidence, and was wired for sound. The conversation described in the prior question then occurred. Would it be a violation of

Osmond's Sixth Amendment rights for his incriminating statement on the tape to be played before his jury? ________________

105. Same basic fact pattern as the prior two questions. Now, however, assume that Osmond was already indicted, and had retained a lawyer. Both Osmond and his lawyer, Loretta, believed that Paula was a true co-defendant; that is, neither realized that Paula had secretly turned state's evidence and was planning to plead guilty and testify against Osmond in return for a lighter sentence. Loretta asked Paula to come to a strategy meeting with herself and Osmond. Paula came to the meeting. At the meeting, Osmond volunteered several self-incriminating statements. Paula did not report these statements to the prosecution. At Osmond's trial, Paula testified against Osmond, but did not report any statements made at the strategy session. Osmond was convicted. On appeal, he argues that Paula's presence at the meeting between Osmond and Loretta constituted a violation of Osmond's Sixth Amendment rights, thus requiring a new trial. Should Osmond's new trial motion be granted on this ground? ________________

106. Rafael was arrested for robbing First Bank, a crime that the police believed was committed by at least two perpetrators. No one other than Rafael was initially charged. Rafael was arraigned, and because he was indigent, the arraignment judge appointed Lawt, a legal aid lawyer, to represent him. Rafael was then released on his own recognizance. The day after the arraignment, the police visited Rafael at his house. They asked him whether he had had a chance to consult with Lawt yet, and he said that he had not. They then said to him, "We know you weren't the only robber. If you tell us who helped you, we'll ask the prosecution to go easy on you." Rafael thought about this proposition for a while, and agreed to talk to the police. They asked him to sign a waiver of his right to consult counsel, a document that he understood and signed. They then emphasized to him that he was not in custody, that he was free to discontinue the questioning at any time, and that if he did so the police would immediately leave. Rafael answered the police's questions about the robbery, explaining how he and his friend Justin had carried it out. Later at his trial, the prosecution offered these statements as evidence against him. Rafael sought to have the statemetns excluded as fruits of a violation of his Sixth Amendment right to counsel. Should the court grant his suppression motion? ________________

Answers

97. Yes. An indigent person must be given court-appointed counsel for her trial, if she is to be sentenced to prison for any length of time upon conviction. It does not matter that the offense is classified as a "misdemeanor" under state law, or that the jail term actually imposed is very brief. *Argersinger v. Hamlin.*

98. No. As long as an indigent defendant is not sentenced to imprisonment, the state is not required to appoint counsel for her, even if the offense is one which is punishable by imprisonment. This rule seems to apply even where the offense charged is a felony under state law, so long as the judge does not in fact impose a jail sentence. *Scott v. Illinois.*

99. No. The Sixth Amendment right to appointed counsel applies only at "critical stages" in the prosecution. The fact that Lester was confined over the weekend, due to the unavailability of a magistrate, did not make this confinement a "critical stage," so he was not entitled to counsel during that time. Typically, the earliest "critical stage" in the prosecution will be the arraignment, at which the defendant enters a plea. So usually, counsel does not have to be appointed for a defendant prior to the arraignment. The fact that a lawyer might have been of some use to Lester — for instance, by getting him released over the weekend — is irrelevant to whether Lester had a Sixth Amendment right to counsel at that time.

100. No. It is true that the Sixth Amendment does not merely entitle the defendant to have a lawyer, but rather, entitles him to the "effective assistance of counsel." However, a defendant whose lawyer has actually participated in the trial must make two showings in order to sustain his "effective assistance" claim: (1) that the counsel's performance was "deficient," in the sense that it was not a "reasonably competent" performance; and (2) that these deficiencies were ***prejudicial*** to the defense, in the sense that there was a "reasonable probability that, but for [the] unprofessional errors, the ***result of the proceeding would have been different***." *Strickland v. Washington.*

Norman can make the first of these showings easily. But he cannot make the second — the proof of his guilt here is so overwhelming that he cannot show a reasonable probability that had he had a competent lawyer, he would have been found not guilty. (All Norman has to do is to show that with competent counsel, there was a reasonable probability that the fact finder would have had a "reasonable doubt" as to Norman's guilt. But Norman almost certainly cannot make even this limited showing.)

101. (a) Yes. In twin 2012 cases, *Missouri v. Frye* and *Lafler v. Cooper*, the Supreme Court held that a defendant has a Sixth Amendment right to the effective assistance of counsel during the plea-bargaining process, even in the situation in which the defendant ends up ***not taking the plea bargain,*** then gets convicted at trial and sentenced to a longer sentence than was available under the plea bargain. So while Otto was deciding whether to accept the 25-to-30-month deal, he was entitled to receive effective advice from Loretta.

(b) Two things: (1) incompetent advice, and (2) resulting prejudice; he has a decent chance of showing these two things. It's pretty clear that Otto can establish point (1), since the facts tell you that any competent criminal defense lawyer would have known that the evidence would be admissible notwithstanding any Fifth Amendment issue. To prove (2) — "resulting prejudice" — however, Otto will have to prove, under the "second prong" of *Strickland v. Washington*, that absent the incompetent advice, there is a reasonable probability that the ***result of the proceeding would have been different.*** In the case of rejection of a plea bargain, the Court held in *Missouri v. Frye* that the defendant must prove ***three different things*** in order to prove the requisite prejudice:

[1] "a ***reasonable probability*** [the defendant] ***would have accepted*** the earlier plea offer had [he] been afforded effective assistance of counsel";

[2] "a reasonable probability the plea would have been ***entered without the prosecution canceling it***" (assuming the prosecution had the power under state law to make such a cancellation); and

[3] "a reasonable probability the plea would have been entered ***without ... the trial court refusing to accept it***" (again assuming the prosecution had the power under state law to refuse to accept the plea).

The odds are pretty good that Otto can establish [1] and [2]. As to [1], if Otto had known that Fred's testimony would be admissible, common sense would have suggested to him that conviction at trial would be likely, and that a 30-month sentence (less than half the 80-month sentence actually imposed, which you are told was in the midpoint of the advisory guidelines range) was a good deal. As to [2], there is no indication that the prosecution would have revoked the deal once accepted, even if she had power under state law to do so (since there is no indication that, for instance, Otto committed any further crimes prior to his trial on robbery charges). [3] poses the biggest hurdle for Otto: you're told that the trial judge has ***discretion*** to ***reject*** any plea bargain that the prosecutor has agreed to. But as long as Otto can show (which he probably can) that the trial judge has tended to rarely exercise his discretion to reject plea bargains, and that there was nothing about the present plea bargain that would likely have struck the judge as being unduly favorable to the defendant, Otto can probably establish [3]. So he's got a decent chance of being entitled to some "relief" (but see (c) below about the likely nature of that relief).

(c) No. The fact pattern here involves "charge bargaining" (i.e., one or more charges are proposed to be dropped under the plea bargain), and *Lafler* sets forth special rules for determining the proper relief in charge-bargaining cases. In fact, *Lafler* expressly indicates that the ***"order of specific performance"*** relief requested by Otto is ***not*** the appropriate remedy. Since the trial judge would have had ***discretion to reject*** the plea bargain, *Lafler* says that the proper remedy for an effective-assistance violation is to (1) require the prosecution to re-offer the original plea deal, ***but*** then (2) allow the trial judge to exercise his ***original discretion***, i.e., to decide whether the correct remedy now is to accept the plea bargain, or reject it (thereby leaving the original conviction in place). So at best, Otto will be entitled to be put back in the position he would have been in had he accepted the plea proposal and was in front of the judge asking him to accept that bargain. Since the judge has already concluded that the two 40-month sentences should run consecutively (not concurrently), Otto's odds of convincing that same judge not to reject a plea bargain calling for less than half as much trial time are not so high — but he'll just have to wait and see what the trial judge does.

102. (a) Yes. Under the Supreme Court's Sixth Amendment case law, some types of decisions in connection with trial are deemed to be matters of "trial strategy," and as to these, the lawyer has the authority to make the decision even if the client objects. (An example would be whether to move to suppress evidence on constitutional grounds.) But there is a category of decisions that are so "***fundamental***" that the Court confers the decision-making power on the *client*, not the lawyer. *McCoy v. Louisiana* (2018). A decision falls into this "fundamental" category if it concerns not how to achieve the client's objectives, but rather, "what the client's objectives in fact <u>are</u>." *McCoy*. In *McCoy*, the Court gave a list of decisions falling into this "fundamental" category, and that list included "whether to testify in one's own behalf." So no matter how stupid Oliver's choice to testify might have been, he had a right to insist on that choice, and Les's refusal to call him so he could exercise that right violated Oliver's Sixth Amendment right to effective assistance of counsel.

(b) Nothing. Normally, even when a defendant shows he has been denied the effective assistance of counsel, he will not be entitled to a new trial unless he also shows that the denial was "***prejudicial***" to him. (That is, the defendant must rebut the presumption that the error was harmless.) This requirement to show prejudice means that the defendant must show that there was "a ***reasonable probability*** that, but for counsel's unprofessional errors, the ***result of the proceeding would have been different.***" But when the error consists of depriving the defendant of the right to make one of the "fundamental" decisions referred to in sub-part (a), the error is deemed to be "***structural.***" When an error is structural, the usual harmless-error analysis does not apply. Instead, the defendant has an ***automatic right to a new trial***, without the need to show anything other than that the structural error occurred. *McCoy*.

103. Yes. An indicted defendant who already has a lawyer has a Sixth Amendment right not to have the police elicit statements from him in the absence of that lawyer. Since Paula was acting as a government agent, and deliberately elicited the incriminating statement from Osmond, Osmond's Sixth Amendment rights were violated. See *Maine v. Moulton*, finding a Sixth Amendment violation on similar facts. The fact that it was Osmond, not Paula, who requested the meeting, will be irrelevant so long as Paula went out of her way to elicit the incriminating statement. (But if Paula had merely listened passively to remarks volunteered by Osmond, there would be no Sixth Amendment violation even though Paula was acting as a government agent and went to the meeting wired, in the hopes of hearing such a statement. See *Kuhlmann v. Wilson*.)

Observe that Osmond wins with his Sixth Amendment argument even though he loses with both a Fourth Amendment argument and a *Miranda* argument. There is no Fourth Amendment violation, because the bugging was done with the consent of one of the participants, and the fact that the participant was a "secret agent" makes no difference. The *Miranda* "self-incrimination" argument loses because Osmond was not in custody. So the Sixth Amendment argument is the difference for Osmond between keeping the damaging evidence out and having it come in.

104. No. The Sixth Amendment right to counsel does not attach until formal judicial proceedings have been commenced against the defendant (e.g., by indictment, arraignment, formal charge, etc.). The mere fact that the police have already focused their investigation on the defendant, and expect to bring charges against him, is not enough. *Hoffa v. U.S.* This is true even though the police know that the suspect has a lawyer with whom he is consulting on the matter. So the fact that Paula was in effect a police agent, and deliberately elicited incriminating material from Osmond, still does not violate Osmond's Sixth Amendment right to counsel.

105. No. The presence of an undercover agent at a conference between a suspect and his lawyer will be a violation of the suspect's Sixth Amendment right to counsel, but only if material from the conference is somehow used by the prosecution. Since no use of the material was made by the prosecution here, Osmond has no Sixth Amendment claim. See *Weatherford v. Bursey*, finding no Sixth Amendment violation on similar facts.

106. No. Rafael's argument for suppression would be based on the idea that since the police knew that he had counsel, the questioning that they initiated, outside the presence of counsel, should be deemed a violation of his Sixth Amendment rights, and that his uncounselled decision to talk to them should not be viewed as a valid waiver of those rights. But Rafael will lose with this argument. As long as the court finds that his decision to speak to the police without first consulting his counsel was a "knowing and intelligent" waiver of the right to have counsel present, the confession will be admissible. And the court *will*, under the circumstances, almost certainly conclude that Rafael's waiver of his Sixth Amendment rights was indeed knowing and intelligent.

Prior to 2009, the Court imposed a bright-line rule that once an arraigned suspect asked for counsel, any police-initiated questioning of the suspect outside the presence of counsel would be deemed involuntary and thus a violation of the Sixth Amendment. See *Michigan v. Jackson* (a case that analogized to the still-valid *Miranda*-derived decision in *Edwards v. Arizona*, under which once a suspect in custody has asked for a lawyer, no results from police-initiated questioning may be used against him until counsel has been furnished). And under *Jackson*, Rafael would have won. But the 2009 decision in *Montejo v. Louisana* overruled *Jackson*, and held that no automatic Sixth Amendment violation occurs when a suspect who is represented by counsel voluntarily submits to non-custodial police-initiated interrogation outside the presence of that counsel. So Rafael's decision to speak to the police will be treated as a valid waiver of his Sixth Amendment right to counsel. (Furthermore, since the questioning was not done in custody, Rafael does not have a valid *Miranda/Edwards* claim either.)

Exam Tips on *THE RIGHT TO COUNSEL*

Here are the issues from this chapter that you are most likely to see on an exam:

Indigent's right to appointed counsel: The right to counsel includes the right of an ***indigent*** defendant to ***appointed*** counsel. Indigence is a vague concept, meaning "lacking funds to hire a lawyer."

Imprisonment actually imposed: The right to counsel exists in any situation in which ***imprisonment***, however short (even one day), is ***actually imposed***.

Prior convictions: One tricky issue about the right to counsel involves the use of ***prior convictions.*** A prior conviction in which the defendant did not have counsel (because no imprisonment was imposed) ***can*** be used under an ***enhancement statute*** to increase the sentence for a subsequent conviction.

Where right attaches: The right to counsel attaches at ***every critical stage,*** that is, any context in which the substantial rights of the accused may be affected. This includes initial appearance, preliminary hearing, trial, sentencing and plea acceptance.

> The filing of ***charges or an indictment*** signals the point at which the right to counsel attaches to all further proceedings. Therefore, questioning or police investigation before that point do ***not*** trigger the right to counsel.
>
> *Example 1:* D is suspected in a bank robbery in which the robber handed the teller a written note demanding the money. Before any charges have been filed against D, police require her, over her objections, to furnish a handwriting exemplar. She asks to have a lawyer present, but the police refuse. There has been no violation of D's right to counsel, because no charges had been filed.
>
> *Example 2:* D is arraigned on charges of burglary. He is then told that he will be appearing in a lineup. He asks to have his lawyer present, but is told that he has no right to have his lawyer present at the lineup. The lineup takes place, and a witness identifies D. This procedure violated D's right to counsel, because once charges are filed, the right to counsel attaches to all further proceedings. Therefore, the identification at the lineup will be excluded from D's trial.
>
> Remember that the right to counsel exists during ***plea-bargaining***. That's true whether the defendant ends up ***accepting*** or ***rejecting*** a plea bargain offered by the prosecution.

Questioning by a secret agent can violate the right to counsel, if that questioning occurs after indictment or the filing of charges. Keep in mind the "active/passive" distinction discussed in Chapter 4: "active" conduct by the secret agent (conduct reasonably likely to elicit an incriminating result) will violate the Sixth Amendment, but "passive" conduct won't.

Example: D has been charged with a crime, and imprisoned. Informer is placed in the same cell as D, with strict instructions not to ask any questions of D, but to listen if D wants to talk. Informer complies, and D confides that she feels guilty about what she has done. D's right to counsel has not been violated in this case. But if Informer had asked leading questions, or had made remarks for the purpose of causing D to incriminate herself, then D's right to counsel would be violated by this post-charge behavior.

Self-representation: A defendant normally has an absolute right to ***represent himself,*** even if the trial judge reasonably believes that the defendant will do an incompetent job. (But that's not true if the defendant has a ***severe mental illness*** that would prevent him from competently putting on a defense.)

Waiver: Anytime the right to counsel is at issue, you should also determine whether the defendant has ***waived*** the right. The right to counsel may be waived if done "knowingly and intelligently." Waiver is judged particularly strictly, though, when it is followed by entry of a guilty plea.

Effective assistance: The right to counsel includes the right to ***effective assistance*** of counsel. To succeed with a claim for ineffective assistance, D must show 2 things (the ***"two prongs"*** of *Strickland v. Washington*):

[1] **First prong:** that counsel's performance fell below an objective standard of "reasonable representation" (below-average representation is not enough to meet this standard); and

[2] **Second prong:** that "but for" such unprofessional conduct there is a ***reasonable probability*** that the ***result*** of the proceedings would have been ***different.*** In practice, this standard is very difficult to meet, and you should probably conclude that D has no viable ineffective-assistance claim.

Example: D's counsel fails to independently interview the only eyewitness, fails to formally request any exculpatory evidence, and fails to raise an available *Miranda* issue. If in fact any investigation or requests would clearly have been fruitless and the *Miranda* argument would not have been successful, D will lose on his ineffective-assistance claim no matter how far below a reasonable standard his counsel's performance fell. That's because D can't meet the second prong of Strickland, that "but for" the unprofessional conduct, there is a reasonable probability that the result of the proceedings would have been different.

Effective assistance during plea-bargaining: The right to effective assistance can be violated during the course of ***plea-bargaining.*** But again, it's hard for D to get actual relief for claims of ineffective assistance during the plea-bargaining.

"Prejudice" standard for bad-plea-bargain cases: Where D's claim is that he was not accurately advised about the potential ***negative consequences*** of a plea bargain, the requirement to show prejudice means that D has to show "a reasonable probability that, but for counsel's unprofessional errors, ***the result of the proceeding would have been different"*** (the second prong of the *Strickland* formulation).

The "I would have insisted on going to trial" standard: This *doesn't* mean that D has to make the difficult showing that had he not taken the bad plea-bargain, he would probably have been *acquitted* at trial. Instead, he ***merely*** has to make a much easier showing: a ***"reasonable probability that,*** but for counsel's errors, he ***would not have pleaded guilty and would have insisted on going to trial."*** [Cite to *Hill v. Lockhart.*]

Example: D is a non-U.S. citizen who pleads guilty to a narcotics crime in order to get a somewhat shorter sentence (the difference between an 18-year sentence and one of 16 or 17 years) than he would get if convicted at trial. Before D takes the plea, his lawyer erroneously assures him that he will not be deported if he pleads guilty. After taking the plea, D discovers that deportation is not just possible but *mandatory* upon conviction.

The issue is whether D can show a "reasonable probability that, but for counsel's errors, he would not have pleaded guilty and would have insisted on going to trial." Even though D would have had no "viable defense" at trial, he can still meet this "reasonable probability" test if there is substantial evidence that because of his circumstances he would have found it attractive to pursue "even the smallest chance of success at trial." There *is* such evidence here. Therefore, D has shown the required "prejudice" — that without the incorrect advice he would probably have gone to trial. Consequently, D is entitled to a new trial. [Cite to *Lee v. U.S.*]

CHAPTER 9

FORMAL PROCEEDINGS

ChapterScope

So far, we have been concerned with the investigatory phase of the criminal justice system. In this final chapter, we briefly examine certain aspects of the system once formal proceedings against the defendant have commenced. We consider:

Grand jury proceedings: Defendants accused of federal felonies, and some state court defendants, are entitled to a ***grand jury indictment***.

Pre-trial release: The Eight Amendment proscribes the setting of ***"excessive" bail.*** Defendants are not entitled to bail, but when bail is set, it may not be excessively high.

Plea bargaining: Most cases are resolved by plea bargaining. A plea bargaining arrangement must be approved by the judge, and will only be approved if the defendant acts in a voluntary and competent way. Plea agreements are generally ***enforceable;*** for instance, once the plea is accepted, the defendant usually cannot change his mind and go to trial.

Right to a speedy trial: The Sixth Amendment guarantees the right to a ***speedy trial.*** However, there is no bright-line rule about how speedy a trial must be.

Discovery: The prosecution must ***disclose*** to the defense ***exculpatory evidence*** within the prosecution's possession.

Trial: The defendant has several important rights relating to how the trial is conducted, including:

the right to a ***public trial***,

the right to ***confront the witnesses*** against him, and

the right ***not to testify***.

Double jeopardy: The Fifth Amendment provides that no person shall "be subject for the same offense to be twice put in jeopardy of life or limb." This is the Double Jeopardy clause.

Acquittal: If the defendant is ***acquitted***, the double jeopardy rule means that he cannot be retried.

Mistrial or reversal of conviction: Usually, the double jeopardy rule does ***not*** prevent reprosecution after a ***mistrial***, or after a ***conviction*** that is reversed on appeal.

I. GRAND JURY PROCEEDINGS

A. **Grand jury indictment generally:** Defendants accused of federal felonies, and some state-court defendants, are "entitled" to a grand jury indictment, that is, to not be prosecuted until a grand jury has indicted them.

1. **Federal practice:** The Fifth Amendment to the U.S. Constitution provides that "no person shall be held to answer for a capital, or otherwise infamous crime, unless on a presentment or indictment of a Grand Jury." This provision has been interpreted to mean that anyone charged with a ***federal felony*** (i.e., a federal crime punishable by imprisonment for more than one year) may only be tried following issuance of a grand jury indictment.

2. **State courts:** The Fifth Amendment's right to a grand jury indictment is one of the two Bill of Rights guarantees that has been held ***not*** binding on the states pursuant to the Fourteenth Amendment's Due Process Clause. (See *supra*, p. 4.) So it is up to each individual state whether to require a grand jury indictment.

   a. **"Indictment states":** Today, about 19 states require a grand jury indictment for all felonies. L&I, v. 2, p. 279. These are commonly called "indictment states."

   b. **"Information states":** The remaining states dispense with the requirement of an indictment in at least some kinds of felonies. Twenty-six states give the prosecutor the option to use an "information" (essentially a complaint prepared by the prosecutor) rather than an indictment in all cases. An additional five states require an indictment only for capital or life-imprisonment cases. *Id.*

B. **Nature of grand jury proceedings:**

1. **Composition:** The grand jury panel is drawn from the same group of ***private citizens*** as the petit jury. Traditionally, the grand jury consisted of 23 members, with a majority needed to indict. Today, most states have moved to ***smaller*** grand juries, and continue to require a less-than-unanimous vote (although as grand juries have gotten smaller, it is more common to find a two-thirds or three-fourths vote, rather than a bare majority, needed to indict).

2. **Procedure:** The grand jury's function is to determine whether there is sufficient evidence to justify a trial. The grand jury hears only evidence presented by the ***prosecutor***. The proceedings are carried out in secrecy, with only the prosecutor, a series of witnesses, and the grand jurors, present.

   a. **Presence of target:** The ***target*** of a grand jury investigation never has the right to be present throughout the proceedings. In fact, in the federal system, and in most states, the target does not even have a legally enforceable right to appear before the grand jury to give testimony. However, a few states, including New York (see N.Y.C.P.L. §190.50(5)) do give the prospective defendant a right to appear. L&I, v. 2, p. 286.

   b. **Result:** In the overwhelming majority of cases, the grand jury votes to indict. If the grand jury refuses to indict, the prosecution must be dropped. See generally L&I, v. 1, p. 25.

C. **Use of evidence:** The grand jury hears witnesses called by the prosecution, and also views documents and other tangible evidence.

1. **Subpoena power:** The grand jury has the power to ***subpoena*** both witnesses (via a *"subpoena ad testificandum"*) and tangible evidence (via a *"subpoena duces tecum"*). A witness who fails to comply with either type of subpoena may be held in ***contempt*** of court.

2. **Use of illegally-obtained evidence:** The grand jury may hear and use ***illegally-obtained evidence***. In other words, there is no exclusionary rule for grand jury proceedings. Thus the fruits of a confession obtained in violation of *Miranda*, or of a search conducted in violation of the Fourth Amendment, may be introduced and relied upon by the grand jury. See, e.g., *U.S. v. Calandra*, 414 U.S. 338 (1974). The grand jury may also hear and rely upon inadmissible ***hearsay***. *Costello v. U.S.*, 350 U.S. 359 (1956).

D. The privilege against self-incrimination, and immunity: The Fifth Amendment privilege against ***self-incrimination*** will frequently entitle a witness who is subpoenaed by a grand jury to refuse to testify. However, this refusal may be overcome by a grant of immunity.

1. **The privilege against self-incrimination:** The Fifth Amendment provides that no person "shall be compelled in any criminal case to be a witness against himself. . . . " This privilege applies in grand jury proceedings — if the witness believes that the testimony he is being asked to give might incriminate him in a subsequent criminal case (whether in the jurisdiction that is conducting the grand jury investigation, or a different jurisdiction), he may decline to testify on Fifth Amendment grounds. *Counselman v. Hitchcock*, 142 U.S. 547 (1892).

   a. **No right not to appear:** At trial, the Fifth Amendment guarantee means that the defendant need not even ***take the stand***. But a different rule applies to grand jury proceedings: the federal courts, and most states, have concluded that the Fifth Amendment does ***not*** allow the witness to refuse to appear at all — the witness must appear in response to the subpoena, and must then state for the record the Fifth Amendment claim. L&I, v. 1, p. 678.

2. **Immunity:** If each witness summoned before a grand jury could simply plead the Fifth Amendment and thereby be relieved of all need to testify, the grand jury's investigative powers would be severely undermined. This does not happen, because the grand jury (acting under the prosecutor's direction) has a powerful weapon to combat this problem: the grand jury may issue ***immunity*** to the witness. Because the grant of immunity means that the witness does not have to worry about his testimony's being used to prosecute him in a later criminal case, the basis for the Fifth Amendment objection is eliminated, and the witness can be required to testify.

   a. **Transactional vs. use immunity:** There are two types of immunity that may be granted: ***transactional*** immunity and ***use*** immunity. Transactional immunity protects the witness against any prosecution for the transactions about which he has testified. Use immunity, by contrast, is much narrower — it merely protects against the direct or indirect use of the testimony in a subsequent prosecution. (For instance, suppose that W testifies under a grant of use immunity that he robbed the First National Bank on April 14, 1988. The prosecution in a later criminal trial of W may not use that testimony as part of the prosecution, but it may nonetheless prosecute W for the robbery if it can prove its case without making any use whatsoever of his testimony.)

   b. **Use immunity sufficient:** For years, it was thought that a person's Fifth Amendment privilege would be nullified only by the grant of transactional, not use, immunity. But in *Kastigar v. U.S.*, 406 U.S. 441 (1972), the Supreme Court held that ***use immunity is sufficient*** to nullify the witness' Fifth Amendment privilege.

i. **No indirect use:** However, the witness must indeed be protected against even ***indirect*** use of his testimony. The burden of proving that there has been no use is placed upon the prosecution at the subsequent trial. The prosecution must prove that it did not use the testimony even to: (1) obtain ***leads*** to information or witnesses, (2) focus the subsequent investigation, (3) interpret the independently-derived evidence, (4) plan cross-examination, or make any other kind of use of the grand jury testimony. (As a practical matter, the subsequent criminal trial must be conducted by prosecutors who did not witness, or read the transcript of, W's grand jury testimony.)

E. **Witness' right to counsel:** Does a witness called before a grand jury have a right to have ***counsel present***? No majority of the Supreme Court has ever squarely ruled on this question. But a plurality of the Court has held that the answer is ***"no."*** See *U.S. v. Mandujano*, 425 U.S. 564 (1976). Most lower courts since *Mandujano* have held that the witness has no constitutional right to have counsel present in the grand jury room, or (in the case of an indigent) to have counsel appointed to assist him with the grand jury proceeding.

1. **Non-constitutionally-required procedures:** Some states, but probably not a majority, do allow the witness to have counsel present in the grand jury room. Those states that do not allow this usually allow the witness to have his lawyer present in the anteroom, though some place limits on how frequently the witness may leave the grand jury room to consult with the lawyer — a court might, for instance, refuse to allow the witness to make a trip to consult with the lawyer prior to each question. L&I, v. 1, pp. 705-07.

II. BAIL AND PREVENTIVE DETENTION

A. **Release pending trial:** When a suspect has been arrested and charged, the government obviously has an interest in making sure that the accused shows up for trial, and an interest in ensuring that the accused does not commit further crimes before trial. At the same time, however, the accused has not yet been convicted of any crime, and has an interest in remaining free until his trial. These two sets of interests conflict. The procedures for bail, for various non-bail forms of release, and for preventive detention, are all ways in which courts and legislatures have tried to balance the competing interests.

B. **Bail:** Traditionally, the system of ***bail*** was the way that courts dealt with the problem of making sure that the defendant showed up for trial. Under the bail system, D is required to post a "bail bond." The bail bond is an amount of money deposited with the court, which D forfeits if he does not show up for trial. In theory, the bail is money belonging entirely to D or his family, but in practice, D and his family come up with only a portion (typically 10%) of the amount, and a bail bondsman supplies the remainder, possibly secured by the family's property.

1. **Eighth Amendment:** The use of bail has been so historically important that it is recognized in the Bill of Rights. The Eighth Amendment (which is applicable to the states through the Fourteenth Amendment's Due Process Clause) provides that ***"excessive bail shall not be required."*** However, the Bail Clause has ***not*** been interpreted so as to give the defendant a right to affordable bail in all situations.

a. **Right to non-excessive bail:** What the Bail Clause does give the defendant is the right, as the wording of the clause itself suggests, to have bail not be "excessive." This appears to mean merely that when the court does set bail, it must not do so in a ***unduly high*** amount. What constitutes an "unduly high" amount is, in turn, to be determined by a number of factors, including "the nature and circumstances of the offense charged, the weight of the evidence against [the defendant], the financial ability of the defendant to give bail and the character of the defendant." *Stack v. Boyle*, 342 U.S. 1 (1951). So, for instance, if a judge were to set a bail of $1 million for a poor defendant accused of the non-violent crime of marijuana possession, the Supreme Court might well hold that this bail was "excessive" (and thus violative of the Eighth Amendment) in the circumstances.

   i. **Right to individualized consideration:** The guarantee against excessive bail means that the judge must consider the defendant's ***individual circumstances*** in fixing bail. The court may not consider the seriousness of the offense as the ***sole*** criterion. Thus in *Stack v. Boyle*, *supra*, 12 defendants were charged with conspiring to violate the Smith Act (which makes it a crime to advocate the forcible overthrow of the government). The trial court set bail at $50,000 for each defendant, apparently without taking into account each defendant's financial status, family ties, or other individualized facts; the court relied solely on the fact that four defendants in a prior Smith Act case had jumped bail. The Supreme Court held that the setting of bail here violated the defendants' Eighth Amendment rights, because bail for each defendant was fixed at a much higher amount than usually imposed for offenses with similar maximum penalties, and because there had been no showing why such high bail was needed on the particular facts here.

b. **Defendant's ability to pay:** The fact that the defendant ***cannot afford*** the bail set in the particular case does ***not*** automatically make the bail "excessive" in violation of the Eighth Amendment. The financial resources of the defendant are one factor to be considered, but not the sole factor.

2. **Right not to allow bail at all:** The Eighth Amendment does not require the judge to set bail in all cases — in recent years, the Supreme Court has approved the concept of "preventive detention" in at least some circumstances. This topic is discussed below.

3. **Decreasing use:** In recent decades, the trend has been away from the use of bail, and towards two other techniques. On the one hand, courts are more likely than ever before to release the defendant on his own recognizance, or by entrusting him to the custody of a private individual (e.g., a parent). On the other hand, courts have become more willing to order preventive detention where the defendant is thought to be dangerous. So the number of situations dealt with by the setting of bail has decreased. This trend has been especially noticeable in the federal system.

C. **Preventive detention:** To what extent may a court's or legislature's decision on whether to grant bail (and the amount) turn on the likelihood that the defendant will ***commit crimes*** while on release? In recent years, it has become clear that the dangerousness of the defendant ***may be considered*** as an important factor in setting the amount of bail, and even in deciding whether any bail at all should be set. In fact, a jurisdiction may set up a ***"preventive detention"*** scheme, whereby the judge is told that under certain circumstances, she may not set bail.

However, a preventive detention scheme may violate the Eighth Amendment if its procedures do not ensure that only those defendants who are genuinely dangerous are denied release.

1. **The federal preventive detention scheme:** The most elaborate preventive detention scheme in existence is that imposed by the ***federal*** system. The federal Bail Reform Act of 1984, 18 U.S.C. §3141 et seq., makes ensuring "the safety of any other person or the community" a relevant consideration in setting bail. A special "detention hearing" is to be held if the case involves a crime of violence, a crime for which the maximum penalty is death or life imprisonment, certain serious drug offenses, or any felony by someone who has twice been convicted of any of the previously-listed felonies. If the judge or magistrate finds that no set of conditions upon release (e.g., release in the custody of another private person, bail, etc.) will eliminate the risk that the defendant will flee or endanger others, then the person is to be detained before trial. If detention is ordered, the defendant gets an immediate appeal.

2. **Federal Act found constitutional:** This federal scheme was found ***constitutional*** in *U.S. v. Salerno*, 481 U.S. 739 (1987). The Court, by a 6-3 vote, rejected both the claim that the Bail Reform Act violated the Due Process Clause, and the claim that it violated the Eighth Amendment's Bail Clause. In particular, the majority found that "nothing in the text of the Bail Clause limits permissible government considerations solely to questions of flight." The government's pre-trial interest in ensuring that the defendant not commit additional crimes or otherwise be dangerous to others was a compelling interest, and was thus entitled to considerable weight. And the extensive procedural safeguards given by the Act — the defendant's right to testify at a hearing, present evidence, cross-examine, receive a written opinion with findings of fact and reasoning, and appeal — were enough to protect his due process rights.

   a. **Individualized determination:** The importance which the *Salerno* Court attached to the procedural safeguards in the federal Act suggests that not every preventive detention act will pass constitutional muster. Any preventive detention scheme must almost certainly contain the opportunity for a ***hearing***, at which the ***individual circumstances*** of the defendant (e.g., his past dangerous tendencies, convictions, community ties, etc.) may be considered. For instance, if a state were to provide that bail should automatically be denied without a hearing, and preventive detention ordered, for any defendant charged with murder, such a mandatory scheme would almost certainly violate the Due Process Clause, the Eighth Amendment's Excessive Bail Clause, or both.

   b. **Dangerousness may be considered:** By the way, the *Salerno* decision also seems to establish that the defendant's dangerousness may be considered in fixing the ***amount*** of bail, not just in deciding whether bail should be allowed at all.

III. PLEA BARGAINING

A. **Plea bargains generally:** Most criminal cases leading to convictions are resolved by ***plea bargain*** rather than by trial. The system of plea bargaining is to the prosecution's advantage, because fewer resources are needed to plea bargain a case than to conduct a full-scale trial. To give the defendant an incentive to "settle" the case rather than insist on a trial, the prosecutor normally gives the defendant an inducement of a *lighter sentence* than that which he would get if he were convicted at trial. Additionally, the plea bargain may enable the defendant to avoid some of the uncertainty inherent in being sentenced by a judge after a conviction at trial.

1. **Three types:** There are three common types of plea bargains:

   a. **Lesser charge:** First, D may be permitted to plead guilty to a ***less serious charge*** than the one which is supported by the evidence. (For instance, he may be allowed to plead guilty to second-degree sexual assault rather than rape.)

   b. **Sentence:** Alternatively, D may plead guilty to the same crime on which he would be charged and tried, but the prosecution may agree to recommend (or at least not oppose) a ***lighter sentence*** than would typically be given by the sentencing judge. In this kind of "lesser sentence" deal, the prosecutor typically does not have the authority to ***guarantee*** that the lesser sentence will be awarded; however, judges usually go along with the prosecutor's recommendation, so there is little practical risk for the defendant in making such a bargain.

   c. **Dropping of other charges:** Finally, D may agree to plead guilty to one charge, in return for the prosecution's promise to ***drop other charges*** that might also have been brought.

   See generally L&I, v. 2, pp. 554-55.

2. **Generally enforceable:** Plea bargains are generally enforceable. For instance, if D pleads guilty to a charge, is sentenced, and then has a change of heart, he is almost always stuck with his bargain.

   a. **Prosecutor may refuse to bargain:** Conversely, the prosecutor has ***no obligation*** to bargain. Even if the prosecutor routinely offers a plea bargain in other, similar, circumstances, she has a right in a particular case to decide to go to trial without offering a plea bargain. See, e.g., *Weatherford v. Bursey*, 429 U.S. 545 (1977) ("There is no constitutional right to plea bargain; the prosecutor need not do so if he prefers to go to trial").

B. Threats and promises by prosecutor:

1. **Threats by prosecutor:** The prosecutor has wide discretion in how to conduct himself during the plea-bargain negotiations. For example, there are relatively few constraints on the prosecutor's right to use ***threats*** during the negotiation. Thus a prosecutor may charge one crime, and then tell the defendant, "If you don't plead guilty to this charge, I'll file more serious charges." So long as the threatened extra charges are reasonably supported by the evidence, the defendant will not be able to plead guilty, then attack the plea on the grounds that he was coerced.

   Example: D is initially charged with uttering a forged instrument, a crime punishable by 2-10 years. The prosecutor tells D that if D does not plead guilty to this charge, he will then charge D under the Habitual Criminal Act, under which D would be subject to mandatory life imprisonment because of his two prior felony convictions. D refuses to take the plea bargain, the prosecutor makes good on his threat, and D is indeed convicted under the HCA and sentenced to life imprisonment.

Held (by the U.S. Supreme Court), the result here does not violate D's due process rights. "There is no . . . element of punishment or retaliation as long as the accused is free to accept or reject the prosecution's offer." *Bordenkircher v. Hayes*, 434 U.S. 357 (1978).

Note: But if the prosecutor in *Bordenkircher* had threatened to bring an extra charge which was, in fact, *not supported* by probable cause, and D had accepted the plea bargain, he might then have been able to attack the plea bargain on the grounds that it was the product of duress. The Court in *Bordenkircher* emphasized that the prosecutor there had probable cause for the more serious charge which he threatened to add and later added.

a. **Threat to treat unusually severely:** The result seems to be the same where the prosecutor threatens to prosecute the case ***more severely than he usually would do.*** For instance, even if D in *Bordenkircher* had shown (as he probably did or could have) that the prosecutor there *never* used the Habitual Criminal Act in other forgery cases like D's, this would presumably have made no difference — so long as the prosecutor had probable cause to bring the more serious charge, he was entitled to do so (or to threaten to do so in an attempt to induce a guilty plea), regardless of the prosecutor's usual tactics in similar cases.

b. **Threats about third person:** If, on the other hand, the prosecutor tries to induce D to plead guilty by offering leniency to a ***third person*** (or, conversely, threatens to prosecute the third person if D does not plead guilty), the courts are somewhat more likely to overturn the plea bargain on the grounds of duress. This is especially true where the third person is a ***spouse***, ***sibling***, or ***child***, because of the greater danger of coercion in such a situation. But even in this situation, the fact that the prosecutor has coupled D's plea with the treatment of third parties does not automatically constitute duress, and it is a rare defendant who will be able to successfully attack the plea later on the grounds that the promise of leniency to, say, his spouse, or the threats of prosecution of the spouse, coerced the plea. L&I, v. 2, p. 581.

2. **Broken bargains:** The plea bargain is essentially a contract, and the rules of contract law generally apply. Consequently, if the prosecution fails to ***honor its part of the bargain***, the defendant may usually either "terminate the contract" (and elect to go to trial), or seek "specific performance" (i.e., insist that the terms as originally agreed upon be carried out).

   a. **Breach by prosecution:** The Supreme Court has held that it is a violation of the Constitution for D to be imprisoned based upon a guilty plea where the prosecution has failed to live up to its promises. *Santobello v. New York*, 404 U.S. 257 (1971). Thus in *Santobello*, D entered a plea to a lesser included offense, based upon the prosecutor's promise to make no recommendation concerning sentence; by the time sentencing occurred, a new prosecutor had taken over, and he recommended the maximum sentence, which the judge imposed. The Supreme Court held that D's constitutional rights were violated here, because D had a constitutional expectation of receiving the benefit of his bargain.

      i. **Judge disagrees:** But the defendant only has the right to receive what the prosecution has promised, and no more. For instance, in the "lesser sentence" scheme (see *supra*, p. 429), the prosecutor promises to ***recommend*** a particular sentence, or not to oppose a particular sentence. If the prosecutor keeps this part of the bargain, but the trial judge ***imposes a more serious sentence***, the defendant's constitutional rights have not been violated, and the defendant may be stuck with the heavier-than-recommended sentence. (But many states and the federal system, although not constitutionally required to do so, would allow the defendant to withdraw his guilty plea at that moment and go to trial.)

ii. **Dropped charges taken into account:** Also, if the defendant pleads guilty to a lesser offense, or pleads to one charge while others are dropped, the sentencing judge may ***take into account*** the dropped charges in deciding on a sentence for the pleaded-to charge. L&I, v. 2, p. 592.

b. **Remedy:** If D can show that the plea bargain promises were broken by the prosecution, normally the court will order specific performance. That is, it will order that the deal be kept (rather than merely giving D the right to go to trial). L&I, v. 2, p. 597.

c. **Breach by defendant:** What's sauce for the goose is sauce for the gander: if *D* fails to live up to the plea bargain, then the *prosecution* has the right to elect to terminate the agreement and try D on the originally-charged offense. This is true even if a judgment of conviction has already been entered as the result of the plea bargain. The problem is most likely to arise where D agrees to ***testify*** against his confederates in return for a lesser charge or lesser sentence, and then reneges.

Example: D is charged with first-degree murder. Under a plea bargain, he is allowed to plead to second-degree murder, in exchange for his promise to testify against his confederates. He testifies against them in an initial trial, and they are convicted; D is then sentenced on the second-degree charge. An appeals court reverses the conviction of the confederates, and the prosecution demands that D testify against them at a second trial. D refuses (on the grounds that the plea agreement did not impose any duty to testify at a second trial); a state court rules against D on this point. D now offers to testify at the new trial, but the prosecution asserts that the plea bargain has been broken and that it has the right to prosecute D for first-degree murder.

Held, for the prosecution. The plea bargain agreement here expressly provided that if D breached, the agreement could be withdrawn and D charged with first-degree murder. Here, the state court decided that D indeed breached. The fact that D may have had a good faith (but erroneous) belief that his refusal to testify at the second trial was not a breach is irrelevant — D gambled that his conduct was not a breach, and lost, so he must bear the consequences. (Four justices dissent, partly on the ground that D always agreed to abide by whatever a court finally determined the plea agreement to mean, and never breached this commitment.) *Ricketts v. Adamson*, 483 U.S. 1 (1987).

C. **Sixth Amendment right to counsel:** The Sixth Amendment right to the assistance of ***counsel applies*** during the plea bargaining procedure. Thus an indigent defendant has the right to have counsel appointed for him to carry out those negotiations. See *Missouri v. Frye* and *Lafler v. Cooper*, both *supra*, p. 391.

D. **Receiving of plea:** The trial judge will not "receive" the plea until she has assured herself that certain requirements, designed to protect defendants, have been complied with:

1. **Competence:** The judge must be satisfied that the defendant is ***competent*** to enter into the plea, and that the plea is truly voluntary.

2. **Understanding of charge:** The judge must determine that the defendant ***understands the charge*** to which he is pleading. The judge tells D that he has a right to a trial and that he is giving up that right by pleading guilty. The judge will then usually explain to the defendant the nature of the charge, and what elements the prosecution would have to prove if the case went to trial. The judge also tells D that he has a right to a trial and that he is giving up that right by pleading guilty.

3. **Understanding of consequences:** The judge will also make sure that the defendant understands the consequences of accepting the plea. This usually means that the judge will explain to the defendant both the maximum possible sentence that might be imposed in response to the plea, and the minimum sentence, if any, which the judge is required by law to impose.

4. **Factual basis:** Most controversially, some states, and the federal system, require that the judge not take the guilty plea unless the judge is convinced that there is a ***factual basis*** for the plea. L&I, v. 2, p. 652. Normally, the judge will not accept the guilty plea unless the defendant says, in effect, "I did the acts that I am charged with committing." Thus if the defendant continues to protest his innocence, and says that he is pleading guilty only to avoid the risk that the trial judge or jury may disbelieve his truthful professions of innocence, the judge will normally ***not accept*** the guilty plea.

   a. **Refusal to take plea is constitutional:** In this scenario — where D desires to plead guilty, but continues to insist upon his actual innocence — it is ***constitutional*** for the trial judge to refuse to take the guilty plea. As the Supreme Court has said, "A criminal defendant does not have an absolute right under the Constitution to have his guilty plea accepted by the court. . . . " *North Carolina v. Alford*, 400 U.S. 25 (1970).

5. **Exculpatory information:** Must the trial court require the prosecution to ***disclose*** to the defense all possibly ***exculpatory material*** in its possession, so that the defendant can accurately ***assess the strength of the prosecution's case*** before deciding whether to plead? The only significant Supreme Court case on point has held that the prosecution need ***not*** disclose ***"impeachment information"*** to the defendant before there is a plea bargain. That is, although D may have a constitutional right to receive exculpatory information from the prosecution ***before trial*** (see, e.g., *Brady v. Maryland, infra*, p. 439), the prosecution may force D to ***waive*** that right in exchange for the plea bargain, at least where the exculpatory information is of a type that would merely be ***helpful to impeach witnesses,*** rather than being direct proof of D's innocence. *U.S. v. Ruiz*, 536 U.S. 622 (2002). (But it remains likely that if the prosecution has ***direct proof*** of D's innocence, it may not withhold that information while making a plea bargain with D.)

E. **Withdrawal of plea by defendant:** Under some circumstances, the defendant may have the right to ***withdraw*** his guilty plea. This is done by a "motion to withdraw" the plea.

   1. **Before sentence:** ***Before sentencing*** has taken place, most jurisdictions give the defendant a relatively broad right to withdraw the plea. For instance, in the federal system, a pre-sentencing withdrawal may be made for "any fair and just reason." L&I, v. 2, p. 658.

2. **After sentencing:** But ***after sentencing***, it is far ***harder*** for the defendant to withdraw the plea. Obviously, courts are reluctant to let the defendant have two bites at the apple, by, for instance, getting one of two charges dropped, and then undoing the arrangement if the sentence on the remaining charge is more severe than the defendant expected. But if the arrangement is that the prosecution will recommend a certain sentence, and the trial judge ignores the recommendation and sentences more severely, many jurisdictions will allow the defendant to withdraw the plea and go to trial (though apparently it is not a violation of D's constitutional rights if he is not permitted to withdraw the plea in this circumstance).

F. **Rights waived by plea:** Normally, a defendant who enters a guilty plea, and undergoes sentencing, is deemed to have ***waived*** any rights, including constitutional ones, that he could have asserted at trial. Therefore, he usually may not ***appeal*** the pleaded-to conviction or the sentence under it. This is true even where D now asserts constitutional rights that were not recognized until ***after*** the plea was entered.

Example: D confesses to a crime during police interrogation. Under state case law prevailing at the time of this confession, the confession would be read to the jury, and it would be up to the jury to decide whether it was voluntary and thus admissible. Because D justifiably fears having the jury hear his confession (even though he believes that it was coerced from him), he pleads guilty. Later, the Supreme Court holds that the state practice of letting the jury decide on admissibility of confessions is unconstitutional, and orders retrials for all defendants who were convicted after juries heard the confession under the forbidden procedures. D argues that his guilty plea should be set aside and a new trial ordered.

Held, for the prosecution. One who has pleaded guilty is in a different position from one who has gone to trial. "The defendant who pleads guilty is . . . convicted on his counseled admission in open court that he committed the crime charged against him. The prior confession is not the basis for the judgment, has never been offered in evidence at a trial, and may never be offered in evidence." Allowing guilty pleas to be reopened based on later decisions concerning admissibility of evidence would impair the state's interest in "maintaining the finality of guilty plea convictions which were valid under constitutional standards applicable at the time." *McMann v. Richardson*, 397 U.S. 759 (1970).

1. **Exception for "non-curable" defects:** However, there is a very limited ***exception*** to the general rule that one who pleads guilty may not later take the benefit of new constitutional or other rulings. The exception has been summarized this way: "A defendant who has been convicted on a plea of guilty may challenge his conviction on any constitutional ground that, if asserted before trial, would ***forever preclude*** the state from obtaining a valid conviction against him, regardless of how much the state might endeavor to correct the defect. In other words, a plea of guilty may operate as a forfeiture of all defenses except those that, once raised, cannot be 'cured'." 75 Mich. L. Rev. 1214, 1226 (1977).

Example: D asserts that the indictment against him is barred by double jeopardy. The trial judge, in a preliminary ruling, holds against him. D pleads guilty, then challenges the indictment on appeal.

Held, D's guilty plea did not waive his "double jeopardy" claim, because the double jeopardy problem, if there was one, could not have been cured by the prosecution. *Menna v. New York*, 423 U.S. 61 (1975).

Note: The important thing to remember regarding D's right to challenge a guilty plea on appeal is that successful challenges are very rare — except for those very few cases where the defense now being asserted by D would have been "uncurable" by the state (and probably not even in all of those situations), once D pleads guilty, he may not challenge his conviction further.

IV. SELECTIVE PROSECUTION

A. Background: Suppose a prosecutor (call her "Pros") decides that in cases where the potential charge is distribution of crack cocaine (with a 10-year minimum sentence), (1) she will charge all ***Black*** defendants with that offense, but (2) she will charge all ***white*** defendants with the ***lesser*** misdemeanor charge of small-scale cocaine possession. When Pros charges a particular Black defendant, D, with crack distribution, may D seek to have the charges dismissed on the grounds that Black defendants including himself are the victim of ***"selective prosecution"?***

In theory, the answer may in some cases be yes, because D can plausibly argue that his Equal Protection rights have been violated. But as we'll see, the Supreme Court has placed such huge procedural obstacles to such a defense that it will be ***exceedingly rare*** for a defendant to succeed with it.

1. **Racial discrimination:** In most cases where defendants have raised claims of unconstitutional selective prosecution, their claim is that the prosecutor's decision to prosecute was ***based on the defendant's race.*** Typically, D is Black, and his argument is that prosecutors either don't prosecute white people at all for the offense in question, or bring lesser charges against whites than against Blacks.

B. Requirements for selective prosecution claim: The Supreme Court has made defense claims that the prosecutor has engaged in unconstitutional selective prosecution ***virtually impossible to establish.*** See ***U.S. v. Armstrong***, 517 U.S. 456 (1996), which we'll discussing immediately below. Indeed, ***no defendant*** in any court seems to have succeeded with a selective-prosecution claim not just since *Armstrong*, but going back to the late nineteenth century.[1]

1. **Two requirements:** In *Armstrong*, the Court said that to bring a successful selective-prosecution claim, the defendant would have to show ***"clear evidence" of two things:***

   [1] **"Discriminatory effect":** First, D must show that the prosecutor's policy "had a ***discriminatory effect***."

   [2] **"Discriminatory purpose":** Second, D must show that that policy was "motivated by a ***discriminatory purpose.***"

---

1. See, e.g., 115 NW. U. L. Rev. 987, 1002-03 (2021): "Since the Court established *Armstrong*'s demanding discovery standard [in 1996], there has ***not been a single successful selective prosecution*** or selective law enforcement claim on the merits." What's more, the last successful selective prosecution claim at either the state or federal level seems to have been the very first one that reached the Court back in 1886.

2. **Hard to establish:** Each of these elements tends to be ***virtually impossible to prove*** by the required clear evidence. We discuss the "discriminatory effect" requirement in Par. 3 immediately below, and the "discriminatory purpose" requirement in Par. 4.

3. **Discriminatory effect:** In *Armstrong*, D claimed that federal prosecuters chose to prosecute Blacks for crack cocaine distribution, whereas in similar cases they charged whites only with much less serious offenses (e.g., possession of cocaine in powdered form, where the sentences are much lower). The *Armstrong* Court first tackled the requirement that D show that the charging decision had a ***"discriminatory effect"*** based on D's race. To meet this requirement, the *Armstrong* Court said, D must "show that ***similarly situated individuals of a different race*** were not prosecuted."

   a. **Strict standard:** The *Armstrong* Court did not say much about what sort of *evidence* of discriminatory effect would satisfy this requirement that "similarly situated individuals" be shown to have been treated with a different effect. But the one example given by *Armstrong* of what evidence *would* suffice suggests ***how hard it will typically be*** for the defendant to amass the required proof of disparate effect. The Court said that the Ds "could have investigated whether similarly situated persons of ***other races*** were ***prosecuted by the state*** of California [and] were ***known to federal law enforcement officers***, but were ***not prosecuted in federal court."***

      i. **Very high bar:** *Armstrong* has been interpreted by lower courts to set an bar that's so high as to be nearly ***impossible-to-satisfy*** when D tries to prove that the unprosecuted individuals of a different race than D were ***"similarly situated"*** to D. These courts have said that D must point to ***particular white persons*** who, faced with potential charges based on the same type of offense (in *Armstrong*, crack distribution), were not charged by the same prosecutor or office. This is generally an insurmountable obstacle, since "it is impossible for a person of color to point to ***similarly situated white individuals*** who were not arrested because ***there is no record of such people."*** 2022 Wis. L. Rev. 825, 831 (2022).

4. **Discriminatory purpose:** Similarly, it is nearly impossible for D to satisfy the second requirement for a selective prosecution claim: proving that the prosecution's charging policies were motivated by a ***"discriminatory purpose."*** That's because, "In the era of colorblindness ... officials in the criminal justice system ***are unlikely to explicitly voice any discriminatory sentiments[.]"*** *Id.* At 832.

C. **Obtaining discovery to show bias:** In most cases involving claims of selective prosecution, the defendant does not even *try* to have the case dismissed on that grounds. Instead, defendants typically ask for the right to ***conduct discovery,*** to help them find evidence that the requirements for a selective prosecution claim have been met.

But the Supreme Court has held that the ***same requirements*** (clear evidence of discriminatory purpose and effect) have to be satisfied before the defendant will even have the right to do such discovery. *Armstrong, supra.* As one observer has noted, "[T]he requirement that defendants moving for discovery present evidence showing the ***same data*** whose existence they are seeking to prove has created a ***'Catch-22' situation.'"*** *Id.* at 830-831.

1. ***Armstrong* case:** The near-impossibility of getting discovery on a selective-prosecution claims is illustrated by *Armstrong, supra.*

a. **Facts:** In *Armstrong*, the Ds, who were Black, were charged with the federal crime of distributing crack cocaine. They asserted that they had been selected for federal prosecution because they were Black, and moved to be allowed to conduct discovery to find evidence supporting their claim. In their motion, they supplied an affidavit from the public defender's office that during the year in question (1991), every one of the crack-distribution charges filed by the relevant federal prosecutor's office was against a Black defendant.

b. **Holding:** But the Supreme Court ***rejected*** the Ds' discovery request. The Court reasoned that if courts were to grant such a discovery motion, the government would have to ***"assemble from its own files*** documents which might corroborate or refute the defendants claim." That document-location process would be unduly burdensome, the Court said, because it would "***divert prosecutors' resources*** and may ***disclose the Government's prosecutorial strategy.***"

i. **What the Ds would need to do:** Therefore, the *Armstrong* Court held, the Ds would not be permitted to obtain discovery unless they could first satisfy the ***same requirements*** (discriminatory purpose and effect) as would be imposed on a defendant seeking outright dismissal for selective prosecution. The Ds would thus need to "***identify individuals*** who were ***not black***, ***could have been prosecuted*** for the [same] offenses for which [the Ds] were charged, but were ***not*** so prosecuted." Since the affidavit submitted by the Ds did not identify any such similarly-situated non-Black potential defendants, the Ds were not entitled to discovery.

V. RIGHT TO SPEEDY TRIAL

A. **The right generally:** The Sixth Amendment provides that "in all criminal prosecutions, the accused shall enjoy the right to a ***speedy . . . trial***." This right applies directly to federal prosecutions, but also applies to state prosecutions by means of the Fourteenth Amendment's Due Process Clause.

1. **Balancing test:** The Supreme Court has not come up with any bright line rules governing how speedy a trial must be. Instead, the Court has adopted a somewhat amorphous ***"balancing test,"*** in which both the prosecution's and the defendant's conduct are weighed. See *Barker v. Wingo*, 407 U.S. 514 (1972). *Barker* sets forth four factors which courts are to consider in deciding whether the trial has been unreasonably delayed:

a. **Length:** The ***length of the delay***. The acceptable length is dictated in part by the nature of the charge. "The delay that can be tolerated for an ordinary street crime is considerably less than for a serious, complex conspiracy charge." *Barker*. Courts have varied as to what kind of delay will typically be prejudicial, but most delays of less than five months are found not prejudicial, and most delays of eight months or longer are found "presumptively prejudicial." 48 Fordham L. Rev. 611, 623 (1980).

b. **Reason:** The ***reason for the delay***. In general, the more culpable the government's conduct regarding the delay, the better the defendant's speedy trial claim. Thus if D were lucky enough to show that the government deliberately delayed the trial to hamper the defense, even a short delay would probably be found prejudicial. Delays due to court congestion are somewhat less damning, but still not to be quickly excused. By contrast, a "valid reason" such as the search for a ***missing witness*** will typically lead the court to find no Speedy Trial violation.

c. **Defendant's assertion of the right:** Whether the defendant ***asserted*** the speedy trial right, and when. If the defendant did not assert that he was ready for trial, and wanted the trial to start immediately, his later claim that the proceedings started too late will not be entitled to as much weight as where he pushed for a quick trial all along.

d. **Prejudice:** The ***prejudice*** that D has suffered by the delay. There are three types of prejudice which D might suffer from delay: (1) oppressive pre-trial incarceration; (2) anxiety and concern while waiting for trial; and (3) impairment of defense. Courts typically do not take types (1) and (2) very seriously. (For instance, in *Barker* itself, D was incarcerated for 10 months prior to trial, but the Court found that this was not enough to constitute constitutionally-significant prejudice.) The third type of prejudice — impairment of the defense — is the most serious. Thus if D can show that witnesses favorable to him have died, moved away where they cannot reasonably be found, or suffered impaired memories, prejudice is likely to be found.

B. **Federal Speedy Trial Act:** In federal prosecutions, the Speedy Trial Clause has been essentially superseded by very elaborate legislation, the ***Speedy Trial Act***, 18 U.S.C. §§ 3161-3174. The Act sets out two separate time limits, one for the period from arrest to charge, and the other for the period from charge to trial.

1. **Ordinary limits:** Ordinarily, the time between arrest and either indictment or information must be no more than 30 days. The time between indictment/information and the commencement of trial must normally be no more than 70 days.

2. **Allowable delays:** However, there are a series of ***"periods of delay"*** which do not count. Some of these are quite elastic. For instance, delay due to the unavailability of an "essential witness" does not count. Similarly treated is a delay due to a continuance granted at the prosecution's request by the trial judge, if the judge puts findings on the record as to why "the ends of justice served by the granting of such continuance outweigh the best interests of the public and the defendant in a speedy trial."

3. **Sanctions:** If the indictment/information is not brought within the 30-day period, or the trial does not commence within the 70-day period following indictment/information (excluding valid "periods of delay"), the court must ***dismiss*** the charges. However, the dismissal does not necessarily have to be "with prejudice" — it is up to the court to decide whether dismissal should be with or without prejudice, based upon such factors as the seriousness of the offense, the circumstances surrounding the delay, and the "impact of a reprosecution . . . on the administration of justice." 18 U.S.C. §3162(a). (Dismissal "without prejudice" means that the prosecutor may obtain a new indictment, and in effect start the prosecution all over again.)

VI. PRE-TRIAL MOTIONS TO SUPPRESS EVIDENCE

A. **Use of a pre-trial suppression motion:** Where the defendant claims that evidence sought to be introduced by the prosecution was illegally obtained, a special procedure is used to decide on the objection. In the typical non-constitutional admissibility situation, the objection is disposed of during the trial at the very moment admission is sought — for instance, if the prosecution tries to put on testimony as to someone's out-of-court declaration, it is at that very moment that the defendant objects. But objections to evidence on the grounds that it was obtained in violation of the Constitution are different; in the vast majority of states, the admissibility of such evidence is determined before the trial even starts, by means of a pre-trial ***motion to suppress***. Thus evidence whose admissibility is questionable based upon any of the chapters of this book — the fruits of an allegedly illegal search or seizure, of an un-*Mirandized* confession, of an unduly suggestive lineup or show-up, for instance — are all determined by a suppression motion.

1. **Writing:** Generally, the motion must be made in writing. The court then holds a hearing on the motion, at which witnesses can testify. In the case of evidence which the defendant claims was seized as part of an unreasonable search, for instance, the court will typically take the testimony of the officers who performed the search, as well as, perhaps, the testimony of the defendant if he was present when the search took place.

B. **Judge/jury allocation:** Except occasionally in cases where the admissibility of a confession is at issue, the judge at the suppression hearing makes the complete decision about admissibility, and leaves no factual issues for the jury relating to admissibility.

1. **Search and seizure:** For instance, if the issue is whether a search and seizure were "unreasonable" and thus violative of the Fourth Amendment, this issue is determined solely by the judge. The judge decides, "Were the search and seizure reasonable?" not merely, "Could a reasonable jury find that the search and seizure were reasonable?" If the judge answers this question "yes," the jury is told to consider the evidence, and not told anything about the issue of reasonableness of the police conduct.

2. **Confessions:** Most states, and the federal system, follow the same rule for a confession which D asserts was involuntary or obtained in violation of *Miranda* — the issue is decided entirely by the judge at the suppression hearing. A substantial minority of states, however, follow a two-step approach, called the "Massachusetts rule," in evaluating claims by the defendant that a confession was ***involuntary***. Under this minority Massachusetts rule, the trial judge rules first on the voluntariness issue. If he finds that the confession was involuntary, the confession is inadmissible, and that is the end of the matter. But if the judge finds that the confession was voluntary, then it is presented to the jury, but with the instruction that the jury must independently find it voluntary or else disregard it. Either the majority or Massachusetts approach is constitutionally allowable. L&I, v. 1, pp. 800-01. (The trial judge makes the sole decision, in virtually all states, as to whether the confession violated the *Miranda* rule.)

C. **Rules of evidence not used:** The suppression hearing is conducted ***without observing the rules of evidence***. For instance, hearsay may be used in determining whether the seizure or confession was illegally obtained. See, e.g., Federal Rule of Evidence 104(a) (In deciding preliminary questions such as the admissibility of evidence, the court "is not bound by the rules of evidence except those with respect to privileges. . . . ").

VII. PRE-TRIAL DISCOVERY

A. **Discovery for the defense:** The defense may be entitled to advance ***disclosure*** by the prosecution of evidence or other material relevant to the case. In some instances, advance disclosure by the prosecution is actually required by the Constitution's Due Process Clause. In a broader set of circumstances, disclosure is likely to be required by statute in the jurisdiction.

1. **The prosecutor's constitutional duty to disclose:** There is no general constitutional duty on the part of the prosecutor to disclose material evidence to the defense. The only respect in which the Constitution plays a major part in pre-trial disclosure is that the prosecution must disclose to the defense ***exculpatory evidence within the prosecution's possession***. This duty derives from the famous case of ***Brady v. Maryland***, 373 U.S. 83 (1963). In fact, a defense request for exculpatory material is frequently called a "*Brady*" request or a "request for *Brady* material." The *Brady* doctrine — that exculpatory material in the prosecution's possession must be disclosed — is founded upon the Due Process Clause.

Example: D and his friend Boblit are charged with felony murder, and the prosecutor seeks the death penalty. Before trial, D's lawyer, L, asks the prosecution to let L examine any statements made by Boblit to the police. The prosecutor shows L several such statements, but doesn't (for reasons that never become clear) show him one statement in which Boblit admits doing the actual killing. At trial, D admits participating in the felony, but denies doing the actual killing. D is convicted and sentenced to death. After trial, L discovers the missing statement, and seeks a new trial.

Held, for D. The prosecutor's failure to disclose Boblit's statement has resulted in a denial of due process to D. This is true even though the statement was relevant not to guilt but to punishment: "The suppression by the prosecution of evidence favorable to an accused upon request violates due process where the evidence is material either to guilt or to punishment, irrespective of the good faith or bad faith of the prosecution." *Brady v. Maryland, supra.*

a. **Good faith irrelevant:** *Brady's* statement about the irrelevance of the prosecution's good faith continues to be good law: even if the prosecution's failure to disclose exculpatory evidence is not motivated by a desire to hamper the prosecution, and is truly the result of negligence or even circumstances beyond the prosecution's control, this makes no difference.

b. **Materiality:** What happens if the prosecution fails to make a required disclosure, and the violation is not determined until after the trial? The defendant gets a ***new trial***, but only if the non-disclosure is found to have been ***"material."*** The non-disclosure will be deemed material if there is a ***reasonable probability*** that, had the disclosure been made, the ***"result of the proceeding would have been different."*** *U.S. v. Bagley*, 473 U.S. 667 (1985).

i. **Specific request:** Where defense counsel has made a ***specific request*** for the type of material in question, and the prosecution falsely responded that there was no such material, the appellate court will be especially quick to find that the omission was material. One reason for this is that here, defense counsel has actually been ***misled*** — not only has the defense been deprived of the material, but it has been falsely led to believe that no such material exists (thereby, perhaps, leading the defense to abandon other efforts to get comparable material). Where the defense has made only a very general request (e.g., a request for "all *Brady* material"), or has made no request at all, the court will be less quick to find that the non-disclosure was material.

ii. **Materiality is decided cumulatively:** When the court decides whether the non-disclosure was "material," it does so by considering all the non-disclosed items ***cumulatively***. So the fact that each item, by itself, is unlikely to have changed the result of the trial is irrelevant if there is a reasonable probability that the entire set of non-disclosed items would have changed the result. *Kyles v. Whitley*, 514 U.S. 419 (1995). (Had the prosecution disclosed prior inconsistent statements made to the police by two eyewitnesses, and disclosed the existence and conduct of a police informant, there was a reasonable probability that the result would have been different.)

c. **Timing:** The *Brady* doctrine does ***not*** require that the disclosure be made ***before trial starts***. All that is required is that disclosure be made under circumstances giving the defendant enough time to make use of the material. Thus disclosure after the trial has started will frequently be sufficient, especially if the court offers the defense a continuance to let it prepare to use the new material. See generally L&I, v. 2, pp. 545-46.

d. **Lost or destroyed evidence:** Suppose that the prosecution is unable to disclose exculpatory evidence because, due to the prosecution's negligence (or worse), the evidence has been ***lost*** or ***destroyed***. Here, the *Brady* doctrine does ***not*** apply unless the defense shows ***bad faith*** on the part of the police. Thus if, due to garden-variety negligence, exculpatory evidence is destroyed, the defendant is not entitled to dismissal of the charges or to a new trial. "Unless a criminal defendant can show bad faith on the part of the police, failure to preserve potentially useful evidence does not constitute a denial of due process of law." *Arizona v. Youngblood*, 488 U.S. 51 (1989).

Example: V, a 10-year-old boy, is kidnapped and sexually molested. A doctor obtains semen samples from V's rectum; the police collect V's clothing. But the police do not perform prompt tests on the rectal samples or refrigerate the clothing, so that it becomes impossible to do blood-group testing on either. D is charged with the crime. Because of the police failures, D is deprived of the possible chance to show that his blood group is different from the blood groups that would have been found in the clothing or rectal samples. D argues that this police wrongdoing amounts to a denial of due process.

Held, there was no denial of due process here. Only if D had shown bad faith on the part of the police would the destruction of evidence here amount to a deprivation of due process. *Arizona v. Youngblood, supra*.

2. **Practice:** Apart from constitutional requirements, most states, and the federal system, have enacted elaborate ***statutory*** pre-trial disclosure schemes.

a. **Types of disclosure:** Here is a very brief summary of the types of disclosure typically covered by state and federal disclosure schemes:

i. **Defendant's statements:** Nearly all states, and the federal system, require the prosecution upon request to give the defense copies of ***prior recorded statements*** by the defendant. See, e.g., Fed. R. Crim. P. 16(a)(1)(A). Many states also require the prosecution to disclose to a defendant any recorded statements made by a ***co-defendant***. L&I, v. 2, p. 488.

ii. **Scientific reports:** The federal system, and most states, also entitle the defense to receive copies of reports of medical and physical ***examinations*** and ***scientific tests*** made for the prosecution. L&I, v. 2, p. 489.

iii. **Documents and tangible objects:** Most states give the defendant the right to information concerning ***documents*** and ***tangible objects*** which will be used by the prosecution at trial.

iv. **Witness lists:** Many jurisdictions require the prosecution to give the defense a ***list of witnesses*** whom the prosecution intends to call at trial. Some, but not as many, states also require the disclosure of any prior written or recorded statements made by witnesses whom the prosecution will be calling at trial.

v. **Police reports:** Most jurisdictions do ***not*** allow the defense to get a hold of ***police reports*** (except where these fall under some other more general provision, such as recorded statements by the defendant or by a witness). Most states treat a police report as being prosecutorial work product and therefore privileged. Thus a police report detailing the results to date of the police investigation would typically not be available to the defense. L&I, v. 2, pp. 498-500.

b. **Taking of depositions:** Most jurisdictions do ***not*** give the defense a broad power to ***take depositions*** of witnesses. On the other hand, if the defense can show that a particular person is a material witness who is not likely to be able to attend the trial, then the court will usually issue an order allowing a deposition to be taken. L&I, v. 2, pp. 508-09.

B. **Discovery for the prosecution:** The prosecution has, of course, no constitutional right to learn of information held by the defense. However, most states, and the federal system, have by statute or court rules given the prosecution some discovery rights. Typically, these are somewhat less broad than those given to the defense.

1. **Alibi disclosure:** Most states, and the federal system, require D to give advance notice of his intent to raise an ***alibi*** defense. These provisions are justified on the grounds that without them, the defense can at the last minute concoct a false alibi defense which would be very hard for the prosecution to rebut. Provisions requiring pre-trial disclosure of alibi defenses generally do not violate the Due Process Clause. See *Williams v. Florida*, 399 U.S. 78 (1970).

2. **Insanity:** Most states, and the federal system, require D to give advance notice if he intends to rely upon the defense of ***insanity***, or to introduce expert testimony that he lacked the mental state necessary for the crime. See, e.g., Fed. R. Crim. P. 12.2.

3. **Reciprocity:** Some states give the prosecution fairly broad discovery rights, but ***condition*** these upon the defendant's exercise of *his* right to discovery. Under these provisions, if the defendant does not seek discovery, then the prosecution does not have it either

(except for specific types covered by other statutory provisions, such as alibi and insanity provisions). L&I, v. 2, p. 518.

4. **Witness lists and statements:** Some states require the defense to disclose the names and addresses of witnesses it intends to call, any prior recorded statements by those witnesses, and/or any anticipated defenses. However, such broad-ranging provisions are somewhat rarer than the specific types discussed above.

VIII. THE RIGHT TO A JURY TRIAL

A. **The right generally:** Criminal defendants have a right to a ***jury trial***. This right is conferred by the Sixth Amendment, which says that "The accused shall enjoy the right to a ... public trial, by an ***impartial jury*** of the State and district wherein the crime shall have been committed[.]"

1. **Applicable to state trials:** This right has always been applied to ***federal*** trials, and has applied to ***state*** trials since 1968, as the result of *Duncan v. Louisiana*, 391 U.S. 145 (1968).

2. **Serious criminal prosecutions only:** The Sixth Amendment right to jury trial applies only to ***criminal prosecutions*** for ***serious*** crimes. This means that the right does not apply in two important categories of proceedings:

   a. **Non-criminal proceedings:** First, the right does not apply to proceedings that are not truly "criminal" proceedings, even though these have a quasi-criminal dimension and can result in the defendant's loss of liberty. For instance, there is no right to jury trial in ***juvenile court proceedings***, even though as a result the juvenile may be committed to a reform school. *McKeiver v. Pennsylvania*, 403 U.S. 528 (1971). The same is true of ***probation revocation*** proceedings (*Minn. v. Murphy*, 465 U.S. 420 (1984)) and ***military trials*** such as courts martial (*Whelchel v. McDonald*, 340 U.S. 122 (1950)).

   b. **Petty crimes:** Second, the right to jury trial does not apply where what is charged is a ***petty*** rather than serious crime. See *Duncan v. Louisiana*, *supra* (stating that "there is a category of petty crimes or offenses which is not subject to the Sixth Amendment jury trial provisions[.]").

      i. **Six-month standard:** As a general rule, the dividing line between a "serious" crime and a "petty" one is a ***potential sentence of greater than six months***. Thus there is automatically a right to jury trial for any crime punish*able* by more than six months in prison, regardless of whether a more-than-six-month sentence is ***actually*** imposed. *Baldwin v. New York*, 399 U.S. 66 (1970).

         (1) **Presumption as to less-than-six-month sentence:** Conversely, if the maximum sentence allowable for the crime is ***six months or less***, there is a strong ***presumption*** that the crime is ***not*** a serious one for which there is a Sixth Amendment jury. However, this presumption can be ***overcome*** if D shows that there are ***additional statutory penalties*** which when taken together with the maximum authorized prison sentence "are so severe that they clearly reflect a legislative determination that the offense in question is a 'serious' one." *Blan-*

ton v. City of North Las Vegas, 489 U.S. 538 (1989). But overcoming this presumption will be difficult; for instance, in *Blanton*, the fact that the not-more-than-six-month maximum prison sentence for driving under the influence was accompanied by a 90-day mandatory ***license suspension*** and a possible fine of $1,000 was ***not*** enough to convince the Court that the legislature viewed the offense in question as a "serious" one.

ii. **Multiple offenses:** Where D is charged with ***multiple offenses*** that are to be tried together, the Court will ***not "aggregate"*** these offenses together for purposes of the six-month test. *Lewis v. U.S.*, 518 U.S. 322 (1996). So if D is charged with two crimes, each of which is punishable by a maximum of five months in prison, there is no right to jury trial, because each offense is to be independently evaluated to determine whether it is a "serious" one, and by this standard neither of the offenses is serious.

B. Issues to which the right applies: To which ***issues*** in a trial does the right of a jury trial apply? The short answer is that as long as the crime charged is a "serious" one (see *supra*), the defendant has the right to have the jury, rather than the judge, decide ***every element*** of the offense. Furthermore, the jury must find each element to exist ***"beyond a reasonable doubt."***

1. **No jury right as to sentencing:** On the other hand, the right to a jury trial does not extend to the area of ***sentencing***. More particularly, the determination of whether particular ***"sentencing factors"*** specified by the legislature do or do not exist in the particular case can be made by the judge. That is, the legislature can choose to leave it up to the judge rather than the jury to evaluate various "aggravating" or "mitigating" factors that will bear on the sentence. For instance, if the legislature authorizes (as it is permitted to do) a greater penalty where D has a certain type of prior conviction, the legislature may leave it up to the judge to determine whether a qualifying prior conviction exists.

Example: Suppose that legislature of State defines the crime of armed robbery, and provides for a standard sentence of between 5 and 10 years' imprisonment upon conviction. Suppose that the legislature further says that in deciding where in the 5-to-10-years range the sentence for a particular armed robbery shall be placed, the decision shall be made by the judge, and that the judge may consider, among other factors, whether D has previously been convicted of a felony (in which case the judge is authorized to increase the sentence up to the 10-year maximum).

The existence of a prior felony conviction here is a "sentencing factor," not an element of the offense. Therefore, the legislature is not violating the Sixth Amendment by letting the judge, rather than the jury, decide whether D has been convicted of a prior felony.[2]

---

2. In fact, unlike other sorts of "aggravating factors," where a *prior conviction* is used as an aggravating factor, the legislature may even provide for a greater maximum sentence (rather than just a slide toward the already-authorized maximum) while allowing the judge rather than jury to find that the prior conviction exists. (When other sorts of aggravating factors are established, the jury rather than the judge must make the finding that the factor exists, if the factor's existence is to be used to impose a longer sentence than would otherwise be authorized. See *Apprendi v. N.J.*, *infra*.)

2. **Fact increases maximum punishment:** The boundary line between an "element of the offense" and a "sentencing factor" may sometimes be blurry. But the basic concept is that if the existence of a particular fact ***increases the maximum punishment*** to which D is subjected, the existence of that fact will be treated as an ***element of the offense***, as to which the jury must make the decision. If, by contrast, the existence of a particular fact merely bears on ***where within the range of possible sentences*** the defendant's sentence should fall, the existence of that fact will merely be a sentencing factor (on which the judge may constitutionally make the decision). For instance, if the legislature tries to enhance the penalties for a particular offense because of the defendant's ***especially-culpable mental state***, like ***racial bias***, it is the jury rather than the judge that will typically have to find that the specified especially-culpable mental state exists.

   Example: New Jersey defines the crime of possession of a firearm for an unlawful purpose as a "second degree" offense. The punishment for a second-degree offense is imprisonment for between 5 and 10 years. A separate statute, however, says that if a second-degree offense is committed "with a purpose to intimidate an individual or group ... because of race, color [or] gender[,]" the crime is punishable by an "enhanced sentence" of between 10 and 20 years. D is charged with possessing a firearm for an unlawful purpose, and pleads guilty. Over his objection, during the sentencing phase the trial judge (not a jury) conducts a hearing on the basis of which the judge concludes that D's unlawful purpose included racial bias. Therefore, the judge sentences D to an enhanced (more-than-10-year) sentence.

   Held, D had a Sixth Amendment right to have the issue of whether he had a race-based purpose decided by a jury, rather than a judge. "Other than the fact of a prior conviction, any fact that increases the penalty for a crime beyond the prescribed statutory maximum must be submitted to a jury, and proved beyond a reasonable doubt." Since D's possession of a race-based motive increased the penalty beyond the 5-10 year maximum that would otherwise apply, the existence of such a motive was required to be determined by a jury. ***Apprendi v. N.J.***, 530 U.S. 466 (2000).

   a. **Death penalty cases:** This principle has important applications to ***death-penalty*** cases. If the legislature says that the maximum penalty for a crime is something less than death in the absence of some statutorily-specified "aggravating factor," then the existence of that factor must be determined by the jury (beyond a reasonable doubt) rather than by a judge. *Ring v. Arizona*, 536 U.S. 584 (2002).

      i. **Significance:** When the result in *Ring* is combined with the results in other cases in which the Supreme Court has placed limits on the circumstances under which the states may impose the death penalty, the consequence seems to be that ***virtually all death penalty determinations must now be made by juries***, not judges.

3. **Sentencing guidelines:** The principle that punishment-increasing facts must be found by a jury also means that schemes involving ***"sentencing guidelines"*** will typically be ***invalid***. In such schemes, the legislature establishes both a maximum sentence for a particular offense (say 10 years), and a standard sentence range for that offense (say 3-5 years). The legislature then orders trial judges to add to or subtract time from the standard range according to various aggravating or mitigating factors found to exist by the judge, with the

result never exceeding the maximum. The purpose of such sentencing guidelines is to ***reduce disparities*** in sentencing from judge to judge, or from region to region.

a. Pair of decisions: In a startling and controversial pair of decisions involving sentencing guidelines, one from 2004 and the other from 2005, the Court has held that (1) ***any increase*** in the sentence given to a defendant — beyond the standard range — by virtue of the judge's finding on a guideline-mandated factor ***violates*** the defendant's right to a jury trial; and (2) this principle means that the influential ***Federal Sentencing Guidelines can no longer be binding on federal judges*** as Congress had wished them to be. We consider each decision separately.

b. *Blakely* (Washington state guidelines): The first of the two cases on sentencing guidelines involved the sentencing guidelines of the state of Washington. The case was ***Blakely v. Washington***, 542 U.S. 296 (2004).

i. Washington guidelines: In *Blakely,* D pleaded guilty to kidnapping his estranged wife, V. The plea agreement reduced the charge to second-degree kidnapping involving domestic violence and use of a firearm. In the agreement, D admitted the facts necessary for the offense (kidnapping, domestic violence and firearm use) but no other facts. Under state law, second-degree kidnapping was a Class B felony, and under the state's general criminal statutes Class B felonies were punishable by a term of up to 10 years. But under Washington's sentencing guidelines, the trial judge was instructed to issue, in the case of second-degree kidnapping with a firearm, a "standard" sentence of 49 to 53 months. But the judge was also permitted to impose a sentence ***above the standard range*** if he found the existence of any of various ***"aggravating factors"*** specified in the guidelines. One of those factors was that the crime was a domestic violence case in which the defendant acted with "deliberate cruelty."

(1) Application to case: The prosecution in *Blakely*, acting in accordance with the plea agreement, recommended to the judge a sentence within the standard 43-53 month range. But the judge, after conducting a three-day bench hearing (which included testimony by V), concluded that D had behaved with deliberate cruelty. The judge therefore imposed a sentence of 90 months, 37 months beyond the top end of the standard range. D appealed, asserting that his right to jury trial was violated by the judge's use of the deliberate-cruelty finding to increase his sentence over the maximum that it could have been without that finding.

ii. Majority finds violation: Five justices agreed with D that this procedure had ***violated the principle of Apprendi,*** *supra*, that a defendant's sentence may not be increased beyond its maximum range except based on facts found beyond a reasonable doubt by a jury. The majority opinion was by Justice Scalia (joined, in an unusual alignment, by Justices Stevens, Souter, Thomas, and Ginsburg).

(2) "Statutory maximum" is the range: The prosecution had argued that for purposes of *Apprendi*, the "maximum punishment" to which D could have been subjected was the 10-year maximum for Class B felonies, so that the judge's finding of deliberate cruelty did not result in a sentence beyond that statutory maximum (in which case there would have been no *Apprendi* violation). But Scalia disagreed: "[T]he 'statutory maximum' for *Apprendi* purposes is the maximum sentence a judge may impose *solely on the basis of the facts reflected in the jury verdict or admitted by the defendant.*" (emphasis in original.) Here, based solely upon the facts admitted by D in his guilty plea, the guidelines meant that the judge could not have imposed a sentence of more than 53 months (the top end of the standard range). So the 90-month sentence violated the *Apprendi* principle, by permitting the judge (rather than the jury) to find a fact — existence of deliberate cruelty — that increased the sentence beyond this otherwise-authorized 53-month maximum.

(3) **"Determinate sentencing" schemes still possible:** Scalia rejected the dissent's argument that the majority ruling would render all "determinate sentencing" schemes unconstitutional. The legislature was free to provide a scheme whereby the existence of each of the allowable aggravating factors was to be found by the jury. (Indeed, Scalia pointed out, Kansas — whose Supreme Court had already held that *Apprendi* required the striking down of that state's sentencing guidelines — had responded by enacting exactly this "let the jury find all the aggravating factors" approach.)

iii. **Dissent:** The four dissenters were represented by two main opinions, one by Justice O'Connor and the other by Justice Breyer.

(4) **O'Connor:** O'Connor believed that the decision would result in "greater judicial discretion and less uniformity in sentencing." She predicted that the sentencing guidelines of a number of states, and those of the federal government, would also be unconstitutional under the majority's approach. Therefore, she thought, "over 20 years of sentencing reform are all but lost, and tens of thousands of criminal judgments are in jeopardy." (As we'll see shortly below in our discussion of the 2005 case, *U.S. v. Booker*, Justice O'Connor's fear that the *Blakely* ruling would lead to a finding that the Fderal Sentencing Guidelines were unconstitutional was quickly borne out.)

(5) **Breyer:** Justice Breyer concluded that the majority was requiring sentencing to take one of three forms, each of which risked either ***impracticality***, ***unfairness***, or ***harm to the very jury trial right*** the majority said it was protecting:

First, the legislature could implement a ***"simple determinate"*** sentencing scheme, in which the sentence was determined totally by a few elements that were part of the charge. For instance, all robberies would be punished by the same sentence, say five years. This scheme would insure uniformity, but at "intolerable costs." First, everyone who committed, say, robbery, would get the same sentence even though the way in which one defendant committed her crime might be very different from that of another. Furthermore, such sentencing ***"gives tremendous power to prosecutors to manipulate sentences*** through their choice of charges."

Second, legislatures might return to the kind of ***"indeterminate sentencing"*** that many states had before the sentencing-guideline reform movement.

That is, there would be a large range of possible sentences for any given crime, and the judge (or the parole board) would keep be given ***virtually complete discretion*** in picking a point within that range. This type of scheme would produce the very sorts of unfair disparities — especially, Breyer said, ***racially-based disparities*** — that had led to reform via determinate-sentencing schemes like Washington's.

Finally, legislatures might try to preserve their multi-factor determinate schemes, but amend them by ***giving the fact-finding authority to the jury*** rather than to the judge. But Breyer believed that any method of carrying out this alternative would be unbearably ***costly*** and ***cumbersome***. If all of the aggravating factors were made part of the underlying offense (e.g., a robbery charge with 17 factors, representing all of the aggravating factors that the prosecution thought might apply), the defendant would unfairly be put in the position of having to contest all of these factors during the main trial. Or, if the legislature required a ***second jury*** (or a second phase for the first jury) to pass on the aggravating factors, this would be so ***costly***, in terms of both money and judicial time, that few states would implement it. And if they did try this approach, states would end up relying more heavily on plea-bargaining rather than trials, and would thus give ***undue discretion to prosecutors*** in deciding what kind of a plea to insist upon.

c. *Booker* (Federal Sentencing Guidelines): One year after *Blakely*, the Court held in ***U.S. v. Booker***, 543 U.S. 220 (2005) that the rationale of *Blakely* meant that the very elaborate ***Federal Sentencing Guidelines***, applicable to federal criminal trials, ***could not be constitutionally applied as written,*** and were instead merely ***"advisory"*** for federal judges.

i. Nature of the Federal Sentencing Guidelines: The Federal Sentencing Guidelines, like the Washington state guidelines struck down in *Blakely*, attempted to reduce disparities in sentencing from judge to judge by curtailing judicial discretion. In the federal Sentencing Reform Act, Congress created a U.S. Sentencing Commission and instructed it to draft extensive Guidelines, under which a "base" sentencing range (say, 18 months to 24 months) was prescribed for each of the hundreds of federal crimes. The Guidelines ***required*** the judge to issue a sentence within the base range unless the judge found by a preponderance of evidence that certain types of facts specified in the Guidelines existed so as to justify either an "upward departure" or a "downward departure."

Under the federal scheme, the minimum and maximum statutory sentences for any crime — originally prescribed by Congress when the offense was defined — were not changed; the Guidelines merely had the effect of specifying *where within that original statutory range* the defendant could be sentenced. For example, Congress might have originally made a particular crime — say possession of cocaine with intent to distribute — punishable by a sentence of "up to 20 years" in prison; enactment of the Sentencing Guidelines did not change this 0-to-20-year statutory range. However, the Guidelines had the effect of limiting the trial judge's sentencing discretion in a particular case of cocaine possession to, say, a range of "60 to

72 months," unless the judge found that some particular aggravating factor was present to justify an upward departure (e.g., that D possessed an unusually large amount, or that he had acted as the organizer of a group pursuing the activity).

ii. Upward departure: *Booker*, like *Blakely*, posed the issue of whether guidelines could be used to increase the defendant's sentence beyond the top of the otherwise-applicable range if the judge — rather than the jury — found the existence of aggravating factors that the guidelines classified as justifying an upward departure.

(1) Facts of the case: *Booker* itself involved two different defendants whose cases had been consolidated for appeal to the Supreme Court. Both cases involved the issue of whether a defendant who had been found by the jury to have possessed *x* grams of cocaine with intent to distribute and who was then found by the judge to have really possessed a ***greater amount*** of cocaine, could be sentenced to an upward departure.

For instance, one of the Ds in Booker, Duncan Fanfan, was found by the jury to have possessed "500 or more grams" of cocaine. The maximum sentence (i.e., the top of the base range) authorized by the federal Guidelines for that amount of cocaine was 78 months. But at a sentencing hearing, the trial judge found — by a preponderance of the evidence — a number of additional facts that under the Guidelines required a much greater sentence, 188 to 235 months. These additional facts included that: (1) Fanfan had possessed a much greater weight of cocaine powder and crack than the jury had found; and (2) Fanfan had been the organizer, leader, manager or supervisor of the criminal activity. So the question was whether Fanfan could be given a sentence in this 15-or-16-year range (rather than the maximum sentence of no more than six years that the facts found by the jury alone would support), given that the additional facts had been found by the judge rather than the jury (and found by preponderance of evidence rather than beyond a reasonable doubt).

iii. Supreme Court strikes Guidelines: By the same 5-4 majority that had decided *Blakely*, the Court decided that the Federal Guidelines as written were ***unconstitutional*** — therefore, the Ds could not constitutionally be sentenced to an upward departure based on facts found by the judge rather than the jury. Then, by a different 5-4 vote, the Court held that the proper remedy for the unconstitutionality was to ***eliminate the mandatory nature of the Guidelines***, and to leave it up to the trial judge whether to follow the Guidelines in a particular case or not. There were two separate opinions for the Court by two different authors; one opinion decided that the Guidelines as written were unconstitutional (which we'll call the "substantive" opinion) and the other decided the proper remedy for this unconstitutionality (which we'll call the "remedial" opinion).

iv. Substantive opinion: The substantive majority opinion was written by Justice Stevens (joined by Scalia, Souter, Thomas and Ginsburg). Stevens believed that *Blakely* was dispositive: there was no constitutionally-relevant difference between the Washington state guidelines invalidated in *Blakely* and the Federal Sentencing Guidelines. For instance, the fact that the federal guidelines were promulgated not by Congress but by an administrative agency (the U.S. Sentencing Commission), whereas the Washington state guidelines were drafted directly by the state legislature, made no difference. The key constitutional defect was the same in both situations: based upon facts found only by the judge, and found by a preponderance of the evidence, in both schemes the judge was required to impose a sentence that was higher than the sentence that the judge would have been allowed to impose had the only facts found been the ones found by the jury.

(2) Substantive dissent: The four dissenters on the substantive question (Breyer, joined by Chief Justice Rehnquist and Justices O'Connor and Kennedy) believed that *Blakely* had been wrongly decided. Breyer asserted that "nothing in the Sixth Amendment ... forbids a sentencing judge to determine (as judges at sentencing have traditionally determined) the *manner* or *way* in which the offender carried out the crime of which he was convicted" (emphasis in original).

But the dissenters *also* believed that even if *Blakely* remained in force, this did not justified invalidating the *federal* guidelines, because those guidelines, unlike the ones in *Blakely*, were ***administrative*** rather than statutory. To the dissenters, this was an important distinction: guidelines written by legislatures posed a risk that the legislature would in effect ***create elements of crimes at will,*** where no jury would have to find that the element was satisfied. But the administrative sentencing commission here was restricted to "rules that reflect what the law has traditionally understood as sentencing factors," a much more limited function that did not pose this same danger of creating new elements of crimes.

v. Remedial opinion: In the ***remedial*** opinion of *Booker*, a different five-justice majority (Breyer, joined by Chief Justice Rehnquist and Justices O'Connor, Kennedy and Ginsburg)[3] concluded that the appropriate "fix" for the Sixth Amendment problem was to ***invalidate the statutory provision that made the Federal Sentencing Guidelines mandatory***. The result was that after *Booker*, federal judges must *consider* the ranges specified by the Guidelines, but the Guidelines are, as the majority put it, ***"effectively advisory."***

(3) Remedial dissent: Four members of the Court dissented from this remedial opinion. The main dissent was by Justice Stevens (joined by Souter and in part by Scalia). Stevens believed that the majority's approach — to completely excise the statutory provision making the Guidelines mandatory — was a solution having ***"extraordinary overbreadth."*** Stevens would have left the Guidelines in force as written, and simply given the government the right to prove to a jury beyond a reasonable doubt any factor required to increase the defendant's sentence beyond the base range.

vi. Response by courts: It it is hard to say what the effect of *Booker* has been on how federal courts sentence criminals. One empirical study, of Massachusetts fed-

3. Only Justice Ginsburg was in the majority in both parts of *Booker*.

eral district courts, concluded that average sentence-length ***climbed***, from 47.7 months before *Booker* to 63.7 by 2008. 63 Stan. L. Rev. 1 (2010), quoted in A,S,H,L,L&M, pp. 1533-34. Also, *Booker* seems to have resulted in ***greater disparity among judges*** in average sentence-length. *Id.*

d. Some post-*Booker* case law: Here are a couple of post-*Booker* developments in how the principle of *Apprendi/Blakely/Booker* — that any fact that changes the maximum sentence under a mandatory guideline or sentencing scheme must be found by the jury — should be interpreted.

i. Appellate review: In the federal system, the ***courts of appeal*** may ***review*** how the district court takes the now "advisory only" Federal Sentencing Guidelines into account in setting a particular sentence. But the appeals courts must be quite ***deferential*** to the trial court's decision about ***how much weight*** to give to the Sentencing Guidelines in the particular case.

(1) Abuse-of-discretion standard: This means that even if the federal district judge's sentence ***diverges greatly*** from that prescribed by the Guidelines, the appeals court may reverse only for ***abuse of discretion***. "[W]hile the extent of the difference between a particular sentence and the recommended Guidelines range is surely relevant, courts of appeals must review all sentences — whether ***inside, just outside, or significantly outside the Guidelines range*** — under a ***deferential abuse-of-discretion standard***." ***Gall v. U.S.***, 552 U.S. 38 (2007).

ii. Mandatory minimums: Recall that under *Apprendi* itself, the Court held that any fact whose existence increased the ***maximum punishment*** to which D is subject is a fact that must be found by the jury. (*Supra*, p. 444.) *Apprendi* left open the issue of whether a fact whose existence increases the ***mandatory minimum sentence*** that the court is ***required*** to impose must, similarly, be decided by the jury. In ***Alleyne v. U.S.***, 133 S.Ct. 2151 (2013), the Court reversed prior law and answered ***"yes"*** to this question.

(2) Consequence: Therefore, *Alleyne* requires the prosecution to plan ahead — if there is any fact whose existence would trigger some (or a higher) ***mandatory minimum sentence*** than would apply without that fact, the issue must be ***submitted to the jury*** to be found (or not found) by that body. And since the *Apprendi* principle is a matter of constitutional interpretation, *Alleyne* applies to ***both federal and state court systems***, and applies anywhere the legislature has set a mandatory minimum that applies only if a certain fact exists. The facts and reasoning of *Alleyne* are set out in the following Example.

Example: D and an accomplice accost a store manager who is on the way to deposit the store's daily receipts into a bank. The accomplice holds a gun, and the two take the receipts. D is charged with the federal crime of carrying a firearm in relation to a crime of violence. The statute says that if the firearm is "use[d] or carrie[d,]" the mandatory minimum sentence is five years; but if the firearm is ***"brandished"*** during the crime, the mandatory minimum becomes seven years. The jury convicts D, and indicates on the verdict form that D "used or carried" a firearm during the crime. But the jury does not put on the form any finding about whether D (or the accomplice) "brandished" a firearm. The trial judge decides that brandishing is a "sentencing factor" that the court can decide by a preponderance of the evidence, not the sort of sentence-determinative fact that *Apprendi* and *Booker* require to be found by the jury. Therefore, the judge imposes a mandatory minimum of seven years rather than five years. D appeals.

Held, for D. Under *Apprendi*, if a fact increases the punishment above what is otherwise legally prescribed, that fact is "by definition an ***element of the offense*** and must be submitted to the jury[.]" Contrary to a prior case, the Court now decides that *Apprendi*'s definition of "elements" includes "not only facts that ***increase the ceiling*** [of permissible sentences] but also those that ***increase the floor***." "Elevating the low-end of a sentencing range heightens the loss of liberty associated with the crime ... [T]he core crime and the fact triggering the mandatory minimum sentence together constitute a ***new, aggravated crime***, each element of which must be submitted to the jury." Therefore, the trial judge erred — since the jury did not find "brandishing," the mandatory minimum sentence applicable to D was five years, not seven years. *Alleyne v. U.S.*, *supra*.

e. **Modification of state sentencing laws:** Partly as a result of *Blakely* and *Booker*, most ***states*** that had mandatory sentencing guidelines have converted them to ***advisory*** status. Others have kept the guidelines mandatory, but now make sure that the jury is required to find any facts needed to determine the applicable guideline sentence or range. About 21 states had sentencing guidelines as of 2008. Cf. www.ncsc.org/~/media/Microsites, accessed 10/18/13.

C. **Waiver:** The defendant may ***waive*** the right to jury trial, provided that the waiver is ***voluntary***, ***knowing*** and ***intelligent***. There are sometimes good tactical reasons why the defendant might want to waive his right to a jury; for example, "some defendants or crimes may be so repulsive that trial by any group of laypeople ... poses more of a risk [of unfair bias] than a proceeding presided over by a less naive judge." W&S, p. 669.

1. **Prosecution may veto:** However, most states, and the federal system, allow the judge or the prosecutor to ***"veto"*** the defendant's waiver of a jury. W&S, p. 670. That is, the judge or (more commonly) the prosecution may ***insist on a jury trial*** even though the defendant does not want one. The Court has held that such a veto does not violate any constitutional right of the defendant, since the prosecutorial or judicial refusal to allow a bench trial merely subjects the defendant to a jury trial, "the very thing that the Constitution guarantees him." *Singer v. U.S.*, 380 U.S. 24 (1965).

D. **Size and unanimity of the jury:** The Sixth Amendment places limits on states' ability to restrict the ***size*** of juries, and forbids ***less-than-unanimous*** verdicts in federal and state felony trials.

1. **Size:** Historically, juries have been composed of 12 persons. However, the Court has held that ***juries of six or more satisfy the Sixth Amendment***. *Williams v. Florida*, 399 U.S. 78

(1970). On the other hand, juries of ***five or fewer violate*** the Sixth Amendment. *Ballew v. Georgia*, 435 U.S. 223 (1978).

2. **Unanimity:** The Sixth Amendment is now interpreted to require that the jury's verdict in ***both state and federal felony*** trials be ***unanimous***. See *Ramos v. Louisiana*, 590 U.S. 83 (2020), reversing prior law allowing non-unanimous verdicts in state felony cases.

E. **Selection of jurors:** Various constitutional provisions limit the procedures by which jurors are ***selected***. There are two distinct areas of concern: (1) the procedures by which the ***"venire"*** (i.e., the panel of available jurors, from which members of any particular jury are selected) is assembled; and (2) the procedures by which the members of a ***particular jury*** (the ***"petit jury"***) are selected from the venire.

1. **The venire, and the requirement of a "cross-section of the community":** Recall that the Sixth Amendment guarantees the accused the right to a trial by "an ***impartial jury*** of the State and district wherein the crime shall have been committed." This requirement of an "impartial jury" has been interpreted to mean that the venire from which petit juries are selected must ***represent a fair cross-section of the community***. Thus in *Taylor v. Louisiana*, 419 U.S. 522 (1975), the Court held that the Sixth Amendment, as applied to the states via the Fourteenth Amendment's due process clause, is violated "if the jury pool is made up of only segments of the populace or if ***large, distinctive groups are excluded*** from the pool." Thus if the state (or, for that matter federal) venire systematically excludes or underrepresents, say, African-Americans or women, the Sixth and Fourteenth Amendments are violated.

a. **Three-part showing needed:** For the defendant to make a *prima facie* showing that the "fair cross-section" requirement has not been met, he must show three things:

> "(1) that the group alleged to be excluded is a ***"distinctive" group*** in the community; (2) that the representation of this group in venires from which juries are selected is ***not fair and reasonable in relation to the number of such persons in the community***; and (3) that this underrepresentation is due to ***systematic exclusion of the group*** in the jury-selection process."

Duren v. Missouri, 439 U.S. 357 (1979).

b. **Purposeful discrimination not required:** The defendant can succeed in showing that a constitutional violation has occurred even if the exclusion or underrepresentation does ***not*** derive from the government's desire to ***discriminate purposefully*** against excluded minority. Thus even if the state grants an exemption from jury service to a particular group for theoretically-laudable reasons, the exemption may violate the fair cross-section requirement if the exemption isn't narrowly-tailored to the state's objective. For instance, in *Taylor v. Louisiana*, *supra*, the state allowed women (but not men) to escape jury service by so requesting on the jury duty summons form, or by simply not showing up. The state defended this treatment on the grounds that women's domestic responsibilities were likely to make it burdensome for them to serve. But the Court rejected this blanket exclusion for women as a violation of the fair-cross-section requirement (though it indicated that an appropriately-tailored exclusion for *anyone* who, regardless of gender, must care for children, *would* be permissible.)

2. **Selection of petit jurors:** The process by which members of the ***petit jury*** (i.e., the regular jury that decides the criminal case) are selected may also raise constitutional and procedural questions.

   a. **Voir dire:** Before individual jurors are placed on the petit jury, each juror's ability to be impartial must be ascertained. This is generally done by the process of ***"voir dire,"*** which means literally "to see what is said." W&S, p. 682. Voir dire is the process by which either the judge or both sides' lawyers ***question the potential*** jurors to eliminate those who ***cannot be impartial.***

      i. **Questions about racial attitudes:** Very occasionally, the trial judge's refusal to ask certain types of questions on voir dire may violate the defendant's Sixth Amendment rights. The main instance in which this can occur involves questions about ***racial attitudes***: if racial attitudes are "inextricably bound up with the conduct of the trial" (*Ristaino v. Ross*, 424 U.S. 589 (1976)), the defendant is constitutionally entitled to have the judge ask about those attitudes, in order to avoid unfair prejudice. For instance, in *Ham v. South Carolina*, 409 U.S. 524 (1973), D was a well-known black civil rights activist who was being tried for marijuana possession in South Carolina. The Court held (unanimously) that in these circumstances the risk of racial prejudice was so great that in order to satisfy D's Sixth Amendment guarantee of an impartial jury, D was entitled to have prospective jurors questioned on the specific issue of their racial attitudes.

         (1) **Limited in scope:** But the ruling in *Ham* has been tightly limited. There is no general right to voir dire questioning on racial attitudes merely because, say, D is Black and is charged with a crime against a white — the right exists only where racial issues are expected to "permeate" the trial. See, e.g., *Ristaino v. Ross*, *supra* (where D, a Black man charged with violent crimes against a white security guard, D was *not* entitled to questioning about racial attitudes, because racial issues did not "permeate" the trial).

      ii. **Questions about media consumed:** Especially in high-profile cases, defense lawyers would often like to be allowed to conduct voir dire that explores in detail ***what pre-trial media covering the case*** each prospective juror has ***consumed.*** But the Supreme Court has held that trial judges have ***wide discretion*** about how to conduct such voir dire, and that a judge's decision to allow only less-comprehensive inquiries than the defense would prefer will be ***reversed only for "abuse of discretion,"*** which is rarely found.

      Example: D (Tsarnaev) is on trial in federal court for capital murder, charged with being one of the two 2013 Boston Marathon bombers. The judge approves most questions on a 100-question form prepared jointly by both sides' lawyers, which is to be filled out by prospective jurors. The form given to the jurors includes questions about whether media coverage might have biased the juror. But the judge rejects D's request for a question that asks each juror to ***"list the facts he had learned about the case from the media and other sources."*** D is convicted and sentenced to death; he appeals in part on the grounds that he had a constitutional right to have this "media consumption" question asked to all jurors. On appeal, the Court of Appeals agrees with D, and vacates his sentence.

Held (by the Supreme Court), D's conviction was ***valid***. A federal district court's questioning of prospective jurors will be reviewed ***only for abuse of discretion.*** Here, the trial judge did not abuse his discretion by declining to ask about each juror's media consumption; the judge reasonably feared that this question would be ***"unfocused,"*** would risk producing ***"unmanageable data,"*** and would at best shed light on "preconceptions" that other questions on the form had already probed. *U.S. v. Tsarnaev*, 142 S.Ct. 1024 (2022).

b. **Peremptory challenges:** Another area in which constitutional issues often arise is that of ***peremptory challenges.*** In nearly all jurisdictions, both the prosecution and defense are given a certain number of peremptory challenges, i.e., the right to have prospective jurors ***excused without cause***.

i. **Race-based challenges:** The most important rule regarding peremptory challenges is that in both federal and state trials, it is a violation of equal protection for the prosecution to exercise its peremptory challenges for the purpose of excluding jurors ***on account of their race***. ***Batson v. Kentucky***, 476 U.S. 79 (1986).

Example: Suppose that D is a black man, accused in a state trial of murdering a white woman. The prosecution reasons that black jurors are likely on average to be more sympathetic to the defense than white jurors would be. Therefore, the prosecution systematically uses all of its eight peremptory challenges to strike black jurors, leaving the final jury with fewer blacks than would have otherwise been the case. D's lawyer objects to this apparently-systematic use of race-based challenges, but the trial court overrules the objection. D is then convicted.

If D can establish on appeal (by the procedures outlined below) that the prosecution indeed used its peremptory challenges in a race-conscious manner, D will be entitled to a retrial on the grounds that (1) the excluded jurors' equal protection rights were violated; and (2) this violation may have impaired D's Sixth Amendment right to an impartial jury.

(1) **D need not be member of excluded group:** D is entitled to make a *Batson* challenge even if he is ***not a member of the excluded racial group.*** For instance, even if D is white, he may challenge the prosecution's exclusion of black jurors. *Powers v. Ohio*, 499 U.S. 400 (1991).

(2) **Gender-based challenges:** It is also an equal protection violation for the prosecution to exclude jurors on the basis of ***gender*** (e.g., the prosecution strikes women because it fears that they tend to favor the defendant more than male jurors would). *J.E.B. v. Alabama ex rel. T.B.*, 511 U.S. 127 (1994).

ii. **Procedure:** The prosecution will virtually never admit that it is intentionally excluding jurors based on their race (or gender). Therefore, D will have to make the requisite showing of race-motivated strikes by ***circumstantial evidence***. The procedure by which D may do so works like this:

(3) **Prima facie case:** First, D must, while jury selection is still proceeding, establish a *prima facie* case of intentional racial (or gender) discrimination. He must do this by showing that: (a) at least some members of a ***particular cog-***

nizable racial group (or gender) have been ***eliminated*** from D's jury; and (b) the circumstances of the case raise an ***inference*** that this exclusion was ***based on race*** (or gender). In demonstrating (b), D can rely on any relevant circumstances, but especially probative are (i) a ***pattern*** of strikes (either as to this particular petit jury, or as to other juries drawn from the same venire) and (ii) ***questions asked by the prosecution*** during voir dire that tend to show race- (or gender-) consciousness.

(4) **Rebuttal by prosecution:** If D makes this *prima facie* showing, the ***burden then shifts*** to the prosecution to ***come forward with a "neutral explanation"*** for challenging jurors of a particular race (or gender). This requires more than a conclusory denial of a discriminatory motive. Nor does the prosecution's belief that jurors of that race would be partial to the defense suffice.

(5) **Decision by court:** If the prosecution comes up with a race-neutral explanation, it is up to the trial court to decide ***whether the defendant has borne his burden*** of establishing that the real reason for the strikes was racial discrimination. That is, the court can conclude that the race-neutral explanation given by the prosecution was the truthful explanation for the pattern of racial strikes; in that event, D loses, and the strikes stand. Alternatively, the court may conclude, as a finding of fact, that the race-neutral explanation proffered by the prosecution was a ***pretext***, rather than the real reason, and that the real reason was some sort of intent to make strikes on race-conscious grounds. In that case, the trial court must order the struck juror to be ***reinstated*** absent a successful for-cause challenge. The trial court's ruling will be reversed on appeal only if it is clearly erroneous.

See *Batson v. Kentucky*, *supra*, as supplemented (as to gender-based strikes) by *J.E.B. v. Alabama ex rel. T.B.*, *supra*.

iii. **Showing pretext:** So how can D make the showing referred to in (3) above, that the prosecution's race-neutral explanation for its strikes was ***pretextual***? This is not an easy showing to make, but defendants usually go about it by trying to show that the prosecution has behaved in a way that is ***inconsistent*** with the genuineness of the race-neutral explanation. For instance, if the prosecution claims that a particular black juror was struck for race-neutral Reason X, D can try to show pretext by demonstrating that the prosecution failed to strike one or more white jurors as to whom the *same Reason X* applied.

Example: In D's capital murder trial, only one of the 20 black members of the 108-member venire is selected to serve, and the prosecution uses its peremptory challenges to strike ten of the blacks. As to one of the struck members, Fields, the prosecution's race-neutral explanation is that Fields said he would not vote for death if rehabilitation was possible, and that this statement caused the prosecution to conclude that Fields might be hesitant to impose a death sentence. D claims that various white jurors who indicated the same second thoughts about the death penalty as Fields were not struck, indicating that the explanation about Fields was pretextual.

Held (by the Supreme Court), for D: the prosecution's strikes violated *Batson*. "If a prosecutor's proffered reason for striking a black panelist *applies just as well to an otherwise-similar nonblack* who is permitted to serve, that is evidence tending to prove purposeful discrimination to be considered at *Batson*'s third step." Here, the fact that there were white panelists who indicated the same hesitation as Fields about whether they would vote for death, but who were permitted to serve, tends to show that the prosecution's explanation about Fields was pretextual. Taken together with other indications of a racially discriminatory purpose in the jury strikes (e.g., the fact that most black panelists, before being asked their opinion of capital punishment, were given a graphic and clinical description of how the death penalty is administered, whereas white panelists usually were not), this establishes that the strikes were racially motivated. *Miller-El v. Dretke*, 545 U.S. 231 (2005).

iv. **Challenges by defendant:** Although most cases raising constitutional objections to the use of peremptory challenges consist of defendants' objections to prosecutors' strikes, the ***converse is also permitted***: the ***prosecution may object*** to the ***defendant's use of race- or gender-based peremptory challenges***, since that, too, violates the equal protection rights of the excluded jurors (and the state has third-party standing to assert those rights). *Georgia v. McCullom*, 505 U.S. 42 (1992).

IX. THE TRIAL

A. **Trial procedure generally:** Procedure at criminal trials is a detailed subject that is beyond the scope of this outline. Here, we consider a few of the major issues.

1. **Right to a "public" trial:** The Sixth Amendment provides that "in all criminal prosecutions, the accused shall enjoy the right to a . . . ***public*** trial." This right does not mean that the trial must be held in a public place big enough for everybody who wants to attend to do so. It does, however, mean that there must be ***some access*** by members of the public. Thus it would be a violation of the defendant's public trial right for the trial to be held against his wishes in a closed judge's chambers, or in a prison. L&I, v. 3, pp. 2-3.

   a. **No right to compel a private trial:** The right to public trial may be waived by the defendant, in the sense that he loses his right to complain. But this does ***not*** mean that the defendant has the right to insist on a ***private*** trial — the court may, without violating the defendant's constitutional rights, order that the trial be conducted publicly over the defendant's objection.

   b. **Limited right to closure:** The defendant's right to a public trial may be ***outweighed*** by a ***compelling state interest***. However, before a trial may be closed, "the party seeking to close the hearing must advance an ***overriding interest*** that is likely to be prejudiced, the closure must be ***no broader than necessary*** to protect that interest, the trial court must consider ***reasonable alternatives*** to closing the proceeding, and it must make findings adequate to support the closure." *Waller v. Georgia*, 467 U.S. 39 (1984).

Examples: Thus if D is being tried for raping V, a minor, the court might order the trial closed during the testimony of V, to protect her interest in confidentiality. But the *Waller* guidelines would probably be violated if the judge closed the entire trial — the judge should instead consider ordering the parties not to refer to V by name. Similarly, if a case involved testimony by an undercover informant, it might be permissible to close that portion of the trial involving the informant's testimony, but not the entire trial.

2. **The opening statement:** All jurisdictions allow each side to make an ***opening statement*** before the evidence is presented. Universally, the prosecution goes first. Some states require the defense to make its opening statement immediately after the prosecution has made theirs; other states give the defense the option of deferring the opening statement until after the close of the prosecutor's case. L&I, v. 3, p. 12.

3. **Presentation of witnesses:** After the opening statement, the prosecution puts on its direct case. The prosecution must establish each element of the crime beyond a reasonable doubt. The defense has the right to cross-examine each prosecution witness (as described further below). At the close of the prosecution's case, the defense puts on its own witnesses. (The defense may instead choose to rest without putting on a direct case, on the theory that the prosecution has failed to carry its burden of proof.)

4. **Motion for directed verdict:** In nearly all states, and in the federal system, the trial judge may ***take the case from the jury*** on the grounds that the evidence is insufficient for a conviction. Typically, this is done in response to a defense motion for dismissal. Most states let the defense make this motion at the end of the prosecution's case and/or after both sides have presented their cases.

   a. **Standard:** The standard for whether to grant a dismissal motion is whether a ***reasonable jury*** could find that the prosecution has proved beyond a reasonable doubt all the material elements of the crime. As one court put it, the judge must determine "whether upon the evidence, giving full play to the right of the jury to determine credibility, weigh the evidence, and draw justifiable inferences of fact, a reasonable mind might fairly conclude guilt beyond a reasonable doubt." *Curley v. U.S.*, 160 F.2d 229 (D.C. Cir. 1947). It is not enough that the judge believes that, if she were sitting on the jury, she would vote to acquit the defendant.

5. **Closing arguments:** After both sides have presented evidence, each side may make a ***closing argument***. In most states, and in the federal system, the prosecution makes the first closing argument, the defense may then reply, and the prosecution may make a rebuttal to the defense's reply. L&I, v. 3, p. 32.

   a. **Limit on prosecution's arguments:** The due process clause places some limits on what the prosecutor may say or imply during the closing argument. If the prosecutor's remarks are found on appeal to be so unfair that they denied the defendant his right to a fair trial, the conviction may be reversed (though this is rare). Here are some of the kinds of things that a prosecutor may typically not say:

      i. **References to unadmitted evidence:** The prosecutor may not refer to specific evidence that was ***not introduced*** at the trial, or that was excluded by the trial court.

ii. **Personal belief:** The prosecutor may not express his ***personal belief*** or opinion as to the ***truth or falsity*** of any testimony or evidence or the ***guilt*** of the defendant. 1 ABA Standards for Criminal Justice, §3-5.8(b).

iii. **Consequences of acquittal or conviction:** The prosecutor may not say that if D is acquitted, he is likely to commit further crimes. Conversely, the prosecutor may not argue that the jury shouldn't worry too much about an erroneous conviction because this can always be taken care of on appeal.

iv. **Inflaming the passions:** The prosecutor may not make arguments for the purpose of catering to the jury's ***prejudices***. Thus comments appealing to racial, religious or class prejudice may be found unfair.

b. **Argument by defense counsel:** There are few practical limits on argument by the defense counsel. The trial judge may declare a mistrial if defense counsel ignores repeated warnings about what not to say. But once the verdict is pronounced, nothing said by the defense counsel makes any difference — if there is an acquittal, the prosecution may not appeal, and if there is a conviction, statements made by the defense counsel will generally be irrelevant on appeal.

B. **Defendant's right to be present:** The defendant has a constitutional right to be ***present*** at his trial. This right derives from the Sixth Amendment's right of the accused "to be confronted with the witnesses against him."

1. **Lost by disruptive behavior:** However, this right can be lost by a defendant's ***disruptive behavior***. Thus if the defendant yells, swears, or refuses to sit still, the court must first warn him, but if the conduct continues the court may order him to be removed from the proceedings. See *Illinois v. Allen*, 397 U.S. 337 (1970).

C. **Defendant's Confrontation Clause rights:** The Sixth Amendment gives any criminal defendant "the right . . . to be ***confronted with the witnesses against him.***" This is the ***Confrontation Clause***. It applies to the states by means of the Fourteenth Amendment. The Confrontation Clause has several main components:

[1] D has the right to ***compulsory process to obtain the testimony of witnesses***;

[2] D has the right to ***cross-examine hostile witnesses***; and

[3] because of [2], if D1 and D2 are on trial together, and D1 refuses to testify on Fifth Amendment grounds, D2 may be entitled to ***block the prosecution from introducing against D2 a confession by D1 that implicates D2.***

We'll consider these aspects separately: compulsory process (in Par. D. below); cross-examination of hostile witnesses (in Par. E); and limits on the prosecution's right to use D1's confession against D2 in (Par. F).

D. **Compulsory process:** The compulsory-process branch of the Confrontation Clause right means that a defendant has the right to have the ***court issue a subpoena*** to compel the testimony of any witness who may have information that would be useful to the defense.

1. **Assistance by the prosecution:** Sometimes, the compulsory-process right means that the prosecution must ***assist*** the defense in finding witnesses. Thus if the prosecution knows the whereabouts or identity of a witness who would be useful to the defense, the

prosecution may be constitutionally compelled to disclose that information. See *Roviaro v. U.S.*, 353 U.S. 53 (1957).

a. **Informant:** For instance, if an undercover ***informant*** has direct information about the crime, the prosecution may be required to disclose the identity, and perhaps even the whereabouts, of the informant. But if the informant is merely a "tipster" who does not have first-hand evidence about the crime, disclosure of his identity is probably not required. (Also, the defendant's Confrontation Clause interest in learning the informer's identity must be weighed against the interest of the state, or the informer himself, in confidentiality to protect ongoing investigations or the informer's safety. See *McCray v. Illinois*, 386 U.S. 300 (1967).)

2. **Right to a witness' testimony:** The Confrontation Clause also gives the defendant a limited right to obtain actual ***testimony*** by a witness. For instance, the state may not establish a blanket rule prohibiting one accomplice from testifying on behalf of another. *Washington v. Texas*, 388 U.S. 14 (1967).

a. **Defense witness immunity:** But the Confrontation Clause does ***not*** prevent the state from ***recognizing common privileges*** on the part of the witness, such as his Fifth Amendment privilege against self-incrimination. Furthermore, a defendant does not seem to have a general constitutional right to ***"defense witness immunity,"*** i.e., no right to force the state to promise W, whose testimony D desires, that the state will not later use the testimony against W. (But if the government introduces testimony by a witness, probably fundamental fairness requires that the witness be given immunity so that the defense may cross-examine him. L&I, v. 3, p. 23.)

E. **D's right to cross-examine witnesses against him:** The Confrontation Clause also places limits on a state's ability to restrict a defendant's right of ***cross-examination***.

1. **Procedural rules:** Thus a state rule of procedure ***limiting cross-examination*** may be found to violate the Confrontation Clause. For instance, a rule preventing a defendant from cross-examining juvenile witnesses based upon their juvenile court records has been found to violate the Confrontation Clause. *Davis v. Alaska*, 415 U.S. 308 (1974).

2. **Limits on hearsay:** Similarly, the Confrontation Clause seems to place some limits on the state's right to use ***hearsay*** evidence against the defendant. The Supreme Court held in *Ohio v. Roberts*, 448 U.S. 56 (1980), that there are two important Confrontation Clause limits on the use of hearsay against a defendant: (1) the prosecution may not admit an out-of-court declaration against D unless the prosecution either produces the declarant or demonstrates her unavailability; and (2) the prior testimony must have been obtained under circumstances providing reasonable ***"indicia of reliability."***

a. **Long-standing hearsay exceptions:** But hearsay that is admitted under long-standing ***common-law exceptions*** to the hearsay rule, such as the dying declaration exception, or the exception for prior testimony taken under circumstances allowing cross-examination, will almost always be found to have sufficient "indicia of reliability."

F. **D1's confession used against D2:** The Confrontation Clause also prevents, in some circumstances, the use of ***one person's out-of-court confession against another.*** The Supreme Court has held that *A*'s Confrontation Clause rights are violated if the confession of *B*, his non-testifying co-defendant, naming *A* as a co-participant in the crime, is introduced without redaction at their joint trial. This is true even if the jury is instructed to consider the confession only against *B*, not *A*. ***Bruton v. U.S.***, 391 U.S. 123 (1968).

> **Example:** D1 and D2 are jointly tried for robbery. Before trial, D1 orally confesses that he and D2 committed the robbery together. At the joint trial, D1's confession is admitted into evidence. The judge instructs the jury that the confession is to be considered only as evidence against D1, not against D2. D1 never takes the stand, so D2 never gets a chance to cross examine him about the confession.
>
> *Held*, D2's Confrontation Clause rights were violated as soon as the jury heard D1's out-of-court confession implicating D2. This is true even though the confession was never admitted into evidence against D2, and even though the jury was instructed to ignore the confession in assessing D2's guilt. In this situation, the risk that the jury would not or could not follow the judge's limiting instruction was so great, and the consequences of failure so enormous, that the limiting instruction was not sufficient to protect D2. *Bruton v. U.S., supra.*

1. **Prosecution's options:** In a situation where *Bruton* applies, D1's confession implicates D2, and the prosecution feels that it needs to use D1's confession against him (D1), the prosecution basically has three choices: (1) it can agree to ***separate trials*** (so that D1's confession is introduced only in D1's trial); (2) it can agree to ***separate juries*** who view a single trial (so that D2's jury can be removed from the courtroom when D1's confession is introduced or referred to); or (3) it can ***redact D1's confession*** sufficiently that the jury won't hear anything to indicate that the confession also implicated D2. Most often, prosecutors attempt to use choice (3), as we'll see shortly.

2. **Confessor takes the stand:** The *Bruton* principle probably applies only where the defendant who allegedly confessed ***declines to take the stand.*** If the confessor takes the stand and denies having made a confession — and perhaps even if he takes the stand and acknowledges the confession, but then opens himself up to the other defendant's cross-examination about it — there is probably ***no*** Confrontation Clause problem. See, e.g, *Nelson v. O'Neil*, 402 U.S. 622 (1971) (no Confrontation Clause problem where co-defendant took the stand, denied making an out-of-court statement implicating D, and testified favorably to D about the underlying events).

3. **Full or partial redaction of D1's confession:** In *Bruton* itself, the part of D1's confession implicating D2 was read to the jury word-for-word, leaving the jury in no doubt about whether D1 had implicated D2. Suppose, however, that in an attempt to avoid a *Bruton* problem, the prosecution ***redacts*** (edits) D1's confession so that ***D2 is not mentioned.***

   This prosecution technique may or may not work; if the redacted confession ***"directly accuses"*** D2, it's inadmissible under the *Bruton* principle. But if D1's confession does *not* "directly accuse" D2, it's admissible against D1; see *Samia v. U.S.*, *infra*, p. 461, where the Court confirmed this as the hard-for-the-defense-to-satisfy standard. .

   a. **Complete redacting:** Where the editing of the confession is ***extensive,*** so that nothing as the jury hears it mentions or even alludes to the involvement of a third person, there is ***no Confrontation Clause problem***, and *Bruton* does not apply. See *Richardson v. Marsh*, 481 U.S. 200 (1987).

b. "Deleted and I" violates *Bruton*: What if D1's confession, when it's read to the jury, is ***redacted only slightly,*** so that the names of any co-defendants mentioned in the original confession are replaced with the word ***"deleted"?*** In such a case, *Gray v. Maryland*, 523 U.S. 185 (1998), the Court held that *Bruton* was violated.

   i. Facts: In *Gray*, Bell and Gray were jointly tried on charges of beating Stacey Williams to death. Before trial, Bell gave a confession, taken by a police officer we'll call "O." Bell decided not to take the stand at the joint trial. The prosecution hoped to get as much of Bell's confession as possible before the jury without violating Gray's *Bruton* rights. Therefore, prosecutors had a member of law enforcement (W) take the stand and read a slightly redacted transcript of the confession to the jury. First, W read from part of the transcript in which O asked Bell, "Who was in the group that beat Stacey?" W then (continuing his reading of the transcript), said that Bell answered, "me, ***deleted, deleted,*** and a few other guys."

   ii. Holding: But the Supreme Court concluded that even this redacted confession ***violated*** Gray's *Bruton* rights: "A redaction that ***replaces a defendant's name*** with an ***obvious indication of deletion***, such as a ***blank space***, the word ***'deleted,'*** or a similar symbol, still falls within *Bruton*'s protective rule." So Gray got a new trial.

c. References to "the other person" allowable: But since *Gray*, the Court has ***dramatically narrowed the protection*** given to defendants by the *Bruton* rule. In ***Samia v. U.S.***, 599 U.S. 635 (2023), the Court held that when D1's confession indirectly refers to D2, *Bruton* applies ***only*** if what's read to the jury contains incriminating statements that are ***"directly accusatory"*** of D2. And the Court found that the redaction there was ***not "directly accusatory of D2,*** even though the redaction seemed highly similar to the "me, deleted and deleted" redaction ruled insufficient in *Gray*.

   i. Facts: The facts of *Samia* illustrate just how extensively the case ***cuts back*** on the protections given by *Bruton* and *Gray*.

      [1] Samia, Hunter and Stillwell were accused of the murder-for-hire of Lee. After the three were arrested by DEA agents, Stillwell gave a confession in which he admitted to participating in the plot, but said he was only the driver and that Samia was the one who actually shot and killed Lee while Stillwell and Samia rode in a van together.

      [2] The prosecution wanted to introduce Stillwell's confession in the joint trial of Stillwell and Samia (as well as of Hunter), even though Stillwell had made it clear that he would not be taking the stand. But the prosecutors realized that if the jury heard Stillwell's full unredacted confession, that confession would directly accuse Samia, and thus violate *Bruton*.

      [3] Therefore, the prosecution ***redacted*** Stillwell's confession before presenting it to the jury. Thus when a law enforcement officer recounted the confession to the jury, he omitted any mention of Samia by name: the officer testified that Stillwell in his confession "described a time when ***the other person he was with*** pulled the trigger on [Lee] in a van that he [the other person] and Mr. Stillwell were driving." The trial judge instructed the jury that the confession was to be admissible only against Stillwell, and not against Samia. The jury

nonetheless convicted Samia.

[4] The prosecution's opening statement at trial had asserted that Stillwell drove the van while Samia was in the passenger seat, and that Samia had fired the fatal shot killing Lee, who was in the back seat. Therefore, Samia argued on appeal that based on this and other evidence in the case apart from Stillwell's confession, when the jury heard the redacted confession, the jury could ***readily infer*** that he, Samia, was the "other person" in Stillwell's confession, thus violating Samia's *Bruton* rights.

ii. Holding against Samia: But the Supreme Court ***rejected*** Samia's *Bruton* claim. The vote was 6-3, with the three liberals in dissent. The majority opinion, by Justice Thomas, said that the *Bruton* rule ***"applies only to 'directly accusatory' incriminating statements,*** as distinct from those that ***do 'not refer directly to the defendant'*** and 'bec[o]me incriminating only when ***linked with evidence introduced later at trial.***' "

(1) Consequence: The redacted confession by Stillwell that the jury heard said merely that "the other person" Stillwell was with "pulled the trigger," Thomas said. That redacted confession, Thomas concluded, was not covered by Bruton's ***"narrow exception,"*** because it ***did not "directly accuse" Samia*** and "became incriminating ***only when linked with [other] evidence."***

iii. Dissent: A ***dissent*** by Justice Kagan (joined by Sotomayor and Jackson) argued that the redacted confession here was ***functionally identical*** to the one in *Gray*, *supra*, which the Court had found violated *Bruton*. Kagan interpreted *Gray* as having held that *Bruton* was violated "when a confession ***'refers directly to the existence' of the non-confessing defendant, even though not by name."***

(2) Rationale: Here, Kagan said, the jury knew from the prosecution's opening statement that there were just three defendants, and that the prosecution was accusing Samia of shooting Lee while both were in the van. Therefore, Kagan argued, when the jury heard the officer testify that Stillwell's confession "described a time when the other person [that Stillwell] was with pulled the trigger," "any reasonable juror would have ***realized immediately*** — and without reference to any other evidence — that ***'the other person' who 'pulled the trigger' was Samia."***

(3) Functionally identical to *Gray* scenario: Consequently, Kagan argued, the redacted confession here was ***functionally identica***l to the redacted one the *Gray* Court had found to have violated *Bruton*.

(4) Consequence: Kagan concluded that the majority's holding in *Samia* meant that "prosecutors can ***always circumvent*** *Bruton*'s protections." *Gray* held that the prosecution may not swap out the name of the person being implicated by the confession by using a blank space or the word ***"deleted."*** But as the result of *Samia*, the prosecution merely needs to replace the name of that person with a reference to ***"the other person"*** who participated in the crime, and the *Bruton* problem goes away. The consequence, Kagan said, is that ***"defendants in joint trials will not have the chance to confront some of the most damaging***

witnesses against them," and the constitutional right of confrontation established by *Bruton* and *Gray* will become ***"a shell of its former self."***

G. Defendant's right to remain silent: The Fifth Amendment provides that no person "shall be compelled in any criminal case to be a witness against himself." This privilege applies to the states via the Fourteenth Amendment's Due Process Clause. The self-incrimination privilege applies in many diverse circumstances,[4] but we are interested here in its effect upon the trial itself.

1. **Right not to take the stand:** The privilege does not mean merely that the defendant may refuse to answer questions asked of him by the prosecution. Instead, it means that the defendant has the right to ***not even take the witness stand***. Indeed, in many if not most criminal trials, the defendant never takes the witness stand.

   a. **Waiver:** But the privilege against self-incrimination may be ***waived***. A defendant who does take the witness stand is universally held to have waived his privilege as to ***any matters within the fair scope of cross-examination***. So once the defendant takes the stand, questions relating to the scope of his direct testimony may be asked, and he may not plead the Fifth Amendment in response.

      i. **Impeachment:** Furthermore, all jurisdictions agree that D may be extensively cross-examined for ***impeachment*** purposes, and may not plead the Fifth. This accounts for the Hobson's Choice faced by every defendant with a criminal record — by taking the stand, the defendant opens himself up to cross-examination about any prior convictions that shed light on his reputation for truthfulness. (For instance, under Federal Rule of Evidence 609(a), D may be questioned based on any prior conviction of a crime involving dishonesty or false statement, whether a misdemeanor or a felony, and may also be questioned about any felony conviction not involving dishonesty or false statement if "the probative value of admitting this evidence outweighs its prejudicial effect to the accused.")

2. **Comment by prosecution:** The privilege against self-incrimination also places limits on the prosecution's right to ***comment*** on the defendant's silence. The general rule is that the prosecution ***may not comment on the fact that the defendant has declined to take the witness stand.*** *Griffin v. California*, 380 U.S. 609 (1965). Sometimes the rule against comment is extended to prevent the prosecution from referring to the state's evidence as being "unrefuted" or "uncontradicted" (especially where the evidence is such that ***only*** the defendant himself could have contradicted it). L&I, v. 3, p. 30.

   a. **Instruction to jury:** The defendant has a right to have the judge ***instruct*** the jury that: (1) the defendant has a constitutional right not to take the stand, and (2) the jury is not to make any inference of guilt from the exercise of this right. *Carter v. Kentucky*, 450 U.S. 288 (1981). (But if the defense "opens the door" by, for instance, saying that D was never given a chance to tell his side of the story, then the prosecution may respond by saying that D could have taken the stand. See *U.S. v. Robinson*, 485 U.S. 25 (1988).)

---

4. See, e.g., Chapter 5, *supra*, p. 239, on confessions made under custodial questioning.

X. DOUBLE JEOPARDY

A. **The guarantee generally:** The Fifth Amendment provides that no person shall "be subject for the same offence to be twice put in jeopardy of life or limb." This is the guarantee against ***"double jeopardy."*** The most classic application of the doctrine is to prevent D from being retried after he has been acquitted by a jury. But the guarantee against double jeopardy may also protect D from being retried after a mistrial (though not usually), and may occasionally limit the prosecution's right to reprosecute if D's conviction at the first trial is set aside on appeal.

   1. **Applicable to states:** The double jeopardy guarantee applies to state as well as federal trials. *Benton v. Maryland*, 395 U.S. 784 (1969).

B. **Proceedings to which guarantee attaches:** The double jeopardy guarantee says that a person can't be twice "put in jeopardy of life or limb." What ***kind of proceedings*** are deemed to put a person "in jeopardy of life or limb"? Clearly ***any felony prosecution*** qualifies, so a person can't be subjected to two felony prosecutions for the same offense (subject to the exceptions discussed below). But the guarantee also applies to at least some proceedings that are ***not felony prosecutions.***

   1. **Issue is whether "punishment" is being imposed:** In general, the concept is that a proceeding whose sole purpose is to ***punish*** the defendant is ***covered*** by the guarantee, but a proceeding which has a significant ***"civil"*** (non-punitive) dimension ***won't*** be covered.

      a. **Misdemeanors:** Thus the guarantee applies to all criminal prosecutions, ***even if for misdemeanors***. So on a particular set of facts, D can't be prosecuted for, say, the misdemeanor of petty theft, acquitted, then retried for that same misdemeanor.

      b. **Civil proceedings:** On the other hand, a proceeding that is solely ***"civil"*** will generally ***not*** trigger the guarantee, even though there may be some punitive aspect to the proceeding.

         i. **Civil fine:** Thus if D is required to pay what the legislature calls a ***"civil fine,"*** this generally won't prevent a later criminal prosecution for the same offense.

            (1) **Really punitive:** But if the "fine" is so ***disproportionate*** to the actual financial damage caused by D's action that the court concludes it's really intended as "punishment," the double-jeopardy guarantee will apply, even though the legislature has labelled the fine "civil."

            Example: D submits 65 inflated Medicare claims, each of which overcharges the government by $9. D is convicted of 65 counts of violating the federal false-claims statute. The government then brings a civil action against D. In this action, the judge fines D $130,000, even though the actual overcharges totalled just $585. *Held*, this "civil fine" was so disproportionate to the actual damages caused by D's conduct that it constituted a second punishment, in violation of the Double Jeopardy prohibition. D's fine must be reduced to a non-punitive level. *U.S. v. Halper*, 490 U.S. 435 (1989).

      c. **Forfeiture:** The same issue arises in conjunction with ***forfeiture*** proceedings. Federal and state statutes typically provide that where an item is either used in, or is the proceeds of, commission of a crime, the item may be seized by (forfeited to) the government. Thus a house in which amphetamines are manufactured, or a car in which marijuana is smuggled, or cash proceeds from drug sales, may be seized by the government. This issue is whether such a forfeiture is "punitive" (in which case it cannot either precede or follow a criminal prosecution for the same offense) or non-punitive (in which case it can).

i. **Normally not punitive:** The Supreme Court has held that forfeitures should normally be viewed as ***non-punitive***. See *U.S. v. Ursery*, 518 U.S. 267 (1996). In *Ursery*, the Court concluded that the federal statutes providing for forfeiture of items used in conjunction with money-laundering or illegal drugs are "civil" and non-punitive, so that forfeiture can either follow or precede a criminal prosecution for the offense.

C. **When jeopardy attaches:** The protection against double jeopardy does not apply until jeopardy has ***"attached."*** Thus if a proceeding is terminated before jeopardy has "attached," the Double Jeopardy Clause does not limit the prosecution's right to try the defendant for the same charge in a new proceeding, no matter how "unfair" this may be to the defendant.

1. **Jury trial:** In a case to be tried by a jury, jeopardy is deemed to "attach" when the jury has been ***empaneled and sworn***, i.e., when the whole jury has been selected and taken the oath. L&I, v. 3, p. 63. This rule as to when jeopardy attaches is constitutionally required. *Crist v. Bretz*, 437 U.S. 28 (1978).

2. **Bench trial:** In a case that is to be tried by the judge sitting without a jury, jeopardy is deemed to attach when the ***first witness has been sworn***. L&I, v. 3, p. 64.

3. **Guilty plea:** In cases terminated by a ***guilty plea***, jeopardy attaches when the court accepts the defendant's plea unconditionally. *Id.* Thus the fact that D has been subjected to a preliminary hearing or even arraigned is not enough. *Id.*

D. **Reprosecution after mistrial:** Suppose that the trial begins, and is then terminated by a ***mistrial***. Most of the time, the prosecution is ***not barred*** from retrying the defendant.

1. **With defendant's consent:** If the mistrial has been brought about by the request of, or with the acquiescence of, the defendant, reprosecution is ***always allowed***. This is true even though the defendant's motion for mistrial is required because of the prosecution's misconduct, and even if that conduct was intentional. See, e.g., *U.S. v. Dinitz*, 424 U.S. 600 (1976) ("A motion by the defendant for a mistrial is ordinarily assumed to remove any barrier to reprosecution, even if the defendant's motion is necessitated by prosecutorial or judicial error").

2. **Without defendant's consent:** Even where the defendant has ***not*** consented, the mistrial will frequently not bar reprosecution. If the court finds that the mistrial is required by ***"manifest necessity,"*** reprosecution will be allowed. But the phrase "manifest necessity" is interpreted less stringently than you might imagine; the Supreme Court has held that the phrase "cannot be interpreted literally," and that a mistrial is appropriate when there is merely a ***"high degree" of necessity.***

a. **Hung jury:** Most commonly, the retrial issue arises in cases where there is a ***hung jury.*** As long as the court is reasonably satisfied that the jury is truly deadlocked, and that additional deliberations will be fruitless, the situation meets the manifest-necessity standard, and the court can declare a mistrial over the defendant's objection. The decision of the trial judge that the jury is hopelessly deadlocked is given ***"great deference"*** by the appellate courts. *Arizona v. Washington*, 434 U.S. 497 (1978).

i. **Time spent in deliberation:** One factor to which trial courts give a lot of weight is whether the jury has ***deliberated*** for a ***significant period of time*** before reaching the apparent deadlock — the longer the deliberation, the more likely the court is to conclude that the disagreement cannot be overcome. Consequently, if the jury reports a deadlock after a relatively brief deliberation period, the trial court is likely to (and should) instruct the jury to ***continue further deliberation***. But because of the great deference given by appeals courts to trial court judgments on the issue of deadlock, a trial judge will typically ***not be reversed*** even if she orders a mistrial following a very brief period of deliberation by the jury, and even if she does not order the jury to make another attempt to break the deadlock.

   Example: D's jury trial for murder lasts less than nine hours, spread over about a week. The jury then starts to deliberate. On the second day of deliberations, the jury sends the judge a note asking what they should do if they can't reach agreement. The judge ascertains, by meeting with the jury, that some but not all of the members believe there is a deadlock. Instead of instructing the jury to make another try at reaching unanimity, the judge summarily declares a mistrial and schedules a new trial; D's lawyer does not object. On appeal, D contends that the mistrial should not have been granted after such brief deliberation, and that the Double Jeopardy Clause therefore prevents the new trial.

   Held, for the prosecution. A mistrial is appropriate when there is a "manifest necessity" for it. But the manifest-necessity test cannot be interpreted literally, and the judge's decision about whether there is a true deadlock is entitled to great deference on appeal. Furthermore, the trial judge is not required, before declaring a mistrial for deadlock, to "force the jury to ***deliberate for a minimum period*** of time, to ***question the jurors individually***, to ***consult*** with (or obtain the consent of) either the prosecutor or defense counsel ... or to consider any other means of breaking the impasse." The Supreme Court has never overturned a trial court's declaration of a mistrial after a jury deadlock under the manifest-necessity standard. Here, the trial judge's decision to grant a mistrial may not have been correct, but it was "not objectively unreasonable," and will therefore be sustained on appeal. ***Renico v. Lett***, 130 S.Ct. 1855 (2010).

ii. **Other problems:** Similarly, retrial will usually be allowed after a mistrial necessitated by there being ***too few jurors left*** on the panel, by the fact that a juror is ***disqualified*** for knowing one of the parties, or for other reasons that are ***not directly attributable to prosecutorial misconduct.*** In general, the more closely the trial court has weighed the alternatives before deciding that a mistrial is the only option, the more likely it is that a retrial will be permitted. L&I, v. 3, pp. 72-73.

iii. **Prosecutorial overreaching:** However, even where there might otherwise seem to be "manifest necessity" for a mistrial, a retrial will not be allowed if the entire episode was brought about by ***"prosecutorial overreaching."*** But this is extremely hard for the defendant to establish — only if he can prove that the government acted with the intent of ***"goading"*** him into moving for a mistrial will he be protected from retrial. *Oregon v. Kennedy*, 456 U.S. 667 (1982).

E. Reprosecution after acquittal: The classic application of the Double Jeopardy Clause is to prevent reprosecution after the defendant has been ***acquitted***.

1. **Acquittal by jury:** Where the case has been tried to a ***jury***, and the jury has come in with a verdict of ***not guilty***, it is clear that the Double Jeopardy Clause prevents the defendant from being retried. *U.S. v. Ball*, 163 U.S. 662 (1896). This is true even though the acquittal was brought about by the admission of what should have been inadmissible evidence, and even if it was brought about by what can later be proved to have been ***perjured testimony*** offered by the defense. For this reason, the prosecution is ***never permitted to appeal a jury acquittal.***

2. **Acquittal by judge:** Essentially the same rule applies to an acquittal by the judge — as long as the judge has found that one or more elements of the offense have not been established by the prosecution, the prosecution may not appeal (even if it is clear that the judge's verdict is based upon a mistake of law, such as the judge's refusal to admit evidence helpful to the prosecution). But if the ***jury*** has first found D guilty, and the judge has then dismissed the verdict as being against the weight of the evidence, an appeal followed by a retrial *will* be permitted.

F. Reprosecution after conviction: Under some circumstances, the fact that the defendant has been ***convicted*** may bar a later prosecution.

1. **Verdict set aside on appeal:** If the defendant is convicted at trial, and then gets the verdict ***set aside on appeal***, the double jeopardy rule normally does ***not*** bar a retrial. *U.S. v. Ball*, 163 U.S. 662 (1896).

   Example: Suppose that D is convicted based upon the fruits of a search and seizure which D contends violated the Fourth Amendment. If the appellate court agrees, the Double Jeopardy Clause does not prevent the state from retrying D on the same charge.

   a. **Insufficiency of evidence:** But there is one important exception to this rule: if the appellate court reverses on the grounds that the evidence at trial was ***insufficient*** to support a conviction (e.g., no reasonable jury could have found D guilty on the evidence presented), then a reprosecution is ***not*** allowed. The theory is that the prosecution gets one chance to assemble all of the evidence it can against D, and if the assembled evidence would not be sufficient to convict, then that is the end of the matter. (But if the conviction is overturned because some evidence was admitted illegally, and the ***remaining*** evidence is not sufficient to support a conviction, then double jeopardy does ***not*** bar a retrial. *Lockhart v. Nelson*, 488 U.S. 33 (1988).)

2. **Conviction of one crime as implied acquittal of another:** If the fact that D is convicted of one crime ***logically implies*** that he is being ***acquitted*** of another crime, then a retrial on the latter is not permitted.

   Example: Suppose that D is charged with both first-degree and second-degree murder on the same set of facts. The jury returns a verdict of guilty of second-degree murder, but says nothing about the first-degree charge. D then gets this second-degree conviction reversed on appeal. D may not now be retried on the first-degree charge, because he was implicitly acquitted of that charge by the second-degree verdict. See *Green v. U.S.*, 355 U.S. 184 (1957).

3. **Resentencing:** Where D is convicted, then appeals and receives a new trial, the Double Jeopardy Clause places some limitations on the ***sentence*** that may be imposed on the new conviction.

   a. **Credit for time served:** The Constitution requires that D be given ***credit*** for the time he served under the first charge before it was overturned. *North Carolina v. Pearce*, 395 U.S. 711 (1969).

   b. **Longer sentence:** On the other hand, the judge hearing the second trial is ***not*** prevented from giving D a ***longer sentence*** than was imposed following the first conviction. "A corollary of the power to retry a defendant is the power, upon the defendant's reconviction, to impose whatever sentence may be legally authorized, whether or not it is greater than the sentence imposed after the first conviction." *North Carolina v. Pearce, supra.*

      i. **Death penalty:** However, if the case is a capital case, and at the first trial the jury recommends against the death penalty, the Double Jeopardy Clause *does* usually bar the court from sentencing D to death if the first conviction is set aside and D is convicted on a retrial. See *Bullington v. Missouri*, 451 U.S. 430 (1981).

G. **Reprosecution by different sovereign:** Under the ***"dual sovereignty"*** doctrine, a conviction or acquittal by ***one jurisdiction*** does ***not*** bar a reprosecution by ***another jurisdiction*** for the ***same act or acts.***

1. **"Same offense":** Recall (p. 464) that the Double Jeopardy clause says that no one shall be subject "for the ***same offence*** to be twice put in jeopardy of life or limb." So the "dual sovereignty" doctrine is based on the idea that even if two jurisdictions prosecute a person for the same conduct, the two prosecutions are ***by definition not for the "same offense."*** As the Supreme Court has put it, "a crime under ***one*** sovereign's laws is not 'the same offence' as a crime under the laws of ***another*** sovereign." *Gamble v. U.S.,* 139 S.Ct. 1960 (2019).

2. **Remains in force:** Although the dual sovereignty doctrine has often been criticized, the Supreme Court has ***refused to abolish it.*** See, e.g., *Gamble, supra* (also discussed *infra*, p. 469), where the Court kept the doctrine in force, saying that each sovereign has a distinct set of interests that it's entitled to vindicate by prosecution.

   a. **Civil rights cases:** The dual sovereignty doctrine has been extensively used in ***civil rights cases***, where an acquittal of D in state court on ordinary violent-crime charges may be followed by a (valid) conviction in federal court on ***federal civil-rights charges.*** As one commentator has explained, "[D]uring the 1950s and the 1960 civil rights era, when a state jury acquitted a defendant of murder or assault upon a civil rights worker, the federal government was still free to prosecute based on the same incident; likewise, the federal courts were not barred from prosecuting the police officers in the Rodney King beating after their state acquittal by a Los Angeles-jury in 1992." D,M&S, Vol. 2, §14.01[B].

3. **Different configurations:** The dual sovereignty doctrine applies to any combination of state and federal charges arising out of the same acts.

   a. **Federal case followed by state case:** Thus acquittal or conviction on ***federal*** charges does not bar a ***later state prosecution*** for substantially the same act(s).

   b. **State case followed by federal case:** Conversely, a ***state*** conviction may be ***followed by a federal prosecution*** for the same act(s).

   Example: D, who has a previous felony conviction for a crime of violence, is driving when he is stopped by a local police officer in Alabama. The officer finds a loaded handgun in the car. D is charged by Alabama for violating that state's law making it a crime for anyone convicted of a crime of violence to possess a firearm. D pleads guilty to this charge. Then, federal prosecutors indict D for the same instance of firearm possession; this indictment charges him with violating a federal statute making it a federal crime for anyone convicted of a felony to possess, "in or affecting commerce," a "firearm or ammunition." D claims that this second prosecution for the same act of possession violates the Double Jeopardy clause; he argues that the dual-sovereignty doctrine is an incorrect interpretation of the clause, and should be overturned.

   Held (by the Supreme Court), for the prosecution. The dual-sovereignty doctrine is a ***valid – and long-established – interpretation of the Double Jeopardy clause***, and will not be overruled here. "Under [the] 'dual-sovereignty' doctrine, a State may prosecute a defendant under state law even if the Federal Government has prosecuted him for the same conduct under a federal statute. Or the reverse may happen, as it did here."

   The rationale for the dual-sovereignty doctrine is that when a single act violates the laws of two sovereigns, each of the sovereigns has a distinct set of interests that it's entitled to vindicate by prosecution. For instance, "[a]n assault on a United States marshal ... would offend against [both] the Nation and a State: the first by 'hindering' the 'execution of legal process,' and the second by 'breach[ing]' the 'peace of the State.' ... That ***duality of harm*** explains how 'one act' could constitute 'two offences, for each of which [the offender] is justly punishable.' " *Gamble v. U.S.*, 139 S.Ct. 1960 (2019).

   c. **State 1 case followed by State 2 case:** Lastly, ***one state*** may prosecute where ***another state*** has already convicted or acquitted for the same offense.

4. **Rationale:** For each of these three results, there's a ***common rationale***: that each jurisdiction ***possesses its own sovereignty***, which would be impaired if the jurisdiction were barred by results in a different jurisdiction. See *Gamble*, *supra*; also L&I, v. 3, pp. 98-102.

5. **Non-constitutional limits:** But many states have ***state-constitutional*** or ***statutory*** provisions protecting the defendant against reprosecution after conviction by some other jurisdiction. Similarly, the U.S. Attorney General's guidelines bar a federal trial "where there has already been a state prosecution for substantially the same act or acts," unless an Assistant Attorney General has approved the reprosecution. *Id.*

a. **Consequence:** In other words, the U.S. Constitution permits two sovereigns to punish the same act, but state-law provisions or federal guidelines may supply a ***non-constitutional rule*** barring the second sovereign from punishing a given act that has already been the subject of a prosecution by the first sovereign.

H. Overlapping offenses: Suppose that one set of facts could prove ***two different offenses***. If the prosecution charges one offense, a conviction or acquittal on this first offense will then bar a prosecution for the second offense. In this situation, the two offenses are said to be the "same" for double jeopardy purposes.

1. **No proofs of additional fact needed:** However, this "overlapping offense" rule is a very narrow one — it applies only where there are ***no additional facts*** needed to prove the second offense beyond what are needed to proved the first offense. The main importance of the rule is that if the prosecution in the first trial gets an acquittal or conviction on a ***lesser included offense***, it cannot bring a subsequent prosecution for the greater offense.

   Example: D steals a car on November 29 from a parking lot in one Ohio county, and is arrested on December 8 for driving the car in another county. D is charged with having "joy rided" on December 8, and pleads guilty. He is then prosecuted for the November 29 act of auto theft and joy riding.

   Held, the prosecution for the November 29 auto theft and joy riding is barred by the Double Jeopardy Clause. Under state law, joy riding consists of taking or operating a vehicle without the owner's consent, and auto theft consists of joy riding plus the intent permanently to deprive the owner of possession. Since the initial guilty plea to joy riding was an offense all of whose elements were contained within the later auto theft charge, the subsequent prosecution for auto theft was for the "same" offense and thus barred. *Brown v. Ohio*, 432 U.S. 161 (1977).

2. **Prosecution for lesser crime:** Conversely, the Double Jeopardy Clause also bars prosecution for the lesser included crime after conviction of the greater one.

   Example: D and his companion rob a store. The companion shoots and kills a clerk during the robbery. D is convicted of felony murder on these facts. He is later tried and convicted of the store robbery.

   Held, the prosecution for the robbery was barred by the Double Jeopardy Clause, because all elements that made up the felony of robbery were necessary for D to have been convicted of felony murder in the first trial. "The Double Jeopardy Clause bars prosecution for the lesser crime after conviction of the greater one." *Harris v. Oklahoma*, 433 U.S. 682 (1977).

3. **Unable to try both at once:** But the rule barring later trial of an included offense does ***not*** apply where the prosecution is ***unable*** to try both cases at once for reasons that are not the government's fault. For instance, if facts needed for proving the second crime had not yet been discovered at the time of the first trial, despite the prosecution's due diligence, the second trial will not be barred. Similarly, if at the time the first case is tried, events have not yet occurred that are needed for the second crime, double jeopardy does not apply.

Example: D is charged with assault and battery on V, and convicted. After the trial, V dies. D may be tried for murder now. *Diaz v. U.S.*, 223 U.S. 442 (1912) (cited approvingly in *Brown v. Ohio, supra*).

I. **Use of prior conviction under "persistent offender" laws:** Many states have enacted ***"persistent offender"*** statutes. These statutes increase the penalty for the present crime if the defendant was ***previously convicted of other crimes***. For instance, California's "three strikes" statute provides that a defendant who has two prior convictions for "serious felonies" will receive a minimum sentence of 25 years to life upon his third conviction. Defendants have sometimes argued that making the sentence for their current crime longer on account of a past conviction violates double jeopardy, on the theory that the person is being punished a second time for the earlier crime.

   1. **Not a double jeopardy violation:** But the Supreme Court disagrees, holding that such persistent-offender statutes ***don't violate*** Double Jeopardy. "An enhanced sentence imposed on a persistent offender . . . 'is not to be veiwed as either a new jeopardy or additional penalty for the earlier crimes' but as 'a stiffened penalty for the latest crime, which is considered to be an aggravated offense because a repetitive one.' " *Monge v. California*, 524 U.S. 721 (1998).

Quiz Yourself on ***FORMAL PROCEEDINGS*** *(ENTIRE CHAPTER)*

107. Dave and Ella burgled the Third National Bank. They left the bank with various jewels and rare coins taken from various safe-deposit boxes. A week later, police officer Orly, acting on a tip from a known, reliable, informant, stopped Dave as he walked down the street carrying a bag. The bag turned out to contain various jewels and coins which Orly recognized as items taken from the heist, so Orly arrested Dave for the burglary and interrogated him back at the station. Dave confessed during interrogation, saying at one point, "me and the person I was with, Ella, broke into the vault, and we each took away about half the loot." In response, police arrested Ella, and tried her together with Dave for the burglary. In the prosecution's opening statement, the prosecutor told the jury, "the evidence will show that Ella and Dave broke into the bank and its vault together, and each took about half of the proceeds." Then, Dave exercised his Fifth Amendment right not to take the stand or testify. Orly, after redacting Dave's confession, testified for the prosecution that "Dave confessed, and said when I interrogated him that "me and the person I was with broke into the bank and its vault, and we divided the loot 50/50."

Ella objected to Orly's testimony, saying that its admission against her violated her Confrontation Clause rights. The judge overruled Ella's objection and admitted the testimony; the judge instructed the jury that "anything that you've just heard about Dave's confession applies only to the case against him, and you shall not consider that confession as bearing at all on the charge against Ella." Both Dave and Ella were convicted, and Ella argued on appeal that the admission of Dave's confession violated her Confrontation Clause rights. Should the appellate court agree with Ella that the admission of this testimony violated Ella's constitutional rights? ________________

108. You work in the Public Defender's Office for the federal Eastern District of Bentley. You represent Darnell, an African-American man, who has been charged in the Eastern District with selling 30 grams of crack cocaine. Under federal narcotics law, the sale of crack is punished much more severely than the sale of an equivalent amount of powdered cocaine. You have checked the Public Defender's Office's records, and you have discovered that during the most recent two years, every person represented by the Office who was prosecuted in the Eastern District for selling more than 20 grams of crack was Black, whereas the Office never represented a single white person who was prosecuted for selling an equivalent amount of crack, apparently because no white person was even arrested for that crime. (A few whites were charged with selling powdered cocaine.)

You have just moved before trial to be allowed discovery into the files of the Assistant U.S. Attorney for the Eastern District, so that you can learn whether this charging discrepancy exists throughout that District's office (not just among the P.D. Office's clients). If discovery shows that the discrepancy does exist, you plan to then raise a "selective prosecution" defense, which if successful may lead to the charges against Darnell being dismissed, or at least changed to the less-severely-punished distribution of powdered cocaine.

According to U.S. Supreme Court precedent,

(a) What showing will you have to make in support of your motion in order for Darnell to be allowed discovery into the charging records of the Eastern District's U.S. Attorney's Office, in order to find evidence to support his claim? ___________________

(b) What are the approximate chances that you will succeed with this motion? ____________

Answers

107. No. It's true that in *Bruton v. U.S.* (1968), the Court said that in the special situation in which a confession by one co-defendant (call him D1), as presented to the jury, ***"directly accuses"*** another co-defendant (D2), D2's Confrontation Clause rights have been violated even though the trial court instructs the jury that it may consider the confession only with respect to D1's guilt, and not at all with respect to D2 — the *Bruton* Court concluded that the risk that the jury would disregard this limiting instruction, and consider D1's confession as bearing on D2's guilt, was simply too great. But a later Supreme Court decision, *Samia v. U.S.* (2023), held that exactly the sort of redacted confession at issue here — where the jury hears merely that D1 confessed that "me and the person I was with" committed the crime together — did ***not*** "directly accuse" D2. Therefore, even though a reasonable juror would likely have combined what she learned from D1's confession with other evidence in the case implicating D2 by name, it was not error to admit the confession, since the confession did not directly accuse D2. Thus *Samia* means that it was not error for the jury to hear Dave's confession and apply it to Ella's guilt.

108. (a) that the prosecutors in the Eastern District followed a charging policy in cocaine cases that had both (i) a *"discriminatory effect"* based on the defendant's race, and (ii) a *"discriminatory purpose"* to treat Darnell and other Blacks less favorably than whites in such cases.

(b) Very low, verging on zero. To prove that the policy had a "discriminatory effect" based on race, the defense will have to show that ***"similarly situated individuals*** of a different race were not prosecuted." [*U.S. v. Armstrong* (1996)] This seems to mean that the defense must point to particular white persons who were known to Eastern District prosecutors as sellers of crack, but were never arrested or charged. But this is a near-impossible burden, since the prosecutor's office would almost certainly not have records of any white person sufficient to show that the person sold crack without even being arrested.

Similarly, to prove that the policy had a "discriminatory purpose" — to treat Blacks less favorably than whites in crack-distribution cases — the defense would have to find in the prosecutors' records a statement that the prosecutors made the conscious decision to treat Black crack-distribution defendants less favorably than white ones. Even if the prosecutors were motivated by a desire to treat Black defendants less well, it is extremely unlikely that they would admit to that motivation in statements contained in their internal records.

Armstrong holds that proof of these two elements (discriminatory effect and discriminatory purpose) must be established just to obtain discovery from the prosecution's files — so the same two elements that would have to be proved to support a selective-prosecution claim on the merits before trial must be proved in order to get discovery, effectively a "Catch-22." That's why there are apparently no state or federal decisions since 1900 that even grant discovery in support of a selective-prosecution claim.

Exam Tips on ***FORMAL PROCEEDINGS***

Here are the most testable concepts from this chapter:

Questions about ***grand juries*** occasionally crop up on exams. When they do, they usually focus on the following three points:

Grand juries may ***consider any evidence***, regardless of its admissibility in a criminal trial.

There is ***no right to have counsel present*** at grand jury proceedings.

A grant of ***use immunity*** with respect to grand jury testimony (the narrower and more common type of immunity) precludes the prosecution from using the testimony or any evidence directly or indirectly ***derived from it*** against the one who gave the testimony. This standard is applied very strictly against the government.

Example: The prosecutor has no information about a bank robbery, other than a rumor that Defendant was involved. The grand jury subpoenas Defendant, who refuses to testify. The prosecutor grants use immunity; Defendant testifies that she and Co-Defendant (who has not previously been under suspicion) robbed the bank. The grand jury indicts both of them. The prosecutor negotiates a plea agreement with Co-Defendant, and Co-Defendant testifies against Defendant at trial. The prosecution's use of Co-Defendant's testimony in its case against Defendant is improper, because Co-Defendant's identity was discovered only because of Defendant's grand jury testimony.

Remember that the Bill of Rights guarantee against ***excessive bail*** (which has never been held to apply to the states anyway) does not amount to a "constitutional right to bail" — the Eighth Amendment guarantees only: (1) the right not to have bail set at an ***excessively high amount*** if and when it is set; and (2) the right to have the court make an ***individualized consideration*** of the defendant's ***particular circumstances*** in setting the amount.

Before the court accepts a ***defendant's guilty plea,*** it must determine that the plea was ***intelligent*** and ***voluntary,*** and that the defendant understands: 1) the nature of the charge, 2) the maximum possible penalty and the minimum mandatory penalty for the offense, and 3) that he is waiving his right to a jury trial.

Guilty pleas can be ***withdrawn*** for any fair and just reason, probably including mistakes about whether items of evidence will be admissible.

Example: D pleads guilty on the mistaken belief that his confession will be admissible at trial. After he learns that his confession is inadmissible, the court will probably let him withdraw his guilty plea and proceed to trial.

Remember that the right to a ***jury trial*** is fundamental. Exam questions frequently require you to explain its parameters.

The Sixth Amendment guarantees all defendants the right to a jury trial if they are charged with a ***felony,*** or with a misdemeanor punishable by more than six months in prison. This right has been incorporated, so it ***applies to states*** as well as the federal government.

Most states give defendants the right to a jury trial in ***lesser misdemeanors*** as well, but they are not required to do so. Defendants in other proceedings do not necessarily have a right to trial by jury.

Sentencing-guideline schemes pose a great risk of violating the Sixth Amendment. If guidelines result in D's being sentenced to a harsher sentence than the facts found by the jury would justify, based on some "aggravating" fact found by the judge, that's a Sixth Amendment violation. (*Example:* The jury finds that D possessed 100 grams of cocaine, for which the maximum sentence under guidelines is 2 years in prison. The judge can't find that D really possessed 300 grams and because of this sentence D to a longer time than 2 years.) Cite to *Blakely* and *Booker* on this point.

Even when there is a right to a jury trial, be on the lookout for express or implied ***waiver***. A knowing and intelligent plea agreement is an example of express waiver. Implied waiver is when the defendant fails to specifically invoke the right or attempts to do so too late in the process of the criminal prosecution.

Be clear that the ***Fifth Amendment*** does not allow defendants to "have their cake and eat it too." Although a defendant has an absolute right under the Fifth Amendment not to testify in his own defense, if he chooses to testify, he has waived his Fifth Amendment right. In other words, he may not take the stand to tell his version, then plead the Fifth Amendment in response to a prosecutor's cross-examination on matters within the scope of his testimony.

However, if D *does* exercise his Fifth Amendment right by not taking the stand, the prosecution ***may not comment*** adversely on this fact to the jury (e.g., the prosecutor may not say, "If he's so innocent, why hasn't he taken the stand to tell you his story?").

Don't forget the ***Confrontation Clau***se of the Sixth Amendment. Remember that this Clause gives any criminal defendant "the right . . . to be ***confronted with the witnesses against him.***"

The aspect of the Confrontation Clause most likely to be tested is that D has the right to ***cross-examine hostile witnesse***s. This matters most in cases where a co-felon gives a confession accusing D, D and the co-felon are tried together, and the co-felon then refuses to take the stand in D's trial. The part of the co-felon's confession that directly names and accuses D of participating can't be admitted against either defendant.

Example: D1 confesses to a crime; the confession says that "D2 and I committed the crime together." Both are tried together. D1 exercises her right not to testify. The confession can't be admitted verbatim against D2 (since D2 can't cross-examine D1). Cite to *Bruton v. U.S.*

But remember that this rule excluding D1's confession is now ***very limited.*** As long as the confession as recounted to the jury ***doesn't directly accuse D2,*** it can be admitted despite D2's Confrontation Clause rights.

Example: D1 and D2 are arrested for robbing a bank together. D1 confesses that "D2 and I robbed the bank together." They are tried jointly, and D1 declines to take the stand. The prosecution reads a redacted version of D1's confession to the jury, in which he is quoted as saying, "I, and another person who was with me, robbed the bank together." Even if the jury would likely infer from other evidence in the case that the "other person" was D2, the confession *can* be admitted as redacted, because it doesn't *directly* accuse D2. Cite to *Samia v. U.S.*

Double jeopardy is an important topic for exam questions. Remember that it involves two important ideas: (1) a defendant cannot be retried on the same charges; and (2) a defendant cannot be tried on two different charges if the defendant's acquittal on Charge A necessarily means the defendant could not be guilty of Charge B (collateral estoppel).

Example: D kills V1 and V2 in the same incident. He is charged with both crimes. He is first tried for the murder of V1. D is acquitted because the jury finds that his intoxication prevented him from forming the necessary intent for murder. In D's trial for the murder of V2, the prosecution is bound by the findings in the first trial about D's intoxication, so he may not be found guilty of this murder either.

In jury trials, jeopardy attaches ***when the jury is sworn.***

Two offenses are not the same for double jeopardy purposes if each requires proof of ***one additional fact*** which the other does not.

If there is a ***mistrial*** (e.g., a ***hung jury***), generally a retrial will not violate double jeopardy.

Typically, a true double jeopardy issue will be obvious from the facts you're given in the question. The most important things to remember about double jeopardy are two situations that seem like double jeopardy, but are ***not***:

Reprosecution by a ***different jurisdiction.*** (*Example:* A state prosecutes D for murder and loses; the federal government then prosecutes D for civil rights violates for the same conduct. The "different sovereign" rule means that the federal prosecution does not violate the double jeopardy clause.)

Reprosecution after a ***hung jury.***

ESSAY EXAM QUESTIONS AND ANSWERS

The following questions are adapted from questions asked on first-year Criminal Law exams at Harvard Law School. The only modification that has been made in the questions is the removal of aspects relating solely to substantive criminal law. The sample answers are not "official," and represent merely one approach to handling the questions.

QUESTION 1: Arn, Bur and Coy were members of PFF (Peace and Freedom Forever), a radical political group. Learning that Shaw, the ruler of an oil producing country, was to make a ceremonial visit to Aubon, oil capital of the United States, they developed the following plan. They would kidnap Shaw when he was at city hall at noon on December 15 to receive the key to the city; and they would hold him in PFF headquarters, which were in the back room of Arn's residence, until he publicly announced a reduction in oil prices. They planned to make good their escape by threatening to detonate, by radio transmitter, thirteen powerful bombs which they would have previously placed in mail boxes on street corners throughout the downtown area.

On December 12, before the explosives were placed, Coy lost his nerve and told Police Inspector Kopp of the plan. Kopp was at first skeptical and asked Coy for evidence of the plan. Coy sent the police detailed charts of City Hall Plaza which he had surreptitiously photographed in the PFF's headquarters. He also sent the original of a letter from Bur to Arn discussing Shaw's visit, which Coy found rummaging through Arn's bed table.

Kopp persuaded Coy to continue working with the group while keeping the police fully informed. Kopp planned to have Coy substitute harmless talcum powder for the explosives sometime before Shaw's arrival.

On December 14, Coy still had not been told where the explosives were kept. When Arn and Bur were absent, Coy asked Kopp to come to the PFF meeting place in Arn's house and help him locate the explosives. Kopp brought with him the police's best bomb-detection device, a dog specially trained to smell dynamite. The dog detected nothing in the headquarters in the back room, but barked insistently at the dresser in the entrance hall. A check revealed a large cache of dynamite which Kopp removed, substituting talcum for it.

As he left Arn's house, Kopp saw on a table near the door a postcard addressed to Arn. Turning it over he read the message: "Let me know if you ever need more dynamite or other building supplies. The deal is good for both of us since I get them wholesale." The card was signed "Dan."

Early the next day, December 15, Arn and Bur planted dynamite charges, which they kept elsewhere, in 13 downtown mail boxes. Arn retained the detonator. Coy was told of their activities without being informed of the specific mail boxes.

Inspector Kopp made his move immediately after hearing of this development from Coy. Kopp took steps at once to locate the bombs. Coy informed Kopp that "Dan" was probably the first name of a building demolition contractor, a cousin of Bur who had sold them the explosives when they had told him about their plan. Coy recalled a tattoo of the word "Mother" high on this contractor's left arm. Hoping that Dan might have been told of the proposed location of the bombs, Kopp went to the offices of all seven demolition contractors in Aubon. Kopp ordered each to roll up his left sleeve. The last had the tattoo. Kopp took the contractor outside to the street where Coy was waiting. Coy took one look at the contractor's face and said, "That's the guy." Instantly Kopp demanded of Dan: "Did you sell dynamite to Arn and Bur?" Dan replied, "Yes."

Furious, Kopp shouted at him, "Damn you! Either you help me find those bombs or you're never going to see daylight again." Dan said he had at his house a postal map of the city on which Arn and Bur had made some marks and maybe that would help. Kopp said, "Can we get it right away?" and Dan, after some hesitation, said, "O.K."

At Dan's house, Dan turned over the map to Kopp. The bomb squad was called, but needed an hour to disarm all of the bombs. Kopp's men, heavily armed, had occupied city hall plaza. When Arn and Bur arrived, they were at once surrounded, but, on Kopp's arrival, he directed that his men stand back with guns drawn in response to Bur's threat to detonate the bombs. Kopp asked Arn and Bur, "Why are you doing this?" Arn replied, "To force a reduction in oil prices." The stand-off remained for several more minutes until Kopp got word that all of the bombs were disarmed. Arn and Bur surrendered when they realized that this was so.

Discuss all issues relating to the admissibility of evidence.

QUESTION 2: A report by a private detective, Breuer, confirmed Walter Jacke's suspicions that his wife, Molly, was having an affair with Walter's old friend, Frank Moreweather. Frank had married a very emotional, extremely jealous woman, Irma. On discovering Frank's infidelities in the past, Irma had reacted almost violently; but she seemed to know nothing about this latest interlude in Frank's life.

Walter loved his wife and wanted her back. He was deeply embittered by Frank's actions, but he was also a careful man. A homicide arrest was the last thing he needed. There is always more than one way to skin a cat, however. For Christmas, Walter insisted that he and Molly give the Moreweathers a pearl-handled pistol.

Soon after Christmas, Irma began receiving a series of phone calls, always when her husband was out. Each involved a lady's voice referring obliquely to Frank's "real reason" for being out and suggesting that it would be wrong, deeply wrong, not to put a stop to this offense. Of course, Irma had no way of knowing that Walter's mistress, Ethel Hogarth, was making the calls at his request.

Suspecting a violation of the harassment and adultery statutes, the Acton police department agreed to Irma's request that they put a tap on the Moreweather phone without Frank's knowledge. The tap picked up conversations between Frank and Molly which would have confirmed Irma's worst suspicions. A trace on the calls to Irma, moreover, showed that they were made from a particular apartment rented to Ethel Hogarth, a woman Irma did not know.

The question, was, of course, who was putting Ethel up to this. The answer required finding first the overlap between her associates and Irma's, and then a motive for one of them to harass Irma. The management of Ethel's apartment building agreed to an arrangement between the police and the maid responsible for Ethel's floor. The maid would, in the course of her regular duties, try to observe anyone coming to and going from Ethel's apartment. If she noted photographs or names when cleaning up in the apartment, she would refer them to the police. Any letters found in the trash would be turned over to the officer in charge of the case.

Meanwhile the calls continued, with Irma becoming increasingly distraught. On January 15 the matter came to a dramatic head. Irma had confronted Frank with her suspicions at dinner. His response had been to slap her and walk out. Another call from Ethel followed his departure. This time Ethel also relayed the information, uncovered by Breuer, as to where Frank and Molly could be found.

Irma had reached the point where she could take no more. She drove to the address of Frank's and Molly's secret rendezvous and waited with gun in hand. An hour later, when she saw them leaving, she fired into their car, wounding Frank and killing Molly. She then called the police who, after arresting her and hospitalizing Frank, set about tying up the loose ends of the case.

The maid had delivered to the police a letter from Walter found in Ethel's trash. The letter included a proposed schedule of telephone calls, and Ethel had put a check mark next to each as she made the call. The maid had also observed other letters apparently from Walter and a picture in the room that looked like a man she had once seen in the corridor. The detective in charge of the case telephoned Walter and asked him to come to the police station, where the maid at once identified him during his fingerprinting as the man seen in the corridor whose picture was on Ethel's dresser.

Next, the police obtained a warrant on the basis of an affidavit alleging that "a reliable informant with no criminal background who has been working with the police in the investigation of the case for several days has advised that she had personally observed in the location to be searched letters from Miss Hogarth's paramour, Walter Jacke, and other incriminating evidence with respect to the crimes of Harassment and Adultery." While she was out, Ethel's apartment was searched for the incriminating picture and letters, which were seized.

Shortly thereafter, she was arrested, informed of Irma's shooting of her husband and Molly, and advised of her rights. Ethel refused to discuss the matter further in the absence of her lawyer.

At the police station Walter was ushered into a seemingly private but secretly bugged room with her where, before he could hush her up, she exclaimed: "Oh Walter, you should have told me who this woman was and what could happen!" Walter's response, "Shut up, you dumb bitch," was elicited before he was advised of his *Miranda* rights. Thereafter, he gave a full account of his involvement and the circumstances that led to his actions. On the basis of Walter's statement, Breuer was arrested.

Evaluate all issues relating to the admissibility of evidence.

ANSWERS

ANSWER TO QUESTION 1

Coy's initial statement to Kopp: Coy's initial statement to Kopp is clearly admissible. It was completely voluntary, and Coy was not in custody at the time it was made. Nor did the police exploit the station-house setting to induce Coy to tell them more than he had originally wished to say. Therefore, the *Miranda* warnings did not have to be given, even though the statement was self-incriminating.

Charts of City Hall: The charts of City Hall provided by Coy are probably admissible. There would be no doubt at all of their admissibility if Coy was found not to have been acting as a police agent at the time he procured them, since the Fourth Amendment (as applied to the states through the Fourteenth Amendment) restricts only the actions of state officials, and of persons acting on behalf of state officials.

However, it seems likely that Coy will be deemed to have been acting as a police agent at the time he surreptitiously photographed the plans, at least if he did not do so until after Kopp had asked him for evidence. If Coy was indeed acting as a police agent, a Fourth Amendment search and seizure may have taken place. The prosecution could argue that Arn and Bur had no justifiable expectation of privacy in the charts, since they shared the charts with Coy; this situation might be analogized to the drugs in the handbag in *Rawlings v. Kentucky* (where D was found to have lost his expectation of privacy in the drugs by putting them in someone else's handbag).

If Arn and Bur had no legitimate expectation of privacy in the charts, Arn, as the owner of the residence where the charts were kept, might argue that he had a legitimate expectation of privacy in his residence which was violated by Coy's search-and-photography-expedition. However, under *Rakas v. Illinois*, mere possession of the premises is probably not sufficient to establish a legitimate expectation of privacy, and Arn might be found to have lost his expectation by giving Coy access to the premises.

Even if Arn and Bur were found to have had a legitimate expectation of privacy in the charts, they might be held to have impliedly consented that Coy use them. If so, Coy's mere examination of the charts did not by itself violate the Fourth Amendment rights of Arn and Bur — the "unbugged agent" cases (*Lewis* and *Hoffa*) make it clear that Arn's and Bur's misplaced trust in Coy as a co-conspirator did not vitiate their implied consent to Coy's access to the charts.

Letter from Bur to Arn: Much the same analysis applies to the letter as to the charts. The chief difference, of course, is that the letter was seized in the private portion of Arn's house. Even assuming that Coy was legitimately in the office part of the house, he almost certainly exceeded his authority by entering Arn's bedroom and rummaging through Arn's personal effects. *Gouled v. U.S.*, holding a similar rummaging to be an unlawful search, seems on point.

Arn certainly seems to have a legitimate privacy expectation in the letter, since it was kept in a private part of the house and as far as we know was not shown to anyone else. Therefore, he should be able to have it kept out of evidence against him. Bur, however, will have difficulty doing the same. He may not keep out the evidence merely on the grounds that its seizure violated the rights of another (Arn). Bur himself seems to have no legitimate expectation of privacy in either the letter or in Arn's bed table (where the letter was found).

Bur might try, as a last-ditch argument, the contention that the introduction of the letter violates his Fifth Amendment right against compulsory self-incrimination. The letter is clearly testimonial, but it is unlikely that Bur can convince the court that the testimony is compulsory, since: (1) the letter was written and mailed in the complete absence of any law-enforcement influence whatsoever; and (2) Bur was not compelled to produce the letter (since it was taken by Coy). This situation seems indistinguishable from the seizure of business records in *Andresen v. Maryland.*

Search of PFF Headquarters by Kopp and Coy: Although Coy's information probably gave Kopp probable cause to believe that evidence (explosives) would be found in the house, there do not appear to have been any exigent circumstances justifying a warrantless entry, particularly since Kopp had ample opportunity to obtain a warrant. Therefore, the search is valid only if Coy had authority to consent to it.

Although the house was not his, Coy might nonetheless have had authority to consent to the search, depending on the extent of his own privileges in the house. Coy himself clearly had authority to be present in the back-room headquarters, but it does not necessarily follow from this that he had the right to invite others (e.g., the police) to search it. The test should probably be whether Arn assumed the risk that by allowing Coy access to the premises, he would invite someone else in. Alternatively, if Kopp reasonably but mistakenly believed that Coy had joint authority over the back room, the search will be upheld. See *Illinois v. Rodriguez*. Most courts would probably hold that Coy had authority to consent at least to the search of the back room.

If Coy did have authority to consent to Kopp's search of the back-room headquarters, the question remains whether Kopp exceeded the scope of the consent, or of Coy's authority to consent, when the dog entered the front entrance. Even if Coy did not have the authority to consent to search of the front hall because he himself did not have the privilege of being there, a variant of the "plain view" doctrine may apply to validate the dog's (and Kopp's) entry into the front hall. That is, if the dog smelled the bomb when he was still in the back room, the government could argue that the bomb was in "plain smell." This situation seems somewhat similar to the police's use of a dog to sniff for drugs in luggage in *U.S. v. Place*, or to sniff for drugs from outside a stopped car in *Ill. v. Caballes*; in both of those cases, the Court held that no search occurred at all. However, the present situation might be distinguished from the ones in *Place* and *Caballes* — in both of those cases, the Court emphasized that the dog was sniffing for *contraband*, which no one has the right to possess, so the sniffing could not have revealed anything as to which the owner had a legitimate expectation of privacy. Here, by contrast, the dog was sniffing for explosives, which may be legitimately possessed. Therefore, the dog's sniffing might be found to have violated Arn's legitimate expectation of privacy in the dresser's contents, in which case the *Place* and *Caballes* precedents may not help the government, possibly making the use of the dog an invalid warrantless search. (The Supreme Court has left open the possiblity that there is a *general* "plain smell" doctrine even outside of the canine-sniffing-for-contraband context, but has never expressly so held. If there were such a general plain-smell doctrine, the dog's use would presumably be valid.)

Even if the entry by Kopp and the dog into the front hall *was* justified on a "plain smell" theory, Kopp might nonetheless have exceeded the scope of that theory by ***opening*** the dresser. If it could be proved that the dog's barking was a very clear indication of the presence of dynamite, a court might be convinced that the opening of the drawer and the seizure of the dynamite were justified by newly-encountered exigent circumstances, namely, the possibility that the dynamite might be used before a warrant could be obtained. Alternatively, the court might hold that the evidence was fully discovered by the dog, and that the opening of the drawer did not constitute a further investigation, but merely a seizure, following naturally from the dog's discovery, and therefore within the scope of the plain view doctrine.

If the "plain smell" doctrine does *not* apply, it seems almost certain that Arn's right of privacy was violated by the opening of the drawer and the seizure of the dynamite. Although the dresser itself may have been in plain view, the dynamite was not, and Arn almost certainly had a justifiable expectation that it would not be opened.

Reading of the post card: The validity of Kopp's reading of the post card found on Arn's table raises similar issues. If Kopp had a right to be near the door by virtue of Coy's consent, the card falls within the plain view exception. However, it is not clear that Kopp had the right to turn the card over and read the reverse side; the situation seems analogous to that in *U.S. v. Catanzaro* (inspector takes rifle off the wall to examine serial number), which was found to fall within the plain view exception. Also, the government might argue that Arn, since he left the card lying on the table, had no justifiable expectation of privacy concerning it, but this argument is unlikely to succeed, since Arn probably had a justifiable expectation that people would not read mail addressed to him in his own house.

It is doubtful whether Dan, the card's sender, can keep the card from being admitted against him, for the same reasons cited previously in connection with Bur's letter to Arn. Bur has no expectation of privacy in the card at all.

Search of Dan for identification purposes: Kopp's order to Dan to roll up his sleeve to determine whether he was the "Dan" who signed the postcard was probably valid in itself, although it may have been the fruit of a previous illegality (the reading of the postcard).

The order to Dan to roll up his sleeve probably constituted a "search" within the meaning of the Fourth Amendment, since it is unlikely that Kopp would have allowed Dan to refuse, and Dan can fairly be said to have been detained. However, the search can probably be justified under either of two theories. First, this confrontation may fall within the *Terry* and *Adams* "stop and frisk" rationale. Since the detainment of Dan was only long enough to establish whether he had the tattoo, the stop fell within the principle that such brief detainments must not be longer than necessary to accomplish their purpose. Also, Kopp had at least the less-than-probable-cause degree of suspicion necessary to support a *Terry-Adams* stop, based on Coy's information — the officer's information in *Adams* was probably less impressive than Kopp's information. Under the "totality of the circumstances" test used for evaluating informants' tips, Coy's information probably provided the "reasonable suspicion" necessary for a stop. See *Alabama v. White*. And although *Terry* involved only questioning, and not an order to the suspect to expose part of his body, dictum in *Davis v. Miss*. indicates that certain reliable identification procedures (e.g., fingerprinting) may sometimes be imposed on a suspect even without probable cause. And whether or not a search warrant would normally be necessary for such fingerprinting, the exigent circumstances of the impending bomb blasts and kidnapping here would excuse the lack of a warrant even if it were ordinarily required.

Secondly, even if the limited intrusions were not justified under the *Terry* rationale, Kopp probably had probable cause for a full-scale arrest by the time he reached Dan, since every other local demolition contractor had been eliminated by prior search. Since Dan could have been arrested and then searched incident to arrest, a search immediately prior to the arrest would also be permitted. (The Court held that warrantless searches made immediately pre-arrest fall under the incident-to-arrest doctrine, in *Rawlings v. Kentucky*.) Therefore, the examination of Dan's arm appears "reasonable" under the Fourth Amendment.

It is true that Kopp's probable cause to believe the last suspect to be Dan was derived in part from earlier searches, probably made without probable cause, and perhaps without even the degree of suspicion necessary for a *Terry* stop. But Dan has no right to complain of these earlier illegal searches, since it was not his own constitutional rights that were violated by them. Nor could he object that the examination of his arm violated his Fifth Amendment right against self-incrimination, since *Schmerber* makes it clear that such physical examinations are not "testimonial" and are therefore not covered by the privilege against self-incrimination.

Show-up of Dan by Coy: The confrontation in which Coy identified Dan as the contractor who sold them the dynamite was a show-up, rather than a lineup, since only the suspect was brought before the witness. While show-ups are considerably more suggestive than lineups, they may be justified where they are not "unnecessarily suggestive." (See *Stovall v. Denno.*) The case for the government here is easily as strong as in *Stovall*. The necessity for acting immediately, rather than taking time to form a lineup, is apparent from the threat of the bombs. Furthermore, Coy's prior exposure to Dan was sufficiently detailed and lengthy to provide him with an "independent basis" for the identification, avoiding intolerable suggestiveness, and also removing the taint of any suggestiveness for purposes of an in-court identification of Dan by Coy.

Dan was not entitled to counsel at this show-up because it preceded formal charges. See *Kirby v. Ill.*

Dan's admission to having sold the dynamite: Dan's admission, at the scene of his arrest, that he sold the dynamite to Arn and Bur, may have been obtained in violation of Dan's *Miranda* rights. Although Dan was not in the station house, he may have been in custody from the moment he was identified by Coy, since Kopp would never have let him leave. (A court would phrase the issue in terms of ***whether a "reasonable suspect" in Dan's position would have known*** that he was not free to leave; if the hypothetical "reasonable suspect" wouldn't have known this, Dan would not have been in custody under this view. See *Berkemer v. McCarty*.)

The government can also plausibly argue that at the time Kopp questioned Dan, there was an emergency, and that the ***"public safety"*** exception to *Miranda* (see *New York v. Quarles*) should apply. Dan could retort that there was no reason for Kopp to believe that use of the bombs was imminent. However, since Kopp knew that the bombs had already been put in the mailboxes, the "public safety" exception will probably be applied.

If, despite the government's public-safety argument, a court found that *Miranda* warnings were required, Dan's admission to having sold the dynamite would not be usable against him. The more interesting question is whether the postal map would also be inadmissible. Dan could argue that the postal map is a "poisonous fruit" of the (possibly) illegal confession, since it is unlikely that he would have given it to the police had he not first implicated himself by confessing to having made the sale. However, this type of argument was expressly rejected by the Supreme Court in *U.S. v. Patane*: even where an unMirandized (but non-coerced) confession leads directly to physical evidence, the physical evidence will not be inadmissible fruit of the poisonous tree. So Dan will not be able to keep the map out of evidence by use of the poisonous-fruit argument.

Arn, like Dan, will try to exclude the map as being the fruit of a poisonous tree. From Arn's point of view, the poisonous tree is the reading of the postcard from Dan to Arn, which was probably an illegal search. Since that card led Kopp to Dan, Arn may be able to argue that Dan's arrest, and his production of the map, were both fruits of the original illegal search and hence not usable against Arn. This is particularly convincing in view of the fact that it is unlikely that Kopp would ever have been put on to Dan had he not read the postcard; even courts applying the "inevitable discovery" extension to the "independent source" rule would be reluctant to apply the extension to a discovery as speculative as the one in the present case.

The government will argue that Dan's production of the map was an independent act of free will, and thus "purged the taint" of the original illegal means by which Kopp was led to Dan. Some support for this position is given by *U.S. v. Ceccolini*'s readiness to find witness' testimony to be untainted. However, Dan produced the map only after insistent questioning by Kopp, and his act does not therefore appear very much more voluntary than Toy's confession in *Wong Sun*. Arn should also try to get Dan's admission of having supplied dynamite excluded; although Arn cannot have this statement excluded from use against himself even if Dan's *Miranda* rights were violated (these rights may only be asserted by Dan himself), Arn can claim, as with the map, that the confession was the "fruit" of the original unlawful reading of the postcard; this contention is likely to be treated the same as is the attempt to exclude the map, whatever that treatment is.

Arn's admission: Arn's admission in the plaza that he was carrying out the scheme in order to force a reduction in oil prices, may have been obtained in violation of *Miranda*. It is hard to say whether Arn was in custody at the time, since he might have been able to use the threat of the bombs to bargain for his escape; as with Dan's initial statement, the existence of custody depends on whether a reasonable person in Arn's position would, at the time he made the statement, have believed that he was free to go. (*Berkemer v. McCarty*.)

ANSWER TO QUESTION 2:

Wiretapping of Moreweather phone: The wiretap on the Moreweather phone was conducted without a search warrant and so is in violation of *Katz v. U.S.* and of Title III of the Omnibus Crime Control Act of 1968, at least with respect to the conversation between Frank and Molly. Frank has the right to object to the introduction against him on an adultery charge of this conversation, since he had a legitimate expectation of privacy concerning it. The conversation between Ethel and Irma, however, was probably not illegally intercepted, since the tap was placed with Irma's consent. The tap was not in violation of Title III, which specifically exempts taps to which one party consents; nor was it in violation of the Fourth Amendment, in all probability, since Ethel would most likely be held to have assumed the risk that the other party to her conversation would betray it. See *U.S. v. White*, in which the Supreme Court held that *Katz* did not render illegal the use of a "bugged agent" to transmit the defendant's voluntary conversations; *White* seems applicable here, even though it involved a transmitter and not a tap.

Maid's search of room and seizure of papers: Despite the apartment manager's agreement to have the maid "keep her eyes open" while in Ethel's room, the maid was working for the police in a sufficiently direct way so that she should be considered a police agent or informer, and her actions must be judged as if they were the actions of the police. The manager's consent to the maid's actions does not by itself prevent them from being a violation of the Fourth Amendment, since by the principle of *Stoner*, such a manager does not have authority to consent to a search of a guest's (or here, a tenant's) room.

The maid may not have conducted a Fourth Amendment search merely by keeping her "eyes open," as long as she performed only the chores which she was supposed to perform, and did not go rummaging; anything she came across while doing her job could probably be turned over to the police under the plain view doctrine. But her rummaging through the wastebasket presents a closer issue. *Cal. v. Greenwood* establishes that a person who puts trash on the sidewalk has no reasonable expectation of privacy in it. But this rule does not necessarily apply to trash within one's residence — a person arguably has a reasonable expectation that her trash will not be scrutinized (at least until it has been carried out of the premises); people often retrieve things that they have inadvertently thrown into the trash, and most of us would feel much more intruded upon by scrutiny of our trash while it was still in our premises than once we had placed it out on the street knowing that scavengers could look through it. In any event, a person almost certainly has a reasonable expectation that the police will not recruit "agents" to scour his residence looking for clues in the trash.

If Ethel did have a justifiable expectation of privacy with respect to the trash, then the maid's action constituted a Fourth Amendment search and seizure. Since there were no circumstances justifying a warrantless search or seizure, Ethel's Fourth Amendment rights were violated, and she has the right to exclude the letter found in the trash.

The maid's scrutiny of the picture of Walter, and the letters from Walter that were not in the wastebasket, might also fall within the plain view exception. Since it is hard to say that Ethel had a justified expectation of privacy as to items which were more or less on display (as the photo probably was), there was probably no Fourth Amendment search as long as the maid discovered these items while she was performing her job. But again, if she found them while rummaging rather than while cleaning, the plain view doctrine does not apply, and her examination of them constitutes a Fourth Amendment search, which in the absence of either a warrant or of circumstances justifying a warrantless search and seizure, is in violation of the Amendment.

If the maid's actions did violate the Fourth Amendment, the items cannot be introduced, since although seized pursuant to a valid warrant they are the fruit of a poisonous tree; the police were able to obtain the warrant only through the maid's illegally-obtained knowledge. Other aspects of the warrant will be discussed below.

If any of the items are found to have been illegally searched for or seized, Ethel will definitely have the right to object, since she had a justifiable expectation of privacy in the premises searched. Walter, however, probably does not have the right to exclude any of the items, since he probably would be held to have abandoned any expectation of privacy in the items by giving them to Ethel. If he pays for the apartment for Ethel, however, and uses it frequently he may be able to assert a sufficient justifiable expectation of privacy in the apartment to allow him to object to the search and seizure occurring there.

The show-up of Walter by the maid: Walter was not entitled to a lawyer when he was identified by the maid because, though the investigation had focused upon him, formal judicial proceedings had not yet been commenced against him. See *Kirby v. Ill.* He was, however, as a matter of due process entitled to an identification free from unnecessary suggestion. *Stovall v. Denno*. Using a show-up rather than a lineup here seems to have been unnecessary, since there was plenty of time to arrange a lineup. On the other hand, the show-up might be found not to have been unduly suggestive, even though unnecessary. In *Neil v. Biggers*, the Court concluded that the inherent suggestiveness of the show-up in question was countered by the good opportunity that the identifier had had on a previous occasion to observe the person now being identified. It is unclear from the facts of the instant case how closely the maid observed the man she later identified as Walter, but it is clear from *Neil* that the Court does not require much. The government can argue that the maid made the connection between the photograph, the man in the corridor, and the suspect being fingerprinted, without being specifically asked if there was any connection. The government can also point out that there were two things, not one, in the maid's mind enabling her to identify Walter — the picture *and* the view she had in the corridor.

An additional difficulty with the show-up is that it occurred while the suspect was being fingerprinted; fingerprinting is such an indication of police suspicion that the show-up might be held intolerably suggestive, to a degree violative of due process, on that ground alone. However, if the government were able to show by "clear and convincing evidence" that the maid had had ample opportunity to examine the photograph and to scrutinize the man in the corridor, she might be permitted to make an in-court identification of the defendant, since that identification would have been shown to be sufficiently independent of the illegal show-up identification to purge the taint of it. See *U.S. v. Wade.*

Even if the show-up was itself valid and not violative of due process, the maid's identification might be excluded on the grounds that it was the fruit of a poisonous tree, the maid's illegal search of the room. The government could argue that the independent source exception applies, since there were two distinct sources for the identification, the picture and the view of Walter in the corridor; only the first could possibly have been illegally obtained. But the government, if it prevailed in this argument, could presumably introduce only the fact that the defendant was identified as having been in the corridor, and not that he was seen to be the man in the photo.

Search warrant: The affidavit submitted by the police to obtain the warrant to search Ethel's apartment was based upon information from a confidential informant. Nonetheless, it provided sufficient information to establish probable cause under the "totality of the circumstances" test of *Illinois v. Gates* — the affidavit contained both information about the reliability of the informant, as well as some information about how the informant obtained the knowledge (personal observation). Taken together, these facts would justify a neutral magistrate in concluding that evidence of crime would probably be found.

The warrant is thus good as to the letters, which were particularly described by reference to their sender and addressee. It is unclear whether it is good as to the picture, which was not particularly described, but which would fall within the catch-all phrase "other incriminating evidence." In *Andresen v. Maryland*, the Supreme Court approved the phrase " . . . other fruits, instrumentalities and evidence of crime . . . ," so the phrase used here may avoid impermissible vagueness. If the phrase is held too vague, the photograph might still be admitted — if the police had probable cause to have listed the photograph and the photograph was in plain view the search will be upheld. See *Horton v. California.*

Even though the warrant may be formally valid, the introduction of the items seized under it might still be excluded by the "fruits of the poisonous tree" doctrine, if Ethel can show that the probable cause for the issuance of the warrant was based on information obtained through violation of her constitutional rights (i.e., the maid's search of her room.) Even if Ethel made such a showing, however, the police may well be able to successfully argue that their reliance on the warrant was ***"objectively reasonable,"*** so that the exclusionary rule should not apply. (See *U.S. v. Leon.*)

"Bug" in the station: Two possibly valid objections may be raised against the bugging of the remarks exchanged between Walter and Ethel in the police station.

(1) *Katz:* The conversation, though within the confines of the police station, was probably initiated with the expectation that it would not be overheard. While this expectation is not as clearly reasonable as the expectation maintained by Katz while in his phone booth, it may be reasonable for a prisoner to expect that electronic devices will not be used to overhear his conversations. The fact that the building is used for police purposes should not automatically mean that no privacy may exist anywhere within it. Furthermore, the police placed the suspects in a room which was designed to convey a false sense of privacy, so the police should not be able to claim now that the expectation was not reasonably maintained. However, *Kuhlmann v. Wilson* indicates that if the police (or their informants) merely listen "passively" to in-custody

conversations, no constitutional violation takes place; this rationale may apply to bugging as well as to the informant-based listening used in *Kuhlmann*.

Assuming that reasonable expectations of privacy were violated, the police would be required to seek a warrant under Title III of the Omnibus Crime Control Act, since this was the electronic interception of an "oral communication." Both Ethel and Walter, as parties to the conversation, have standing to object to its interception under Title III.

(2) *Miranda:* Ethel, having refused to speak in the absence of an attorney, could not have been formally interrogated further or even encouraged to change her mind, according to *Miranda*. She may be able to argue that the arranged meeting with Walter in the confines of the police station was a deliberate attempt to bypass the protections of *Miranda*, and that that decision should apply to exclude any incriminating statements made by her. While the encounter with Walter was not "interrogation" in the strict sense, it did utilize the inherent, subtle, coercive pressures of the police station and the anxiety of the two suspects in meeting each other to induce speech by one who did not want to speak with the police while under restraint by them. However, the police conduct in setting up and monitoring a meeting between two spouses here is similar to that in *Arizona v. Mauro*, where the Court held that no interrogation occurred and that no *Miranda* warnings needed to be given.

Even if each suspect can, by one or both of the arguments set out above, object to the admissibility of his own statements, it is less clear that Walter can also suppress Ethel's remark from use against him, and vice versa. Since the police were counting on the confrontation of the two suspects and then the interactions of their remarks to cause admissions by both, Walter and Ethel might successfully argue that the statements of each are the product of both, and hence that each may object to all statements made. But the court may hold that each statement violated the rights of only the person who made it.

Walter's Confession: Assuming that Walter was given his *Miranda* warnings before making his confession, his only chance to have the confession excluded is to show that it was tainted by earlier illegality. His best bet for this is to show that it was the direct product of the trickery used by the police to induce his incriminating remark to Ethel; he can point out that when he realized how he had incriminated himself, he no longer saw any point in denying the crime, and that he therefore made a confession which he otherwise would have had no reason to make. But *Oregon v. Elstad* establishes that where a confession is preceded by *Miranda* warnings, it will be presumed voluntary (and admissible) even though the suspect may have been influenced by his belief that the "cat's out of the bag." But *Elstad* also holds that the presumption of voluntariness will not apply if the confession derives from "deliberately coercive or improper tactics in obtaining the initial statement," and Walter may be able to persuade the court that the police tactics here were coercive or improper.

Even if Walter is able to exclude his confession, by showing that it was the product of trickery and thus not voluntary under all the circumstances, Ethel will have difficulty in similarly excluding it from use against her. Although she can try to show that it was the direct product of the illegal bugging of her own incriminating remark to Walter, it is unlikely that this argument will be persuasive; two important factors, Walter's own incriminating statement and the *Miranda* warnings, intervened between her remark and Walter's confession.

Breuer's arrest: Breuer will not be able to exclude from the case against him Walter's remarks in the confession incriminating him. Even if the confession was illegally obtained from Walter, Breuer's rights were not thereby violated, and he cannot assert Walter's rights to bar the confession.

TABLE OF CASES

Principal discussion of a case is indicated by page numbers in *italics*.

SUBJECT MATTER INDEX

www.ingramcontent.com/pod-product-compliance
Lightning Source LLC
LaVergne TN
LVHW082010200926
848481LV00010B/2830
9798894109787